BOTTOM LINE'S TREASURY OF
HEALTH SECRETS
FOR SENIORS

1,937 Remarkable Secrets from

America's Very Best Doctors and Health Experts

www.BottomLinePublications.com

Bottom Line's Treasury of Health Secrets for Seniors:
1,937 Remarkable Secrets from America's Very Best Doctors and Health Experts

Copyright © 2012 Boardroom® Inc.

10 9 8 7 6 5 4 3 2

ISBN 0-88723-671-5

Bottom Line Books® publishes the advice of expert authorities in many fields.
These opinions may at times conflict as there are often different approaches to
solving problems. The use of this material is no substitute for health, legal,
accounting or other professional services. Consult competent professionals
for answers to your specific questions.

Telephone numbers, addresses, prices, offers and Web sites listed in this book
are accurate at the time of publication, but they are subject to frequent change.

Bottom Line Books® is a registered trademark of
Boardroom® Inc.
281 Tresser Boulevard, Stamford, CT 06901

www.BottomLinePublications.com

Bottom Line Books® is an imprint of Boardroom® Inc., publisher of print periodicals,
e-letters and books. We are dedicated to bringing you the best information from the most
knowledgeable sources in the world. Our goal is to help you gain greater wealth,
better health, more wisdom, extra time and increased happiness.

Printed in the United States of America

Contents

8 • BEAT THE BLUES & REVITALIZE

9 • HEALING RELATIONSHIPS

PART 2: TREATING EVERYDAY AILMENTS

14 • LOOKING YOUR BEST

15 • ALLERGIES, IMMUNE SYSTEM & RESPIRATORY HEALTH

16 • DIGESTIVE DISORDERS

21 • HEART DISEASE

Preface

We are proud to bring you *Bottom Line's Treasury of Health Secrets for Seniors: 1,937 Remarkable Secrets from America's Very Best Doctors and Health Experts*. We trust that you'll find the latest discoveries, best treatments and money-saving solutions to your health concerns.

Whether it's quality medical care, new heart therapies, breakthrough cancer treatments or cutting-edge nutritional advice, our editors talk to the people—from top research scientists to consumer health advocates—who are creating the true innovations in health care.

How do we find all these top-notch medical professionals? Over the past two decades, we have built a network of literally thousands of leading physicians in both alternative and conventional medicine. They are affiliated with the premier medical institutions and the best universities throughout the world. We read the important medical journals and follow the latest research that is reported at medical conferences. And we regularly talk to our advisers in major teaching hospitals, private practices and government health agencies.

Treasury of Health Secrets for Seniors is a result of our ongoing research and contact with these experts, and is a distillation of their latest findings and advice. We trust that you will enjoy the presentation and glean new, helpful and affordable information about the health topics that concern you and your family.

As a reader of a Bottom Line book, please be assured that you are receiving reliable and well-researched information from a trusted source.

But, please use prudence in health matters. Always speak to your physician before taking vitamins, supplements or over-the-counter medication...changing your diet...or beginning an exercise program. If you experience side effects from any regimen, contact your doctor immediately.

The Editors, Bottom Line Books, Stamford, Connecticut.

PART 1

Living the Healthy Life

1

Get the Best Medical Care

Hey Doctor, Treat Me...
Not My Age

It's not surprising that older adults have more health problems than young people. What is surprising is how poorly this older population is served by our health-care system.

This is partly due to medical ageism, a subtle type of age discrimination that makes it harder to navigate the health-care system as you get older. In a Duke University survey, nearly 80% of respondents older than 60 had been told at least once by their doctors that their ailments were due to age—the implication being that the ailment is simply a result of getting older, so the doctor isn't going to treat it.

Many of the conditions that get more common with age, such as pain, hearing loss and depression, are never fully investigated. Similarly, a doctor might feel that a little knee pain or the leakage of urine is "normal" in older adults. This attitude means that underlying problems might never be diagnosed.

Undertreatment is one consequence of medical ageism...overtreatment is another. Doctors who practice what is known as "cookbook medicine" tend to recommend the same tests and procedures for everyone.

Your doctor should treat you, not your age. *Here's what to watch out for—and what to do to make sure that medical ageism doesn't hurt you or a loved one...*

UNDERTREATMENT

Rationing health care is among the most common forms of medical ageism. A doctor looks at the patient's medical record, notes the birth date and then makes certain assumptions.

Example: A patient who complained that he hurt his knee during a tennis match

Mark Lachs, MD, MPH, professor of medicine and co-chief of the division of geriatrics and gerontology at Weill Cornell Medical College in New York City. He is director of Cornell's Center for Aging Research and Clinical Care and director of geriatrics for the New York-Presbyterian Health System. He is author of *Treat Me, Not My Age* (Viking). *www.treatmenotmyage.com.*

might be advised to take up a less physically demanding sport, such as golf. Or he might simply be told to "take it easy."

I know plenty of 70- and 80-year-olds who are in great shape and play a tough game of tennis, and a few 40-year-olds who are frail. The doctor's job is to address the problem, not to ignore the problem with age-based assumptions.

Self-protection: Don't let your doctor brush off any health issue with a reference to age. Be wary if he/she performs a perfunctory exam or rushes through your history. You should be asked detailed questions such as, "When did the pain start?"…"How many days are there when it doesn't hurt?"…"How's your range of motion?" etc.

It's possible that there won't be an easy solution, or any solution, for your problem. If that's the case, make sure that your doctor tells you why. "You're just getting older" is not an acceptable answer.

OUTDATED EXAM

The traditional office exam is not effective for older adults. It was created more than 100 years ago, when people didn't live as long. Information about blood pressure, reflexes, heart sounds, etc., is helpful, but it tells little about how well you function in daily life.

Example: A patient who appears perfectly healthy based on the standard medical exam might be falling every day at home.

Self-protection: Don't wait for your doctor to discover things. Make a list before you go, which might include balance problems, declines in muscle strength, poor hearing or even social isolation, which can lead to depression. These and other functional issues often are more important for long-term health than what is revealed by an exam.

Ideally, your doctor also will perform tests to see how you actually function. He might speak at different volumes to check your "real-life" hearing. You might be asked to walk or to stand up and then sit down. You might be given a list of words and numbers and asked to repeat them.

Helpful: Ask friends and family members if they've noticed things that you haven't. Maybe you keep turning up the volume on the television or asking people to repeat themselves. You might be getting tired more easily or forgetting names more often.

ARE YOU DEPRESSED?

Depression is common in the elderly, but doctors often fail to diagnosis it. This is partly because it takes time to perform a mental health evaluation, so most doctors don't routinely do it. It's also because older adults often experience different symptoms of depression than those who are younger.

Self-protection: Tell your doctor if you've been feeling more irritable lately…have been losing weight…or are eating less regularly. These are common signs of depression in older adults.

Important: If you're suffering from depression, ask for a referral to a gerontologist (an internist who specializes in treating older patients) or a geriatric psychiatrist. Medicines can be helpful, especially when used in conjunction with supportive psychotherapy, but older people respond differently to antidepressants. They may require different doses and/or durations of treatment than younger adults.

OVERCARE

Too much medical care is just as dangerous as too little, particularly for those who are taking multiple medications, have underlying health problems and generally are frail.

Example: The mother of a friend of mine has Alzheimer's disease and dementia, as well as diabetes. The doctors and nurses who care for her always track her blood sugar. This requires multiple daily blood sticks…which she thinks is a sign that they're trying to kill her, making her agitated and unhappy. For a patient like this, treating the diabetes this aggressively doesn't make a lot of sense.

Similarly, I would hesitate to subject an 82-year-old woman to the inconvenience and stress of a mammogram, particularly if she has had many negative mammograms in the past, no history of breast problems and no family history of breast cancer.

Self-protection: Don't agree to any test or procedure without asking your doctor if the results will change or improve your outcome.

You also should ask questions such as, "What will happen if I do nothing?"..."Will the results of this test lead to more tests?"..."What are the side effects of testing?"

A patient might reasonably decide that he wants every possible test and treatment—it's just as reasonable to do the opposite in some cases.

AVOID THE ER

According to 2007 data from the National Center for Health Statistics (the most recent data available), about 25% of Americans older than 75 went to the emergency room at least once that year. That's the last place that you want to be except in a real emergency.

In the ER, there's too much care—and too little. Examinations are rushed. There's often a lack of communication among doctors. Patients may be given tests that they don't really need. It's an extremely stressful environment.

My advice: Ask your doctor how you can contact him, or an assistant, at any hour. Certainly don't delay in getting to the ER if you have serious symptoms, such as those of a stroke or heart attack, but other conditions might wait until the next day if you can get the over-the-phone OK from your doctor.

Be Sure to Ask Your Doctor…

Charles B. Inlander, health-care consultant and founding president of People's Medical Society, a consumer advocacy organization active in the 1980s and 1990s. He is the author of 20 books, including *Take This Book to the Hospital with You: A Consumer Guide to Surviving Your Hospital Stay* (St. Martin's).

It's easy to be intimidated by a doctor, especially when it comes to asking questions. All too often, we're afraid that we might sound silly or ignorant or insult our physician by seeming to question the wisdom of his/her diagnosis or suggested treatment. But studies have shown that patients who ask the most questions often get better care. Here are five important questions that doctors should be asked—but rarely are. *Each question can improve the quality of care you receive (and perhaps save you money)...*

1. What is the cost of the drug(s) you are prescribing? A study found that nearly 90% of doctors surveyed said they were concerned about the cost of their patients' medications, but fewer than half knew the cost of the drugs they commonly prescribed. Asking your doctor what a drug costs lets him know that you are concerned about your health-care expenses and forces him to find out about medication prices. The question can open a discussion on the availability of a generic drug or a less expensive brand-name drug.

2. Why are you referring me to that particular specialist? When your doctor refers you to a specialist, he probably will suggest a particular doctor. But is this doctor the best qualified to treat your problem? Doctors often refer patients only to specialists who are affiliated with their own health system or insurance plan networks or to those who refer patients back to them. To ensure that you are getting a range of opinions and treatment options, ask for the names of at least two or three specialists and schedule appointments to see them.

3. Is this the right hospital for me? Research has shown that smaller, community-based hospitals often are just as good as big-name teaching hospitals for most routine surgeries or treatments, such as a gallbladder removal, but usually a lot cheaper. This is crucial when a portion of the costs is coming out of your own pocket in the form of copayments and deductibles. If you need treatment that requires a hospital stay, ask your doctor if a community hospital is an option.

4. Does Medicare cover this treatment? A little-known provision of the Medicare law stipulates that if a doctor fails to inform you in writing that a service or treatment is not covered by Medicare, the doctor cannot charge you for it. If you are a Medicare beneficiary, always ask the doctor if the treatment he is proposing is covered by Medicare.

5. Are there going to be more tests? I recently saved money by receiving a *magnetic resonance imaging* (MRI) scan. How? My doctor wanted me to have a series of X-rays, but he mentioned that he might also order an MRI at a later date. I found out that the series of X-rays was going to cost more than $1,000 versus $800 for the MRI. My copay would be 20% of either treatment. Before scheduling the appointment, I called my doctor and asked if we could skip the X-rays and go right to the MRI. He agreed. Ask your doctor whether a single comprehensive test might be an option.

More from Charles Inlander...

Choosing the Treatment That's Right for You

Millions of Americans are confronted each year with complex treatment options for a variety of conditions. Unless patients are fully informed about the available treatments, the decision-making process can be daunting, adding to the anxiety of the diagnosis itself.

Over the last 30 years, the treatment of serious medical conditions has been transformed by new and improved techniques, often giving patients a variety of treatment options. Whatever your medical condition, your physician will make treatment recommendations, but the ultimate decisions are yours. *My advice...*

• **Get to the right doctors.** Start with the doctor who diagnosed your problem. Ask him/her to fully explain your condition and its severity. Ask your doctor to then refer you to specialists who treat the condition—for cancer, for example, a medical oncologist (for advice on chemotherapy), a surgeon (for recommendations on surgery) and a radiation oncologist (for advice on radiotherapy).

Trap: Studies show that most specialists tend to recommend the treatments associated with their areas of expertise, often omitting different approaches offered by other specialists who treat the same condition. Don't be silent in these sessions—ask what all your treatment options are, including those outside the doctor's own specialty.

• **Do your research wisely.** Doing an online search of your condition will bring up hundreds—even thousands—of articles about treatment options, some of which are sure to be out of date or just flat-out wrong. To

ensure that you are getting reliable information, consult the Web sites of organizations that provide information, not treatment, for your condition—for example, the American Cancer Society (*www.cancer.org*)...the American Heart Association (*www.americanheart.org*)...and the National Institutes of Health's PubMed (*www.pubmed.gov*).

• **Make a list.** Find out the benefits and the risks associated with each treatment option, including side effects and possible long-term complications. For example, some people experience blood clots after angioplasty (even months later) that require follow-up treatment, such as surgery. As you gather this information, make a list of each treatment's benefits and risks. Then review all of your treatment options with your doctors and family. This approach helps to ensure that you make the decisions that are right for you.

Also from Charles Inlander...

How to Get the Medical Care You Need Now

An older woman in Philadelphia contacted me some time ago because her doctor had told her to schedule heart-valve surgery with a surgeon he recommended, but she wasn't able to get an appointment to see this surgeon for three weeks. She didn't feel well and wondered why she couldn't get a quicker appointment. What should she do? I told her to call the referring doctor and have him call the surgeon. But before the referring doctor could intervene, the woman's daughter found her unconscious on the floor. She was rushed to the hospital for emergency heart-valve surgery—and survived. But not everyone is so lucky when such scheduling problems occur.

Waiting for appointments with specialists, long delays in getting scheduled for surgery and even interminable waits for test results are some of the most frequent complaints I hear from medical consumers. For example, the average waiting time to get an appointment with an orthopedic surgeon in Boston is 40 days ...a gynecologist 70 days...and 21 days to see a cardiologist, according to a recent survey.

The numbers aren't much better across the country.

My advice on expediting appointments and test results…

• **Ask your doctor to make the appointment.** Anytime your doctor recommends that you see a specialist, you should ask if the doctor will call to make the appointment. The referring doctor usually can get you squeezed in if the problem needs quick attention. Even if your problem can wait, a delay of weeks often creates anxiety—so if you're still not satisfied with the appointment date, call the specialist's office and ask to be contacted if there is a cancellation. Then call the office as early as possible each week to ask if a cancellation has occurred. Chances are good that you'll get a quicker appointment.

• **Be willing to travel.** If you are flexible about when and where you receive medical tests (my father once had an outpatient MRI at midnight because the time was available), you'll have far less waiting time.

• **Choose the right day of the week.** Most medical labs are closed on weekends. To get your test or biopsy results sooner—without having to wait over the weekend—schedule your appointments on Monday or Tuesday whenever possible.

Insider secret: Since blood tests for cholesterol levels are usually scheduled early in the morning (because you are required to fast), those tests results are usually back the same day. Call your doctor's office that afternoon to see if your results are in.

Medical Myths That Can Wreck Your Health

Nancy Snyderman, MD, chief medical editor for NBC News. She is a head and neck cancer surgeon and associate clinical professor in the department of otolaryngology/head and neck surgery at the University of Pennsylvania, and author of *Medical Myths That Can Kill You* (Three Rivers).

Americans know more about health issues than ever, yet certain medical myths persist.

Examples: You can't really catch a cold by going outside without a coat in the winter (colds are caused by exposure to a virus)…you don't have to drink eight glasses of water each day to remain healthy (the best guide is to drink when you're thirsty—you'll need to drink more if you're mowing the lawn on a hot summer day than if you're sitting quietly indoors)…and stress does not cause ulcers (ulcers are usually caused by the *Helicobacter pylori* bacteria).

Most medical myths are relatively harmless, but a few endanger the health of those who subscribe to them. Even medical professionals might believe these myths, which could put their patients at risk. *Five of the most widespread and dangerous myths…*

Myth 1: **Vaccinations are only for kids.** American adults rarely receive vaccinations, except perhaps a flu shot and a tetanus booster. Some vaccines for pneumonia and meningitis are very appropriate for older people—and Zostavax, a shingles vaccine, is specifically designed for those age 60 and older.

Vaccinations you may need…

• **Shingles vaccination.** Ninety percent of today's adults had chicken pox as a child. And while this gives them lifetime immunity to chicken pox, it does not protect against shingles (both shingles and chicken pox are caused by the same virus).

Note: Since people may not know or remember whether they had chicken pox, the vaccination is usually given anyway.

• **Tetanus booster.** Get a tetanus booster every eight to 10 years.

• **Pneumonia (pneumococcal) vaccination.** Get this if you have never had one…or if you had one more than five years ago and were under age 65.

• **Meningitis vaccination.** Get this if you have not already had one.

• **Polio vaccination.** This is given on an as-needed basis, even if you were immunized as a child, particularly before traveling to a Third World country.

Important: Some adult vaccinations, including the shingles vaccine and tetanus boosters, usually are covered by health insurance. Others often are not, so discuss coverage with your insurer.

***Myth 2:* Annual checkups are unnecessary.** The US Preventive Services Task Force, an expert panel set up by the US Public Health Service, argued in 1995 that annual checkups are not cost-effective because they only rarely reveal serious diseases. This has encouraged many Americans to stop scheduling checkups.

The task force failed to consider that annual checkups do more than catch major diseases. *They also...*

• **Establish a relationship between patient and doctor.** Patients who feel comfortable with a primary care physician are more likely to seek timely care for future health concerns.

• **Give patients a chance to receive treatment for nagging problems that they otherwise would have endured.**

• **Provide doctors with an opportunity to discuss fitness and lifestyle issues with patients.** Many cases of cancer, heart disease and stroke could be avoided if patients simply followed the exercise, diet and lifestyle advice offered by doctors during routine physicals.

The Congressional task force was correct about one point—annual health exams are most effective when they are targeted to a patient's specific health risks based on his/her lifestyle and family history. So, if a parent had heart disease or cancer, especially at an early age, discuss with your doctor whether you should be tested more vigilantly than standard recommendations.

***Myth 3:* My heart is fine as long as my cholesterol reading is below 200 milligrams per deciliter (mg/dl).** Your total cholesterol reading is relatively unimportant. Your level of one particular type of cholesterol, called low-density lipoprotein (LDL), is a much better indicator of heart disease risk. If your LDL level is below 130, your risk for heart disease is likely to be low. However, if you suffer from high blood pressure, obesity, a family history of heart disease or other heart disease risk factors, your LDL reading might have to be below 100 or even lower to be considered safe.

Helpful: If you have trouble lowering your LDL cholesterol, don't drink unfiltered coffee, such as espresso, cappuccino, Turkish coffee and coffee brewed in French press coffeemakers—they contain naturally occurring oils called terpines that can increase LDL cholesterol levels.

***Myth 4:* My doctor will identify cancer before I ever could.** Certain types of cancer, including skin cancer, testicular cancer and breast cancer, are usually first spotted by patients. Waiting for your next doctor's exam to turn up suspicious spots or lumps could greatly decrease the odds of a successful outcome if you do have one of these forms of cancer.

A second common cancer belief—that cancer is almost always a death sentence—is also a myth. There are many types of cancer, and medical science has made tremendous progress in treating some of them, such as Hodgkin's lymphoma and acute lymphocytic leukemia.

Progress has also been made with many forms of cancer that still have distressingly high fatality rates. Where patients once died in months, they might now live for years.

***Myth 5:* A natural product is a safe product.** Many people assume that the natural supplements sold in health-food stores are great for their health. But because natural supplements are exempt from government safety and effectiveness testing, it is difficult to know which ones are good for us and which are bad.

Example: The naturally occurring compounds ephedra and tryptophan have been found in "natural" over-the-counter products—but they have proven to be unsafe.

We can't even be certain that natural supplements contain the ingredients and dosages that they claim. Further, what is safe for one person can be dangerous for someone else.

This doesn't mean that all natural products should be avoided, just that natural supplements should be purchased only from trustworthy stores and upon the advice of a knowledgeable alternative health practitioner.

Give your doctor a list of any natural supplements that you are considering taking—there might be basic health risks, or the supplement might interact poorly with your prescription medications.

Top-Rated Hospitals In the US

2010-2011 rankings from *US News & World Report*, Washington, DC.

The best hospitals in the US are Johns Hopkins in Baltimore…Mayo Clinic in Rochester, Minnesota…Massachusetts General, Boston…Cleveland Clinic…Ronald Reagan UCLA Medical Center, Los Angeles…New York-Presbyterian, University Hospital of Columbia and Cornell, New York City…University of California at San Francisco Medical Center…Barnes-Jewish Hospital, Washington University, St. Louis…Hospital of the University of Pennsylvania, Philadelphia…Duke University Medical Center, Durham, North Carolina…Brigham and Women's Hospital, Boston…University of Washington Medical Center, Seattle…University of Pittsburgh Medical Center…University of Michigan Hospitals and Health Centers, Ann Arbor.

These hospitals earned high scores in at least six specialties, such as cancer care, heart treatment and children's health. For the complete list of hospitals, their specialties and their rankings, go to *www.usnews.com/besthospitals.*

In the Hospital? Know Your Rights

Marjory Abrams, president, BottomLine newsletters, Boardroom Inc., 281 Tresser Blvd., Stamford, Connecticut 06901.

Did you know that hospital patients can request to be treated by a full-blown doctor rather than just a resident? Or that hospital charts are no longer secret? Thanks to the Health Insurance Portability and Accountability Act (HIPAA), patients may ask for their own copies instead of trying to sneak a look at their progress.

Trisha Torrey is a patient advocate and author of the book *You Bet Your Life! The 10 Mistakes Every Patient Makes (www.everypatients advocate.com).* Here are some of the rights that she and other advocates encourage hospital patients to assert…

•**You have the right to refuse to be observed, examined or treated by anyone and to ask for someone else.** For example, if a technician is unable to draw your blood after repeated attempts, ask for someone with greater expertise.

•**You have the right to refuse any treatment and to be told what the ramifications of refusal may be.** You can refuse any medication, too—but be sure to ask about possible consequences.

•**You (and your loved ones) have the right to receive an ethics consultation upon request—for example, if family members disagree about life support.** Ethics consults may include a physician, nurse, patient representative or other professionals, along with the patient and/or family members.

•**You have the right to visitors you choose.** A new federal regulation allows the patient to designate anyone he/she wants to visit, as long as you provide signed documentation to the hospital and your request complies with the hospital's visitors policy.

•**You have the right to be made as comfortable as possible.** If nighttime lighting is too bright for you, ask for it to be switched off or dimmed. People who aren't ready to walk should be helped into a chair for an extended sitting period several times daily.

•**You have the right to have an advocate by your side 24/7.** You may ask a friend or loved one to fill that role or hire someone. You can find professional advocates at *www. AdvoConnection.com.*

•**You have the right to be moved to a different room if and when the hospital has a vacancy if a roommate keeps you up at night or otherwise hinders your recovery.**

Torrey urges patients and their loved ones to invoke their rights, when appropriate, as respectfully as possible rather than confrontationally. Try to reach a mutually acceptable solution. You don't want to create animosity, but you want to make sure—very sure—that you get what you need.

Naturopathic Doctors and Hospital Visits

Most naturopathic physicians (NDs) do not have hospital privileges and cannot treat hospitalized patients. If your primary health-care provider is an ND, ask him/her to recommend an MD (Doctor of Medicine) or a DO (Doctor of Osteopathic Medicine) who can take an integrative approach and work with you while you are in the hospital. The MD or DO also can consult with your ND to advise on natural treatments.

Charles Inlander, health-care consultant and founding president, People's Medical Society. He is author of 20 books, including *Take This Book to the Hospital with You* (St. Martin's).

How to Get Out of the Hospital Alive

Peter J. Pronovost, MD, PhD, professor in the departments of anesthesiology, critical care medicine and surgery at Johns Hopkins University School of Medicine in Baltimore. He is coauthor, with Eric Vohr, of *Safe Patients, Smart Hospitals* (Hudson Street).

Hospital-acquired infections are among the most common preventable causes of death due to medical errors, but hospitals still aren't doing enough to prevent these and other mistakes.

New research: A recent survey of hospitals found that 87% don't always follow infection-prevention guidelines—including basic hand-washing protocols.

Result: As many as one in 10 patients will acquire a potentially deadly hospital infection.

Most doctors know what they need to do to prevent unnecessary mistakes. The challenge is to consistently implement proven safety measures. Until this occurs, there are steps you can take to help protect yourself if you are hospitalized.

The following is an interview with Peter J. Pronovost, MD, PhD, patient-safety researcher at Johns Hopkins University School of Medicine, about hospital risks—and what patients can do to stay safe.

You refer to the "toxic" culture in hospitals. What does this mean? Most patients assume that medical care is guided by scientific principles—that doctors do things in ways that are safe as well as effective.

But it's not that simple. Doctors are human. They often are overconfident and have strong personalities and big egos that cause them to do things that conflict with the patient's best interests.

Recent example: At our hospital, an otherwise healthy patient suffered serious complications after kidney surgery. It was clear that the patient needed to return to the operating room, but the surgeon refused because a CT scan indicated that there was nothing wrong.

We all know that test results can be misleading. Even though the patient had serious complications, the surgeon wouldn't admit the possibility of error. And surgeons often have complete authority in such cases.

As the intensive care physician on call, I explained the situation to another surgeon and he agreed to operate. It turned out that the first surgeon had accidentally cut the pancreas and intestine during the procedure—an error that could be lethal.

Surgery is not a perfect science—even the best surgeons make mistakes. Had systems been in place to keep personality issues (such as a surgeon's insistence that he couldn't make a mistake) out of the equation, much of this patient's suffering could have been prevented.

What kinds of systems can help? Teamwork is a big one. Johns Hopkins researchers did a study that looked at errors and liability claims at a number of hospitals. We found that in nearly 90% of cases, at least one of the team members knew that something was wrong but was either afraid to speak up or was ignored by the person in charge.

At Johns Hopkins, we created a system in which nurses must attend rounds with the attending physician and head resident. This helps prevent subsequent errors in communication and has caused medication errors to drop to almost zero. It also cut the time that

10

patients spent in intensive care units (ICUs) by about half.

Patients also should be active team members. Speak up and ask questions if you do not understand something. Always ask all health-care practitioners who enter your room to please wash their hands.

You've pioneered the use of checklists. How do they help? A checklist virtually eliminates the hierarchal mind-set that I discussed above. A doctor or surgeon can't get away with merely saying, "Because I said so." He/she is required to follow step-by-step procedures that have been shown to improve safety.

Example: About 31,000 Americans a year die from infections caused by central lines (catheters placed in a vein in the neck, groin or chest). We examined data from the CDC in order to summarize the most important points in developing the checklist. Our checklist included things like hand-washing…cleaning the patient's skin with the disinfectant chlorhexidine…draping the patient…and the use of a surgical mask, hat, gown and gloves.

In Michigan, where the checklist was first adopted, the incidence of central-line infections dropped by 66% within 18 months after the protocols were implemented—a reduction that has now been sustained for more than three years.

If you're planning a surgery: Ask what the hospital's rate is for catheter-related bloodstream infections—and be concerned if it is much above one out of every 1,000 catheter days. If you or a family member has a catheter, ask every day whether it is still needed.

Should patients ask about checklists before choosing a hospital? Absolutely. Virtually every procedure can be done more safely when the medical staff follows clear and consistent guidelines.

Checklists don't have to be complicated. Take hand-washing. It's among the most effective ways to prevent hospital infections. Yet even doctors and other health-care workers in hospitals working on infection prevention do not do it about 30% of the times that they should. It's perfectly reasonable for a patient who is scheduled to undergo surgery to ask

his surgeon whether he follows an infection-prevention checklist.

Another example: Wrong-site surgery. Nearly 3,000 times a year in the US, surgeons operate where they shouldn't. There are cases in which the surgeon has operated on the wrong side of the body (such as amputating the left leg instead of the right) or even on the wrong patient.

The Joint Commission (a nonprofit group that regulates hospital standards and safety) now mandates that operating room teams perform a "time-out" before surgery. During this time, the surgeon marks the surgical site. The case is then reviewed both by surgeons and nurses to confirm the patient's name and the nature of the surgery.

If you're planning a surgery: Prior to the operation, ask your surgeon if he uses the time-out period. If so, ask him to perform the step before you're sedated so that you can participate. That way, you can confirm your name and other details. For example, the surgeon might touch your right knee and say something like, "This is where we're operating, right?" When you're awake, the risk for error is further reduced.

Hospital-acquired pneumonia is a big risk for patients. What can patients do to prevent it? If you spend time in an ICU, there's a good chance that you'll be put on mechanical ventilation to help you breathe. We've found that elevating the head of the bed so that it's raised at least 30° will help mucus from the mouth and nose drain into the stomach instead of the lungs. Yet the beds in ICUs are often kept in a horizontal position. Inhaling mucus is one of the main causes of ventilator-associated pneumonia.

Also important: A family member should ask each day whether mechanical ventilation is still needed for the patient.

How can patients who are allergic to latex—widely used in many hospitals—protect themselves? We went latex-free at Johns Hopkins three years ago. Some hospitals, however, continue to use latex gloves during surgery even though about 1% of Americans are allergic and could experience a life-threatening ana-phylactic reaction.

The allergy tends to occur in people who have had frequent exposure to latex in the past. This includes health-care workers (who often wear the gloves) or patients who have undergone multiple surgical procedures in which latex gloves were used.

My advice: Before having a procedure, tell your surgeon that you don't want to be exposed to latex. Latex-free gloves are readily available—hospitals should use them.

How to Have a Smooth Hospital Stay

Charles B. Inlander, health-care consultant and founding president of People's Medical Society, a consumer advocacy organization active in the 1980s and 1990s. He is the author of 20 books, including *Take This Book to the Hospital with You: A Consumer Guide to Surviving Your Hospital Stay* (St. Martin's).

I recently had to put all my years of experience as a medical-consumer advocate to the test when I found myself in the hospital recuperating from surgery for an enlarged prostate gland. My surgery was a success—in part because I chose a surgeon who had done the procedure, a transurethral resection of the prostate (TURP), more than 1,000 times. But my hospital stay went without major incident also because I knew what to do to avoid problems. *Here's what you—or a loved one—can do to have an equally successful hospital stay...*

• **Bring a list of your medications.** I always advise people to bring a list of all their medications—and the dosages—when they go to the doctor, but the same applies if you're headed to the hospital. Coming prepared with your medication list is one of the best steps you can take to protect yourself against medication errors. I brought my medication list and kept it on the adjustable table by my bedside. One nurse thanked me and used it to be sure that her records were correct.

• **Hang signs.** The 84-year-old man in the bed next to mine was nearly deaf and couldn't understand the questions that the doctors and nurses asked him. He would just nod and say "yes" to everything. When I realized this was happening, I made a sign with bold print that read, "You have to speak directly into my ear!" and hung it on the wall above his head. It worked. Once my roommate was able to hear the staff, they got real answers. You can make a sign for a variety of messages, such as "Contact my son/daughter (and give phone number) for any medical permissions."

• **Use the phone.** One night, I needed the nurse but was getting no response when I pushed the call button. I waited 20 minutes and finally picked up the phone, dialed "0" and asked for the nurses' station on my unit. A nurse answered on the first ring. I asked her to come to my room, and she showed up about 10 seconds later. I never had a problem again when I pushed the call button.

• **Bring earplugs.** Hospitals are noisy places. Knowing this, I brought earplugs with me and slept peacefully. A portable music player with earphones or noise-canceling headphones can provide the same escape.

• **Call home.** Twice during my three-day hospitalization, my doctor visited when no one from my family was around. So when my doctor entered the room, I got on the phone, called my wife and had the doctor talk to her at the same time he was talking to me. This is the best way to keep your family informed, and it is especially helpful if you are physically weak and need help asking questions.

• **Check the bill.** I received a bill from the hospital that said I owed $2,600. I knew this was wrong. By going over the itemized bill (which I had requested at my discharge), I discovered that I had been inadvertently charged for services received by another patient. Because I was diligent and made a lot of calls, the insurer found the error. Since an estimated 85% of all hospital bills have errors in them, it's buyer beware!

7 Things Doctors Don't Tell You About Anesthesia

David Sherer, MD, an anesthesiologist in the suburbs of Washington, DC, and former physician-director of risk management for a major HMO. He is author of *Dr. David Sherer's Hospital Survival Guide* (Claren).

All forms of anesthesia can cause side effects or complications, yet doctors don't always take the time to address these issues with patients. *What you must know...*

• **Your supplements can increase your risk.** Some herbs and nutritional supplements can be lethal when they're combined with anesthesia. Ginkgo, for example, can elevate blood pressure. Because some anesthetic drugs have the same effect, patients taking both can experience sharp rises in blood pressure. This increases the risk for stroke and heart attack.

Risks from supplements are greatest with general anesthesia, but even with regional anesthesia (such as spinal or epidural), there are dangers.

Example: Garlic supplements thin the blood, which can cause additional bleeding with regional anesthesia.

During the presurgery interview with your anesthesiologist, mention everything that you're taking. Also, talk with the doctor or naturopath who prescribed the supplements about any possible interactions.

• **Nausea can be controlled.** Many forms of anesthesia stimulate the chemoreceptor trigger zone, a part of the brain involved in nausea. Older anesthetic drugs, such as nitrous oxide (laughing gas), are far more likely to cause nausea than newer agents. But postoperative nausea and vomiting still are among the most common side effects of anesthesia.

Better control: A relatively new class of drugs, known as 5-HT3 antagonists (such as Zofran), may reduce postsurgical nausea more effectively than their predecessors. Scopolamine patches, which are commonly used to prevent motion sickness, also can be helpful.

Important: If you've had surgery and experienced nausea in the past, tell the anesthesiologist during the presurgery interview. He/she will make sure that you get the appropriate kinds and doses of medication.

• **Constipation and urinary retention are likely.** Analgesic narcotics, such as codeine, Demerol and Percodan, have a tendency to make it difficult for patients to urinate or have a bowel movement—problems that can persist for days or even weeks after the surgical procedure.

Helpful: Ask the anesthesiologist if your procedure can be done with an ultrasound-guided nerve block instead of general anesthesia. Patients given this type of anesthesia typically require lower doses of narcotics, which can reduce the side effects.

• **Snoring is a danger sign.** Patients who snore or make snoring sounds during sleep may suffer from sleep apnea, a condition in which breathing may stop and start, leading to the lowering of oxygen levels.

The danger: Patients with sleep apnea tend to have more complications during intubation, the insertion of an endotracheal tube into the patient's windpipe (trachea) that delivers oxygen and many inhaled anesthetics. Problems with intubation can be the riskiest part of anesthesia—diminished airflow can cause brain damage or death.

• **Dantrolene should be on hand.** It's the only drug that can reverse malignant hyperthermia, an anesthesia-related complication that can lead to increases in body temperature and a breakdown of multiple organ systems. This occurs in perhaps one in every 65,000 patients. Without treatment, it is fatal in more than 80% of cases. When *dantrolene* (Dantrium) is administered, the death rate is less than 10%.

Hospitals are required to stock dantrolene, but some outpatient facilities might not have it. Don't undergo any procedure involving general anesthesia unless this lifesaving drug is available and can be administered if necessary.

• **A "local" prior to an IV reduces pain.** Most procedures start with the insertion of a large-bore intravenous (IV) needle into a vein.

The IV is used to deliver some forms of anesthesia and/or other drugs during surgery.

Because these needles are so large, they can cause a lot of pain. An injection of lidocaine works to numb the skin before an IV is inserted. Many hospitals don't do this, so be sure to ask for it.

• **The anesthesiologist should be board-certified.** Anesthesia can legally be administered by a medical doctor (anesthesiologist), an anesthesia assistant or a certified registered nurse-anesthetist. Except for the simplest procedures, it's always best to have a board-certified anesthesiologist administer the anesthetic. He/she has the most experience and training. He can administer the anesthesia alone or in conjunction with other professionals. You can find out if the doctor is board-certified by contacting your state board of medicine or the American Board of Anesthesiology (*www. theaba.org*).

How to Get the Best Emergency Care

Joel Cohen, MD, medical director of DoctorCare, a house call practice in Cave Creek, Arizona, *www. doctorcareaz.com*. He has practiced emergency care, urgent care and internal medicine for 20 years and is author of *ER: Enter at Your Own Risk—How to Avoid Dangers Inside Emergency Rooms* (New Horizon).

Emergency rooms are overcrowded and understaffed. You may be treated by an overworked medical student, an exhausted intern or a doctor trained in a field unrelated to your problem.

Find the best ERs: Ask your primary care doctor, pulmonologist, cardiologist or other specialist where to find local high-level trauma or teaching hospitals. Ask the public relations departments at nearby hospitals for brochures promoting the hospitals' areas of expertise. Read hospital Web sites. Consult Castle Connolly Medical Ltd., a guide to top doctors and hospitals (212-367-8400, ext. 16, *www.castle connolly.com*).

Cost: $24.95 for a one-year membership.

KNOW WHEN TO GO

For flu, a twisted ankle, longtime bad back or repeat kidney stone pain, call your doctor for an appointment. Consider going to a good walk-in urgent-care center (their quality varies tremendously) if your doctor isn't available and your insurance covers it. If you can, avoid ERs on Mondays and on Friday and Saturday nights, the busiest times.

Do head for the ER if you're experiencing unbearable or worst-ever pain…profuse bleeding…unfamiliar or severe chest pain, shortness of breath or abdominal pain…sudden arm or leg numbness or weakness…any other signs of a stroke or heart attack (see below).

STEALTH SYMPTOMS

If you are having a stroke or heart attack, the sooner you reach an ER that has the appropriate technology and expertise, the better. When given within about three hours for stroke, six hours for a heart attack, clot-busting drugs may save your life or reduce disability. Optimal stroke treatment can make the difference between paralysis and a little weakness.

Little-known symptom: In older women, shortness of breath is a more common primary heart attack symptom than chest pain.

Other subtle heart symptoms: Weakness… fatigue…unfamiliar indigestion…jaw or upper back pain.

Information: American Heart Association (800-242-8721, *www.heart.org*)…National Heart, Lung, and Blood Institute (301-592-8573, *www. nhlbi.nih.gov/actintime*).

Subtle stroke symptoms: Severe headache…facial tingling…drooping mouth…unexplained dizziness.

Information: American Stroke Association (888-478-7653, *www.strokeassociation.org*).

THE BEST CARE ONCE THERE

At the ER, contribute to the quality of your care. *Be sure to…*

• **Enter riding.** Patients arriving by ambulance get much faster attention than walk-ins. Don't let a friend drive you unless waiting for an ambulance would take too long.

• **Focus on one or two chief complaints.** The more vague you are, the less seriously your problem will be taken.

Example: Mention the new sharp pain in your side, not your arthritic hip.

• **Help the staff to help you.** Don't accept every test or treatment suggested without a discussion. Ask the doctor treating you in the ER to help you decide whether the potential gains of any proposed intervention justify possible risks.

• **Identify yourself and your circumstances often.** Ask what you're being given and why. To a nurse adding medication to your IV line, say, "Do you know about my drug allergies?" Don't assume that everyone has read your chart.

• **Be wary.** Reject medications and prescriptions proposed without logical, compelling reasons. Refuse any risky or unnecessary test or treatment.

Reasons: Older people are especially vulnerable to complications from invasive procedures…standard adult drug dosages can be too strong for older people.

If you are sensitive to drugs or you have kidney or liver problems, tell every ER staff member who treats you.

• **Don't leave too soon.** An ER staff eager to "clear the board" may want to send you home although you feel the same as or worse than when you arrived. Explain that you still feel bad. Ask the person discharging you, "Are you an attending physician here? Will you discuss my case with my family doctor?" You can also ask to speak to the attending physician yourself, but he/she may not be available.

TAKE AN ADVOCATE

It's hard to advocate for yourself in the midst of a health emergency. A relative, friend or neighbor can make sure your needs are met…scrutinize your care…discuss options…make phone calls…take detailed notes. Staff are more vigilant when someone is watching.

Your advocate can request the business card of every doctor who sees you…the name of every nurse who treats you…the name of every test that you're given. You may need these details later in the day or for your records.

Self-defense: With an "ER buddy," visit ERs together and compare notes. Show each other where your relevant medical papers are kept, such as health-care proxies naming the person who can make health decisions for you. Agree to accompany each other to the ER if needed.

Delirium—A Common Hospital Danger

Malaz Boustani, MD, MPH, associate professor of medicine at the Indiana University School of Medicine and scientist at the Indiana University Center for Aging Research.

If you are admitted to a hospital, you're at greater risk for a disorder that very few doctors recognize and treat appropriately…delirium.

Frightening statistic: Delirium—a condition characterized by confusion and changes in memory and emotion—affects 60% of patients age 65 and older recovering from major orthopedic surgery and 80% of intensive care unit (ICU) patients.

What's more, research now shows that the brain trauma associated with delirium also can have significant negative effects on long-term mental and physical health.

Important finding: A meta-analysis published in *The Journal of the American Medical Association* found that older patients with delirium were, on average, more likely to die within 22 months…at increased risk of entering a nursing home within 14 months…and more likely to develop dementia within four years. These patients also are more likely to suffer a serious physical disability.

Equally disturbing: Up to about 60% of delirium cases go unrecognized by the patients' doctors.

The good news: Protocols now exist to help doctors and patients' families prevent delirium in people who are at highest risk and to detect the condition when it occurs. Various approaches to treating and reversing delirium also are now being studied.

WHAT IS DELIRIUM?

Delirium is an acute mental state that is typically characterized by confusion, inattention and disorientation. Delusions (false beliefs) or hallucinations (perceiving something that is not there) also may occur with delirium.

ARE YOU AT RISK?

Delirium is most prevalent among adults age 65 and older. At particular risk are older adults with existing mild cognitive impairment, such as early-stage Alzheimer's disease or some other form of dementia, who are undergoing major vascular surgery, such as abdominal aneurysm repair, or orthopedic surgery. Hearing or vision loss is another risk factor since this can result in diminished sensory input (a trigger for delirium).

Also at risk are people who take anticholinergic medications, such as *diphenhydramine* (Benadryl), *paroxetine* (Paxil) and *amitriptyline,* on a regular basis. These drugs inhibit the neurotransmitter acetylcholine, which is crucial for memory and coherent thought. Disruption of acetylcholine production, which is already reduced in older people, is what causes delirium.

Particularly troublesome are drugs called benzodiazepines, which act on the central nervous system and are used as sedatives. These include *lorazepam* (Ativan), *alprazolam* (Xanax), *chlordiazepoxide* (Librium), *clorazepate* (Tranxene), *diazepam* (Valium) and *oxazepam.* It's now believed that such sedatives—which are widely used for ICU patients on ventilators to keep them from "fighting" the machine—play a major role in triggering or exacerbating delirium.

PREVENTING DELIRIUM

For at-risk patients, a variety of stressors can nudge them into delirium. These include pain, infection, disturbed sleep patterns, dehydration or a fall. Starting a new anticholinergic drug also can trigger delirium.

Prevention focuses on doing everything possible to avoid such triggers. *Steps typically include...*

• **Not disturbing the patient's sleep unnecessarily.**

• **Preserving normal body rhythms.**

How: Turn lights on at 7 am and dim them at 7 pm.

• **Managing pain effectively.**

• **Keeping the patient well-hydrated.**

• **Making sure that the patient's hearing and vision aids are being used.**

• **Keeping the patient oriented to the time of day.**

• **Reducing the use of ventilators.**

Also: Minimizing the use of sedatives when a patient is on a ventilator.

Implementing these measures has been shown to reduce hospital-wide incidence of delirium by 60%.

DETECTING DELIRIUM

Even when preventive steps are taken, delirium remains a risk. That's why hospital staff and patients' families need to be alert to its symptoms, which can arise over a period of just a few hours. *Symptoms include...*

• **Sudden confusion,** change in personality, disorientation and/or memory problems.

• **Difficulty sleeping.**

• **Speech disturbances.**

• **Delusions (false beliefs).**

• **Visual and/or auditory hallucinations.**

These symptoms tend to come and go, so even a brief occurrence is cause for alarm.

Important: While patients with delirium may be agitated, they also can be very quiet and still be suffering from these symptoms.

Many hospitals now use a structured interview called Confusion Assessment Method (CAM) to evaluate at-risk patients. It takes only a few minutes to administer and has proven highly effective at identifying delirium when it occurs. If you think a loved one might have delirium, ask a nurse or doctor to administer the CAM interview.

TREATING DELIRIUM

If delirium is suspected, the goal is to identify and treat the medical condition, such as infection, that triggered the delirious state as soon as possible. Any agitation that may be induced by the delirium also is treated.

Recent research: A program that involves immediately stopping all use of benzodiazepines or anti-cholinergic drugs and administering a very low dose of the antipsychotic medication *haloperidol* (Haldol) is undergoing controlled studies at Indiana University.

In addition, researchers are looking at ways to reduce the use of ventilators in ICUs. In one study, patients were taken off sedatives briefly and encouraged to breathe on their own each day to wean them off the ventilator—an approach shown to shorten time in the ICU by four days, on average, and reduce one-year risk for death by 32%.

Important to remember: Some doctors tend to focus too much on medicating the body without taking into account a drug's effects on the brain. When it comes to delirium, the less medication, the better.

More Care Is Not Always Better Care

David C. Goodman, MD, professor of pediatrics and of health policy, Dartmouth Medical School, Hanover, New Hampshire.

A recent report at Dartmouth Medical School uncovered startling regional variations in the intensity and cost of chronic conditions and end-of-life care.

Their findings: Though some parts of the country offer older patients more costly and aggressive care than other regions *(for example:* The average Medicare cost per patient in the last 24 months of life ranged from over $57,000 in Manhattan to $15,000 in Dubuque, Iowa), there is generally no difference in mortality and in some cases patients even die slightly sooner.

MORE CARE IS NOT ALWAYS BETTER CARE

Problems arise as more hospitalizations expose people to more hospital-acquired infections and medical errors. The risk of harm can multiply when a patient is seeing numerous doctors. Also, more diagnostic tests can find "abnormalities" that turn out to be harmless after many more tests, some of them with their own risks.

INCREASE YOUR ODDS OF BETTER CARE

According to David C. Goodman, MD, a professor of pediatrics and of health policy at Dartmouth Medical School, the remedy to this "needless variability in care and cost" is for the medical profession to develop and institute evidence-based guidelines on best practices. He believes reimbursement for care should reward better outcomes, not just higher volume of services. *Until these reforms are in place, concerned health-care consumers can take these steps to increase the odds of getting the best medical care...*

• **Make sure your doctor understands and agrees with your philosophy about aggressiveness of care,** both overall and at every stages of your illness.

• **Ask questions.** Inquire about the pros and cons, benefits and risks, for all recommended tests and procedures.

For example, ask questions such as: Will the results of this test change my treatment? If not, why should I have it? What is the evidence that this intervention will help me? How will it affect my quality of life? What will happen if I decide not to have it? The fact that something can be done doesn't mean it should be done.

• **Fill out an advanced directive and inform your doctor that you have done so.** (Free forms are available at *www.caringinfo. org.*) Spell out your preferences for care in situations in which you may no longer be able to express your wishes. Think about whether you want invasive life-support treatments, such as a feeding tube or cardiopulmonary resuscitation, and under what circumstances.

• **Compare hospitals.** Check how the Dartmouth group rates your local hospital's management of chronic diseases at *www.dart mouthatlas.org.* In addition to the fact that there are regional trends toward more or less intense care, Dr. Goodman adds that there are also striking variations hospital to hospital, within regions. For example, if you live in Miami, which has a high health-care intensity, go to the above Web site to find Miami hospitals that deliver relatively less intense, but still high-quality, care.

● **Take charge of coordinating your care or assign a trusted and assertive family member to the task.** To avoid the consequences of fragmented care, send reports of all specialists' visits, tests and treatments to your primary care provider. Also, make sure that he/she advises you on preventive measures—diet, exercise, etc.—to forestall complications and hospitalizations.

The high cost of medical equipment and the need for doctors to protect themselves from lawsuit provide motivating factors to prescribe treatments beyond patient wellness. In the end, medicine is a business and more care often means greater profits for health-care providers, from the physician to the hospital to the drug and device manufacturers. Be sure that what your doctor is recommending is truly in your best interest.

Finding the Best Home Care

Charles B. Inlander, health-care consultant and founding president of People's Medical Society, a consumer advocacy organization active in the 1980s and 1990s. He is the author of 20 books, including *Take This Book to the Hospital with You: A Consumer Guide to Surviving Your Hospital Stay* (St. Martin's).

Are you scheduled for surgery and know that you will need help caring for yourself while you recover? Do you or a loved one have a chronic condition, such as advanced Parkinson's disease or Alzheimer's, and need long-term assistance to help with medications and chores of daily living? Home-care services are one way to help you meet these needs.

Beware: Choosing the right home-care service is not easy. *What to ask about…*

● ***What services are available?*** A good home-care agency should offer services from registered nurses (RNs) or licensed practical nurses (LPNs), who can provide wound care, injections, condition management (for example, checking diabetics' blood sugar) and even intravenous treatments…physical therapists, who can help you regain or maintain mobility…speech pathologists to help you regain communication skills after stroke or surgery…occupational therapists to assist you in regaining or improving skills such as dressing, bathing or eating…dietitians to evaluate and suggest nutrition programs…and home health aides, who assist in daily activities such as bathing. Some agencies also can arrange for housekeeping and companion services for those who live alone.

Wise idea: To lower the cost of housekeeping and/or companion services, ask your friends and family members if they could provide those services. Home care can range from about $20 an hour for basic services to $100 an hour for professional services provided by nurses and therapists.

● ***Is the agency licensed and certified?*** Most states require home-care agencies to be licensed by the state health department. Call that department to see if the license of the agency you are considering is current and to confirm that there are no restrictions because of past problems. More than 7,200 agencies are "Medicare-certified"—they meet federal standards and Medicare will pay for some or all of the services provided to Medicare beneficiaries.

Wise idea: Use only Medicare-certified agencies, even if you are not eligible for Medicare, since they are scrutinized closely.*

● ***Is the home care covered by private insurance?*** If you have private health insurance, check to see if home-care services are covered. Are you limited to specific agencies? (Some managed-care plans do restrict the agencies you can choose.) Also consider long-term-care

*To locate Medicare-certified home-care agencies near you, call 800-MEDICARE. Ask for "home-care compare data" (or consult *www.medicare.gov/home healthcompare/search.aspx*).

insurance, since many policies written today include provisions for home-care services. But look carefully at any restrictions on the services you can use. Shop around, because plans vary widely. To learn more, contact your state insurance department.

•*Can you trust the caregiver?* There have been many horror stories of individual home-care providers abusing or taking advantage of patients. Make sure any agency you use does criminal background checks on all employees.

Wise idea: If you are hiring someone on your own, ask for at least five references from people for whom he/she has worked. Firms on the Internet or in your local phone book can perform a criminal check starting at about $20.

More from Charles Inlander...

Can a Rehabilitation Therapist Help You?

When my wife developed a rather severe case of vertigo that caused dizziness, blurred vision and nausea, her neurologist recommended a physical therapist who specialized in vestibular rehabilitation therapy, which focuses on inner-ear problems—the source of the particular type of vertigo she was experiencing. By using head-rolling exercises done while lying down, she was able to make the vertigo go away. Before this experience, my wife had never known that there was a type of physical therapy that treated conditions such as vertigo.

Rehabilitation therapy is a major area of medicine that includes a number of disciplines besides physical therapy. *Rehab therapists work in hospitals, clinics and rehab centers and often will come to a person's home as part of a health-care regimen. Main types of rehab therapists...*

•**Physical therapists** (PTs), who are perhaps the best known in the field of rehab therapy, use hands-on techniques and exercises to treat people who have conditions that limit their abilities to move (such as injuries or diseases affecting muscles, joints, nerves and bones).

When to ask your doctor about PT: If you need help regaining mobility after hip, knee or ligament surgery—or if you've suffered a heart attack, stroke or broken limb. For more information, contact the American Physical Therapy Association (800-999-2782, *www.apta.org*).

•**Occupational therapists** (OTs) develop customized treatment plans to improve a person's ability to perform daily activities—often with the help of special equipment.

When to ask your doctor about OT: If you are recuperating from knee- or hip-replacement surgeries, for example, and need equipment to help you climb stairs or use your bathroom safely. For more information, contact the American Occupational Therapy Association, Inc. (301-652-2682, *www.aota.org*).

•**Speech therapists** specialize in a variety of speech, voice and language disorders.

When to ask your doctor about speech therapy: If you are recovering from a stroke or other disabling condition, such as throat or tongue cancer. For more information, contact the American Speech-Language-Hearing Association (800-638-8255, *www.asha.org*).

•**Recreational therapists** use a variety of techniques, including sports, dance and movement, drama, music and community outings, to treat and maintain a person's physical, mental and emotional well-being.

When to ask your doctor about recreational therapy: If you or a loved one has a disabling condition, such as Alzheimer's disease (mind-stimulating activities, such as games and arts and crafts, may be recommended) or you are wheelchair bound (appropriate sporting activities, such as wheelchair basketball, may be recommended). Relaxation techniques also are taught. For more information, consult the American Therapeutic Recreation Association (601-450-2872, *www.atra-online.com*).

All of these therapies are covered by insurance if the care is related to a medical condition or injury.

"Star System" Rates Nursing Homes

Medicare.gov rates nursing homes as having from one to five stars overall, and also separately on (1) the results of health inspection reports, (2) the level of staffing per resident and (3) "quality or performance," based on 10 different physical and clinical measures. To learn and compare the star ratings of nursing homes by name or geographic location, go to *www.medicare.gov/nhcompare*.

Are In-Store Health Clinics Any Good?

A growing number of retail establishments—including big-box stores, drugstores and supermarkets—have contracted with outside firms to offer on-site health services. In-store clinics typically are reliable and convenient for diagnosing and treating minor complaints, such as colds, earaches, sore throats and urinary tract infections. They operate on a walk-in basis and usually are staffed by nurse practitioners, who can write prescriptions that can be filled on site. Most will accept insurance.

Charles Inlander, health-care consultant and founding president, People's Medical Society. He is author of 20 books, including Take This Book to the Hospital with You *(St. Martin's).*

Do You Really Need Surgery?

Dennis Gottfried, MD, associate professor of medicine at the University of Connecticut School of Medicine, Farmington, and a general internist with a private practice in Torrington, Connecticut. He is the author of Too Much Medicine *(Paragon House).* www.drdennis gottfried.com.

Up to 30% of surgical procedures in the US are unnecessary. This shocking statistic was recently released by the respected nonprofit, nonpartisan policy analysis group The Rand Corporation.

The analysis confirms why it's so crucial to request a second opinion from a physician who is not associated with your doctor before agreeing to any elective surgery.

Procedures that may not be necessary—and alternatives to consider...

STENTS

Each year, more than one million heart patients are treated with angioplasty and stents, which restore normal circulation to the heart and reduce angina (chest pain).

With angioplasty, a deflated balloon is threaded into the coronary artery. It's then inflated to flaten plaque (fatty deposits), and a metal stent is placed inside the artery to prevent arterial deposits from reblocking the opening.

Problem: Angioplasty and stents are overused. A study of more than 2,300 patients presented at a recent meeting of the American College of Cardiology found that patients with stable angina, in which discomfort occurs in a consistent pattern (such as during exertion), who were treated with medications (such as nitroglycerine to dilate the blood vessels) had the same outcomes as those treated with stents—without the dangers of an invasive procedure.

Who is helped by stents: Patients with a recent worsening of chest pain (unstable angina). For people with a significant blockage in the left main coronary artery or with three coronary arteries blocked and a weakened heart muscle, bypass surgery (which involves grafting a vein from another part of the body to bypass the blockage) improves life expectancy.

Who isn't helped by stents: People with stable angina. These patients usually should be treated with medications to control the pain and to reduce blood pressure and cholesterol. Medications are just as effective at preventing future heart attacks and preventing death as stenting in these patients—without the risks of a surgical procedure. Stenting and bypass surgery should be used only in patients for whom medication fails to adequately control chest pain.

CAROTID ENDARTERECTOMY

About 20% of all strokes are related to blockages in the carotid arteries in the neck. With a procedure known as carotid endarterectomy, the blockages are surgically peeled away to improve circulation to the brain and potentially prevent a stroke.

Problem: Severe carotid blockages (generally blockage of 80% or more) occasionally can lead to "ministrokes"—transient ischemic attacks (TIAs), which often precede a full-blown stroke. But if a person has a severe obstruction and no TIA symptoms, the likelihood of having a major stroke is very small. Performing a carotid endarterectomy in those people decreases the chance of having a stroke by only 0.7%.

Who is helped by carotid endarterectomy: People with severe carotid blockage and TIAs have a 13% risk of having a disabling stroke over the next two years. When a carotid endarterectomy is performed, the risk drops to 2.5%.

Who isn't helped by carotid endarterectomy: People with a blockage of less than 60% even if they have a history of ministrokes. In this group, the risk for stroke is higher after surgery—perhaps because the risk of stroke-producing plaque being dislodged during the operation may exceed the patient's initial stroke risk.

In groups of people with severe obstruction and no TIA symptoms, more than 140 endarterectomies must be performed to prevent one stroke. For obstructions of 60% to 79%, there is no convincing scientific evidence for surgery. Nonsurgical treatment, including the use of aspirin and cholesterol-lowering drugs, is preferable in all of these cases.

PROSTATECTOMY

About 180,000 American men are diagnosed with prostate cancer each year and about 30,000 die from the disease. Surgical removal of the prostate (prostatectomy) often is recommended, but risks include infection, impotence and incontinence.

Problem: The majority of prostate cancers grow slowly. Most men with the disease would eventually die from an unrelated condition even if the prostate cancer weren't treated.

In a recent study published in *The New England Journal of Medicine*, older men with early prostate cancer who were treated with prostatectomy died at about the same rate as older men with similar cancers who had no surgery.

Who is helped by prostatectomy: Men who are in their 50s and younger with biopsy findings that show an aggressive form of prostate cancer are generally candidates for prostatectomy.

Who isn't helped by prostatectomy: Men whose life expectancy is less than 10 years at the time of diagnosis. They're less likely than younger men to die of their cancer and face a high risk for surgical complications. Older men with prostate cancer often do better with hormone therapy and/or radiation.

BACK SURGERY

Surgery for a herniated (ruptured) disk is among the most commonly performed orthopedic procedures in the US.

Problem: A herniated disk that presses on a nerve can be excruciatingly painful. But in 80% to 90% of cases, enzymes secreted by the body break down disk material and the nerve pain disappears in time. This can take many months, so surgery promises faster relief.

Disk surgery, however, has serious potential risks, including nerve injuries, buildups of scar tissue, infection and chronic back pain. A recent study in the *Journal of the American Medical Association* compared the long-term outcomes of back patients who had surgery with those who didn't. The likelihood of recovery was virtually the same.

Who is helped by back surgery: People with severe, intractable back pain that radiates into a leg (sciatica) or those with a progressive neurological deficit, such as foot weakness, or a loss of bowel or bladder control, which indicates compression of a spinal nerve, require prompt surgical treatment.

Who isn't helped by back surgery: People whose only symptom is low back pain. Studies have shown that individuals with local symptoms do better with nonsurgical treatment, including anti-inflammatory drugs, acupuncture, massage therapy and physical therapy.

For most people with mild sciatica, the pain usually disappears within a few months as the disk breaks down.

KNEE REPAIR

You shouldn't assume that you need surgery if you suddenly develop pain, inflammation and swelling in one or both knees. Sometimes the pain is from a medical problem such as gout or Lyme disease.

Problem: Even with knee injuries, many surgeons want to repair or remove damaged tissue without waiting enough time to see if normal healing will take place.

Who is helped by knee surgery: People in whom a ligament or tendon is completely severed. For these patients, the knee will rarely heal well enough on its own to restore adequate function and reduce pain. For people who engage in intensive sports, arthroscopic surgery (using a "keyhole" incision) for lesser injuries often is recommended since they may not be willing to wait for healing to occur.

Who isn't helped by knee surgery: For most people with knee injuries, surgery—even arthroscopic—is the last resort. First, rest the leg, use anti-inflammatory drugs and try physical therapy and braces. Follow this approach for at least one to two months before considering knee surgery.

How to Have Successful Hip Surgery

Andrew A. Shinar, MD, chief of the division of joint replacement, and an assistant professor of orthopedics and rehabilitation at Vanderbilt University Medical Center in Nashville. Dr. Shinar is a principal investigator of a clinical trial to determine the safety of weight bearing after total hip replacement.

If you suffer from hip pain due to arthritis or some other condition that damages the joints, you may at some point find yourself among the roughly 200,000 adults in the US who opt for a hip replacement each year. This procedure is considered only when other options, such as pain medications, physical therapy and/or the use of a cane or walker, don't provide adequate relief.

Before you or a loved one contemplates a hip replacement: Be sure you're well informed about several recent advances that can help give you the best possible results...*

IS MINIMALLY INVASIVE BETTER?

Most people who are considering hip replacement now assume that minimally invasive surgery, which is reported to cause less pain and allow faster recovery than a traditional operation, is preferable.

With a minimally invasive procedure, the surgeon uses special instruments and one or two incisions (one to six inches long) rather than the one 10- to 12-inch incision most commonly used in the past. It's logical to think that a large incision causes more discomfort than a smaller one. It's not true, however, that hip-replacement patients who undergo minimally invasive procedures automatically do better.

Latest thinking: Studies comparing minimally invasive with traditional hip-replacement procedures have failed to show that one approach is consistently superior to the other. Researchers speculate that other factors, including the choice of painkillers and the type of physical therapy used after surgery, make a bigger difference.

People who are relatively lean are generally the best candidates for a minimally invasive approach...obese patients often require a larger incision because subcutaneous fat makes it difficult for the surgeon to see within the joint.

Regardless of the size of the incision, most patients leave the hospital in roughly the same amount of time—minimally invasive, two to three days...and traditional, three to five days. Those who are relatively fit usually resume most of their normal activities within four to six weeks. Older or frailer patients might take three months or more to fully recover.

*When exploring any of the surgeries mentioned in this article, remember that surgeons are best at performing procedures that they do frequently. You may benefit by choosing the approach the surgeon commonly uses when performing hip replacement.

BETTER MATERIALS

As the materials used in hip replacements have become more durable—and now that a significant amount of time has passed since the earliest surgeries—it appears that many artificial joints can last the rest of a person's life (20 or more years). In the past, artificial joints generally lasted no more than 10 to 15 years.

In the past, there also was greater concern that vigorous activities and movements could cause the artificial ball to pop loose (dislocate) from the artificial socket —the main complication of hip replacement and a common reason that patients sometimes require a second or even third operation.

Now: Dislocations are rare. At one time, about 3% of patients who had hip replacement would eventually suffer a dislocation. Now, only about 1% do. *Here's why…*

•**Bigger ball joints.** The size of the ball joint has increased from about an inch to an inch and a half in diameter. The larger surface area creates a bigger jump distance—how far the hip can move without the risk that the ball will "jump" from the socket.

New procedure: With anterior hip replacement, the surgeon makes an incision on the front of the hip rather than on the side (lateral) or back (posterior). Studies show that patients who have this type of surgery are only about half as likely to suffer a dislocation as those who don't.

However, the anterior procedure can have a higher risk for other complications, such as nerve injuries or bone fractures. It's possible that surgeons haven't yet developed the expertise that they have with older procedures. More research must be done before we will know whether the anterior approach is better than other techniques.

POSTSURGICAL ADVANCES

•**Movement.** In the past, people undergoing hip replacement were told to avoid putting pressure on the joint for up to six weeks after surgery.

Now: Patients are encouraged to stand up and bear as much of their weight as they would by walking within just a few hours of leaving the recovery room.

Resuming activity soon after surgery reduces the risk for potentially deadly blood clots, one of the most dangerous complications. A Swedish study showed that double the number of patients on a fast-track rehabilitation protocol felt well at three months after surgery.

•**Better pain relief.** A decade ago, patients who had undergone hip replacement were given oral and intramuscular narcotics for pain.

Now: More potent combinations of drugs, including slow-release *oxycodone* (OxyContin) to control pain…and injections or pills of advanced anti-inflammatory drugs—such as *ketorolac* (Toradol) or *celecoxib* (Celebrex)—to reduce inflammation, are typically used.

•**Quicker physical therapy.** With hip replacement, physical therapy has traditionally begun the dayafter surgery. Patients weren't discharged from the hospital until they could perform certain movements, such as a straight-leg raise or get in and out of bed without help.

Now: The same type of physical therapy is used, but it's often started within four hours of leaving the recovery room. A study reported in the *Journal of Arthroplasty* found that joint-replacement patients who received modified anesthesia and painkillers and quickly started physical therapy were able to complete straight-leg raises in eight hours, compared with 73 hours for those following older protocols.

QUICK FACTS—HIP REPLACEMENT

Most people who undergo a hip replacement are over age 60. That's when the main reasons for the procedure, including hip pain caused by osteoarthritis or a broken hip due to a fall, are most likely to occur.

During a hip replacement, the surgeon removes damaged bone, then presses or cements an artificial hip socket into place. A metal stem with a ball on top is inserted into the top of the thigh bone. The ball is then fitted snugly into the socket. Most artificial hip joints last 20 or more years.

Better Stitches, Less Infection

Researchers reviewed six papers analyzing infection rates of 673 joint-surgery patients whose wounds were closed with nylon sutures or metal staples.

Result: Infection risk was three times higher after staple closure than after suture closure. In hip surgeries specifically, infections were four times more likely when staples were used instead of stitches.

If you're considering orthopedic surgery: Ask your doctor which closure method he/she recommends for your procedure.

Toby O. Smith, university lecturer, University of East Anglia, Norwich, UK.

Newer Hip Implants Last Longer

Hip implants can last 20 years, according to Craig Della Valle, MD. In an analysis of data for 124 hip replacements, 96% of the cement-less metal components used in newer-generation hip implants remained in place for 20 years after surgery. These implants have a porous structure that allows bone to grow into the device, forming a more durable bond than implants using cement, which can crack and loosen over time.

Craig Della Valle, MD, associate professor of orthopedic surgery, Rush University Medical Center, Chicago.

Beware of Sleep-Deprived Doctors

Regulations limit working hours of doctors in training but not practicing physicians.

Recent study: Patients who had non-urgent surgery with surgeons who slept fewer than six hours the previous night while on call had an 83% higher risk for complications, including bleeding and organ damage. Research shows that lack of sleep can impair surgeons as much as alcohol intoxication.

When scheduling non-urgent surgery: Check to ensure that the proposed day is not following a night your surgeon will be on call.

Michael Nurok, MD, PhD, intensive care physician, Hospital for Special Surgery, New York City.

Before Surgery, Read This...

Rebecca Shannonhouse, editor, *Bottom Line/Health*, Boardroom Inc., 281 Tresser Blvd., Stamford, Connecticut 06901.

Until recently, if you were scheduled for surgery, most likely your doctor did not have much research to estimate your personal risk for complications.

Now available: Risk calculations based on data from millions of patients evaluate the "risk variables," such as age, obesity, smoking and alcohol use, that predict how well—or poorly—a particular person will do during surgery.

Example: Someone with diabetes is more likely to suffer from post-surgical infection than a person without diabetes.

It's estimated that risk calculations, if used by every US hospital, could help prevent potentially millions of surgical complications annually. Risk calculations prior to surgery "give patients an idea of where they stand," explains Karl Y. Bilimoria, MD, surgery instructor at Northwestern University.

Risk calculations are now used to estimate the risks associated with colon and pancreas surgeries in addition to cardiac surgeries. Programs for other procedures are in development. *Before you have surgery...*

•**Find out if the hospital performs risk calculations.** If it does, be sure you know your risks for the surgery you're considering. Your primary care physician may be able to provide risk calculations for heart, colon or pancreas surgeries.

• **Delay the surgery if it isn't urgent and you have controllable risk factors, such as smoking.** You can reduce your risks for surgical complications by quitting smoking.

Best Time for Surgery

Schedule surgery for 9 am or earlier, if possible. According to recent findings, people who are operated on early in the day may need less pain medication and be less likely to have postoperative vomiting and nausea than patients whose surgery is done in late afternoon.

Reason: Unknown—research is continuing.

Melanie Wright, PhD, assistant professor of anesthesiology, Duke University Medical Center, Durham, North Carolina.

Best Choices for Outpatient Surgery

Charles B. Inlander, health-care consultant and founding president of People's Medical Society, a consumer advocacy organization active in the 1980s and 1990s. He is the author of 20 books, including *Take This Book to the Hospital with You: A Consumer Guide to Surviving Your Hospital Stay* (St. Martin's).

The next time you need surgery, chances are you will not be admitted to a hospital. Instead, you will most likely show up at an outpatient surgery center in the morning, have your procedure and go home that same day. Each year, about 35 million outpatient surgeries are performed in the US—and the number keeps growing.

For consumers, this shift from inpatient (in a hospital, typically with at least an overnight stay) to outpatient surgery (in a hospital or freestanding facility with same-day release) has many benefits, including lower total costs and reduced risk of contracting a hospital-acquired infection. Because you return home from outpatient surgery the same day, you also get to recover in your own bed!

But outpatient surgery also comes with risks. Not all outpatient surgery centers are alike, and for certain patients, the type of outpatient center you choose may determine whether you have a good or poor outcome— or even die. *What you need to know about surgery centers...*

• **Hospital-affiliated centers.** These surgery centers have several advantages. Because they are part of—or affiliated with—a hospital, the doctors and nurses are supervised by hospital medical and nursing directors. When a hospital is inspected by agencies that accredit it based on the safety and quality of its patient care, they also include the outpatient surgery programs.

Insider secret: If something goes wrong with your procedure, hospital outpatient facilities have direct access to the hospital's emergency and other departments that can quickly be called in.

• **Freestanding surgical centers.** Non-hospital-affiliated surgery centers typically are owned by doctors. About 15 million procedures are performed in these settings each year. And more are coming. Freestanding, non-hospital-affiliated surgery centers can be a good choice—especially for common outpatient procedures, such as cataract surgery, colonoscopy, knee surgery and other frequently performed, low-risk surgeries.

Insider secret: If you go to a surgery center that is not affiliated with a hospital, make sure that it is accredited by one of these organizations—the Joint Commission (formerly known as Joint Commission on Accreditation of Healthcare Organizations)...Accreditation Association for Ambulatory Health Care (AAAHC)...or the American Association for Accreditation of Ambulatory Surgery Facilities (AAAASF).

• **How to make the right choice.** If you have multiple health problems (regardless of your age) and need outpatient surgery, it's safer to use a hospital-affiliated facility that can respond more quickly to emergencies. Otherwise, a freestanding facility can be fine—as long as it's accredited. If you opt for an outpatient surgery facility that's not affiliated with a hospital, be sure to ask the staff if the center has an arrangement with an ambulance service and a local hospital in case an emergency arises.

Insider secret: Since many non-hospital-affiliated facilities are doctor-owned, check out that doctor with your state medical licensing board.

Post Surgery Blood Clot Prevention

D angerous blood clots are likely up to 12 weeks after surgery. Patients who have recently undergone surgery are up to 110 times more likely to be admitted to a hospital because of potentially fatal thromboses (blood clots) than people who have not had surgery.

Self-defense: Anticlotting drugs and physical measures, such as compression stockings, can reduce risk.

Jane Green, MD, PhD, group head and principal investigator, Cancer Epidemiology Unit, University of Oxford, England, and coauthor of a study of thromboses in 947,454 women, published in *BMJ Online First.*

If You Receive Poor Medical Care…

Charles B. Inlander, health-care consultant and founding president of People's Medical Society, a consumer advocacy organization active in the 1980s and 1990s. He is the author of 20 books, including *Take This Book to the Hospital with You: A Consumer Guide to Surviving Your Hospital Stay* (St. Martin's).

I n my almost 40 years of helping consumers with health-care problems, the number-one reason that people have contacted me is to find out where to file a complaint about a doctor, hospital, nurse or pharmacist. In most cases, the individual is not interested in filing a medical malpractice lawsuit. Rather, he/she simply wants to report shoddy business practices, including billing problems, or poor health care.

Filing a complaint is relatively easy. But knowing where to file can be tricky. All complaints are investigated. Results vary from state to state, and from board to board, but you will be notified of the outcome, which could include suspension or revocation of the health-care provider's license. Here's how and where to file a complaint when you have a gripe against a health-care practitioner or a facility…

•**State licensing board.** If you have a complaint against a doctor, contact the state medical licensing board in the state where the problem occurred. All doctors must be licensed by the state in which they practice. You can find the address, phone number and Web site of the medical licensing board in your state at *www. aimmembers.org/boarddirectory.*

•**Filing a complaint against a nurse or a pharmacist also is done at the state level.** The National Council of State Boards of Nursing lists all the boards and their contact information at *www.ncsbn.org.* Click "Boards of Nursing" on their home page. The National Association of Boards of Pharmacy also lists each state board at *www.nabp.net.* Click "Board of Pharmacy" on the home page. Hospitals and nursing homes are usually licensed by a division of a state's health department. If you do not have access to a computer, call your state's governor's office for the phone number of the board you are trying to reach.

•**Attorney general's office.** If you have a complaint about a doctor's bill or you suspect fraudulent billing, you also should file a complaint with your state's attorney general's office. You can find contact information from the National Association of Attorneys General at *www.naag.org.* The attorney general investigates and litigates all business and criminal charges that might need to be brought against a licensed doctor or facility. The attorney general's office may refer some criminal complaints to your local district attorney's office.

•**Medicare.** If you are a Medicare or Medicaid beneficiary and have a complaint against a doctor or hospital for matters relating to your insurance, call Medicare at 800-633-4227 to file your complaint. They will pass it along to the appropriate government agency.

All complaints should be made in writing. To ensure a proper investigation, include the full name of the offending party...tell where, when and what time the incident occurred... and include statements of witnesses, if available. Also include copies of bills and other pertinent paperwork, if requested.

Supplements That Speed Healing After Surgery

Supplements can help speed recovery after elective surgery by promoting development of healthy tissue...reducing inflammation, swelling and bruising...and/or minimizing scarring. Before you begin, consult your surgeon and have a nutrition-oriented physician prescribe dosages suitable for you (even for over-the-counter products).

Reason: Some supplements can thin the blood, interact with medications or other supplements, or make you sensitive to lasers.

Supplements your doctor may consider include sublingual vitamin B-12 (to dissolve under the tongue)...a vitamin B complex that includes B-1, B-2, B-3 and B-6...vitamin A... vitamin C...and/or selenium. Typically supplementation would begin about one month before surgery and continue for several weeks afterward—but again, your doctor should make this decision.

Andrew Rubman, ND, medical director, Southbury Clinic for Traditional Medicines, Southbury, Connecticut.

2

Health Care &
Your Money

How to Hunt for Medical Bargains

Recent reports show that doctor visits are down by as much as 7%, which means many medical professionals may be willing to negotiate. But medical bargains can be found in any economy. *Here are the best ways to find good deals on high-quality services in your community and beyond...*

•**Ask the right question.** Many times, getting a discount is as easy as asking for it. Don't be afraid to ask a surgeon (if you are contemplating surgery) or any type of health provider if he can "do better" after discussing the cost of a medical procedure or service. This is especially helpful if a big out-of-pocket cash outlay is involved because you have no insurance or your insurance does not cover a particular service, such as dental care or cosmetic surgery.

Insider secret: Don't worry about getting lower-quality care if you pay a discounted price. Research shows that price does not affect quality when it comes to medical care.

•**Get the ammunition you need to negotiate.** When my wife recently needed a dental implant, our dentist and the surgeon he recommended quoted her a price of more than $3,000. But we shopped around and found two other highly recommended surgeons and dentists who were offering the same procedure at a price of $2,000. When we told that to our dentist, he and the surgeon matched the price.

Insider secret: When negotiating for a discount, you'll have the best luck if you comparison shop and are able to quote a lower price from a competitor.

•**Don't forget about discounts on equipment.** You've probably seen those TV commercials for motorized scooters and wheelchairs. If you're insured, the deal may look good. But

Charles B. Inlander, health-care consultant and founding president of the People's Medical Society, a consumer advocacy organization active in the 1980s and 1990s. He is the author of 20 books, including *Take This Book to the Hospital with You* (St. Martin's).

if you are not covered, you may be able to match the price or do even better at a local medical equipment shop that's looking for customers. And even if you are insured, many local stores will throw in a maintenance contract at no additional charge just to get your business. Hearing aids also are being sold at the steepest discounts in years. With a few phone calls, you often can find deals at 20% to 50% off retail price.

Remember: Hard times mean good deals for those who look for them. So don't put off what you thought you couldn't afford. Like all other businesses these days, medical and health providers badly need your patronage and very often will reduce their prices to get it.

Low-Cost Doctor And Vision Care

Jim Miller, an advocate for senior citizens, writes "Savvy Senior," a weekly information column syndicated in more than 400 newspapers. Based in Norman, Oklahoma, he is a contributor to the NBC *Today* show. *www.savvysenior.org.*

There are a variety of programs and services that provide free or low-cost medical care…

• **Health centers.** Federally funded by the Health Resources and Services Administration (HRSA), these health centers provide low-cost health and dental care. You pay what you can afford based on your income. 888-275-4772, *http://findahealthcenter.hrsa.gov.*

• **Hill-Burton facilities.** There are about 200 Hill-Burton health-care facilities around the country that offer free or reduced-cost health care. Eligibility standards vary by facility, but most require your income to be at or below two times the US poverty guideline (see *http://aspe.hhs.gov/poverty*). 800-638-0742 (800-492-0359 for Maryland residents), *www.hrsa.gov/hillburton.*

• **Free clinics.** Nationwide, there are about 1,000 privately funded, non-profit, community-based clinics that provide care to those

in need at little or no cost. To locate a clinic in your area, call your local hospital or go to *www.freemedicalcamps.com.*

• **Indian Health Service (IHS).** An agency within the Department of Health and Human Services, IHS provides free medical care to approximately 1.5 million American Indians and Alaska Natives. *www.ihs.gov.*

• **Remote Area Medical.** A nonprofit, all-volunteer, charitable organization that provides free health, dental and eye care to uninsured or underinsured people in remote areas of Kentucky, Tennessee, and Virginia. *www.ramusa.org.*

EYE CARE

• **EyeCare America.** This program, coordinated by the American Academy of Ophthalmology, provides a medical eye exam and up to one year of treatment at no out-of-pocket expense for seniors and diabetics. 800-222-3937, *www.eyecareamerica.org.*

Mission Cataract USA provides free cataract surgery to people of all ages who don't have Medicare, Medicaid or private insurance and have no other means to pay. 800-343-7265, *www.missioncataractusa.org.*

• **Vision USA.** Coordinated by the American Optometric Association (AOA), Vision USA provides free eye-care services to uninsured and low-income workers and their families who have no other means of obtaining care. 800-766-4466, *www.aoa.org.*

• **New Eyes for the Needy.** A not-for-profit eyeglass program that accepts donations of used prescription eyeglasses and distributes them to people in need. 973-376-4903, *www. neweyesfortheneedy.org.*

• **Lions Club.** Your local Lions Club can help you find free or discounted eye-care and eyeglasses programs, including the OneSight program (*www.onesight.org*), along with other local services. Call 800-747-4448 to get the number of your state Lions Club office, which can refer you to your community representative, or go to *www.lionsclubs.org.*

What the New Health-Care Law Means for Your Wallet

Maura Carley, MPH, CIC, the CEO of Healthcare Navigation, LLC, a patient advocacy company with offices in New York City, Chicago and in Shelton and Darien, Connecticut, *www.healthcarenavigation.com.*

T he recent federal law overhauling the US health-care system will have far-reaching financial effects for millions of consumers. *Here, a top expert describes what the new law means for you—and how you can best prepare for the dramatic changes to insurance coverage over the coming years...*

FOR INSURANCE COVERAGE
Maura Carley, MPH, CIC

•**If the Medicare "doughnut hole" has kept you from buying some prescribed drugs, relief is on the way.** Previously, Medicare recipients with more than $2,830 in annual drug costs had to pay 100% of drug costs out of pocket up to $4,550. In 2012 the gap starts when drug costs exceed $2,930 and ends when they reach $4,700, but there's a 50% discount on brand-name drug purchases in the "doughnut hole." This discount increases until it reaches 75% in 2020.

•**If you have a Medicare Advantage Plan,** consider whether to switch to a Medicare Supplemental Plan during the next open-enrollment period (usually mid-October to early December). The new health-care law is likely to lead to premium increases and/or benefit reductions for Medicare Advantage Plans, which are offered by private insurers and serve as alternatives to standard Medicare coverage. Medicare Supplemental Plans, or "Medigap policies," also are sold by private insurers, but they supplement standard Medicare rather than replace it. New Supplemental Plans M and N, available through private insurers since June 1, 2010 are worth a look.

•**If you have a long-term-care insurance policy, keep it.** The health-care law includes an optional long-term-care insurance program, which started in 2011, but the benefits offered by this program are capped at $50 per day—not nearly enough to pay what might cost several hundred dollars a day for long-term care if you are disabled. If you're considering obtaining a new long-term-care policy, don't assume that the best option is to go with this federal plan.

•**If you have an adult child younger than 26,** you can provide coverage for that child under your group or family health policy, but explore other options first if your adult child is not already covered.

Currently, each state has its own rules for how long children can remain on their parents' policies. Some force children off the policies when they graduate college...others allow children to remain on their parents' health insurance policies well into their 20s—but only if the children remain unmarried and often only if they are in college or living under the parents' roof. The new rules will not have these restrictions—though remaining on the parents' plan will not be an option if the adult child is eligible for a group plan through his/her own employer or spouse's employer.

In many states, healthy people in their 20s can obtain private health insurance on the open market for as little as $150 per month, less than it might cost to keep these young people on family policies. However, these inexpensive individual policies often have high deductibles, no coverage for maternity care and other restrictions.

Helpful: Starting in 2014, those in their 20s can buy "catastrophic" coverage with lower premiums and very high deductibles.

•**If you have put off going to a doctor** for fear that having any major health problems on your record would make it difficult to obtain insurance in the future, it may be time to make the appointment. Between the high-risk pool that was created in 2010 and the rules prohibiting insurers from turning down applicants because of preexisting conditions, which go into effect in 2014, the new law greatly increases the odds that acceptable coverage will be available to you even if there are health problems on your record.

Special Savings For the Disabled

David Squar, founder of DisabledDiscounts.com, an online resource guide owned and operated by people with disabilities and their caregivers. Squar has researched disability-related issues for more than two decades, ever since his wife, Mara, was diagnosed with multiple sclerosis. *www.disableddiscounts.com.*

Living with a disability, including a chronic illness, presents many physical challenges. And the ever-increasing financial burdens make daily life even more complicated.

Good news: There are discounts available to help people with disabilities bridge the financial gap—discounts that can save hundreds, maybe even thousands, of dollars per year.

Unfortunately, very few of these discounts are publicized. *Here's how to find discounts in your area...*

•**Contact local Community Action programs and Area Agencies on Aging.** These nonprofit organizations are not specifically designed to help the disabled. Community Action programs primarily assist low-income individuals, while Area Agencies on Aging aid seniors. However, a significant percentage of low-income individuals and seniors are disabled, so the employees and volunteers who work for these organizations often know about savings opportunities for the disabled, too. *To help you find the organizations that serve your area, contact...*

•**The Community Action Partnership,** 202-265-7546, *www.communityactionpartnership.com.*

•**National Association of Area** Agencies on Aging, 202-872-0888, *www.n4a.org.*

•**Locate nonprofit groups associated with your disability or disease.** These associations—and their local chapters—often know where to find discounts on the medical supplies, mobility equipment and support services that those suffering from the condition require. Some of these organizations have negotiated special discounted rates with suppliers, and a few even provide subsidized equipment directly.

Associations that do a particularly good job with this include...

•American Liver Foundation, 212-668-1000, *www.liverfoundation.org.*

•ALS Association, 800-782-4747, *www. alsa.org.*

•Hemophilia Foundation, 800-424-2634, *www.hemophilia.org.*

•Muscular Dystrophy Association, 800-572-1717, *www.mdausa.org.*

•National Kidney Foundation, 800-622-9010, *www.kidney.org.*

•National Multiple Sclerosis Society, 800-344-4867, *www.nationalmssociety.org.*

Example: The Muscular Dystrophy Association's Equipment Assistance Program can help MD sufferers registered with that organization obtain free secondhand wheelchairs, hospital beds, patient lifts and other equipment if they lack the financial means and insurance to obtain these things on their own.

If there is no large organization for your disability, contact local chapters of the organizations listed earlier and ask if they can provide guidance on locating discounts for someone with your specific condition.

•**Visit the Web site E-Bility.com to download accessibility software.** The software can make personal computers easier for disabled people to use. Some software is free. (On *www. e-bility.com,* click "Resources," then "Links," then "Software" for a list of programs.)

Example: Camera Mouse, a free download, lets those with limited use of their hands control the mouse pointer on their computer screens simply by moving their heads. A Webcam is required (*www.cameramouse.com*).

•**Sign up for a pair of federal government discounts for the disabled.** *The two excellent programs...*

•"That all may read" program from the Library of Congress mails audiobooks to people whose vision or physical impairments make it difficult for them to read printed books. The program is free—you even can borrow an audiobook player for free and return the audiobooks that you have borrowed postage-free when you're done with them. More than 60,000 audiobooks are available (*www.loc.gov/nls*).

•The National Park System's Access Pass offers those who are permanently disabled free admission for life to national parks and other federal recreational lands. The pass also provides free admission to up to three accompanying adults. (Admission is always free for children.) Expanded amenities, such as camping and boat launching, are not free but often are discounted by 50% (*www.nps.gov/findapark/passes.htm*).

•**Contact your utility providers.** Power companies and communications companies sometimes offer special discounts to customers who have special needs. If the customer service representative you speak with does not know of any such discounts, ask to speak with a manager—disabled customer discounts often are unknown even to the company's own reps.

Examples of discounts...

•Pacific Gas & Electric customers who rely on life-support equipment or whose health conditions make them especially dependent on heating or air-conditioning can purchase power at the lowest available household rate through PGs Medical Baseline Allowance program (800-743-5000, *http://pge.com*).

•AT&T and Verizon Wireless customers whose disabilities make it difficult for them to use a telephone directory often qualify for free directory-assistance calls. Contact AT&T (800-464-7928 or 800-772-3140 in California, *www.att.com* and type "Customers with Disabilities" in the search box) or Verizon Wireless (800-922-0204, *http://aboutus.verizonwireless.com/accessibility*) for details.

•**Ask your veterinarian if he/she knows of any discounts or financial assistance programs for service animals or pets belonging to the disabled.** If he doesn't, ask regional animal-focused nonprofits the same question. Veterinarian professional associations, animal lovers' groups and even state governments sometimes discount or subsidize the cost of animal care for disabled pet owners with limited financial means. *Examples...*

•The Feline Veterinary Emergency Assistance Program provides financial assistance when cats belonging to disabled people require

surgery that their owners cannot afford (no phone number available, *http://fveap.org*).

•The Pet Project offers low-cost pet food, veterinary services and animal care to pets belonging to residents of Broward County, Florida, who suffer from severely disabling conditions or terminal illnesses (954-568-5678, *www.petproject forpets.org*).

•The state of California's Assistance Dog Special Allowance provides $50 per month to the disabled owners of service animals if certain conditions are met (916-657-2628, *www.cdss.ca.gov* and type "Assistance Dog Allowance" in the search box).

Get Dental Care For Less Money

Jordan Braverman, MPH, former director of legislative and health policy analysis at Georgetown University's Health Policy Center, Washington, DC. He is author of several books on health-care policy and financing, including *Your Money & Your Health* (Prometheus).

D ental care is rarely covered by Medicare...few retirees have dental insurance...and those who have dental insurance often find that their coverage is very limited.

Dental bills average around $677 per year for the typical senior, and a major procedure, such as a root canal or a dental implant, can push that tab into four or even five figures.

Exception: Medicare usually will pay dental bills if they are related to a medical incident that requires a hospital stay, such as jaw reconstruction following a car accident.

Some resources that could help you dramatically reduce your dental bills or even provide dental care for free...

HEALTH INSURANCE

Insurance can help pay dental bills. Options to consider...

•**Dental insurance.** If you have access to subsidized group dental insurance through an employer or former employer, it likely is worth having. If not, the case for dental insurance is less compelling.

Dental insurance typically features copayments as high as 50%...annual benefit caps in the low four figures...often long waiting periods before expensive procedures are covered...and usually only 80% coverage if your dentist is out of network. Dental insurance premiums for seniors are about $430 per year for individual plans. That's a steep price for such limited coverage, but not necessarily an awful deal if you have reason to believe that you will require significant dental work within a few years, perhaps because your dentist has warned you that a major procedure cannot be put off too much longer.

If you do decide to sign up for dental insurance, consider the policies offered through AARP. Rates on AARP dental policies often are a bit lower than what comparable individual dental coverage would cost elsewhere.

More information: Visit *www.deltadental ins.com/aarp/.*

If you do have dental insurance, confirm that your dentist will accept it before agreeing to any procedure. Work with him/her to get the most out of the insurance if he does.

Example: If the dental work you require is not an emergency and significantly exceeds your coverage's annual benefits cap, ask your dentist if the work—and the bill—could be spread out over two or more plan years.

●**Private health insurance.** If you do not have dental insurance but have private health insurance in addition to Medicare, this health insurance could include some basic dental benefits. Read the plan literature or call the insurance company's customer service department to find out.

●**Health Savings Accounts (HSAs).** If you and/or your employer contributed to a pretax Health Savings Account while you were employed, you can use available HSA money for most dental services. Unfortunately after retirement you are no longer eligible to make contributions to an HSA.

HAGGLING

Dentists' bills often are negotiable—but only if you discuss costs before having the dental work done. Ask if you can get a senior discount or a cash discount if you pay in cash. Either of these appeals could net you savings of 5% to 10%.

Call other dentists' offices to ask their prices for the procedure. If you find a better rate, tell your dentist that you are on a tight budget and ask if he can match the lower price.

Get a second opinion before agreeing to any major procedure. There's a chance that your dentist could be recommending an expensive procedure that is not necessary. Have your dental files, including the most recent test results and X-rays, forwarded to the dentist who will provide this second opinion so that you do not have to pay to have these repeated. You will have to pay for the second opinion, but the cost of a simple office visit is so much lower than the cost of an elaborate dental procedure that it can be a smart investment if there is any chance that the original dentist was wrong.

IF YOU HAVE A LIMITED INCOME

You probably can get dental care even if your financial resources are very limited...

●**Medicaid.** Medicaid is available only to those with low incomes and limited assets. Eligibility rules and program benefits vary by state. In most states, Medicaid provides at least basic dental care for those living near or below the poverty line.

To find out if you qualify, contact your state's Medicaid Office. (Visit *www.benefits.gov*, type "Medicaid/Medicare" into the search box, then choose your home state. Or call 800-333-4636 for a contact phone number for your state's Medicaid office.)

Helpful: Nursing homes are legally required to arrange for dental care for residents who use Medicaid to pay for their stays. That typically means that they must either bring a dentist to the nursing home or transport the resident to a dentist's office to receive care.

●**Local and state dental associations.** Many have programs that provide dental services for free or reduced rates to those in financial need. Services are provided by dentists who volunteer their time. Eligibility requirements vary.

State and local dental associations can be found on the Web site of the American Dental Association (ADA)—at *www.ada.org*, click on "About ADA," then "National, State & Local Organizations" to find relevant associations. Or call the ADA at 312-440-2500 and ask for your state dental association's phone number.

Example: The Connecticut State Dental Association sponsors an annual "Mission of Mercy" program that provides free cleanings, extractions and fillings on a first-come, first-served basis. Unlike most programs of this sort, Connecticut's Mission of Mercy does not require proof of limited income. See the Connecticut State Dental Association's Web site for more information (*www.csda.com/ctmom/ctmom4.html*).

• **Public or nonprofit dental clinics.** Available in many regions, these typically charge very low rates, perhaps linked to the patients' ability to pay. In some cases, treatment is free.

Your area Agency on Aging should be able to direct you to any dental clinics in your region and might know of other local low-cost dental options for seniors. (Call the US Administration on Aging's Eldercare Locator, 800-677-1116, or use the Locator on the Web at *www.eldercare.gov* to find your local Agency on Aging if you cannot locate it in your phone book.) Your local or state dental association also might know of area clinics.

MONEY-SAVING OPTIONS

If you are too well off to qualify for low-income dental programs, consider these options…

• **Local dental colleges.** Performed for perhaps half the usual cost, the work is done by dental students under the supervision of qualified instructors. The quality of the dental care tends to be good…however, a dental school might not provide a full range of dental services.

The American Dental Education Association Web site can help you find dental schools in your region. (At *www.adea.org*, click "About ADEA" then "Who We Are," and "Predoctoral Dental Education Programs.") Typing

"dental schools" and the name of your state into Google.com also can help you find any schools in your region.

• **Retail dental centers.** Usually located in shopping malls, they typically charge 10% to 20% less than traditional dentists' offices.

Dental Discount Programs

A dental discount program can be worthwhile if you suddenly face a costly procedure. The plans usually give you 10% to 60% off within a few days of your signing up.

Cost: Generally $80 to $160/year for individuals, $130 to $200/year for families.

What to do: Call your dentist's office to find out which plans it accepts and which ones give the best benefits for the type of procedure you need. Do not join a plan based on its advertising.

Alternative: Ask your dentist if he/she will give you a discount if you pay in advance by check rather than with a credit card—some dentists may give you 10% off.

Money, Time-Life Bldg., Rockefeller Center, New York City 10020.

Watch Out for Coding Errors

Look for coding errors on medical bills. Mistakes in current procedural terminology (CPT) codes can change your diagnosis and lead to higher charges both for your insurance company and for you.

What to do: Carefully examine the explanation of benefits or Medicare summary notice you receive when bills are processed. If the charges or procedures seem wrong, call the provider or your insurer for an explanation.

Check CPT codes for accuracy by searching online for theetters CPT and the code number.

Consumer Reports Money Adviser, 101 Truman Ave., Yonkers, New York 10703. *http://ConsumerReportsMoney Adviser.org.*

New Twists on Long-Term-Care Insurance

Scott LeBauer, CLU, ChFC, founder of LeBauer Estate and Retirement Strategies, LLC, and an expert in long-term-care insurance. He is vice president of Prestige Brokerage, Ltd, an insurance brokerage firm based in Denver, and associate general agent at Capitas Financial, LLC, a network of insurance brokerages. *www. capitasfinancial.com*

About 60% of Americans who reach age 65 will need long-term care at some point in their lives. The cost can be the single largest health-care expense they face in retirement. A nursing home bill averages $200 a day—that's $73,000 a year—and often is more than double that in some parts of the US. Assisted-living facilities, which provide help for daily activities such as eating and doing laundry but limited medical support, average $35,000 per year and often cost more than double that. Home health care also adds up quickly.

Long-term-care (LTC) insurance might help make those bills manageable, but it also is expensive, costing thousands of dollars per year in premiums for something that you may never need.

Responding to concerns about the drawbacks of traditional LTC insurance, more and more insurance companies are introducing a "blended product," or "hybrid," approach, offering annuities and life insurance policies that are packaged with LTC benefits. With this approach, the LTC policy is there if you need it—but if you don't need it, the annuity or life insurance benefits can be passed on to your heirs and/or the cash values can be used for other needs. These alternatives may have higher upfront costs than traditional LTC insurance, but they provide more options.

Hybrids generally are best for people in their 60s and early 70s, partly because they don't provide inflation adjustments as strong as those available for stand-alone LTC insurance.

Recent tax rule changes make these alternatives even more tempting. Under the old rules, any payouts of LTC benefits from an annuity or life insurance policy were fully taxed, but under new federal rules, those payouts are distributed tax-free as long as they are used to purchase LTC benefits.

Depending on your tax rate at the time you start to draw on benefits, this will preserve perhaps 25% or more of the value of your life insurance or annuity payouts for LTC.

Here are some alternatives to traditional LTC insurance and ways to identify which might be right for you or someone close to you...

DEFERRED ANNUITY HYBRID

At least six insurance companies, including Genworth Financial, Prudential and Transamerica, now offer deferred annuity hybrids. These typically are basic deferred annuities assuring certain levels of asset growth that are packaged with an LTC option. They work best for people who already have determined that a deferred annuity fits well into their portfolio of investments but who also are seeking LTC protection.

With a deferred annuity, you typically make investments over a long period—often 10 to 30 years. During this time, earnings accumulate tax-deferred with protection against any loss and a guaranteed income stream that starts at a specified date.

What annuities do well is create a specific income, but what if your income needs sharply increase because you require long-term care? That's where the hybrid feature comes in, providing LTC benefits when needed.

Features and levels of protection can vary from plan to plan even more dramatically than with traditional LTC policies. These differences include details of what triggers LTC coverage, what exactly is covered, how long the benefits last and how much is paid per day or month.

A good hybrid product should offer features similar to those of a traditional LTC insurance policy, including coverage for in-home care as well as nursing home care. The waiting period should not be too long, say no more than six months, before benefits start.

Example: A 61-year-old man invests $100,000 in a deferred annuity that earns 2% a year. That annuity may provide up to $450,000 in LTC benefits if he needs them. If he never has to tap into the LTC account and dies at age 80, his beneficiary would get a modest $128,000 payout.

Caution: There can be surrender penalties on these annuities, meaning that if you cash out before a specified date, then you'll pay a fee, which could be as high as 10% of the withdrawal.

Any withdrawals before you need LTC benefits will end up reducing the amount that you have available for LTC costs. Thus, if you use $50,000 of your cash in the annuity cited in the example above (50% of $100,000), you will have $225,000 of LTC benefits remaining (50% of $450,000).

Whether this works out to be the best deal for you depends on whether you will ever need the coverage and for how long…how much you would have to pay in traditional coverage premiums…and how much you will be saving on taxes by using the deferred-annuity approach. (It's best to consult a trusted financial adviser to determine which approach is right for you.)

If you are already invested in a deferred annuity but you still would like to purchase a traditional LTC policy, consider using withdrawals from that annuity to pay premiums for an LTC insurance policy.

Advantage: The recent tax law allows you to make the transfers from a deferred annuity to pay LTC premiums without paying taxes on the withdrawals.

LIFE INSURANCE HYBRID

Another alternative to traditional LTC insurance is life insurance with a linked LTC benefit. At least 10 insurers are offering fairly similar hybrid products. These allow your spouse and/or heirs to be protected by some life insurance policy death benefits whether or not you end up needing the LTC benefit.

Attractive hybrid policies are available from John Hancock, Lincoln Financial, Nationwide, Genworth Life and OneAmerica, some with very flexible LTC benefits, including compensating a family member for parental care.

Let's look at John Hancock's LifeCare product. If a 61-year-old man in reasonable health chooses a traditional LTC policy, he would pay $3,111 every year in premiums. By age 85, he would have paid $74,664 out of pocket and by age 90, $90,219.

With the John Hancock hybrid, he makes a onetime payment of $100,000, which secures a policy with a LifeCare rider that provides six years of LTC coverage—a typical time span in such products—starting with his first claim. (Most people don't live more than two years after going into a nursing home, and a policy covering an unlimited period of coverage is tremendously expensive, so most people don't opt for that.)

One of three things will happen under this 61-year-old man's coverage…

1. If he ever changes his mind and doesn't want the policy anymore, after year three, he is guaranteed to be able to get back his original $100,000. In 20 years, if he wants to quit, he could get back a guaranteed $120,340. The gain above the $100,000 would be taxable as ordinary income. (Before year three, there may be surrender charges.)

2. If he dies never needing the LTC protection, his beneficiaries receive a death benefit of $168,385, exempt from income tax. But be aware that this amount starts to be spent down if he does need LTC payouts. If all the LTC money is used up, there is a residual death benefit of $5,000 for burial costs.

3. The greatest value comes in the form of LTC protection. Our 61-year-old has up to $84,192 available each year for six years for LTC expenses, a total of $505,152. If the $505,152 is not used up in six years, it simply lasts longer. In addition, as noted above, there is $5,000 for burial expenses.

Advantages: It's typically easier to qualify for this type of LTC coverage than for a traditional LTC or life insurance policy. Unlike with traditional life underwriting, no blood testing or medical exam is required and no medical records are pulled.

If you suddenly find yourself in a financial bind—your spouse gets sick or your grown child is in a jam, etc.—and you need money, you can get your principal back without paying a surrender charge or penalty. And unlike with some stand-alone LTC policies, there is no risk that the cost of the coverage will go up in the future—all prices are locked in and guaranteed for life.

Caution: Using up your LTC benefits will leave very little or maybe nothing for your beneficiary in life insurance benefits. If leaving a legacy is critical and/or additional life insurance protection is needed for a spouse, it may be advisable to have a separate life insurance contract.

Long-Term-Care Rates Soar

Long-term-care policy rates due to soar. Companies including AIG, MetLife and Lincoln National have applied for or received approval to raise rates anywhere from 10% to 40%.

Example: John Hancock has recently raised rates by an average of 40%. The exact increase will depend on a policyholder's age and when the policy was purchased. Increases will not apply to Leading Edge or Custom Care II Enhanced policies or to federal workers, whose premiums already rose 25%. Rates were last raised in 2008, by 13% to 18%. The companies say that the number and length of claims have been higher than expected, increasing costs.

What to do: Keep your existing policy if you can afford the rate increase. If not, consider reducing the benefit period to keep premiums about the same.

The Kiplinger Letter, 1729 H St. NW, Washington, DC 20006, and *The Wall Street Journal.*

When a Medicare Claim Is Denied

Judith Stein, JD, founder and executive director of The Center for Medicare Advocacy, Inc., a nonprofit advocacy organization that provides assistance with the Medicare system. It is based in Willimantic, Connecticut, with an office in Washington, DC. *www.medicareadvocacy.org.*

Many seniors assume that they have no choice but to pay when their Medicare claims are declined in whole or in part. In fact, denied or underpaid claims can be appealed—and more than half of these appeals are successful.

APPEALS THAT WORK

When your Medicare claim is denied or approved for less than the full amount, you have 120 days to request a "redetermination" of the decision. The Medicare Redetermination Request Form (Form CMS-20027) is available on the Medicare and Medicaid Web site (*www.cms.hhs.gov*) or by calling 800-633-4227.

The written claim denial that you originally received includes instructions for where and how to submit this form. The claim denial includes an explanation as to why your claim was denied or why payment for your treatment wasn't covered in full. You will need to contest this explanation to win your appeal. Ask your doctor to write a letter responding to the points raised in the denial and explaining why the health care is necessary. Include a copy of this letter with your appeals form, and keep a copy for your records.

Common reasons for denial of treatment and how to fight them...

Reason for denial: The treatment, prescription or medical service is unlikely to cause your health condition to improve. (The denial likely falls into this category if the notice you received includes words or phrases such as "stable," "chronic," "not improving" or "no restorative potential.")

How to fight: The Medicare program is required to look at your total condition and health-care needs, not just a specific diagnosis or your chance for full or partial recovery. Ask your doctor to write a letter explaining why the medical care is needed.

Example: Medicare denied home health care to a patient with Lou Gehrig's disease, an incurable degenerative condition, because the care would not help her improve. The patient successfully appealed, arguing—with her doctor's help—that while having a nurse visit her home would not improve her condition, it could slow the disease's progression and is needed to otherwise care for her various health issues.

Reason for denial: You are likely to require care for a very long time…or have already received treatment for a very long time without a resolution of the problem.

How to fight: Point out that Medicare coverage is not limited to treatments that work quickly. As long as your doctor continues to order this treatment for you, Medicare should continue to cover it. Include a letter from your doctor explaining that the treatment is having some positive effect or expressing an expectation that it will. (Medicare rules do limit how many days' coverage is available in a nursing home or a hospital but not for home care.)

Reason for denial: You do not qualify for Medicare-covered home care because you are not homebound.

How to fight: According to Medicare rules, "homebound" does not mean that you are completely unable to leave your home, nor does it mean that you are confined to a bed. You can be considered homebound even if you leave your home to obtain medical care or attend occasional family gatherings. You must require assistance and considerable effort to get out of the house.

Ask your care provider (which could be a family member, a home health professional or a doctor) to write a letter describing in detail how difficult it is for you to leave your home, and include this with the appeals form.

Reason for denial: The dosage level of a prescription is greater than the dosage normally prescribed…or the drug prescribed is not normally prescribed for your health problem.

How to fight: Have your doctor write a letter explaining why the unusual dosage or drug is medically necessary for you. If possible, have the doctor cite published reports of similar usage.

Example: Your doctor might explain that you are allergic to the drug normally prescribed for your health problem.

Reason for denial: Technical errors were made in the original Medicare claim. The rejection might cite a "coding error" or "incorrect Medicare recipient number."

How to fight: Ask the health-care provider that submitted the claim to correct the problem and resubmit.

DON'T GIVE UP

If your Medicare appeal is denied, you have the right to file as many as four more appeals. Your odds of success improve the further you pursue the fight. While the initial "redetermination" appeal is made to the same group that initially denied your claim, later appeals are made to increasingly independent arbiters.

Appeal #2: You have 180 days from the date your redetermination request is denied to request that a Qualified Independent Contractor (QIC) make a "reconsideration determination." You will have to complete the Medicare Reconsideration Request Form (Form CMS-20033, available at *www.cms.hhs.gov*).

If the redetermination denial includes any reasons for denial not mentioned earlier, ask your doctor to write a new letter. Otherwise, attach a copy of your doctor's earlier letter.

Appeal #3: If your second appeal is denied as well and the amount in dispute is at least $120 ($200 for a hospital inpatient claim), then you have 60 days to file a third appeal, this time with an Administrative Law Judge (ALJ) of the US Department of Health and Human Services. Filing instructions are included with the denial.

ALJ appeals are presented to the judge via telephone (or videoconference if you have the necessary technology). At the beginning of the hearing, confirm that the judge has a copy of any letters of support written by your doctors. Then explain your situation and why you require the care in dispute.

Helpful: Judges are supposed to rule based on the evidence and the law, but they are human. It never hurts to remind the judge that you are living on a fixed income and that you would face major financial problems or even health problems if Medicare fails to pay this bill and/or approve the treatment.

Appeal #4: If the judge turns down your third appeal, you have 60 days to request that the Medicare Appeals Council (MAC) review the decision. The ALJ denial will include instructions on how to do this.

Appeal #5: If the MAC turns down your appeal, you have 60 days to determine if you wish to hire an attorney and file a judicial review in Federal District Court. The amount in dispute must be greater than $1,180 ($2,000 for a hospital inpatient claim) to qualify. (This amount may change each year.) For more information, contact the Department of Health and Human Services at 877-696-6775 or *www.hhs.gov/omha*.

Where to Find Free Expert Medical Advice

Charles B. Inlander, health-care consultant and founding president of the People's Medical Society, a consumer advocacy organization active in the 1980s and 1990s. He is the author of 20 books, including *Take This Book to the Hospital with You* (St. Martin's).

Even though there is an abundance of health information online, you may not find answers to specific questions related to your personal medical diagnosis or treatment. For those questions, you may want to speak to an expert other than your own doctor. The good news is that it's often easy to reach an expert—and, in many cases, that medical information is free! *Clever ways to get information from top-notch medical experts...*

• **Contact a medical school.** Faculty members at medical schools, such as physicians and researchers, know about the latest treatments for rare or complicated medical problems and can be good sources of referrals to doctors and hospitals that specialize in your medical condition. First, check the listings of medical schools at the Web site of the Association of American Medical Colleges, *www.aamc.org/medicalschools*, and look for the school closest to you (in case you need to meet directly with the expert). When you call a medical school, ask for the chairperson of the department most closely related to your medical condition—for example, cardiology or endocrinology.

Insider tip: When you call, don't go into detail about your medical condition. Instead, get right to your question. For example, you may ask, "Where would you recommend I get a second opinion for this problem?"...or "Is the treatment my doctor recommended the only option?"

• **Call a teaching hospital.** Because medical students are taught in these hospitals, the physicians who head the specialty departments are often considered leaders in their field. You can get a list of teaching hospitals in your state at *www.healthguideusa.org/teaching_hospitals.htm*. Follow the steps described above in contacting the specific person best able to help you. Because department heads typically have busy schedules, chances are you will have to leave a message.

Insider tip: Most of these doctors have private practices, so you should be prepared to schedule an appointment if you have a complicated question or problem. But if you are looking for a referral or source of information (such as studies) about a disease or treatment, the doctor or his/her staff often will get back to you with a suggestion at no charge.

• **Go to your insurance carrier.** You may be surprised to learn that your insurance company may have the answer to your medical question. If you have questions about your medical care, call your insurer's nurse/medical expert hotline. More and more insurance companies are putting in hotlines that allow you to speak to health-care practitioners directly. In addition, members of many health plans can discuss their medical conditions and treatment issues with experts such as nurses, respiratory therapists and dietitians, known as case managers or disease management specialists. Check to see if your insurer has such a program.

Yes, You Can Cut Big Medical Bills Down to Size

Susan Dressler, president of Health Claim Assistance, Inc., a medical billing advocacy company located in West Chicago, Illinois (*www.healthclaimassistance.net*).

Major medical problems can turn into major financial problems for those who lack Medicare or health insurance. They can be just as costly for those who do have health coverage if Medicare or insurance won't cover the bills.

There may be a way out. Insurance or Medicare can be convinced to pay up, or health-care providers can be convinced to pare down charges.

BEFORE AND DURING TREATMENT

Before receiving any potentially expensive nonemergency medical treatment...

• **Ask your insurance company to confirm that the health-care provider is in its provider network.** If you have Medicare, ask the provider to confirm that it has a participation agreement with Medicare and accepts Medicare's approved amount as payment in full. If it doesn't, find a health-care provider that does.

• **Read your insurance plan's benefits booklet** (or online benefits summary). Pay special attention to the section labeled "Exclusions" or "Not Covered." If you have any doubt that the procedure will be covered, contact your insurance company.

• **Don't agree to the treatment without knowing how much it will cost** if you do not have insurance or Medicare or if the treatment is not covered by your plan. Confirm with your doctor that the treatment is necessary.

• **Keep a log of every drug, test and procedure.** Do this yourself, or ask a family member to remain on hand throughout your treatment and keep the log for you. When your bill arrives, this log will help you confirm that your bill is accurate.

DON'T PAY WHAT YOU DON'T OWE

Health-care providers, insurance companies and Medicare sometimes bill patients improperly. *What to do...*

• **Compare the bills you receive from providers with the "Explanation of Benefits" (EOB) statements** you receive from your insurance company or "Medicare Summary Notices" (MSNs) you receive from Medicare. The amounts that these EOBs or MSNs say you were charged should match the amounts on the health-care providers' bills. If they don't, call the provider's patient financial services department. It might be a simple billing error. Or it could be a case of "balance billing," where you're billed for the uncovered portion of the provider's charges. (Sometimes charges are combined and it isn't always clear what's been paid for.)

• **Request itemized bills from health-care providers.** Standard medical bills don't always fully break down charges. With an itemized bill, you can spot double billing and charges for services not rendered. Note: You must get these from the provider—Medicare and insurance companies will not provide itemized bills.

• **Scan the paperwork sent to you by Medicare or your insurance company** to determine why a procedure or product was not covered or was only partially covered. Often the explanation will be that a procedure wasn't "medically necessary," that the bill was larger than is "reasonable and customary" or that you were outside the age range for which the procedure is covered.

Your doctor might be able to convince your insurance company or Medicare that the refusal is incorrect. Ask the doctor to write a letter explaining why the procedure was medically necessary in your case or to provide a reason why the bill was larger than usual. You can continue to appeal this decision if it isn't initially reversed.

• **Ask the health-care provider to confirm that the procedure was coded properly.** Insurance and Medicare claims sometimes are rejected simply because someone in the provider's office entered the wrong billing code.

• **Determine whether an out-of-network charge is justified.** If you visited a health-care provider that is not part of your insurer's network (or one that does not have a participation agreement with Medicare), you might have to pay a significant share of the bill. If you visited this health-care provider because of a medical emergency, however, the bills should be treated as if they came from an in-network or participating provider. Sending copies of emergency room reports or police accident reports to the insurance company or Medicare could convince them that this was a legitimate emergency.

Helpful: Out-of-network bills also should be covered if no in-network provider was qualified to provide the type of care required.

NEGOTIATE A LOWER BILL

The amount a health-care provider charges is not chiseled in stone. *To get a better price...*

• **Discuss money before the procedure.** Your negotiating power is strongest before receiving treatment, though it still might be possible to haggle afterward.

• **Ask the provider's patient financial services department for a "charity case application"** if you are financially unable to pay a large health-care bill. If your application is approved, your bill might be dramatically reduced or waived entirely.

Helpful: If you have a stack of bills from hospitals, doctors, labs and other health-care providers, request this hardship discount from the largest company first—typically, the hospital. Once you have written evidence that the hospital has granted you a discount, the smaller medical providers might match this discount.

• **Ask for a discount from the health-care provider's patient financial services department in exchange for prompt out-of-pocket payment.** Some health-care providers are willing to cut their prices by anywhere from 10% to 50%, though others never budge.

Tip: Stress that you want to pay, but the bill is so large that you are financially unable to do so. This is likely to be more effective than creating an adversarial relationship by arguing that the bills are exorbitant and unfair.

• **Hire a professional claims advocate to assist with your negotiations** if the provider won't lower your bill. The Alliance of Claims Assistance Professionals (888-394-5163, *www.claims.org*) or Medical Billing Advocates of America (540-904-5872, *www.billadvocates.com*) can help you find assistance in your region.

Make sure that the advocate you hire has at least 10 years of experience in claims assistance or medical billing, is familiar with the health-care providers that you are dealing with and can provide at least three former clients as references.

Expect to be charged between $30 and $120 an hour, depending on region and experience level, or around 15% to 35% of the amount that the claims assistance professional saves you.

Mail Order or Drugstore? How to Choose...

Charles B. Inlander, health-care consultant and founding president of the People's Medical Society, a consumer advocacy organization active in the 1980s and 1990s. He is the author of 20 books, including *Take This Book to the Hospital with You* (St. Martin's).

Not long ago, I asked one of my good friends, who is a retired pharmacist, what he thought of mail-order pharmacies. Are they as reliable as my neighborhood pharmacy? And what about price?

Here's what he said: "I get most of my prescriptions via mail order. But you must do your homework so you'll know how to best use a mail-order or local pharmacy."

Important pros and cons to help you decide when to use a mail-order or local pharmacy...

• **Neighborhood pharmacies.** If you are filling a onetime prescription, such as an antibiotic for an infection or a painkiller after recent surgery, your local pharmacy is the way to go.

Pros: Your prescription can often be filled while you wait, and you can speak face-to-face with a pharmacist when you pick up the prescription. Some pharmacies will deliver your medication to your home the day the prescription is filled, which is handy when you are ill or housebound.

Cons: Some pharmacies, especially small, "mom-and-pop"–type stores, will not accept your discount prescription drug insurance. Since many smaller pharmacies may not have the drugs your doctor ordered on their shelves, it may take a day or two to get them. Drugs at local pharmacies also are usually more costly than those bought via mail order, and many chain drugstores will not dispense a greater-than-30-day supply even if your doctor writes the prescription for 90 days. (This allows the pharmacy to collect a copay or dispensing fee each time you refill.)

• **Mail-order pharmacies.** They are ideal for medications you take on a regular basis.

Pros: Mail-order prices are usually lower than those charged by local or chain pharmacies because mail-order overhead is lower. Mail-order pharmacies routinely fill up to 90-day prescriptions with a onetime copay, saving you more money. Most major online pharmacies, such as Medco Health Solutions (*www.medco.com*)...CVS's Caremark (*www. caremark.com*)...and AARP's prescription discount program, Walgreen Health Initiatives (*www.walgreenshealth.com*), have pharmacists available 24 hours a day to answer questions, so there's no waiting for information.

Cons: Mail-order pharmacies are not practical for drugs you need quickly, although some have overnight delivery options at a steep price. You must plan your refill orders well in advance (typically 15 days before your prescription runs out). Also, if you need to speak to a pharmacist often, you'll likely get a different person each time you call.

Caution: Some online mail-order companies are bogus. For this reason, the FDA recommends buying only from US mail-order pharmacies that are licensed to sell in your state. Find your state board at the National

Association of Boards of Pharmacy, *www. nabp.net*, and check out the mail-order company you want to use.

Get Your Drugs at 50% Off—or Even Free

Edward Jardini, MD, a family physician at Twin Cities Community Hospital in Templeton, California, where he has served as chair of the pharmacy and therapeutics committee. He is the author of *How to Save on Prescription Drugs: 20 Cost-Saving Methods* (Celestial Arts).

Anyone who regularly uses prescription medication knows how pricey drugs can be.

Fortunately, there are places where you can buy your drugs for less—or even get them for free. The key is knowing where to look.

Important: Although most low-cost drug programs have income eligibility requirements, do not assume that you won't be accepted into a program just because your income is officially too high. Many programs will consider applications on a case-by-case basis.

Best resources for finding low-cost or free medications...

DRUG DISCOUNT NETWORKS

Some groups connect patients with public and private assistance programs that provide discounted or free drugs to eligible patients. *These include...*

• **Partnership for Prescription Assistance** (888-477-2669 or *www.pparx.org*). This large collaborative network of professional medical organizations, including the American Academy of Family Physicians, and private groups links patients with more than 475 public and private patient assistance programs that offer more than 2,500 drugs at reduced cost or no charge. Income qualifications vary by state.

• **Together Rx Access Program** (800-444-4106 or *www.togetherrxaccess.com*). Backed by a consortium of big pharmaceutical companies, this program provides a 25% to 40% discount on more than 300 brand-name and generic prescription drugs. The program targets patients who do not have prescription drug coverage with annual incomes of $45,000 or less for individuals...$90,000 for a family of four (income eligibility is adjusted for family size).

PHARMACEUTICAL PATIENT-ASSISTANCE PROGRAMS

Major pharmaceutical companies have their own patient-assistance programs that provide many—though not all—drugs for a discount, or even for free, to people who cannot afford them. Eligibility requirements vary—even families earning up to $70,000 a year can qualify. Some companies evaluate the applications on a case-by-case basis.

For a comprehensive directory of patient assistance programs, visit *www.pparx.org* or call 888-477-2669. To determine the manufacturer of a particular drug, ask your pharmacist or go online. *Among the pharmaceutical companies with programs...*

• **Abbott Patient Assistance Program** (800-222-6885, *www.abbott.com*). Click on "Global Citizenship."

• **AstraZeneca's AZ&Me Prescription Savings Program** (800-292-6363, *www.astrazeneca-us.com*).

• **GlaxoSmithKline** (888-825-5249, *www.gskforyou.com*).

• **Lilly Cares Patient Assistance Program** (Eli Lilly) (800-545-6962, *www.lillycares.com*).

• **Merck Patient Assistance Program** (800-727-5400, *www.merck.com/merckhelps/patient assistance/home.html*).

• **Novartis Patient Assistance Foundation** (800- 277-2254, *www.pharma.us.novartis.com*).

• **Pfizer Connection to Care** (866-706-2400, *www.pfizerhelpfulanswers.com*).

• **Roche Patient Assistance Foundation** (877-757-6243, *www.rocheusa.com*). Click on "Corporate Responsibility."

Some pharmaceutical companies also offer coupons that can be printed from their Web sites, as well as discount card programs offering savings on some products. Check the drug manufacturer's Web site for details.

PHARMACY BENEFIT MANAGERS

Because of their size, large companies that act as third-party managers of prescription drug programs can provide discounted medications. *Ones to consider...*

• **Caremark: RxSavings Plus** (877-673-3688, *www.rxsavingsplus.com*). This program offers a card that is accepted at more than 59,000 US pharmacies and provides an average savings of 20%. You can use the card as long as you're not receiving insurance reimbursement, including Medicare. For up to a 50% discount, order a 90-day supply by mail.

• *Express-Scripts:* Outreach Rx (800-769-3880, *www.rxoutreach.com*). Designed for low-income patients, this program sets annual income limits of less than $32,670 for most individuals or less than $44,130 a year for couples. A 90-day supply of most medications costs $20, $30 or $40, depending on the drug.

GOVERNMENT PROGRAMS

Federal, state and local governments also offer eligible patients access to low-cost drugs...

• **US Department of Veterans Affairs** (877-222-8387, *www.va.gov*). For people who were honorably discharged from active duty in a branch of the military, the VA will provide prescription drugs at a cost of $8 a month. The prescription must be written by a doctor in a VA clinic. To qualify, you must fill out application form 10-10EZ (available at local VA offices and medical centers or online at *www.va.gov/healtheligibility/application*) and provide a copy of your discharge document.

The VA also offers a separate health-care program, called CHAMPVA, for family members of a veteran who has a permanent disability or who died in the line of duty or due to a service-connected disability—as long as they're not eligible for TRICARE (see below).

• **TRICARE** (*www.tricare.mil*). TRICARE is a healthcare benefit for active-duty service members, reserve members, retired uniformed armed services members, their families and survivors. Widows and widowers of active-duty members also may qualify unless they remarry. The plan includes prescription coverage.

If the medication is obtained at a military treatment facility, it is free. Medications obtained at retail network pharmacies or by mail cost $3 to $22 for a 90-day supply.

•**National Conference of State Legislatures** (202-624-5400, *www.ncsl.org/programs/health/drugaid.htm#discount*). The programs vary widely—and the information is available through state departments of health or social services.

PATIENT ADVOCACY GROUPS

Some groups charge a set fee to help patients find free or low-cost medications. This works well for people who don't want to deal with the application process required for most drug-assistance programs.

•**The Free Medicine Foundation** (573-996-3333, *www.freemedicine.com*). This group will search for programs that can provide your drugs for little or no charge. The onetime fee of $10 is reimbursed if the group fails to find your medication for free. The service is available to people with incomes up to $88,000 for a family of four...$58,280 for couples...and $43,320 for individuals.

•**Indigent Patient Services Inc.** (727-521-2646, *www.ipsc.cc*). A onetime registration fee of $25 per person is required for this program, and each prescription (usually three months' worth of medication) costs $20.

MASS-MARKET RETAILERS

Some large retail stores, such as Walmart, Target, Costco and Kmart, offer low-price prescriptions on generic and some brand-name medications. Walmart, for instance, offers a program that covers many brand-name, and over-the-counter generic drugs at a cost of $4 for a 30-day supply and $10 for a 90-day supply. For information, go to store Web sites or ask at your local store's pharmacy.

Financial Help for Older Americans

Get help paying for prescription drugs, health care, utilities and more. At Benefits-CheckUp (*http://benefitscheckup.org*), sponsored by the National Council on Aging, older Americans can get information about more than 1,500 programs to help with health care, taxes, energy costs and more. Once you find a program, you can print out application forms or apply online for benefits.

James Bragg, founder, FightingChance.com, Long Beach, California.

Important Medical Tests

Jim Miller, an advocate for senior citizens, writes "Savvy Senior," a weekly information column syndicated in more than 400 newspapers nationwide. Based in Norman, Oklahoma, he offers a free senior newswire service. *www.savvysenior.org*.

In addition to a nutritious diet, regular exercise and not smoking, health screenings are the best way to stay healthy as you age. But for the approximately 46 million Americans living without health insurance and millions more who are underinsured, health screenings may be a luxury they can't afford.

Fortunately, free or low-cost health screenings for a wide range of medical conditions are provided through various national, state and local organizations, government agencies and even businesses.

The best way to find these screenings in your area is by calling the health department of your city, county or state. Also check with hospitals, pharmacies, senior centers and your "area agency on aging."

National and local health associations that focus on particular diseases also may help you. For example, to search for free or low-cost cancer screenings, call the American Cancer Society (800-227-2345) or the National Cancer Institute (800-422-6237).

Other national and regional screening programs and services...

CARDIOVASCULAR DISEASE

•**Legs for Life.** This program offers free screenings for peripheral arterial disease (PAD), a "hardening of the arteries" condition that affects an estimated 8 million to 10 million

Americans. Individuals with PAD have much greater risk for heart attack, stroke and even leg amputation. Some screening sites also can test for related diseases, such as abdominal aortic aneurysm and carotid artery disease. Most screenings take place in September and require an appointment. 800-488-7284, *www. legsforlife.org*.

• **Society for Vascular Surgery** offers a list of 23 clinics and health-care facilities around the country that provide a variety of free or low-cost vascular screenings. *www.vascular web.org* (click on "Patients and Families," then "Vascular Screenings").

• **WISEWOMAN Program.** For low-income, uninsured and underinsured women between the ages of 40 and 64, the Centers for Disease Control and Prevention (CDC) offers free blood pressure and cholesterol tests in 20 states. Some sites also offer testing for diabetes and osteoporosis. 800-232-4636, *www.cdc. gov/wisewoman*.

• **Sister to Sister Foundation** sponsors National Women's Healthy Heart Fairs in 12 major cities around the country each year. The fairs offer women free screenings for blood pressure, body mass index (BMI), cholesterol, glucose (blood sugar), triglycerides (blood fats) and waist circumference. 888-718-8033, *www.sistertosister.org*.

SKIN CANCER

• **American Academy of Dermatology** offers free skin cancer screenings by volunteer dermatologists across the US. 888-462-3376, *www.aad.org/* (type "screenings" in search box).

• **Skin Cancer Foundation** operates a nationwide "Road to Healthy Skin Tour" that starts in April and runs through September. 800-754-6490, *www.skincancer.org*.

BREAST AND CERVICAL CANCER

• **National Breast and Cervical Cancer Early Detection Program.** This CDC program is for low-income, uninsured and underinsured women. It offers free or low-cost mammograms and Pap tests year-round in all 50 states, the District of Columbia and five US territories. 800-232-4636, *www.cdc.gov/cancer*.

• **National Mammography Day.** On the third Friday of October every year, hundreds of hospitals and clinics across the country offer free or low-cost mammograms to women in need. To locate a screening site, visit the National Breast Cancer Awareness Month Web site at *www.nb cam.org* (click on "Find a Mammography Center Near You"). Then call the site to find out if it is offering free screenings.

PROSTATE CANCER

• **Prostate Cancer Awareness Week.** Each year, during the third full week of September, the Prostate Cancer Educational Council coordinates with hundreds of sites across America to offer free or low-cost screenings to all men over age 45 and to high-risk men (African-Americans and men who have a family history of the disease) over age 40. The screening consists of a prostate-specific antigen (PSA) blood test and digital rectal exam. 866-477-6788, *www.pcaw.org*.

• **Zero, the Project to End Prostate Cancer** offer free screenings from mobile screening units that tour the country. 888-245-9455, *www.zerocancer.org*.

COLORECTAL CANCER

• **CDC** currently provides funding for 25 state programs that give free or low-cost colon and rectal cancer screenings to people ages 50 and older who have no insurance and low incomes. Specific state contact numbers include Maryland (800-477-9774)...Washington (888-438-2247)...Nebraska (800-532-2227)... and New York (866-442-2262). *www.cdc.gov/ cancer/colorectal*.

• **Fight Colorectal Cancer** offers free information about colorectal cancer research, free or low-cost screenings, diagnoses and treatment options. *www.fightcolorectalcancer.org*, 877-427-2111.

KIDNEY DISEASE

• **Kidney Early Evaluation Program** (KEEP). Sponsored by the National Kidney Foundation, this program offers free screenings for those at elevated risk, including adults with high blood pressure, diabetes or a family history of kidney disease. It also offers free screenings in at least 20 cities on World Kidney Day, the second Thursday in March. 800-622-9010, *www.keeponline.org*.

• **American Kidney Fund** offers free kidney screenings to anyone age 18 and older in the Atlanta, Chicago and Washington, DC, metropolitan areas. 866-300-2900, *www.kidneyfund. org/get-tested/*

ASTHMA

• **American College of Allergy, Asthma & Immunology** sponsors free asthma screenings, mostly done in May, in more than 250 locations across the US as part of National Asthma and Allergy Awareness Month. *www. acaai.org* (click on "Patients & Public", then "Asthma", then "Screening").

MEMORY

• **National Memory Screening Day.** On the third Tuesday in November, the Alzheimer's Foundation of America offers free, confidential memory screenings. 866-232-8484, *www.nation almemoryscreening.org*.

VISION

• **Prevent Blindness America** offers free vision screenings in 24 states and the District of Columbia. 800-331-2020, *www.preventblind ness.org*.

MENTAL HEALTH

• **National Depression Screening Day.** Screening for Mental Health Inc. offers free confidential screenings nationwide for depression, suicide risk, bipolar disorder, chronic anxiety and posttraumatic stress disorder, usually first week of October. *http://mentalhealth screening.org*.

SEXUALLY TRANSMITTED DISEASES

Most health departments and many hospitals and other health-care facilities provide free or low-cost screenings for HIV, AIDS and other sexually transmitted diseases. 800-458-5231, *www.hivtest.org*.

WALGREENS SCREENING TOUR

National retail pharmacy chain Walgreens is sponsoring a free health-screening program across the US called the AARP/Walgreen Wellness Tour. This 3,000 community, two-year tour offers six free screenings—cholesterol…blood pressure…bone density…glucose levels…body mass index…and waist circumference. 866-484-8687, *www.waytowelltour.com*.

3

Drug Updates & Alerts

Dangerous Medication Risks for Seniors

Modern medications are so powerful that they both save lives and endanger them. Individuals 50 and older become increasingly vulnerable to adverse drug reactions. This is when people are most likely to take several medications prescribed by multiple health professionals who often don't communicate with each other.

Additional reasons: Aging slows reaction time and recovery…diminished liver and kidney functions result in altered metabolism and excretion.

Also: Reapportionment of fat and lean body tissue changes drug distribution.

Surprising: The drugs most commonly implicated in adverse drug reactions are time-honored medications prescribed for chronic conditions.

Examples: Diuretics (water pills), such as *hydrochlorothiazide* and *furosemide* (Lasix), to reduce fluid retention and blood pressure… oral anticoagulants (blood thinners), such as *warfarin* (Coumadin), to limit clotting after a heart attack or stroke.

DANGEROUS INTERACTIONS

An often-quoted 1998 study published in the *Journal of the American Medical Association* found that in the US, more than 2.2 million people a year have serious adverse reactions to prescribed drugs and 100,000 of them die, making drug interactions one of the leading causes of hospitalization and death. *Watch out for these…*

• **Drug-food interactions.** Some labels say, "Take with food." Which food? Grapefruit juice often triggers a drug-food interaction that may

The late Robert N. Butler, MD, professor of geriatrics, Mount Sinai School of Medicine, and president, International Longevity Center (*www.ilcusa.org*), both in New York City. He won the Pulitzer Prize for his book *Why Survive? Being Old in America* (Johns Hopkins University).

be good (helps the body absorb certain AIDS drugs) or bad (deactivates some blood pressure drugs and cholesterol-lowering drugs). Oat bran also can make blood pressure medication less effective.

Solution: Ask your doctor or pharmacist which foods might affect the actions of your medications and how.

Although taking drugs with a meal may reduce stomach upset, food may delay the drug's absorption, alter its characteristics or make its actions less predictable. Speak up—ask whether this applies to any medication you take.

Reduced body mass and increased fat make older people more sensitive to alcohol, which interacts with many commonly prescribed drugs and many commonly prescribed sleep aids, such as sedatives and hypnotics.

Danger: Alcohol is a major ingredient in many liquid medications, especially cough syrup.

• **Drug–drug interactions.** Prescription drugs known for interacting with other drugs include cholesterol-lowering statins, such as *atorvastatin* (Lipitor) and *pravastatin* (Pravachol), and blood pressure–lowering antihypertensives, such as *furosemide, propranolol* (Inderal) and *clonidine* (Catapres).

Self-defense: Find out which potential interactions apply to each medication you take now…and whenever a new one is prescribed, ask your doctor and/or pharmacist which drugs or foods not to take with it. Perhaps just separating the food and the drug by two or three hours would be safer.

• **Over-the-counter (OTC) drugs can wreak as much havoc as prescription drugs.**

Examples: Antacids, antihistamines and heavy use of nonsteroidal anti-inflammatory drugs (NSAIDs), such as aspirin and *ibuprofen* (Advil, Motrin). According to an estimate by James Fries, MD, professor emeritus at Stanford University School of Medicine, NSAID-induced gastrointestinal bleeding sends about 76,000 Americans to the hospital each year… and kills about 10% of them.

Antacids (Milk of Magnesia, Tums, Amphojel) can reduce the effectiveness of antibiotics, such as *tetracycline* and *ciprofloxacin*

(Cipro)…antihypertensive drugs, such as *propranolol* and *captopril* (Capoten)…and heartburn drugs, such as *ranitidine* (Zantac) and *famotidine* (Pepcid AC). But antacids can also increase the potency of *valproic acid* (Depakote/Depakene), for seizures and bipolar disorder…*sulfonylurea* (Glucotrol), for diabetes…*quinidine*, for arrhythmias…and *levodopa*, for Parkinson's disease.

The older (first-generation) antihistamines, taken widely for allergies, colds and flu, can have dangerous interactions when taken with other drugs that cause drowsiness, such as antidepressants, alcohol, pain relievers, muscle relaxants and medications for seizures or anxiety.

Examples: *Brompheniramine* (in Robitussin Allergy & Cough) and *doxylamine* (in NyQuil).

The examples listed above are drops in the bucket. Check your own medications.

PERILOUS FALSE ALARM

Some drugs can drain certain vitamins from the body. If these vitamins aren't replaced, resulting symptoms may mimic those of dementia or other age-related conditions.

Examples: Tuberculosis drugs can deplete vitamin B-6, leading to amnesia, and vitamin-B complex, leading to apparent senility. Seizure drugs (anticonvulsants) can deplete vitamin D, leading to hearing and walking problems and general weakness. An older person displaying characteristics that are associated with dementia may just have an easily corrected vitamin deficiency.

MEDICATION ERRORS

As it happens, the drugs found by the United States Pharmacopoeia* to be most frequently implicated in medication errors are commonly taken by seniors.

Examples: Insulin (for diabetes)…*warfarin* and *heparin* (to control clotting, such as in cardiovascular disease)…*albuterol* (Proventil, for asthma or bronchitis).

The Joint Commission (formerly the Joint Commission on Accreditation of Healthcare

*The nonprofit public standards–setting authority for prescription and OTC medicines, dietary supplements and other health-care products made and sold in the US.

Organizations) recently asked hospitals to start providing every hospital patient with a list of all his/her prescribed medications and instructions for taking new ones. Patients, the Joint Commission said, should be encouraged to show the list to everyone providing care in and out of the hospital.

Have an advocate—a family member or friend—with you when you're in the hospital. Anyone hospitalized in my family is attended by a relative night and day.

Potentially fatal danger: Poor communication about meds when a patient is moved, such as from a critical care unit to a general medical unit or from one health-care facility to another...or when nurses or other caregivers change shifts.

Self-defense: If you don't get a list from the hospital, maintain and hand out a list of your own. A free form is available online at *www.jointcommission.org*. Under "Topics," click on "Speak Up", then "Help Avoid Mistakes with Your Medicines." Also, question every drug you're given by anyone, anywhere, anytime.

Vitamins and Herbs That Don't Mix with Common Medications

George T. Grossberg, MD, the Samuel W. Fordyce Endowed Chair in Geriatric Psychiatry at St. Louis University School of Medicine in St. Louis, Missouri. He is the coauthor of *The Essential Herb-Drug-Vitamin Interaction Guide* (Broadway).

Most doctors warn their patients about the potential dangers of combining some medications, but few take the time—and some are not well-informed enough—to offer guidance on the harmful effects of taking certain vitamins and/or herbs with prescription drugs.

Recent study: Among 132 pharmacists surveyed, 47% had seen a patient with a suspected side effect from a vitamin-drug or herb-drug interaction, according to research published in the *Annals of Pharmacotherapy*.

Hidden danger: The problem is particularly common among Americans over age 65, who comprise about 14% of the US population but take 40% of all drugs, vitamins and herbs. Older people also are more sensitive to the side effects of vitamin-drug or herb-drug interactions due to changes in metabolism and the brain.

HARMFUL INTERACTIONS

When some vitamins and/or herbs are taken with certain drugs, the supplement can...

• **Weaken the effectiveness of the drug.**

Example: The herb astragalus, which is used to boost immunity, may reduce the immunosuppressive effects of such drugs as *cortisone.*

Strengthen the effectiveness of the drug, causing a type of drug overdose.

Example: Black cohosh, an herb used to control the symptoms of menopause, can lower blood pressure. If taken with an antihypertensive medication, it can cause hypotension (severely low blood pressure) with symptoms such as dizziness and fatigue.

VITAMIN-DRUG INTERACTIONS

Vitamins that are among the most likely to cause dangerous interactions with drugs...*

• **Vitamin A promotes immunity, proper bone growth and healthy skin.** It also plays a role in night vision and the growth and maintenance of cells of the gastrointestinal tract.

Recommended Dietary Allowance (RDA): 2,300 international units (IU) for women...3,000 IU for men.

Supplemental vitamin A may interact with drugs including: The anticoagulant warfarin—vitamin A can increase the risk for bleeding and bruising.

• **Vitamin B-6** is involved in digestion, the production of red blood cells and the maintenance of a healthy brain and nervous system.

RDA: 1.3 mg for all adults ages 19 to 50...1.5 mg for women over age 50...1.7 mg for men over age 50.

*Multivitamins or individual supplements containing nutrients that exceed the RDA may cause interactions.

Supplemental vitamin B-6 may interact with drugs including: Amiodarone (Cordarone), taken for heart arrhythmias—B-6 may increase skin sensitivity to sunlight…*carbidopa* and *levodopa* (Sinemet), taken for Parkinson's disease—B-6 may interfere with the medication's effectiveness…*theophylline* (Elixophyllin), taken for asthma—B-6 may increase the risk for seizures induced by theophylline.

• **Vitamin C** is important for immunity and helps the body manufacture and repair blood vessels, skin, muscles, teeth, bones, tendons, ligaments, hormones and neurotransmitters.

RDA: 75 mg for women…90 mg for men.

Supplemental vitamin C may interact with drugs including: The anticoagulants *heparin* (Hepalean) or warfarin, taken for cardiovascular disease—vitamin C may reduce the effectiveness of these drugs.

• **Calcium** helps build strong bones and assists in wound healing, blood clotting, cellular metabolism and muscle contraction.

Adequate intake (AI):** 1,000 mg for adults ages 19 to 50…1,200 mg for adults over age 50.

Supplemental calcium may interact with drugs including: Digitalis drugs, such as *digoxin* (Lanoxin), which improve the heart's strength and efficiency—calcium can decrease digitalis levels…*aminoglycoside* antibiotics—calcium can increase the risk for kidney failure.

HERB-DRUG INTERACTIONS

Herbs that are among the most likely to cause dangerous interactions with drugs…

• **Valerian,** a mild sedative, is used to treat insomnia and anxiety.

Lowest effective dose: 400 mg, up to two hours before bedtime.

Valerian may interact with drugs including: A selective serotonin reuptake inhibitor (SSRI), such as *sertraline* (Zoloft), or tricyclic antidepressant, such as *desipramine* (Norpramin)—valerian can cause excessive sedation, depression and mental impairment.

**AI is sometimes used in place of RDA.

• **Grapeseed extract** is rich in powerful antioxidants called *procyanidolic oligomers* (PCOs). It is used to treat high blood pressure, heart disease, varicose veins and macular degeneration.

Lowest effective dose: 75 mg daily.

Grapeseed extract may interact with drugs including: A blood-thinning medication, such as aspirin or warfarin—grapeseed extract can increase the risk for bleeding and bruising.

• **Yohimbe** is an African herb that improves blood flow. It is sometimes prescribed for men who have erectile dysfunction.

Lowest effective dose: 5.4 mg daily.

Yohimbe may interact with drugs including: The allergy medication phenylephrine, found in over-the-counter products, such as Vicks Sinex Nasal Spray…or the asthma medication *albuterol* (Proventil)—yohimbe can cause a potentially dangerous increase in heart rate and blood pressure.

• **Apple cider vinegar** is a popular folk remedy that has been used to treat arthritis, high blood pressure and leg cramps.

Lowest effective dose: One tablespoon daily.

Apple cider vinegar may interact with drugs including: Medication for congestive heart failure and/or high blood pressure, such as *digoxin, furosemide* (Lasix) and *hydrochlorothiazide* (Microzide)—apple cider vinegar can increase the risk for *hypokalemia (*low potassium levels), which can further complicate heart disease.

• **Evening primrose oil** is derived from the seed of the evening primrose plant. This herbal supplement delivers high levels of gamma-linolenic acid (GLA), an essential fatty acid. It is used to treat premenstrual syndrome, hot flashes, high blood pressure (during pregnancy) and rheumatoid arthritis.

Lowest effective dose: 540 mg daily.

Evening primrose oil may interact with drugs including: Antiseizure medications, such as *clonazepam* (Klonopin)—evening primrose oil can lower the effectiveness of such drugs, making a seizure more likely.

More from Dr. George Grossberg...

How to Stay Safe

You can take vitamins and/or herbs safely and effectively if you use them with the supervision of your primary care physician.

Talk to your doctor about using a vitamin or an herbal supplement before taking the product.

Helpful: Take a bottle of the supplement to your next appointment to help your doctor determine whether it is likely to cause adverse interactions with any of your medications. If you don't have an appointment scheduled, call your doctor and read the supplement's ingredient list to him/her. Also, check the Web site of the National Institutes of Health's Office of Dietary Supplements, *www.ods.od.nih.gov*, for information about vitamins and herbs that interact with prescription medications.

Safest approach: The lower the dose of the vitamin and/or herb, the less likely it is to interact with a drug. Ask your doctor about taking the recommended dietary allowance (RDA) for vitamins or minerals and/or the lowest dose listed on the label of an herbal supplement.

Avoid Dangerous Supplement–Drug Interactions

Catherine Ulbricht, PharmD, senior attending pharmacist at Massachusetts General Hospital in Boston. She is coeditor of *Natural Standard Herb & Supplement Handbook: The Clinical Bottom Line* (C.V. Mosby).

An increasing number of American adults now take herbs or nutritional supplements for a wide range of ailments, including arthritis, depression and nausea.

Problem: Unlike prescription drugs, herbal supplements are not regulated by the FDA, so there are no labeling requirements regarding potential interactions with prescription or over-the-counter (OTC) drugs.

Whether they are used in capsules, extracts, liquid, cream or tea, many herbal products can be harmful when combined with prescription or OTC medication.

What happens: Some herbs can interact with medications by affecting their absorption, metabolism or by other mechanisms. As a result, drug levels may become too high or too low.

Catherine Ulbricht, PharmD, a pharmacist at Massachusetts General Hospital and one of the country's leading experts on herb-drug interactions, offers her advice on commonly used herbs...*

CAYENNE

Cayenne is also known as chili or red pepper. Cayenne's active component, capsaicin, which is used as a spice in food, is commonly used as a pain reliever in prescription medicine, often for osteoarthritis, rheumatoid arthritis and diabetic neuropathy (nerve pain resulting from diabetes).

Possible interactions: When combined with aspirin, *ibuprofen* (Advil) or any other nonsteroidal anti-inflammatory drug (NSAID), cayenne may increase these drugs' side effects, especially gastrointestinal (GI) upset. In some people, cayenne also may enhance the pain-relieving action of NSAIDs.

Like NSAIDs, cayenne can have a blood-thinning effect, increasing the risk for bleeding. (When used topically, this risk is lessened because lower doses of cayenne are absorbed.) Do not use cayenne if you take a *monoamine oxidase* (MAO) inhibitor antidepressant, such as *phenelzine* (Nardil).

Caution: Avoid getting cayenne (in any form) in your eyes, nose, etc., where it can cause burning or stinging.

GINGER

Ginger is a popular antidote for nausea and/or vomiting. Research suggests that ginger also may help prevent blood clotting and reduce blood sugar levels.

Possible interactions: If you take an NSAID or antiplatelet drug, such as *clopidogrel* (Plavix), ginger may further increase bleeding risk.

*Check with your doctor or pharmacist before taking any herbal product.

51

GREEN TEA

As scientific evidence has revealed the disease-fighting benefits of antioxidant-rich green tea, an increasing number of Americans have begun drinking it—or, in some cases, taking it in capsules or extracts. Although new research questions the health benefits of green tea, some studies have found that it may help prevent cancer, especially malignancies of the GI tract, breast and lung. More investigation is needed to confirm these findings. To read more about clinical trials on green tea, go to the National Institutes of Health's Web site, *www.clinicaltrials.gov.*

Possible interactions: Most forms of green tea contain caffeine, which may intensify the effect of any medication that increases blood pressure and/or heart rate, such as the decongestant *pseudoephedrine* (Sudafed). Decaffeinated green tea is available, but this form still contains some caffeine and may not have the same health benefits.

Caution: People with arrhythmia (abnormal heart rhythm) should consume no more than moderate amounts of green tea, determined by their personal sensitivity to caffeine.

LICORICE

Licorice contains a compound known as *glycyrrhizin*, which has antiviral properties. For this reason, licorice is often used to treat the common cold and herpes infections (including cold sores). However, some studies have shown that topical licorice cream does not help genital herpes.

Possible interactions: Licorice can interact with diuretics, such as *chlorothiazide* (Diuril) and *furosemide* (Lasix), and any medication that affects hormone levels, such as birth control pills.

Caution: It also may increase blood pressure and bleeding risk.

MILK THISTLE

This popular herb is used for liver problems, including cirrhosis and hepatitis. These benefits are well documented by research.

Possible interactions: Milk thistle may interfere with how the liver breaks down certain drugs, such as antibiotics and antifungals.

Milk thistle also may interact with the *anticonvulsant phenytoin* (Dilantin). The herb may lower blood sugar and cause heartburn, nausea and vomiting or other GI upset.

Caution: If you take diabetes medication, do not use milk thistle unless you are supervised by a health-care professional.

ST. JOHN'S WORT

St. John's wort is commonly used for depression. Several studies show that it may work as well as a prescription antidepressant, such as *paroxetine* (Paxil), for mild to moderate depressive disorders. More research is needed before St. John's wort can be recommended for severe depression.

Possible interactions: St. John's wort may interact with drugs that are broken down by the liver, including birth control pills, the blood thinner *warfarin* (Coumadin) and migraine medications. People who take St. John's wort may experience stomach upset, fatigue, sexual dysfunction, dizziness or headaches.

Caution: St. John's wort should not be taken with prescription antidepressant medication.

More Supplement–Drug Combinations to Avoid

Joe Graedon, MS, pharmacologist, Durham, North Carolina, and author of *Best Choices from the People's Pharmacy* (NAL Trade).

Dangerous supplement-medication interactions to look out for...plus healthful alternatives.

• **Licorice,** taken for digestive problems such as heartburn, does not go well with diuretics for high blood pressure—the combination can cause potassium levels to drop, interfering with normal heart rhythms.

Better: Ginger tea.

• **Turmeric,** taken for arthritis pain, can react with blood thinners, increasing the possibility of bleeding.

Better: Antioxidant-rich juices, such as grape, pomegranate and cherry.

• **Feverfew,** a migraine remedy, also should not be taken with blood thinners.

Better: Get enough magnesium through supplements—people with low levels of it are more prone to migraines.

Note: Doses of more than 300 milligrams (mg) of magnesium a day can cause diarrhea.

Medication Mix-Ups Can Be Deadly

Milap C. Nahata, PharmD, a professor and chairman of pharmacy practice and administration in the College of Pharmacy at Ohio State University and associate director of pharmacy at the Ohio State University Medical Center, both in Columbus.

When you take a drug, you expect it to ease your symptoms or cure your medical problem. However, the drugs you take can sometimes cause serious harm—or even death—if there is a medication "error" (such as taking a wrong dose or an inappropriate drug).

Frightening statistic: Each year, up to 1.5 million Americans are affected by preventable errors involving both prescription and over-the-counter (OTC) drugs, according to the Institute of Medicine. Most of these errors are minor and unlikely to cause serious problems—with dangerous exceptions.

Example: A baby in one hospital needed 0.5 mg of morphine for sedation and/or pain relief. The doctor who wrote the prescription didn't put a "0" before the decimal point. A nurse who didn't see the decimal point gave the child 5 mg. This tenfold error was doubled when the child, who later died as a result of the overdose, was given an additional excessive dose.

WHAT'S GOING WRONG?

Medication errors can occur in several ways. Often, patients skip doses, stop a drug without medical advice or neglect to tell their doctors about other drugs and/or supplements they are taking, exposing themselves to the possibility of a dangerous interaction.

But health-care professionals also can play a role in medication errors. *Common reasons for medication errors that occur in doctors' offices and at pharmacies and hospitals...*

• **Incorrect doses.** Most prescription drugs come in standard doses, such as 10 mg or 100 mg. On occasion, doctors may accidentally omit a "0" or jot down a decimal point that's difficult to see.

Self-defense: When your doctor hands you a prescription, confirm the dose (the specific number of milligrams, for example) before leaving his/her office.

ABBREVIATIONS

When writing prescriptions, doctors use abbreviations that can be easily misread by pharmacists.

Example: The abbreviation "QOD" means every other day..."QD" means every day... "BID" means twice a day...and "QID" is four times a day. If the pharmacist reads "QD" as "QID," the patient will be taking four times the recommended dose, which can lead to side effects.

Self-defense: Make sure you understand the intended dosing instructions (for example, once or twice daily) before leaving your doctor's office. Then confirm the drug and dose with the pharmacist before leaving the pharmacy to ensure that you're receiving both the correct medication and dose.

WRONG DRUGS

There are more than 10,000 prescription drugs and as many as 300,000 OTC medications on the market. Some of these drugs have similar names that are easily confused—either by the doctor who is writing the prescription or by the pharmacist who's filling it.

Example: It's easy to confuse *bupropion,* an antidepressant, with *buspirone,* an anti-anxiety drug.

Self-defense: Know the exact name of the drug you're supposed to be taking (both the generic name and the brand name)...why you're taking it...and what it looks like—consult the *Physicians' Desk Reference* online at *www.pdrhealth.com* to view photographs of commonly prescribed drugs.

Check the drug name before you leave your doctor's office. Repeat the name out loud when you order the drug at the pharmacy. In the example above, bupropion is the generic name for the brand-name drug Wellbutrin. Buspirone is the generic name for Buspar.

Helpful: Prescription tablets and capsules are imprinted with numbers that are specific to particular drugs and doses from specific manufacturers. When you first fill a prescription, write down the manufacturer's number and keep it in a safe place. When you get the prescription refilled, double-check to ensure that it has the same number.

OTHER PRECAUTIONS TO TAKE

If you take medication…

• **Consult the pharmacist.** About 95% of patients don't ask questions about how to use their medication, according to research published by the California Board of Pharmacy and other groups. These patients may not understand not only how much of the medication to take or when and how often to take it, but also what side effects might occur or how to tell if the drug is working.

Self-defense: Consult with the pharmacist every time you start a new prescription—particularly if you're also taking other drugs with which it might interact.

Important: Many people who work behind the counter are pharmacy technicians. When asking questions about a medication, make sure that you're talking to a pharmacist. Look for the title "Pharmacist" or "RPh" (Registered Pharmacist) on the person's jacket (or nameplate)—or ask the person's title.

Helpful: A patient who takes multiple drugs can prevent many errors by buying them all at the same pharmacy. Virtually all pharmacies now have computers that track medications and will automatically give an alert if a patient adds a new drug that might interact with others that he is taking.

• **Tell your doctor about everything you take.** Adults over age 65 account for 13% of the US population but take one-third of all prescription drugs. Anyone taking numerous drugs may experience side effects and/or drug interactions—many of which could be avoided

if patients periodically reviewed medication use with their doctors and/or pharmacists.

Doctors usually ask patients what medications they're currently taking. They don't always ask about—or patients fail to mention—supplements and/or OTC drugs.

Self-defense: Every time you see your doctor, bring a list that includes everything you're taking. Don't assume that supplements, including herbs, don't count. Many of these products can interact with prescription drugs.

Can I Crush My Pills to Make Them Easier to Swallow?

Not always. Crushing a pill makes it easier to swallow when mixed with food or liquid but may reduce its effectiveness. A crushed pill releases its active ingredients immediately, which may not be appropriate for some extended-release drugs. Also, some tablets contain a coating for easier swallowing and to help mask the taste. If the pill is crushed, it may be more difficult to swallow due to the bitter taste. If your pill has a small line called a score etched in it, this indicates that you can split the tablet, and it is probably safe to crush. Ask your pharmacist first to be sure.

Susan C. Winckler, RPh, president and CEO, Food and Drug Law Institute, Washington, DC.

Pay Attention to Expiration Dates

Manufacturers guarantee product potency only until the expiration date. The medicine may be good later—but you can't be sure. Over-the-counter products in the original unopened manufacturers' packages kept under optimal conditions may last two years or more. Most prescription medicine is dispensed by pharmacists in patient-specific packaging and probably won't last as long.

Storage conditions also affect potency.

Example: If you keep medicine in a so-called medicine chest—a bathroom cabinet—it will degrade more quickly than if you store it away from bathroom heat and humidity.

Bottom line: After the expiration date, medicine should be discarded.

Susan C. Winckler, RPh, president and CEO, Food and Drug Law Institute, Washington, DC.

The Awesome Healing Power of "Blended" Medicine

Brent A. Bauer, MD, director of the Complementary and Integrative Medicine Program and a physician in the department of internal medicine at the Mayo Clinic in Rochester, Minnesota.

With more and more Americans embracing elements from both worlds, an increasing number of physicians are prescribing a combination of conventional and complementary treatments—an approach known as "blended" medicine.

Blended treatments that you should know about...

HIGH CHOLESTEROL

Every year, about 1 million Americans have a heart attack, and nearly half a million die from heart disease—in part, because of uncontrolled high cholesterol.

Conventional approach: The use of cholesterol-lowering statin drugs, such as *pravastatin* (Pravachol) and *atorvastatin* (Lipitor). People who take these drugs and modify their diets can sometimes reduce their risk for a heart attack by 25% to 50%.

Drawbacks: Statins, particularly at high doses, can cause severe muscle pain and other side effects in up to 30% of patients. Also, statins have little effect on triglycerides, another type of blood fat that's linked to heart disease.

Blended approach: By using plant stanols and sterols (modified plant extracts found in a number of "functional" foods, including butter substitutes such as Benecol and Promise activ Light), people with mildly elevated cholesterol often can control their cholesterol levels.

Those with higher cholesterol levels can combine one of the butter substitutes described above with a statin drug for better results than from either treatment alone. In some cases, the medication dosage can be reduced, which lowers the risk for drug side effects.

For example, people who eat the equivalent of three pats of one of these butter substitutes daily can achieve reductions of 10% to 20% in LDL "bad" cholesterol—in addition to the reductions achieved with medications.

Helpful: Many people with high cholesterol also have elevated triglycerides—fish oil (1,000 mg to 3,000 mg daily from a supplement) reduces triglycerides by up to 50% in some patients.*

Remember: When striving to reduce cholesterol levels, start by exercising regularly and following a healthful diet, such as the Mediterranean diet.

BACK PAIN

Four out of five Americans suffer from back pain (due to injury, back strain or a herniated disk, for example) at some time in their lives.

Conventional approach: A combination of short-term rest, mild exercise (such as stretching) and nonsteroidal anti-inflammatory drugs (NSAIDs), such as *ibuprofen* (Motrin). Less often, surgery is required for conditions such as a herniated disk.

Drawbacks: Conventional treatments are only modestly successful for most patients.

Blended approach: Acupuncture—combined with the use of other medical treatments, including physical therapy and pain medications. Patients who have six to eight acupuncture treatments, usually given once or twice a week, often have long-lasting relief—although some require monthly "tune-ups" to stay pain-free.

*Consult your physician before trying any of the dietary supplements described in this article.

Good news: Many insurance companies cover the cost of acupuncture as a treatment for back pain.

Also helpful: An herb known as devil's claw is very popular in Europe for low-back pain. More than a dozen reputable studies show that it's effective—and it's less likely than ibuprofen or other drugs to cause side effects, including gastrointestinal upset. Follow the label directions.

To relieve osteoarthritis: Consider trying devil's claw alone or in conjunction with a regimen that includes heat and cold therapy…exercise…*glucosamine* and *chondroitin* supplements (typical dose: 1,500 mg of glucosamine and 1,200 mg of chondroitin daily)…and over-the-counter anti-inflammatory medication.

When buying devil's claw, look for a product that is standardized to contain 50 mg to 100 mg of *harpagoside* (the active anti-inflammatory ingredient). Check the product label for dosage instructions.

ANXIETY DISORDERS

One of the most common psychiatric problems in the US, anxiety disorders can lead to a variety of symptoms, including heart palpitations and a persistent fear and worry in situations that would not feel threatening to most people. Only a minority of patients ever seek treatment—and those who do often have limited success.

Conventional approach: In addition to counseling, some patients may be advised to take a benzodiazepine tranquilizer, such as *diazepam* (Valium) or *lorazepam* (Ativan). Or they might be given a prescription for an antidepressant, a beta-blocker or another drug to help relieve anxiety.

Drawbacks: Many psychiatric drugs cause side effects, including unwanted sedation, weight gain or problems with libido and sexual function. Some anxiety medications can be addictive.

Blended approach: Meditation—with or without drug therapy—has a strong record of success in treating anxiety. Studies show that people who meditate for 20 minutes at least once a day experience less anxiety (and less depression).

All forms of meditation seem to be effective. One of the easiest involves breathing exercises, in which patients take a series of deep breaths, hold them briefly and then slowly exhale.

What to do: Inhale through the nose for a count of four…hold your breath for a count of seven…then exhale through the mouth for a count of eight.

Important: People who meditate for longer periods—and more often—tend to experience less anxiety overall than those who do it for less time.

Also helpful: Kava, an herbal supplement. Some studies show that it's about as effective as benzodiazepines for anxiety. Follow the dosage instructions on the label.

Important: The FDA issued a warning in 2002 that kava had been linked to liver damage. Although it can be effective for many patients with anxiety disorders, kava should be used only under a doctor's supervision.

FATIGUE

Often due to stress or poor sleep habits, fatigue also can be caused by underlying health problems.

Conventional approach: Patients who experience severe and frequent fatigue should get a complete medical workup (your doctor will recommend specific tests) because it can be caused by literally hundreds of disorders.

Drawbacks: Unless your doctor can identify a specific underlying cause for fatigue, the treatment options are limited. People usually are advised to exercise more and get sufficient sleep—but that doesn't work for everyone.

Blended approach: Ginseng, an herb that has traditionally been used by athletes to improve stamina, seems to help many patients with fatigue.

Look for the American form of ginseng with at least 5% ginsenosides (the active chemical ingredient). Follow the dosage directions on the label.

Site Spells Out Drug Safety

Find out if your medications are safe at a new Web site run by the Food and Drug Administration. The Postmarketing Drug Safety Evaluations site gives information about what the FDA has learned 18 months after a drug or vaccine is approved or after 10,000 patients have used it, whichever comes later. The list of currently available information is at *www.fda. gov* (click on "Drugs," then "Postmarket Drug Safety," "Index to Drug-Specific Information").

Warning! Never Combine These Medications

Cynthia Kuhn, PhD, professor in the department of pharmacology at Duke University School of Medicine, Durham, North Carolina. She is a coauthor of *Buzzed: The Straight Facts About the Most Used and Abused Drugs from Alcohol to Ecstasy* (W.W. Norton).

The office of the chief medical examiner of New York City reported that the death of 28-year-old actor Heath Ledger was caused by a combination of prescription drugs—two narcotic pain relievers combined with antianxiety medication and sleep aids.

The use of multiple drugs is inherently risky. The FDA has identified thousands of potential drug interactions, many of which are minor. Serious problems tend to occur when patients take two or more drugs that affect the same body system. Each of the drugs used by Ledger, for example, can potentially affect cellular receptors that regulate breathing. Taken together, they had additive effects—the combination was more powerful than the effects of any one of the drugs taken alone.

According to the federal Substance Abuse and Mental Health Services Administration, more than 3 million emergency room visits in 2009 (the most recent year for which data is available) involved prescription or over-the-counter drugs or supplements.

Caution: The risk for drug interactions is highest among the elderly. They tend to use the most drugs, and their bodies metabolize (break down) drugs more slowly than younger adults.

HOW INTERACTIONS HAPPEN

Patients who use medications appropriately—taking the prescribed doses for only particular conditions and regularly reviewing drug use with a physician—are unlikely to have serious problems.

Main risks: Different drugs prescribed by more than one doctor...using drugs to treat conditions for which they weren't originally prescribed (many people stockpile leftover drugs and use them later, possibly for unrelated conditions)...or using a drug that was appropriate initially but might be dangerous when combined with drugs a patient has subsequently started taking.

Protect yourself by frequently updating a list of the drugs and supplements you take. Review the list with every doctor at every office visit and whenever a new drug is prescribed.

Most common dangerous drug interactions...

OPIOID PAINKILLERS/SEDATIVES

Opioid painkillers, such as *hydrocodone* and *oxycodone*, have powerful effects on the central nervous system. Even on their own, they can suppress breathing when taken in high enough doses. The risk is much higher when they're combined with sedating drugs, such as those used to treat anxiety or insomnia. These include the benzodiazepine class of medications, such as *diazepam* (Valium) and *alprazolam* (Xanax).

Many people take these drugs in combination. For example, someone might take alprazolam for chronic anxiety, then add hydrocodone following an injury. The drugs often are prescribed by different doctors who don't know the patient's drug history.

What to do: Never combine prescription painkillers and sedatives without your doctor's okay.

WARFARIN/ANTIBIOTICS/NSAIDS

The blood thinner *warfarin* (Coumadin) is notorious for interacting with other drugs. It has a narrow "therapeutic index," the difference between a helpful and a toxic dose.

Drugs that increase the effects of warfarin can lead to uncontrolled bleeding.

Many antibiotics and antifungal drugs, including *erythromycin, ciprofloxacin* and *ketoconazole*, are broken down by the same liver enzyme that metabolizes warfarin. Taking warfarin and any of these drugs together may deplete the enzyme, leading to higher levels of warfarin in the body.

What to do: If you have an infection, your doctor can prescribe an antibiotic that is less likely to interact with warfarin. Antibiotics that are less likely to cause an interaction include *penicillin, amoxicillin, ampicillin* and *tetracycline*.

Caution: Warfarin may cause gastrointestinal bleeding when combined with aspirin, ibuprofen or other nonsteroidal anti-inflammatory drugs (NSAIDs). If you take warfarin and need a painkiller, acetaminophen (Tylenol) might be a better choice.

MULTIPLE ANTIDEPRESSANTS

Patients who combine selective serotonin reuptake inhibitor (SSRI) antidepressants, such as *fluoxetine* (Prozac) and *sertraline* (Zoloft), or who combine an SSRI with another type of antidepressant may experience serotonin syndrome, a rare but potentially fatal reaction.

Many antidepressants increase brain levels of serotonin, a chemical produced by some neurons (nerve cells). Patients who combine antidepressants or take too much of one can accumulate toxic levels of serotonin. This can cause dangerously elevated blood pressure, known as a hypertensive crisis.

Serotonin syndrome usually occurs when patients switch from an SSRI antidepressant to a monoamine oxidase inhibitor (MAOI), an older type of antidepressant, without allowing time for the first drug to wash out of the body.

What to do: Follow your doctor's instructions exactly when discontinuing an antidepressant. Most of these drugs have to be tapered—slowly decreasing the dose over a period of weeks—before starting a new drug.

VIAGRA/NITRATES

Men who take nitrate drugs (such as nitroglycerine) for heart problems should never take *sildenafil* (Viagra) without a doctor's supervision.

Viagra and similar drugs for treating erectile dysfunction cause blood vessels to relax. Nitrate drugs do the same thing. Combining them can cause a dangerous drop in blood pressure.

What to do: Men who take nitrates for heart problems can talk to their doctors about safer alternatives for treating erectile dysfunction, including vacuum devices or penile injections.

ACETAMINOPHEN FROM MULTIPLE PRODUCTS

Taken in excessive doses, the pain reliever *acetaminophen* (Tylenol) can cause liver damage.

Main risk: Combining acetaminophen—for treating arthritis pain, for example—with unrelated products (such as cold/flu remedies) that also contain acetaminophen.

What to do: When using acetaminophen, don't exceed the dose listed on the product label—and check labels to ensure that you don't take another product that contains acetaminophen simultaneously.

Find Out the Latest Drug Recalls

To stay up to date about drug recalls, regularly visit the Web site *www.recalls.gov*. The free site compiles information from federal government agencies that initiate or announce recalls, including the Food and Drug Administration, Environmental Protection Agency, US Department of Agriculture and Consumer Product Safety Commission. You also can go to individual agency sites to sign up for e-mail alerts that will be sent directly to you.

Examples: *www.fda.gov* or *www.epa.gov*. The e-mails may include safety advice in addition to recall announcements.

Donald L. Mays, senior director of product safety and technical policy, Consumers Union, Yonkers, New York, which publishes *Consumer Reports*.

Free Drug Samples May Cost You

Patients who get drug samples from doctors end up spending more on drugs overall than patients who don't.

Reason: Patients fill prescriptions for drugs they initially got free—and drugs given as samples often are newest and most expensive. Free samples do not save money when a drug is used long-term instead of equally effective, cheaper drugs.

G. Caleb Alexander, MD, assistant professor of medicine, University of Chicago Medical Center.

Are Your Medications Making You Sick?

Hyla Cass, MD, board-certified psychiatrist and nationally recognized expert in nutritional and integrative medicine. She is the author of several books, including *8 Weeks to Vibrant Health* (McGraw-Hill) and *Supplement Your Prescription* (Basic Health). *www.cassmd.com.*

Then we think of drug side effects, what usually comes to mind are headache, dizziness, dry mouth and other such complaints.

Commonly ignored side effect: Many popular medications can deplete your body of crucial nutrients—an unintended effect that can increase your risk for diseases ranging from cancer to heart disease. *What you need to know...*

ARE YOU AT RISK?

•**Nutrient depletion,** which causes such symptoms as fatigue, muscle cramps and even a rapid heartbeat, can potentially occur within weeks after starting a medication.

More often, such symptoms occur gradually, over months or even years—and, as a result, often are dismissed by people taking the drugs as mere annoyances or mistaken for signs of aging.

In some cases, a hidden nutrient deficiency increases one's risk for other illnesses—for example, a deficiency of folate (a B vitamin) may raise your risk for cancer or cause physiological changes that can set the stage for heart attack or stroke.

Important: If you take one or more medications regularly, ask your doctor about nutrient depletion—and whether you should be tested. Doctors can do a basic blood screening profile for low blood levels of vitamins and minerals, such as B-12, folate, calcium, magnesium and potassium. (See page 61 for more details.)

However, to more accurately measure your levels of all the important nutrients, your doctor should consider more sophisticated testing.

For example, SpectraCell's micronutrient test measures more than 31 vitamins, minerals, amino acids and antioxidants. Not all doctors are familiar with the test, but you can go to *www.spectracell.com* and click on "Find a Clinician" to locate a physician in your area who is. The panel costs around $325, and insurance may pay some of the cost. Or try the Metametrix Nutrient and Toxic Elements Profile, which costs from $79 to $164, depending on the specific tests (800-221-4640, *www.me tametrix.com*).

Helpful: Be sure to eat foods that are rich in nutrients that may be depleted by your medications. To ensure adequate levels of these nutrients, ask your doctor about taking the supplements described below. *Drugs that can deplete nutrients...*

ASPIRIN AND OTHER NSAIDS

Well-known nonsteroidal anti-inflammatory drugs, (NSAIDs), such as aspirin, are used to reduce pain and inflammation. Millions of Americans also take aspirin to "thin" the blood, reducing the risk for a heart attack or stroke.

Nutrients depleted: Folate and vitamin C. Insufficient folate is thought to increase the risk for a variety of cancers, including malignancies of the breast and colon. Low folate also has been linked to elevated levels of homocysteine, an amino acid that can raise risk for heart attack and stroke.

People who are low in vitamin C get more colds, flu and other infections than those with normal levels. A deficiency of vitamin C also can impair the body's ability to produce and repair cartilage—which may explain why people with osteoarthritis who regularly take an NSAID often suffer more joint pain in the long run.

My recommendation: Take 1,000 mg of vitamin C daily if you take an NSAID regularly. A Boston University study found that people who got the most vitamin C were three times less likely to develop osteoarthritis, or have an increase in symptoms, than those who got lower amounts.

Caution: High-dose vitamin C can cause loose stools in some people—if this occurs, reduce your dose to 500 mg daily.

In addition, take a 400-mcg to 800-mcg folic acid (the man-made form of folate) supplement daily. Take vitamin B-12 (1,000 mcg daily) with folic acid—taking folic acid alone can mask a B-12 deficiency.

Also helpful: 1,000 mg to 2,000 mg of fish oil daily. One study found that 60% of people with osteoarthritis who took fish oil improved their joint pain within 75 days. Half improved so much that they no longer needed to take an NSAID.

CALCIUM CHANNEL BLOCKERS

When it comes to blood pressure medication, most people know that diuretics (water-excreting drugs) can deplete important nutrients, including potassium. It's less well-known that blood pressure drugs known as calcium channel blockers, including *amlodipine* (Norvasc) and *nicardipine* (Cardene), can have the same effect.

Nutrient depleted: Potassium. People with low potassium may experience muscle weakness and fatigue. Their blood pressure also may rise, which offsets the drug's effectiveness.

My recommendation: Take a 100-mg potassium supplement daily. Because many foods contain significant amounts of this mineral, you can eat a single extra serving of a high-potassium food as an alternative. A medium baked potato with the skin, for example, provides 850 mg of potassium...and a large banana has 487 mg. Check with your physician if

you have kidney disease—extra potassium can worsen the condition.

GEMFIBROZIL

People who can't control elevated cholesterol with a statin, or who suffer muscle pain or other side effects when taking a statin, may be given a prescription for *gemfibrozil* (Lopid). This and similar drugs, known as fibrates, raise levels of HDL (good) cholesterol and reduce harmful LDL cholesterol and triglycerides.

Nutrients depleted: Vitamin E and the naturally occurring nutrient coenzyme Q10 (CoQ10). A deficiency of vitamin E, a potent antioxidant, can increase risk for cancer, heart disease and other conditions, such as nerve disorders. Inadequate CoQ10 often results in muscle pain and weakness...and can impair the heart's ability to beat efficiently.

My recommendation: Take 200 mg of CoQ10 and 100 mg of natural vitamin E (mixed tocopherols) daily.

METFORMIN

Metformin (Glucophage), the most popular oral diabetes drug, reduces blood sugar by making cells more responsive to insulin. It also causes less weight gain and fewer episodes of hypoglycemia (excessively low blood sugar) than other diabetes drugs.

Nutrients depleted: Vitamin B-12. A study in *Archives of Internal Medicine* found that patients taking metformin had average vitamin B-12 levels that were less than half of those in people who weren't taking the medication. Metformin also reduces levels of folate. A deficiency of these nutrients can cause fatigue, forgetfulness and depression.

My recommendation: Take 1,000 mcg of vitamin B-12 daily. Since many multivitamins have only 200 mcg (or less) of B-12, you'll have to supplement to reach the 1,000-mcg daily dose. For folic acid, take 400 mcg to 800 mcg daily.

Important: When increasing levels of vitamin B-12, people with diabetes may be more likely to experience episodes of hypoglycemia. Ask your doctor about getting an A1C blood test, which measures blood sugar levels over a period of weeks rather than at a single point in time.

Your Drugs May Deplete Vital Nutrients

Mark A. Stengler, NMD, licensed naturopathic medical doctor and leading authority on the practice of alternative and integrated medicine. He is founder and medical director of the Stengler Center for Integrative Medicine, Encinitas, California. He is author of the newsletter *Bottom Line Natural Healing, www.drstengler.com.*

Here are several common drugs and what they take from us. Talk to your doctor about whether you need to supplement.

- **Acetaminophen**—depletes glutathione
- **Acid blocking medications,** including proton-pump inhibitors and H2 blockers—deplete vitamin B-12 (When supplementing, look for the type known as methylcobalamin, which is better utilized by the body than others.)
- **Antibiotics**—deplete B vitamins and healthy gut flora (which can be replaced by probiotics)
- **Diabetes medication**—depletes coenzyme Q10 (CoQ10) and folic acid
- **Diuretics** (both regular and potassium-sparing) for high blood pressure—deplete vitamin B complex and trace minerals
- **Estrogen**—depletes B vitamins, calcium, magnesium, zinc
- **Ibuprofen**—depletes folic acid
- **Laxatives**—deplete calcium, zinc, iron, magnesium
- **Sleep medications**—deplete melatonin, the hormone that maintains a normal circadian cycle, including sleep
- **Statin drugs** (cholesterol-lowering medications)—deplete CoQ10
- **Steroids (prednisone)**—deplete calcium, vitamin D, vitamin C, potassium.

Evaluate Prescription-Drug Ads

The Food and Drug Administration Web site, *www.fda.gov* (in the search box insert "ad"), provides information on which drug ads are believable and which are misleading. The site also has information on advertising for certain medical devices.

Drugs and Gray Hair

Drugs may cause hair to turn gray. People with substance abuse problems are twice as likely to turn prematurely gray as people who do not overindulge. Along with illegal drugs, alcohol also damages the production process of melanocytes, the cells that give hair its color.

Stuart Reece, MD, University of Queensland Medical School, Brisbane, Australia, and leader of a study of the effect of drug consumption on hair color, published in *Archives of Dermatology.*

Counterfeit Drug Alert

Buy online drugs only from established US companies.

Why: Counterfeit drugs are increasingly common. More than 50% of Internet drug outlets that conceal their physical addresses sell counterfeit drugs. Consumers lured by low prices and well-designed Web sites are the most common victims. Drugs sold at these sites may have the wrong amounts of active ingredient, or none at all, and may contain dangerous additives. Buy from companies approved by the National Association of Boards of Pharmacy with a Verified Internet Pharmacy Practice Sites (VIPPS) logo.

World Health Organization, Geneva, Switzerland, *www.who.int.*

Save Money With Older Generic

Expensive osteoporosis drug is no more effective than older generics. The medicine *ibandronate* (Boniva) can be taken monthly. Other cheaper drugs in the same class, called bisphosphonates, must be taken weekly or daily. But they all are about equally effective at preventing bone fractures—and Boniva costs 10 times as much as *alendronate* (Fosamax). Ask your doctor to consider price when prescribing an osteoporosis medication for you.

Consumer Reports, 101 Truman Ave., Yonkers, New York 10703.

Common Drugs And Memory Loss

Common drugs can cause memory loss, warns Noll L. Campbell, PharmD. Anticholinergics are used as sleep aids and to fight allergies. They are sold over the counter under such brand names as Benadryl, Dramamine, Excedrin PM, Nytol, Sominex and Tylenol PM. Prescription versions include Paxil, Demerol and others. Anticholinergics are known to have short-term effects on memory and cognitive function.

Recent finding: Anticholinergics also have long-term effects, such as gradual memory loss.

Noll L. Campbell, PharmD, FASCP, BCPP, is research assistant professor with Purdue University School of Pharmacy and clinical specialist in geriatrics, Wishard Health Services, both in Indianapolis. She is author of a six-year study published in *Neurology*.

Off-Label Drug Danger

Off-label drug danger. Although the FDA allows doctors to prescribe drugs for conditions for which they were not originally given approval, a recent survey showed doctors knew the "approved" status of a drug only 50% of the time.

Problem: Many "off-label" uses for drugs are not supported by scientific evidence.

Safest: Ask your doctor if he/she is prescribing a drug off-label—if so, ask why he expects it to be effective.

G. Caleb Alexander, MD, assistant professor, department of medicine, University of Chicago Medical Center.

Hope for Advanced Skin Cancer

New drug for advanced skin cancer is available, we hear from Keith Flaherty, MD.

Background: About half of melanoma patients have a BRAF gene mutation that promotes tumor growth.

Recent study: When 49 adults with advanced BRAF-positive melanoma took PLX4032, an oral BRAF inhibitor, 81% of their tumors shrank by at least one-third within two months. In three patients, tumors disappeared. Relapse occurred after nine months, on average, compared to about two months with standard treatment.

If you have advanced melanoma: Visit *www.clinicaltrials.gov*. Search "PLX4032" to find trials that are recruiting patients.

Keith Flaherty, MD, director of the developmental therapeutics section of the cancer center at Massachusetts General Hospital, Boston.

Heartburn Drug Danger

Don't mix heartburn drugs with the blood thinner *clopidogrel* (Plavix). Taking Plavix along with certain drugs that reduce acid reflux, such as *omeprazole* (Prilosec) or *lansoprazole* (Prevacid), may raise the chance of a cardiac event, such as a heart attack or stroke, by 50%. But some doctors suggest taking this combination to lower the risk for stomach bleeding.

Self-defense: Ask your doctor about alternative heartburn drugs, such as *famotidine* (Mylanta and Pepcid) and *rantidine* (Zantac). Consider avoiding such medicines completely if your doctor says that your risk for stomach bleeding when taking Plavix is low.

David Flockhart, MD, PhD, chief, division of clinical pharmacology, Indiana University School of Medicine, Indianapolis.

ER Drug Danger

Some drugs prescribed in ERs, such as pro-poxyphene for pain, may be dangerous for older adults who already are taking a variety of drugs. The medications prescribed may have a larger and longer-lasting sedating effect on older adults and may increase the risk for falls at home and other complications.

Self-defense: Carry a list of all medicines and supplements that you use with you at all times, including dosage information. If someone is bringing you to the hospital, be sure that person has a copy of the list to give to hospital personnel. Consider asking the physician if there are safer alternatives to the drugs prescribed, especially pain medications.

William J. Meurer, MD, assistant professor, department of emergency medicine, University of Michigan, Ann Arbor, and coauthor of a study of 1.5 billion emergency room visits, published in *Academic Emergency Medicine.*

"Dementia" May Be a Drug Side Effect

Don't assume that a diagnosis of dementia is accurate. Up to 10% of seniors diagnosed with Alzheimer's or other forms of dementia may really be suffering from drug side effects.

Most likely culprits: Sleeping pills, tranquilizers and beta-blockers used to treat high blood pressure, among other ailments. When you take several drugs of any kind (including over-the-counter drugs), unexpected interactions can cause dementia-like symptoms.

Safety: Call your doctor at the first sign of memory problems arising after taking a new drug.

Samuel Gandy, MD, PhD, professor, Alzheimer's disease research, Mount Sinai School of Medicine, New York City, *www.mountsinai.org.*

Cholesterol Drugs Can Make You Sick

Cholesterol drugs may lower immunity to bacterial infections, warns researcher Cosima T. Baldari, PhD. In lab experiments, the statin *simvastatin* (Zocor) inhibited the activity of macrophages (immune cells that destroy bacteria) and increased production of cytokines (substances that trigger and sustain inflammation).

Result: Bacterial infections may last longer, though there is no evidence that the drug makes people more susceptible to infection. Other statins are likely to affect immunity in a similar way.

Cosima T. Baldari, PhD, is professor of molecular biology, University of Siena, Siena, Italy, and senior author of a study published in *Journal of Leukocyte Biology.*

Asthma Drug Warning

Long-acting *beta agonists* (LABAs) now must carry an FDA warning label saying that they should be used for the shortest possible time and not on their own but with an inhaled corticosteroid. Long-term use actually may worsen asthma. This is particularly the case for LABAs that are single-agent drugs, such as Serevent and Foradil. (Other LABAs, such as Advair and Symbicort, contain inhaled corticosteroids.)

Norman H. Edelman, MD, is chief medical officer of the American Lung Association and professor of preventive medicine, internal medicine, physiology and biophysics at Stony Brook University, Stony Brook, New York.

Heartburn Meds Raise Food-Poisoning Risk

Stomach-acid drugs raise food-poisoning risk. Medicines that lower production of stomach acid, such as Prevacid and Prilosec, can increase food-poisoning risk by reducing the acid that is the body's natural defense.

Self-defense: If you use these drugs, be especially careful when handling raw meat and poultry, and avoid foods associated with food poisoning, such as raw oysters, raw eggs and unpasteurized milk.

Leo Galland, MD, internist, founder and director, Foundation for Integrated Medicine, New York City, *www.mdheal.org.*

Extra Help for RA

A relatively new drug for rheumatoid arthritis (RA) called *Actemra* (tocilizumab) may help patients with moderate-to-severe RA who have not done well with previous drugs. Most other RA drugs—such as *Enbrel, Humira* and *Remicade*—are TNF inhibitors. They block the activity of tumor necrosis factor, which promotes the inflammation that causes many symptoms. Actemra blocks the interleukin-6 (IL-6) receptor, also associated with inflammation.

Beth L. Jonas, MD, rheumatologist and director of Rheumatology Fellowship Training Program, Thurston Arthritis Research Center, University of North Carolina at Chapel Hill.

Bone Drug Causes Hip Fractures?

Taking osteoporosis drugs may cause brittle bones, warns Joseph Lane, MD. Bisphosphonates such as *Actonel, Boniva, Fosamax* and Reclast can lead to deterioration in bone quality and increased hip fractures. The drugs are extremely effective in the first years of use. But after four or five years, if bone density is no longer improving, talk to your doctor about taking a "drug holiday" from bisphosphonates.

Joseph Lane, MD, chief of Metabolic Bone Disease Service, Hospital for Special Surgery, New York City, and leader of a study of women and long-term bisphosphonate use.

Shop Around for Generics

The price of a generic drug can vary dramatically, says health economist Devon Herrick, PhD.

Example: In one California town, a 30-day supply of the statin *simvastatin,* the generic version of Zocor, sold for $7.71 at Costco...$19.87 at an independent drugstore...$24.36 at Walmart...$63.59 at CVS...and $89.99 at Walgreens.

Self-defense: Check prices at several stores—you usually don't need to be a member of wholesale clubs to get prescriptions from them.

Devon Herrick, PhD, is a health economist at National Center for Policy Analysis, Dallas.

Drug Alert for Kidney Patients

When researchers analyzed data for 578 patients receiving the blood-thinning drug *warfarin* (Coumadin) for stroke prevention or other conditions, they found that those who also had severe chronic kidney disease (CKD) required significantly lower dosages of warfarin and were at higher risk for bleeding complications than were patients with mild or moderate CKD or no kidney disease.

Nita A. Limdi, PhD, PharmD, associate professor of neurology, University of Alabama, Birmingham.

Disposing of Drugs

When and how should you get rid of unused medication?

Dispose of unused medication when your doctor switches you to a different drug or when a product passes its expiration date.

How: Ask your doctor, pharmacist and local recycling service if there is a program for collecting unused medication. Or mix unused pills with coffee grounds or kitty litter to discourage kids and pets from sampling them… then seal them inside a plastic bag before placing them in the trash.

Exception: The FDA recommends that certain powerful narcotics, such as prescription pain relievers, be flushed down the toilet to avoid intentional abuse by people for whom the drugs were not prescribed.

Best: Flush a drug only if directed on the label.

Jack M. Rosenberg, PharmD, PhD, professor of pharmacy practice and pharmacology, Long Island University, Brooklyn.

"Dirty" Drugs

James Rudolph, MD, geriatrician and director of the Postoperative Delirium Service at the Veterans Affairs Boston Healthcare System and the Boston Geriatric Research Scholars Program.

If you're like most Americans, you have probably taken—or may currently take—an over-the-counter (OTC) allergy or cold drug, pain reliever or sleep aid containing *diphenhydramine*. This generic medication has become widely available without prescription in such products as Benadryl, Excedrin PM and Tylenol PM.

What you may not know: These drugs, as well as dozens of others that are used by millions of Americans, block the action of *acetylcholine*, a neurotransmitter that controls several critical functions in the body ranging from body secretions to cognitive function.

Why is this a potential problem? Cells in virtually every part of the body have molecular openings (receptors) that respond to acetylcholine. A drug that's used to treat a condition in one part of the body invariably affects receptors somewhere else.

Result: A high incidence of unintended effects. In some cases, people who use these so-called anticholinergic drugs suffer side effects such as constipation, urinary retention, blurred vision, dry mouth or even symptoms that mimic Alzheimer's disease.

"DIRTY" DRUGS

Medications that cause a high rate of unintended effects are known in the health-care community as "dirty" drugs. The same active ingredient that reduces bladder spasms, for example, might also cause constipation by reducing intestinal contractions or eye dryness by blocking acetylcholine at the receptors that constipation by reducing intestinal contractions or eye dryness by blocking acetylcholine at the receptors that control body secretions.

Important finding: A study published in the *Journal of the American Geriatrics Society* looked at 544 men with high blood pressure, some of whom were taking anticholinergic drugs for relatively minor conditions such as allergies. Over a two-year period, the men taking the drugs were significantly more likely to suffer impaired memory and other cognitive declines.

Most cognitive effects will clear once a person discontinues the drug, but full recovery is not a certainty, depending on your age and other health conditions. What's more, many anticholinergic drugs are taken indefinitely for chronic conditions.

COMMON USES AND ALTERNATIVES

Popular anticholinergic drugs...

•**Allergies.** Many of the older allergy drugs, including Benadryl, are effective at relieving irritated eyes, sneezing and runny nose. That's not surprising, since one of the main anticholinergic effects is to reduce mucus and other secretions. But the side effects, such as drowsiness and a dry mouth and eyes, are pronounced. Few can take these drugs and function well the next day.

My advice: Take Benadryl or a similar drug only if you have occasional allergy symptoms and need to get a good night's sleep. To reduce daytime drowsiness, take such a drug only at bedtime.

Better: Avoid allergens in the first place. If this is not possible, take a nonsedating antihistamine, such as *fexofenadine* (Allegra) or *loratadine* (Claritin). These drugs have relatively mild anticholinergic effects—most people can take them without experiencing side effects. If you have seasonal allergies, take one of these drugs daily throughout the allergy season. They aren't designed to control single flare-ups.

Also effective: Nasal steroids. Consult your doctor.

•**Depression.** Before selective serotonin reuptake inhibitor (SSRI) antidepressants were developed, doctors often prescribed *amitriptyline* for depression. This drug has fallen out of favor because it tends to cause strong anticholinergic side effects. But some of the newer drugs, such as *paroxetine* (Paxil), the most anticholinergic of the SSRIs, have similar effects.

My advice: If your doctor is going to prescribe an antidepressant, ask him/her about SSRI antidepressants with the least anticholinergic effects, particularly those with a shorter "half-life," such as *sertraline* (Zoloft). These drugs are eliminated from the body more quickly, so they're less likely to cause side effects. This is particularly important for older adults, who metabolize drugs more slowly.

•**Insomnia.** Most OTC drugs taken for insomnia, including the allergy medication Benadryl and sleep aid Sominex, contain *diphenhydramine*. It can cause constipation, difficulty concentrating, urinary retention and trouble with eye focus—and stays active in the body for 12 to 18 hours, which can lead to next-day grogginess.

My advice: Avoid taking diphenhydramine for insomnia.

Better: Practice good sleep habits.

Examples: Go to bed at a reasonable hour, and maintain the same schedule every night. Exercise regularly but not within two hours of your bedtime—it will make falling asleep more difficult. Take a warm bath before bed to help you relax.

Important: Make the bedroom a peaceful place—no TV, computer, etc. If you don't fall asleep within a half hour, get up and do something else until you're ready to try to sleep again. Avoid the computer and all electronics—their glow delays release of the sleep-inducing hormone melatonin.

•**Motion sickness.** Many anticholinergic drugs prevent and/or relieve motion sickness. However, the doses needed to reduce motion sickness can also cause drowsiness or confusion as a side effect.

My advice: Avoid motion sickness drugs such as *dimenhydrinate* (Dramamine).

Better: Use a prescription scopolamine patch (such as Transderm Scop). The active ingredient enters the body slowly and is less likely to cause side effects than oral dimenhydrinate. The patches deliver about 1.5 mg of scopolamine over three days. Apply the patch to a hairless area at least four hours before traveling/sailing.

•**Urinary incontinence.** People who suffer from an unusually intense and frequent need to urinate, known as urge incontinence, are often treated with overactive bladder medications such as *oxybutynin* (Ditropan) or *tolterodine* (Detrol).

These drugs may cause dry mouth, blurred vision, constipation and/or cognitive impairments.

Adults age 65 and older have the highest risk for side effects. This is partly because the blood-brain barrier becomes more porous with age. These drugs are not supposed to enter the brain—but often do.

My advice: After discussing dosages and potential side effects with your physician, you may want to consider taking one of these drugs if incontinence is preventing you from living a normal life. It may be better to cope with drug side effects than to become housebound due to fear of having an "accident."

Even better: Bladder training, in which a doctor or therapist teaches you to gradually increase the intervals between urinating by waiting longer than you think you can. Most people can gradually increase their "holding" time by several minutes to several hours.

If urgency/frequency occurs during the night, see your doctor. Nighttime urination may especially be a problem for men with enlarged prostates, but incontinence drugs are unlikely to help—and may even be harmful.

AN ADDED DANGER

The cognitive state of a person taking an anticholinergic drug can affect the severity of the side effects from these medications.

Example: If a person with no cognitive issues takes *diphenhydramine* (Benadryl), he/she might not experience any significant anti-cholinergic side effects. However, a cognitively impaired person on the same medication at the same dose might sleep for two days or even develop delirium (a condition causing a confused mental state and behavioral changes).

Every kind of medication causes side effects in some people, but the anticholinergic drugs are especially problematic because their target—the neurotransmitter acetylcholine—is present in so many different types of cells.

Ask your doctor to review all of your medications. People who take two or more anticholinergic medications are far more likely to experience side effects than those who take just one.

Avoid This Common Drug-Dosing Error

Rebecca Shannonhouse, editor, *Bottom Line/Health*, Boardroom Inc., 281 Tresser Blvd., Stamford, Connecticut 06901.

D on't reach into your kitchen utensil drawer the next time you need to portion out prescriptions or other medications. If you take a spoonful of medicine, you may be getting more—or less—than you need.

Recent finding: When 195 cold and flu sufferers were asked to pour one teaspoon of medicine into kitchen spoons of differing sizes, they tended to underdose by as much as 8%…or overdose by up to 12%.

Since the average kitchen spoon holds more—or less—liquid than an official, 5-milliliter teaspoon, people who "guesstimate" the correct dose often get too much or too little of the active ingredient, says Jack M. Rosenberg, PharmD, PhD, professor of pharmacy and pharmacology at Long Island University in Brooklyn, New York. Such errors in dosing can have significant cumulative effects when a medicine is taken for several days.

To protect yourself, Dr. Rosenberg advises that you…

• **Talk to the pharmacist.** Ask him/her if it is okay to use a kitchen spoon to measure the dose of a liquid medicine. A kitchen spoon could be fine for some medicines, such as a liquid antacid, but for many others, you might think that you're pouring the correct amount—but you'll probably be wrong.

• **Use a precision device when needed.** Always use the calibrated cap or measuring device that's supplied with some medications. If no such device is provided, use a measuring teaspoon, oral syringe or a dropper.

• **Read the label.** Some over-the-counter medications have age and body-weight guidelines for dosing. Follow the label advice exactly, unless otherwise specified by your physician.

Generic Drug for Enlarged Prostate

The FDA recently approved a generic form of *tamsulosin* (Flomax) to treat benign prostatic hyperplasia (enlarged prostate). Tamsulosin is an alpha-blocker that relieves symptoms such as frequent or urgent need to urinate and/or weak urine stream by relaxing prostate and bladder muscles. Side effects may include sleepiness and/or diarrhea.

If you take Flomax: Ask your doctor about switching to this budget-friendly generic medication.

Brenda Stodart, PharmD, senior supervisory health promotion officer, FDA Center for Drug Evaluation and Research, Silver Spring, Maryland.

Bone Loss Drug Cut Breast Cancer Risk

Recent studies showed that postmenopausal women taking bisphosphonates, primarily Fosamax, to protect against bone loss and fractures had one-third fewer cases of invasive breast cancer than women not taking the drugs. Ask your doctor whether a bisphosphonate is right for you.

Richard Theriault, DO, a bisphosphonates expert, is a professor in the department of breast medical oncology, The University of Texas MD Anderson Cancer Center, Houston.

Breast Cancer Drug Underused

Trastuzumab (herceptin) blocks a protein that promotes tumor growth. It is currently given primarily to early-stage patients whose tumors have a lot of the protein.

But: Two federally run studies suggest that some women who test negative for the protein actually may have enough of it to benefit from herceptin.

JoAnne Zujewski, MD, head of breast cancer therapeutics, Clinical Investigations Branch, National Cancer Institute, Bethesda, Maryland.

Warning on Aluminum

Jack E. Fincham, PhD, RPh, professor of pharmacy practice and administration, School of Pharmacy, University of Missouri, Kansas City.

As the third most commonly occurring element, aluminum is present in food, water, air, various cooking utensils and even some medications (such as antacids, buffered aspirin and/or intravenously administered fluids). This is typically not a problem for people with normal kidney function—unless you consume high doses of aluminum. Because the body eliminates aluminum through urine, feces and by breathing, there is usually little accumulation in the body.

However, individuals on kidney dialysis or who have chronic kidney disease should not consume aluminum-containing products. Also, aluminum is contained in cigarette smoke, secondhand smoke and thirdhand smoke residues (on clothes or curtains, for example). When combined with toxins and/or carcinogens, the presence of aluminum in the bloodstream can be dangerous.

Medical Privacy

You do not have to disclose your medications to airport security screeners—and you can conceal their names on bottles by putting tape over them. The Transportation Security Administration considers medication use a matter of medical privacy—but screeners have the right to test medication bottles to be sure that they do not contain explosives or anything that is not allowed on aircraft.

Wired, 520 Third St., San Francisco, California 94107.

Painkillers Can Kill

Amanda Risser, MD, MPH, assistant professor of family medicine at Oregon Health and Science University (OHSU), Portland. She practices family medicine at OHSU Family Medicine at Richmond, a community health center in Portland.

Nonsteroidal anti-inflammatory drugs, known as NSAIDs, are not as safe as people think. In 2004, an NSAID known as *rofecoxib* (Vioxx) was withdrawn from the market after it was found to increase the risk for heart attack and stroke. Other NSAIDs, including aspirin, have a high risk for side effects, including internal bleeding.

The occasional use of NSAIDs is unlikely to cause serious problems. The risks start to rise when people use these drugs too often or if people have certain risk factors. *Main dangers...*

CARDIOVASCULAR RISKS

Low-dose aspirin therapy (100 mg or less daily) has been shown to decrease the risk for heart attack and stroke in high-risk patients. Other NSAIDs, however, don't fare so well.

People who regularly take NSAIDs other than aspirin have an average increase in blood pressure of about five points. These drugs also can worsen congestive heart failure and increase risk for heart attack. The Cox-2 inhibitor Celebrex is believed to increase these risks more than other NSAIDs.

Self-defense: Avoid Celebrex if you have cardiovascular risk factors, such as hypertension or high cholesterol, or if you've previously had a heart attack. With other NSAIDs, I advise patients to check their blood pressure within a week or two after starting the drug. If blood pressure is going to rise, it usually does so during that time.

Also important: Don't exceed the dose recommended on the label. People who take high doses of ibuprofen or diclofenac, for example, are more likely to have cardiovascular "events" than those who take the amounts recommended on the label.

While it would be easy to assume that people who regularly take a non-aspirin NSAID may reduce cardiovascular risk by taking low-dose aspirin as well, studies have shown that this isn't the case and that this combination of medications is risky, especially for gastrointestinal (GI) complications.

ASTHMA

About 21% of adults with asthma experience a worsening of symptoms when they take aspirin. In rare cases, aspirin can cause respiratory problems, such as difficulty breathing, in people without a history of asthma.

Warning: People who experience respiratory problems when they take aspirin usually have a high cross-reactivity to similar drugs—they'll experience similar symptoms when they take ibuprofen, indomethacin or other NSAIDs. The risk for aspirin-exacerbated asthma is highest in patients who also have nasal polyps and/or recurrent bouts of sinusitis.

Self-defense: In general, asthma patients should avoid aspirin and other NSAIDs, particularly if they also have polyps or sinusitis. These patients can safely substitute acetaminophen. Asthma patients who need additional pain relief should ask their doctors about such prescription non–NSAID drugs as *gabapentin* (Neurontin) and *nortriptyline* (Aventyl, Pamelor).

KIDNEY COMPLICATIONS

Up to 2% of patients who regularly take NSAIDs will have to stop taking them because of kidney problems.

Self-defense: Patients undergoing dialysis or those with kidney disease should not take NSAIDs—acetaminophen is a better choice.

I advise patients with diabetes or other risk factors for kidney disease to have a baseline creatinine test when they start NSAID therapy and then subsequent monitoring. Creatinine is a metabolic by-product that indicates how well the kidneys are working. Patients can keep using NSAIDs if their creatinine remains stable.

Important: Patients who have developed kidney disease as a consequence of liver disease should never take NSAIDs. They have a high risk for complications, including total kidney failure.

LIVER DISEASE

Some studies have shown that patients who take the painkillers *sulindac* (Clinoril) or *diclofenac* have an increase in liver enzymes circulating in the bloodstream. This increase is less likely to occur with other NSAIDs.

Self-defense: Stop taking NSAIDs if your doctor determines there's an increase in liver enzymes. The complications usually reverse when the drugs are discontinued.

Important: NSAID-related liver damage is rare. It usually occurs in patients who already have a liver disease, such as hepatitis C or cirrhosis. (Liver problems are rare with acetaminophen as well, but be sure not to take too much—follow directions on the label.)

CENTRAL NERVOUS SYSTEM

Older adults who take NSAIDs will sometimes develop central nervous system problems. Aspirin, for example, can cause or worsen tinnitus (ringing or other sounds in the ears). Indomethacin has been linked to cognitive changes, including psychosis in rare cases.

Self-defense: Follow the dosing instructions on the label. These disorders mainly occur when people take NSAIDs in excessive doses—and will resolve when the drugs are discontinued or are taken in a lower dose.

GI COMPLICATIONS

It's estimated that at least 10% to 20% of people who regularly take one or more NSAIDs experience GI irritation. Many eventually will develop ulcers in the stomach, duodenum (the part of the small intestine nearest the stomach) and/or esophagus.

What happens: The NSAIDs reduce levels of prostaglandins, substances that help maintain the protective linings of the digestive tract. These drugs also are acidic—they can irritate tissues and potentially cause internal bleeding.

An analysis of data from the 1990s showed that NSAID-related bleeding was responsible for 32,000 hospitalizations and 3,200 deaths annually. The risk for bleeding is especially high among people 75 years old or older.

Self-defense: Older adults, particularly those with ulcers, should avoid NSAIDs—so should anyone who also is taking an anticoagulant, such as warfarin. The risk for bleeding in those who take both types of drugs is five to six times higher than for those who are taking only an anticoagulant.

Patients with a high risk for NSAID-related bleeding can take acetaminophen. It rarely causes GI irritation. People with arthritis also might try the supplements glucosamine and chondroitin or capsaicin cream.

4

Brain Health & Super-Aging Secrets

The Real Truth About Alzheimer's Prevention

We all want to do everything possible to avoid Alzheimer's, the irreversible, progressive brain disease that affects more than 5 million Americans.

The problem: Experts disagree on whether anything we do to change our lifestyles will actually help.

The news media has recently reported a statement made by a panel of 15 scientists in the *Annals of Internal Medicine* that there's not enough evidence to recommend any particular lifestyle habits to prevent Alzheimer's.

How could they make such a statement?

What the headlines missed: There is, in fact, a large body of scientific evidence suggesting that certain strategies help protect against Alzheimer's disease—it's just that these interventions have yet to be definitively proven

in clinical settings. Instead, the evidence we have at this time is basic scientific research, such as cellular and animal studies, as well as epidemiological research that analyzes large groups of people to discover factors that may be linked to increased or decreased risk for Alzheimer's.

Clinical research, which tests a specific agent such as medication along with a placebo, always lags behind basic and epidemiological research because it is costly and difficult to conduct.

My advice: Follow well-known Alzheimer's prevention strategies. To begin, eat healthfully—ideally a Mediterranean diet that emphasizes brain-healthy omega 3–rich fish and antioxidant-rich fruits, vegetables and nuts.

Marwan Sabbagh, MD, a geriatric neurologist and founding director of the Cleo Roberts Center for Clinical Research at the Banner Sun Health Research Institute in Sun City, Arizona, one of 29 NIH-sponsored Alzheimer's Disease Centers in the US. Dr. Sabbagh is the author or coauthor of more than 120 scientific articles on the disease and is author of *The Alzheimer's Answer* (Wiley).

71

And get regular aerobic exercise to stimulate blood flow to the brain. The most recent research links 45 to 60 minutes four days a week to reduced Alzheimer's risk. Pace yourself, and consult your doctor before starting any exercise program. In addition, keep up with the latest research, and consult your doctor about incorporating simple, underrecognized strategies such as those described below...

AVOID COPPER

Current evidence: In basic research on animals and on the brain cells of people who have died of Alzheimer's, scientists at the University of Rochester Medical Center in New York recently found that copper damages a molecule that shuttles beta-amyloid out of the brain. Beta-amyloid is a protein that forms toxic chunks (plaque) in the brains of people with Alzheimer's, and it may play a key role in the development of the disease. This research builds on a decade of research linking excessive levels of copper in the body to Alzheimer's.

What to do: According to research published in *Chemical Research in Toxicology*, people over age 50 should avoid nutritional supplements that contain copper...take a 15-mg zinc supplement daily—zinc helps the body remove excess copper...limit intake of red meat, which contains a lot of copper...and use an effective filtering system to remove copper from drinking water.

My personal approach: Depending on the water source, tap water may contain significant amounts of copper even if the water isn't flowing through copper pipes. For this reason, I have stopped drinking unfiltered tap water. To remove copper from my drinking water, I use a reverse osmosis waterfilter to separate the water from potentially harmful substances.

Reverse osmosis filtration systems are found at home-improvement stores and online in tap or under-the-sink models (about $150) or whole-house models (up to $3,000).

GET ENOUGH VITAMIN E

Vitamin E has been studied for Alzheimer's for more than a decade, with a landmark study in *The New England Journal of Medicine* in 1997 showing that high doses of vitamin E were more effective than a placebo at delaying specific outcomes of Alzheimer's disease, such as nursing home placement. Now, a recent new study links high dietary intake of vitamin E to a reduced risk for the disease.

Current evidence: In a 10-year study involving more than 5,000 people, those with the highest dietary intake of vitamin E were 25% less likely to develop Alzheimer's than those with the lowest intake, reported Dutch researchers in *Archives of Neurology*.

What to do: Eat vitamin E-rich foods, which supply the full range of vitamin E nutrients. Most vitamin E supplements do not contain the entire class of these nutrients. The data now clearly support dietary sourcesof vitamin E over supplements. Aim to get 15 mg of vitamin E daily.

Best sources: Wheat germ oil (20 mg per tablespoon)...almonds (7 mg per ounce)...sunflower seeds (6 mg per ounce)...and spinach (4 mg per cup, boiled).

BEWARE OF HOSPITALIZATION AND ANESTHESIA

Doctors have long known that some older adults develop Alzheimer's symptoms soon after being hospitalized.

Current evidence: Researchers conducted a six-year study involving nearly 3,000 people age 65 and older who didn't have dementia (cognitive decline most commonly caused by Alzheimer's). As reported in *The Journal of the American Medical Association*, those who were hospitalized for a noncritical illness, such as broken bones, had a 40% higher risk of developing dementia.

The researchers speculated that several factors might play a role in increasing dementia after hospitalization, such as hospital-acquired infections...general anesthesia, tranquilizers and painkillers taken in the hospital...and the blood pressure and blood sugar problems that frequently arise during hospitalization. Research has linked each of these factors, in varying degrees, to the development of Alzheimer's.

What to do: If you are hospitalized, try to stay in the hospital for as short a period as possible. If you need anesthesia and have a choice between general anesthesia or local or spinal anesthesia, opt for the local or spinal. As much as possible, minimize the use of optional psychoactive medications, such as tranquilizers and sleeping pills.

HAVE A PURPOSE IN LIFE

No one knows why people who feel that they have a purpose in life tend to be less likely to develop Alzheimer's, but it does seem to help.

Current evidence: In a study published in *Archives of General Psychiatry*, researchers at the Rush University Medical Center in Chicago found that older adults with a high score on a questionnaire evaluating one's sense of purpose in life (feeling that life has meaning and having goals that guide behavior) were 2.4 times more likely to remain free of Alzheimer's than adults with a low score.

What to do: Look for ways to add meaning to your life—for example, volunteer for your neighborhood association or for local organizations that strive to improve your community. The social involvement associated with volunteering also may help guard against Alzheimer's. Research has linked social connectedness to decreased risk for the disease.

The Alzheimer's Question

Rebecca Shannonhouse, editor, *Bottom Line/Health*, Boardroom Inc., 281 Tresser Blvd., Stamford, Connecticut 06901.

Would you want to know if you were going to get Alzheimer's disease? The brain changes that accompany this disease start 10 years or more before symptoms develop.

Breakthrough finding: Researchers were able to predict, with 100% accuracy, which individuals with mild cognitive impairment (a condition that often precedes Alzheimer's) would develop full-blown Alzheimer's within five years.

Historically, Alzheimer's has been definitively diagnosed only during an autopsy. But a recent study shows that two proteins, amyloid

beta and tau, can be markers for Alzheimer's disease when found in a person's spinal fluid. Researchers speculate that even people without signs of memory loss who have these proteins may develop Alzheimer's.

It will now be possible to enlist people who have mild cognitive impairment and these proteins in studies to develop new Alzheimer's medications, explains Samuel Gandy, MD, PhD, a professor of neurology at Mount Sinai School of Medicine in New York City.

People with memory problems who now choose to get the test and learn that they're likely to develop Alzheimer's will also have time to put their affairs in order while their minds are still relatively sharp.

Catch: Right now, there are no effective treatments for Alzheimer's—and the spinal tap can be painful for some and carries risk for headache, back pain and bleeding. A new diagnostic PET scan is in late-stage trials. With such complex issues in play, anyone who is worried about Alzheimer's should have a long talk with his/her doctor.

Concerned About Memory Loss?

Majid Fotuhi, MD, PhD, director of the Center for Memory and Brain Health at Sinai Hospital and assistant professor of neurology at Johns Hopkins University, both in Baltimore. He is the author of *The Memory Cure* (McGraw-Hill).

If you or members of your family are concerned about your memory, a thorough neurological exam can determine with 90% to 95% accuracy whether you have normal age-related memory loss or some form of dementia.

Good news: People who are alert enough to worry about their memories are less likely to have significant problems. Declines in memory or cognition that are apparent to others—but not to the patient—are usually more serious.

Key parts of a neurological exam...

YOUR MEDICAL HISTORY

Neurologists who specialize in memory loss usually can identify underlying problems from a person's medical history alone.*

Important: A friend or family member should accompany the patient to a neurological exam to help provide information regarding the patient's memory and/or lifestyle.

Questions typically asked...

• **Does the memory loss occur often?** People who repeat themselves frequently or repeatedly ask the same question during conversations are more likely to have a significant memory impairment than those who forget only occasionally.

• **Are there recent triggers?** A patient who recently had surgery might be taking a prescription painkiller or sedative that impairs memory. A head injury—even one that occurred years ago—also can result in memory loss, particularly if the patient also has high blood pressure, diabetes or other health problems. These factors—in combination with an old head injury—can have additive effects on the brain that can result in dementia.

• **Is the patient depressed?** Depression can cause trouble with attention and focus, both of which can lead to memory problems.

• **Is the problem progressing?** Memory loss that keeps getting worse or occurs with confusion—such as getting lost in a familiar area—usually indicates an underlying problem, such as dementia.

MENTAL STATUS EXAM

The Mini-Mental Status Exam (MMSE), which is commonly used to assess memory, evaluates...

• **Recent versus long-term memory.** The doctor may name three common objects, such as an apricot, a flag and a tree, and ask the patient to repeat the objects three minutes later.

What the results may mean: In the early stages of Alzheimer's, a patient might not remember the three objects that were named

just minutes earlier, but is probably able to recall details, such as a favorite childhood song or beloved pet, from the distant past.

• **Orientation.** The patient will be asked to state his/her name, the year, season, day of the week and the date. Such questions test a patient's general awareness.

What the results may mean: Orientation can be impaired by medication side effects or substance abuse as well as different types of dementia, such as Alzheimer's. A patient is more likely to have dementia if he can't remember major details such as the name of the city where he lives.

• **Attention span.** The patient will be asked to count backward (by sevens) from, say, 100...or to spell a short word, such as "holiday" or "pitcher," backward.

What the results may mean: These tests measure alertness and mental focus. A poor score indicates that a patient might have delirium (a usually temporary decline in mental function due to an acute problem, such as a urinary tract infection) rather than, or in addition to, dementia.

Example: I recently saw in my practice a 102-year-old patient who didn't know where she was. I ordered a urine test, and it turned out that she had a urinary tract infection. I gave her antibiotics, and two days later she was back to normal.

PHYSICAL EXAM

The neurologist also will perform a physical examination that tests, among other things, reflexes and muscle movements to determine whether the patient has had a stroke or has thyroid problems, heart problems, Parkinson's disease or other conditions that can contribute to dementia.

DIAGNOSTIC TESTS

Depending on the results of the medical history and clinical exam, other tests, including the following, may be performed...

• **Imaging tests.** A magnetic resonance imaging (MRI) scan can show evidence of a stroke, bleeding in the brain, a brain tumor or brain shrinkage.

• **Blood tests.** Low levels of thyroid hormone and vitamin B-12 (both are detected by blood tests) may contribute to dementia.

*Ask your doctor to refer you, if possible, to a neurologist affiliated with an academic medical center. He/she will be more likely to be up-to-date on the latest research.

More from Majid Fotuhi, MD, PhD,

Simple Brain-Boosting Exercises Cut Your Risk for Alzheimer's

Anyone who has ever done a sit-up or bicep curl knows that exercises are generally targeted to specific parts of the body.

But what about brain exercises?

What most people don't realize: Even though it's common to assume that a daily crossword puzzle or game of bridge or chess gives your brain a full workout, that's not true.

There are, in fact, specific activities that can be done on a regular basis to "exercise" all parts of your brain so that you have the best possible chance of retaining your mental capacities as you age.

Brain-boosting exercises are most effective when performed as part of an overall brain-health regimen that also includes regular aerobic exercise to increase blood flow to the brain.

TOP 10 BRAIN BOOSTERS

The brain exercises described below are not only fun to do, but also challenge a person's reasoning, planning, memory and spatial skills.

1. Challenge your powers of navigation. If you have a GPS navigation device in your car, turn it off when driving to an unfamiliar destination and use a map to find your way. If you don't have a GPS and use maps anyway, concentrate on remembering the route so that you can make most of the return trip by memory.

Also helpful: When you're walking inside a large building, keep track of where north and south are.

Good for: Right parietal lobe, the part of your brain that's responsible for judging your orientation in space.

2. Engage in math on the fly. While grocery shopping, tally the cost of your purchases in your head.

Also helpful: When driving a distance of any length, keep track of your elapsed time and miles covered, and use this information to periodically calculate your average speed.

Good for: Left parietal lobe, the part of your brain used to make mathematical calculations.

3. Play mind games. When you have some "downtime"—if you're stuck in traffic, for example, or waiting on line at the store—memorize your credit card numbers or phone numbers of friends.

Also helpful: Spell the names of cities and states backward.

Good for: Frontal lobes, used in planning and abstract thinking...left parietal lobe...and left temporal lobe, specialized for language functions, including speech, language comprehension and verbal memory.

4. Take a class in ballroom dancing. You must pay attention to the sequence of steps, memorize them and then perform them while following the rhythm of the music and the movements of your partner.

Good for: Parietal lobes (spatial awareness)...frontal lobes (planning of movement)... and cerebellum (balance and physical movement). The right frontal lobe and cerebellum are activated with the music component of dancing.

5. Prepare new recipes. Preparing an unfamiliar dish forces you to carefully follow instructions and coordinate the order and timing of each step, thereby strengthening the parts of your frontal lobes used for following directions and planning. Be adventurous—the more unfamiliar the ingredients and cooking style, the more you'll have to focus.

Good for: Both frontal lobes.

6. Do tai chi. In addition to giving a workout to the cerebellum and frontal lobes on both sides, remembering sequences of the slow-motion movements used in tai chi relaxes the brain. Added bonus: Tai chi reduces levels of the stress hormone cortisol.

Good for: Cerebellum...and frontal lobes.

7. Purchase furniture you have to assemble yourself. Or fix things at home, such as malfunctioning remote controls and clogged sinks. Having to figure out the parts and steps required is certain to give your brain's frontal lobes a stimulating workout.

Good for: Both frontal lobes…and the cerebellum.

8. Learn to play a musical instrument. Mastering the technique of any new instrument exercises parts of your brain used for fine motor control, auditory processing and procedural thinking, among others. If you already play a musical instrument, challenge yourself by learning a new song.

Good for: Both parietal lobes…both frontal lobes…and the cerebellum.

9. Enroll in a drawing, painting or sculpture class. Learning a new art form exercises your "right brain," which is responsible for visual memory, as well as creative imagination. People who already practice an art form should push themselves with new works.

Good for: Right parietal lobe…and right frontal lobe.

10. Read the news actively every day. Reading about political events—not just in the US but around the world—requires and activates "attention" centers of the brain, mostly the frontal lobes.

Remembering scores of sports events also heightens and sharpens the frontal lobes.

Good for: Both frontal lobes.

Stress Raises Risk for Cognitive Decline

Stress raises risk for cognitive decline in older people with diabetes.

Recent finding: Brain function is slowed among patients with type 2 diabetes who have high levels of the stress hormone cortisol. Researchers hope that regulating cortisol levels may reduce cognitive decline in people with diabetes.

Study of 1,066 people between ages 60 and 75 by researchers at University of Edinburgh, Scotland, published in *Diabetes Care*.

Lessons for Living Longer from the People Who Live the Longest

Dan Buettner is founder of Blue Zones, an organization that studies the regions of the world where people commonly live active lives past the age of 100, and author of *The Blue Zones* (National Geographic). *www. bluezones.com.*

The average life expectancy in the US is 78.1 years, an age that is far less than our potential maximum life spans.

On the Japanese island of Okinawa, there are approximately 50 centenarians (those who reach 100 years or more) per 100,000 people. In the US, at most 20 per 100,000 people reach this impressive milestone.

A long life is not an accident. Writer and longevity expert Dan Buettner, in conjunction with the National Institute on Aging and the nation's top gerontologists, has studied what he calls the world's Blue Zones, areas where people live unexpectedly long and healthy lives. In addition to Okinawa, the Blue Zones include Sardinia, Italy…Loma Linda, California (home to many Seventh-day Adventists)…and the Nicoya Peninsula in Costa Rica.

Important finding: Only about 25% of longevity is determined by genetics. The other 75% is largely determined by the choices that we make every day. The average American could live up to 14 more good years by putting the following habits to work.

CHOOSE ACTIVITY, NOT "EXERCISE"

In Sardinia, where the rate of centenarians is 208 per 100,000, many men work as shepherds. They hike for miles every day. Similarly, people in Okinawa get hours of daily exercise in their gardens. California's Seventh-day Adventists, one of the longest-living groups in the US, take frequent nature walks.

What these groups have in common is regular, low-intensity physical exercise. They don't necessarily lift weights or run marathons. They merely stay active—and they do it every day throughout their lives.

Daily physical activity improves balance and reduces the risk for falls, a common cause of death among seniors. It lowers blood pressure and improves cardiovascular health. It increases the odds that people will be functionally independent in their later years.

Recommended: 30 to 60 minutes of moderate physical activity daily. This could include riding a bicycle or walking instead of driving.

EAT LESS

Okinawan elders intone this adage before eating—*hara hachi bu*—a reminder to stop eating when their stomachs are 80% full.

People who quit eating when they're no longer hungry (rather than eating until they feel full) find it easy to maintain a healthy weight, which reduces the risk for heart disease. This approach is more natural than conventional diets. *Helpful...*

• **Serve yourself at the kitchen counter, then put the food away.** People who do this tend to eat about 14% less than those who don't.

• **Use smaller plates and bowls.** Doing so makes servings look larger, which helps you eat less. In one study, people who ate from a 34-ounce bowl took in 31% more than those who used a 17-ounce bowl. Similarly, people drink at least 25% more when they use short, wide glasses instead of tall, narrow ones.

• **Buy small.** Most people consume about 150 more calories when they take food from large packages than when they take it from smaller ones.

LIMIT MEAT

In every Blue Zone, meat is consumed, at most, a few times a month. People in these communities live mainly on beans, whole grains, vegetables and other plant foods. These foods are high in fiber, antioxidants and anticancer compounds. Traditional Sardinians, Nicoyans and Okinawans eat what is produced in their gardens supplemented by staples—durum wheat (Sardinia), sweet potato (Okinawa) and maize (Nicoya). Strict Adventists avoid meat entirely.

Studies of Seventh-day Adventists show that a relatively high proportion eat nuts (any kind). Those who eat about two ounces of nuts five or more times a week have heart disease rates that are only half those who rarely eat nuts.

CONSIDER WINE

Studies of long-lived people suggest that drinking alcohol in moderation is a powerful factor in living longer. It is consumed in three of the Blue Zones (Okinawa, Sardinia and Costa Rica). In Sardinia, the shepherds drink about one-quarter bottle of red wine a day. Their wine has two to three times more flavonoids than other wines (because of the hot climate and the way the wine is made). Flavonoids reduce arterial inflammation. Inflammation has been linked to atherosclerosis, diabetes and Alzheimer's disease.

CULTIVATE A SENSE OF PURPOSE

A study funded by the National Institutes of Health (NIH) found that people who are excited by life and feel that they're making a difference tend to live longer (and healthier) lives than those who just "get by."

Okinawans call it *ikigai* and Nicoyans call it *plan de vida*, but in both cultures, the phrase essentially translates to *why I wake up in the morning*. Anything that gives you a sense of purpose—even taking pleasure in watching your children or grandchildren grow up well—can add years to your life.

DE-STRESS

Many people don't realize that the 24/7 American lifestyle is literally toxic. It produces a chronic increase in stress hormones that triggers inflammation throughout the body.

Most of the world's longest-lived people incorporate some form of meaningful downtime into their daily lives. Nicoyans take a break every afternoon to socialize with friends. For Adventists, the Saturday Sabbath is a time to rest.

EMBRACE YOUR SPIRITUAL SIDE

Faith is a key element that most centenarians have in common. The Sardinians and Nicoyans are mostly Catholic. Okinawans have a blended religion that stresses ancestor worship. The Adventists form a strong religious community. People who attend religious services are about one-third less likely to die in a given period than those who don't. Even among people who don't go to church, those with spiritual beliefs have less depression, better immunity and lower rates of heart disease.

PUT FAMILY FIRST

In the Blue Zones, a great emphasis is placed on family—and people who live with or maintain close ties with their families get sick less often than those without these ties. They also are more likely to maintain better mental and social skills throughout their lives.

The Ultimate Brain Foods

Alan C. Logan, ND, naturopathic physician and author of *The Brain Diet* (Cumberland House), and scientific journals. *www.drlogan.com.*

If you are trying to do everything possible to keep your brain in good health, chances are your diet includes well-known brain-boosting foods, such as salmon (with its beneficial fatty acids) and blueberries (with their high antioxidant and anti-inflammatory content).

Here are some less well-known options that can also confer significant brain-protecting effects (because these foods contain a wide variety of important nutrients, it's wise to consume them even if you take brain-boosting supplements, such as fish oil or vitamin B-12)…

• **Purple sweet potatoes.** Like yellow or orange sweet potatoes, the purple variety is loaded with antioxidants. But purple sweet potatoes also have special antioxidants—purple pigments called *anthocyanins*. These pigments help preserve the integrity of blood vessels that transport oxygen to the brain and improve signaling between nerve cells in the brain (neurons).

As we age, the integrity of the tiny blood vessels delivering nutrients and energy—in the form of blood sugar (glucose)—to the brain diminishes. But our mental sharpness is dependent on a healthy blood supply.

For the greatest benefits: Aim to eat one medium purple sweet potato (available in gourmet supermarkets and Asian grocery stores) or one yellow or orange sweet potato twice a week. Instead of topping them with butter and/or salt, try eating oven-roasted sweet potatoes with the nutrient-rich skins.

• **Sardines.** When it comes to fish that provide the most brain-boosting omega-3 fatty acids, most people think of salmon, mackerel and herring.

Even better: Sardines (along with salmon, mackerel and herring) are less likely than large fish, such as swordfish, shark and tilefish, to have high amounts of mercury and polychlorinated biphenyls (PCBs). Plus, sardines are budget-friendly and convenient because they are typically canned and require no cooking.

For the greatest benefits: Eat three to four servings of omega-3–rich fish, including sardines—about 3.5 ounces per serving (the size of a deck of cards) weekly. When cooking fish, trim the skin—this practice significantly reduces PCB content.

• **Omega-3–enriched eggs.** As a rich source of a valuable nutrient known as choline, eggs help protect against cognitive decline by facilitating efficient communication between neurons.

For the greatest benefits: Try omega-3–enriched eggs, which have an anti-inflammatory effect that also promotes brain health. Eat four to five omega-3 eggs per week.

Important: The omega-3 content of eggs remains generally stable during scrambling and poaching, according to research. Hard-boiling may be somewhat less beneficial due to the breakdown of brain-boosting fats within eggs during boiling.

• **Ginger.** As an anti-inflammatory, ginger can preempt the manufacture of inflammatory brain chemicals and potentially can delay or slow down the progression of inflammation-related brain conditions, such as Alzheimer's disease.

For greatest benefits: Add one teaspoon of freshly grated ginger to your meals two or three times a week…or about one-half teaspoon of powdered ginger. If you prefer pill form, take one 500-mg ginger capsule daily.

• **Green tea.** Green tea contains *epigallocatechin-3-gallate* (EGCG), an antioxidant that curbs brain-damaging inflammation.

Promising research: A recent study found that mice that drank water with EGCG for six months showed a 50% decrease, on average, in the amyloid plaques characteristic of Alzheimer's disease.

For the greatest benefits: Drink three to four (eight-ounce) cups daily. Decaffeinated green tea also promotes brain health but is less potent than caffeinated.

• **Coffee.** Regular consumption of caffeinated coffee can reduce risk for cognitive decline and neurodegenerative diseases, such as Alzheimer's and Parkinson's.

This brain-protective effect may be due to coffee's ability to protect the fat component of cells against oxidative stress. Since the brain is 60% fat, this could account for the positive link between coffee consumption and lower risk for neuro-degenerative diseases.

For the greatest benefits: Consider drinking two to four (eight-ounce) cups daily of home-brewed coffee, which tends to have less caffeine than coffee bought at a coffee shop.

Helpful: If you are especially sensitive to the effects of caffeine or you suffer from insomnia, anxiety, high blood pressure or irregular heartbeat, moderate your intake of caffeine and/or try decaffeinated coffee, which still is a good, though somewhat less potent, source of antioxidants.

Eat Your Way To a Better Memory

Oranges are a great source of folate, which boosts recall and information processing. Aim for one medium-sized orange per day. Black beans are rich in fiber and vitamin B-1, which helps memory by synthesizing acetylcholine, a neurotransmitter that is crucial for memory. Aim for one-half cup a day. Sage improves recall for up to four hours after consumption. Add one teaspoon of sage-infused olive oil to canned or homemade soup, or use it in a meat marinade.

Natural Health, One Park Avenue, New York City 10016, *www.naturalhealthmag.com*.

Chromium and Memory

When 26 adults with mild memory loss took a 1,000-mcg chromium picolinate supplement or a placebo daily for 12 weeks, the supplement group performed better on memory tests while the placebo group showed no change.

Theory: This trace mineral reduces insulin resistance, a condition in which the body's cells don't use insulin properly. Too little insulin in the brain may contribute to poor memory.

If you're concerned about your memory: Ask your doctor about taking 400 mcg of chromium picolinate daily.

Caution: This supplement may affect dosage requirements for diabetes medications.

Robert Krikorian, PhD, associate professor of clinical psychiatry, University of Cincinnati, Ohio.

Treatments May Ease Behavioral Problems

Noll L. Campbell, PharmD, clinical pharmacy specialist in geriatrics, Wishard Health Services, Indianapolis.

Cholinesterase inhibitor drugs, such as *donepezil* (Aricept) and *rivastigmine* (Exelon), which are prescribed to help slow the progression of cognitive impairment in Alzheimer's disease patients, also curb such symptoms as aggression, paranoia and wandering, with no major side effects, according to a recent review of nine studies.

Important: Cholinesterase inhibitors typically are prescribed for less than 10% of Alzheimer's patients seen in primary care practice—and for fewer than three months, on average—even though 90% of patients have behavioral and psychological symptoms.

Possible reasons: Dementia often goes unrecognized by primary care physicians…and because of the stigma attached to a dementia diagnosis, many patients and doctors may not pursue treatment options. If a family member has Alzheimer's disease, ask his/her doctor whether a cholinesterase inhibitor might be helpful. A growing body of evidence shows that atypical antipsychotics, such as *risperidone* (Risperdal) and *quetiapine* (Seroquel), which have been used for behavioral problems in elderly dementia patients, may hasten their death (due to cardiovascular events or pneumonia).

Brain Stimulation for Alzheimer's

Ten Alzheimer's patients received a placebo or repetitive transcranial magnetic stimulation (rTMS), which applies magnetic pulses to the brain at high frequencies.

Result: The rTMS group improved sentence-comprehension test scores by 11%, while the placebo group showed no change. Benefits lasted for up to eight weeks.

If a loved one has Alzheimer's: Ask the patient's doctor about rTMS—it is available at several US hospitals and research centers.

Maria Cotelli, PhD, researcher, Centro San Giovanni di Dio Fatebenefratelli, Brescia, Italy.

Apple Juice May Curb Alzheimer's Symptoms

Twenty-one adults (ages 72 to 93) with moderate-to-severe Alzheimer's disease who consumed eight ounces of apple juice daily for one month showed a 27% improvement in behavioral and psychotic symptoms (including decreased anxiety, agitation and delusions).

Theory: Apple juice may boost production of the neurotransmitter acetylcholine, which declines as a result of Alzheimer's.

If a loved one suffers from Alzheimer's: In addition to giving prescribed medications, try serving apple juice to enhance his/her comfort.

Thomas Shea, PhD, professor and director, Center for Cellular Neurobiology and Neuro-degeneration Research, University of Massachusetts Lowell.

Infections and Alzheimer's

Infection may accelerate Alzheimer's progression, we hear from Clive Holmes, PhD.

New study: In 222 Alzheimer's patients who were followed for six months, those with inflammation due to infections (such as respiratory or gastrointestinal) had twice the rate of memory loss as those who hadn't suffered such inflammation.

Theory: Tumor necrosis factor-alpha, a protein involved in the inflammation process, may play a role in brain functioning.

If a loved one has Alzheimer's: Make sure he/she is promptly treated for infections.

Clive Holmes, PhD, professor of biological psychiatry, University of Southampton, UK.

Not Just for Kids...

Musical video games can sharpen the mind. People who play along with the beat of the songs develop new connections between neurons and synapses, building up the brain. Music games such as Guitar Hero and Rock Band can be played alone or with a partner.

Ezriel E. Kornel, MD, FACS, neurosurgeon, Brain & Spine Surgeons of New York, White Plains.

Online Games That Improve Your Mind

Andrew Carle, an expert on technology for older adults. He is assistant professor at the College of Health and Human Services at George Mason University in Fairfax, Virginia.

Electronic games have been around for many years, but they recently reached a new level with computer programs designed specifically to help older adults hone their mental abilities.

These games—including some that are better described as mental exercises—are aimed at improving several important abilities, including memory, eye-hand coordination, audio perception and visual acuity. And they're fun!

The best of these programs continually offer new challenges to customers via the Internet, so games you played last week won't necessarily be the same as those you play this week. That's a big advantage over bridge, chess and other classic games that are challenging but require the same skill regardless of how long you play them.

NEW CHALLENGES

The new mental exercises generally fall into two categories. "Brain Gyms" are designed to be personalized and comprehensive, which gives you an incentive to play—just as working out at an actual gym may be more enjoyable than, say, just using a treadmill in your den. They're also likely to adjust more often according to your performance.

"Brain Trainers" usually have a smaller selection of games—though many can be very entertaining—and they're aimed at a broad range of users, not just older adults.

Most new training games are sold on a subscription basis, but some can also be purchased on a CD.

A potential drawback of the new games is that few of them can be played directly against an opponent, although two or more people can sometimes challenge each other by playing separately and then comparing scores.

Before making a purchase...

• **Try out the program,** which most companies let you do online for free.

• **Even if a trial game seems to work well, check the "system requirements" page of the manufacturer's Web site** to make sure that your computer can play the game you're interested in. The new games typically require a computer with at least 256 megabytes (and preferably 512 megabytes) of random access memory (RAM) and 500 megabytes (and preferably 1 gigabyte) of free disk space on your hard drive. You may also need headphones for some of the games that involve auditory skills.

WORKING OUT IN THE "GYM"

Popular brain gyms include...

• **CogniFit.** Dozens of entertaining exercises are aimed at improving reaction time, short-term memory, eye-hand coordination and the ability to recognize signs and symbols.

In one game, a room with different-colored walls is displayed on the screen. A colored ball bounces off one wall and then another. The object is to make sure that the ball bounces off only the wall that's the same color as the ball. The game is more difficult than it first appears.

Price for the gym: $99.95 for six-month subscription.

Information: 866-669-6223, *www.cognifit. com.*

• **Posit Science.** One exercise program sharpens your eyesight while another is aimed at improving your hearing.

Eyesight exercises are designed to widen your field of view and improve your ability to locate certain colors and shapes. Auditory games give you practice in telling sounds apart, responding to different sounds and remembering what you hear. Exercises of this kind are helpful in many ways, from improving driving skills to enjoying a Broadway show. Combined audio and visual programs also available.

Price for the gym: $395 for a two-user version. $690 for combined programs.

Information: 866-599-6463, *www.posit science.com.*

• **Vigorous Mind.** I'm on the advisory board of this company, which provides a variety of entertaining games designed to improve memory as well as skills in language, perception, mathematics, reasoning and eye-hand coordination.

Price for the gym: $39.95 for three months, $64.95 for six months and $119.95 for one year.

Information: 888-769-6463, *www.vigorous mind.com.*

"TRAINERS" ON THE WEB

Some of the most popular brain trainers...

• **Lumosity.** By accessing a Web site, you can play games designed to improve attention span, speed at performing tasks and other cognitive abilities, such as concentration and memory for both names and numbers.

The games are colorful and entertaining, and as your skill improves, tasks become progressively difficult.

Price: $14.95 for one month or $80.40 for one year.

Information: *www.lumosity.com.*

• **MyBrainTrainer.** The company's 21-day online training program aims to help you process information, perform simultaneous tasks, retrieve information from memory and improve concentration. The program records daily and monthly scores so that you can keep track of improvements and know where you still need practice. Exercises include dozens of games that require you to respond to visual and/or audio signals.

Price: $9.95 for three months or $29.95 for one year.

Information: *www.mybraintrainer.com.*

NO COMPUTER NEEDED

If you don't want to rely on a computer for playing mind-expanding games, consider…

• **Big Brain Academy.** Each of the 15 games is played on a Nintendo DS handheld device. You can play alone to improve your score or with as many as seven other competitors. The games are designed to test your ability to think logically, analyze, compute, visually identify and memorize. At the end of a game, you receive a label that describes your brain—from "caveman" to "Isaac Newton."

Typical price: $19.99 plus about $110 for a Nintendo DS, on which you can play dozens of other games suitable for adults, including Crosswords DS and Scrabble.

Information: 800-895-1672, *www.ninten do.com.* Games and the DS device are also available from such retailers as Amazon.com and Office Depot.

• **Platinum Solitaire 3.** A dozen variations of the game can be played on many cell-phone models, including BlackBerry, Nokia, Samsung and Sony Ericsson. In its "casino mode," Platinum Solitaire 3 lets you place simulated bets on your talent.

Note: The higher the bet, the more difficult the game becomes.

Typical price: $3 and up. The game is also available free with some cell-phone subscriptions that include a Nokia phone.

Information: 212-993-3000, *www.gameloft. com.*

Memory Robbers That Are Often Overlooked

Cynthia R. Green, PhD, assistant clinical professor of psychiatry at Mount Sinai School of Medicine in New York City and president of Memory Arts, LLC. *www. memoryarts.com.* She is the author of *Total Memory Workout* (Bantam).

Alzheimer's disease is such a dreaded diagnosis that you may be filled with panic if you experience occasional memory loss. But these worries may be unnecessary.

As people age, the brain undergoes changes that may lead to some decline in short-term memory. This is normal.

Of course memory loss that truly concerns you is another matter. *Ask your primary care physician to refer you to a neurologist or geriatrician for an evaluation if…*

• **You have noticed a significant change in your everyday memory over the past six months.**

• **Friends or family members have expressed concern about your memory.**

• **You have begun forgetting recent conversations.**

In the meantime, consider whether your occasional forgetfulness may be due to one of the following causes, all of which can be easily corrected…

NOT ENOUGH SLEEP

Poor sleep is probably the most common cause of occasional memory lapses. The ability to concentrate suffers with insufficient rest. Sleep also appears to be essential for consolidating memory—whatever information you learn during the day, whether it's the name of a colleague or the street where a new restaurant opened, you need sleep to make it stick in your mind.

Self-defense: If you're not sleeping seven to eight hours nightly, make it a priority to get more sleep. If you are unable to improve your sleep on your own, talk to your doctor.

WIDELY USED DRUGS

Impaired memory is a potential side effect of many medications. Obvious suspects include prescription sleeping pills…opiate painkillers, such as *meperidine* (Demerol)…and anti-anxiety drugs, such as *diazepam* (Valium) and *alprazolam* (Xanax).

Certain blood pressure–lowering medications, such as beta-blockers, and antidepressants also cause memory problems in some people. Even over-the-counter antihistamines, such as *diphenhydramine* (Benadryl), can have this effect.

If you're taking multiple medications, more than one may cause impaired memory, making it even more difficult to identify the culprit.

Timing is often a tip-off: When impaired memory is an adverse drug effect, it's most likely to appear when you start taking a new medication or increase the dose. But not always.

As we grow older, our bodies become less efficient at clearing medications from the body, so the same dose you've been taking safely for years may cause problems you never had before.

Self-defense: If you think medication might be affecting your memory, do not stop taking the drug or reduce the dosage on your own. Talk to your doctor or pharmacist for advice.

EMOTIONAL UPSET

When you're anxious, stressed or depressed, your ability to concentrate suffers. Whatever it is that worries or preoccupies you keeps your mind from focusing on facts, names, faces and places, so they aren't absorbed into memory.

Self-defense: To keep everyday tensions from undercutting your memory, practice some form of relaxation or stress reduction. Yoga, meditation, deep breathing—or something as simple as allowing yourself a soothing time-out to walk or chat with a friend—can relieve accumulated stress and bolster your recall.

True depression is something else: Even mild-to-moderate depression can sap your energy, take pleasure out of life and affect your memory. If you suspect that you may be depressed, be alert for other symptoms—such as difficulty sleeping, sadness, apathy and a negative outlook—and see your doctor or a mental-health professional.

TOO MUCH ALCOHOL

Moderate red wine consumption has been shown to promote the health of your heart and arteries. Because of this cardiovascular health benefit, red wine also may reduce risk for dementia.

Excessive drinking, on the other hand, is harmful to the brain. Among its devastating toxic effects is a severe and often irreversible form of memory loss called Korsakoff's syndrome, a condition that occurs in alcoholics.

Alcohol's effect on memory can be subtle. Some people find that even a glass or two of wine daily is enough to interfere with learning facts and recalling information. Pay attention to how mentally sharp you feel after having a drink. If you think your alcohol intake may be causing forgetfulness, cut back. Remember, tolerance for alcohol generally declines with age, giving the same drink more impact.

Self-defense: There is more scientific evidence supporting red wine's brain-protective effect than for any other form of alcohol. If you are a man, do not exceed two glasses of red wine daily, and if you are a woman, limit yourself to one glass daily.

ILLNESS

A simple cold or headache is enough to interfere with your concentration and recall.

Illnesses that commonly go undiagnosed also may play a role. For example, when the thyroid gland (which regulates metabolism) is underactive, the mind slows down along with the body. (Other signs of an underactive thyroid include weight gain, constipation, thin or brittle hair and depression.) An overactive thyroid can affect your memory by making you anxious, "wired" and easily distracted.

Memory impairment also may be a symptom of other disorders, such as Parkinson's disease, multiple sclerosis or Lyme disease.

NUTRITIONAL DEFICIENCY

An easily overlooked memory robber is a vitamin B-12 deficiency, often marked by general fatigue and slowed thinking. Older people are especially at risk—as we age, our ability to absorb vitamin B-12 from foods diminishes.

Self-defense: If you have occasional memory lapses, ask your doctor for a blood test to check your vitamin B-12 level.

SAFEGUARDING YOUR MEMORY

Even if you've identified a relatively harmless cause for occasional forgetfulness, it's still wise to take steps to guard against cognitive decline in the future. *My advice…*

•**Get enough exercise.** Exercise helps prevent a wide range of serious health problems, including heart disease, diabetes and some types of cancer. The evidence also is strong that exercise protects against dementia—and enhances everyday memory performance by improving overall circulation and lowering risk for disorders that can affect memory, such as high blood pressure and obesity.

Self-defense: A leisurely stroll around the block may be relaxing, but you must get 30 minutes of moderate exertion (such as brisk walking or swimming), three to four days a week, to keep your memory intact.

•**Stay on top of chronic health problems.** Studies have shown repeatedly that people with high blood pressure, atherosclerosis (fatty buildup in the arteries), obesity and/or diabetes are at dramatically increased risk of developing dementia in their later years.

The effect of these chronic medical conditions on day-to-day memory is less clear. Research shows that memory declines when blood sugar rises in people with diabetes and improves when they take dietary steps to stabilize it.

Self-defense: If you have a chronic health problem, work with your doctor to keep your symptoms under control.

•**Give your brain a timed workout.** A growing body of research shows that mental exercise helps fend off everyday age-related cognitive changes that contribute to occasional forgetfulness.

Self-defense: Crossword puzzles and the number game Sudoku have gotten a lot of attention as "brain" workouts, but I prefer timed games, such as the word game Boggle or the card game Set (both available online or at discount stores). Racing against the clock gives your mental muscles a real workout by challenging such intellectual skills as attention, speed and multitasking.

Dementia: When It's Not Alzheimer's

Muriel R. Gillick, MD, an associate professor of population medicine at Harvard Medical School/Harvard Pilgrim Health Care, and staff geriatrician at Harvard Vanguard Medical Associates, all in Boston. She is the author of *Tangled Minds: Understanding Alzheimer's Disease and Other Dementias* (Plume).

Memory-robbing Alzheimer's disease is the most common form of dementia, affecting more than five million Americans.

What you may not know: One-third to one-half of patients with dementia suffer from a non-Alzheimer's neurological disease that typically starts with symptoms other than memory loss.

In advanced stages, the symptoms of these other dementias resemble those of Alzheimer's disease. Besides suffering from memory loss, patients eventually have minimal ability to speak and/or limited ability to move.

Anyone who has problems with walking, planning activities or mood (such as apathy or depression) should be evaluated by a neurologist or geriatrician, who may suggest treatments that can help improve symptoms.

Non-Alzheimer's dementias…

VASCULAR DEMENTIA

It's the second most common form of dementia in older adults, and the one that's potentially the most preventable.

Key symptoms: Difficulty performing mental tasks, such as balancing a checkbook or planning an activity, and problems with walking, bladder control and/or vision. Although memory loss is one of the first symptoms experienced by people with Alzheimer's disease, it typically occurs later in most patients with vascular dementia.

Vascular dementia can be caused by a single large stroke, multiple small strokes or narrowing of small blood vessels to the brain due to plaque formation (atherosclerosis).

Some patients experience symptoms of vascular dementia abruptly—for example, immediately after a stroke. More often, damage to the brain occurs over a period of years. A magnetic resonance imaging (MRI) scan of the brain often shows abnormalities in people with vascular dementia.

The same conditions that increase the risk for stroke—elevated blood pressure, diabetes and high cholesterol—also increase the risk for vascular dementia. Treating these conditions won't reverse cognitive changes but can play a significant role in prevention.

Recent finding: European researchers followed a group of patients age 60 and older for four years. All had hypertension, but none had signs of dementia. Those who were given the drug *nitrendipine*—a calcium channel blocker similar to the US drug *nifedipine* (Procardia)—to control hypertension were half as likely to develop vascular dementia over a four-year period as those who weren't given the drug.

Treatment: Alzheimer's drugs known as cholinesterase inhibitors, such as *donepezil* (Aricept) and *rivastigmine* (Exelon), may reduce symptoms of vasculardementia in some patients.

LEWY BODY DEMENTIA

Lewy body dementia, which typically occurs in adults age 65 and older, is named for Dr. Friederich H. Lewy, the scientist who discovered the disease's characteristic abnormal protein deposits that form inside nerve cells in the brain.

Key symptoms: Some are typical of Alzheimer's disease, such as memory loss and confusion...others resemble those caused by Parkinson's disease, such as muscle rigidity. Lewy body dementia also causes visual hallucinations (seeing objects or people that are not really there)...delusions (a false belief that cannot be altered by a rational argument)... and fluctuations in alertness.

No one knows exactly what causes Lewy body dementia. The protein deposits are often present in patients with Alzheimer's and Parkinson's diseases, suggesting that the conditions may be linked in some way.

To diagnose Lewy body dementia, doctors look for a progressive decline in cognitive abilities, along with intermittent episodes of hallucinations, a lack of alertness and Parkinson's-like symptoms.

Treatment: Parkinson's disease drugs, such as *carbidopa* and *levadopa* (Sinemet), to improve motor symptoms.

Warning: In some Lewy body patients, Sinemet may worsen hallucinations.

For hallucinations and delusions, low doses of antipsychotics, such as *quetiapine* (Seroquel) or *olanzapine* (Zyprexa), if necessary.

Warning: The antipsychotic drugs *haloperidol* (Haldol) and *risperidone* (Risperdal) worsen Parkinson's-like symptoms in patients with Lewy body dementia.

FRONTOTEMPORAL DEMENTIA

This is a rare form of dementia in which portions of the brain shrink, causing extreme changes in personality. Unlike other forms of dementia, which are most common in older adults, frontotemporal dementia typically appears between ages 40 and 60.

Key symptoms: Inappropriate public behavior, such as getting undressed in public...rude comments...lack of inhibition...apathy or a loss of interest in everyday life...short-term memory loss...and compulsive behavior, such as constantly shutting doors.

No one test can diagnose frontotemporal dementia. Imaging studies of the brain, such as MRI, will sometimes show shrinkage of the frontal or temporal lobes. There are no treatments that can stop frontotemporal dementia or slow its progression. Most patients die within two to 10 years after the initial diagnosis.

Treatment for symptoms: Antipsychotic drugs (preferably low-dose) may be used to reduce agitation or compulsive behavior. However, research shows that these drugs are not very effective for this purpose and may even hasten death in older dementia patients.

Do Your Hands Shake?

Elan D. Louis, MD, professor of neurology and epidemiology and associate chairman of neurology at the College of Physicians and Surgeons and the Mailman School of Public Health at Columbia University, New York City.

Many diseases can cause tremors, involuntary shaking or muscle movements that can make it hard to drink a glass of water, hold a knife or fork, or write a note. The most common is essential tremor, a difficult-to-treat disorder that causes uncontrollable shaking of the hands, head and/or other parts of the body.

An estimated 10 million Americans have the disorder, as did the late Katharine Hepburn. According to the National Institutes of Health, essential tremor may affect as many as 14% of people over the age of 65.

Essential tremor can be so mild that it is merely an inconvenience, or it can progress to the point that patients struggle with any activity that requires hand control, such as buttoning a shirt.

Little was known about essential tremor until recently. Elan D. Louis, MD, a pioneering neurologist and epidemiologist, discusses what we know now about the disorder...

RECENT FINDINGS

We have learned from recent brain studies that patients with essential tremor have about a 40% reduction in Purkinje cells. These are brain cells that produce an inhibitory neurotransmitter known as *gamma-aminobutyric acid* (GABA).

Lower-than-normal levels of GABA could cause, or contribute to, a loss of muscle control.

Healthy Purkinje cells are packed with protein structures (neurofilaments) that are linearly shaped and neatly arranged. In patients with essential tremor, these structures more often look messy and chaotic. The disruption in these structures could inhibit the transport of essential substances within the nerve cells.

About half of all cases of essential tremor are thought to be due to a genetic mutation. Exposure to lead may be a factor. Also, a substance called *harman* could contribute to the disorder. Harman is naturally produced in the body—it also is present in many foods, especially meat. We have found, in some studies, that patients with essential tremor sometimes have levels of harman that are 50% to 100% higher than in people without the disease.

Levels of harman rise when meat is cooked at high temperatures or for long periods of time. However, the research is too preliminary at this stage to advise people to change their cooking and/or eating habits to avoid essential tremor.

IS IT PARKINSON'S?

Essential tremor usually is easily distinguished from Parkinson's disease. In patients with Parkinson's, the hands mainly shake when they are at rest. With essential tremor, the shaking occurs when the hands are in use. With Parkinson's disease, shaking often occurs in the legs as well, whereas in essential tremor, the head and voice often shake.

Until recently, doctors mainly looked for action tremors (shaking while the hands were being used) to diagnose essential tremor. We have learned in the last few years that these patients tend to have other issues as well, including abnormal eye movements, problems with coordination and possibly cognitive changes (such as memory loss).

Though essential tremor is different from Parkinson's disease, the underlying causes may be linked in some fashion. We have found that Parkinson's disease occurs about four times more often in those with essential tremor than in those without it.

Postmortem (after-death) studies show that patients with Parkinson's disease as well as some patients with essential tremor have abnormal clumps of proteins (Lewy bodies) in the brain. However, the clumps occur in different areas depending on the disease.

TOP TREATMENTS

There is nothing we know that individuals can do to prevent essential tremor. Nor can it be cured. Treatments can help but, due to side effects, are recommended only when the tremor is severe enough to interfere with daily life or cause embarrassment.

Propranolol (Inderal) or other beta-blocker drugs. Commonly used to treat cardiovascular diseases such as hypertension, these drugs interfere with adrenaline and can reduce the severity of tremors by 10% to 50%. Only about half of patients who take a beta-blocker will achieve a significant reduction in essential tremor symptoms. These drugs cause side effects in many patients, including inability to exercise (due to a slower heart rate), a worsening of asthma and sometimes depression/fatigue.

Primidone (Mysoline), an anti-seizure drug, is about as effective as a beta-blocker. It is used as frequently as beta-blockers. Again, it is effective only in about half of cases. The main side effects are nausea and drowsiness—the drowsiness, though, often diminishes over time.

Deep-brain stimulation can reduce tremors in most patients by 70% to 90%. Slender electrodes are surgically implanted in the brain and powered by a battery-run unit, implanted under the collarbone, that a patient can control. This is the best treatment that we now have for essential tremor, but patients often are reluctant to undergo brain surgery. There is a risk for stroke (if the surgeon accidentally nicks a blood vessel) during the procedure, but this is extremely rare. The operation is performed with "waking" anesthesia.

Any patient who can't control essential tremor with medications (assuming that the symptoms are significant) should talk to his/her doctor about this procedure.

Brain Risks and PTSD

Veterans who have suffered post-traumatic stress disorder (PTSD) have nearly twice the risk for dementia as ones who have not had PTSD. Some studies have shown PTSD to be connected to lower volume in a brain area involved with memory and stress response. Further research is needed to determine if there are any steps that veterans with PTSD can take to preserve brain function, though stress reduction and exercise may help.

Kristine Yaffe, MD, associate chair for clinical and translational research, professor, departments of psychiatry, neurology and epidemiology, University of California, San Francisco.

Brain Surgery Breakthrough

Surgeons at the Johns Hopkins University School of Medicine can now perform some types of brain surgery through a small incision in the eyelid. Known as a minicraniotomy, it's less traumatic than conventional procedures, which involve opening the top half of the skull.

Journal of Otolaryngology–Head and Neck Surgery

H2 Blockers And Brain Health

Stomach-acid medications can lead to mental decline, warns Malaz Boustani, MD, MPH. Mental decline can range from mild cognitive problems (such as confusion) to severe dementia.

Recent finding: People who used prescription and over-the-counter H2 blockers, such as Axid, Pepcid, Tagamet and Zantac, for more than two years were nearly two-and-a-half times more likely to develop cognitive difficulties than people who had not used them.

Self-defense: Talk to your doctor about safer alternatives.

Malaz Boustani, MD, MPH, is a geriatrician at Indiana University School of Medicine, Indianapolis, and leader of a study of 1,558 people, published in *Journal of the American Geriatrics Society.*

Alcohol Kills Brain Cells...and Other Myths About the Brain

Sandra Aamodt, PhD, and Sam Wang, PhD, coauthors of *Welcome to Your Brain* (Bloomsbury). Based in northern California, Dr. Aamodt is editor in chief of *Nature Neuroscience*, a scientific journal on brain research. Dr. Wang is associate professor of neuroscience at Princeton University, Princeton, New Jersey.

We use our brains every moment of our lives, but a lot of what we accept as fact about our brains is really just folklore. Now cutting-edge scientific techniques are helping us unravel the secrets responsible for everything from creating and storing memories to avoiding jet lag and senility. *The truth behind common myths...*

Myth: You can't reverse memory loss.

Some of the memory erosion that comes with aging can be slowed or even reversed. For example, when aging cells in the front part of your brain, known as the prefrontal cortex, shrink, it causes a loss of "executive function," skills that let you multitask and focus intently on what you are doing. You can improve executive function through physical exercise, which increases the blood flow and the availability of oxygen and glucose to your brain cells.

To do this, you need at least 30 minutes of cardiovascular exercise, such as aerobics or fast walking, three times a week. Even if you have been sedentary for a while, your ability to focus can improve markedly within a few months of starting an exercise program.

Myth: We use just 10% of our brains.

This myth is based on the erroneous and simplistic view of the brain as a single unified structure, like a computer hard drive. The brain actually consists of various parts, and you use every part every day. There are no large, unused or unexplored reserves of gray matter waiting to be tapped.

Myth: Alcohol kills brain cells.

Chronic heavy drinking can cause your brain to shrink, and that is associated with many disorders, ranging from an inability to concentrate to a form of dementia in which you lose old memories and can't form new ones. But the shrinkage isn't caused by brain cells dying. Heavy drinking shrinks *dendrites*, the microscopic, highly branched connections between brain cells. The distinction is important because, unlike brain cells, dendrites are capable of expansive regrowth. Alcoholics who give up drinking can improve their cognitive abilities.

A more relevant question for most people is whether moderate drinking damages the brain. The answer is no. In general, men can have up to three drinks a day and women up to two without adversely affecting brain function long-term. In fact, the widely held belief that red wine is beneficial for your brain's health as you age is true. For example, as little as one glass every three or four days decreases stroke risk.

Myth: Jet lag can be cured only by time.

When you travel across time zones, it often takes several days to feel normal again. Meanwhile, you're falling asleep at 7 pm or waking up at 4 am. This is because the internal clock in your brain, known as the circadian rhythm, needs time to resynchronize.

There's a reliable way to speed up this process. Doses of bright sunlight can resynchronize your internal clock more quickly than time.

Rule of thumb: Plan ahead to determine the best arrival time for light exposure. On the first day at your destination, it is optimal to get as much bright sunshine as possible. This fools your body into speeding up its circadian rhythm. For example, if you fly east—say, an overnight trip from the US to Europe—get bright light for a few hours after you arrive.

Exposure to sunlight around noon will help you get up more easily the next day without feeling so sluggish.

Myth: Blind people have sharper hearing.

The blind are no better at detecting faint sounds than sighted people. However, the blind do have much better spatial memory because they can't rely on vision to tell them things, such as "Did I set the glass down on the counter?"

The blind also are better at recognizing where sounds originate, which is another way of keeping track of where things are.

Little-Known Ways to Keep Your Brain Healthy

Jamison Starbuck, ND, a naturopathic physician in family practice, Missoula, Montana.

Everybody wants as much brain power as possible. To achieve that goal, large numbers of Americans have started eating more omega-3-rich fish (or taking fish oil supplements) and begun daily exercise routines, such as walking, biking, swimming or aerobic dancing. But there are other lesser-known strategies that you also can adopt to maximize your brain power. *What I recommend for my patients in addition to fish consumption and exercise...*

1. Consider taking ginkgo biloba and bacopa monnieri.* Ginkgo is widely recommended for its brain-boosting effects. However, a lesser-known herb—*bacopa monnieri*—is also an excellent choice. Both herbs support cerebral circulation and mental focus. For my patients who want to maximize their ability to retain new information, I recommend 120 mg of each herb daily.

*Caution: If you are pregnant, breast-feeding or take any medication—especially for anxiety, depression, a mental disorder or dementia—consult your doctor before using the supplements described here or adding them to your treatment regimen. Ginkgo, in particular, should not be used with blood thinners, including aspirin.

Also helpful: Phosphatidylserine (PS). Research has shown that this protein-derived nutrient is helpful in slowing the progression of dementia and improving focus and concentration. A typical dose is 300 mg per day. PS may be taken alone or in addition to the herbs described above.

Caution: People with a soy allergy should not take PS—most formulas are made from soy.

2. Watch out for anxiety. Many people fail to recognize the degree to which anxiety can interfere with focus and concentration. If you suspect that anxiety may be compromising your brain function, ask your doctor about taking *gamma amino butyric acid* (GABA), an amino acid that is naturally present in our brains. Optimal amounts of GABA allow the mind to both relax and focus, without causing sleepiness or sedation. A typical dose is 100 mg one to three times a day.

3. Try Kundalini yoga. All forms of yoga involve stretching and focused breathing, but Kundalini (the word refers to concentrated life force, according to Indian philosophy) is my favorite because it incorporates a variety of deep breathing exercises that simultaneously wake up and calm the brain. I recommend practicing this form of yoga for 45 minutes at least once weekly. To find a Kundalini yoga teacher near you, consult the International Kundalini Yoga Teachers Association, 505-629-1708, *www.kundaliniyoga.com.* As an alternative, you can improve your brain health by practicing deep breathing. Sit quietly in an erect position with a straight back and breathe in and out through your nose. Inhale as slowly and as deeply as you can, extending your abdomen outward...exhale as fully as possible, trying to push all of the air out of your lungs. Do this for five minutes daily, setting a timer if necessary.

4. Keep your whistle wet. Adequate water intake is crucial for optimal brain health. Drink one-half ounce of water per pound of body weight daily.

Brain Bruises— Concussion Risk Increases with Age

Barry Willer, PhD, professor of psychiatry and rehabilitation medicine, New York State University at Buffalo.

Whether mild, moderate or severe, all concussions temporarily disrupt how the brain works, affecting memory, judgment, reflexes, speech, balance and coordination. Typical symptoms include headache, dizziness, ringing in the ears, nausea and slurred speech...additional symptoms may appear hours or days later and include mood changes, sensitivity to light and noise and sleep disturbances.

Concussion expert Barry Willer, PhD, professor of psychiatry and rehabilitation medicine at New York State University at Buffalo, explains that concussions occur when the brain bangs against the skull. If you bump your head into a low-hanging door frame you may get a doozy of a bruise, but because the brain is protected by fluid and the movement was slow, the brain usually remains undisturbed and concussion free.

CONCUSSION RISK INCREASES WITH OLDER BRAINS

Complicating matters for older people, the brain shrinks slightly as we age, leaving more space between it and the skull, and more opportunity for a higher impact collision. Falling backward can be especially dangerous, says Dr. Willer, since there's little opportunity to break the impact of the fall and the skull on pavement or the floor. Anyone with concussion symptoms should seek medical evaluation, Dr. Willer urges, since bleeding in the brain can result (although it is rare). This is a medical emergency.

POST-CONCUSSION SYNDROME

The likelihood of concussion having long-term effects also increases as we age...so seniors who hit their heads must be double aware. In about 10% of patients with concussions, a problem called post-concussion syndrome (PCS) develops, says Dr. Willer, in which concussion symptoms linger longer than two or three weeks, as you gradually feel worse with a headache, fatigue, depression and sometimes confusion. PCS symptoms are often intermittent. Physical or mental effort will often make these symptoms much worse, leading the person to gradually cut back on activities he/she enjoys. A problem with older patients, according to Dr. Willer, is that effects of post concussion syndrome are often confused with other cognitive problems associated with aging. Ignoring them is a mistake.

UNIQUE PCS TREATMENT

Rest and non-aspirin analgesics such as acetaminophen are what's historically recommended for treatment, but Dr. Willer has pioneered a very different and promising approach. While rest is mandatory immediately following concussion, his research shows that low-impact aerobic exercise, such as walking, carefully calibrated to match an individual's ability and health status, can actually help PCS patients heal. He says that at a certain point in exertion, PCS symptoms recur, so it's important to be careful and exercise under trained supervision. While PCS recovery often takes many months, Dr. Willer has seen complete PCS recovery in as little as six weeks with proper exercise.

Dr. Willer cautions that exercise of any kind during the first three weeks after a concussion inhibits recovery. He suggests that if walking is your chosen method once you do begin to exercise, do it on a treadmill so you can stop the moment symptoms (especially headache) start to increase. To learn more about his program for PCS treatment, call 716-829-2070 or go to the University at Buffalo's Concussion Clinic Web site at *www.ubortho.buffalo.edu/ concussion/information.htm*.

Get Your Memory Back in Gear

Gary Small, MD, professor of psychiatry and bio-behavioral sciences, and director, University of California, Los Angeles, Center on Aging. He is author of *The Memory Bible* and *The Longevity Bible* (both from Hyperion). *www.drgarysmall.com.*

Age is the biggest factor for memory loss. We all have memory problems of some sort by age 60, such as momentarily forgetting someone's name, or briefly wondering why we just walked into a room. We can't stop the effects of aging, but we can slow them down.

MEMORY TECHNIQUES

Some people are so good at memorizing things that they test their talent in competitive matches involving knowledge of trivia or the recall of remarkably large numbers. Scientists have found that those people are no different from the rest of us. There is nothing out of the ordinary in their brain structure nor are there any indications of unusual intelligence. They simply often tap into a memory technique used since antiquity called the Roman Room method.

This method is simple. Visualize yourself walking a familiar route, such as the rooms of your home. Mentally place images of the items to be remembered on specific points on the route. It may be helpful to place items where they may logically be—if you want to remember to buy coffee beans, mentally place them on the kitchen counter. When you want to recall them, mentally retrace your steps.

Over time, you can add more objects to the rooms. If one day you want to remember to pick up the newspaper, add it next to the coffee beans on the counter. If it's airline tickets, visualize them taped to the fridge door. Extend your route or even add other familiar locations for certain kinds of memory tasks.

The Roman Room method is a very useful technique. Orators back in Ancient Rome would remember lengthy speeches this way, imagining each progression of a speech by mentally walking through rooms where they had placed objects to remind themselves of lines. *Yet since today we have much more clutter coming at us, I also teach my patients an additional memory technique that I call Look, Snap, Connect…*

•**LOOK reminds us to focus our attention.** The most common explanation for memory loss is that the information never gets into our minds in the first place. Because we are distracted, we don't take in the information or don't allow ourselves to absorb it. Simply reminding ourselves to focus our attention will dramatically boost memory power.

•**SNAP stands for creating a mental snapshot or visual image in your mind's eye** of the information to be remembered. For most people, visual images are much easier to remember than other forms of information.

•**CONNECT means we need to link up the visual images from snap in meaningful ways.** These associations are key to recalling memories when we want them later. When linking your mental images, create a story that has action and detail.

Example: Say that you want to remember five words on your "to do" list: Mail, gasoline, grandson, sweater, airline. Come up with a story linking them. For instance, I imagine a grandson knitting a sweater on a plane, then mailing it at the airport, when the plane lands to refuel. Whatever the story ends up being, having detail, action and, for me, humor, all help to imprint the information.

When trying to remember faces and names, create an image either linked to the person whose name you need to remember or a distinguishing feature of his/her face. A redhead named Lucy could be remembered by noting that the red hair reminds you of Lucille Ball. You could remember the last name of a woman named Potvin by imagining that she landscaped her yard with pots full of vines.

MENTAL AEROBICS

It's never too late to improve your memory. Recent studies show that even people in the early stages of Alzheimer's can be taught significant face and name retention under the guidance of a professional. For those of us looking to overcome the common forgetfulness in daily life, we can tackle much of that ourselves by doing activities that involve lateral thinking.

Lateral thinking means that we are trying to solve a problem from many angles instead of tackling it head on. Here are some mental aerobic exercises to get you started and, hopefully, suggest further how to invoke lateral thinking in your life.

QUIZ TIME

A lot of memory loss is simply being too busy to absorb what people are saying. These exercises are meant to remind you to slow down, focus and consider what is at hand. *In doing so, your memory will improve...*

1. Brush your hair using your nondominant hand. You may find it awkward at first, but over a few days notice how much easier it gets. This and other exercises don't directly help your memory (after all, how often will any of us need to remember to brush with the opposite hand?). What these mental aerobics do is challenge your mind to think differently and examine tasks we often do without thinking, and which lead to our minds getting "flabby."

2. Fill in a grid so that every row, column and two-by-two box contains the numbers 1, 2, 3 and 4.

3. Say "silk" six times. Then answer the following question: What do cows drink?

This exercise will help you be more thoughtful about things, which in turn is conducive to better memory.

4. See how many words you can spell from these letters: LIGOBATE

No letter may be used twice in any given word, and each word must contain the letter L.

5. How many months have 28 days?

6. All of the vowels have been removed from the following saying. The remaining consonants are in the correct sequence, broken into groups of two to five letters. What is the saying?

STRK WHLTH RNS HT

How well did you do? Regardless, this is just a start to remembering more and living better.

ANSWERS TO QUIZ

Q2: Across row 1: 1, 2, 3, 4 or 1, 2, 4, 3. Row 2: 4, 3, 1, 2. Row 3: 2, 1, 4, 3 or 2, 1, 3, 4. Row 4: 3, 4, 2, 1.

Q3: Cows drink water. If you said "milk," you need to focus your attention.

Q4: agile, ail, aale, bagel, bail, bale, blog, boil, el, Gail, gale, gel, glib, glob, globe, goal, goalie, lab, lag, lea, leg, lib, lie, lob, lobe, log, loge, oblige.

Q5: All of them. (If you say only one month has 28 days, it's an example of not paying attention to the matter at hand—all months have 28 days, after all.)

Q6: Strike while the iron is hot.

Lessons from The "Super-Agers"

Daniel James Berlau, PhD, an adjunct assistant professor in the department of neurology at the University of California, Irvine, School of Medicine. He specializes in neurobiology and memory and is a principal investigator in the ongoing 90-Plus Study.

Want to live a long, healthy life? To learn how, just ask a "super-ager." That was the thinking of researchers at the University of California, Irvine, who recruited more than 1,000 residents from a retirement community to study what exactly caused these people to live to age 90 and beyond.

Known as the "oldest-old," this group of individuals who are 90 years old or over is comprised of about two million Americans and is the fastest growing segment of the US population. What the researchers have learned from this group may surprise you.

The 90-Plus Study, which is ongoing, holds important lessons for all of us who hope to reach advanced age with our mental and physical faculties intact.

What's been discovered so far...

THROW OUT YOUR SCALE

Obesity is harmful for everyone, but older adults who carry a few extra pounds are more likely to live longer than those who are lean.

Surprising result: Adults in the 90-Plus Study with a body mass index (BMI), which is weight relative to height, of 25 to 29.9—a range that is considered "overweight"—lived longer, on average, than those with BMIs of 18.5 to 24.9, the "normal" range.* (Participants' average age was 72 when their BMIs were measured.)

It is not clear why these extra pounds appear to be protective in older adults. It is possible that people who are somewhat overweight have better nutritional status overall than those who are lean.

In addition, people with extra fat reserves may be better able to circumvent "wasting," the age-related loss of muscle tissue and strength that can lead to frailty and an increased risk for illness.

Caution: In our research, being obese (a BMI of 30 and higher) at any age was not associated with a longer life span. And being overweight or obese at age 21 was associated with a shorter life span.

EXERCISE WORKS

Study participants who exercised for 45 minutes or more a day, most days of the week, were 27% less likely to die within an eight-year period than those who exercised less than 15 minutes daily. Their activities included swimming, biking, tennis, vigorous walking and dancing. They also were more likely to retain more of their memory and other cognitive functions.

Striking research finding: Even participants who got very little exercise—as little as 15 minutes a day—lived significantly longer than those who were completely sedentary.

Dementia risk is quadrupled: Among the oldest-old, those who scored in the lowest 20% in physical performance—which measured such factors as balance and the ability to walk a certain distance—were four times more likely to have dementia than those who scored in the highest 20%.

*To learn your BMI, go to the Web site of the National Heart, Lung and Blood Institute, *www.nhlbisupport.com/bmi/*.

Physical activity not only improves cardio-vascular and cerebral blood flow, but also increases circulation so that brain cells receive more nutrients. There is also strong evidence that exercise promotes neurogenesis, the growth of new brain cells (neurons) and the connections between these cells.

MONOPOLY, ANYONE?

The onset of Alzheimer's disease is one of the greatest fears of older adults. The incidence of dementia from all causes, including Alzheimer's disease, doubles every five years between ages 65 and 85.

Key finding: Participants in the 21-year Bronx Aging Study who spent three hours daily engrossed in mental activities, including playing board games, reading, dancing or playing a musical instrument, were significantly less likely to develop dementia than those who spent less (or no) time doing these activities.

Examples: Specifically, participants who spent hours playing board games had a 75% lower risk of developing dementia...and those who spent a similar amount of time playing a musical instrument had a 70% lower risk.

For optimal results: Aim for three hours of such activities daily. Shorter periods of mental focus can also decrease the risk for dementia, but three hours a day seems to be optimal.

Calculate Your Chance Of Living to 100

Estimate your chance of living to 100 by visiting *www.livingto100.com* and answering 40 questions about family history, health, diet and lifestyle. Have your cholesterol and blood-pressure numbers handy—you need to enter them. The site, created by Thomas Perls, MD, who is the founder of the New England Centenarian Study, lets you see how your answers influence longevity, so you can change life-shortening habits if you want to.

Thomas Perls, founder, New England Centenarian Study. *www.livingto100.com*.

5

Nutrition Tips for a Long, Healthy Life

Good and Easy…Eating the Mediterranean Way

There is abundant scientific evidence on the health benefits of the so-called Mediterranean diet, which promotes the traditional eating habits of long-lived people in such countries as Greece and Italy.

Landmark research: Among the most compelling evidence is one long-term European study of healthy men and women ages 70 to 90.

It found that following the Mediterranean diet as part of an overall healthful lifestyle, including regular exercise, was associated with a *more than 50%* lower rate of death from all causes over a decade. Numerous studies have associated this type of eating with reduced risk for heart disease, cancer, cognitive decline, diabetes and obesity.

But many Americans are reluctant to try the Mediterranean diet for fear that it will be difficult or costly to follow because it emphasizes such foods as omega-3–rich fish, vegetables and nuts.

Surprising findings: Mediterranean eating does not increase food costs, according to a recent study—and this style of eating need not be complicated.

Below, Wendy Kohatsu, MD, an assistant clinical professor of family medicine at the University of California, San Francisco, and a chef who conducts cooking demonstrations for patients and doctors, explains the best ways to incorporate Mediterranean eating into your daily diet…

EASY WAYS TO GET STARTED

To effectively tap into the Mediterranean diet's powerful health benefits, it's important

Wendy Kohatsu, MD, assistant clinical professor of family medicine at the University of California, San Francisco, and director of the Integrative Medicine Fellowship at the Santa Rosa Family Medicine Residency Program in Santa Rosa, California. Dr. Kohatsu is also a graduate of the Oregon Culinary Institute.

to know exactly which foods should be eaten—and in what quantities.

Start by getting four to five daily servings of *whole* grains (one serving equals one-half cup of cooked quinoa, brown rice or whole-wheat pasta, for example, or one slice of whole-wheat bread) and two to three daily servings of low- or nonfat dairy products (such as yogurt, cottage cheese or milk), which are an important source of bone-protecting calcium. *In addition, be sure to consume…*

•**Oily fish.** This high-quality protein contains abundant omega-3 fatty acids, which help fight the inflammation that plays a role in cardiovascular disease, Alzheimer's disease and asthma.

Best choices: Follow the acronym SMASH— salmon (wild)…mackerel (Spanish, not king, which tends to have higher levels of mercury)…anchovies…sardines…and herring.

How much: Three ounces (the size of a deck of cards), twice a week.

Chef's secret: Drain canned sardines (the large size), grill briefly, sprinkle with fresh lemon juice and chopped parsley.

Beware: Some fish—such as shark, swordfish, golden bass (tilefish), king mackerel and albacore tuna—can be high in mercury. Avoid these. If you eat tuna, choose the "light" version, which contains less mercury than albacore tuna does.

If you don't like fish: Take a fish oil supplement (1,000 mg daily). Choose a brand that guarantees that no lead or mercury is present.

My favorite brands: Carlson's and Nordic Naturals.

Vegetarians can get omega-3s from flaxseed, walnuts and other nonfish sources. However, nonfish food sources of omega-3s are largely in the form of *alpha-linolenic acid* (ALA), which is not as potent as the more biologically powerful fatty acids found in fish. Algae-derived *docosahexaenoic acid* (DHA) capsules contain the omega-3s found in fish. The recommended dose of DHA capsules is 1,000 mg daily.

What most people don't know: A small but important study shows that eating oily fish

with beans, such as lentils and chickpeas (also known as garbanzo beans), improves absorption of the iron found in beans.

•**Olive oil.** Olive oil contains about 77% healthful monounsaturated fats. Olive oil is also high in sterols, plant extracts that help reduce LDL "bad" cholesterol and increase HDL "good" cholesterol.

Best choice: Look for extra-virgin (or "first-press") olive oil. ("Extra virgin" means that the oil is derived from the first pressing of the olives.)

How much: Use olive oil as your primary fat—in salad dressings, marinades and sautées. To minimize your total daily intake of fat, do not exceed 18 g to 20 g of saturated fat and 0 g of trans fat from all food sources.

Chef's secret: If you dislike the "grassy" taste of some extra-virgin olive oils, look for Spanish and Moroccan versions, which tend to be more mellow. One good choice is olive oil made from the *arbequina* olive, which has a buttery taste.

What most people don't know: Nutrients in extra-virgin olive oil may offer some pain-relieving qualities over the long term.

•**Nuts.** Like extra-virgin olive oil, nuts are high in healthful monounsaturated fats. In fact, a recent Spanish study found that a Mediterranean diet that included walnuts significantly lowered risk for heart disease.

What kinds: Besides walnuts, best choices include almonds and peanuts. Choose plain raw nuts—not salted or honey-roasted.

How much: One-quarter cup daily.

Beware: A quarter cup of nuts contains about 200 calories. Eat only a small handful daily—for example, about 23 almonds or 35 peanuts. If you're allergic to nuts, try pumpkin, sunflower or sesame seeds instead.

Chef's secret: Store nuts in your freezer to prevent them from going rancid.

•**Fruits and vegetables.** Many of the most healthful vegetables—including those of the brassica family, such as cabbage, kale, broccoli and cauliflower—originated in the Mediterranean area.

What kinds: Choose brightly colored fruit, such as citrus and berries, and vegetables, such as spinach, watercress, beets, carrots and broccoli.

How much: Five to nine servings daily. (A serving is one-half cup of cooked vegetables, one cup of leafy greens, one medium orange or one-half cup of berries.)

Contrary to popular belief, frozen vegetables, which are often far less costly than fresh produce, are just as nutritious—if not more so because they're frozen at their peak level of freshness and don't spoil in the freezer.

Chef's secret: Cooking tomatoes in olive oil concentrates the tomatoes' levels of *lycopene*, a powerful antioxidant that has been associated with a decreased risk for prostate, lung and stomach cancers.

The Ultimate Health Food—Beans

Jo-Ann Heslin, RD, CDN, a Douglaston, New York–based registered dietitian. She is co-author of 30 books, including *The Healthy Wholefoods Counter* (Pocket) and two college textbooks on nutrition.

You may want to name blueberries as the food that is richest in disease-fighting antioxidants. Few people are aware that red beans actually have more antioxidants than these nutrition-packed powerhouses.

WHAT MAKES BEANS SO SPECIAL?

Some foods are rich in protein, while others provide healthful unsaturated fats, vitamins and minerals or fiber.

Beans (in a class of vegetables known as legumes) are all of the above—the ultimate "combination food," providing maximum nutritional value, including about 15 g of protein and about 13 g of fiber per cup cooked. (A typical serving is one-half cup cooked.)

Compelling scientific evidence: In a landmark study of nearly 800 people (ages 70 and over) from Japan, Sweden, Greece and Australia, the risk for death over a seven-year period

dropped by 7% to 8% for each 0.7 ounces (about one-quarter cup cooked) of beans consumed daily.

Bonus: It's especially important to eat beans as we grow older. As we age, our metabolism slows, and we tend to eat less—even though we need more vitamins, minerals and other food-based chemicals to support a weakening immune system…fiber to keep digestion functioning smoothly…and protein to offset the age-related loss of muscle tissue. Beans provide all these benefits—and they're economical and easy to eat for those who have difficulty chewing or swallowing.

BEAN STANDOUTS

More than 100 types of beans are grown worldwide and offer similar basic nutritional advantages. *However, some varieties stand out…*

• **Red beans** not only have more antioxidants than blueberries, but also are a good source of iron (5.2 mg iron per cup cooked).

• **Kidney beans** are also rich in antioxidants and are an especially good source of fiber (13 g fiber per cup cooked).

• **Pinto beans** have been shown to reduce markers for heart disease, including total cholesterol, when one-half cup cooked was consumed daily for eight weeks, according to research published in the *Journal of the American College of Nutrition*.

• **Lima beans** are a good source of potassium and have been shown to reduce blood glucose levels.

• **Navy beans**, which also are a rich source of potassium as well as calcium and magnesium, have been linked to reduced risk for high blood pressure and heart attack.

• **Black beans** are another excellent source of antioxidants—one cup cooked offers the same antioxidant levels as a six-ounce glass of red wine.

• **Garbanzo beans** (also known as chickpeas) have been shown to reduce LDL "bad" cholesterol by nearly 5%.

• **Soybeans** have higher-quality protein—it closely matches that of eggs, meat and milk—

and more of it (60% of your daily needs in a single cup) than other types of beans.

Important: Soybeans are the richest source of isoflavones—phytochemicals with estrogen-like properties. Although research findings have been mixed, there is some concern that high intake of isoflavones may promote the growth of precancerous or malignant breast cancer cells. The American Cancer Society recommends that women who are at high risk for breast cancer or with a history of the disease eat no more than moderate amounts of soy foods and avoid isoflavone supplements.

BEST WAYS TO ADD BEANS
TO YOUR DIET

Aim for at least three cups of cooked beans (six servings) per week. *For example, you can try...*

•**Garbanzo or kidney beans in lettuce salads.**

•**Navy beans or black beans in soups.**

•**Roasted soybeans (soy nuts) and edamame (fresh soybeans)** as convenient snack foods.

•**Three-bean salad containing more dried beans** (such as chickpeas and kidney beans) than yellow or green string beans.

For even more variety: Try adzuki beans in rice dishes...anasazi beans in Southwestern soups...and fava beans in stews. These varieties are available at health-food stores and most supermarkets.

NO MORE GAS!

Many people avoid beans because they can cause intestinal gas. To minimize gas, add beans to your diet gradually—start with one-quarter cup on top of a salad, for example... and increase your intake to half-cup and full-cup servings over a period of weeks.

Other gas-control secrets: Get dried beans when they're fresh (otherwise, the beans' natural starches degrade and become more difficult to digest). Look for a "best by" date or buy dried beans at a store where business is brisk. Soak them overnight, then rinse them thoroughly before cooking.

SODIUM-REDUCING TRICKS

The high salt content of canned beans (it's added to preserve texture) is a problem if you're on a low-sodium diet. Canned beans typically contain 300 mg of sodium per one-cup serving. By washing the beans, you can lower the sodium content by 40% or more. Rinsing canned beans thoroughly also helps prevent intestinal gas.

When cooking dried beans, it is not necessary to add salt. However, seasonings, including salt (in moderation), can be added once the beans are cooked. For convenience, freeze serving-size portions for later use. Frozen cooked beans also are becoming increasingly available at supermarkets and are nearly sodium-free.

TOP 10 ANTIOXIDANT FOODS

1. Red beans
2. Wild blueberries
3. Red kidney beans
4. Pinto beans
5. Cultivated blueberries
6. Cranberries
7. Artichokes
8. Blackberries
9. Prunes
10. Raspberries

Source: US Department of Agriculture

Good Nutrition on a Tight Budget

David Grotto, RD, LDN, a registered dietitian and former spokesperson for the American Dietetic Association. He is the author of *101 Foods That Could Save Your Life* (Bantam). To read his nutrition blog, go to *http://davidgrotto.wordpress.com.*

Food prices in the US have recently soared, increasing at the fastest rate since 1990. Many households need to cut corners at the grocery store.

Problem: You may find that you need to choose less expensive—but less nutritious—food to make ends meet.

Solution: With smart food choices, you can eat well without breaking the bank or sacrificing taste.

Eight extremely nutritious yet economical foods...

ALMONDS

Rich in fiber, vitamin E and healthful mono-unsaturated fats, almonds are widely known to help fight heart disease. Few people are aware, however, that almonds contain more bone-building calcium than any other nut.

Recommended portion size: One ounce (about 23 nuts) daily.

Typical cost per portion: 32 cents to 53 cents.*

BEANS

Beans are an excellent source of fiber, protein and B vitamins—and they are rich in cancer-fighting antioxidants called anthocyanins.

Recommended portion size: One-half cup (cooked or canned) daily.

Typical cost per portion: 35 cents.

How to choose: All beans are similar in nutritional value, but the varieties with darker colors—such as black, red, kidney and adzuki beans—contain more disease-fighting antioxidants. Dried and canned beans have similar nutritional value. To reduce the sodium content of canned beans by about 40%, rinse them in water for 40 seconds before cooking.

CHARD

Chard is a dark green, leafy vegetable that is very low in calories but high in fiber. It is an excellent source of the antioxidants vitamin A and vitamin C...vitamin K, which promotes blood health...vitamin D and magnesium, which are necessary for bone health...and potassium, which helps minimize the negative effects of excessive sodium. Chard also contains the antioxidants lutein and zeaxanthin, which help prevent eye disease.

Recommended portion size: One cup raw...or one-half cup cooked, daily.

Typical cost per portion: 50 cents.

*Typical cost per portion is based on national food price estimates. Prices may vary.

How to choose: Swiss chard, red chard and rainbow chard offer similar levels of nutrients.

EGGS

Eggs are a good source of protein, providing all the essential amino acids. They also contain vitamin D for bone health...vitamin B-12, which helps maintain energy...choline, which improves brain function...and eye-protecting lutein and zeaxanthin.

These important nutrients are found in egg yolks, which contain cholesterol. However, there is not a strong correlation between dietary cholesterol and blood cholesterol levels, so it's safe for most people to eat eggs daily.

Helpful: To limit saturated fat intake, cook eggs in a nonstick pan coated with vegetable spray and make scrambled eggs with nonfat milk.

Recommended portion size: One or two eggs daily. If you have heart disease, check with your doctor or a registered dietitian before eating this number of eggs.

Typical cost per portion: 15 cents per egg.

How to choose: Brown or white—free-range or not—all eggs provide similar levels of nutrients.

MUSHROOMS

Mushrooms, such as white button or cremini, are a good source of vitamin D, as well as the mineral selenium and the phytochemical ergothionine, both of which have cancer-fighting properties. With their meatlike texture, mushrooms are an inexpensive supplement to beef—for example, you can use mushrooms to replace some of the beef in hamburgers or meatloaf.

Recommended portion size: One-half cup (about 1.5 ounces)...or four to five small mushrooms daily.

Typical cost per portion: 25 cents to 50 cents.

How to choose: All edible mushrooms have nearly the same nutritional profile.

OATS

Oats can significantly reduce cholesterol—people who eat one-and-a-half cups daily for one month can lower total cholesterol by up to 14 points. In addition, oats contain healthy amounts of vitamin E, calcium, magnesium, potassium, selenium, zinc and iron.

Recommended portion size: Up to three-quarters cup dry (one-and-a-half cups cooked) daily.

Typical cost per portion: 35 cents.

How to choose: There is no health benefit to eating steel-cut oats over whole oats.

POTATOES

Of all vegetables, potatoes are among the richest sources of potassium, which is important for controlling blood pressure and reducing risk for stroke and dementia. Potatoes are highly "satiating"—meaning they effectively reduce hunger.

Important: The nutritional value of a potato is almost equally divided between the flesh and the skin, so eat the skin whenever possible.

Recommended portion size: One medium potato (about eight ounces) daily.

Typical cost per portion: 40 cents.

How to choose: Potatoes with purple or red skins and sweet potatoes have more antioxidants.

PRUNES

The antioxidant compounds in prunes help prevent hardening of the arteries—perhaps by protecting the lining of the blood vessels from plaque formation. Prunes also may help lower LDL cholesterol. The laxative effect provided by prunes is due not only to their high fiber content, but also to a natural compound in the fruit called sorbitol.

Recommended portion size: Five or six prunes daily.

Typical cost per portion: 30 cents to 40 cents.

How to choose: Consume the dried fruit, not the juice, which contains more concentrated sugars and less fiber per serving.

Nutritional Supplements For Seniors

Alan H. Pressman, DC, PhD, CCN, author of numerous books on nutrition and health, including *The Complete Idiot's Guide to Vitamins and Minerals* (Alpha). *www.drpressman.com.*

Many older adults regularly take vitamins, minerals and other dietary supplements. But just because something is "natural" or "drug free" doesn't mean that it's always safe. As a senior, if you take any sort of supplement, you need to be aware of the risks and be sure to take the right dosage.

YOUR DAILY MULTIVITAMIN

Most doctors agree that taking a daily multivitamin with minerals is good insurance against those times when you can't eat as well as you should. Doctors often also recommend daily multis to people older than age 50 because the ability to absorb some nutrients in food, such as the B vitamins, declines as people get older. Your doctor may also recommend specific B vitamins, such as B-12, in addition to a multivitamin, if he/she thinks you need it. Check for a good brand on Consumerlab.com or ask your pharmacist.

Also look for a formulation designed for the nutritional needs of older adults. These multis generally contain the same amounts of vitamins A, C, D, E and K as those formulated for younger adults, but may contain higher amounts of the B vitamins. Multis made for seniors may also contain some ingredients that are helpful for older adults, such as *lutein* and *zeaxanthin* (they can help prevent sight-robbing age-related macular degeneration) and lycopene (which may be helpful for preventing prostate cancer).

Important: Your multivitamin should not contain iron. Even without taking supplements, older adults can start to build up higher than normal levels of iron in their bodies. This isn't an issue for most people. But, if you have the hereditary disease hemochromatosis (iron overload disease), iron builds up in the body to dangerously high levels. You may not find that you have this disease until you start to exhibit serious symptoms, such as liver problems or diabetes, because there is no direct test for it.

Bottom line: Take an iron supplement only if your doctor tells you to for some specific reason.

Dosage: Doubling up on your daily multivitamin probably won't hurt—but it probably won't give you any extra benefit. Get more of the vitamins and minerals that are in your daily supplement, as well as extra fiber, antioxidants and other valuable nutrients, by adding more whole grains, fresh fruits and vegetables to your diet.

CALCIUM

Most daily multivitamin supplements contain from 100 milligrams (mg) to 300 mg of calcium—considerably less than the recommended daily intake of 1,200 mg for men and women older than age 50. If you can't get the additional calcium from your diet (dairy products, sardines and spinach are good sources), consider taking calcium and vitamins D and K—all nutrients you need to maintain strong bones.

One good choice: Viactiv, which combines all three nutrients.

Interactions caution: If you're taking a *cycline antibiotic* (tetracycline, doxycycline or another) or the antibiotic *ciprofloxacin* (Cipro), skip the calcium supplements until you finish the course of antibiotics—calcium blocks your absorption of the drug. You can continue taking a daily multivitamin while on a course of antibiotics, but take the drug and the multi several hours apart.

Dosage: 1,000 to 1,500 mg a day of calcium is safe for most people. More than that can cause constipation and could interfere with prescription medications. Calcium in the form of calcium carbonate is effective—and inexpensive. When taking calcium, take a total of 500 mg of magnesium daily for proper calcium absorption. And, be sure to get the recommended dietary allowance of vitamin D (400 IU) and the daily adequate intake of vitamin K (90 mcg for women, 120 mcg for men).

HERB CAUTIONS

Herbal supplements should be used with caution at any age, but there are some herbs that can be especially dangerous for older adults...

• **St.-John's-wort.** Also called hypericum, this herb is usually taken at a dosage of 900 mg to 1,800 mg daily, and can help mild depression.

Problem: It can interact badly with a number of drugs commonly prescribed for older adults, including blood thinners and medications for depression, epilepsy, Parkinson's disease, heart disease—even heartburn.

What to do: Because the list of drugs that interact with St.-John's-wort keeps growing, don't take it if you take any prescription drug. If you think you might benefit from treatment for depression, ask your doctor what will be best for you to take.

• **Ginkgo biloba** can help age-related memory problems by improving blood flow to the brain.

Beware: Ginkgo biloba is a mild blood thinner. Don't use it at all if you take a prescription blood thinner, such as *warfarin* (Coumadin). If you take a daily low-dose aspirin, you can use ginkgo, but take it 12 hours apart from the aspirin. If you take a daily regular-dose aspirin, ask your doctor about taking ginkgo.

Dosage: All reputable brands are standardized to contain 24% of flavonoids (chemical compounds with antioxidant properties). The usual dose is 60 mg, taken one to three times a day. Take with meals to avoid stomach upset.

• **Ginseng.** Ginseng is an adaptogen, a naturally occurring substance found in plants that helps strengthen your body's ability to handle stress and fight off illness. Ginseng is especially helpful as you grow older. Studies have shown that ginseng can improve thinking and learning.

Side effects: Ginseng can lower blood sugar, which could be a problem if you have diabetes. Ginseng also can cause headaches—stop taking it if that happens.

Quality caution: Be sure to use only American ginseng root (Panax quinquefolius), which is the species that has been most thoroughly studied and is believed by herbal practitioners to be most effective, and select a product from a well-known, brand-name manufacturer.

Dosage: Ginseng is traditionally made into a tea—have no more than one cup a day. If you prefer capsules, stick to no more than 100 mg a day. Start with a low dose—half a cup of tea or 50 mg in capsule form. If you don't notice any negative effects, such as itching, skin rash, diarrhea or insomnia, gradually increase the daily dose to one full cup or 100 mg over a week's time.

• **Saw palmetto** helps relieve symptoms of benign prostatic hyperplasia (BPH), also called enlarged prostate. Check with your doctor to be sure that your symptoms (frequent urination or difficulty urinating) aren't caused by something more serious.

Interaction cautions: Do not take saw palmetto if you're taking any prescription drug to relieve the symptoms of BPH, such as *finasteride* (Proscar) or *tamsulosin* (Flomax). Saw palmetto lowers levels of testosterone, as do the drugs, and levels may get lowered too much. Don't use saw palmetto if you take a blood-thinning drug such as warfarin. (Saw palmetto is safe to take with a daily aspirin.)

Quality caution: Saw palmetto products vary in quality, so look for a product from a well-known manufacturer.

Dosage: 320 mg daily.

The One Vitamin That Can Save Your Life

Michael F. Holick, MD, PhD, professor of medicine, physiology and biophysics at Boston University School of Medicine. He is the author of *The Vitamin D Solution* (Hudson Street). Dr. Holick has been an outspoken critic of dermatologists' standard advice to avoid all sun exposure. *www.DrHolick.com*

The health benefits of vitamin D have been making news for some time now, but roughly two-thirds of Americans still are not getting enough of this vital nutrient.

Even though vitamin D has long been known to promote bone strength—it enables bone-building calcium to pass through the small intestine and into the bloodstream and the bones—many other health benefits are being discovered. *Most recently, research findings have shown that low vitamin D also is linked to chronic diseases, such as...*

• **Cancer.** For example, about half of colorectal cancers in the US are believed to be preventable by raising vitamin D levels in people who are deficient.

• **Dementia.** Adults age 65 and older with the lowest levels of vitamin D were found to be more than twice as likely to suffer cognitive impairment (which often precedes dementia) than those with optimal levels of the vitamin.

• **Diabetes.** People who get more than 800 international units (IU) of vitamin D daily may be about one-third less likely to develop type 2 diabetes.

• **Heart disease.** Risk for heart disease was reduced by 31% in women who took vitamin D supplements as part of a study on osteoporosis related fractures.

How could one vitamin have such a profound effect on overall health? Research now shows that vitamin D helps facilitate cellular health in virtually every cell in the body including those in the brain. If this cellular health is interrupted due to a vitamin D deficiency, health problems, such as those described earlier, may occur.

LITTLE-KNOWN FACTS

What you may not know about vitamin D...

• **Few doctors recommend a blood test to measure 25-hydroxyvitamin D,** a form of vitamin D that acts as a marker for vitamin D status. Adults over age 60 should ask to be tested.* They are at increased risk for vitamin D deficiency since the skin becomes less able to manufacture the vitamin from sunlight as the body ages.

Recommended blood level of vitamin D: Thirty to 100 nanograms of 25-hydroxyvitamin D per milliliter (ng/mL) of blood. I like to keep patients between 40 ng/mL and 60 ng/mL, but up to 100 ng/mL is safe.

*Vitamin D testing is covered by most health insurers, including Medicare.

Helpful: It's best to get tested in the winter, when levels are likely to be lower than in the summer. If you are deficient, your doctor will prescribe therapeutic doses of vitamin D. Get retested eight to 12 weeks later, then follow up once a year.

• **Low energy, bone pain (especially in the arms and legs) and/or lack of muscle strength can indicate a vitamin D deficiency.** A condition known as *osteomalacia*, which causes softening of the bones, can result from vitamin D deficiency. Unlike osteoporosis, which occurs when existing bone is weakened, osteomalacia is an abnormality in the bone-building process. People with osteomalacia complain of throbbing and aching bone pain.

Simple self-test: Press firmly with your thumb or forefinger on your breastbone or your shins. If you feel pain in either of those areas, you're probably low in vitamin D and may have osteomalacia. See a doctor to have your vitamin D status tested.

• **The US recommendations for vitamin D are too low.** The Office of Dietary Supplements, part of the National Institutes of Health, advises Americans to get 600 IU of vitamin D daily from food and/or supplements if you're age 50 to 70…and 800 IU daily for those over age 70.

My advice: If you don't think you can get enough timed sun exposure without sunscreen (see below), get 1,500 IU to 2,000 IU of vitamin D daily. Foods that contain vitamin D (such as wild-caught salmon, mushrooms and vitamin D–fortified milk and breakfast cereals) do not provide significant amounts of the vitamin. Many people will also need to take a vitamin D supplement.

Important: A supplement is especially critical if you don't get much sun due to your distance from the equator—for example, you live in Seattle rather than Miami.

Supplements also are required for people who have been tested and are low in vitamin D…and are more frequently necessary for dark-skinned people because dark skin pigmentation naturally filters vitamin D–producing sun rays.

• **The vitamin D produced from sunlight is superior to that provided by supplements.** Sun-produced vitamin D has been shown to last at least twice as long in the blood as vitamin D from supplements.

There are no simple formulas to determine the amount of sun exposure needed to produce adequate amounts of vitamin D.

My general guideline: Three times a week—during the period of 10 am to 3 pm (virtually no vitamin D is produced at other times)—spend one-quarter to one-half the amount of time in the sun that it takes you to get the beginning of a sunburn.* For someone with dark skin, this might be 30 minutes three times weekly. If you're fair-skinned, five to 10 minutes might be enough. Expose your arms and legs—and, if possible, your abdomen and back—to sun. During timed exposures, put sunscreen on your face to help prevent sun damage. When you're not doing a timed exposure, cover all exposed skin with sunscreen to prevent sunburn.

Note: If you live above 33° latitude (roughly any area north of Atlanta), you cannot produce any significant vitamin D from sun exposure during the winter.

• **Inadequate sun exposure may increase your risk for melanoma and other cancers.** Sunburn increases the risk for skin cancer, but there is no scientific evidence that moderate sun exposure has the same effect. In fact, most melanomas (the most lethal form of skin cancer) occur on parts of the body that receive little sun. Research published in the *Journal of Investigative Dermatology* shows that people who get regular, moderate sun exposure are less likely to develop melanoma than those who get little or no sun. Melanoma kills about 8,600 Americans annually. Colon, prostate and breast cancers combined claim about 115,000 lives. Each of these cancers has been linked to insufficient vitamin D.

Important finding: A study in the journal *Cancer* reported that insufficient sun exposure in the US accounted for 85,000 more

*If you take a prescription drug or are at high risk for skin cancer or have a history of the disease, consult your doctor.

cancer cases than would have occurred had the same people gotten more sun.

- **Certain medications reduce vitamin D levels.** Antiseizure drugs, such as *phenytoin* (Dilantin), the steroid prednisone, AIDs medications and some other drugs destroy vitamin D and increase one's risk for osteomalacia and other conditions associated with vitamin D deficiency. People taking such drugs may need double or triple the usual amounts of vitamin D. Other medications that reduce vitamin D include the cholesterol-lowering drug *cholestyramine* (Questran)...the weight-loss medication *orlistat* (Xenical)...and the herb St. John's wort.

If you take one of these products, you may need to take a vitamin D supplement to maintain adequate blood levels of the vitamin.

Reduce Copper and Iron Intake After Age 50

Copper and iron are useful to the body— but high levels after age 50 can damage cells and are associated with Alzheimer's disease, heart disease and other age-related illnesses. To reduce consumption, eat less red meat and do not take vitamin or mineral pills containing copper or iron. You also may want to donate blood regularly to reduce iron levels and take zinc supplements to lower copper levels. Talk to your doctor first.

George Brewer, MD, professor emeritus, human genetics, University of Michigan Medical School, Ann Arbor, and author of a review paper on iron and copper toxicity, published in *Chemical Research in Toxicology.*

Multivitamins And Blood Thinners

Multivitamins may change how blood thinners work. Vitamin K, which helps blood to clot and can be found in many multivitamins, can impact the effectiveness of blood thinners, such as *warfarin* (Coumadin).

Important: Talk to your doctor if you are taking a blood thinner and a multivitamin with vitamin K. It is important to keep your levels of vitamin K consistent.

Sarah L. Booth, PhD, director, Vitamin K Laboratory, Jean Mayer USDA Human Nutrition Research Center on Aging at Tufts University, Boston.

Where to Store Your Vitamins

Vitamins and supplements lose potency when stored in kitchens and bathrooms.

Reason: Humidity in these rooms can cause slight chemical changes in vitamins and dietary supplements, making them less effective.

Self-defense: Store bottles away from humid areas.

Lisa Mauer, PhD, associate professor of food science, Purdue University, West Lafayette, Indiana, and leader of a study published in *Journal of Agricultural and Food Chemistry.*

Raisins Have More Antioxidants Than Grapes

Raisins have nearly three times more antioxidants than red or green grapes, making them one of the best sources of antioxidants. When fruits are dried, their compounds are highly concentrated. Raisins are a good source of fiber, potassium and some minerals.

But: Raisins also have a higher concentration of sugar and more calories than grapes. One-half cup of grapes has nearly 50 calories...one-half cup of raisins has about 220 calories.

Best: 60 raisins, or one ounce, once a day is a healthy snack with just 85 calories.

University of California, *Berkeley Wellness Letter,* 500 Fifth Ave., New York City 10110, *www.wellness letter.com.*

Chickpeas Curb Cholesterol

In recent research, 45 adults with high total cholesterol levels (250 mg/dL, on average) ate at least 25 ounces (about three cups) of canned chickpeas (garbanzo beans) weekly for 12 weeks.

Result: The participants' total cholesterol levels dropped by 7.7 points, on average.

Theory: Chickpeas are high in fiber and polyunsaturated fats, which help reduce total cholesterol when they replace saturated fats.

Self-defense: Enjoy chickpeas in salads, hummus and other dishes.

J.K. Pittaway, researcher and lecturer in health and biomedical science, University of Tasmania, Launceston, Tasmania, Australia.

Grab a Can of Sardines

Sardines may be the healthiest seafood. They are nearly the richest in heart-healthy omega-3 fat—richer than tuna and many fish-oil supplements. And, they contain fewer contaminants than tuna, swordfish, farmed salmon and most other fatty fish. They are also a good source of calcium if you eat the bones.

Caution: Canned sardines may be high in salt, so if you are on a sodium-restricted diet, check the can label.

UC Berkeley Wellness Letter, *www.wellnessletter.com.*

Is Wild-Caught Fish Better Than Farmed?

Farmed and wild-caught fish are equally healthful for most people. Despite reports that farmed fish contain more contaminants

than wild, both generally are safe and nutritious to eat.

But: Pregnant women, nursing mothers and young children should be careful about which fish they eat. See the list at *www.fish4health. net,* and click on "Wallet Card" for a printable card that you can carry when dining out.

Charles R. Santerre, PhD, professor of food toxicology, department of foods and nutrition, Purdue University, West Lafayette, Indiana.

Are You Cooking the Health Out of Your Food?

Richard E. Collins, MD, director of wellness at South Denver Cardiology Associates in Littleton, Colorado. He is author of *The Cooking Cardiologist* (Advanced Research) and *Cooking with Heart* (South Denver Cardiology Associates). *www.thecookingcardiologist.com.*

Inflammation is the body's natural, temporary, healing response to infection or injury. But if the process fails to shut down when it should, inflammation becomes chronic—and tissues are injured by excess white blood cells and DNA-damaging free radicals.

Result: Elevated risk for heart disease, cancer, diabetes, osteoporosis, arthritis and other diseases.

Richard E. Collins, MD, "the cooking cardiologist," offers his advice on how to prevent chronic inflammation.

His advice: Follow a diet that is rich in immune-strengthening nutrients...and use cooking techniques that neither destroy food's disease-fighting nutrients nor add inflammatory properties to it.

SMART WAYS WITH VEGETABLES

Deeply colored plant foods generally are rich in antioxidants that help combat inflammation by neutralizing free radicals.

Examples: Healthful flavonoids are prevalent in deep yellow to purple produce...carotenoids are found in yellow, orange, red and green vegetables.

Exceptions: Despite their light hue, garlic and onions are powerful antioxidants.

Unfortunately, these nutrients are easily lost.

For instance: Boiling or poaching vegetables causes nutrients to leach into the cooking water—and get tossed out when that potful of water is discarded. The high heat of frying causes a reaction between carbohydrates and amino acids, creating carcinogenic chemicals called acrylamides. And even when healthful food-preparation techniques are used, overcooking destroys nutrients. *Better...*

• **Microwave.** This uses minimal water and preserves flavor (so you won't be tempted to add butter or salt). Slightly moisten vegetables with water, cover and microwave just until crisp-tender.

• **Stir-fry.** In a preheated wok or sauté pan, cook vegetables over medium-high heat for a minute or two in a bit of low-sodium soy sauce.

• **Steam.** This beats boiling, but because steam envelops the food, some nutrients leach out. To "recycle" them, pour that bit of water from the steamer into any soup or sauce.

• **Stew.** Nutrients that leach from the vegetables aren't lost because they stay in the stew sauce.

• **Roast.** Set your oven to 350°F or lower to protect vegetables' nutrients and minimize acrylamides.

THE RIGHT COOKING OILS

Do you cringe when the Food Network chefs sauté in unrefined extra-virgin olive oil? You should. This oil has a very low smoke point (the temperature at which a particular oil turns to smoke) of about 325°F—and when oil smokes, nutrients degrade and free radicals form.

Best: Sauté or stir-fry with refined canola oil, which has a high smoke point. Or use tea seed cooking oil (not tea tree oil)—its smoke point is about 485°F.

Try: Arette Tea Seed Oil (*www.aretteorganic. com*) or Republic of Tea (800-298-4832, *www. republicoftea.com*).

Rule of thumb: If cooking oil starts to smoke, throw it out. Use a laser thermometer (sold at kitchenware stores) to instantly see oil temperature—so you'll know when to turn down the heat.

Easy, Healthful Flavor Boosts

To make food taste better without adding fat or salt, use citrus—lemons, limes and oranges—to bring out food flavors. Cook with herbs—then sprinkle on fresh herbs just before serving. Try unusual spices, such as cumin and cloves—alone or in combination—to produce varied flavors. If a salad dressing or cooking liquid tastes a little flat, add dried or fresh herbs to the dressing as well as an acid, such as lemon or vinegar, to brighten the cooking liquid.

Linda Gassenheimer, award-winning author and food columnist, Coral Gables, Florida. *www.dinnerinminutes. com*

Spices That Lower Cholesterol, Boost the Brain and More

Ann Kulze, MD, a primary care physician and founder and CEO of Just Wellness, LLC, which specializes in corporate and group wellness seminars, Mt. Pleasant, South Carolina. She is author of *Dr. Ann's 10-Step Diet: A Simple Plan for Permanent Weight Loss and Lifelong Vitality* (Top Ten Wellness and Fitness). *www.dranns10steps.com*.

Spices and herbs not only boost the flavor of your food, they also boost your health. Powerful plant compounds known as phytochemicals are found in high concentrations in many spices and herbs. Phytochemicals help fight heart disease, cancer, Alzheimer's, type 2 diabetes, arthritis and other diseases.

Here are the seasonings to add liberally to your food as often as possible. Unless otherwise noted, fresh herbs and spices offer a higher concentration of phytochemicals, but dried still are powerful.

SUPER SPICES...

The following spices have been shown to be particularly beneficial to our health...

• **Cinnamon.** Cinnamon has an almost medicinal power. Recent studies have shown that cinnamon enhances the metabolism of glucose and cholesterol and thus may provide protection from type 2 diabetes and cardiovascular disease.

A study reported in *Diabetes Care* highlighted cinnamon's favorable impact on the blood fat levels of people with type 2 diabetes. After eating one to six grams (about one-quarter to one-and-one-quarter teaspoons) of cinnamon daily for 40 days, overall levels of unhealthy blood fats dropped significantly—up to 26% for total cholesterol and 30% for triglycerides (a type of blood fat).

Even healthy people can benefit from cinnamon's impact on blood sugar, according to a study in *The American Journal of Clinical Nutrition.* Adding cinnamon to rice pudding significantly decreased the test subjects' normal, post-dessert elevations of blood sugar.

Interestingly, at least some of this effect was related to the spice's ability to delay how quickly food leaves the stomach and enters the intestines. In this regard, cinnamon also may be helpful in reducing appetite and hastening weight loss by enhancing satiety (the feeling of fullness).

Suggested uses: Cinnamon can be added to oatmeal, cereal and yogurt...coffee and tea...pumpkin and apple dishes...and rice and beans for an Indian touch.

• **Turmeric.** Curcumin (turmeric's active ingredient) is one of the most potent, naturally occurring anti-inflammatory agents ever identified and thus may be one of the best all-round spices for disease protection and antiaging. Inflammation plays a central role in most chronic diseases.

Turmeric also can be considered "brain health food." Research studies on mice demonstrate turmeric's ability to reduce the buildup of plaque in the brain that is associated with Alzheimer's and cognitive decline. Laboratory research has shown that turmeric also has potent anticancer properties.

Suggested uses: Add turmeric to your favorite bean, poultry, seafood, tofu and rice dishes, as well as to soups and stews. Turmeric often is used in classic Indian dishes, such as curries.

MORE HEALTH HELPERS

• **Cilantro.** Cilantro is high in the vitamins A and K and beta-carotene, and like any dark, leafy green, it is full of beneficial phytochemicals, including a natural antibiotic called *dodecenal*. In a University of California, Berkeley, laboratory study, dodecenal killed the bacteria Salmonella more effectively than a powerful prescription antibiotic.

Suggested uses: Add fresh, chopped cilantro to salsa, guacamole, omelets, salads, soups and stews.

• **Ginger.** Ginger is an anti-inflammatory superstar. It suppresses the action of inflammatory cytokines and chemokines. And for people plagued with motion sickness or morning sickness or experiencing postoperative nausea and vomiting, ginger—fresh or dried—has proved to be an effective and safe option. The phytochemicals in ginger also are valuable for boosting immunity, especially to combat viral infections.

Suggested uses: Dried powdered ginger is even more potent than fresh. Add it to sauces and salad dressings, or sprinkle it on salad, poultry or seafood. You also can add a thumbnail-sized piece of raw ginger to hot tea. Ginger is delicious in its candied form, and pickled ginger is perfect with sushi.

• **Parsley.** One tablespoon of fresh parsley provides more than half of the daily recommended value of vitamin K. It's also rich in vitamin A, lutein and zeaxanthin (which promote eye health) and provides nature's most concentrated source of flavonoids, plant pigments that provide health benefits. Parsley is among those plants that may be particularly useful for combatting cancer, allergies and heart disease.

Suggested uses: Add fresh chopped parsley to salads, pasta and rice dishes, soups and stews. Parsley is a main ingredient in the Mediterranean cracked-wheat dish tabouli.

• **Rosemary.** This savory herb contains phytochemicals that can reduce the formation of cancer-causing compounds known as *heterocyclic amines* (HCAs). HCAs can form when the proteins in meat are heated to high temperatures.

Preliminary research also indicates that rosemary may enhance insulin sensitivity, improving the action and efficiency of insulin in the body, aiding in a healthy metabolism and slowing the aging process. And it turns out that Shakespeare's Ophelia wasn't all that far off when she said that rosemary is for remembrance. According to a study in *Journal of Neurochemistry*, rosemary contains the compound *carnosic acid* (CA), which helps protect the brain.

Suggested uses: I always add one teaspoon of dried rosemary or a tablespoon or two of fresh to a pound of ground meat before grilling burgers. Rosemary also is good in lamb and potato dishes, soups and stews.

Eat Your Way to Low Cholesterol

Kenneth H. Cooper, MD, MPH, founder of The Cooper Clinic and The Cooper Institute for Aerobics Research, both in Dallas. A leading expert on preventive medicine and the health benefits of exercise, he is author of *Controlling Cholesterol the Natural Way* (Bantam). *www.CooperAerobics.com*

If you have high cholesterol, your primary objective should be to find a way to lower it without drugs and their side effects. The good news is that just eating the right foods often can reduce cholesterol by 50 points or more.

Most people know to eat a low-fat diet, but there are certain foods that can help lower cholesterol that may surprise you…

MACADAMIA NUTS

Macadamia nuts are among the fattiest plant foods on the planet, about 76% total fat by weight. However, nearly all of the fat is monounsaturated. This type of fat is ideal because it lowers LDL (bad) cholesterol without depressing HDL (good) cholesterol.

A team at Hawaii University found that study participants who added macadamia nuts to their diets for just one month had total cholesterol levels of 191 mg/dL, compared with those eating the typical American diet (201 mg/dL). The greatest effect was on LDL cholesterol.

Macadamia nuts are higher than other nuts in monounsaturated fat, but all nuts are high in vitamin E, omega-3 fatty acids and other antioxidants. Data from the Harvard Nurses' Health Study found that people who ate at least five ounces of any kind of nut weekly were 35% less likely to suffer heart attacks than those who ate less than one ounce per month.

Caution: Moderation is important because nuts—macadamia nuts, in particular—are high in calories. Limit servings to between one and two ounces daily—about a small handful a day.

RHUBARB

Rhubarb is ideal for both digestive health and lowering cholesterol because it contains a mix of soluble (see "Oats" on page 108) and insoluble fibers.

A study reported in *Journal of the American College of Nutrition* found that participants who ate a little less than three ounces of rhubarb daily for four weeks had an average drop in LDL cholesterol of 9%.

This tart-tasting vegetable isn't only an ingredient in pies. You can cut and simmer the stalks and serve rhubarb as a nutritious side dish (add some low-calorie strawberry jam for a touch of sweetness).

RICE BRAN

It's not as well-known for lowering cholesterol as oats and oat bran, but rice bran is just about as effective and some people enjoy it more. A six-week study at University of California, Davis Medical Center found that people who ate three ounces daily of a product with rice bran had drops in total cholesterol of 8.3% and a reduction in LDL of 13.7%.

You can buy rice bran in most supermarkets—it's prepared like oatmeal. Or you can try prepared rice-bran breakfast cereals, such as Quaker Rice Bran Cereal and Kenmei Rice Bran.

RED YEAST RICE

Made from a yeast that grows on rice, red yeast rice contains monacolins, compounds that inhibit the body's production of cholesterol.

One study found that people who took red yeast rice supplements and did nothing else had drops in LDL of 23%. When the supplements were combined with healthy lifestyle changes, their LDL dropped by about 42%.

Red yeast rice may be less likely than statins to cause the side effect myopathy (a painful muscle disease).

Recommended dose: 600 milligrams (mg), twice daily. It is available online and at health-food stores.

GREEN TEA

Green tea is a concentrated source of polyphenols, which are among the most potent antioxidants. It can lower LDL cholesterol and prevent it from turning into plaque deposits in blood vessels. In one study, men who drank five cups of green tea daily had total cholesterol levels that were nine points lower than men who didn't drink green tea.

Three to five cups daily are probably optimal. Black tea also contains polyphenols but in lower concentrations than green tea.

VITAMINS C AND E

These vitamins help prevent cholesterol in the blood from oxidizing. Oxidized cholesterol is more likely to cling to artery walls and promote the development of atherosclerosis, the cause of most heart attacks.

I advise patients with high cholesterol to take at least 400 international units (IU) of d-alpha-tocopherol, the natural form of vitamin E, daily. You might need more if you engage in activities that increase oxidation, such as smoking.

For vitamin C, take 1,000 mg daily. People who get the most vitamin C are from 25% to 50% less likely to die from cardiovascular disease than those who get smaller amounts.

THE BIG THREE

In addition to the above, some foods have long been known to reduce cholesterol, but they are so helpful that they bear repeating again…

• **Cholesterol-lowering margarines.** I use Benecol every day. It's a margarine that contains stanol esters, cholesterol-lowering compounds that are extracted from plants such as soy and pine trees. About 30 grams (g) of Benecol (the equivalent of about three to four pats of butter) daily will lower LDL by about 14%.

Similar products, such as Promise Buttery Spread, contain sterol esters. Like stanols, they help block the passage of cholesterol from the digestive tract into the bloodstream. We used to think that sterols weren't as effective as stanols for lowering cholesterol, but they appear to have comparable benefits.

• **Oats.** They are among the most potent nutraceuticals, natural foods with medicine-like properties. Both oat bran and oatmeal are high in soluble fiber. This type of fiber dissolves and forms a gel-like material in the intestine. The gel binds to cholesterol molecules, which prevents them from entering the bloodstream. A Harvard study that analyzed the results of 67 scientific trials found that even a small amount of soluble fiber daily lowered total cholesterol by five points. People who eat a total of 7 g to 8 g of soluble fiber daily typically see drops of up to 10%. One and a half cups of cooked oatmeal provides 6 g of fiber. If you don't like oatmeal, try homemade oat bran muffins. Soluble fiber also is found in such foods as kidney beans, apples, pears, barley and prunes.

Also helpful: Psyllium, a grain that's used in some breakfast cereals, such as Kellogg's All-Bran Bran Buds, and in products such as Metamucil. As little as 3 g to 4 g of psyllium daily can lower LDL by up to 20%.

• **Fish.** People who eat two to three servings of fish a week will have significant drops in both LDL and triglycerides, another marker for cardiac risk. One large study found that people who ate fish as little as once a week reduced their risk for a sudden, fatal heart attack by 52%.

I eat salmon, tuna, herring and sardines. Other good sources of omega-3 fatty acids include walnuts, ground flaxseed, tofu and canola oil.

Fish-oil supplements may provide similar protection, but they are not as effective as the natural food, which contains other beneficial nutrients as well.

Pistachios Reduce Cholesterol

Pistachios contain healthy fats and are rich in plant sterols, which inhibit cholesterol absorption. The nuts also are high in antioxidants—even higher than other nuts. Substituting one or two one-and-a-half-ounce servings of pistachios a day for fatty meats or other sources of saturated fat can lower LDL (bad) cholesterol by 10% to 12%.

Penny M. Kris-Etherton, PhD, is Distinguished Professor, department of nutritional sciences, Penn State University, University Park, Pennsylvania, and leader of a study published in *The Journal of Nutrition*.

Sugar Can Be Deadly

Nancy Appleton, PhD, a clinical nutritionist in San Diego. She is author, with G.N. Jacobs, of *Suicide by Sugar: A Startling Look at Our #1 National Addiction* (Square One). *www.nancyappleton.com*

The phrase "addictive white powder" probably makes you think of illegal drugs. Add sugar to that addictive group. Americans consume vast quantities—and suffer withdrawal symptoms when they don't get it. In fact, animal studies indicate that sugar is more addictive than cocaine.

Excess sugar has been linked to obesity, cancer, diabetes and dementia. *What to do...*

SUGAR, SUGAR EVERYWHERE

In the US, the average person consumes about 142 pounds of sugar each year, the equivalent of 48 teaspoons a day. Of that amount, 74 pounds is "added" sugar—about 23 teaspoons every day. Added sugars are defined as those sugars added to foods and beverages during processing or home preparation as opposed to sugars that occur naturally.

People who want to cut back on sweeteners usually start with the sugar bowl. They spoon less sugar on their breakfast cereal, for example, or use a sugar substitute in their coffee.

This doesn't help very much. The vast majority of added sugar in the diet comes from packaged foods, including foods that we think are healthful.

For example, eight ounces of one brand of sweetened apple yogurt contains 44 grams of sugar, according to the nutrition facts label. Four grams equals one teaspoon, so that's 11 teaspoons of sugar. (You cannot tell from the label how much sugar is from the yogurt, how much is from the apples and how much is added sugar.)

Most of the added sugar that we consume comes from regular soft drinks (there are about 10 teaspoons of sugar in 12 ounces of nondiet soda), candy, pies, cookies, cakes, fruit drinks and milk-based desserts and products (ice cream, sweetened yogurt).

If you look carefully at ingredients labels, which list ingredients in order of quantity, you will see that the first two or three ingredients often are forms of sugar, but many have innocuous-sounding names, such as barley malt, galactose and agave nectar. Other forms of sugar include honey, maple syrup, corn syrup, corn sweetener, dextrine, rice syrup, glucose, sucrose and dextrose.

DANGEROUS IMBALANCE

The difference between sickness and health lies in the body's ability to maintain homeostasis, the proper balance and performance of all of the internal functions. Excess sugar disturbs this balance by impairing immunity, disrupting the production and release of hormones and creating an acidic internal environment.

It's not healthy to maintain a highly acidic state. The body tries to offset this by making itself more alkaline. It does this, in part, by removing calcium and other minerals from the bones.

Result: People who eat too much sugar experience disruptions in insulin and other hormones. They have an elevated risk for osteoporosis due to calcium depletion. They also tend to have elevated levels of cholesterol and triglycerides (blood fats), which increase the risk for heart disease.

BREAK THE CYCLE

Sugar, like drugs and alcohol, is addictive because it briefly elevates levels of serotonin, a neurotransmitter that produces positive feelings. When a sugar addict doesn't eat sugar, serotonin declines to low levels. This makes the person feel worse than before. He/she then eats more sugar to try to feel better—and the vicious cycle goes on.

For the best chance of breaking a sugar addiction, you need to ease out of it. This usually is more effective than going cold turkey. Once you've given up sugar entirely and the addiction is past, you'll be able to enjoy small amounts of sugar if you choose, although some people find that they lose their taste for it. *How to break the habit...*

• **Divide sugar from all sources in half.** Do this for one week.

Examples: If you've been drinking two soft drinks a day, cut back to one. Eat half as much dessert. Eat a breakfast cereal that has only half as much sugar as your usual brand, or mix a low-sugar brand in with your higher-sugar brand.

• **Limit yourself to one sweet bite.** The second week, allow yourself to have only one taste of only one very sweet food daily. This might be ice cream, sweetened cereal or a breakfast muffin. That small "hit" of sugar will prevent serotonin from dropping too low, too fast.

After about two weeks with little or no sugar, your internal chemistry, including levels of serotonin and other neurotransmitters, will stabilize at a healthier level.

• **Eat fresh fruits and vegetables.** These foods help restore the body's natural acid-alkaline balance. This will help reduce sugar cravings and promote better digestion. Be sure to substitute fresh fruits for juices. Whole fruit is better because the fiber slows the absorption of sugars into the bloodstream. The fiber also is filling, which is why few people will sit down and eat four oranges—the number you would need to squeeze to get one eight-ounce glass of juice.

Helpful: All fruits are healthful, but melons and berries have less sugar than other fruits.

The Darker the Better

Dark-roasted coffee is gentler on the stomach than light-roasted coffee. People who get heartburn or stomach irritation from most coffees often find dark roasts less bothersome.

Possible reason: Dark-roasted coffee contains more N-methylpyridinium, a compound created in the roasting process that limits stomach acid.

Veronika Somoza, PhD, professor and chair of the research platform of molecular food science at the University of Vienna and researcher of different coffee blends, presented at a recent meeting of the American Chemical Society.

Supercharged Food Combinations

Lisa R. Young, PhD, RD, adjunct professor of nutrition at New York University and a dietitian in private practice, both in New York City. She is author of *The Portion Teller Plan: The No Diet Reality Guide to Eating, Cheating and Losing Weight Permanently* (Broadway), *www.portionteller.com.*

Good nutrition depends not only on what you eat, but also on how well your body absorbs or uses vitamins and minerals in your food. Some nutrients are best absorbed or utilized when consumed with certain other nutrients. Here are easy dishes that combine complementary foods for a synergistic nutritional bonanza—and taste great.

BOOST BETA-CAROTENE

• **Beta-carotene** provides antioxidants that protect cells from harmful free radicals. It also enhances your immune function.

• **Eat with polyunsaturated fat** to support cognitive function and fight inflammation.

Easy recipes to combine beta-carotene and polyunsaturated fat…

• **Steam sliced butternut squash or carrots** just until soft…to combine with polyunsaturated fat, serve the vegetables with tuna or herring.

• **Bake a sweet potato or half an acorn squash**…for polyunsaturated fat, drizzle with flaxseed oil.

BOOST CALCIUM

• **Calcium** builds bones and helps control blood pressure.

• **Eat with vitamin D** to strengthen bones and teeth, and to protect against various cancers.

Easy recipes to combine calcium and vitamin D…

• **Toss together chopped fresh collard greens and shredded Swiss cheese**…to combine with vitamin D, stir into beaten eggs for an omelet or a quiche.

• **Broil salmon or perch and serve on a bed of spinach or dandelion greens**…for vitamin D, top with mushrooms.

BOOST FOLATE

• **Folate** reduces your risk for Alzheimer's disease and protects against birth defects.

• **Eat with vitamin C** to neutralize the toxic by-products of fat metabolism. Vitamin C also improves your absorption of iron, which is needed for red blood cells.

Easy recipes for folate and vitamin C…

• **Make a spinach and asparagus salad**…to combine with vitamin C, toss with orange slices, strawberries and lemon vinaigrette.

• **Cook great northern beans or black-eyed peas**…for vitamin C, stir in chopped tomatoes and red or orange bell peppers.

BOOST LUTEIN

• **Lutein** protects eyesight and combats skin damage.

• **Eat with monounsaturated fat** to lower cholesterol and blood pressure. Monounsaturated fat deters cancer-causing cell damage.

Easy recipes to combine lutein and monounsaturated fat…

• **Make a salad of romaine lettuce, green peas and hard-boiled egg**…to combine with monounsaturated fat, add avocado slices, shredded low-fat mozzarella and olive oil.

• **Mix up a fruit medley of sliced peaches, papaya and oranges**…for monounsaturated fat, stir in chopped hazelnuts, slivered almonds and pumpkin seeds.

BOOST POTASSIUM

• **Potassium** promotes function of nerve and muscle cells, while it maintains normal blood pressure and heart function.

• **Eat with magnesium** to regulate heartbeat and strengthen bones.

Easy recipes to combine potassium and magnesium…

• **Mix together lentils and lima beans**…to combine with magnesium, stir the legumes into quinoa or bulgur.

• **Toss together dried apricots and dried banana chips**…for magnesium, add bran cereal, pumpkin seeds and Brazil nuts to make trail mix.

BOOST ZINC

• **Zinc** strengthens the immune system and speeds wound healing.

• **Eat with protein** to help build and repair body tissues. Protein also produces hormones and essential body chemicals.

Easy recipes to combine zinc and protein…

• **Stir-fry diced chicken with chickpeas**…to pump up the protein, sprinkle with chopped cashews.

• **Mix wheat germ into enriched breakfast cereal**…for protein, top with low-fat yogurt.

Beyond Broccoli—the Healthiest Foods You Haven't Heard About

Tonia Reinhard, RD, a registered dietitian and professor at Wayne State University, Detroit. She is author of *Superfoods: The Healthiest Foods on the Planet* (Firefly).

We all have heard about so-called superfoods—like blueberries and broccoli—that have high levels of nutrients and healthful phytochemicals.

Here are some less-known foods that are loaded with health benefits and that can jazz up meals. Unless otherwise noted, they are available at most supermarkets.

BILBERRY

Bilberries are high in phytochemicals, including a class of compounds known as anthocyanins. A 2010 laboratory study published in the *Journal of Medicinal Foods* found that bilberry extract inhibited the growth of breast cancer cells. The berries also may improve blood glucose levels, helping to prevent diabetes.

During the Second World War, British pilots who had eaten bilberries prior to evening bombing raids noticed improvements in their night vision. Some compounds in bilberries may help prevent macular degeneration, a common cause of blindness.

Helpful: You can substitute fresh bilberries for blueberries. Or look for bilberry juice. It won't provide the fiber that you would get from fresh berries, but it still has the phytochemicals. Bilberries are available online and in health-food stores.

TROUT

Salmon gets all the publicity, but like salmon, trout is a fatty fish with large amounts of omega-3 fatty acids. These "good fats" have been linked to a reduced risk for heart disease, rheumatoid arthritis, dementia and other chronic conditions.

Scientists have recently discovered that a *peptide* (short strands of amino acids) in trout reduced both cholesterol and triglycerides in rats. It may do the same in humans. Trout also is high in vitamins B-6 and B-12, selenium, thiamine and riboflavin.

Helpful: Trout is just as easy to prepare as salmon because the fat keeps it tender, making it less likely to suffer from overcooking than a leaner fish.

One delicious recipe: Combine the juice of three lemons (about six tablespoons of bottled lemon juice) with three tablespoons of olive oil, one-quarter cup of chopped parsley and ground pepper to taste. Dip trout fillets in the mixture…place them on a baking sheet…and bake at 400°F for about 15 minutes.

BITTER MELON

Also known as goya, bitter melon is a fruit that often is combined with pork or other meats and used in stir-fries in Asian restaurants. Many people love it, but its bitter taste takes some getting used to. The payoff is worth it. A report in *Nutrition Review* noted that a diet high in bitter melon (three or more servings per week) helps reduce insulin resistance, a condition that can progress to type 2 diabetes.

Also, bitter melon is high in anti-viral compounds, which can keep you healthier in cold-and-flu season. And bitter melon is among the best sources of vitamin C, with about 60 milligrams (mg) in a one-cup serving, about the same amount as in one orange. It is available in Asian grocery stores.

Helpful: The bitterness can be tempered by adding sweetness to a recipe. For example, you could add dried cranberries or one tablespoon of apricot jam to a bitter melon stir-fry.

JICAMA

This crunchy, juicy vegetable (the "j" is pronounced like an "h") is as popular throughout Mexico and Central and South America as iceberg lettuce is in the US.

Researchers in Thailand identified antiviral activity in jicama. It is rich in vitamin C and potassium and also high in fiber, with 5.9 grams supplying 24% of the recommended daily amount.

Helpful: Jicama usually is eaten raw—it's the best way to preserve the vitamin C content. You can add slices or cubes to a garden salad or serve it alone, drizzled with lime juice (and chili powder if you like), as a tangy counterpoint to richer dishes.

ENOKI

Unlike the standard white button mushrooms sold in every American supermarket, enoki mushrooms have long, threadlike stalks, each topped by a delicate white dome.

A Singapore study found that enoki contains a protein that boosts immune function. It's also a powerful antioxidant that can suppress free radicals, important for reducing inflammation in arteries, joints and other parts of the body.

Helpful: The mushrooms have a mild, almost fruity taste. In Japan, they're added to miso soup. Or you can eat them raw, sprinkled on salads or in side dishes. They are available in Asian grocery and specialty stores.

NONI

This is not a fruit that you want to take a bite out of—in its unadulterated form, it has a singularly nasty taste. (Its nickname is "vomit fruit.") It's usually juiced and then combined with other fruit juices. After it's blended, it adds a sharp, but not unpleasant, taste, similar to the taste of unripened pomegranate.

Noni is rich in many phytochemicals, including some with potent antioxidant effects. A 2010 animal study found that noni may help to lower blood pressure. It also appears to inhibit the growth of melanoma, a deadly form of skin cancer.

Helpful: In health-food stores, look for a product that is 100% pure noni juice. Then mix one to two ounces of noni juice with other fruit juices, such as apple or pear juice. Experiment to determine what tastes best to you.

GOJI BERRY

Dried goji berries are popular in Australia and Asia, where they are enjoyed as a slightly tangy-sweet snack. Goji also can be used to make juice or a fruity spread.

Gojis are high in antioxidants. In a study published in *Nutrition Research*, participants who drank four ounces of goji juice daily for 30 days had significantly reduced free radical activity in the blood. The berries also are

thought to help protect against diabetes and atherosclerosis. And they're high in fiber, with three grams in one-quarter cup. They are available online and in some health-food stores.

Helpful: Munch them as a snack, or add them to muffins or other baked goods.

Caution: If you're taking a blood-thinning medication such as *warfarin* (Coumadin), talk to your doctor before eating goji berries. They may change the drug's effects.

Edible Flowers Can Boost Health

Most contain antioxidants, including vitamin C.

Edible flowers: Violets in garnishes and desserts are a source of rutin, which may strengthen capillaries…borage, good in salads, can help relieve a cold or cough…lavender petals, which taste sweet, may help protect the central nervous system…roses, which taste both sweet and astringent, may fight cardiovascular disease…nasturtiums, lemon gold marigold and calendula petals are good in salads and improve eyesight and fight cancer.

James Duke, PhD, ethnobotanist, Green Pharmacy Garden (*www.greenpharmacy.com*) and former USDA researcher, Fulton, Maryland.

Alcohol and Your Health

Don't start drinking alcohol for your health. Research shows that moderate alcohol consumption has cardiovascular benefits—but claims of other benefits for alcohol are uncertain.

Example: A six-and-a-half-year follow-up on a study that initially linked alcohol to improved mobility found that it was lifestyle factors that were beneficial—not the alcohol.

Bottom line: Weight control and regular exercise are far more important for health maintenance and improvement than alcohol consumption.

Cinzia Maraldi, MD, department of clinical and experimental medicine, University of Ferrara, Italy, and leader of a study of 3,061 people, ages 70 to 79, published in *Journal of the American Geriatrics Society.*

The Beer/Bone Connection

Beer is high in dietary silicon which has been linked to bone health. Beers with the highest levels of malted barley and hops are richest in silicon. The silicon content of 100 commercially available beers was found to range from 6.4 to 56.4 milligrams per liter. The India pale ale category generally had the most silicon.

Charles Bamforth, PhD, professor, department of food science and technology, University of California, Davis, and leader of a study of the silicon in beer, published in *Journal of the Science of Food and Agriculture.*

Coffee Protects the Liver

Among people who had developed chronic liver disease from heavy alcohol intake, those who drank one to three cups of coffee per day were about 40% less likely to develop cirrhosis (characterized by a scarred liver with diminished function) than those who did not drink coffee. Those who drank more than four cups per day reduced their risk by 80%. It is unclear whether the benefit is due to caffeine or another ingredient.

Arthur Klatsky, MD, is a cardiologist and adjunct investigator, division of research, Kaiser Permanente, Oakland, California, and leader of a 14-year study of 125,580 people.

Juice vs. Fruit

Pomegranate juice is healthier than the fruit itself.

Reason: Most of the fruit's antioxidants are found in the inedible rind of the fruit—but the rind is typically used to create the juice. Pomegranate juice helps protect the heart and prevent arthritis and gingivitis.

Best: Choose pure pomegranate juice with no added sugars or fillers (such as apple or pear juice).

Steven Pratt, MD, ophthalmologist, Scripps Memorial Hospital, La Jolla, California, and author of *SuperHealth* (Signet).

For Citrus Lovers

Don't remove the white pith of an orange or grapefruit peel from the fruit. Called the *albedo*, it is a good source of vitamin C and other compounds that may help reduce inflammation and prevent cancer. It also contains the soluble fiber pectin, which helps lower cholesterol.

Prevention, 33 E. Minor St., Emmaus, Pennsylvania 18098.

How to Eat Meat Without Risking Your Health

Barry Popkin, PhD, Carla Smith Chamblee Distinguished Professor in the department of nutrition at the University of North Carolina Gillings School of Global Public Health in Chapel Hill. He is the author of *The World Is Fat: The Fads, Trends, Policies and Products That Are Fattening the Human Race* (Avery).

For years, a growing body of scientific evidence has linked diets that contain excessive amounts of red and/or processed meats to health problems ranging from heart disease and cancer (especially of the colon) to diabetes.

Landmark findings: A National Institutes of Health (NIH)-AARP study of about 500,000 adults ages 50 to 71 found that those who ate the most red meat (five ounces daily, on average) had a 30% higher risk for death—mostly from heart disease or cancer—than those who ate the least (two-thirds ounce daily, on average). Those who ate the most processed meat (about one-and-one-half ounces daily) had a 20% higher risk for death than those who ate the least.

In addition, researchers who analyzed data from the Women's Health Study (of about 37,000 women) found that those who ate at least five servings of processed meat (mostly bacon and hot dogs) a week for nine years were 38% more likely to develop diabetes than those who had less than one serving weekly.

Yet scientists point out that it is possible that other factors were responsible for the meat eaters' increased health risks. For example, people who eat little meat may eat large amounts of fruits and vegetables, and those nutrients—not the lack of meat—may be what protects them against heart disease.

Ultimately, you don't have to swear off meat entirely to have a healthful diet. But before you sharpen the steak knives, consider these six secrets to enjoying meat while staying healthy…

1. Choose wisely. When shopping for red meat, opt for lean cuts. If possible, choose meat from cattle that are "range-fed"—that is, the animals roam the range and are not confined to small spaces, and they eat grass instead of grain meal.

Animal meat takes on characteristics of the foods eaten by the animal. For example, the muscle tissue of grass-fed animals has levels of beneficial omega-3s that are 10 to 15 times greater than the levels found in grain-fed animals. Plus, the physical activity that occurs with range-fed animals changes the composition of the animals' fat.

Important: Labeling guidelines have been hotly debated in recent years. Many food scientists believe that guidelines have been diluted. For instance, a package labeled "grass-fed" may mean the animal ate grass for only part of its life. In terms of best nutritional value,

I recommend meat that is lean and, ideally, range-fed.

Also important: If the meat is marbled or has a large rind of fat, keep looking. Best choices include filet mignon and "loins," such as sirloin and tenderloin, instead of rib eyes, which usually are fattier.

2. Buy meat directly from farms if possible. There are farms across the US that sell range-fed meats. To find a supplier of such meat, consult the Web site *www.EatWild.com*, owned and operated by Jo Robinson, a journalist who has investigated the differences between animals raised in feedlots and range-fed farms for nearly a decade.

3. Eat whole instead of processed meats. Avoid bacon, bologna, deli meats, hot dogs, pepperoni, salami, Spam, canned hash, sausages and other processed meats. These products have little nutritional value and are full of additives, fats, preservatives and salt.

4. Prepare meat wisely. When proteins in meat (found not only in red meat but also in fish, pork and poultry) are exposed to high heat, the carcinogen *heterocyclic amine* (HCA) forms from a chemical reaction among amino acids (protein building blocks), sugars and creatine (found in muscles).

To avoid this risk, reduce gas heat from high to medium and avoid grilling for long periods of time (the browner the meat, the more likely that HCAs are present). Grill meat over embers instead of flames. Check the meat temperature with a thermometer. Remove beef, pork and lamb from the grill at 160° F, and chicken and hot dogs at 165° F.

One study found that marinating meat before grilling for 40 minutes reduced HCA production by 92%.

Key marinade ingredients: Apple cider vinegar, garlic, lemon juice, mustard, olive oil, salt and spices—especially of the antioxidant-rich mint family (thyme, basil and oregano). Reduce the amount of time meat is high-temperature grilled by first heating meat in the microwave. Or instead of grilling, try baking, roasting or stir-frying, all of which create fewer HCAs.

5. Reduce saturated fat intake elsewhere in your diet. It is primarily the saturated fat in red meat that increases blood levels of cholesterol and, therefore, risk for heart disease. If you wish to continue eating red and processed meats (even in limited amounts), reduce your intake of other sources of saturated fat in your diet (such as sour cream, butter and whole dairy products). Generally, you want to limit saturated fat in your diet so that it makes up 10% or less of your total daily calories.

6. Limit meat consumption. Aim to eat no more than an average of one ounce of red meat per day and no more than one ounce of processed meat per week. Keep in mind that red meat includes pork as well as beef.

Also helpful: If you crave the texture of meat, consider replacing some or all red and processed meats with white meat (whole lean chicken, turkey and fish). Fish, in particular, has higher levels of heart-healthy omega-3 fatty acids than red and processed meats.

A surprising finding of the NIH-AARP study described earlier is that regular consumption of white meat did not increase risk of dying at all. In fact, those who ate the most white meat actually had a lower risk of dying than those who ate the least.

Choose Coconut Water Over Energy Drinks

Coconut water is healthier than most energy drinks. The clear liquid inside coconuts contains vitamins, minerals, amino acids and phytohormones, which have antioxidant and antiplatelet properties that help prevent cancer and have positive effects on neurological diseases, such as Alzheimer's. It also can help the body replenish electrolytes lost during a workout. One cup of coconut water has 46 calories. Available in grocery stores and online.

Environmental Nutrition, 800 Connecticut Ave., Norwalk, Connecticut 06854. 12 issues. $24/yr. *www.EnvironmentalNutrition.com*

Whole Grains Linked to Lower Blood Pressure

Researchers who reviewed health and nutrition data for 31,684 men found that those who consumed the most whole grains (about 52 g daily) were 19% less likely to develop high blood pressure than those who consumed the least whole grains (about 3 g daily).

Best sources: Oatmeal (instant or cooked)—one cup, 30 g to 35 g…popcorn—one cup, 10 g to 12 g…whole-wheat bread—one slice, about 15 g…and bran cereal—one cup, 5 g to 10 g.

Alan Flint, MD, DrPH, research scientist, department of nutrition, Harvard School of Public Health, Boston.

Five Rules for Healthful Snacking

Jamison Starbuck, ND, a naturopathic physician in family practice in Montana, both in Missoula. She is past president of the American Association of Naturopathic Physicians and a contributing editor to *The Alternative Advisor* (Time Life).

Do you like to eat a little something between meals? Here's a set of rules for healthful snacking—and a list of tasty, fun foods that make good snacks.

Rule 1. Drink water first. Often, we head for a snack when we're actually thirsty. Drink a 12-ounce glass of water and wait 10 minutes. If you are still hungry, select a healthful snack.

Rule 2. Choose a snack food that still bears a resemblance to its original form. Natural food—the most healthful food—comes from the earth or an animal. Lettuce grows in the dirt. Oranges and nuts hang from trees. Corn, wheat and oats grow in fields. The fillet or steak you're having for dinner was part of an animal before it landed on your table. When you apply this concept to snacks, it's fairly easy to make healthful choices. Cheetos, for example, are a long, long way from the corn from which they are made—many synthetic ingredients are added.

Rule 3. Avoid fat- and sugar-laden snacks. If a sweetener or oil is the first or second ingredient on the label list, skip this snack.

Rule 4. Keep portions small. The more fat or sugar in the snack (cheese, nuts and dried fruit), the smaller the portion should be. Recommended snack size is one ounce of cheese…eight nuts…or two tablespoons of dried fruit. Watery, fiber-rich snacks, such as fresh fruit or vegetables, can be eaten in larger portions—½ cup to one cup is reasonable.

Rule 5. Drink a cup of hot mint tea with your snack. It aids your digestion, promoting absorption of nutrients, which improves the satisfaction you derive from the food. *My snack suggestions…*

Raw almonds, hazelnuts or pecans…whole fruit…celery sticks, carrots or a rice cake covered with a tablespoon of nut butter (almond, sesame, cashew) or hummus (mashed chickpeas flavored with lemon juice, garlic and oil)…whole-grain muffin (no bigger than a tennis ball) containing fruit, nuts and/or ground seeds and made with honey or cane sugar—not corn syrup…vegetable salads, such as cooked and chilled beets drizzled with olive oil and a sprinkle of goat cheese or cole slaw made with oil and vinegar rather than mayonnaise…air-popped popcorn—plain or seasoned with garlic or a pinch of sea salt… small baked potato, seasoned with herbs and a sprinkle of oil (put extra potatoes in the oven when you make dinner and refrigerate them for snacks that can be eaten later)…and rice—½ cup, with nuts and a dash of oil..

Surprise! Popcorn Is Good for You

In a recent study, researchers found that popcorn is the richest source of antioxidants among whole-grain snack foods, including tortilla chips and crackers.

Self-defense: In addition to regularly consuming fruits and vegetables, you can increase your antioxidant intake by enjoying popcorn as a snack (with little or no salt and no butter).

Joe Vinson, PhD, professor of chemistry, University of Scranton, Pennsylvania.

Calorie Counts Are Often Wrong

Do not believe calorie counts on restaurant menus or frozen meal labels.

Recent study: At 10 chain restaurants, calories in 29 meals averaged 18% higher than listed on menus. For 10 frozen supermarket meals, calories were 8% more than labels said.

Reasons: Variations in ingredients and portion sizes. For example, the amount of mayonnaise may vary from sandwich to sandwich.

Self-defense: Use nutrition labels as guidelines, but do not consider them to be scientifically precise.

Susan B. Roberts, PhD, professor of nutrition and professor of psychiatry, Tufts University, Boston, author of *The "i" Diet* (Workman) and leader of a study published in *Journal of the American Dietetic Association. www.instinctdiet.com*

Vegetable Juice Aids Weight Loss

Overweight adults with metabolic syndrome—characterized by excess fat in the midsection, high blood sugar and high blood pressure—who followed a diet rich in fruits, vegetables and whole grains lost an average of four pounds in 12 weeks when they also drank eight ounces of low-sodium vegetable juice daily. People who did not drink vegetable juice lost an average of one pound.

Possible reason: The juice—usually tomato juice mixed with juices from a variety of vegetables—may fill you up so that you eat less.

Study of 81 adults with metabolic syndrome by researchers at Baylor College of Medicine, Houston, presented at an *Experimental Biology* meeting.

Healthful Hot Cereals

Lisa R. Young, PhD, RD, is a nutritionist in private practice and an adjunct professor of nutrition at New York University, both in New York City. She is the author of *The Portion Teller Plan* (Morgan Road).

A delicious hot bowl of cereal is a great way to start the day. An excellent source of fiber, most hot cereals are also low in fat and contain whole grain (be sure the first item in the ingredient list is whole wheat, oats, rye or barley).

Here are my top picks for hot cereals—nutritional breakdown is based on one-quarter cup dry cereal, which yields one cup cooked cereal...

MCCANN'S
STEEL-CUT IRISH OATMEAL

Chewy with a wholesome, grainy taste: 150 calories...2 g fat...0 g saturated fat...0 g trans fat...0 mg sodium...0 g sugar...and 4 g fiber.

BOB'S RED MILL
10 GRAIN HOT CEREAL

A flavorful mixture of 10 different grains: 140 calories...1 g fat...0 g saturated fat...0 g trans fat...5 mg sodium...0 g sugar... and 5 g fiber.

HODGSON MILLS
OAT BRAN HOT CEREAL

Delicious taste with the heart-healthy benefits of oat bran: 120 calories...3 g fat...1 g saturated fat...0 g trans fat...0 mg sodium...0 g sugar...6 g fiber.

To liven up your hot cereal...

•**Cook using skim milk or soymilk instead of water for a creamier texture.**

•**Sprinkle ground cinnamon, allspice or nutmeg on the plain varieties.**

•**Mix in ground flaxseed or wheat germ to add omega-3s and vitamin E, respectively.**

•**Add blueberries, bananas or other fruit.**

•**Top off with chopped nuts.**

Is Sauerkraut a Cancer Fighter?

Marji McCullough, ScD, RD, strategic director, nutritional epidemiology, American Cancer Society, Atlanta.

Yes, according to some studies. As a cruciferous vegetable, cabbage (and, therefore, sauerkraut) is high in compounds such as *indoles*—shown in laboratory and animal studies to have cancer preventive properties. Indoles detoxify carcinogens by activating enzymes that cause a shift in estrogen metabolism, which may protect against certain estrogen-related cancers, such as breast cancer.

Some (but not all) human studies have found that people who eat cruciferous vegetables daily, or even a few times weekly, are also at lower risk for certain other cancers, including gastrointestinal and lung cancers. Although some people believe that the fermentation used for sauerkraut plays a role, this has not been proven in human studies.

When buying sauerkraut, be sure to look for "low sodium" on the label. If you don't like sauerkraut's somewhat sour taste, cook it with an apple...or try other cruciferous vegetables, including broccoli, cauliflower, Brussels sprouts and kale.

Snacks That Fight Fat

To prevent fat around your middle, eat a snack containing protein, fat and low-glycemic carbohydrates every day between 3 pm and 4 pm—perhaps a protein bar, such as the Simply Bar or ProteinFusion Bar...or a serving of high-protein low-fat cheese and 12 almonds. This type of snack boosts metabolism and balances blood sugar—keeping the body's insulin level lower. A lower insulin level helps protect against midbody weight gain.

Natasha Turner, ND, naturopathic doctor, Toronto, and author of *The Hormone Diet* (Rodale). *www.the hormonediet.com*

The Skinny on Olive Oil

Did you know olive oil has more fat than butter? Also, it has 20% more calories per tablespoon.

But: Olive oil has less unhealthy saturated fat than butter.

Bon Appétit, 6300 Wilshire Blvd., Los Angeles 90048.

Bananas Fight Depression, Heartburn And More

Ara DerMarderosian, PhD, professor of pharmacognosy (the study of natural products used in medicine) at the University of the Sciences in Philadelphia.

Most people know that bananas are an excellent source of potassium (one ripe banana supplies more than 10% of an adult's daily requirement of the mineral). That's important because people with a low dietary intake of potassium are 28% more likely to suffer a stroke than those who consume higher levels, according to a study conducted at Tulane University.

Lesser-known medicinal uses of bananas…

• **Depression.** Bananas are a good source of tryptophan (a precursor to serotonin, a brain chemical that helps regulate mood).

• **Diarrhea.** Unripe bananas and plantains (high-starch, green bananas that are typically cooked) are a rich source of tannins, astringent plant compounds that help stop water accumulation in the intestines, thus diminishing diarrhea.

• **Heartburn and ulcers.** Bananas neutralize acidity and soothe and coat esophageal tissue with pectin (a substance used as a thickener and stabilizer in jellies).

Important: In rare cases, bananas may cause an allergic reaction. Bananas with blackened skin can increase blood sugar levels. Because bananas have high levels of potassium, people with kidney problems should check with their doctors before eating this fruit.

Trans Fat Alternative Dangerous, Too

Many products once made with trans fats now contain palm oil, which has been praised for its high levels of vitamin E and oleic acid, thought to reduce risk for cardiovascular disease and protect against certain types of cancer. But palm oil also is high in saturated fats and can raise levels of LDL (bad) cholesterol.

Better: Stick to foods containing olive or canola oil.

Prevention, 33 E. Minor St., Emmaus, Pennsylvania 18098.

Keep Your Weight Down with Calcium And Vitamin D

Combat postmenopausal weight gain by taking daily supplements of calcium (1,000 mg) and vitamin D (400 international units).

Recent study: Among 36,282 women ages 50 to 79, those who took these supplements over a seven-year period were less likely to gain weight than those who did not.

Theory: These nutrients may stimulate breakdown of fat cells and reduce absorption of fat by the intestines.

Important: Diet and exercise still are key to maintaining a healthy weight.

Bette Caan, DrPh, senior research scientist, Kaiser Permanente, Oakland, California, and leader of a study published in *Archives of Internal Medicine*.

Popular Herbs with Unexpected Health Benefits

Holly Phaneuf, PhD, expert in medicinal chemistry and author of *Herbs Demystified* (Avalon). She is a member of the American Chemical Society and is currently conducting research on exercise and herb use.

You may know that the tiny, fiber-rich seeds of the flax plant can be used as a laxative and that ginger helps ease nausea. But can you name any of the other health benefits provided by these plant-derived remedies?

Few people can. However, credible scientific evidence shows that many herbs that are well-known for treating a particular ailment have other important—but little-known—uses.* *For example...*

ARTICHOKE LEAF

Artichoke leaf extract is used by some people with mildly elevated cholesterol levels as an alternative to prescription statin drugs. Exactly how the herb works is unknown, but animal studies suggest that it inhibits HMG CoA-reductase, an enzyme that plays a key role in the liver's production of cholesterol.

In a placebo-controlled, randomized study conducted at the University of Reading in England, adults who took 1,280 mg of artichoke leaf extract daily for three months reduced their cholesterol levels by 4.2%, on average, while levels increased by 1.9%, on average, in those taking a placebo.

What else artichoke leaf can do: Calm indigestion. In a placebo-controlled, randomized study, patients rated their chronic indigestion as significantly improved after taking artichoke leaf extract twice daily for six weeks. Tests on rats suggest that the herb stimulates the gallbladder's production of bile, which helps facilitate the digestion of dietary fat.

*If you use prescription drugs and/or have a chronic medical condition, such as diabetes, cancer or heart disease, speak to your doctor before trying herbal remedies. In some cases, herbs may interfere with medication or cause an undesired effect on a chronic medical problem. Women who are pregnant or breast-feeding also should consult a doctor before taking herbs.

Typical dose: About 320 mg daily of artichoke leaf soothes digestive complaints. This dosage can be taken until the indigestion is no longer a problem.

Caution: Avoid artichoke if you are allergic to plants in the daisy family or if you have gallstones (artichoke appears to make the gallbladder contract).

FLAX

Often used as a gentle laxative, the seed of the flax plant (flaxseed) contains fiber and phytonutrients known as lignans—a combination that helps draw water into the gut to speed digestion. For laxative effects, eat one tablespoon of whole or ground seeds (sprinkled on cereal, for example) daily. Be sure to drink at least eight ounces of water when eating flaxseeds to prevent them from forming a temporary blockage in the intestines.

What else flaxseed can do: Help prevent breast and prostate cancers. Lignans form estrogen-like compounds that inhibit the body's production of the hormone in women and men. This effect is believed to reduce risk for estrogen-dependent malignancies, including some breast and prostate cancers.

Typical initial dose: One to two tablespoons of ground flaxseed daily, which can be increased gradually to as many as five tablespoons daily.

Grinding flaxseed (in a coffee grinder, for example) rather than eating it whole releases more of its cancer-fighting compounds. Also, ground flaxseed is better than flaxseed oil, which lacks the plant's beneficial lignans unless they are replaced during the manufacturing process.

Helpful: Be sure to refrigerate flaxseed to prolong freshness and preserve potency.

Caution: Do not consume flaxseed within two hours of taking an oral medication—flaxseed may interfere with absorption of the drug.

GARLIC

With its powerful blood-thinning effects, garlic is widely used to help prevent artery-blocking blood clots that can lead to a heart attack or stroke. The typical recommendation for this purpose is one clove of fresh garlic or one-half to three-quarters of a teaspoon of garlic powder daily.

What else garlic can do: Help prevent stomach and colorectal cancers. The National Cancer Institute funded an analysis of 23 clinical studies that linked garlic consumption (raw, cooked or from garlic supplements) to a 10% to 50% decrease in risk for these types of cancers. This cancer-fighting effect is believed to result from the antioxidant activity of garlic's sulfur-containing molecules. Garlic also is a popular remedy to stave off the common cold, but research on its virus-fighting properties has shown mixed results.

Recommended: A fresh crushed garlic clove four to seven times a week.

GINGER

Ginger is widely used to treat nausea, including that due to motion sickness (one-quarter to one-half teaspoon of ginger powder)…and chemotherapy (one to two teaspoons daily of ginger powder). Ginger is believed to quell queasiness by stopping intense stomach motions that can interfere with digestion.

What else ginger can do: Relieve arthritis pain. With its aspirin-like effects, ginger inhibits both COX-1 and COX-2 enzymes, two substances that are involved in the production of inflammatory hormones known as prostaglandins.

Typical dose: One-quarter to one-half teaspoon daily of ginger powder.

TURMERIC

In India, turmeric is a popular remedy for indigestion. It contains curcumin, an oily, yellow pigment that appears to prevent gut muscles from contracting and cramping.

What else turmeric can do: Relieve arthritis, morning stiffness and minor sprains. Turmeric reduces levels of an inflammatory, hormone-like substance known as PGE2. In lab studies, researchers also are finding that turmeric helps prevent colorectal and skin cancers, but its cancer-fighting mechanism has not yet been identified.

In addition, turmeric is being studied for its possible role in decreasing risk for Alzheimer's disease. Test tube and animal studies suggest that turmeric interferes with the formation of amyloid plaque, a hallmark of this neurodegenerative disease.

Recommended: Consume turmeric powder regularly by adding it to food, such as Asian dishes.

Caution: Because turmeric can cause gallbladder contractions, people with gallbladder problems should avoid the herb.

A Food Label to Follow

To identify foods that have been verified as natural—and that have no genetically modified organisms—look for the "Non-GMO Project" label. Foods that pass the project's tests have a label showing an orange butterfly on top of two blades of grass in the form of a check mark. The project, which went public in the fall of 2009, has certified several hundred products so far. Genetically modified foods originate from crops whose DNA has been altered to create organisms that not only grow faster than natural crops but also are pesticide resistant. While qualities such as these are advantageous, there is a possibility that GMOs can harm plants, animals and people.

More information: *www.NonGMOProject. org.*

E Magazine, 28 Knight St., Norwalk, Connecticut 06851.

How to Protect Against Killer Food Allergies

Steve L. Taylor, PhD, professor of food science and codirector of the Food Allergy Research and Resource Program at the University of Nebraska, Lincoln. He is a leading expert on food allergies and serves on the editorial boards of the *Journal of Food Protection and the Journal of Natural Toxins.*

Many people with food allergies have mild symptoms, such as a rash, runny nose or itchy eyes, when they eat small amounts of a problem food. But they may still be at risk for a potentially deadly reaction.

In the US, food allergies cause up to 30,000 emergency room visits and 200 deaths annually due to *anaphylaxis*, an acute reaction that can cause respiratory distress and/or a heart arrhythmia (irregular heartbeat).

The Food Allergen Labeling and Consumer Protection Act, which went into effect in January 2006, requires food manufacturers to list eight major allergens on food labels to help people with food allergies identify and avoid problem foods.

IS IT REALLY AN ALLERGY?

Not all reactions to food are due to allergies. Tens of millions of Americans suffer from food intolerance. A food intolerance, such as a sensitivity to the lactose in milk, can begin in childhood. The most common symptom of lactose intolerance is gastrointestinal discomfort, including diarrhea, cramping and flatulence.

Food allergies affect about 11 million to 12 million Americans. With a food allergy, the immune system mistakenly identifies as harmful the various proteins—or even a single kind of protein—within one or more foods. This triggers a cascade of events that causes immune cells to respond to the "threat" by releasing large amounts of histamine and other chemicals that produce the allergic symptoms.

The most common food allergen is shellfish. Up to 2% of Americans are allergic to shrimp and/or other shellfish, such as lobster, crab and crayfish. This type of allergy often is ignored—primarily because most people tend to eat shellfish far less often than other allergenic foods, such as eggs, peanuts and fish.

TESTING FOR ALLERGIES

A food allergy usually can be diagnosed with a thorough medical history taken by an allergist.

The doctor will want to know...

• **When do symptoms occur?** Food allergies typically cause symptoms within a few minutes to several hours after exposure. Symptoms include stomach cramping, hives, lip swelling, runny nose, congestion and asthma. With a food intolerance, symptoms may not occur until the next day.

• **How much did you eat?** With food allergies, any exposure can trigger symptoms. For some patients, 1 mg—an amount that's almost impossible to see—will provoke an allergic response. A reaction can even be triggered by kissing—or sharing utensils with—someone who has eaten a substance to which you are allergic. A skin reaction can occur from touching the substance.

With a food intolerance, symptoms usually are linked to the amount consumed. Someone who's sensitive to milk, for example, can often drink a small amount without a reaction.

Two tests can identify most food allergies. *They are...*

• Skin prick. Extracts of suspected foods are pricked into the skin with a needle. The appearance of a rash within a few hours—or even a few minutes—indicates a food allergy.

Caution: The skin-prick test isn't advisable for patients with severe allergies. The tiny amounts of food used in the test could trigger a life-threatening reaction.

• Radioallergosorbent test (RAST). This blood test detects antibodies to specific food proteins. The test occasionally produces false positives—indicating an allergy where none is present. It's often combined with the skin-prick test for more accurate results.

TREATMENT

People with a history of serious food reactions must carry an EpiPen. Available by prescription, it's a self-injector that delivers a dose of epinephrine. Epinephrine stimulates the heart and respiration and helps counteract deadly anaphylaxis.

Important: Use the EpiPen immediately if you experience difficulty breathing or throat constriction. Even if you take the shot promptly, get to an emergency room as soon as possible for follow-up treatments.

Also helpful: Take an antihistamine, such as Benadryl, according to label instructions. It can lessen the severity of symptoms while you get to an emergency room.

Omalizumab (Xolair), a medication currently used for asthma, appears to significantly blunt reactions in food–allergy patients who receive a monthly injection of the drug. In an early study, patients who reacted to trace amounts of peanuts were able to eat eight to 10 nuts without experiencing problems. Further studies must be completed to determine whether the FDA deems it an effective—and safe—therapy for food allergies.

AVOIDING PROBLEM FOODS

Because there isn't a cure for food allergies—and even trace amounts of a protein can trigger reactions—strict avoidance is the best defense...

• **Always read food labels**—even if you've safely eaten that product in the past. Manufacturers frequently change or add ingredients.

• **Ask about "hidden" ingredients in medications.** Some prescription and over-the-counter (OTC) drugs, as well as vitamins and supplements, contain milk proteins or other common food allergens. This information should be on the label, but check with your doctor or pharmacist before taking any medication or supplement.

• **Talk to the chef or restaurant manager when eating out.** The waiter or waitress doesn't always have accurate information about food ingredients and preparation. Ask to speak to the chef or manager instead and tell him/her what you're allergic to. Explain that any contact with the offending food can be life-threatening.

• **If you're allergic to shellfish,** for example, tell the chef or manager you can't eat a hamburger that was cooked on the same grill used to cook shrimp.

Other hidden sources of food allergens: Cooking oils that are used to cook different foods...knives and cutting boards that aren't washed clean between uses.

• **Wear a medical alert bracelet/necklace.** Anaphylaxis can potentially cause a loss of consciousness within minutes. A medical alert bracelet/necklace lets medical personnel know that you require urgent treatment for your allergy.

For Travelers with Food Allergies...

Travelers with serious allergies to peanuts, shellfish and other foods can order allergy emergency cards in several languages at *www.selectwisely.com*. The cards can be used at restaurants and hotels in other countries to communicate what you are allergic to.

Cost: Starting at $6.50.

Arthur Frommer's Budget Travel, 530 7th Ave., New York City 10018, *www.frommers.com*.

Eggs, Greens Fight Vision Loss

A study sponsored by the National Eye Institute examined the link between nutrients and age-related macular degeneration (AMD), a leading cause of vision loss in people over age 65.

Results: Among 4,519 adults ages 60 to 80, those whose diets were highest in the carotenoids lutein and zeaxanthin had a 35% lower risk for developing "wet" AMD (the most severe form) than those with the lowest intake.

Wet AMD is difficult to treat, so prevention is key. Lutein and zeaxanthin may protect the macula (part of the retina) from damaging ultraviolet rays.

Self-defense: Eat at least one daily serving (two servings if over age 50) of eggs, kale, spinach, turnip greens, collard greens, romaine lettuce, broccoli, zucchini, peas or Brussels sprouts.

Mark A. Stengler, NMD, licensed naturopathic medical doctor in private practice, Stengler Center for Integrative Medicine, Encinitas, California...and author of many books, including *The Natural Physician's Healing Therapies*.

Egg Allergies and Flu Shots

People with egg allergies can get flu shots, says Matthew Greenhawt, MD. People allergic to eggs have long been told that they should not get flu shots because the vaccine contains egg protein. Recent finding: Most people who are allergic to eggs are able to get an influenza vaccination safely, but talk to your doctor and allergist before doing so.

Matthew Greenhawt, MD, a clinical lecturer at University of Michigan Health System, Ann Arbor, and coauthor of guidelines for vaccinating people with allergies to eggs.

Allergy-Free Baking Mixes

Baking mixes for people with food allergies: Cherrybrook Kitchen makes cake, cookie, brownie, pancake and frosting mixes that are dairy-free, egg-free, peanut-free and nut-free. Different products are available for people with different allergies.

Example: Chocolate cake and chocolate-chip cookie mixes are available in gluten-free versions. Costs vary.

Information: 866-458-8225, *www.cherry brookkitchen.com.*

Samir S. Shah, MD, infectious diseases physician, Children's Hospital of Philadelphia, and leader of an analysis of the medical records of more than 355,000 children, ages 18 or younger, admitted to 31 US hospitals during 2004, published in *Archives of Pediatrics & Adolescent Medicine.*

Sensitive to Gluten?

What grains are safe to eat if you are sensitive to gluten (a substance present in wheat)?

You can eat brown rice, corn, wild rice and buckwheat (also called kasha), all of which are easy to find. Less common grains that also are fine—but you may have to hunt a bit for them—are amaranth, millet and quinoa.

Caution: If you have a gluten sensitivity, it is not enough to avoid wheat. You also must stay away from products containing rye, barley and spelt. Gluten can cause digestive problems in people who are sensitive to it.

Thomas Brunoski, MD, a specialist in food and environmental allergies and nutritional medicine in private practice in Westport, Connecticut.

6

Exercise Equals a Healthier You

How the Father of Modern Aerobics Stays Motivated

D r. Kenneth Cooper is widely recognized as one of the world's leading authorities on fitness and preventive medicine. His work on the importance of cardiovascular health has led to a worldwide revolution in physical fitness. His first book, the international best seller *Aerobics*, was published in 1968. *Here he advises on how anyone can get healthy and fit...*

I've participated in regular, scheduled exercise for more than 50 years. What keeps me motivated after all this time? The same thing now as when I first began—better health, improved quality of life and increased happiness.

When I broke my leg a couple of years ago in a skiing accident, for the first time in decades I couldn't have regular activity. I became depressed, I gained weight, I felt my quality of life had gone downhill. As I gradually was able to return to my normal level of activity, I started feeling better and better. I've had to substitute fast walking for running, but that doesn't really make any difference. Once I was moving again, my heart rate went down...I returned to my normal weight...my depression lifted. I felt great again.

What this proved: Even seniors like me can modify their exercise programs to compensate for injuries and other health problems and continue to stay active. I'm still working 50 to 60 hours a week and exercising at least an hour a day. You can get healthier as you get older. What's more, to a great extent, you control whether this happens—not your doctor, not your insurance company, not the government.

Kenneth H. Cooper, MD, MPH, founder and head of the Cooper Aerobics Center in Dallas and CooperLife, a residential healthy-living community, in McKinney, Texas. His latest book, written with his son, Tyler C. Cooper, MD, MPH, is *Start Strong, Finish Strong* (Avery).

BENEFITS OF FITNESS

Positive things motivate us—and fitness brings a lot of positives. *At the Cooper Institute (the research division of Cooper Aerobics Center), we've pinpointed important benefits that go along with increased fitness, no matter how old you are…*

• **The longevity benefit.** Being fit can add three years to your life—and you are 65% less likely to die prematurely than someone who is unfit.

• **The mental health benefit.** Exercise more and you'll improve your mental health, with less likelihood of depression.

• **The physical function benefit.** Establish good health habits, and you'll delay by several years the age at which you develop even minimal disability.

• **The cancer protection benefit.** Exercise lowers your risk for every cancer.

• **The strong bone benefit.** Weight-bearing exercise, such as walking or running, lowers your risk of excessive bone loss after age 50.

• **The healing benefit.** If you're an older adult who exercises regularly, skin wounds heal faster. It might also help you recover from other ailments.

THE SIX MOTIVATION "NO'S"

In my many years of medical practice, I've heard, over and over again, the same six reasons for not exercising, to the point where I've developed an acronym for them—TEMMPF.

TEMMPF stands for six "no's": No time… no energy…no motivation….no money…no place…no fun.

The good news: All these no's can easily be overcome. Let's take the six no's one by one and turn them into "yes's"…

• **No time.** You can easily work exercise into your daily routine, what I call "activity add-ons."

Examples: Take the stairs instead of the elevator…walk or pace while you're talking on the phone…do exercises while watching TV…park farther from a store's entrance than you have to, then don't use a shopping cart for manageable loads.

Smart move: Make a point of spending time with people who have the same health goals as you—you can swap ideas about new activity add-ons.

• **No energy.** Just take the first few steps. It will energize you to take the next steps—and to keep on going. You'll be amazed at how your energy level goes up.

• **No motivation.** A sincere decision on your part that you don't want to lose your quality of life will be a big motivator to get you moving.

Motivation strategy: Think about what makes you feel good. Getting fit and staying fit means that you're more likely to be able to continue doing the things you enjoy as you get older. You might even be able to return to a favorite activity that you gave up because it was too physically demanding.

• **No money.** You don't have to join a gym or health club, or hire a trainer or buy expensive equipment to get fit. All you have to do is get out and go for a 30-minute walk just three times a week.

Stick with it: Walk with a friend or listen to music on headphones—you'll enjoy it and the time will pass quickly.

• **No place.** You can walk anywhere. Try walking in a mall—not just to avoid inclement weather, but also if you don't have safe or lighted places to walk outdoors. Walk in circles in your house or march in place while you watch TV if that's what it takes.

Strategy: Many of my patients enjoy the companionship of a walking group—members motivate each other to keep going. Your local hospital or Y may be able to help you find a group.

• **No fun.** Fitness can be a lot of fun—just ask anyone in a walking group. Saying you're bored by your fitness program is a cop-out. It's easy to vary your routine and find ways to make fitness enjoyable.

Example: Use a pedometer and add steps every day until you reach your target—then see if you can surpass that number.

Bottom line: My real message here is that you can…

• **Start your fitness program at any age.**

• **Continue your program as you age.**

• **Adjust your program to meet changing needs and interests.**

Fitness is a journey, not a destination. If you keep it up for the rest of your life, you'll find that you can build muscle mass and improve your overall fitness at any age, even if you've never exercised before.

The Key to Muscle and Bone Strength

Vikram Khanna, MHS, PA, clinical exercise specialist, health educator and chief executive officer of Galileo Health Partners, based in Ellicott City, Maryland. He is coauthor, with Henry Brinton, of *Ten Commandments of Faith and Fitness: A Practical Guide for Health and Wellness* (CSS).

No form of exercise is more essential to muscle and bone strength than strength training. Strength training involves lifting weights and/or using exercise bands or tubing. Strength training improves just about every measure of health, including the ability to stay active and independent in your later years.

Many people think that strengthening is less important than walking or other forms of aerobic exercise. Not true. Aerobic exercise is important, but people with weak muscles don't have enough strength to adequately work the cardiovascular system.

Other strength-training myths…

Myth: **I'll get too bulky if I lift weights.** Just about every woman with whom I've worked has said something like, "I don't want to look like Arnold Schwarzenegger."

You won't. That kind of physique is largely determined by testosterone. Few women produce enough testosterone to produce bulky muscles. For that matter, few men will ever look like Arnold in his heyday no matter how much they work out.

Genetics has more to do with bulking up than how much you lift. I'm a good example. I've been lifting weights for more than 30 years. I weigh 150 pounds, exactly the same as when I started.

When you start strength training, about 30% of the initial improvement occurs because of improved efficiency between your muscles and central nervous system. After that, your muscles start growing—but maximizing muscle size requires specific training, which most people don't need.

Myth: **Strength training takes too much time.** Actually, it's among the most efficient forms of exercise. People are told, for example, to walk or get other forms of aerobic exercise for at least 30 minutes most days of the week. With strength training, you need to spend only about 20 minutes twice a week.

Many of my clients are busy executives. I typically advise them to go to the gym, warm up with five to 10 minutes of light cardio work (such as walking or running on a treadmill) and then strength train for 15 to 20 minutes. That's long enough to work all of the main muscle groups.

Myth: **I can get just as strong with yoga or Pilates.** No, you can't. These activities are beneficial, but they provide only light-to-moderate workouts. They're useful if you're just starting to exercise after being sedentary. After that, people tend to "top out" within a few months because the exertion levels don't change.

With strength training, you can constantly change the intensity of workouts by changing the weight and/or repetitions as your strength increases. People who lift weights can double their strength within a year.

Myth: **"Free weights," such as barbells, give a better workout than machines.** They give a different workout. When you lift a barbell or dumbbell, you have to balance the weight in multiple planes. For example, you not only have to lift the weight but also have to prevent it from swaying from front to back or from side to side. This brings additional muscle groups into play.

Weight machines allow you to lift in a more controlled manner. There's no side-to-side or front-to-back movement. There is less stress on the joints, which generally is preferable for older or less fit adults. The machines isolate particular muscle groups, which can give notable gains with less stress.

Easy Way to Build Strength, Fight Weakness

Are you losing strength in your leg muscles? Do you find it hard to climb a set of stairs?

First, see your doctor to determine whether you have a medical condition that is causing weakness. While you're there, ask him/her about performing wall squats to strengthen your thighs.

What to do: Stand facing away from the wall with your feet about two inches away from the wall. Bend your knees, sliding your back down the wall to a "sitting" position. Hold the position for a few seconds, then slide your back up the wall to the starting position. Do 15 wall squats, rest briefly, then do another 15, every other day. If you have balance problems, ask someone to assist you as you perform wall squats. If you have knee problems, swimming may be a better option.

The late Robert Butler, MD, president and CEO of the International Longevity Center, New York City.

Lift Weights Twice A Week

People over age 65 who engage in weight-bearing exercise for one hour twice a week for six months may increase muscle strength by 50%.

Bonus: Participants went from being 59% weaker than their younger counterparts to being only 38% weaker.

Simon Melov, PhD, associate professor and director of genomics, Buck Institute for Age Research, Novato, California, and coauthor of a study of 25 people, published in the online journal PLoS One.

Supplements for Strong Muscles

Mark A. Stengler, NMD, licensed naturopathic medical doctor in private practice, Stengler Center for Integrative Medicine, Encinitas, California…and author of many books, including The Natural Physician's Healing Therapies *(Bottom Line Books).*

Strong muscles make it easier to perform tasks of daily living, maintain balance and avoid falls. Reducing body fat lowers blood pressure and improves blood sugar regulation. Canadian researchers examined the effects of two supplements—*creatine monohydrate* (CrM), a compound found in meat, and *conjugated linoleic acid* (CLA), a fatty acid in dairy products and plant oils—believed to have a synergistic effect in boosting muscle while cutting fat. For six months, 39 men and women, ages 65 to 85, did two hours of muscle-building resistance exercises twice weekly and took either placebos or 5 g of CrM plus 6 g of CLA daily.

Results: On average, supplement users lost 4.2 pounds of body fat, compared with a loss of 0.88 pounds of body fat for placebo users. Supplement users also showed greater increases in muscle mass, strength and endurance.

Helpful: Seniors should ask their doctors about resistance training. Adults over age 65 who are overweight or who have muscle weakness should also inquire about taking 5 g of CrM plus 6 g of CLA daily for six months, continuing indefinitely if strength improves. Both are sold at health-food stores. Do not take CrM if you have kidney or liver disease—you may have problems metabolizing it.

Throw Away Your Scale

Older people who are overweight live longer than those of normal weight.

Recent finding: People age 70 and older who were overweight but not obese had 13% lower risk for death from all causes.

Theory: Extra fat provides a metabolic reserve, which older people need to help them recover from illness.

Leon Flicker, PhD, director, Western Australia Centre for Health and Ageing, The University of Western Australia, Perth, and leader of a study of 9,240 people, published in *Journal of the American Geriatrics Society.*

Aerobic Exercise Slows Mental Decline

The brain starts to shrink during middle age, so it processes information more slowly.

Recent finding: As little as three hours a week of walking triggers biochemical changes that increase the volume of brain regions responsible for memory and cognitive function.

Arthur Kramer, PhD, department of neuroscience and psychology, University of Illinois, Urbana, and leader of a study published in *Journal of Gerontology.*

An Olympic Trainer's Secret to Improving Your Balance in Just 10 Minutes a Day

Joel Harper, a New York City–based personal trainer who designs equipment-free workouts for Olympic athletes and business executives. The exercises described in this article are included in his DVD *Fit Pack: Better Balance,* available at *www.JoelHarperFitness.com.*

Health experts have long advocated doing aerobic exercise and strength training on a regular basis, but a new type of activity is now being added to that prescription—balance training.

Startling statistic: Declining balance skills as people age are thought to be a major factor in the 450,000 hospitalizations that occur in the US each year due to falls. Research suggests that up to half of those falls could be prevented with the help of balance exercises.

Good news: Five easy exercises will begin to improve your balance, ankle flexibility, leg strength and overall agility—within days for many people. For best results, spend about 10 minutes performing these exercises every day. If the basic exercises seem too easy, try the advanced versions.

BETTER BALANCE WORKOUT

You can strengthen all the key muscles that are critical to your overall sense of balance by simply using the force of your body weight.

When beginning these exercises, stand next to a sturdy chair for added support when necessary. Keep your stomach taut throughout, pretending there's a string pulling up from the top of your head and lengthening your spine. This helps center your body and engages and strengthens your stabilizer muscles (which support your trunk, limit movement in joints and control balance). Be sure to breathe naturally rather than holding your breath, which can throw off your balance. Also, it's ideal to do the exercises barefoot in order to use the muscles in your feet.

Note: These exercises, designed by leading fitness expert and Olympic trainer Joel Harper, are unique in that they help decrease the imbalance that most of us have—we all carry more tension in one side of our bodies—but also simultaneously strengthen the muscles that support our skeletal structure.*

• **The Hippie**

Purpose: Stretches hips and hamstrings (that run along the back of the thighs).

What to do: Stand with your feet together and bend forward at your waist as far as you comfortably can. Let your arms hang down. If your lower back is stiff or your hamstrings are tight, place your hands on your hips instead of letting them hang down. Let your head hang down to help release tension.

Next, alternate bending one knee slightly for 15 seconds while keeping the other leg straight (keeping both feet flat). Perform a total of three bends per leg. If you feel light-headed

*Consult you doctor before starting this or any other exercise program.

from the blood rushing to your head from this position, put your hands on the ground and look straight ahead.

• Quad Sways

Purpose: Strengthens your core (abdominal and back muscles) and quadriceps (located at the front of the thighs).

What to do: Stand with your left palm flat on your stomach and the top of your right hand on your lower back. Next, lift your right knee in front of you until your thigh is parallel to the floor—if this is too hard, simply go as high as you comfortably can.

While keeping your chest lifted and your stomach pulled in, let your ankle dangle down and sway your lower leg from your knee to your foot from side to side 20 times. Switch legs and repeat.

Advanced version: Do this with your eyes closed.

• Tight Rope

Purpose: Improves mental focus. For this exercise, use a stretched-out, 10-foot string or some other straight line on the floor that you can easily feel and follow with your bare feet, such as a line of tile grout.

What to do: Stand with arms out to your sides at shoulder height, palms up. Next, walk along the line, imagining that you're walking along a tightrope. Try to look straight ahead the entire time. Walk to the end of the line, then turn and walk back, keeping the line in the middle of your feet. With each step, focus on not shifting your body weight until you feel the string below your foot. Don't move forward until you are centered on the line. Do five times.

Advanced version: Perform the exercise walking backward or with your eyes closed.

• North and South

Purpose: Strengthens your legs and core.

What to do: With your arms out to your sides at shoulder height and palms facing down, lift your left leg in front of you as far and as high as you can while holding it straight and keeping your toes pointed forward. Next, without touching the ground, sweep your leg under your body and extend it straight back

behind you as high as you can, this time with your foot flexed (your toe pulled in toward your knee). Do 10 times. Then switch legs and repeat.

Advanced version: Reach out your arms and hands at shoulder height directly in front of you while simultaneously reaching your leg directly behind you. Switch directions. Aim to be horizontal while balancing on your supporting leg.

• Floating Chair

Purpose: Strengthens lower abdominals, hip flexors (muscles that bring the legs and trunk together in flexion movement) and quadriceps.

What to do: Sit on the floor with your knees bent and your feet flat on the ground. Place your hands underneath your legs behind the backs of your knees. Next, pull in your stomach and lift your feet off the ground so that you're balanced on your buttocks. Hold for 30 seconds, keeping your back straight and breathing normally.

Advanced version: Perform this exercise with your palms facing up, one inch from the sides of your knees.

Best Walking Buddy

Seniors who take walks with shelter dogs get more health benefits than seniors who walk with a friend or spouse. Walking speed, balance and confidence improve more when older adults take regular walks with dogs kept at local shelters.

Possible reason: Awareness that the dogs need the seniors' time and attention. Check with a local shelter to see if volunteers are needed.

Rebecca Johnson, PhD, associate professor and Millsap Professor of gerontological nursing and public policy, University of Missouri, and director, Research Center for Human-Animal Interaction, both in Columbia, Missouri.

Improve Your Posture...
For Better Health

Steven Weiniger, DC, chiropractor and certified posture exercise professional (CPEP) in private practice in Roswell, Georgia. He is author of *Stand Taller—Live Longer: An Anti-Aging Strategy* (BodyZone).

Is bad posture harming your health? According to recent research published in the *Annals of Internal Medicine*, poor posture is linked to...

- **Reduced breathing capacity.**
- **Less overall strength.**
- **Slower walking speed.**
- **Increased risk of falling.**

These problems are dangerous primarily because they interfere with a person's ability to exercise, which, in turn, may increase risk for health conditions ranging from cardio- vascular disease to dementia.

THE SECRET TO GOOD POSTURE

Distortions in posture—which typically include a forward-thrusting head, hunched shoulders and a pelvis that is rolled forward—evolve over many years.

It's a mistake to strive for "perfect" posture, standing ramrod straight with shoulders back. To improve posture, it's more effective to focus on balance, alignment and motion.

Simple test: Stand straight and lift your left knee so it's bent at a 90° angle with your thigh parallel to the floor. If this is too high, lift your leg as high as you can. Do this in a doorway so you can catch yourself if necessary. Slowly count, stopping as soon as you must put your foot down or wave your arms to help you stay balanced. Switch legs and repeat. If you can't balance securely on each leg for at least 20 seconds, your muscles may be too weak to maintain balance.

IT TAKES JUST "THREE A DAY"

By practicing the three simple exercises below on a daily basis (each takes just a minute or two), you're likely to start to improve your posture, and your overall health, within a matter of weeks.

Exercise 1: **One-leg balance.** This exercise strengthens the balancing muscles on both sides of the body and improves your sense of your body's position.

Do this exercise at least three times daily—and near a wall in case you need help staying balanced. Wear any shoes and clothing you like. *What to do...*

- Stand with your shoulders back and down and belly in.
- Next, lift your left knee as you did in the balance test so it's bent at a 90° angle with your thigh and foot (toes pointing forward) parallel to the floor.
- Hold this position for 30 seconds, keeping your right leg perfectly straight, knee locked but not pushed backward. Don't wave your arms, twist or hop around to keep your balance. If you find that you must do any of these things, put your right hand on a nearby wall. Then switch legs and repeat to build symmetry of control and balance.

As your balance improves over time, touch the wall with just one finger...then tap the wall...then let go and balance unaided.

Exercise 2: **Alignment.** Performed at least once a day, this exercise helps improve your awareness of your body alignment and helps correct a forward-head posture. *What to do...*

- Lie down on the floor, face-up with your arms at your sides, palms up and shoulders flat.
- Keeping your head level, look straight up at the ceiling. If you cannot comfortably keep your head level, place a thin pillow or rolled towels underneath.
- Relax, take a deep breath and maintain this position for at least two minutes while being conscious of the alignment of your head, shoulders and pelvis.

Exercise 3: **Sitting posture.** This exercise is especially useful if you sit for much of the day. Perform it at least three times daily.

To do the exercise, you'll need an inflatable exercise ball (available at discount stores and sporting-goods stores for about $20). The ball should be inflated so that when you sit on it, your knees are bent at a 90° angle and your thighs are parallel to the floor. *What to do...*

• Sit a third of the way back on the ball with your feet slightly apart, noting the position of your feet, pelvis, shoulders and chest.

• Next, slowly lift your right heel off the ground for 30 seconds, keeping your right toes on the floor. (If you start to wobble, touch a nearby wall with your left hand.)

• Return to the starting position and repeat with your left heel.

As this exercise becomes easier, try doing it with your feet pressed together. Once that becomes easy, progress to lifting each foot entirely off the ground for 30 seconds or as long as you can.

Caution: If you feel unstable on the ball, have someone stand next to you or do the exercise near a wall or in a doorway.

The Extreme Dangers Of Sitting

James A. Levine, MD, PhD, head of endocrinology, University Hospitals Case Medical Center, Cleveland, and former director of the Non-Exercise Activity Thermogenesis (NEAT) Laboratory at the Mayo Clinic in Rochester, Minnesota. He is coauthor of *Move a Little, Lose a Lot* (Crown).

B eing a couch potato has long been known to threaten a person's health. But now researchers are discovering that it's much more dangerous than previously thought.

Troubling statistic: Americans spend more than half their waking hours sitting—primarily watching TV, driving and working at a desk.

THE PROBLEM WITH SITTING

Our bodies are programmed to move. When we spend most of our waking hours sitting, our health suffers in various ways. *Examples...*

• **Sluggish central nervous system.** Sitting causes your central nervous system to slow down, leading to fatigue. Three weekly sessions of low-intensity exercise, such as walking at a leisurely pace, which stimulates the central nervous system, reduced fatigue by 65% after six weeks, according to one study.

• **Weakened muscles.** Sitting weakens your muscles (especially those that support posture and are used to walk) and stiffens joints, leading to a hunched posture and increased risk for back and joint pain.

• **Poor fat burning.** The walls of your capillaries are lined with lipoprotein lipase, an enzyme that breaks down certain fats in the bloodstream. Sit for a few hours, and these enzymes start switching off. Sit all day, and their activity drops by 50%.

• **Increased heart risks.** Sitting for long periods, even in people with healthy body weight, will have negative effects on blood sugar and blood fat levels, which may contribute to diabetes and heart disease.

THE "NEAT" SOLUTION

Fortunately, the dangers of prolonged sitting can be countered by engaging in simple, low-intensity movement throughout the day.

Non-exercise activity thermogenesis (NEAT) is the term that is used for the energy that is expended (calories burned) doing everyday activities.

While in previous generations our work and recreational activities involved regularly standing up and moving the body's muscles, today's world of cars, desk jobs, TVs and computers has reduced our daily NEAT dramatically.

The solution is to add small amounts of non-exercise-related activity into your daily routine. For example, simply standing up triples your energy expenditure compared with sitting. And since a slow (1 mile per hour) walk triggers more than half the metabolic activity of a brisk (3 mph) walk, a leisurely hour-long stroll burns more calories than an intense 30-minute power walk.

Interesting: We burn just five calories an hour while sitting and 15 while standing.

TO COUNTERACT SITTING AT HOME

With a little forethought, it's possible to significantly raise your activity level without stepping foot in a gym. Not surprisingly watching TV and long hours at the computer are among the biggest traps when you're at home. *To develop your own NEAT lifestyle in your home...*

• **Stand up and walk around.** Do this every time an advertisement comes on the TV.

• **Keep a stability ball handy.** Since sitting on this kind of large, inflatable ball requires you to shift slightly from side to side to keep your balance, it engages more muscles (especially those in your abdomen and back) than sitting in a regular chair does. Strong abdominal muscles help fight back pain and enhance stability and balance. Stability ball chairs are available from Gaiam (877-989-6321, *www. gaiam.com*, $99)…and Isokinetics, Inc. (866-263-0674, *www.IsokineticsInc.com*, $65).

• **Place exercise equipment near your TV.** Good choices include a treadmill, stationary bike and/or elliptical trainer. If you watch TV, choose a half-hour show every day and begin using the equipment as the theme music comes on. Continue until the show ends.

Another option: Try a "mini stepper," a small device with two footpads that lets you step in place against resistance. These machines can be tucked away when not in use. Mini steppers are widely available from such companies as Stamina Products, Inc. (800-375-7520, *www.staminaproducts.com*, $40 to $170)…and NordicTrack (*www.nordictrack. com*, 888-308-9616, $120).

• **Put your computer on an elevated surface, such as a shelf or stand.** This way, you can stand while typing or surfing the Web.

• **Follow the 10-minute rule.** Whenever you're working at a computer, get up for 10 minutes every hour to stretch your back and legs. Use this time to perform tasks that can be done while standing, such as making phone calls.

• **Choose action-oriented video games.** If you play video games, opt for an active game (including Wii, which allows you to mimic motions used in sports such as tennis) instead of more sedentary games.

• **Stand up when you answer the phone.** If possible, pace near your desk for the duration of the call.

• **Take the stairs.** Avoid the elevator as much as possible.

• **Park your car a distance (half a mile, for example) from your destination.** If you take mass transit, get off the bus or subway one or two stops before you usually get off.

• **Take a midday walk.**

• **Use a standing desk.** It allows you to stand while working. Ernest Hemingway used such a desk. They are available from such companies as Ergo Desk (800-822-3746, *www. ergodesk.com*)…and Anthro (800-325-3841, *www.anthro.com*).

Cost: About $240 to more than $2,000.

• **Engage in "active intimacy."** Catch up with your spouse or other family members or friends by talking with them while you stroll around the neighborhood together.

Use Yoga to Treat High Blood Pressure, Insomnia and More

Beryl Bender Birch, founder of The Hard & The Soft Yoga Institute and the nonprofit Give Back Yoga Foundation, *www.givebackyoga.org*, both based in East Hampton, New York. She is the author of *Power Yoga* (Simon & Schuster), *Beyond Power Yoga* (Fireside) and *Boomer Yoga* (Sellers).

Yoga has long been known to reduce stress while also boosting strength, flexibility and overall well-being.

Now: More and more scientific studies are showing that yoga helps treat specific medical conditions ranging from high blood pressure to asthma. Unfortunately, many people never even try yoga because they assume that it's too difficult or unconventional.

What you should know…

YOGA FOR EVERYONE

Yoga is easy to do at home and requires a minimal investment in special equipment. It is best performed in your bare feet (so your feet won't slide) while wearing comfortable clothing. A yoga mat keeps your feet even more secure (available in some sports-equipment stores and from online retailers such as *www. yogadirect.com*, 800-331-8233…and *www.jadeyo ga.com*, 888-784-7237. Typical cost is $25 to $40).

133

For the introductory postures below:
Hold for at least five "slow breaths" (close your mouth and breathe in through your nose for a few seconds as your lower belly rises…exhale slowly for about six seconds). Each pose can be repeated two to three times at each session (one to three per week).

FOR HIGH BLOOD PRESSURE

A single 10-minute session of "slow breathing" can result in a temporary lowering of both systolic (top number) and diastolic (bottom number) blood pressure. How much depends on such factors as diet, stress level and genetics.

My recommendation: Do Face Up Dog Posture and Face Down Dog Posture followed by Child's Pose.

What to do: For **Face Up Dog**, start by lying facedown on the floor with your feet (tops flat on floor) in line with your hips. Place your arms at the sides of your chest and hands directly under your shoulders. While keeping your knees on the floor, push into your arms straightening them, roll your shoulders back, arch your back slightly and keep your neck aligned with your spine. Hold for five breaths. Then exhale into **Face Down Dog** (by turning your feet so that your heels are flat on the ground, and pushing up and back into an upside-down V). For **Child's Pose**, kneel with your feet folded under flat and extend your arms straight in front of your head, palms flat on your mat. Touch your forehead to the ground if possible.

ASTHMA

In a recent study of 20 people with asthma, those who took two one-hour yoga classes plus a half-hour home class weekly for 10 weeks reported reduced symptoms.

My recommendation: Do the Extended Side Angle Posture. It increases lung

capacity by stretching and activating the intercostal muscles between each rib, which expand when you inhale and contract when you exhale.

What to do: From a standing position at the top of your mat, inhale and step back with the right foot, taking your feet wide apart, about four to five feet. Turn your left foot out and your right foot in about 45°, and raise your arms parallel to the floor. Exhale while bending your left knee directly over your ankle as you rest your left forearm on your left thigh. Reach your right hand out over your head and ear. Keep your head in alignment with the spine and your abdomen pulled in. Look up and take five breaths. Inhale, come up out of the posture. Reverse your feet and arms and exhale down to the other side, repeating the stretch.

INSOMNIA AND ANXIETY

Yoga is excellent for insomnia and anxiety—breathing slowly and deeply through your nose slows your brain waves and calms the nervous system.

My recommendation: Try the Warrior I Posture.

What to do: From a standing position, inhale and step your left foot out in front of you three to four feet. Turn the back heel inward about 45° toward the midline of your body, the outside edge of the foot flat on the floor. Use a wall or back of a chair to help with balance if necessary. Bend your left knee directly over your left ankle. Keep the belly pulled in and inhale deeply.

Exhale, raise your arms overhead as high as you can, touching your palms over your head if possible. Take five breaths. Repeat with the opposite leg in front.

LOW BACK PAIN

In a recent study, people with chronic low back pain who practiced yoga (two 90-minute sessions weekly for six months) reported less pain and disability than those receiving conventional treatment, such as medication and surgery.

My recommendation: Do the Locust Posture.

What to do: Lie on your stomach with your legs and feet together, arms back at your sides, facedown and chin on the floor. Inhale, then exhale while raising your head, shoulders and legs into the air. Press your hands into the floor for balance.

More from Beryl Bender Birch...

Yoga Safety 101

If you have a chronic medical condition, check with your doctor before beginning a yoga program, and consider consulting a qualified yoga teacher for a customized "prescription" of yoga poses.*

Caution: While doing yoga, don't hold your breath! That may raise your blood pressure. If you have high blood pressure, any eye condition where increased pressure should be avoided or neck injuries, forgo postures in which your head is inverted, such as headstands—these poses can significantly increase blood flow to the brain, increasing your risk for a stroke or other cardiac event.

To find out how yoga can keep you young, see page 147.

*To find a qualified yoga therapist, consult the International Association of Yoga Therapists, 928-541-0004, *www.iayt.org*.

A Better Way to Walk— Boost Calorie Burn by Nearly 20%

Timothy S. Church, MD, MPH, PhD, professor and director of preventive medicine research at Pennington Biomedical Research Center in Baton Rouge, Louisiana.

You can turn a walk into a whole-body workout with a pair of Nordic fitness poles—long, handheld poles modeled after cross-country ski poles. Pole (or Nordic) walking is a low-impact aerobic activity that strengthens the upper body...improves posture...minimizes back and leg strain...and boosts your calorie burn by almost 20%.

• **Picking poles.** One-piece poles are safest, especially for seniors and people with balance problems, because they won't collapse the way adjustable-length telescoping or twist-locking poles might.

Test for size: Grasp the pole handle and place the tip on the ground a few inches in front of you, elbow bent and tucked into your side. If your elbow makes a 90-degree angle, the pole is the proper length.

Or: Multiply your height in centimeters by 0.68—the resulting number is your pole size. Choose poles with interchangeable tips—metal for trails, grass, sand or snow...rubber for pavement and mall walking. Poles are sold at sporting-goods stores and online (check 877-754-9255, *www.skiwalking.com*).

Cost: $70 to $130.

• **Correct technique.** To get started, swing your arms normally as you walk—left arm moving forward as the right foot takes a step and vice versa. As the right foot lands, bend your left elbow to 90 degrees and plant the left pole tip across from your right heel...then push the pole against the ground to help propel yourself forward. Keep poles angled rearward—they should never be farther forward than the front foot.

Goal: Walk at a moderate to brisk pace for at least 30 minutes five times a week. Pole-walking is safe for just about everyone—but it's best to check with your doctor before starting any exercise program.

A Foolproof Walking Program

Jamison Starbuck, ND, naturopathic physician in family practice in Missoula, Montana. She is a past president of the American Association of Naturopathic Physicians and a contributing editor to *The Alternative Advisor* (Time-Life).

A significant body of scientific research shows that walking promotes weight loss and reduces the risk for cardiovascular disease (including heart attack and stroke) as well as diabetes, breast cancer and colon cancer. Walking also helps fight osteoporosis, anxiety, depression and memory problems. It even improves immune health, reducing the frequency and duration of colds and flu.

For thousands of years, walking—at a speed of about three miles per hour, on average—was our primary mode of transportation. Now, nearly 40% of Americans don't walk beyond the bare minimum needed to get through the day. If this describes you, you are not letting your body do what it was designed to do. *My advice...*

• **Make walking a priority.** Set aside specific times to walk five days per week. If you keep a daily calendar, write down when you plan to walk. Also, invest in a good pair of walking shoes. Depending on where you live, you also may need rain gear as well as warm, but not restrictive, clothing and a head covering for cold weather. In hot weather, try to avoid the hottest part of the day—and wear a hat to avoid excessive sun exposure. In harsh weather, you can walk in a shopping mall.

• **Start slowly.** Many people are far too ambitious when they first start walking. In the beginning, walk only five minutes up to five days a week. Then increase your time by five minutes per session each week. If possible, work up to 30 minutes per day, five days per week within six weeks.

• **Walk outside whenever possible.** Walking is most enjoyable when it exposes you to fresh air, sunlight and views of nature—even urban trees and flower boxes. The varied terrain of outdoor walking, including uneven sidewalks or the slope of a trail, improve *proprioception*—the brain's awareness of body position and balance—and will make you more agile and less vulnerable to falls. To prevent injury, pay attention to the terrain, your surroundings and to how your body feels as you walk. If your balance is poor, invest in a walking stick, available at most outdoor-sports stores starting at $20.

• **Get the right amount of fluid and take supplements.** Drink one-half ounce of water per pound of body weight throughout the day—and at least 12 ounces of water just before walking. In addition, ask your doctor about taking daily mineral supplements containing 300 mg of magnesium and 99 mg of potassium. Following these steps will help you avoid muscle cramps, which are usually caused by dehydration, a deficiency of magnesium and/or potassium or lack of strength.

Caution: If you are taking blood pressure medication or have kidney disease, be sure to discuss potassium supplementation with your doctor before trying it.

Even if you don't need to lose weight, it's a safe bet that walking will make you feel healthier and stronger.

Prevent Foot Pain After You Walk

An exercise called "foot dome" strengthens the muscles of the transverse arch, which extends across the pads of your toes. Strengthening the arch helps the feet to absorb impact.

What to do: In bare feet, take a half step forward with your left foot. Keep most of your weight on your right foot. With your left heel firmly planted on the floor and your toes as straight as possible, raise the top of your left foot so that it looks like a dome. Hold the position for a count of 10. Repeat with your right foot. Perform five times daily.

Peggy W. Brill, PT, a board-certified clinical specialist in orthopedic physical therapy with a New York City–based private practice.

Tai Chi Helps You Stay Young and Vital

Roger Jahnke, OMD, tai chi expert and trainer, Institute of Integral Qigong and Tai Chi. www.iiqtc.org.

If you don't like to exercise, try tai chi—a Chinese martial art consisting of very slow controlled movements. It's great for stress reduction and for maintaining muscle tone and balance.

Tai chi expert Roger Jahnke, OMD, author of *The Healer Within* (HarperOne) and *The Healing Promise of Qi* (McGraw-Hill), trains teachers of tai chi at the Institute of Integral Qigong and Tai Chi (*www.iiqtc.org*). Here he describes easy-to-do beginner exercises that will help you find out immediately how great tai chi can make you feel.

Exercise 1: Raise Hands

(This exercise also can be performed in a seated position with only the arm movements.)

Do 10 repetitions 1 to 2 times daily.

Helps: Develop a calm awareness of the body. Builds leg and arm strength.

1. Stand with feet shoulder-width apart or slightly wider (toes pointing forward). Bend your knees slightly. Don't let your knees extend past the front of your toes.

2. Rest your palms on the front of your thighs. Inhale as you straighten your legs (don't lock them). Keep your fingers slightly down (so that your wrists are bent) as you let your arms float up to shoulder level.

3. Bend your knees and let your arms float down—fingers pointed up—as you bend your elbows and sink further into the bent-knee position. Then slowly straighten your wrists so that your outstretched hands (palms facing down) are aligned with your arms.

4. Exhale as you slowly sink down, bending your knees as much as is comfortable. Keep your palms parallel to the ground as you come back to the starting position.

Exercise 2: Swaying Bear

(If this exercise is difficult, try it holding on to a chair. When you get stronger, you can try it without the chair.)

Do 10 repetitions on each side.

Helps: Develop a sense of balance and strengthen the leg muscles.

1. Stand with your feet a little wider than shoulder-width, toes facing forward. Bend your knees slightly.

2. Place your hands at your sides (at waist level) with your palms facing down and your elbows bent. Imagine your arms floating on top of water.

3. Very, very slowly shift your weight from side to side, keeping your knee over your foot and not bending your knee past your toes. Slowly shift to the right by bending and putting your weight onto your right leg—then slowly shift back and put more weight onto your left leg. Go to the point where the other leg is straight but not locked. As you advance, you can take a wider stance and bend your knees farther.

Should You Start Using A Heart Monitor?

Because heart rate is directly related to intensity of physical activity (how hard you are exerting yourself), a heart rate monitor can provide a reliable indication of your effort.

Good brands: Polar, Nike and Garmin. If you purchase a monitor, you'll need to determine your target heart rate. Maximal heart rate for cardiovascular exercise can be predicted by subtracting your age from 220. A conservative range at which to exercise is 50% to 60% of your maximal heart rate.

Example for a 65-year-old: 220−65=155. 50% to 60% of 155 is 77.5 to 93 beats per minute.

Important: Certain medications, including blood pressure drugs, can affect your heart rate. Consult your doctor before beginning a new exercise program.

Julie Frey, clinical instructor of kinesiology and adult fitness program coordinator, Indiana University, Bloomington.

Aerobic Exercise Slows Mental Decline

The brain starts to shrink during middle age, so it processes information more slowly.

Recent finding: As little as three hours a week of walking triggers biochemical changes that increase the volume of brain regions responsible for memory and cognitive function.

Arthur Kramer, PhD, department of neuroscience and psychology, University of Illinois, Urbana, and leader of a study published in *Journal of Gerontology*.

Push-ups Great For Seniors

Push-ups are excellent exercise for seniors. The ability to do them is more than an indicator of fitness—the exercise increases upper-body strength, which helps protect against injury from falls.

Why: When people fall, they instinctively reach out to catch themselves in a manner similar to the push-up motion. Upper-body strength helps break the weight of a fall safely. Those who don't have the strength to do a push-up are at heightened risk of suffering a broken wrist or other injury in a fall—and of not being able to push or lift themselves up, even if not injured.

Fitness: At age 60, men should be able to do 17 push-ups...women should be able to do six of them.

James Ashton-Miller, PhD, director, biomechanics research laboratory, University of Michigan, Ann Arbor.

Simple Diet Strategies

Adopt easy, healthful eating habits that work well with your exercise schedule...

• **Have a small snack before exercising.** If you exercise on a completely empty stomach, your blood sugar will drop and you will feel hungrier afterward...and will be more likely to overeat.

• **Keep a food diary before eating, not after.** Writing down what you plan to eat encourages you to decide whether you are really making good food choices.

• **When you have a full meal, eat it soon after your workout.** People served 15 to 30 minutes after exercise tend to eat less than those who wait an hour or more for food.

• **Drink water regularly.** Water drinkers eat almost 200 fewer calories a day than people who drink only coffee, tea or soda.

Leslie Bonci, MPH, RD, CSSD, LDN, director of sports nutrition, Center for Sports Medicine, University of Pittsburgh Medical Center.

Working Out Is Better With a Friend

Cedric X. Bryant, PhD, chief science officer, American Council on Exercise, San Diego. He has authored or coauthored numerous books, including *Strength Training for Women* (Human Kinetics).

Whether you plan to walk briskly around the neighborhood each morning or train for a triathlon, an exercise partner may be just what you need. *Advantages of working out together...*

• **Exercising is more fun when you play, chat or engage in friendly competition with another person.**

• **You're less likely to skip a workout when someone is counting on you to show up.**

• **A partner minimizes your risk for injury** —spotting as you lift weights, correcting your body alignment in yoga poses.

• **You work muscle groups and deepen stretches in ways that are difficult to do on your own.**

• **You save money by sharing equipment,** swapping fitness DVDs or carpooling to the tennis court.

The key to success is to make a good match —so your best friend or nearest neighbor may not be the optimal choice. *Ask yourself if you and a potential partner are similar enough in these key areas…*

• **Fitness level.** Is she interested in a leisurely bike ride around the park, while you want to train for a cycling trip through France? That's not a fit.

• **Schedule.** If you're a morning exerciser and she's a night owl, can you find a compromise —such as lunch hour?

• **Temperament.** Do you both like to talk while you lift weights, or would one of you find the other's chatter distracting?

• **Commitment.** Is she game to jog in any weather, while you run for shelter when clouds roll in?

There are no right or wrong answers to the questions above—it's just a matter of compatibility. *If you have doubts, keep looking…*

• **Check the bulletin board at a local community center, spa or gym.**

• **Ask a personal trainer for a referral.** She even may offer you and your new partner a two-for-one discount.

• **Search** *www.exercisefriends.com…*or *www.craigslist.org* (look under "community" for your city) for a match.

Important: Always check with your doctor before beginning a new exercise program.

STRENGTH TRAINING FOR TWO

Many strength-training moves can be adapted for partners. Here are examples of exercises for the upper, mid and lower body. For more techniques, experiment with your buddy or consult a trainer.

• **Medicine ball push.**

Equipment: A four- to 10-pound medicine ball (a weighted ball about the size of a basketball, sold at sporting-goods stores, about $20).

Partner 1: Stand facing your partner, about three feet apart. Hold the ball between your hands at chest level, a few inches in front of you, elbows bent and pointing out to the sides (Figure A). Step forward with the right foot and gently throw the ball, using a pushing motion, so it arcs just above head height (Figure B).

Partner 2: Extend arms to meet the ball, bending elbows as you catch it to bring the ball toward your chest.

Both partners: Take turns throwing and catching 10 to 15 times, alternating the foot that steps forward as you throw.

Modification: If you have bone loss or wrist problems, use a ball no heavier than six pounds.

• **Stability ball crunches.**

Equipment: A 21-inch-diameter inflatable stability ball (about $20 at sporting-goods stores). If you are shorter than five feet tall, use a 17-inch ball…if taller than five feet, seven inches, use a 25-inch ball.

Partner 1: Kneel and face your partner, one arm extended forward at chest height, palm facing away from you to create a "target" for your partner to clap. Between each of her "crunches," move your palm to a slightly different location—giving her a moving target.

Partner 2: Recline face-up, low to mid-back pressed against the ball, knees bent at a 90-degree angle, feet shoulder-width apart and close to where your partner is kneeling. Hold your hands a few inches in front of your chest, elbows bent. Using abdominal muscles, do a crunch by lifting your upper body up and away from the ball…at the top of your crunch, straighten one arm and clap your partner's palm…lower back down. Do 10 to 15 crunches, alternating the hand that claps.

Both partners: Switch positions.

Modification: If balance is a problem, lie on the floor instead of the ball to do crunches.

• **Squats.**

Both partners: Stand back-to-back, keeping your torso firmly pressed against your partner's from shoulder blade to hip throughout the exercise. Together, slowly bend knees and lower hips while moving feet forward until thighs are parallel to the floor (as if sitting on a chair) and knees are directly above ankles. Hold for about 30 seconds. Then slowly straighten knees and raise hips while walking backward until you are standing once again. Rest for about 15 seconds. Repeat five to 10 times.

Caution: If you have knee problems, limit the depth of your squat to your pain-free range.

TANDEM STRETCHING

For safety, always move slowly and gently, clearly communicating when your stretch has reached the desired level of intensity. Do the stretches below after your aerobic or strength-training workout, as part of your cooldown. Finish with the breathing exercise.

● **Chest-opening stretch.**

Partner 1: Stand erect, arms reaching behind you, elbows straight but not locked, palms facing each other.

Partner 2: Stand facing your partner's back, just beyond her outstretched hands. Grasping her wrists, pull gently and steadily toward yourself to open your partner's chest...hold for 15 to 30 seconds...rest...repeat two to four times.

Both partners: Switch positions.

● **Straddle stretch.**

Both partners: Sit on the floor facing each other. Holding hands, spread legs as wide as possible, knees straight, toes up, feet pressed against your partner's feet. As one partner slowly leans forward, the other leans back... then switch, continuing the forward-and-backward movements. After about 30 seconds, widen your straddle if possible. Repeat several times.

● **Yoga breathing.**

Both partners: Sit cross-legged on the floor, facing away from each other, backs touching, spines straight. Breathing through the nose, inhale deeply, pause for a few seconds, then exhale slowly. Continue for one minute, matching the rhythm of your partner's breathing. Then switch, so that one partner inhales as the other exhales, continuing for

another minute. Use this meditative breathing technique to calm your mind and prepare for the rest of your day.

Better Exercise for Older Women

Few studies have looked at postmenopausal women's response to exercise.

Recent study: When 10 healthy but sedentary women (average age 55) performed one hour of vigorous cycling five days a week, their markers for cardiovascular health improved (for example, resting heart rates dropped by four beats per minute).

Implication: Whenever possible, postmenopausal women should work their way up to five vigorous, one-hour workouts (such as swimming, cycling or jogging) a week—but even less strenuous exercise is likely to provide some benefits.

George Brooks, PhD, professor of integrative biology, University of California, Berkeley.

If You're Starting to Exercise, Expect to be Miserable...It'll Pass

Tyler C. Cooper, MD, MPH, a preventive medicine specialist at the Dallas–based Cooper Aerobics Center (*www.cooperaerobics.com*). He is coauthor, with his father, Kenneth H. Cooper, MD, MPH, founder and chairman of Cooper Aerobics Center, of *Start Strong, Finish Strong* (Avery).

We all know that exercise is perhaps the single most beneficial action we can take to protect our health, and millions of people vow each January 1 to start—and stick with—a program of regular physical activity.

So why are two of every three American adults still "sedentary"—meaning they get little or no exercise?

The following are answers from Tyler C. Cooper, MD, MPH, a preventive medicine physician at the renowned Cooper Aerobics Center in Dallas. This health and wellness organization was founded by his father, Kenneth H. Cooper, MD, MPH, the physician responsible for coining the term "aerobics," who now serves as chairman of the center.

LIVE THREE YEARS LONGER!

Most people who want to start exercising do so because it's "good" for them. But to stay motivated, you should know exactly why you want to start exercising.

For example, compared with people who exercise regularly, sedentary people are three times more likely to develop metabolic syndrome—a constellation of risk factors including high blood pressure (hypertension), elevated "bad" cholesterol, high blood sugar and obesity. Regular physical activity also has been found to reduce risk for cognitive decline.

And if that doesn't keep you motivated, consider this: People who regularly exercise briskly live an average of three years longer than those who are sedentary. "Briskly" means exercising at an intensity that makes you perspire and breathe a little heavily while still being able to carry on a conversation. This is known as the "talk test."

HOW MUCH EXERCISE?

It's a common misconception that you must exercise daily to achieve significant health benefits.

In a study of 10,000 men and 3,000 women conducted at the Cooper Aerobics Center's clinic, we found that walking just two miles in less than 30 minutes three days a week is all that's needed to achieve a "moderate" level of fitness, which lowers risk for all causes of death and disease.

For a less demanding workout that confers the same benefits, you could walk two miles in 35 minutes four days a week…or walk two miles in 40 minutes five days a week. If you prefer other forms of exercise, such as biking or swimming, use these frequency guidelines, plus the talk test (described above) to achieve a moderate fitness level. By increasing the frequency and/or intensity, you'll achieve even greater health benefits.

HIT THE SIX-WEEK MARK

If you have not exercised regularly in the last six months and/or are overweight (for women, having a waist size of 35 inches or more…for men, 40 inches or more), the basic exercise requirement described above may be too much. You may want to start by walking only to the end of the block for a few days, then gradually increase the distance. Aim for an increase of up to 10% weekly—for example, from 10 minutes per week to 11 minutes the next week and so on.

Helpful: Expect the first few weeks to be miserable—you'll feel some muscle soreness for a while. Accept it—but make the commitment to keep going.

Important: If your muscle pain doesn't go away within several weeks, see your doctor to rule out an underlying condition, such as arthritis.

We've found at the Cooper Aerobics Center that few people quit after they've performed a program of physical activity for six weeks. Once people reach the four- to six-month mark, adherence to an exercise program approaches 100% for the long term.

DETERMINE YOUR BASELINE

If you've been sedentary, be sure to get a comprehensive medical checkup before starting an exercise program. This is particularly important for men age 40 and older and women age 50 and older—cardiovascular disease risk rises at these ages.

People of any age with underlying health problems or a family history of diabetes, hypertension, high cholesterol or heart disease also should get a checkup before starting to exercise.

Ask your doctor—or a fitness trainer—to give you baseline measurements for strength, flexibility and aerobic capacity, which will enable you to track future changes.

Checking these measurements (along with such markers as blood pressure, cholesterol and blood sugar) again in about three months will give you tangible evidence of your progress and can motivate you to keep exercising.

Treat Eating and Exercise Guidelines as Goals

Don't be intimidated by recent eating and exercise guidelines. Federal recommendations suggest that Americans eat nine servings of fruit and vegetables a day—up from five servings. Consider the recommendations a goal, not a requirement. The biggest dietary health improvement comes to people who increase their intake of fruit and vegetables from one serving a day to two. Everything above that brings a smaller benefit. The same applies to new exercise guidelines, which call for 60 minutes of exercise most days to avoid gaining weight. Consider 60 minutes a goal. The old recommendation of 30 minutes still brings substantial health benefits.

Consensus of nutrition researchers, reported in The New York Times.

The 10-Minute Total Body Workout

Sean Foy, MA, exercise physiologist and behavioral and nutritional coach in Placentia, California. He is author of *The 10-Minute Total Body Breakthrough* (Workman). *www.4321Fitness.com.*

You don't need extended workouts to strengthen muscles, increase cardiovascular fitness or lower your blood pressure, blood sugar and triglycerides. You can achieve these and other fitness benefits with 10 minutes of exercise a day.

The secret is High Energy Aerobic Training (HEAT), my take on high-intensity interval training.

HOW IT WORKS

For decades, trainers argued that effective aerobic exercise required elevating your heart rate to 65% to 80% of its maximum rate and keeping it there for 30 minutes or longer.

The problem with this approach—besides the fact that few people are willing to dedicate this much time to exercise—is that it's not as effective as higher-intensity movements. For example, high-intensity interval training has been shown to not only accelerate your metabolism during exercise but also long after the workout is over. Research shows exercise is most effective when it challenges the muscles, including the heart and lungs, at higher levels of intensity.

With HEAT, you alternate intense 30-second bursts of exercise with 30-second periods of moderate exercise. This means that your muscles and organs are repeatedly pushed to their limits. But because the intense phase lasts only 30 seconds, it's achievable even for those who are new to exercise.

A study at the University of New South Wales and Garvan Institute found that overweight women who alternated high-intensity with moderate activity lost three times more weight than those who exercised at a continuous pace for twice as long. The HEAT method also improves levels of lipids (blood fats) and increases endurance.

THE EASY 4-3-2-1 PROGRAM

I developed a program that packs every type of beneficial exercise into one 10-minute session. It's called 4-3-2-1 because it includes four minutes of aerobic exercise…three minutes of resistance exercise (such as body-weight exercises)…two minutes of core strengthening…and one minute of stretching and deep breathing.

To keep time, you can use a large wall clock with a second hand…a wristwatch with a second hand…a digital sports watch…a stopwatch…or a cell phone with a stopwatch feature.

As you advance, you can repeat sections or the entire circuit. *For beginners, I recommend the following…*

4 MINUTES OF AEROBIC TRAINING

•**Chair jogging.** Sit upright on the edge of a sturdy chair with your arms bent at a 90° angle. Warm up by gently moving your arms and legs as though jogging slowly, raising your knees as high as you comfortably can. Do this for 30 seconds. Next, bend forward slightly from the waist, and perform the same motion, but faster. Move as quickly as you comfortably can. Maintain this brisk pace for 30 seconds. Alternate between fast and slow "running" every 30 seconds for four minutes.

3 MINUTES OF RESISTANCE TRAINING

• **Wall squat.** Lean your back against a wall with your feet hip-width apart and your arms at your sides. Walk your feet out from the wall two to three feet. Bend your knees slightly. Keeping your back against the wall, bend your knees more and slowly slide down. Go as low as you comfortably can, but not so far that your knees extend over your toes. Try to hold the squat for one minute. *Then, without resting, do a wall push-up...*

• **Wall push-up.** Face the wall. Place your hands against the wall, with your hands a little wider than shoulder-width apart. Walk your feet back from the wall two to three feet. Rise onto the balls of your feet, and lean into the wall. With your knees slightly bent, lower your face and chest slowly toward the wall. Go as far as you comfortably can. Now press your hands into the wall to push yourself back to the starting position. Repeat as many times as you can in one minute. *Then, without resting, move on to a stationary lunge...*

• **Stationary lunge.** Stand straight (next to the wall or a chair for balance, just in case) with your arms hanging loosely at your sides. Step backward three to four feet with your left foot. Press into the floor with the heel of your right foot (in front) and the ball of your left foot (in back). Make sure that your weight is balanced. Bend both knees, lowering your right thigh until it's parallel to the floor. "Lunge" down as low as you can—but don't let your left knee rest on the floor. Hold for 30 seconds. Return to the starting position. Reverse the sequence, and repeat with the other leg, again holding for 30 seconds.

2 MINUTES OF CORE STRENGTHENING

• **Chair plank.** Place your hands shoulder-width apart on the back of a sturdy chair, desk or table at waist level. Keep your feet close together, and lean forward. Imagine that you're a long, strong board that's leaning against a table. While holding this position and keeping your body straight, rise onto the balls of your feet, keeping your arms extended, elbows slightly bent. Try to hold the position for one minute. Without resting, do a chair side bend...

• **Chair side bend.** Sit upright on the edge of a sturdy chair, with your feet hip-width apart and your knees at a 90° angle. Let your arms hang down, with your hands below your waist. Slowly lean your upper body to the left, lowering your left hand toward the floor, while keeping your buttocks firmly in place. Lean as far as you comfortably can without raising your buttocks off the chair. As you lean, let your head move in alignment with your upper body. Tighten the abdominal muscles, and stay in the side-bend position for two seconds. Return to the starting position, then repeat on the other side. Repeat as often as you can in one minute.

1 MINUTE OF STRETCHING

• **Chair forward bend.** Begin the same way you did in the exercise above but with your feet about shoulder-width apart. This time, lower your arms so that they're between your thighs. Relax your shoulders. Bend forward from the waist. Lower your chin to your chest, and let your hands drop toward the floor. Let your weight pull your upper body toward the floor. Hold this position for 30 seconds, breathing deeply throughout the stretch. Without resting, do a chair spinal twist...

• **Chair spinal twist.** Stay in the same chair, with your feet hip-width apart. Cross your hands and arms over your chest. Twist your upper body to the left, rotating from the waist and allowing your head and shoulders to move as one unit. Rotate as far as you can without bouncing or straining. Try to hold the stretch for 15 seconds, breathing deeply. Then repeat the movement in the other direction.

Photos: Used by permission of Workman Publishing Co., Inc., New York. All Rights Reserved

Exercise Greatly Cuts Heart Disease Risk

Men at high risk for heart disease (due to hypertension, high cholesterol and/or other risk factors) who exercised for 30 minutes four to five days per week reduced their risk of dying from a heart attack or stroke by 50%.

Self-defense: Everyone—especially those who are at risk for heart disease—should perform aerobic exercise, such as walking or swimming, for at least 30 minutes four to five days a week.

Peter T. Katzmarzyk, PhD, professor, and associate director for population science, Pennington Biomedical Research Center, Baton Rouge, Louisiana.

Exercises That Help with Everything You Do

Larkin Barnett, an adjunct professor of exercise science at Florida Atlantic University in Boca Raton, and the author of *Functional Fitness: The Ultimate Fitness Program for Life on the Run* (Florida Academic).

Functional training is a form of exercise that strengthens the muscles that we use in everyday activities, such as standing, walking, sitting, doing chores and carrying packages.

How it works: Functional training helps integrate the limbs and the trunk muscles for fluid, powerful movements...puts your body

into proper alignment...improves posture and balance...and promotes deep breathing for relaxation.

A functional fitness routine can be incorporated into cardiovascular and strength-training workouts. The exercises described below are designed for people of all fitness levels and should be performed daily...

SIT UP AND TAKE NOTICE

Benefits: Corrects trunk alignment, including weak abdominal muscles that don't provide sufficient support for the lower back...and enhances stamina and endurance.

Good for: Carrying objects...walking and running...and relieving muscle tension caused by working at a desk or a computer.

What to do: While sitting in a straight-backed chair, scrunch your shoulders up toward your ears, then relax them. Inhale slowly while you raise your shoulders, then exhale slowly as you lower them. Do this three to five times, feeling tension drain out of your shoulders and neck.

Next, sit tall, perched on your sit-bones (you can find these by rocking side-to-side) and concentrate on stacking your hips, ribs, chest and head on top of each other like building blocks. Exhale powerfully while pulling your abdominal muscles inward toward your spine. Then pull your shoulders back gently. Take several deep breaths.

Finally, sit up tall, while picturing the tops of your ears stretching upward. This elongates the spine and improves respiratory function. Tighten your abdominals inward and upward toward your spine while exhaling forcefully three to five times.

THE COMPASS

Benefits: Strengthens your postural muscles (to improve coordination and balance)... and reduces fatigue and stress on the legs, hips and back.

Good for: Relieving muscle soreness from extended standing as well as improving performance in all sports and physical activities.

What to do: With your feet flat on the ground about 12 inches apart, pretend you're standing in the middle of a large compass. With exaggerated movements, shift your entire body toward each of the four main points on the compass—north (forward), south (backward), east (to the right) and west (to the left)—pausing momentarily at each point. Do this three to five times. Contract your abdominal muscles and notice how your control improves.

Gradually make your movements smaller and smaller. Do this for 30 seconds. End by standing still and feeling your body weight evenly distributed.

THE PELVIS AS A FISH BOWL

Benefits: Centers the hips and places the pelvis in neutral alignment, reducing stress on the legs, back and neck.

Good for: Lifting…getting in and out of bed …and swinging a golf club or tennis racket.

What to do: Standing with your feet about 12 inches apart, contract your stomach muscles and draw them inward and up toward your spine. Picture your hips as a fish bowl filled with water, with the bowl's rim at your waistline.

Now tip your hips forward slightly and visualize water spilling out of the front of the fish bowl. Next, tip your hips backward slightly and visualize water sloshing out of the back of the bowl. Finally, balance the fish bowl so that the rim is perfectly level. This is your pelvis's "neutral" position. Throughout the day, assume this position as you stand up, walk and sit.

SHOULDER BLADE, ARM, FINGERTIP

Benefits: Teaches you to initiate arm movements from your trunk muscles (including your shoulder girdle muscles) for more power and control.

Good for: Relieving muscle tension caused by driving a car or speaking on the telephone…and playing golf and racket sports.

What to do: While standing, lift your arms to your sides at shoulder level. Then lift your arms higher, in the shape of a "U," while sliding your shoulder blades downward. Imagine that you have a balloon next to each ear. Initiate these movements from the shoulder blades. Lower your arms, then repeat three to five times.

Feel-Good Exercises You Can Do in Bed

Genie Tartell, DC, RN, a New York City–based chiropractor and registered nurse who focuses on physical rehabilitation. She is coauthor of *Get Fit in Bed* (New Harbinger).

Think about the last time that you really stretched your body. Didn't you feel great afterward?

Unfortunately, most individuals—including many who are physically active—just don't do enough to improve their muscle tone, flexibility and strength. To help people incorporate a simple workout regimen into their daily routines, I have devised a program that can be performed in a comfortable setting you are bound to visit each day—your bed.

These bed exercises not only increase your strength, flexibility and endurance, but also stimulate production of the mood-enhancing brain chemical serotonin, leaving you feeling calm and relaxed. As a result, most people find that they sleep better when they do these exercises at night, and feel invigorated if they do the routine in the morning.

The following exercises are designed for anyone but are particularly helpful for people who are confined to bed (while recovering from an illness or injury) and for those unable to find time during the day to exercise. They can be completed in just 10 minutes a day.

Important: When performing each movement, breathe in slowly for a count of four… hold for a count of one…then exhale through pursed lips for a count of four.

ALTERNATE LEG LENGTHENER

Purpose: Tones and stretches the spine and pelvis, which bears much of the upper body's weight.

What to do: While lying on your back with your body centered on the bed and your hips and legs flat on the bed, stretch your right leg forward by pushing with the heel of your right foot. Return your leg to the starting position. Do the same stretch with your left leg. Repeat five times with each leg.

HIP SIDE TO SIDE

Purpose: Tones and stretches the hips and low back.

What to do: While lying on your back with your hips flat on the bed, rock your hips gently—as far as comfortable—to the right and then to the left. Keep your upper body stable. Repeat five times in each direction.

ARMS-SHOULDER SEESAW

Purpose: Tones and stretches the shoulders and upper back.

What to do: While lying on your back, place your arms at your sides. Slide your right arm and shoulder toward your right foot. Next, raise your right shoulder toward your head, while at the same time sliding your left arm and shoulder toward your left foot. Then raise your left shoulder toward your head, while lowering your right arm and shoulder toward your right foot. Repeat five times on each side, moving your shoulders up and down like a seesaw.

ARMS TOWARD THE HEADBOARD

Purpose: Stretches the shoulders and rib cage, allowing for deeper, much more relaxed breathing.

What to do: While lying on your back, extend your arms behind your head. Stretch your right arm toward the headboard of your bed or the wall behind you. Return your right arm to your side and then extend your left arm behind you. Repeat five times on each side.

ELBOW-KNEE PISTON

Purpose: Strengthens your abdominal muscles while increasing your heart rate (improves heart muscle strength and endurance).

What to do: While lying on your back, raise your knees and, using your stomach muscles, lift your upper body toward them. Bend your arms so that your elbows are pointing at your knees. Bring your left elbow toward your right knee, then return to the starting position. Then bring your right elbow toward your left knee, maintaining a continuous pumping motion. Repeat six times.

COBRA

Purpose: Builds upper body strength (important for daily activities such as bathing and cooking).

What to do: Lie on your stomach with your elbows bent and palms flat on the bed next to your shoulders. Fully straighten your arms to lift your upper body so that it curves into a cobra-like position. Hold for a few seconds, then return to the starting position. Repeat three times.

MODIFIED BOW

Purpose: Tones and strengthens the back and improves muscular coordination.

What to do: Lie on your stomach with your arms at your sides. Raise your legs and upper body simultaneously (only to a level that is comfortable), then reach back with your arms as if you are trying to touch your raised feet. Hold for a few seconds, then return to the starting position. Repeat three times.

SWIMMING IN BED

Purpose: Strengthens the arms and legs, while increasing heart rate and stimulating blood flow throughout the body.

What to do: While lying on your stomach, move one arm forward, then move it back while moving your other arm forward, simultaneously kicking your legs. Repeat 20 times, counting each arm movement as one repetition.

BRIDGE

Purpose: Cools down the body and directs blood flow away from the legs to the heart, reducing risk for blood clots in the legs.

What to do: Lie on your back with your knees bent, feet flat on the bed and your arms at your sides. Tighten up your buttock muscles as you lift your pelvis toward the ceiling—until your pelvis is in line with your thighs. Then gently lower your body back to the bed. Repeat five times.

Important: If you think any of these exercises may be too strenuous for you, check with your doctor before trying them.

Illustrations by Shawn Banner.

Inactivity Raises Disease Risk—Quickly

Researchers asked 18 healthy men to reduce the number of steps they took daily from either 6,000 or 10,000 steps to about 1,400 steps by using a car or elevators.

Result: After two weeks, the men had higher levels of blood sugars and fats that raise risk for diabetes, heart disease and other diseases.

Theory: When excess blood fats and sugars don't clear the bloodstream quickly—a process promoted by exercise—they can adversely affect metabolic functions.

Self-defense: Aim to exercise for at least 30 minutes (in at least five-minute segments) most days of the week.

Frank Booth, PhD, professor, department of physiology, University of Missouri College of Medicine, Columbia.

Yoga Can Keep You Young!

Mary Louise Stefanic, certified yoga and qigong instructor with a focus on therapeutic yoga. She is a staff member at the Loyola Center for Fitness and Loyola University Health System, both in Maywood, Illinois.

Not that long ago, yoga was viewed primarily as an activity for "youngish" health nuts who wanted to round out their exercise regimens. *Now:* Older adults—meaning people in their 60s, 70s, 80s and beyond—are among the most enthusiastic practitioners of this ancient healing system of exercise and controlled breathing.

To learn more about the unique benefits you can derive from yoga, we spoke with Mary Louise Stefanic, an 80-year-old yoga instructor who has taught the practice for more than 40 years.

YOGA IMPROVES HEALTH

Yoga's varied health benefits are largely what's making the practice so popular now with older adults. More than 1,000 scientific studies have shown that yoga can improve conditions ranging from arthritis, asthma, insomnia and depression to heart disease, diabetes and cancer (see pages 133–34).

You look better, too: Yoga is quite useful in helping to prevent rounding (or hunching) of the back, which occurs so often in older adults. This condition can lead to back pain and breathing problems as the rib cage presses against the lungs.

GETTING STARTED

If you want to see whether you could benefit from yoga, ask your doctor about trying the following poses, which address common physical complaints. These poses are a good first step before taking a yoga class.* Yoga is best performed in loose, comfortable clothing and in your bare feet, so your feet won't slip. *Poses to try…*

• **Knees to chest pose.** For low back pain and painful, tight hips.

What to do: Lie on your back (on carpet or a yoga mat, available at sports-equipment stores for about $25). With your arms, hug both knees in to your chest. Keep your knees together and your elbows pointing out to each side of your body.  Slowly rock from elbow to elbow to massage your back and shoulders. Take deep, abdominal breaths while holding your thighs close to your chest and hold for six complete inhales and exhales.

• **Mecca pose.** This pose also relieves back pain.

What to do: Begin by kneeling on the floor with your knees together. For added comfort, place a small towel behind your knees.  Sit back on your feet, and lean forward from your waist so that your chest and stomach rest atop your thighs.

*To find a yoga class near you, check your local community center and/or consult the International Association of Yoga Therapists, *www.iayt.org.*

Reach your arms out in front of you, resting your forehead to the floor while stretching your tailbone to your heels. Hold for six complete inhales and exhales.

•**Leg rotation.** For sciatica, a cause of back, pelvic and leg pain.

What to do: Lie on your back with both legs extended. Slowly bring your right knee to your chest and inhale. Rest your right ankle on the front of your left thigh, and exhale as  you slowly slide it down along your left knee, shin and ankle to toes. This helps "screw" the top of your right thighbone into the hip socket, easing lower back and leg pain. Repeat on other side. Do three times on each side.

To conclude your session: While in a sitting position, press your palms together. Bring your thumbs into your breastbone. Tuck your elbows in and down, press your breastbone to your thumbs, lifting and opening your chest. Hold for six breaths.

Important: Even when you're not doing yoga, don't forget your breath. Slow, thoughtful, deep breathing is most effective, but don't perform it too quickly. I find the technique to be most effective when you hold the inhalation and exhalation for a certain number of counts.

What to do: Lie on your back, resting your hands on your belly so that your middle fingers touch across your navel. Inhale through your nose for a count of six, pushing your navel out so that your fingertips separate. Pause, then exhale for a count of nine, pulling your navel back in. Perform these steps two more times (more may make you dizzy). Do this in the morning and at night (deep breathing improves mental focus and can be energizing in the morning and calming at night).

Check Equipment Safety

Make sure at-home exercise equipment is safe before you sign on the dotted line. Try out the machine in the store—if it grinds, clicks, squeaks, doesn't move smoothly or is built poorly, don't buy it. Make sure there is a customer service hotline in case you have problems assembling, maintaining or using the equipment. Check the manufacturer's and retailer's reputations with the Better Business Bureau. For more information, read the Federal Trade Commission's advice about fitness equipment at *www.ftc.gov.*

Cedric Bryant, PhD, chief exercise physiologist, American Council on Exercise, San Diego.

Get Aerobic Benefits... Even If You Can't Move So Well

Karl Knopf, EdD, professor of adaptive/older adult fitness at Foothill College, president of Fitness Educators of Older Adults Association, and director of adaptive fitness at the International Sports Sciences Association and an adviser to Sit & Be Fit.

Everyone knows about the multitude of benefits of aerobic exercise. But what if you are confined to a wheelchair or have limited mobility because of a recent physical trauma, such as stroke? *Fortunately, there are many practical options...*

IN THE SWIM

According to Karl Knopf, EdD, professor of Adaptive/Older Adult Fitness at Foothill College in Los Altos Hills, California, water can be a lifesaver—literally—for the person whose mobility is limited. There are a variety of therapeutic pools designed exactly for this purpose—some where you can use a walker or wheelchair in the water, and also commercially available "swim spas" (also called "counter current" pools) where you can adjust the water flow to swim in place or walk with more of a challenge.

Water walking is another option. By using a pool "noodle" (children use these brightly colored, foam-covered tubes as pool toys) under their arms while in the water, a mobile wheelchair user (someone who uses a wheelchair, but has some leg mobility) can actually float in one place while moving his/her legs, gaining aerobic benefits without impact.

Note: Exercise caution and never go in the water unsupervised. A life jacket or an Aqua-Jogger for added safety.

BICYCLES BUILT FOR YOU

Pedal exercisers (like bicycle pedals but without the bicycle) are easy to find, and easy to use for the mobility-challenged person who retains some (even if not much) ability to move his or her legs. This unobtrusive, relatively inexpensive (prices typically range from $15 to $40, depending on the materials with which they are made) device is widely available through medical supply stores or online from Amazon. It consists of a small frame with pedals on which a "rider" can place his feet while sitting in a regular chair and pedal away, just like a regular bicycle.

ARM-ONLY AEROBICS

For people with absolutely no use of their legs, there are several ways to get aerobic exercise. Many gyms are equipped with a device called an arm ergometer. Somewhat like riding an inverted bicycle. The user sits in a seat while grasping a set of "handlebars" which rotate exactly like bicycle pedals. "This provides an excellent aerobic workout with no leg motion necessary whatsoever," said Dr. Knopf, with one warning. "Arm exercises generally elevate heart rate more than leg exercises, so if you're using one of these devices, don't rely on exercise heart rate to determine your intensity level." Instead, he recommends using the "rate of perceived exertion. Ask yourself, *How hard is this on a level of one to 10*, with one being the least possible effort (like sleeping) and 10 being the most effort you could possibly manage for a few seconds." Dr. Knopf suggested aiming for a workout that feels moderately challenging. (It's best to get specific advice from your physical therapist or health-care provider on how hard to push yourself.) Another option would be the talk test. If you can't carry on a conversation, you are training too intensely.

YOU CAN DO THIS AT HOME

There are video options, as well. Sit and Be Fit (*http://www.sitandbefit.org*) is a non-profit organization that produces a television show for seniors and the mobility-challenged (it appears on PBS stations) and also sells a variety of video workouts for people facing physical challenges. With workout videos specifically for people with Parkinson's disease, arthritis, osteoporosis and MS, as well as for those who are mobility impaired, the organization and its products come highly recommended by Dr. Knopf.

7

Women's Health

The Authoritative Breast Cancer Update

When the US Preventive Services Task Force (USPSTF) recently issued updated recommendations for less frequent breast cancer screening than has been previously used for many women, it sparked an immediate controversy.

The debate focused mainly on two of the USPSTF's recommendations—that there is insufficient evidence to support routine mammography for women ages 40 to 49 with an average risk for breast cancer...and that women ages 50 to 74 with an average risk should undergo screening mammography only every two years (biennial).* For women age 75 and older, the USPSTF concluded that there was

*To read a summary of the USPSTF's recommendations (including a clarification of the task force's intent), go to the Web site of the Agency for Health Care Research and Quality, *www.uspreventiveservicestaskforce.org/uspstf/uspsbrca.htm.*

insufficient evidence to advise for or against breast cancer screening.

Many doctors disagreed with the new recommendations, claiming that reducing the frequency of mammography would increase deaths from the disease.

How can women make the best choices for themselves?

Here are some important details that weren't widely reported in the press—and what you need to know about breast cancer tests besides mammography...

WHY THE CONTROVERSY?

The USPSTF is an independent panel of doctors and scientists that bases its recommendations on an analysis of the benefits and harms associated with preventive services such as screening for the early detection of various diseases.

Robert Smith, PhD, director of cancer screening for the American Cancer Society, *www.cancer.org,* and an adjunct professor of epidemiology at the Rollins School of Public Health at Emory University in Atlanta.

In reviewing the evidence for breast cancer screening, the USPSTF analyzed several studies and mathematical simulations of women undergoing regular mammography screening. The task force found that while most of the studies did show a greater benefit with annual versus biennial mammography—as many as one-third of cancers would be missed with biennial versus annual screening—the harms, including false-positive test results, inconvenience, anxiety and unnecessary biopsies of noncancerous abnormalities, were judged to outweigh the benefits.

Doctors who object to the USPSTF's recommendations argue that although the majority of women will experience a false-positive test result for breast cancer at some point in their lives (resulting in a follow-up mammogram, ultrasound or, less often, a biopsy), the risk is worth the potential benefit of detecting a malignancy earlier. That's why the American Cancer Society (ACS), the American College of Obstetricians and Gynecologists and several other groups believe that the guidelines that existed prior to the USPSTF's updated recommendations should continue to be followed.**

For most women, this means that yearly mammography should begin at age 40 and continue as long as the woman is in good health. Women of any age who are at increased risk for breast cancer (due to such risk factors as a family or personal history of the disease) should talk to their doctors about the appropriate age and frequency for screening.

How can medical experts interpret the data so differently?

The ACS, in particular, analyzed the same data reviewed by the USPSTF but also looked at supplemental data because some of the trials examined by the USPSTF screened women with procedures that are no longer used today, such as single-view mammography. The more recent data studied by the ACS found that when women in their 40s were screened annually with high-quality mammography, there were two to three times fewer breast cancer deaths than what the USPSTF estimated.

**To read the ACS's guidelines for breast cancer, go to the ACS Web site, *www.cancer.org.*

OTHER IMPORTANT TESTS

What you should know about other tools that can be used in addition to mammograms to help detect breast malignancies—and the ACS's position on each…

•**Magnetic resonance imaging (MRI)** uses a magnet and computer technology to create highly detailed images of the breast without exposing the patient to radiation.

Women at high risk for breast cancer—such as those who have a known BRCA1 or BRCA2 gene mutation…a first-degree relative (mother, sister or daughter) with a BRCA1 or BRCA2 gene mutation…or a history of radiation treatments to the chest for childhood cancer—should get an annual MRI plus mammography.

Women at moderately increased risk—including a personal or family history of breast cancer or other breast conditions, such as extremely dense breasts—should talk with their doctors about the benefits and risks of adding MRI screening to their yearly mammography.

•**Ultrasound** produces an image by bouncing nonradiation-producing, ultra-high frequency sound waves off of breast tissue.

Ultrasound is mainly used in women with unusually dense breast tissue to help determine whether a questionable image on a mammogram is a noncancerous, liquid-filled cyst or a solid mass that might be a cancerous tumor.

•**Breast self-exam (BSE)** involves a woman inspecting her own breasts for changes, such as hard lumps or thickening. Most women do not perform frequent BSEs, or they use poor technique (such as failing to inspect the entire breast).

Since BSE has not been found to reduce deaths due to breast cancer, women should consider this an optional technique. (For advice on the proper way to perform a BSE, go to *www.cancer.org* and type "breast self-exam" in the search field.)

Women should always be attentive to the look (color, size and shape) and feel of their breasts while changing clothes or showering and report any changes to their physicians right away.

Digital mammography uses a computer so the image can be sharpened for greater clarity.

Digital mammography has been shown to be equal to—not better than—film mammography in detecting cancers in most women. For premenopausal women and women with dense breasts, however, digital mammography appears to provide more accurate results. And it may be able to reduce the rate of false-positives.

The latest statistics indicate that more than half the breast-imaging facilities in the US now have digital technology. For postmenopausal women, either technology is acceptable.

Drug Combo Helps Breast Cancer Patients

Many women who have HER2 positive tumors—an aggressive type that accounts for about 20% of all breast cancers—take the drug *trastuzumab* (Herceptin).

Recent study: Women with advanced cancer who also took the drug *lapatinib* (Tykerb) survived 19 weeks longer than women using trastuzumab alone—an increase of almost 50%.

Kimberly Blackwell, MD, associate professor of medicine and director of the breast cancer clinical trials program, Duke University Medical Center, Durham, North Carolina, and leader of a study of 296 women, presented at the recent San Antonio Breast Cancer Symposium.

Better Mammograms

When scheduling a mammogram, ask if the imaging center's accreditation is current. The federal Mammography Quality Standards Act (MQSA) requires imaging centers that provide mammograms to have their equipment inspected annually to ensure that it meets the act's stringent criteria. Faulty mammography equipment can produce inaccurate test results.

Joseph Daniels, MBA, RT (radiological technologist), imaging director, Baylor Regional Medical Center, Plano, Texas.

Reduce Unnecessary Breast Biopsies with An Elastogram

After a suspicious mass is detected in the breast through mammography or an MRI, patients typically are sent for an ultrasound. An elastogram, which looks at the stiffness of tissue, can be taken at the same time. Benign (noncancerous) masses tend to measure smaller on elastograms in comparison with the standard ultrasound image...suspicious ones usually are larger. Not all offices that do ultrasounds offer elastograms—ask your doctor.

Stamatia V. Destounis, MD, diagnostic radiologist at Elizabeth Wende Breast Care, LLC, Rochester, New York, and leader of a study of 193 patients who underwent elastograms and ultrasounds.

Soy for Breast Cancer— Villain or Protector?

Mark A. Stengler, NMD, licensed naturopathic medical doctor and leading authority on the practice of alternative and integrated medicine. He is founder and medical director of the Stengler Center for Integrative Medicine, Encinitas, California, and associate clinical professor at the National College of Natural Medicine, Portland, Oregon. He is author of *The Natural Physician's Healing Therapies* (Bottom Line Books).

There has been a lot of controversy about the benefits of soy as it relates to cancer. There are some doctors who believe that soy should be avoided because it can cause cancer or a hormone imbalance, while others believe that it is a healthful protein-rich vegetarian food that can prevent cancer.

For the past 20 years, researchers have studied soy as a potential anticancer food. Soy contains weak estrogen-like compounds called phytoestrogens (or plant estrogens). The theory is that these compounds attach to cells and block the potent cancer-promoting effect of the real hormone.

Although research has sometimes been contradictory, the most recent and comprehensive studies demonstrate that a soy-rich diet does seem to reduce the risk of developing breast, prostate, endometrial, colon and lung cancers. Most of the research, however, has focused on breast cancer.

The question about soy and breast cancer that has been most unclear: Does soy help or harm women who already have been diagnosed with breast cancer? Researchers weren't sure about the estrogen-like effect of soy on breast cancer survivors or soy's potential interaction with the breast cancer drug tamoxifen.

But a study from Vanderbilt University Medical Center in Nashville examined soy consumption among 5,000 Chinese women who had been successfully treated for breast cancer. Even though the women in the study ate a diet that is different from women's diets in the US (the researchers did not specify the type of soy consumed), there is important information to be gleaned from this study.

Study findings: The women who ate the most soy protein—and therefore consumed the greatest amount of specific phytoestrogens called isoflavones—were about one-third less likely to have a recurrence of breast cancer or to die during four years of follow-up.

A study from the National Cancer Institute found that soy consumption early in life conferred protection against breast cancer later. The women studied were of Chinese, Japanese and Filipino ancestry and were living in California or Hawaii.

PRACTICAL ADVICE

If you have had breast cancer, these studies don't mean that you should start eating as much soy food as possible—because excessive amounts of any one food to the exclusion of others is unhealthful. But the evidence does suggest that soy is safe for women with breast cancer. *Based on the research so far, here's my thinking on eating soy foods...*

• **Pay attention to the type of soy you eat.** Soy foods do seem to protect against breast cancer recurrence and death from the disease. But the specific types of soy foods may be the real key. Asians tend to eat a diet high in fermented soy foods, such as miso (fermented soy paste used in miso soup and other dishes), tempeh, natto, soy sauce, tamari and tofu. (Tofu is available in fermented and unfermented forms. Fermented is more healthful than unfermented.) The beneficial bacteria (also known as probiotics) involved in fermentation seem to provide other health benefits, including aiding nutrient digestion and enhancing immunity. In contrast, Americans tend to eat many unfermented soy foods, which aren't healthful—for example, soy turkey (a form of processed soy) or soy chips. I recommend consuming fermented soy foods...minimally processed soybeans (such as edamame) in moderate amounts...and small amounts of nongenetically modified (the label should say "organic") soy products, such as soy milk.

• **Minimize exposure to synthetic estrogens.** We are surrounded by synthetic estrogens—in the estrogen-mimicking chemicals in pesticides and soft plastics containing bisphenol A.

Important: Soy phytoestrogens are very weak when compared with many of these synthetic estrogens. I think it's imperative to minimize exposure to synthetic estrogens. Use caution with pesticides, and heat food in glass (not plastic) containers.

• **Avoid isoflavone supplements.** The jury is still out when it comes to the benefit of isoflavone supplements for those with cancer. I recommend that patients with cancer avoid them.

Lentils May Prevent Breast Cancer

A recent study found that women who ate one-half cup of lentils at least twice a week were 24% less likely to develop breast cancer, compared with women who ate the same amount of lentils less than once a month or not at all.

Theory: Lentils' protective effects may be due to particular types of phytochemicals. One-half cup of lentils has 9 grams (g) of protein, 8 g of fiber, 3 milligrams of iron and only 115 calories. And they are inexpensive. Add lentils while cooking soups and whole grains, and use cooked lentils in salads.

Clement A. Adebamowo, MD, ScD, associate professor of epidemiology, department of epidemiology and preventive medicine, Institute of Human Virology, member of the Greenebaum Cancer Center, School of Medicine, University of Maryland, Baltimore, and coauthor of a study of 90,630 women, published in *International Journal of Cancer.*

Pomegranates May Help Prevent Breast Cancer

The hormone estrogen causes certain breast cancer cells to proliferate.

Lab finding: Compounds called *ellagitannins*, which are plentiful in pomegranates, inhibit the aromatase enzyme that converts androgen to estrogen—and thus may help prevent the growth of hormone-dependent breast tumors. More research is needed...but in the meantime, women may benefit from adding pomegranates or pomegranate juice to their diets.

Shiuan Chen, PhD, director of tumor cell biology and co-leader of the breast cancer program at the City of Hope Helford Clinical Research Hospital in Duarte, California, and principal investigator of a lab study.

Taking Calcium Cuts Breast Cancer Risk by 40%

In a recent study, women who took calcium supplements daily for five years had 40% lower risk for breast cancer than women who did not take calcium...women who took a multivitamin daily had 30% lower risk.

Jaime Matta, PhD, professor of pharmacology and toxicology, Ponce School of Medicine, Ponce, Puerto Rico, and coauthor of a study of 725 women, presented at the American Association for Cancer Research's 2010 annual meeting.

Longer Life After Breast Cancer Recurrence

Women with recurring breast cancer who took part in a psychological intervention program to lower stress reduced their risk of dying from the disease by 59%. Women in the program met weekly and learned progressive muscle relaxation, how to cope with fatigue and additional stress-reducing techniques. After the program, they met monthly for eight months.

Result: Patients who attended the intervention had better immune system function.

Barbara L. Andersen, PhD, professor, department of psychology, The Ohio State University, Columbus, and principal investigator and coauthor of a study of 227 women, published in *Clinical Cancer Research.*

Natural Breast Cancer Weapon?

In laboratory studies using breast cancer cells, researchers have found that the dietary supplement bitter melon reduced the growth and division of cancer cells and caused the cells to die more quickly. More research is needed.

Cancer Research.

Weight Lifters Less Likely to Develop Lymphedema

Breast cancer survivors who lift weights are less likely to develop arm and hand swelling. That condition, lymphedema, occurs after women have breast cancer surgery. In the past, doctors told women not to lift weights—or even carry children or bags of groceries—after breast surgery, to avoid making symptoms worse.

Recent finding: Women who lifted weights regularly after surgery, first under the guidance of trained fitness instructors and then on their own, developed stronger arms and were less likely to have lymphedema.

Kathryn Schmitz, PhD, MPH, associate professor of epidemiology and biostatistics, University of Pennsylvania School of Medicine, Philadelphia, and leader of a study of 141 breast cancer survivors with lymphedema, published in *The New England Journal of Medicine*.

Shorter Course of Radiation for Breast Cancer

Timothy J. Whelan, BM, BCh, is a professor and head of the radiation therapy program at the Juravinski Cancer Centre at McMaster University in Hamilton, Ontario, and leader of a study of 1,234 breast cancer patients.

Early-stage breast cancer patients often undergo radiation after a lumpectomy to reduce the risk for recurrence.

Recent study: One group of patients received the standard 25 sessions of radiation, at the typical dose, over 35 days…a second group received 16 sessions of higher-dose radiation over 22 days. Both groups received the same total dose overall and experienced similar side effects during treatment.

Results: Both groups had nearly identical five-year survival rates (96.8% in the standard group and 97.2% in the short-course group)…and approximately the same 10-year recurrence rates (6.7% in the standard group and 6.2% in the short-course group). Radiation toxicity and adverse cosmetic effects (skin changes, breast tissue firmness), were uncommon and were similar in both groups.

Summary: A shorter course of radiation can be more convenient and cost less than the standard course—so ask your oncologist about both treatment options. But note that short-course radiation may not be best for all patients…for instance, women with large breasts are more likely to experience adverse cosmetic effects.

Breast Thermography as Screening Tool

Mark A. Stengler, NMD, licensed naturopathic medical doctor and leading authority on the practice of alternative and integrated medicine. He is founder and medical director of the Stengler Center for Integrative Medicine, Encinitas, California, and author of many books, including *The Natural Physician's Healing Therapies* (Bottom Line Books).

Breast thermography is a screening technique that uses infrared cameras to detect variations in body heat in the breast. The technology is based on the premise that diseased tissue (including precancerous, cancerous and fibrocystic tissues) produces metabolic activity and vascular circulation that increases temperature in this tissue.

Thermography produces an image that is then evaluated for abnormalities.

Important: Thermography is used to complement—not replace—accepted conventional tests, such as ultrasound, mammography and magnetic resonance imaging. It might be used during the years in which a patient does not get a mammogram or for patients who refuse to use mammography. (One of the positive aspects of thermography is that it does not involve any radiation.) Thermography can identify breast tissue that is showing signs of a tumor starting to form, whereas mammography can show only that a precancerous tumor already

155

has formed. In this way, thermography helps physicians identify—and possibly treat—abnormal breast tissue before it's detected by other screening techniques. Thermography is not yet widely accepted by conventional medicine. Further studies are needed before it becomes part of mainstream medicine's arsenal of screening techniques.

More from Mark Stengler, NMD...

Cool Hot Flashes with Rhubarb Extract

The health benefits of rhubarb have long been recognized. Now German researchers are investigating the use of an extract derived from rhubarb to cool the hot flashes of perimenopause and menopause.

In their recent study, they found that ERr 731, the name of the extract derived from rhubarb, significantly reduced the number and intensity of hot flashes in perimenopausal women, compared with women who were taking a placebo. The women took one tablet of ERr 731 daily for 12 weeks.

Scientists don't fully understand how or why this rhubarb extract works, but it does contain a unique phytoestrogen (naturally occurring chemical in plants that acts like estrogen), which is a possible key to its efficacy. No harmful side effects have been associated with the extract.

Brand to try: Estrovera, a tablet that has ERr 731. Distributed by Metagenics (800-692-9400, *www.metagenics.com*), it is available through health-care professionals and online. (A list of practitioners by region is available on the manufacturer's Web site.)

Better Hot Flash Therapy

Hot flashes are a common side effect of the hormone therapy that is typically used to treat breast cancer.

Recent study: When 50 breast cancer patients (average age 54) received acupuncture

or the antidepressant *venlafaxine* (Effexor), a drug often prescribed for breast cancer patients who have hot flashes, both groups reduced the incidence of their hot flashes by half—but only the antidepressant group had side effects (including dry mouth and constipation). Hot flashes increased again two weeks after the medication group stopped treatment and 12 to 14 weeks after the acupuncture group stopped.

Eleanor Walker, MD, division director, Breast Radiation Oncology, Henry Ford Hospital, Detroit.

Progesterone for Hot Flashes

Progesterone may help relieve hot flashes and night sweats, say University of British Columbia researchers. Healthy postmenopausal women suffering from hot flashes and night sweats took either 300 milligrams (mg) of oral progesterone or a placebo. Those who took progesterone experienced a 56% reduction in the intensity of hot flashes and night sweats and a 48% reduction in the number of hot flashes and night sweats, versus 28% and 22%, respectively, in those taking a placebo. The progesterone did not cause any side effects. Talk to your doctor about using bioidentical progesterone to control hot flashes.

J. Prior, et al., "Progesterone Is Effective for Hot Flash Treatment and Provides an Alternative to Estrogen," presented at The Endocrine Society's annual meeting in San Diego.

Hormone Therapy Cuts Colon Cancer Risk

Menopausal hormone therapy (HT)—in the form of estrogen alone or with progestin—can ease symptoms of menopause, such as hot flashes and vaginal dryness.

Recent finding: Perimenopausal or post-menopausal women who were using HT at the start of a 10-year study were 36% less likely to be diagnosed with colon cancer during the decade-long study period than women who had never used HT. The benefit was strongest in women who used HT for a total of five to 15 years.

But: Other studies associate HT with increased risks for breast cancer and cardio-vascular disease. So, if you are considering or already using HT and are at risk for colon cancer, discuss the new study findings with your doctor when weighing HT's benefits versus risks.

Katherine DeLellis Henderson, PhD, assistant research professor in the division of cancer etiology at City of Hope National Medical Center in Duarte, California, and an investigator on the California Teachers Study, a prospective longitudinal study of more than 100,000 women.

Dangerous Menopause Medication Puts Kids and Pets at Risk

Andrew L. Rubman, ND, founder and medical director, Southbury Clinic for Traditional Medicines, Southbury, Connecticut. *www.southburyclinic.com.*

Getting rid of your hot flashes may lead to trouble for any children or pets you snuggle with. The FDA has issued a warning that accidental exposure in the form of skin-to-skin contact to Evamist, a prescription spray medication for hot flashes, may cause serious health problems in kids and pets.

"Women using Evamist need to be aware of the potential risks to children who come in contact with the area of skin where this drug is applied," Julie Beitz, MD, director of the FDA's Office of Drug Evaluation III, said in an agency news release. "It is important to keep both children and pets away from the product to minimize exposure."

SPRAY-ON TROUBLE

Hot flashes can be the result of plummeting estrogen levels at menopause. Evamist is just one of many prescription drugs that can be used to address this problem. It was approved by the FDA in 2007 as treatment for moderate-to-severe hot flashes and contains *estradiol*, a potent form of estrogen. Evamist gets sprayed on a woman's forearm between the elbow and wrist once a day.

Problems for children: To date, the FDA has received eight reports of adverse events in children between the ages of three and five who were accidentally exposed to Evamist. *These included...*

- **Premature puberty,** breast development and nipple swelling in girls.
- **Breast enlargement in boys.**

These problems (which may not be permanent) occurred several weeks or months after the children first came into contact with Evamist.

Pet problems: Two dog owners complained about adverse events, including mammary or nipple enlargement, genital problems, liver failure and elevated estrogen levels caused by pet contact with treated skin. Small pets may be especially vulnerable.

KEEP LOVED ONES SAFE

If you use Evamist, the FDA now recommends taking measures to protect those around you...

- **Don't let children or pets come into contact with treated skin** (until it has been washed) and, most especially, don't let them lick it.
- **Cover up.** If you cannot avoid contact, wear long sleeves.
- **Do not use the spray** in the same room with children or pets.
- **If a child inadvertently touches your arm after you apply Evamist,** promptly wash his/her skin with soap and water.
- **Contact your pediatrician or vet if accidental exposure occurs** or if you notice unusual symptoms such as breast enlargement in children or pets.

Even better is to consider other treatment options, advises Andrew L. Rubman, ND. In

157

his view, it's not just children and pets who should avoid Evamist—everyone should. He calls it "a simplistic solution to a complex problem," noting that it fails to address key issues such as the vast individual variations in hormonal sensitivity. In his practice, Dr. Rubman prescribes supplements such as black cohosh and individually balanced bioidentical hormonal preparations.

Should You Quit Taking Calcium to Protect Your Heart?

JoAnn E. Manson, MD, DrPH, professor of medicine and women's health at Harvard Medical School and chief of the division of preventive medicine at Brigham and Women's Hospital, both in Boston. She is one of the lead investigators for two highly influential studies on women's health—the Harvard Nurses' Health Study and the Women's Health Initiative. Dr. Manson is the author, with Shari Bassuk, ScD, of *Hot Flashes, Hormones & Your Health* (McGraw-Hill).

Did you toss your calcium pills in the trash—and then worry about getting osteoporosis—after a recent study concluded that calcium supplementation could increase heart attack risk? Let's not be too hasty. Here's what that widely publicized study really showed…and what we women should do with the information.

As reported in the journal *BMJ*, investigators analyzed data from 11 clinical trials in which nearly 12,000 patients—mostly women age 70 or older—were randomly assigned to receive calcium supplements or placebos for an average of nearly four years.

The shocker: People who took 500 milligrams (mg) or more of calcium daily were about 30% more likely to have a heart attack than those who did not take calcium.

Many physicians, including me, were surprised by these findings, as other research (detailed below) suggests that calcium generally has a neutral or even protective effect on the heart. Still, this study raises the possibility

that calcium supplements should not be used as widely as they are now.

The concern: In recent years, researchers have discovered that vascular calcification (calcium buildup in atherosclerotic plaques in the arteries) is a risk factor for heart attacks…and it may be that overzealous consumption of calcium can contribute to vascular calcification or even to the development of atherosclerosis itself. But before you panic, consider the following facts…

The *BMJ* study's results do not necessarily apply to dietary calcium. Indeed, a high intake of calcium from foods, including calcium-rich low-fat dairy products, has been associated with lower risks for various heart attack risk factors, including diabetes…high blood pressure…and metabolic syndrome, a cluster of symptoms that includes abdominal obesity, high triglycerides, high blood pressure, high blood sugar and low HDL (good) cholesterol.

Why might dietary calcium have more favorable effects than supplemental calcium? Because dietary calcium may interact with other nutrients in food to yield health benefits…and because calcium from food may be absorbed into the bloodstream more slowly than calcium from supplements, thus reducing the likelihood of high blood calcium levels.

The *BMJ* study findings do not necessarily apply to calcium supplements taken in combination with vitamin D. The *BMJ* study focused on calcium supplements taken alone, without vitamin D. However, many calcium supplements sold in the US also contain vitamin D. Available research suggests that the same heart risks are not found with such combination supplements because vitamin D regulates calcium metabolism, the mechanism by which the body maintains appropriate calcium levels.

Example: The Women's Health Initiative—in which about 36,000 postmenopausal women were randomly assigned to take either placebos or 1,000 mg of calcium plus 400 international units (IU) of vitamin D per day—did not find an increased risk for either vascular calcification or heart attack.

According to the *BMJ* study, calcium supplementation did not increase heart attack risk in people whose dietary calcium intakes were less than about 800 mg per day. This bolsters the idea that excess calcium might be responsible for the *BMJ* study results. It may be especially true for older people who have decreased kidney function.

WHAT WOMEN SHOULD DO

To me, this study has a clear take-home message. For bone health, I advise that you get the currently recommended amount of calcium each day, taking into account both your dietary and supplemental calcium sources—but avoid ingesting more than this amount. Many experts recommend 1,000 mg of calcium per day up to age 50 and 1,200 mg per day thereafter…as well as about 800 IU per day of vitamin D from food and/or supplements.

Bottom line: If you get this much calcium from food alone, skip the supplements. If you do not get sufficient calcium from your diet, make up the difference by supplementing (and take care to get enough vitamin D, too).

To estimate the amount of calcium in your diet, check the calcium content of specific foods on the USDA Web page at *www.ars. usda.gov/services/docs.htm?docid=18877*…on the National Institutes of Health Web page at *http://ods.od.nih.gov/factsheets/calcium*…and/or on food labels.

Rich dietary sources of calcium include…

Yogurt, plain, low-fat: 415 mg per cup.

Sardines, canned with bones: 325 mg per three-ounce serving.

Milk, low-fat: 305 mg per cup.

Cheddar cheese: 204 mg per ounce.

Salmon, canned with bones: 181 mg per three-ounce serving.

Collard greens: 178 mg per ½ cup chopped and cooked.

Figs: 155 mg for five figs.

Cottage cheese (1% milk fat): 138 mg per cup.

Unless you consume a lot of dairy products, you are unlikely to get too much calcium from food alone.

But: It is easy to get too much supplemental calcium—so check labels not only on your calcium tablets but also on your multivitamins, calcium-plus-vitamin-D supplements and any calcium-containing medications that you may be taking.

"White Foods" and Heart Disease

Women who eat "white foods"—white bread, white rice, pasta—have more heart disease.

Recent finding: Women who consume a lot of carbohydrates that cause fast increases in blood sugar—that is, foods with a high-glycemic index (GI)—have a higher risk for heart disease than women who eat carbs with a low-glycemic index. Women who ate the most high-glycemic foods had twice the risk for heart disease as women who ate the least. Low-glycemic foods include most vegetables and whole-grain products. The effect was seen only in women, not in men.

Study of 15,171 men and 32,578 women by researchers at Italy's National Cancer Institute and other Italian institutes and universities, published in *Archives of Internal Medicine.*

Menopause Raises Cholesterol, Increasing Heart Disease Risk

The average LDL (bad) cholesterol count jumps by about 9% in the two-year window surrounding the final menstrual period. Total cholesterol levels also increase by about 6.5%.

Important: Women undergoing menopause should take steps to keep cholesterol under control.

Among the strategies: Regular exercise… maintaining a healthy weight…not smoking… and taking cholesterol-lowering medications.

Karen A. Matthews, PhD, distinguished professor of psychiatry and professor of epidemiology and psychology, University of Pittsburgh School of Medicine. She is lead author of a study of menopausal transition in 1,054 women, published in *Journal of the American College of Cardiology.*

Abused Women Are Prone to Unexpected Ailments

A recent study compared women who were never abused with women who had experienced domestic violence in the previous year.

Worrisome finding: Abused women were significantly more likely to have been diagnosed with health problems not typically regarded as being associated with abuse—such as chest pain, headaches, acid reflux and urinary infections.

If you are being abused: Help your doctor recognize the real problem behind your symptoms by confiding in him or her...and contact the National Domestic Violence Hotline (800-799-7233, *www.thehotline.org*) for assistance with this issue.

Amy Bonomi, PhD, associate professor of human development and family science at Ohio State University in Columbus, and lead author of a study of 3,568 women.

Ovarian Cancer Slowed

Women with advanced ovarian cancer given *bevacizumab* along with chemotherapy, followed by continued use of bevacizumab, showed no worsening of their cancer for 14.1 months, compared with 10.3 months for women given only standard chemotherapy. Women receiving bevacizumab did have more frequent side effects, including high blood pressure. Discuss the risks and benefits with your oncologist.

Robert A. Burger, MD, director of Women's Cancer Center, Fox Chase Cancer Center, Philadelphia, and leader of a study presented at an annual meeting of the American Society of Clinical Oncology.

Dual Therapy Best for Cervical Cancer

Some cervical cancer patients may get radiation...others also get chemotherapy.

Recent analysis: Women who got both treatments had higher five-year survival rates and lower recurrence rates than those who had radiation alone. There was some suggestion that continuing chemotherapy after radiation ended might further improve outcomes, but more research is needed.

Patients: Discuss these findings with your oncologist.

Claire Vale, PhD, a research scientist at the Medical Research Council Clinical Trials Unit in London, England, and leader of an analysis of 15 studies involving 3,452 women.

Important News About Genital Skin Cancer

Andrew Bronin, MD, associate clinical professor of dermatology at Yale School of Medicine in New Haven, Connecticut. A dermatologist in private practice in Rye Brook, New York, he also is editor in chief of *DermClips*, an American Academy of Dermatology (AAD) continuing medical education publication, and a recipient of the AAD's Presidential Citation award.

Remember back in the 1960s, at the height of the feminist movement, when women were encouraged to look at their vulvas (external genitalia) in a hand mirror in order to learn about their bodies? Turns out there's a medical rationale for this, too—because such self-exams help detect genital skin cancer.

It can be surprising to learn that women can get skin cancer "down there." Though men also get genital skin cancer, a recent study found that women are almost three times more likely to die of the most common type of this disease. It's not clear why women's mortality rates are higher—it might be that women are more susceptible or that this cancer is more aggressive in women...or just that growths are easier to find on male genitalia, so men get treated earlier in the progression of the disease.

The vulva includes the clitoris, labia (vaginal lips) and opening to the vagina. There are several types of vulvar cancer. Andrew Bronin, MD, is associate clinical professor of dermatology at Yale School of Medicine in New Haven, Connecticut, and a dermatologist in private practice in Rye Brook, New York. *Here are his prevention and early detection strategies for protecting yourself from...*

•**Squamous cell vulvar cancer.** This skin cancer arises in the squamous cells (the layer of cells on the surface of the skin) and accounts for nearly 90% of vulvar cancers. Risk factors include age (85% of women who contract the disease are over age 50)...chronic vulvar or vaginal inflammation...infection with HIV (the AIDS virus)...or a history of cervical cancer or *lichen sclerosus* (a disorder characterized by thin, itchy vulvar tissues).

Squamous cell cancer can be linked to certain strains of human papillomavirus (HPV). The HPVs are a group of more than 100 related viruses, some of which are also associated with genital warts and cervical cancer. The sexually transmitted strains of HPV usually spread during vaginal, anal or oral sex via skin-to-skin contact (rather than via bodily fluids). Though the virus sometimes clears up on its own, there is no surefire way to eradicate HPV—so prevention is important. *To reduce your risk...*

•Get tested for HPV. Like a Pap smear, the HPV test analyzes cervical cells. If you are not infected, ask your doctor whether you should get the Gardasil vaccine, which protects against four of the most troublesome strains of HPV. "Although the vaccine is currently FDA-approved for women age 26 and under, it also may benefit older women," Dr. Bronin said. "Even if you are infected with one strain of HPV, consider vaccination—because it may protect you against three other strains."

•Even if a man has no visible genital warts, he could have a "preclinical" HPV infection—meaning that the virus is present and contagious

but hasn't yet produced visible symptoms. So if you enter a new relationship, have your partner use condoms. But understand that this is not foolproof since it protects you from infections only in areas covered by the condom.

Also: Be aware that the more sexual partners you've had—and the more partners your partner has had—the higher your likelihood of having been exposed to HPV.

•**Don't smoke!** Smoking increases vulvar cancer risk, especially if you have HPV.

•**Vulvar malignant melanoma.** This type accounts for only about 4% of vulvar skin cancers, but it is the most deadly because it spreads rapidly. Melanoma develops in the *melanocytes*, the skin's pigment-producing cells. You probably know that sun exposure increases the risk for malignant melanoma—but sun is not a requirement for the development of this disease. In fact, melanoma has the potential to occur anywhere that you have pigment cells...and that's every square inch of your skin, including your vulva. You can get malignant melanoma even where the sun never shines.

"Having moles that are atypical—in other words, funny-looking to the eye and under the microscope—anywhere on your body increases your risk for vulvar malignant melanoma. So does a personal or family history of any malignant melanoma," Dr. Bronin said. Unfortunately, vulvar melanomas have some of the worst prognoses of all malignant melanomas, with a five-year survival rate of only 50%...precisely because they often are not caught until it is too late.

•**Vulvar adenocarcinoma.** This type begins in the gland cells just inside the vaginal opening or in the top layer of vulvar skin. It accounts for about 8% of vulvar cancers. Though less deadly than melanoma, it has a relatively high recurrence rate.

Concern: Diagnosis often is delayed because a cancerous growth may be easily mistaken for a cyst.

KEY: EARLY DETECTION

Catching vulvar cancer early offers the best chance for a good outcome. *Potentially life-saving strategies…*

•**Give yourself periodic vulvar self-exams.** The frequency depends on your personal risk factors, so ask your gynecologist to recommend a schedule.

What to do: "Use a mirror to check the inner and outer labia, vaginal opening, clitoris and perineal area between the vagina and anus. Look for abnormal lumps or growths…red, white or grayish lesions…changes in pigmentation…swelling…or sores that don't heal," Dr. Bronin suggested. If you spot any such signs, see your gynecologist or dermatologist as soon as possible.

•**Also be on the lookout for unexplained itching,** tenderness, pain or nonmenstrual bleeding—and again, alert your doctor without delay.

•**Get an annual gynecologic checkup.** Your doctor will be watching for the disease (among other things)—but it doesn't hurt to ask, "Do you see any signs of vulvar cancer?"

Diagnosis and treatment: When suspicious growths are found, the tissue is biopsied. If the precancerous condition *vulvar intraepithelial neoplasia* is diagnosed, laser therapy or surgery can keep it from turning into a squamous cell cancer. If the biopsy does reveal squamous cell cancer, treatment options include laser therapy, surgery, radiation and/or chemotherapy.

If a pigmented skin lesion is suspected of being malignant melanoma, it should be surgically removed by a dermatologist or gynecologist and examined at a pathology lab. Early recognition and removal of a malignant melanoma can be lifesaving.

For vulvar adenocarcinoma, treatment is also surgical, with the extent of the surgery depending on the extent of the disease. Again, Dr. Bronin emphasized, early detection offers the best chance for limiting the necessary surgery and enhancing the prognosis.

Drug-Free Incontinence Cure

Larissa V. Rodríguez, MD, associate professor of urology, codirector of Pelvic Medicine and Reconstruction, and director of Female Urology Research, all at the David Geffen School of Medicine at the University of California, Los Angeles.

You've probably heard a hundred times that Kegel exercises are key to halting urinary incontinence. But did you know that there are different ways to Kegel—and that the right way depends on which type of incontinence you have? Or that other exercises also help prevent bothersome leaks? This could be the information you need to put the problem behind you.

Of course, you should alert your doctor if you're experiencing incontinence. But chances are good that you won't need drugs or surgery if you practice the exercises below, recommended by urologist Larissa V. Rodríguez, MD, of the David Geffen School of Medicine at the University of California, Los Angeles. *What to do…*

•**Identify your problem.** If a little urine escapes when you exercise, sneeze, cough or laugh, you have stress incontinence. It occurs when weakness develops in the muscles of the pelvic floor (the hammock-like structure that supports the uterus and bladder) and the sphincter of the urethra (the tube that carries urine out of the bladder), causing the bladder's position to drop and preventing the urethra from closing properly.

If you experience a sudden, urgent need to urinate in response to a trigger (such as sipping a drink or hearing running water) or at random, you have urge incontinence. This occurs when abnormal nerve signals cause the bladder to contract involuntarily.

•**Pick the correct Kegel.** With either type of incontinence, step one is to identify your pelvic floor muscles. Insert a finger into your vagina and try to contract the muscles that allow you to feel the squeeze on your finger…or instead, try to stop your urine midstream. The muscles you use to accomplish these tasks are the ones that need strengthening. (*Note:* Do not make a habit of interrupting your urine stream—try it just once or twice to isolate the correct muscles.)

For stress incontinence: Squeeze your pelvic floor muscles and hold for five seconds…relax…repeat 10 times. Throughout the day, do 10 sets of 10 squeezes each—for a total of 100 squeezes daily. Also squeeze those muscles whenever you cough or sneeze.

For urge incontinence: Do a chain of 10 Kegels very quickly, holding for one second and then releasing for one second. Do this 10 times daily. Also do it whenever you feel a sudden urge to go—fast Kegels activate nerves that tell the bladder to relax.

• **Try weighted vaginal cones.** These exercise aids, which further strengthen the pelvic floor, are especially helpful with stress incontinence. A set of cones typically includes several softly tapered cones weighing from about 0.7 ounce to about 2.5 ounces. [Editor's note: Vaginal cones are readily available online (for instance, see *www.vaginalweights.org*) starting at about $60.]

To use: Gently insert the lightest cone into the vagina…then, using your pelvic floor muscles, try to keep the cone inside for at least one minute as you walk around. Practice daily—as your muscles get stronger, try a heavier cone.

• **Practice timed voiding.** This exercise retrains your bladder, helping mostly with urge incontinence. The idea is to urinate on a schedule—for instance, starting at intervals of every two hours. If you feel an urge to go sooner, try to wait until the end of the two hours…or decrease your starting interval to whatever amount of time allows you to void without urgency or incontinence. Once you can easily manage the starting interval, gradually lengthen the time between bathroom trips —for example, to every three hours. As your bladder adjusts, you gain more control over its contractions…and are less likely to leak.

• **Keep it up.** Dr. Rodríguez said, "With daily practice, both types of incontinence typically improve significantly within three to six weeks—but to keep muscles strong, you must make a lifetime commitment to pelvic floor exercise."

Bleeding After Sex?

Bleeding after sex should be looked into. Postcoital bleeding could be related to abnormal (precancerous or cancerous) cells on the cervix…a cervical polyp…an intrauterine device (IUD)…a sexually transmitted disease, such as gonorrhea, chlamydia or trichomoniasis…a uterine fibroid…a yeast infection…or some kind of trauma to the vagina, cervix or perineum. If you experience bleeding after intercourse, it may be a warning sign to see your gynecologist.

Lissa Rankin, MD, obstetrician/gynecologist, Mill Valley, California, and author of *What's Up Down There? Questions You'd Only Ask Your Gynecologist If She Was Your Best Friend* (St. Martin's).

Better Sex? Try Yoga

Forty healthy women who practiced a series of yoga poses one hour daily for 12 weeks reported significant improvements in sexual functioning (including increased arousal, lubrication and frequency of orgasm).

Theory: Yoga improves functioning of the hormone secretion glands and strengthens pelvic muscles—both of which can lead to satisfying sexual activity.

To enhance sex: Consider a yoga class. To find a certified teacher, visit the International Association of Yoga Therapists Web site, *www.iayt.org*, or call 928-541-0004. Consult your physician before trying yoga.

Vikas Dhikav, MD, research officer, neurology department, Guru Gobind Singh Indraprastha University, New Delhi, India.

High Cholesterol Harms Women's Sex Lives

In a recent study of 556 women, researchers found that women with *hyperlipidemia* (elevated cholesterol levels in the blood) reported significantly lower sexual satisfaction than those without the condition.

Theory: Accumulation of fats in blood vessel walls (already linked to erectile dysfunction in men) also may reduce blood flow to female genitals.

If you have experienced a loss of sexual function: Ask your doctor to check your total cholesterol levels.

Katherine Esposito, MD, PhD, researcher, department of geriatrics and metabolic disease, Second University of Naples, Italy.

What the "Drink More, Weigh Less" Study Really Means

JoAnn E. Manson, MD, DrPH, professor of medicine and women's health at Harvard Medical School and chief of the division of preventive medicine at Brigham and Women's Hospital, both in Boston. She is one of the lead investigators for two highly influential studies on women's health—the Harvard Nurses' Health Study and the Women's Health Initiative. Dr. Manson is the author, with Shari Bassuk, ScD, of *Hot Flashes, Hormones & Your Health* (McGraw-Hill).

Don't drink alcohol"—to avoid empty calories—is routine advice given to dieters. But surprising new research suggests that, compared with nondrinkers, women who drink alcohol in moderation are actually less likely to gain weight and are at lower risk of becoming obese.

Does this mean that we should drink more—or that more of us should drink? No, it doesn't. Here's what the study really showed and what we can learn from it...

As reported in *Archives of Internal Medicine*, my colleagues and I assessed the drinking habits of 19,220 US women age 39 and older who were of normal weight (body mass index between 18.5 and 24.9). About 59% of the women were light or moderate drinkers, consuming fewer than two drinks per day...3% were heavy drinkers, consuming two or more drinks per day...and 38% were nondrinkers. By the end of the 13-year study, 41% of the women had become overweight or obese.

What surprised us: Compared with nondrinkers, women who drank one to less than two drinks per day had a 30% lower risk of becoming overweight or obese...heavier drinkers had a 27% lower risk than nondrinkers. So among all these women, it was the nondrinkers who were the most likely to have excess weight!

Even so, the absolute changes in weight were relatively modest. On average, over the 13 years, nondrinkers gained about eight pounds...light-to-moderate drinkers gained five to six pounds...and heavy drinkers gained about three and a half pounds. Why did these modest average weight gains bump 41% of study participants from the normal weight category to overweight or obese? Some women gained more than the average amount...and many had started the study in the high-normal weight range.

Previous studies of men had found the opposite—that nondrinkers gain less weight than drinkers. So how do we explain these new findings in the study of women? *Theories...*

While male drinkers tend to add alcohol to their daily calorie intake, females tend to substitute alcohol for food without increasing total calories.

Due to metabolic differences, women appear to use up more calories in breaking down alcohol than men do.

Alcohol may rev up women's metabolism more than men's.

THE TAKE-HOME MESSAGE...

For normal-weight women who already drink, continued light-to-moderate drinking may provide a modest weight-control benefit.

Bonus: Other studies suggest that moderate alcohol consumption lowers heart disease risk.

But: Women who are already overweight should not use alcohol as a weight-loss strategy. Other research suggests that already overweight women may use up fewer calories in metabolizing alcohol—and so may be more likely than lean women to gain weight from a given amount of alcohol.

Furthermore: I do not advise using the new study as a reason to start drinking if you currently abstain, because even moderate alcohol consumption increases the risk for hemorrhagic stroke and certain cancers.

Better: Keep pounds off by exercising regularly and maintaining a healthful diet.

If you drink: Even one drink per day (five ounces of wine, 12 ounces of beer or 1.5 ounces of liquor) can boost cancer risk, so limit yourself to one drink no more than three or four times per week or, alternatively, to half a drink per day.

Red Wine Boosts Women's Sex Drive

Women who drank red wine in moderation had more sexual interest and lubrication than ones who drank little or none.

Possible reason: The antioxidants and alcohol in the wine may increase production of nitric oxide, a gas that helps artery walls relax—increasing blood flow to genitals.

Caution: Drink no more than one to two glasses of red wine a day—any more decreases sexual response.

Study of 798 women by researchers at University of Florence, Italy, published in *The Journal of Sexual Medicine.*

Could You Develop a Drinking Problem?

Stephanie Brown, PhD, a licensed psychologist and director of the Addictions Institute in Menlo Park, California. She also is the author of 10 books on addiction and recovery and was the founder of the Alcohol Clinic at Stanford University in Stanford, California.

It's heartbreaking to watch a loved one slide down that slippery slope from social drinking to problem drinking to alcoholism—or to slide down it yourself. But did you know that this can happen to almost anyone, at almost any point in life? And women in midlife or beyond are certainly not immune.

But: Because many people do not realize this, it is easy for an older woman's descent into addiction to go unrecognized until the problem is very advanced...or until a tragedy occurs.

Psychologist Stephanie Brown, PhD, director of the Addictions Institute in Menlo Park, California, explained, "Aging brings new and different stresses that may cause a woman to turn to alcohol even if she did not do so in the past."

Examples: In midlife, a woman may feel lonely when children leave home...disappointed if a career stalls...strained by providing care for elderly parents...or adrift if a marriage ends in divorce. Later in life, she may experience a sense of purposelessness or financial insecurity after retirement...anxiety about health problems...or grief when loved ones pass away.

Certain physiological factors of aging also contribute to a woman's risk, according to the book *Women Under the Influence* from the National Center on Addiction and Substance Abuse (CASA) at Columbia University. Physical tolerance for alcohol diminishes as her lean muscle mass ebbs, metabolism slows, and liver and kidney function decline. This leaves an older woman with a higher blood alcohol level than a younger woman who drinks the same amount.

Consequence: A level of drinking that appeared to be safe and moderate in earlier adulthood can become addicting as the years pass.

Some research has shown that women experience higher rates of late-onset alcoholism than men do, the CASA researchers reported, perhaps due to higher rates of stress. About half of all cases of alcoholism among older women begin after age 59—compared with only one-fourth of cases among older men.

HOW ALCOHOL SUCKS WOMEN IN

A mature woman who honed her natural coping skills as a younger adult may be less likely to develop an alcohol problem than one who sometimes relied on outside substances to relieve stress. But even a woman who usually copes well can slide into abuse.

Dr. Brown explained, "It's subtle, but sometimes a person just begins to turn toward alcohol. For instance, a woman accustomed to a daily glass of wine might notice that having a little more helps her feel better. She thinks, So what's a little more?" Gradually the habit grows...until it is much more than a habit.

An alcoholic is drawn to alcohol the way a person is drawn to a lover—she feels excited when they are together and wants that experience every day. Once that love is established, the alcoholic makes lifestyle changes that allow her to drink more. She may socialize only with friends who enjoy drinking...bring wine to a party as a "gift" or carry little bottles in her purse to ensure that alcohol is available...or spend increasing amounts of time drinking alone at home. Despite this, she may insist that she does not have a drinking problem—because denial is a common characteristic of addiction.

Meanwhile, people around her may fail to recognize the situation.

Reasons: An older woman's drinking is less obviously disruptive to the family than it is when young children live at home. Doctors often neglect to screen older women for alcoholism—according to CASA researchers, only 17% of female patients age 65 and over said that their doctors asked about alcohol during a checkup. And when possible symptoms of alcohol abuse (memory problems, fatigue, headache, insomnia) are present, older wom-

en often are misdiagnosed with depression, anxiety or age-related cognitive decline.

Result: Among the estimated two million American women over age 59 who might benefit from treatment for alcohol abuse, less than 1% receive such treatment.

SPOTTING THE WARNING SIGNS

Moderate drinking for women typically is defined as no more than one serving of alcohol per day—that's 12 ounces of beer, five ounces of wine or 1.5 ounces of liquor. But people in denial about their drinking may dismiss that limit as absurdly strict. Often this denial continues until—or even after—they pass out at a party, get arrested for drunk driving, wake up in a stranger's bed or cause a serious accident.

But quantity doesn't tell the whole story. Dr. Brown said, "Getting hooked psychologically is independent from the quantity of alcohol consumed. If that one drink per day becomes the focus of a person's life or if she feels like she cannot enjoy dinner without a drink, that is a warning of psychological dependence."

Reason: The defining characteristic of addiction is loss of control—over when you drink...or how much you drink...or the way in which you think about drinking.

Bottom line: A woman should seek help from her doctor or a therapist if she frequently drinks more often or in greater quantity than she intended...or if she experiences cravings for or obsessive thoughts about alcohol. Does this describe you or a loved one? Remember that there is always hope—because just as a woman is never too old to develop a drinking problem, she is never too old to recover.

Older Women Need an Hour of Activity—Every Day

To avoid gaining weight over time, older women at a healthy weight need about one hour of moderate-intensity activity per day. This includes going for a brisk walk, riding a bicycle, playing golf, gardening and playing with grandchildren.

I-Min Lee, MD, associate professor, department of medicine, Brigham and Women's Hospital, Harvard Medical School, Boston, and leader of a study of 34,079 women, average age 54, published in *The Journal of the American Medical Association.*

Female? Over 65? Some Extra Weight Can Prolong Your Life

Chantal Matkin Dolan, PhD, MPH, a consultant for the Health Economics and Outcomes Research Group at Genentech, Inc.

Here's a bit of supposedly good news for many women—a recent study found that women over 65 deemed "overweight" according to the government in fact had lower mortality rates than thinner women in the same age group.

The study, published in the *American Journal of Public Health*, used data from the *Study of Osteoporotic Fractures* funded by the National Institutes of Health. The study included more than 8,000 women aged 65 and older who were tracked over an eight-year period. The researchers examined each woman's BMI (body mass index), which is calculated based on height and weight (*http://www.nhlbisupport.com/bmi/*). Those with BMIs ranging from 24.6 to 29.8—the middle distributions of BMIs examined, meaning they were neither the fattest nor the thinnest of those tested— had the lowest mortality rates. The optimum survival was estimated to be in women scoring 29.2, which is considered "overweight" on the BMI scale.

Based on the National Heart Lung and Blood Institute (NHLBI) BMI categories, the women in this study with BMIs between 25 and 29.9 are overweight. And, according to the NHLBI guidelines, being overweight and obese increases the risk for various diseases.

Experts note that it would be important to closely examine the methodology for the study before drawing any conclusions from the "counterintuitive findings," but lead study author Chantal Matkin Dolan, PhD, MPH, says that in her view the study results suggest that current BMI guidelines are not appropriate and perhaps need to be adjusted for age. Until recently, she said, few studies have examined the association between obesity, body size and mortality in older women. She said that further research needs to be done to better understand the apparently protective effect of a few extra pounds after age 65…and emphasized that the results for older women cannot be extrapolated to younger women or to men without further research.

Improve Your Health and Appearance with Silicon

Mark A. Stengler, NMD, licensed naturopathic medical doctor and leading authority on the practice of alternative and integrated medicine. He is founder and medical director of the Stengler Center for Integrative Medicine, Encinitas, California, and associate clinical professor at the National College of Natural Medicine, Portland, Oregon. He is author of *The Natural Physician's Healing Therapies* (Bottom Line Books).

Patients often are surprised when I recommend silicon for their thinning hair or brittle nails. I believe that this mineral is a well-kept secret in the medical world. Note that silicon, the mineral, is different from silicone, the synthetic compound that (in gel form) is used in some medical applications and products, including breast implants.

Silicon is the second most common mineral in the Earth's crust and is found in sand on beaches. While it was once believed to be an inert contaminant, researchers discovered more than a century ago that silicon was concentrated in many of the body's tissues. What's more, silicon plays a role in keeping us healthy by strengthening bone and joint cartilage and maintaining the health of hair, skin and fingernails. How silicon can help you…

HEALTH BENEFITS OF SILICON

You may have heard silicon referred to as a "trace mineral," a mineral needed by the body in only very small amounts. But there is growing evidence that silicon could eventually be regarded as a macro mineral, which is required in amounts larger than that provided by food alone.

We have silicon in every cell off our bodies. Concentrations of silicon are highest in bone, connective tissues, skin, fingernails and hair, as well as the trachea, tendons and aorta—tissues that need strength and/or resilience. *Silicon's main role is to enhance the structural integrity of specific tissues, such as...*

• **Collagen.** Scientific evidence points to silicon being involved in the synthesis and "stability" of collagen, the body's chief protein. We need collagen to make most of our organs, bone and the fibrous tissues of the skin, tendons and ligaments. Without adequate collagen production, bones and ligaments weaken and skin tissue is compromised.

• **Joint cartilage.** Collagen and noncollagen proteins are needed to make joint cartilage, the role of which is to protect the joints and enable bones to move freely.

• **Bone.** Silicon is a major constituent of bone-making cells. Concentrations of the mineral are especially high in cells actively forming new bone. The mineral enhances the absorption of calcium, and a lack of silicon reduces the calcium content of bone. High intake of silicon is associated with better bone-mineral density and stronger bones.

Several studies have found that taking supplemental silicon increases the mineral density of bones.

Example: A study of postmenopausal women published in *BMC Musculoskeletal Disorders* found that adding a silicon supplement improved bone-mineral density above and beyond what was achieved with just calcium and vitamin D supplementation.

• **Skin, hair, fingernails.** Several small but promising studies have found that supplemental silicon often can restore a younger- and healthier-looking appearance. This is probably related to collagen and elastin production. Elastin is a protein that, as the name suggests, gives skin the ability to stretch. One study found that a commercial silicon oral supplement called RegeneMax reduced microwrinkle depth by 30%. It also improved the youthful look, or elasticity, of the skin. Other studies have found that silicon supplements can increase the thickness of hair strands and strengthen fingernails, making them more resistant to breaking.

GETTING SILICON INTO YOUR BODY

While silicon was once plentiful in herbs and grains, farming methods have depleted silicon from the ground, so many plant foods are not as rich in silicon as they could be. Because of this, most people have suboptimal levels of silicon. We need 5 grams (g) to 20 g daily of silicon—and the best way to get this amount is to take supplemental silicon.

DOSING

For those people who have thinning hair or lackluster, aging skin and want a more youthful appearance, I recommend taking 5 milligrams (mg) daily of choline-stabilized *orthosilicic acid*, which is biologically active and much better absorbed than silicon derived from herbal sources. It is available in liquid and capsule form. If you have severe osteoporosis or osteoarthritis or brittle nails or hair, consider taking 10 mg daily. If your body takes in more silicon than it needs, you excrete the excess (so taking in more than you need at these doses is not a problem).

Brands to try: JarroSil by Jarrow Formulas (310-204-6936, *www.jarrow.com*) and Xymogen's RegeneMax (800-647-6100, *www.xymogen.com*, available through health-care professionals).

There are no side effects, and silicon is safe to take with other medications. Silicon supplements should be avoided by people with chronic kidney disease (excess silicon could result in further kidney damage) and women who are pregnant.

What Your Hair Says About Your Health

Stefan Kuprowsky, ND, a professor at the Boucher Institute of Naturopathic Medicine in New Westminster, British Columbia, Canada, and a private practitioner with the Vancouver Naturopathic Clinic in Vancouver, British Columbia. He is a board member and chairman of the Quality Assurance Committee of the College of Naturopathic Physicians of BC. *www. vancouvernaturopathicclinic.com.*

A series of bad hair days usually signals nothing more serious than a lousy haircut or inappropriate styling product.

But: Sometimes troubles with tresses suggest an underlying health problem, according to Stefan Kuprowsky, ND, a professor at the Boucher Institute of Naturopathic Medicine in Canada—and a new stylist or styling technique won't help when the real reason for your hair problem lies inside your body.

Dr. Kuprowsky said, "When the 100,000 or so hairs on your head are unhealthy, chances are that you are unhealthy, too. That's why it is important to include hair problems in your discussions with your doctor as part of an overall assessment of your health." Here's what you need to know if you have...

• **Thinning hair.** An adult woman typically loses up to about 100 hairs a day, Dr. Kuprowsky said, and it is normal for this number to go up with age. Even so, no matter what your age, you should tell your doctor if there seem to be more hairs than usual in your shower drain, if your hairstyle feels skimpier than it used to or if your scalp becomes more visible—because there may be an underlying medical cause.

Possible conditions your doctor may investigate include thyroid problems...an autoimmune disorder...low iron stores in the body...starting or discontinuing birth control pills or hormone therapy...or use of certain medications, such as beta-blockers, the blood thinner *warfarin* or nonsteroidal anti-inflammatory drugs. Treating the underlying cause or switching medications often halts or reduces hair loss.

Also: With a condition called *telogen effluvium*, a sudden severe stress or shock (for instance, from a serious illness, major surgery or childbirth) triggers hair loss that begins a few weeks after the event. Fortunately, hair usually starts to grow back after about six months.

• **Bald patches.** When clumps of hair fall out and leave bald patches, the condition is called *alopecia areata*. Often, women who experience this have a family history of the problem. An autoimmune disorder may be to blame. In most women, hair grows back on its own. In some cases, the condition later recurs...minimizing stress may reduce this risk.

• **Hair breakage.** This could signal a protein deficiency. Possible causes for such a deficiency include a strict vegan diet...impaired ability to properly digest and absorb proteins and other nutrients...or low levels of stomach acid (as can occur when taking antacid medication for heartburn). Your doctor can assess your diet and medication use and order blood work and other tests to help pinpoint the problem, Dr. Kuprowsky said.

• **Dry hair.** This suggests a dietary deficiency of omega-3 essential fatty acids.

Recommended: Boost your omega-3 intake by eating more oily fish, walnuts and flaxseeds and/or by taking fish oil supplements.

• **Flaking, itchy scalp.** This can signal an allergic reaction to hair products, so if you recently tried a new shampoo, gel or other product, stop using it and see if the flakes go away. If you also have a painful and/or inflamed scalp, see your doctor—this may signal a severe allergic reaction or chronic inflammatory condition (such as *seborrheia dermatitis*) that could result in hair loss.

Another possible cause for flaking is a topical yeast imbalance on the scalp, which also may be accompanied by an internal yeast imbalance in the digestive tract. This often is triggered by oral antibiotic use. According to Dr. Kuprowsky, additional possible symptoms of a yeast imbalance include excessive sugar cravings, gas, bloating, skin rashes and fatigue. To restore balance, ask your doctor about taking daily supplements of live probiotics, *caprylic acid* or grapefruit seed extract.

If these natural yeast inhibitors aren't strong enough, the antifungal medication *nystatin*, for oral or topical use, is an option.

Topical help: Use an antifungal shampoo containing selenium sulfide, such as Selsun Blue.

• **Very oily hair.** If your hair "gloms" together and you need to shampoo frequently, you might be ingesting too much saturated fat (found in meat and dairy products) or trans fat (found in many processed foods). These fats not only are unhealthy for your heart, but they also tend to make hair greasy, Dr. Kuprowsky said.

His recommendation: Cut back on saturated and trans fats, focusing instead on foods with healthful unsaturated fats, such as olive oil, flaxseed oil and hemp seed oil. Your hair (and your heart) will be better for it.

Best Mascara for Contact Lens Wearers

Robert Abel, Jr., MD, an ophthalmologist with Delaware Ophthalmology Consultants in Wilmington, founder of *www.eyeadvisory.com* and author of *The Eye Care Revolution and Lethal Hindsight* (Xlibris).

Soft contact lenses are about 50% water and designed to be permeable—their surface is basically a very fine mesh—so any material that is water-soluble can get lodged in the fabric of the lenses and cause irritation. For this reason, water-resistant mascaras are most appropriate for contact wearers because they are made of materials that are less likely to flake and permeate the mesh. To further minimize potentially irritating flaking, apply your mascara before you insert your contacts (if you can see well enough to do so)…and take the lenses out before you remove your mascara. Wearing mascara and contacts simultaneously also brings a small risk for infection of the eye, since the contact lenses and the mascara wand can harbor harmful bacteria. To minimize this risk, clean the wand at least once a month by washing with baby shampoo (and rinsing

afterward)…and replace your mascara every three months whether or not it's used up.

Helpful: Blinc, a type of water-resistant mascara, forms tiny tubes around each eyelash, minimizing flaking and irritation for contact lens wearers.

Cost: $25 (877-454-7763, *www.blincinc.com*).

The Secret to Keeping Spider Veins Away

Karen Burke, MD, PhD, assistant clinical professor of dermatology and a research scientist at Mount Sinai Medical Center in New York City. She has a private practice for dermatology and dermatologic surgery, also in New York City. Dr. Burke is the author of several books, including *Thin Thighs* (Hamlyn).

Nobody wants to see spider veins—those tiny, twisty, red or blue blood vessels—spring up on her legs or face…or anywhere else, for that matter.

To the rescue: *Rutin*, an antioxidant flavonoid naturally found in buckwheat, citrus fruits, apple peels and black tea. According to Mount Sinai Medical Center dermatologist Karen Burke, MD, PhD, supplementing with 500 milligrams (mg) of rutin daily (continuing indefinitely) helps prevent spider veins, possibly by reducing inflammation.

Taking rutin won't get rid of existing spider veins—for that, you'll need treatment from a dermatologist (for instance, injections of a sclerosing solution to close the blood vessels, making them fade away). However, the supplements can lower your risk for recurrence once spider veins have been treated. Rutin supplements are sold over the counter in health-food stores and online. Having recommended rutin to hundreds of adult patients over more than 15 years, Dr. Burke has had no reports of allergic reaction or adverse side effects.

Additional prevention strategy: Heat promotes spider vein formation—so avoid sitting with your legs near a radiator or fireplace. If you want to soak in a hot bath or Jacuzzi, put your legs up on the edge of the tub, out of the water.

Running and Cycling May Worsen Varicose Veins

Strenuous exercise that puts pressure on the legs may make varicose veins more noticeable.

Better: Low-impact, moderate exercise, such as swimming and walking, can ease symptoms by stimulating circulation without increasing pressure. Consult your physician.

University of California, Berkeley Wellness Letter, 500 Fifth Ave., New York City 10110.

Rash on Your Ring Finger?

Wedding-ring dermatitis can cause red, scaly welts on the ring finger, underneath a person's wedding band. It can be caused by moisture and soap trapped under the ring—or by an allergy to nickel, which is usually present in small amounts even in costly rings made of gold, silver or platinum. You can develop a rash even after wearing a ring for years because its protective coating wore away and the nickel has come to the surface.

Self-defense: Stop wearing the wedding ring until the rash heals—one to two weeks. A hydrocortisone cream, such as Cortaid, may help. If you start wearing the ring again and the rash reappears, see a dermatologist to get an allergy test to determine if the rash is caused by a reaction to nickel. You may need to have the ring recoated or buy a new one.

Jeffrey Benabio, MD, dermatologist, Kaiser Permanente, San Diego.

Discharge? What's Normal, What's Not

Cherie A. LeFevre, MD, is an associate professor of gynecology and director of the Vulvar and Vaginal Disorders Specialty Center at St. Louis University School of Medicine.

Have you ever sat on the toilet, peeked at your panties and said, "Yuck"? Join the club—because vaginal discharge is a fact of life for most women.

Still, it's not always easy to tell what's normal and what's not. "Being aware that 'normal' can change with age and other factors helps prevent unnecessary anxiety when everything's fine…and alerts you to the need for medical attention when there's a problem," said Cherie A. LeFevre, MD, director of the Vulvar and Vaginal Disorders Specialty Center at St. Louis University School of Medicine. *Here's what you need to know…*

WHEN NOT TO WORRY

Vaginal discharge—a combination of fluid, cervical mucus and cells from the vaginal walls—helps keeps the vagina healthy as new cells replace old ones that are shed.

Typically, discharge has a creamy texture and yellow-white hue. You probably know that discharge tends to get more abundant and slippery when you're sexually aroused and thinner and more scant after menopause.

But: You may not realize that vaginal discharge can change and yet be no cause for concern when you…

• Take certain antibiotics that can make discharge thinner.

• Experience emotional stress, which can increase discharge.

• Use hormone replacement therapy, which increases vaginal secretions.

• Wear silk or nylon underpants or tight-fitting pants, which restrict airflow and increase sweating and other secretions in the genital area.

If you are bothered by your normal abundant discharge: Two or three times a day, wash your genital area with unscented soap, pat dry and put on fresh underwear. This won't reduce discharge, but it will make it less annoying. Dr. LeFevre cautioned, "Do not try to deal with discharge by douching, wearing panty liners (even unscented ones) or using feminine hygiene spray. These can cause irritation, encourage bacterial growth and increase discharge."

If you are bothered by scant discharge: To relieve postmenopausal vaginal dryness that causes itching and makes sex uncomfortable, rub a dab of olive oil or other natural vegetable oil product in and around the vagina twice daily and before intercourse. Dr. LeFevre explained, "This won't cause irritation the way over-the-counter vaginal moisturizing products sometimes can."

WHEN TO SEE YOUR DOCTOR

Of course you would contact your doctor if you had obvious signs of vaginal trouble, such as truly foul-smelling discharge, itching, burning or pain. But by staying alert to more subtle signs of trouble, you can catch a developing problem before it has time to progress. Watch for changes in the discharge's odor (such as a fishy or yeasty smell)...color (greenish or grayish)...and consistency (very thick, frothy or cottage cheese-like). *If any such symptoms start to appear, call your doctor. You may need to be tested and treated for...*

• **Bacterial vaginosis,** an infection that develops when the vaginal environment becomes too alkaline, allowing bacteria to thrive.

Treatment: Oral or topical antibiotics.

• **Yeast infection,** an overgrowth of the candida fungus that is a normal part of the vaginal environment.

Note: Some women are more prone to yeast infections when taking antibiotics.

Treatment: Nonprescription topical or prescription oral antifungal medication. Taking a daily oral probiotic supplement also may help treat or prevent vaginal yeast infections.

• **Trichomoniasis,** a sexually transmitted disease caused by a single-celled parasite that burrows under the vaginal lining.

Treatment: Antibiotics for you and your sex partner—so he doesn't reinfect you.

Could Those Bumps Be Genital Warts?

Shobha S. Krishnan, MD, a family physician and gynecologist at Barnard Health Services at Columbia University in New York City. She is founder and president of the Global Initiative Against HPV and Cervical Cancer and author of the award-winning book *The HPV Vaccine Controversy: Sex, Cancer, God and Politics* (Praeger). *www.thehpvbook.com.*

Have you ever had genital warts? If so —whether or not you noticed them or knew what they were—there's a good chance that they will return.

Genital warts are caused by the human papillomavirus (HPV)—primarily by two HPV strains called type 6 and type 11, according to Shobha S. Krishnan, MD, author of *The HPV Vaccine Controversy*. There are actually more than 100 different strains of HPV, several of which cause cervical cancer—but the strains that cause warts are not the same as those linked to cancer.

The virus is transmitted primarily via sexual contact or skin-to-skin contact...and this can occur even when the infected partner has no sign of warts. Dr. Krishnan explained that risk of contagion is elevated among people who have multiple sex partners, unprotected sex or impaired immunity (for instance, due to stress, cigarette smoking, poor eating habits, lack of sleep or chronic illness). Typically warts appear six weeks to nine months after sexual contact with an infected partner, but it can take much longer—so you may not know exactly when you got infected or by whom.

• **Recognizing the symptoms.** Typically genital warts are small, soft, fleshy bumps or groups of bumps in the genital area. In some cases, they are painless, tiny, few in number and easily overlooked. In other cases, they are quite clearly visible and/or cause noticeable irritation, itching or bleeding. Genital warts can appear on a woman's vulva (external genitals), vaginal walls and cervix...on a man's penis and scrotum...and, in either gender, on or near the anus and in the mouth or throat from oral sex.

If you suspect that you have genital warts, see your doctor. Diagnosis is based on a visual examination. Two-thirds of patients diagnosed with genital warts are women.

•**To treat or not to treat?** In up to 30% of cases, genital warts go away on their own without treatment, typically within four months—so talk to your doctor about whether a wait-and-see approach is appropriate for you. According to Dr. Krishnan, the decision about whether or not to treat genital warts is best made on a case-by-case basis after discussion between a patient and her doctor.

Note: Even when warts do go away without treatment, there is no test that can reveal whether the immune system has completely gotten rid of the virus or whether the virus is still lying dormant in the body.

•**Treatment options.** Many people choose to treat genital warts, especially if the growths are increasing in size or number and/or causing physical discomfort or emotional distress. But it is important to realize that, while treatment can get rid of the existing warts, it does not get rid of the virus itself—so warts may and often do reappear. It is not known whether treating the warts reduces the risk of passing the virus on to a sex partner.

The choice of treatment depends in part on the number, size and location of the warts. Talk to your doctor about the pros and cons of various therapies. According to Dr. Krishnan, options include a botanical ointment made from green tea extract which has antiviral properties…topical antiviral medication, such as *podofilox* (Condylox)…or in-office procedures such as cryotherapy (freezing) or laser therapy.

•**Prevention strategies.** Unless you are celibate or in a mutually monogamous relationship with an uninfected person, it is best to use condoms consistently to reduce (but not eliminate) your risk for HPV contagion. Also, Dr. Krishnan recommended talking to your doctor about the benefits and risks of the Gardasil vaccine, which protects against HPV types 6 and 11 (as well as two other HPV strains linked to cervical cancer). Gardasil is FDA-approved for females and males age nine to 26, but it can be given to older women and men.

8

Beat the Blues & Revitalize

How to Design Your Perfect Retirement

People nearing or in retirement can benefit from a personal mission statement to "redesign" a period of life that often lasts decades. Retirement does not come with instructions—you must write your own training manual.

The best part of retirement is having control over your time and the freedom to pursue your interests. But you need to devote time and deep thought to figure out what you want now, where you are going and how you will get there. A well-crafted statement can help you develop a plan that will unify your identity, life's purpose and core values. As a retired physician and volunteer at the small-business counseling agency SCORE, I see many people flounder in retirement. That's why a personal mission statement is so important at this stage of life. It will provide the needed structure and strategies to get you where you want to go.

FIVE KEYS TO A HAPPY RETIREMENT

Personal mission statements are just that—personal. Yours will not look like mine or anyone else's. *However, your statement should address the following five keys to a happy retirement...*

• **Health.** Your number-one priority should be a commitment to a healthful lifestyle. Without it, your retirement plans will be foiled. In preparing your mission statement, include strategies to promote regular exercise, a more healthful diet and quitting bad habits, such as smoking or drinking too much.

• **Giving back.** Ponder ways to share your intellectual, social and economic capital with others. This could mean becoming a coach or mentor to younger people.

Richard G. Wendel, MD, MBA, Cincinnati-based author of *Retire With a Mission: Planning and Purpose for the Second Half of Life* (Sourcebook). Dr. Wendel is a retired urologist with a business background who volunteers at SCORE, Counselors to America's Small Business, *www.score.org*.

174

Inheritance issues should also be thought through and included in your mission statement. Many retirees do not give sufficient thought to a fair distribution of family assets, keepsakes and heirlooms. Lack of clear instructions may create discord and hurt feelings among heirs.

• **Renewing family life.** One of the windfalls of retirement is time available to strengthen family ties. Consider ways to reach out to children and grandchildren, settle old arguments with siblings or aged parents and renew ties with your extended family. You might organize a reunion, dig into genealogy or look up long-lost first cousins.

• **Personal interests.** How often have you said, "I'd like to study guitar or take up woodworking or go to cooking school, but I just don't have the time"? Well, in retirement, you do. A side benefit of cultivating new interests is a growing circle of friends. One of the most positive predictors of a satisfying retirement is a large social network.

• **Finances.** Money will provide the options and flexibility to carry out your plans, so include a financial strategy in your mission statement.

Best: Consult a financial planner, tax adviser or other qualified professional to be sure that your resources are adequate and to develop strategies for a financially secure retirement.

HOW TO GET STARTED

To write an effective document, you'll need to set aside enough time to sit down and think deeply as you write the bulk of your statement. Naturally, you will add to it and revise it over time as more ideas occur to you…and show all or parts of your statement to some of your family and friends to get their insights. *Start by answering these questions…*

• **How do I stay healthy and active?**

• **How can I share my experience with others?**

• **How will my family relationships change?**

• **Which new and old friendships do I wish to nurture?**

• **Which new social and athletic activities might I like?**

• **What do I want to leave to my heirs and charity?**

• **Do I want to work part-time?**

Your mission statement may be just a few succinct paragraphs or it may run to several pages. Just be sure to address your goals, objectives, values and a vision of where you want to be in three to five years. *Some examples to get you started…*

• **Mission…**

• Help my daughter, a single mother, raise her three small children.

• Share my financial-planning expertise by teaching a personal-finance class at the local community college.

• Explore my creative side by signing up for evening painting classes.

• Develop a healthful eating plan by consulting a nutritionist.

• Become more active in my place of worship.

• **Vision…**

• In three to five years, move to Vermont and make new friends.

• Grow my new e-commerce business by 50%.

• Have an established, part-time consulting practice.

• **Values…**

• Always be guided by caring and giving, not jealousy or intolerance.

• Focus on my spiritual life. Practice the habit of gratitude, giving thanks daily for the good things in my life.

• Acknowledge that the human body is my most valuable possession and vow to become the primary caretaker, focusing on a healthful lifestyle.

• **Identity…**

• Replace the accolades earned at work with pride in personal development.

• Feel proud of my primary career but excited about new ventures ahead. Enjoy new roles as caregiver, nurturer and homemaker.

• Rejoice in the new freedom of retirement.

NOW PUT IT IN ACTION

A well-tailored mission statement may take months or even a few years to evolve. Corporations consider this a living document and so should you. You might tape it above your desk for daily reflection or put it in a drawer for an occasional fresh look. Either way, a personal mission statement will be an indispensable tool in helping you pursue your passions in this new phase of life.

Paradise or Purgatory? Is a Retirement Community Right for You?

Andrew D. Blechman, an award-winning investigative newspaper reporter and feature writer based in Berkshire County, Massachusetts, who made numerous trips around the country to research this rapidly expanding retirement lifestyle. He is author of *Leisureville: Adventures in America's Retirement Utopias* (Atlantic Monthly).

Americans have retired in droves to age-restricted communities ever since six model homes opened in Sun City, Arizona, in 1960—the first such development in the world. Today, as Sun City celebrates its 50th-anniversary with more than 40,000 inhabitants, some 1,500 "leisure retirement communities" have become a way of life for nearly 12 million people.

While age-restricted communities tend to cluster in sunny states, they're proliferating everywhere. You may be surprised to learn that 60% of new retirement communities are being built in the North. Massachusetts, where I live, contains 150, with about 200 more proposed.

The largest age-restricted (and gated) retirement community in the world is The Villages in central Florida. One-and-one-half times the square mileage of Manhattan and currently housing 70,000, this flock of "villages" lured former neighbors of mine, the Andersons, several years ago. In a one-month stay at The Villages, two weeks of which were spent at their new home, I did my preliminary research for *Leisureville: Adventures in America's Retirement Utopias*, a study of retirement communities around the country.

My goal: To understand the appeal of a unique way of living that has been luring our elders away.

INDEPENDENCE AND COMMUNITY

The most prominent type of retirement community, and the one I studied for my book, focuses on recreation. The amenities are plentiful, with little waiting for a tennis court or tee time...and a constant influx of new residents that encourages bonding and creates instant community.

Grown children feel relieved that Mom and Dad are busy and happy. Some communities contain continuing-care facilities for residents who become unable to care for themselves.

While these communities vary widely, they share attributes that say "paradise" to some—and "purgatory" to others.

A CERTAIN AGE

Designed for those who prefer a child-free environment, retirement communities address the needs and desires of the older set. Minimum age requirements—usually age 55—are strictly enforced. At least one member of each household must be the minimum age or older. (Filling the house with unrelated roommates is not allowed.) Guests, including relatives, under age 18 or 19 may visit for only a predetermined number of days per year.

Pros: Residents relish the novelty of having their needs treated as a top priority. A child-free environment ensures more peace and quiet than ordinary neighborhoods provide. Seniors feel safe surrounded by age peers.

Cons: Grandchildren's visits are limited. They can never move in, whatever the family situation. People who enjoy mingling with others of all types and ages might find the setting too limiting.

RECREATION 24/7, INCLUDING SEX

Golf, tennis, swimming, Bingo, dances and hobby groups dominate daily activities in leisure-oriented communities. An active singles scene includes the never married, the divorced, the previously widowed and those widowed after moving in. A relaxed social atmosphere with no work responsibilities tends to encourage sexual freedom. I have observed that a good number of older gentlemen, and some women, regularly seek and find sex partners.

Pros: Life can be all play—a common retirement fantasy. Tennis courts, swimming pools and gyms aren't overrun by the young. Recreational facilities are designed for less-than-perfect eyesight and physiques.

Cons: People who are less focused on sports and hobbies may feel alienated, as may retirees who derive significant pleasure from high culture—opera, theater, classical music, a superb public library. Widows and widowers who haven't dated in 50 years and who dismiss the use of condoms as solely for contraception are unaware that sexually transmitted infections, including herpes, syphilis and AIDS, have infiltrated the senior singles scene.

LOTS OF RULES

Home owners must respect many rules ("deed restrictions").

Examples: Exterior paint colors and even the height of shrubs may be prescribed…pets limited to two…lawn ornaments and window air conditioners banned.

Pros: Modern amenities, including plenty of bathrooms and closets. Homes designed with few stairs and universal accessibility.

Deed restrictions ensure that neighborhoods remain clean and neat. Many home owners consider mandatory conformity a small price to pay for knowing that they'll never see their neighbors' car on blocks, swing sets in the yard or gnomes on the lawn.

Cons: Each community's success hinges on perpetual investment and care by the managing owner. You may never know whether the developer is about to declare bankruptcy, as some have, leaving behind partially completed, thinly populated "communities" with houses that will probably become increasingly difficult to sell.

PRIVATE OWNERSHIP

The communal areas of most recreational retirement communities—the golf courses, the downtown, the streets—as well as the empty lots and unsold houses are owned by their builders (or whomever the builders sell them

to). Special zoning arrangements (these communities bring in lots of tax revenue for local jurisdictions) may permit community rules to sidestep state and county laws in many aspects of life.

Pros: Many residents, delighted with their low per-home property taxes, feel confident that the owners have a personal stake in meeting community needs.

Cons: Residents trade the ballot box for the suggestion box. Residents with a gripe plead their cases before a corporate board, not elected officials. Don't look in the local paper or at public meetings for discussions of serious issues.

Expect to live under a form of "taxation without representation." Through steadily increasing maintenance fees, the owners can charge residents for, say, new golf courses and recreation centers.

ADVICE FOR POTENTIAL BUYERS

If age-restricted retirement community living attracts you, visit several, staying for a while if you can arrange it. I learned far more during my four weeks with the Andersons than any official tour could have shown.

Generally, these communities have wonderful recreational amenities. But is the intellectual spark bright enough for you? Can you find a group that reads the kinds of books you like? *Other questions to consider…*

•**Where do you want to be in 20 years?** How would you feel about being far from your family and old friends later in life?

•**Can you imagine aging happily there?** Might you "age in place" instead, perhaps having your current home retrofitted?

•**Will your house purchase be a good investment, bringing decent value if you sell?**

Working After Retirement Protects Against Sickness

Postretirement work helps guard against illness.

Recent finding: Researchers who interviewed 12,189 adults found that those who took "bridge jobs"—full-time, part-time or self-employment—after official retirement had fewer major diseases (such as diabetes, cancer and arthritis) and performed better at daily tasks than those who stopped working.

Theory: The increased physical and mental activity—as well as social interaction—required for working protects against chronic illness and functional decline.

Yujie Zhan, researcher, department of psychology, University of Maryland, College Park.

Before You Buy a Retirement Home

Before buying a home in a retirement community, ask if you can stay over one or two nights. A short stay will give you a better idea of how it would be to live in the community and whether the facilities meet your needs. Many adult communities now are letting potential home buyers stay two or three nights for as little as $99 per night.

AARP Bulletin, 601 E St. NW, Washington, DC 20049.

New Approaches to Elderly Depression

George S. Alexopoulos, MD, founder and director, Weill Cornell Institute of Geriatric Psychiatry, NewYork-Presbyterian/Weill Cornell Medical College, Westchester Division, and director, NIMH-supported Advanced Center for Interventions and Services Research (ACISR) in Late-Life Depression, White Plains, New York.

Medical advances that help people live long lives are not really "advances" if those extra years are miserable ones. Depression is a problem among America's elderly and awareness of this condition is an important first step to greater understanding and better treatments, so life not only lasts longer, but is also happier and more rewarding up until the very end.

George Alexopoulos, MD, founder and director of Weill Cornell's Institute of Geriatric Psychiatry at New York-Presbyterian/Westchester, discusses new directions for research and how elderly patients with depression can be helped now.

BRIGHTER DAYS ARE HERE

Among recent developments that provide hope for senior citizens suffering from depression…

• **New approaches in psychotherapy can be tailored to provide what elderly patients need most.** According to Dr. Alexopoulos, that means specifically helping them to address and find solutions for their new mental and/or physical limitations. For instance, effective therapy for an elderly patient may focus less on personal growth or relationship issues and more on achieving a better understanding of their nutritional needs so they'll eat better, which will improve mood and energy level. And they may need to explore other ways to adjust their living circumstances so that they can feel better emotionally and physically.

• **It's now known that inadequate blood supply to the brain can cause chemical changes associated with depression**—and doctors can use modern brain imaging techniques to identify specific regions where this is occurring. They can then utilize corrective treatment if blood flow is found to be blocked or insufficient among elderly patients when they first show signs of depression.

• **Doctors have gotten better at fine-tuning medications for their elderly patients**—for example, it's now known that elderly patients do better with certain antidepressants (such as sertraline, citalopram and esctitalopram) that aren't as likely to interact dangerously with other medications.

According to Dr. Alexopoulos, the goal is to help elderly patients with depression to take an honest look at what they used to be able to do that they can no longer do…explore how they feel about these limitations…and then to learn better ways to work around them, with the ultimate goal of finding a way to accept them. If you or someone you love faces this problem and these new approaches aren't being incorporated into treatment, bring this article along to your next appointment and ask to discuss whether they can be. These are heartening steps in the right direction toward a brighter future…the hope is that we can all, indeed, look forward to living long and happy lives.

One Step at Time

Robert Maurer, PhD, associate clinical professor of clinical psychology at David Geffen School of Medicine at the University of California, Los Angeles. He is author of *One Small Step Can Change Your Life* (Workman). *www.scienceofexcellence.com.*

Contemplating big changes triggers feelings of fear, and that fear prods the *amygdala*—the primitive fight-or-flight part of the brain—into action. The amygdala does not weigh the benefits of bold changes or consider how these changes could be accomplished—it simply interprets our fear as evidence that we face danger and encourages us to either run away or resist.

If we can prevent the amygdala from taking charge, we greatly improve our odds of implementing major changes. *The best way to do this is in small, incremental steps…*

TINY STEPS

Small steps feel insignificant and carry little risk of catastrophic failure, so we don't feel fear…the amygdala does not sense danger…and our fight-or-flight response is not triggered.

Taking small, incremental steps rather than bold leaps also helps train the brain to view change as normal. Major changes feel unnatural and difficult in part because they're uncommon. Make incremental changes each day, and change feels comfortable.

In some instances, small steps might be all that's needed. We tend to think that important changes require bold action, but seemingly minor changes can have a greater-than-expected impact.

Here's how to put the power of small steps to work…

TO START EXERCISING

Your mind and your body are likely to rebel if you shift quickly from inactivity to a rigorous exercise program. And you don't need to. The Mayo Clinic studied thin and overweight people. They found that thin, fit people often did not go to the gym. They simply moved more during the day—they took stairs, paced in their offices, etc. This resulted in burning 300 to 350 calories per day more than sedentary people—which resulted in a 30-to-40-pound difference in weight per year.

Instead of a rigorous exercise program, start with one that's so quick and easy that your mind and body have no cause to resist. *Small-step strategies…*

• **Walk one block and back.** Add one house to the distance each day.

• **Next time you watch TV, stand up and walk around the room for a single 30-second commercial.** The following day, stand and walk for an entire commercial break. Continue slowly expanding your walk time until you're walking during every commercial.

• **Stand on your treadmill for a few minutes each morning while you read the newspaper.** After a few days, turn the treadmill on, and walk for a minute or two. Then add a minute or two more every week.

TO MANAGE STRESS

Traditional stress-reduction techniques, such as meditation, feel unnatural to many people. Some people actually become more stressed when they try to meditate because they feel that they are wasting time. These people would be better off using smaller, quicker stress-reduction strategies. *Small-step strategies…*

• **Try to speak more slowly for a few minutes.**

• **Consider which part of your body is "holding stress"**—it often is the neck, the lower back or the shoulders. Focus on that body part, then take one deep breath. Thinking about the body forces the mind to stop obsessing over problems and pressures for a moment.

• **When you are working, schedule three-minute breaks every 90 to 120 minutes.** Working nonstop for longer than this increases stress and reduces productivity.

TO CLEAN YOUR HOUSE

Cleaning a house can seem overwhelming. To get past this, tackle the task in stages so small that they don't seem daunting and don't deprive you of doing something you enjoy. *Small-step strategy…*

• **Select a five-minute segment of your day that you could spend cleaning without giving up an activity you enjoy.** Pick a single part of the house, set a timer for five minutes and stop cleaning the instant the time is up.

After a month or two of quick-and-easy short-burst cleaning, the idea of cleaning should no longer conjure up such deeply negative associations in your mind, making extended cleaning sessions more tolerable. In the meantime, five minutes of cleaning each day usually can keep a home clean.

TO GET MORE SLEEP

If you try to go to bed an hour earlier than usual, you'll either think of things that need to get done and skip this earlier bedtime…or you'll go to bed but be unable to fall asleep. Instead, let your mind adjust gradually to a new sleep schedule. *Small-step strategy…*

• **Go to bed one minute earlier than usual.** Then move your bedtime an additional minute earlier each day until you wake rested. This might not take as long as you think—researchers have found that even a few minutes of extra sleep per night can make a difference.

TO REDUCE SPENDING

Unless your financial problems are so pressing that drastic change is necessary, spend a month training your brain to search for small savings before attempting big ones. This reduces the odds that the mind will rebel against the economizing. *Small-step strategies…*

• **Remove one item from your shopping cart before checking out.**

• **Set a goal of trimming $1 from your budget each day.**

• **Allow yourself your favorite daily indulgence, but purchase it in a smaller size or split it with a friend.**

• **Try the store brand of one brand-name item you usually buy.**

Set Aside Worry Time

Relieve anxiety by setting aside "worry time." During the worry time, confront an issue that is weighing on your mind and think of a constructive action you can take to improve the situation. Even if you can't resolve the problem, you'll likely feel better for having confronted it and done something about it.

University of California *Berkeley Wellness Letter*, 500 Fifth Ave., New York City 10110. *www.wellnessletter.com.*

Seeing a Shrink For the First Time?

If you are going to a psychiatrist for the first time, here's what to expect. Be ready for a thorough review of your previous history—medical and emotional as well as psychiatric—before discussing your current issues and concerns. Try to be as open, unguarded and as complete as you can. Bring as many medical records as possible. Have a list of all medicines you currently take, plus those you have taken in the past—especially psychiatric medicines—and include notes on what worked and what did not. Be prepared to discuss social, family, educational and work history…living situation…marital and sexual history…and any risky behaviors, from unprotected sex to failure to use a seat belt.

Richard O'Brien, MD, spokesperson for the American College of Emergency Physicians and clinical instructor, Temple University School of Medicine, Philadelphia.

The Very Best Stress-Fighting Foods

Susan Mitchell, PhD, RD, a registered dietitian based in Winter Park, Florida. She has coauthored three books, including *Fat Is Not Your Fate* (Simon & Schuster), and hosts a nutrition and health podcast on WDBO.com.

Powerhouse foods, such as salmon (with its heart-protective omega-3s) and spinach (with its cancer-fighting flavonoids), win lots of praise for their ability to help fight diseases.

Few people realize, however, that these foods—and some others—also help reduce and protect against the harmful effects that ongoing stress can have on the body, be it from a chronic illness or a hectic work schedule. By consuming a variety of foods that work synergistically, you can help prevent many of the negative effects of stress.

Powerful stress-fighting foods…

• **Black-eyed peas.** These are an excellent source of folate, a B vitamin crucial to fighting stress.

My advice: Eat one-half cup daily of black-eyed peas (or other folate-rich legumes, such as chickpeas, red beans, black beans or lentils).

Also good: Try one ounce of sunflower seeds (toasted kernels) or one-half cup to one cup of cooked broccoli daily.

• **Mangoes.** Antioxidants, such as vitamin C, help repair the damage that occurs to our cells when we are under stress. Oranges are one option, but mangoes may be an even better choice because they not only contain vitamin C but also disease-fighting carotenoids, including beta-carotene and vitamin E.

My advice: Enjoy mango at least once a week when in season. Because frozen fruit is picked at the height of the season and promptly frozen, it is a great substitute if fresh fruit is not available. Mango can be cubed and eaten alone or tossed in a mixed fruit salad. Use frozen mango in smoothies or chopped mango in salsa.

If you don't like mangoes (or you are allergic): Try other vitamin C sources, such as kiwi (two small fruits daily)…or cranberry, orange, blueberry, pomegranate or grape juice (six to eight ounces of 100% juice daily).

• **Nuts.** Almonds, pistachios and walnuts are rich in vitamin E, another antioxidant that helps curb stress-induced cell damage.

My advice: Eat a handful (one ounce) of almonds, pistachios or walnuts daily or every other day. Be sure to keep the portions small—nuts are relatively high in calories. If you have high blood pressure, choose nuts that are unsalted or low in sodium.

If you don't like nuts (or you are allergic): Try avocado. One or two thin slices daily (or one-quarter cup cubed) has the same beneficial fats found in nuts plus potassium, a mineral that has been shown to help lower elevated blood pressure.

• **Sweet potatoes.** These creamy, almost dessertlike root vegetables are brimming with antioxidant carotenoids, such as beta-carotene. In addition, sweet potatoes provide vitamin C, potassium and an appreciable amount of fiber (five to six grams for a medium potato), which contributes to the widely recommended 25- to 30-gram-per-day goal.

If you don't like sweet potatoes (or you are allergic): Eat carrots (one-half cup daily)…cantaloupe (one-quarter cup daily)…apricots (three to five dried or one fresh daily)…or acorn squash (one-half squash daily).

• **Yogurt or kefir.** Stress can lead to elevated levels of the stress hormone cortisol, which, in turn, wears down the immune system. Although it's not widely known, a significant amount of immune system activity takes place in the gastrointestinal tract.

When a person is under chronic stress, he/she is more susceptible to infections and, as a result, may take an antibiotic. These drugs destroy not only the harmful bacteria that are making you sick, but also the "good" bacteria in your gut.

By consuming yogurt or kefir (a tangy, yogurtlike drink), you can replace those healthful bacteria, which are key to maintaining a vital immune system.

My advice: Add one serving a day (a single-serving container of yogurt or a cup of kefir) to your diet. Choose a yogurt or kefir product that says "live and active cultures" on the label—and be sure that it contains the following strains of healthful bacteria—Lactobacillus casei…and/or Lactobacillus acidophilus. If you're taking an antibiotic, look for S. boulardii or Lactobacillus GG—these strains are most effective in people who take these medications.

Good news: Many people who are lactose-intolerant are able to consume yogurt and/or kefir. Start with only one-quarter cup of yogurt or kefir once or twice a week and slowly increase the amount as your body adjusts. Naturally fermented foods, such as sauerkraut, also contain healthful bacteria—try one-half cup serving daily.

Here's How to Get Your Vitality Back…and Feel Great Again

Frank Lipman, MD, founder and director of the Eleven Eleven Wellness Center, a healing center in New York City that combines Western and alternative medicine. He is coauthor of *Spent: End Exhaustion and Feel Great Again* (Fireside). *www.spentmd.com.*

Modern life depletes the energy of many of us. If you are exhausted, overwhelmed by your life and feeling older than your years, then you know what I'm talking about.

I grew up in South Africa and went to medical school there. The first patients I treated were in an impoverished rural area that had no electricity. These people had their share of poverty-related diseases but had no symptoms of insomnia, depression, anxiety or the stress-related indigestion, headaches, back pain or fatigue that I see in so many of my patients in the US now.

Reason: They lived according to the rhythms of nature—going to sleep when the sun went down, eating natural foods and entertaining themselves with community music and dance.

People in our modern society live in exactly the opposite way—disconnected from the natural rhythms of the days and seasons, over-loaded with stress, eating processed foods, not getting enough exercise and exposed to artificial light well into the night before trying to fall asleep.

Result: The body's hormones get thrown off kilter, leading to tension and fatigue—the condition I call "spent."

To counter this syndrome, I've devised a program to remove these modern-day stresses from your life and put your body back in sync with its natural rhythms. *To help you revitalize your energy…*

DON'T EAT REFINED SUGAR

Removing all refined sugar and artificial sweeteners from your diet is essential to feeling your best. Sugar makes blood sugar shoot up and then quickly drop as the body produces insulin to process it. This crash causes the adrenal glands to produce the stress hormone cortisol, which is linked to weight gain and chronic inflammation.

Refined sugar (or added sugar) is listed on food labels in many ways, including as cane or brown sugar…date, beet or grape sugar… fructose, sucrose, glucose, maltose or corn syrup…fruit juice concentrate…barley malt, caramel, carob or sorghum syrup.

To make it easier to remove added sugar from your diet, drink lots of water (add mint or lemon to make it more palatable). Often, sugar craving is actually hunger, and drinking water helps you feel full. Replace sugary foods and drinks with a smoothie (see pages 183 and 185), fruit, salad, nuts, a piece of chicken or fish. If you feel you must have something sweet, one ounce of dark chocolate is a good, reasonably low-sugar treat.

To reduce sugar cravings, you can take 1,000 milligrams (mg) of the supplement glutamine (an amino acid that makes the body think it's getting glucose) every four to six hours on an empty stomach. (Take it with cold or room-temperature liquid since heat destroys glutamine.) Take glutamine for as long as you need to. It is available in health-food stores and has no side effects.

If you must have something sweet in your coffee or tea, try natural sweeteners made from plants, such as stevia, agave and xylitol, which are sold at health-food stores. These natural sugars do not affect blood sugar levels as radically as refined sugar does.

Do not use artificial sweeteners. While they don't cause the harmful hormonal cascade that refined sugars do, they contain unhealthy chemicals. Cut out all aspartame (NutraSweet and Equal), saccharin (Sweet'N Low), sucralose (Splenda) and acesulfame potassium (Ace-K), including any diet sodas or other food and drinks containing them. After three or four days without refined sugar or sweeteners, you'll feel lighter and less "spent," and your craving for sugar will start to diminish.

REINVENT YOUR BREAKFAST

The typical breakfast is dominated by carbohydrate-rich cereals and baked goods and has little of the healthy proteins and fats that are essential for energy. To reestablish your body's natural rhythm, make a smoothie for breakfast. In a blender, mix one-and-a-half cups of fresh or frozen fruit, preferably organic to avoid pesticides…one cup of unsweetened nut milk (such as almond milk)…four ice cubes…three to four tablespoons of whey protein powder…and two teaspoons of greens powder—a powder of mixed plant sources that is full of healthful phytonutrients. (Whey and greens powders are sold in health-food stores.)

SUPPLEMENT WITH "ADAPTOGENS"

"Adaptogens" are tonic herbs that simultaneously calm you and boost your energy.

Note: It's a good idea to check with your doctor before taking supplements. *The three best…*

• **Rhodiola is an herb that modulates cortisol levels.** Take 200 mg to 600 mg daily of a standardized extract or 2 grams (g) to 3 g of the dried root. Do not take if you have bipolar disorder, since rhodiola can increase brain levels of serotonin, a chemical that affects mood.

• **Asian ginseng boosts immunity and promotes a sense of well-being.** Take 100 mg to 200 mg daily of a standardized ginseng extract or 1 g to 2 g of the dried, powdered root in capsule form. Ginseng can cause palpitations or insomnia. Consult your doctor before taking it if you have high blood pressure.

• **Ashwangandha is an Indian herb that promotes vitality, energy and stamina.** Take 3 g to 6 g daily of the dried root. Don't take it if you have gastric irritation or ulcers, are taking sedatives or have kidney or liver disease. Since ashwangandha is a member of the nightshade family (tomatoes, eggplant, etc.), people who have reactions to these plants, such as joint pain or gastric distress, should start with the smallest dose and stop if they get a bad reaction.

If you take just one of these, I recommend rhodiola—but I've found that they work best together. Take every morning for three months, then stop for three weeks, then repeat this cycle. As a general rule, it's best to let the body have a rest from supplements and work on its own for a while.

GET A GREAT NIGHT'S SLEEP

One reason people feel exhausted is that they don't get restorative sleep each night. The hormone melatonin plays a key role in inducing sleep and regulating your internal body clock. But nighttime light, especially bright light from a TV or computer screen, stops melatonin from kicking in because your body thinks it's still daytime.

Solution: Switch the TV and computer off no later than 10 pm. Take a warm bath, listen to relaxing music or do some yoga stretches before turning in. Keep your bedroom as dark as possible for adequate melatonin production. Use window shades if needed, and cover up lights from clocks, cell phones and other devices. If you can't darken your room sufficiently, wear an eye mask.

ENTRAIN YOUR NATURAL RHYTHMS

"Entrainment" is the ability to mimic a "pulse" different than our own. When you listen to music, your internal rhythms actually shift to match the tempo of whatever you're listening to.

You can slow down your pulse (body) and mind (thoughts) by the steady beats of slow-paced music—or energize yourself with music that has a fast beat. Listen to slow-paced music while sitting and relaxing. Or get up and move to a faster beat for 10 to 15 minutes. Listen to music at the start and end of the day…when exercising…while cooking dinner…or any time that feels right for you.

Eat Your Way to a Better Mood

Susan Kleiner, PhD, RD, author of *The Good Mood Diet: Feel Great While You Lose Weight* (Springboard) and *Power Eating* (Human Kinetics). Based on Mercer Island, Washington, she is a nutritionist who has worked with athletes, professional sports teams and executives, *www.goodmooddiet.com*.

Food can put you in a good mood. When you eat, the nutrients in the food are quickly absorbed into your bloodstream. One organ that's affected by those nutrients is your brain—which is why your mood, mental energy, focus and memory are all directly affected by the foods you eat. When you feel down or sluggish, think about what you have eaten. When you eat junk, you feel like junk.

HOW FOOD LIFTS YOUR MOOD

Your brain is an intricate structure, complete with a set of chemicals—neurotransmitters—that control all facets of your body, including mood. At the center of this is the neurotransmitter serotonin, which is linked to feelings of well-being. What you eat—particularly the relationship between the proteins and carbohydrates—has a direct impact on your serotonin levels.

For your body to make enough serotonin, you need to have plenty of the amino acid tryptophan in your diet. Especially good sources are protein foods, such as turkey, fish, chicken, beef, milk, eggs and cheese. Other good sources are nuts and beans. For tryptophan to get carried into your brain efficiently, you need to eat proteins along with healthful, complex carbohydrates, such as whole grains. Avoid refined carbohydrates, such as white flour, and salty and sugary snack foods, such as potato chips and cookies.

Complex carbohydrates make other amino acids move out of the way, enabling tryptophan to cross out of the bloodstream into the brain. Eating small amounts of healthful carbohydrates throughout the day helps to maintain blood sugar levels, and that in turn maintains insulin, which also helps tryptophan get to the brain. Conversely, when blood sugar levels fall, the hormone cortisol rises. Cortisol's role is to break down protein, which disperses more amino acids into the blood—making less room for tryptophan.

CARBS, PROTEIN AND FAT

To feed your brain the right way, do the following…

• **Eat carbohydrates and proteins together.** The best mood-food combinations are meals that are high in complex carbohydrates and low in protein. Aim to get 40% of your daily calories from high-quality carbohydrates and 30% of your daily calories from protein. (The rest will come from fat.) At every meal or snack, combine high-quality carbohydrates, such as whole grains, fruit, sweet potatoes, or beans or other vegetables, with a protein, such as fish, lean meat, chicken, cheese or tofu. *Suggested meals…*

Breakfast: One serving of whole-grain cereal with one tablespoon of ground flaxseed, fruit, one cup of fat-free milk and an egg.

Lunch: A sandwich with whole-grain bread, three ounces of turkey, reduced-fat mayo and vegetables.

Dinner: One-half cup brown rice, vegetables, fruit, four ounces of broiled wild salmon rubbed with one teaspoon of extra virgin olive oil and eight olives.

• **Don't forget about fats.** The omega-3 fatty acids found in fish are known to improve mood in those who are depressed. In addition, certain kinds of fats help to keep brain cell membranes fluid and able to communicate well with one another. Aim to get 30% of your daily calories from these "good" fats, including omega-3 fatty acids and omega-9 fatty acids that come from plant sources. The fats found in nuts, nut butters, seeds, avocados, olives and olive oil also make it easier for serotonin to pass in and out of your brain cells.

Caution: Avoid low blood sugar. When you get hungry, your blood sugar drops. You feel tired and grouchy and lose your concentration. I ask my clients to eat a meal or healthful snack every 2½ to three hours. By eating regularly, you avoid the low mood caused by low blood sugar.

Bonus: Eating frequent small meals stops you from overeating and can help you lose weight.

TOP FEEL-GREAT FOODS

My favorite good-mood foods, in order of importance...

• **Fat-free milk is a lovely combination of carbohydrate and protein in one easy package.** Milk is naturally high in tryptophan and is a great dietary source of vitamin D, another nutrient that increases serotonin. I recommend three eight-ounce servings of milk daily.

For those who can't drink milk: Try soy milk fortified with calcium and vitamin D, although it doesn't contain as much tryptophan as milk. If you have trouble digesting lactose, the sugar found in milk, try using isolated whey protein powder, which contains a protein that is separated from milk and has little or no lactose or fat, but is a rich source of tryptophan. Whey protein powder is available in health-food stores. Mix into juice, smoothies or yogurt.

• **Fish is another feel-great food.** Cold-water fish, such as salmon and mackerel, have the most omega-3 fatty acids and are known to raise mood. (The most healthful cooking methods are baked and broiled, not fried.) Sole, flounder and cod also contain omega-3 fatty acids and can lift mood. And try a fish oil supplement. Even my clients who eat fish also take a daily supplement of fish oil—one that combines about 500 mg total of *eicosapentaenoic acid* (EPA) and *docosahexaenoic acid* (DHA).

• **Eggs (with the yolks) are a great source of protein and other nutrients, including vitamin D.** Yolks are full of choline, a B vitamin that's essential for making *acetylcholine*, one of the most abundant neurotransmitters in your body. You need acetylcholine to send messages along your nerves and to keep your memory strong, among other things. I recommend an egg a day (or up to seven a week but no more than one yolk daily). Don't worry about eggs raising your cholesterol. Studies show that one egg a day has no effect on the cholesterol levels of healthy people.

• **Cocoa sends your brain a nice mix of carbohydrates, protein and tryptophan that can help raise your mood and relax you for a good night's sleep.** (Don't worry about the caffeine in cocoa. There are only about seven milligrams in a tablespoon of cocoa powder.) I suggest that you use your third milk serving of the day to make the cocoa.

Best: Make it with alkaline-free or natural cocoa powder, which should be noted on the label. This designation refers to a processing technique for cocoa beans that leaves more of the antioxidants called flavonols in the cocoa. Add fat-free milk and a sweetener. Sugar is OK if it doesn't disturb your sleep and you're not trying to lose weight. Agave syrup is a good alternative because it doesn't raise blood sugar levels. If you want a noncaloric sweetener, stevia and Splenda are sound choices.

More from Dr. Kleiner

Good Mood Smoothie

Try this healthful smoothie in place of a meal—or as a snack. It combines many of my favorite mood-boosting ingredients.

1 cup fat-free milk

½ medium banana

14 grams (about a tablespoon) isolated whey protein powder*

1 tablespoon organic peanut butter

1 tablespoon alkaline-free cocoa powder

1 rounded teaspoon Omega-3 Brain Booster powdered supplement (optional) **

4 to 6 ice cubes

Combine all the ingredients in a blender and process until smooth, about one minute.

Makes one serving.

*If your whey protein is sweetened, you don't need to add any additional sweetener. If your supplement is unsweetened, add about one packet of Splenda.

**Omega-3 Brain Booster supplement is a flavorless fish oil powder (800-788-0808, *www.omega3powder.com*). One rounded teaspoon is equal to 500 mg of fish oil—and can be taken in addition to eating fish. If you already take fish oil, skip the powder.

Easy Ways to Reduce Stress

Controlled breathing helps reduce stress. Close your eyes, take in a deep breath while thinking the word *calm*, then exhale while thinking the word *down*. Repeat several times—giving yourself the message to calm down.

Alternative: Chew a piece of sugar-free gum. This can increase blood flow to the brain, increasing the feeling of being calm and in control.

Prevention, 33 E. Minor St., Emmaus, Pennsylvania 18098. $15.85/yr.

A Happy Diet

In a study of more than 10,000 men and women without depression, those who most closely adhered to the Mediterranean diet (rich in fruits, vegetables, legumes, nuts, olive oil, fish and whole grains) over an average 4.4-year period were about half as likely to develop depression.

Theory: The diet enhances function of the endothelium (the blood vessels' inner lining), which is needed to support the brain-cell development that helps prevent depression.

If you are at risk for depression (due to family history or recent stressful life events): Try the Mediterranean diet. Learn more at *www. oldwayspt.org/mediterranean-diet-pyramid.* (See also page 94 for more information.)

Miguel A. Martínez-Gonzalez, MD, PhD, professor and chair, department of preventive medicine, University of Navarra, Pamplona, Spain.

Better SAD Cure

Recent research: Sixty-nine adults with seasonal affective disorder (SAD) received *cognitive behavioral therapy* (CBT) and/or light therapy. CBT required twice-weekly meetings for six weeks. Light therapy involved sitting beside a light box 30 minutes daily throughout winter.

Results: The next winter, the combination group had a 6% recurrence rate compared with 7% for the CBT group and 37% for the light therapy group.

If you have SAD: Consider a combination of CBT and light therapy. To find a practitioner, visit the Academy of Cognitive Therapy site, *www.academyofct.org.*

Kelly Rohan, PhD, associate professor of psychology, University of Vermont, Burlington.

Drug-Free Ways to Overcome Depression

Hyla Cass, MD, a board-certified psychiatrist and nationally recognized expert on integrative medicine based in Pacific Palisades, California. She is author or coauthor of 10 books, including *Natural Highs: Feel Good All the Time* (Penguin) and a board member of the American College for Advancement in Medicine. *www.cassmd.com.*

Everyone feels blue occasionally, but for many Americans who are depressed, feelings of sadness and hopelessness persist for months or years.

Conventional treatment for depression includes medication, most often with a *selective serotonin reuptake inhibitor* (SSRI), such as *fluoxetine* (Prozac), or a *selective serotonin/ norepinephrine reuptake inhibitor* (SSNRI), such as *venlafaxine* (Effexor). The mechanism is unclear, but these drugs may work by blocking reabsorption of the brain chemicals serotonin and/or norepinephrine, leaving more of these mood-lifting neurotransmitters in the brain.

Problem: Antidepressants' side effects can include lowered libido, weight gain, headache, fatigue, anxiety, zombie-like moods and even suicidal tendencies.

New finding: An analysis of numerous clinical studies concluded that SSRIs were not significantly more effective than a placebo against mild-to-moderate depression. Other studies are more favorable for antidepressants, and medication is a vital part of treatment for some patients—but given the concerns about antidepressants, many experts believe that these drugs are overprescribed.

Better: A natural approach that treats depression with minimal side effects. *How it works…*

GETTING STARTED

Research demonstrates the mood-elevating effects of regular exercise, proper diet, sufficient sleep and moderate sunshine—yet depression can erode motivation to pursue healthful habits.

What helps: Certain dietary supplements are natural mood enhancers, combating depression by correcting biochemical imbalances and increasing motivation to make healthful lifestyle changes.

Important: Before using supplements, check with a doctor knowledgeable about natural medicine, especially if you take medication, have a medical condition or are pregnant or breast-feeding. *Best…*

• **If you are not depressed, take the nutrients listed below under "Mood Boosters for Everyone"** to maintain healthful neurotransmitter levels.

• **If you are depressed but are not taking an antidepressant,** try natural remedies before considering drugs.

• **If you take an antidepressant but see no improvement in mood and/or suffer from side effects,** ask your doctor about weaning off the drug and starting natural therapies. Do not discontinue drugs on your own!

• **If an antidepressant is helping you and side effects are minimal,** continue your medication and ask your doctor about also taking supplements.

Supplements below are available in health-food stores and online.

Guideline: Begin at the low end of each recommended dosage range. If symptoms do not improve within a week, gradually increase the dosage.

MOOD BOOSTERS FOR EVERYONE

The following supplements are appropriate for most adults. Take all of them indefinitely to prevent or treat depression. They are safe to take while on antidepressants.

• **Omega-3 fatty acids.** These are essential for production of neurotransmitters that affect mood and thinking. Most effective are *eicosapentaenoic acid* (EPA) and *docosahexaenoic acid* (DHA), found in fish oil. Take 1,000 milligrams (mg) to 2,000 mg of combined EPA/DHA daily.

Caution: Fish oil may increase bleeding risk in people taking a blood thinner, such as *warfarin* (Coumadin).

• **B vitamins and magnesium.** The B vitamins help carry oxygen to the brain and produce neurotransmitters. They work best together and are absorbed best when taken with magnesium. Take a daily multivitamin or a vitamin-B complex that includes the following—25 mg each of vitamins B-1 and B-2…20 mg each of vitamins B-3 and B-6…50 mg each of B-5 and magnesium…and 100 micrograms (mcg) each of B-12 and folic acid.

Caution: Avoid supplements of B-3 if you have diabetes, gout or liver problems…avoid B-6 if you take *L-dopa* for Parkinson's disease.

• **Vitamins C, D and E.** These aid neurotransmitter production and/or protect brain cells. Take a daily multivitamin that includes 500 mg to 1,000 mg of vitamin C…2,000 international units (IU) of vitamin D…and 400 IU of vitamin E.

FOR EXTRA HELP

If you still are depressed after taking the nutrients above for seven to 10 days, also take either of the following supplements. If symptoms do not improve within two weeks, switch to the other supplement. If you still see no improvement, take both.

Important: Though many patients are successfully treated with a combination of these supplements and antidepressants, this requires close medical supervision. Theoretically, the combination could lead to the rare but potentially fatal serotonin syndrome, caused by excess serotonin. Symptoms include headache, increased body temperature, fast heart rate, blood pressure changes, hallucinations and/or kidney damage.

Once you find an effective regimen, continue for several months. Then reduce your dose by one-quarter for one week. If symptoms return, resume the former dose. Otherwise, continue reducing until you find an effective maintenance dose or can stop completely.

•**St. John's wort.** This herb raises serotonin and possibly the neurotransmitter dopamine, and may calm nerves. With breakfast, take 300 mg to 900 mg daily of a standardized extract of 0.3% hypericin (the active constituent).

Caution: Side effects may include digestive distress and a sun-sensitivity rash. St. John's wort may interact with some drugs, including warfarin, the heart drug *digoxin* (Digitalis) and birth control pills.

•**5-HTP** (5-hydroxytryptophan) or L-tryptophan. These are forms of the amino acid tryptophan, which converts to serotonin. With fruit juice, take either 50 mg to 100 mg of 5-HTP or 500 mg to 1,000 mg of L-tryptophan once or twice daily.

Caution: Occasional side effects include nausea and agitation.

TO REV UP...

If your symptoms include low energy and sleepiness, add either of the following to your regimen for as long as necessary. They may be taken with an antidepressant under close medical supervision.

•**Tyrosine.** This amino acid aids production of energizing adrenaline, dopamine and thyroid hormone. Take 500 mg to 1,000 mg before breakfast and in mid-afternoon.

Caution: Tyrosine may raise blood pressure—talk to your doctor. Do not use tyrosine if you have melanoma—it may worsen this cancer.

•**SAMe (s-adenosyl-methionine).** This compound boosts neurotransmitters and energy. Take on an empty stomach no less than 20 minutes before or after eating or taking any other supplement.

Dosage: Take 200 mg to 400 mg once or twice daily.

Caution: It may cause irritability and insomnia. Do not take SAMe if you have bipolar disorder—it could trigger a manic phase.

TO WIND DOWN...

If depression symptoms include anxiety and/or insomnia, try...

•**Valerian.** This herb enhances activity of *gamma-aminobutyric acid* (GABA), a calming neurotransmitter. Take 150 mg to 300 mg one-half to one hour before bed. After one to two months, stop for a week. If insomnia returns, resume use. It is safe to take with an antidepressant.

Caution: Don't take valerian while using sedatives, such as muscle relaxants, antihistamines or alcohol.

Secret of Happiness?

Happiness in old age is not just a matter of good health and a high standard of living—although those things help. It is more a matter of feeling in control of your environment—and older people are generally better at feeling that way than younger ones.

Example: Figuring out what makes you angry and finding ways to avoid it. In general, older people become sad and angry less often than younger people, and the feelings tend not to last as long.

Important: Continue to engage in pleasurable and substantive activities, such as part-time work, volunteer activities and taking care of grandchildren.

Laura Carstensen, PhD, founding director, Stanford Center on Longevity, Stanford, California.

Work Longer, Live Longer

People who retire at age 55 are twice as likely to die by age 65 as those who keep working. Until recently, it was generally thought that retiring early increased longevity.

Shan P. Tsai, PhD, manager, department of epidemiology, Shell Health Services, Shell Oil Company, Houston, and leader of a study of 3,500 Shell Oil retirees, published in *British Medical Journal*.

Don't Let Grief Endanger Your Health

Phyllis Kosminsky, PhD, a clinical social worker specializing in grief, loss and trauma at the Darien, Connecticut–based Center for Hope/Family Centers. She is the author of *Getting Back to Life When Grief Won't Heal* (McGraw-Hill).

When someone close to you dies, it's natural to grieve. The ache may never go away entirely, but you gradually accept that your loved one is gone, and you find a new way for life to feel normal.

But for up to 15% of bereaved people, intense grief can linger for years or even decades. This so-called complicated grief is powerful enough to disrupt the bereaved person's ability to work, get along with others and/or to find much pleasure in anything. Although elements of depression are present, complicated grief also is marked by chronic and persistent yearning and longing for the deceased…and an inability to accept the loss.

Especially in older adults, complicated grief can go undetected by doctors and family members—or even the sufferers themselves. Regardless of age, the condition can contribute to chronic depression, drug and alcohol abuse and certain infectious diseases (by weakening the immune system). In people who have heart disease, the emotional stress created by complicated grief can worsen their condition.

HURT BUT HEALING

A person who is grieving is bound to experience feelings of sadness, emptiness, loss—and often anger. Physical symptoms are also common. You lack energy and feel fatigued. You may have trouble sleeping—or do nothing but sleep. You find it hard to concentrate and may even wonder about the meaning of life. Some people lose their appetites, while others eat uncontrollably. Headaches, digestive problems, and other aches and pains often occur.

These grief responses may actually serve a purpose. The psychological pain and physical symptoms force you to slow down, giving your mind and body the opportunity to heal.

Important: There's no fixed timetable for grieving. No one can say "you should be over it" in three months, six months or even a year. As long as the general trend is toward feeling better, it's normal to have ups and downs.

GRIEF CAN BE COMPLICATED

If painful feelings last for more than a few months—and don't seem to be getting better—something may have gone wrong with the grieving process.

Red flags: Thoughts of the lost person constantly intrude throughout the day…or you're simply unable to speak about your loss…or normal life seems impossible, and you feel you can't survive without the person.

Complicated grief is more likely to occur if your relationship with the person you lost was characterized by…

• **Dependence.** We all depend on those we love. But such dependence is excessive when you can't let yourself acknowledge that the person you need so badly is dead and no longer there for you.

• **Ambivalence.** Virtually all relationships have some degree of ambivalence. For example, it's common to love a parent for his/her strength and reliability, but resent that person's tendency toward harsh judgment. Even in the most loving of marriages, anger comes up from time to time. Recognizing our negative feelings toward the deceased person can trigger guilt, so we instinctively push away those thoughts. However, the negative thoughts invariably find their way back into our consciousness, until we acknowledge them.

Regardless of the nature of the relationship, a sudden or otherwise traumatic death can complicate the task of grieving. You relive the moment—or keep trying to push it out of your mind. Problems also arise when death follows an extended illness, triggering both grief and guilt-inducing relief that the person is no longer suffering—and perhaps that you no longer have to take care of him.

ALLOWING YOURSELF TO GRIEVE

Grieving involves experiencing your full range of emotions, including anger, resentment and relief as well as sadness. Some of these feelings may be hard to bear, especially if you have no one with whom to share them. Most people find it helpful to have the emotional support of others.

What to do...

• **Don't isolate yourself.** Spend time with compassionate, understanding friends and family members who are willing to listen, and tell them how you feel.

If you need to talk more than these people are willing to listen, consider joining a grief support group. Local hospitals, hospices and mental-health facilities can help you find a support group.

Online support groups can be helpful if you live in a remote area, prefer not to deal with others face-to-face or lack transportation. Visit the Internet community GriefNet, *www.grief net.org.*

• **Be active.** For many people, doing is better than simply talking. Volunteer work can be especially healing—helping others diverts you from your own sadness and is a powerful way to help yourself.

Physical exercise also is a potent mood-lifter and a general aid to mental health. Anything that gets your body moving is a step in the right direction.

• **Take time to grieve.** Particularly if you have a busy schedule, spend five to 10 minutes a day in a quiet, private place where you feel safe and comfortable experiencing your grief. Focus on your feelings and on thoughts about the deceased. This way, if your grief intrudes during the day, you can remind yourself that you will have a chance to grieve at some point later.

WHEN TO GET HELP

If your own efforts to deal with grief aren't enough, a professional can help you find where and why you're stuck.

Consider therapy or counseling if you're showing signs of depression—you can't work, can't sleep, can't eat, can't get interested in anything or can't deal with other people. Ask your physician to direct you to a therapist or counselor with experience in dealing with grief. Or you can find a list of "thanatologists"—grief specialists—from the Association for Death Education and Counseling, 847-509-0403, *www.adec.org.*

You also may want to consult your doctor about short-term use of medication to help you function in your day-to-day activities.

Shore Up Your Strength During a Health Crisis

Brenda Shoshanna, PhD, a clinical psychologist in private practice in New York City. She is author of several books, including *Journey Through Illness and Beyond* (*www.journeythroughillness.com*).

Illness is as much a part of life as health—and brings with it opportunities for personal growth.

It is difficult to remember this in the midst of a crisis, but you do have a say. Instead of giving in to feelings of hopelessness and withdrawing from life, it is possible to actually improve the quality of your life—by repairing fractured relationships, making positive changes and embracing the love of family and friends. *Important steps...*

PUT GUILT ASIDE

Everyone has regrets, which are often magnified during a prolonged or end-of-life illness. Patients may feel guilty because they don't want to be a burden and because they want to maintain self-respect. Some feel that they can no longer contribute to others.

Family members, on the other hand, may experience guilt simply because they're healthy and their loved ones are not. It's difficult to go forward in life while a person they love is no longer able to.

Guilt is a toxic emotion that damages relationships. It can make a patient's final days (or years) less fulfilling than they could be.

Advice for the patient: Every family has regrets from the past. Take this time to ask for apologies and to offer them...tell your loved ones what they've meant to you...and thank them for all they've done and given.

Advice for family members: Don't stop living. By going forward in your life and maintaining a positive attitude, you can uplift your family members and bring more energy and hope to your ill loved one. Those who give up on their lives, who make themselves martyrs, exude a sense of despair, which has a bad effect on everybody.

MAINTAIN YOUR POWER

The fear that accompanies illness can make us feel timid and childlike. When that happens, it's natural to look for an authority figure—usually a doctor—to make decisions for us.

No matter who your doctor is, you're the one in control. You might not be able to change the course of your illness, but you can take charge of the way you respond to it, the decisions you make and the actions you take. It is important to make your own decisions during the course of the illness. If you cannot do this, have a family member ask for details about a treatment and possible alternatives. Those who engage actively with their illness and maintain a sense of control feel less like victims.

Many people live for years with a serious illness. The ways in which you approach the illness, your emotions, beliefs, actions and sense of self-esteem all affect the quality of your days and often the outcome.

REDUCE STRESS

Try meditation and/or visualization. Both techniques help reduce pain as well as stress and depression. *They can also improve the quality of your life—and you can do them on your own, and in all circumstances...*

- **Visualization.** Patients imagine, in as much detail as possible, a scenario in which they're happy and at peace: Sitting by a lake in the woods...walking in a meadow...a moment with special friends, etc.

Other forms of visualization involve picturing the illness dissolving and other parts of the person growing stronger.

- **Meditation.** There are many forms of meditation, all of which develop balance and focus. Concentration on the breath, or on a phrase that is meaningful, or repetition of a prayer, calms the system and quiets turbulent feelings and thoughts.

LISTEN TO YOUR ILLNESS

Research has shown that negative emotions, such as depression and anxiety, can manifest themselves as physical symptoms or even disease. It's common, for example, for a spouse who has lost a long-term partner to die shortly afterward.

It can be very helpful to look a little more deeply into your life and see what stress might be creating or fueling your illness. Sometimes when we are depressed or feel hopeless, our immune systems are weakened and do not fight disease as well as they might. When some individuals make personal changes in their lives, they notice that the pain and symptoms they experience can decrease or dissolve completely. Illness can be used as an opportunity for emotional healing, and emotional healing can impact illness.

EMBRACE THE CHANGE

Although no one wants to be sick, the more we resist and deny what's happening, the less energy we have available to heal. The more we engage in catastrophic thinking, the worse we feel.

Better: Stay in the present. Rather than dwell on what could or will happen, experience each day as it is.

Helpful: Focus on what is good and enjoyable. Reflect on your life—those things that give you pleasure, what is meaningful, what you would like to do next. Be especially aware of all of the love that you've given and received.

When you are able to, it is beneficial to resume as much of your usual activities as possible. If possible, stay in touch with friends, invite them to visit, and plan outings and trips that are enjoyable and meaningful.

People who view illness as a spiritually transforming experience have more peace of mind and less fear and anger. They often grow to realize that all of life is impermanent and that, ultimately, they're part of that which is greater than themselves. This promotes serenity.

FOR FAMILY MEMBERS

Family members are often afraid to talk honestly with patients. They tend to pretend that everything will be fine...to act cheerful when they are upset and sad. Sometimes they even withhold medical information.

Better: Be real. Patients know intuitively when those around them are "faking it." What they need most is to feel close and connected, to be treated with honesty, which is another way of saying "with respect."

Don't laugh when you feel like crying. It's OK to express feelings of sadness and to share moments of concern. It's also important to allow the patient to say what he/she really thinks and to feel what he really feels. Don't keep trying to cheer someone up if he wants to express doubt and fear. Just be there for him and listen. This will mean a great deal.

It's important to be honest with patients, but this does not mean that you can say everything to everyone. Most patients let you know what they really want to know and what they prefer to have kept from them. It's important to listen and respect where the patient is coming from and to be sensitive to his feelings.

Phone Therapy Can Be Effective

Researchers recently analyzed 12 studies on psychotherapy for adults that was conducted by telephone and involved at least four sessions (typically 45 to 50 minutes each).

Result: About 8% of patients discontinued treatment soon after its start compared with an average dropout rate of nearly 47% for those receiving traditional face-to-face psychotherapy. Telephone therapy also appeared to be as effective at treating depression as office visits.

Theory: Telephone psychotherapy transcends barriers to office sessions, such as transportation problems or juggling appointments with work and family obligations. Anyone who is considering discontinuing psychotherapy treatments because of time constraints or transportation problems should ask his/her therapist if phone therapy is an option.

David Mohr, PhD, professor of preventive medicine, Feinberg School of Medicine, Northwestern University, Chicago.

Why Doesn't Everyone Keep a Journal?

Linda Senn, author of The Many Faces of Journaling: Topics & Techniques for Personal Journal Writing *(Pen Central). Based in St. Louis, Senn is also a publisher, writing coach and business consultant.* www.pencentralonline.com.

Putting subjects that are difficult to talk about into words on paper—a pending divorce, the loss of a loved one—can help you deal with these issues. Keeping a journal can also be a highly effective way to remind yourself of personal goals, such as losing weight or spending more time with a family member.

Problem: Despite the advantages, most people don't keep journals because they believe it's too time consuming.

Reality: It can take as little as 10 to 15 minutes every few days or so.

Frequent question: What's the difference between a journal and a memoir? The difference isn't always clear-cut, but a journal is usually written for one reader—you. In contrast, a memoir is typically written to be shared with others. Many times, however, a journal will evolve into a memoir, such as Anne Morrow Lindbergh's collection of essays *Gift from the Sea* (Pantheon) or Walt Whitman's *Specimen Days* (Kessinger), which includes some of the poet's essays and journaled notes.

GETTING STARTED

The best ways to keep your journal…

• **Set aside a specific time of day to write in your journal.** A particularly effective time is just before you go to bed in the evening, when you can write about your worries—and then literally close the book on them. On the other hand, if writing about your worries keeps you from sleeping, try ending your entry with a sentence or two about your reasons for gratitude. In other words, count your blessings.

Scientific fact: Psychologist Robert Emmons at the University of California at Davis has determined that regularly writing down the things in our lives that we are grateful for promotes better, more restorative sleep, increased psychological well-being and better general health. Emmons explains the process in his recent book, *Thanks! How the New Science of Gratitude Can Make You Happier* (Houghton Mifflin Harcourt).

Evening can also be a time to write about your goals and aspirations for the next day. The following morning, you can consider what you wrote. If you find that journaling doesn't come easy in the evening, experiment with other times of day. Many people enjoy writing in their journals as soon as they get up in the morning or right after breakfast.

•**Write as much or as little as you want.** Include anything that you might want to refer to in the future—recipes, ball game scores, the weather, observations about the neighbors and events that have made you happy or proud. This journal is for you—nothing in it is too trivial if you wanted to write it down.

Caution: Never feel obligated to journal. If you force yourself to make daily entries even when the day's events have been boring, you'll soon lose interest in the project. And don't get in the habit of writing so much that you look at the journal as a chore.

•**Write a recap of the news of the day.** This is especially useful if you have trouble starting a day's entry. Writing a sentence or two about what went on in Washington or your hometown often leads to comments about related events…and then to comments that are unrelated.

•**Keep a separate "travel journal" when you are away from home.** It can be lots of fun, and a travel journal is a kind of writing that's often shared with others. If you're traveling with the grandchildren or other young people, encourage them to keep journals, too.

•**Journal about your dreams.** We often forget our dreams soon after waking up. Not even psychologists agree on how to interpret dreams, but by writing about them, you can see how the subject matter of your dreams changes. That gives you insights that might otherwise be lost.

Example: Several years ago, I dreamed I was in a helicopter over a desert, where I was trying to help my in-laws. As I flew closer, my in-laws started firing guns. In the dream, I first thought that they were trying to protect me, but it became apparent that they were shooting at me.

If I hadn't written about the dream, I might easily have forgotten it. But as I wrote about the dream in my journal, I realized that there was hostility on the part of my in-laws that I had previously ignored. Understanding that hostility gave me the courage to make important life changes.

WHEN TO SHARE

Though not many people let others see their journals immediately after they're written, you'll eventually realize that your journals are a trove of personal and family history. If you don't want your children or others to ever read your journals, burn them. Otherwise, assume that future generations will cherish your words long after you're gone.

Younger generations almost always discover important facts about their families when they read an elder's journal. In my case, for instance, I had assumed that I was the first entrepreneur in the family. But after reading an old family journal, I discovered that there were several other entrepreneurs before me, including a great-grandfather who was a publisher and author. Having this information helped bolster my self-confidence.

As you keep your journal today, you will never know what entries might inspire future generations.

Important exception: Many journals, especially those that deal with very personal matters, are truly not meant to be seen by others. If you believe that your journals fall into this category, reread your entries after a few months or years. If you still feel that others shouldn't read your entries, destroy your journals. They will have served their purpose.

KEEPING HISTORY SAFE

If you use old-fashioned notebooks for your journals, designate a safe place to store the notebooks after they're full. For added safety, consider making a copy of the pages when you finish a notebook, and then store the copies in another place.

Another alternative is to scan the pages into a computer and save them as portable document format (PDF) files, which can then be stored on a computer disk. If you can't create PDF files from your journal on your computer, have the files made at a FedEx Office store or ask a tech-savvy friend to do it. FedEx Office can also copy and bind your journal pages into a book.

If you prefer writing on your computer, save your journal both on the hard drive and a removable disk. And to guard against a computer crash, also print out hard copies of the pages.

Online blog sites offer another way to keep a journal, especially one that you want to share immediately with family and/or friends. But unless you want others to read your entries, choose a blog site where you can limit the Internet users who have access to them, such as Blogger.com.

When you journal on a blog, don't forget to guard against the possibility that the blog site itself will crash. You can do this by saving your entries on your computer and making hard copies.

Journals Online

Online journal Web sites boost commitment. 750Words (*www.750words.com*) encourages members to write 750 words every day. The words can be whatever is on your mind, your first novel, plans for a new business or anything else you want. The site makes writing every day fun and addictive. It gives you little electronic badges for writing every day for 10 days…writing an entry without taking any breaks…writing a series of entries very early or late in the day, etc. OhLife (*http://ohlife.com*) sends you an e-mail every night asking how your day went. You just respond to the e-mail and that becomes your entry for the day in this online journal. Memiary (*www.memiary.com*) also asks what you did today and gives you space for five answers. All of the sites are free and private. You can access past entries for help writing memoirs or finding the brilliant idea that you had a week ago.

Secrets from the Memoir Coach: How to Write Your Life Story

Ina Hillebrandt, founder and president of Los Angeles–based Pawpress (*www.inaspawprints.com*), which offers a wide range of services to writers, including editing, coaching and help with self-publishing. She is author of *How to Write Your Memoirs* (Pawpress).

More people may be interested in your memoirs than you think—not just family and friends but also people in the same profession or with similar experiences, or those who have lived in the same parts of the country. And memoir writing is easier than ever before thanks to new technology and the availability of professionals who can help you, usually at a reasonable price.

BEFORE YOU START

Throughout my experience in helping writers, I have found that once they are assured that people will actually want to read what they write, authors' next concerns are where to start and how to organize their life stories. But it's really easier than it seems.

•**Structure.** Writing about events in chronological order is the simplest structure to follow. If you're dealing with a shoe box full of notes that have accumulated over the years, it's usually not difficult to sort them by date. Also consider variations in structure, such as flashbacks, which can be useful in adding interest and in showing readers how recent events relate to much earlier ones. You can also structure memoirs by topics or by milestones in your life.

Example: I recently helped a client write memoirs that were structured according to the many houses that she had lived in.

Mistake: Thinking of your memoir as a novel in which all the events have to be woven together. In fact, memoirs can be structured as a collection of short stories that aren't necessarily related—or if they are, readers will make their own connections.

• **Audience.** If you're writing for family members, you may not need to describe in detail relatives whom readers are likely to know. On the other hand, if your memoir is also aimed at former business colleagues, more thorough descriptions will probably be necessary.

TO FIND INSPIRATION

As you start writing, it's helpful to remind yourself of past events, which can be a great source of inspiration. *Examples...*

• **Old pictures, scrapbooks, home movies and letters.**

• **Classmates, old friends and relatives you may not have spoken with in many years.**

• **Your earliest memories.** In my case, it was when I was two years old and my father came home from World War II. (My aunt told me to say, "Hubba-hubba," when he walked in the door.)

HELP FOR WRITERS

There are many resources available to aspiring memoirists today...

• **Learn from the pros.** One of the best ways to learn about memoirs is to read what others have written.

Two of my favorites: Steve Martin's *Born Standing Up: A Comic's Life* (Scribner) and Michael Caine's *What's It All About?* (Random House).

Though it's not a memoir in the conventional sense of the term, Laura Hillenbrand's *Seabiscuit: An American Legend* (Ballantine), about the legendary racehorse, is written in an excellent narrative style.

• **Computer assistance.** Today, people do most of their writing on a computer with a word-processing program that checks spelling and grammar. But if you dislike typing, consider using a speech-recognition software program that lets you dictate into a microphone attached to your computer. The program converts what you dictate into a text file.

If your computer doesn't have a speech-recognition program, you can buy one for about $50 to $200 from Staples, Office Depot and other retailers. The leading program is Dragon

Naturally Speaking made by Nuance Communications (*www.nuance.com*).

• **Typists.** If you prefer writing in longhand, you can hire a typist to transcribe what you write for about $3 to $5 per page, depending on where you live. And depending on how legibly you write, a typist can usually transcribe 1,000 to 1,500 words an hour.

• **Writers groups.** In most parts of the country, there are groups of amateur writers who constructively criticize each other's work and who often invite professional authors to offer advice and inspiration. To find a group, enter "writers group" plus the name of your city into your Internet search engine. Most groups welcome new members and are either free or charge about $100 or less in yearly dues.

Caution: Not all writers groups are helpful. A client of mine showed a memoir to a writers group only to be criticized for writing about the South and using Southern expressions in her dialogue. In fact, those were key strengths of her memoir.

Best: Attend a few meetings. If, after each session, you feel energized and inspired, it's probably a good group for you.

• **Editors.** Should you hire an editor to assist you before you start writing or publish? Probably not, if your memoirs are meant only for family and close friends. But if you have a wider audience in mind, an editor is almost a necessity because even the best writers make errors.

Friends with editing experience will often help out free of charge. Otherwise, you can find an editor for hire by phoning the English departments at local colleges, contacting a local writers group or searching for "editors for hire" on the Internet. Also, the Independent Writers of Southern California (877-799-7483, *www.iwosc.org*) can often put people in touch with an editor regardless of where you live.

Before hiring an editor, talk with three or four references to make sure that the editor has worked satisfactorily on memoirs similar to yours.

Cost: About $2,000 a book, half of which is usually paid up front and the remainder on completion of the editing.

PUBLISHING OPTIONS

When you are ready to publish your book…

• **Have the typewritten manuscript copied and bound** at retailers such as FedEx Office for a typical price of $13 to $15 per book.

• **Self-publish by one of the companies that specialize in this type of printing,** including Infinity Publishing (*www.infinitypublishing.com*), LightningSource.com, Lulu.com and UPublish.com.

Cost: About $8,000 for 1,000 copies of a 200-page paperback book.

• **Create a Web site for your memoirs.** This has the advantage of letting others comment on your work.

Cost: $250 to $1,500 or more to set up a Web site (includes producing three designs for approval, and should be easy to use and have tools that bring visitors to your site) and $25 to $50 a month to maintain it—update information, forward or handle e-mail and forward book orders to the author.

To find a Web site designer, look for a site you like and contact the Web designer. Or ask friends who have a site to give a recommendation.

Important: To prevent others from profiting from your memoirs, copyright them.

Cost: $35 from the US Copyright Office (202-707-3000, *www.copyright.gov*).

Also, be aware that there can be consequences if you criticize or discuss the private lives of people who aren't public figures (and sometimes even if they are).

Safeguard: If your memoir is critical of any living person, retain a lawyer familiar with publishing to review the book.

Cost: $5,000 to $10,000. Ask what the cost will be before engaging an attorney.

Free Yourself From Clutter

Julie Morgenstern, founder of New York City–based professional organizers Julie Morgenstern Enterprises, *www.juliemorgenstern.com*. Clients include the Office of the Mayor of New York, Time Warner and the Miami Heat. Morgenstern is author of *Organizing from the Inside Out* (Henry Holt).

Problems created by a cluttered home go far beyond the difficulty of keeping it clean. Looking for simple objects can be a painfully time-consuming experience. You and your friends and family can't enjoy spending time in the house as you should. Even worse, messy houses and apartments are environments for accidents waiting to happen.

With so much at stake, consider a massive shedding of possessions—getting rid of more than you ever imagined that you could do without.

Result: Your life will be less stressful, but also invigorated—and probably safer, too.

My experience shows that in the average household, 80% of belongings that have cluttered desks, drawers, tabletops, closets, trunks, shelves, attics, basements, garages, etc., are candidates for tossing. In many cases, people will enjoy life more by discarding an even higher percentage of possessions.

HOW TO DO IT

You might be able to jettison unneeded possessions on your own by going through your house room by room, examining each item and tossing out those that you don't actually treasure or use. But even people who are motivated often need help. When you do it on your own, there's a risk of being distracted—when you come across unexpected items, for example.

Another person at your side can keep you motivated and, in some cases, help with the physical work required in discarding what may be many stacks of possessions. *Steps to success…*

• **Detach.** For most people, sentimentality gets in the way of successfully uncluttering. You certainly don't want to throw out all of those items that inspire wonderful memories.

But the truth is, you probably have many more of these items than you really need.

Strategy: Keep only the very best reminders you have of a particular person, time or event.

Example: One or two photos from your high school prom—not the dozen that you stashed away and haven't looked at for decades.

• **Put most of your old possessions in storage for two or three months** if you have serious doubts about whether you can live without them. At the end of that time, go to the storage facility. Then take back the items you can't do without, and either discard or give away the rest.

Whether you use a self-storage facility or hire a company to pick up and store your goods, the cost shouldn't be more than a few hundred dollars.

Trap: Believing that you can unclutter your house by putting pictures, documents, letters and other written memorabilia on computer disks. In fact, scanning documents onto disks can be a very lengthy process, and you're still faced with the question of what to do with the originals. Unless you have lots of spare time, disk storage usually makes sense just for pictures, E-mail and other documents that are already in digital format.

• **Ask a friend or relative to help.** The best candidates are people that you trust and who understand why you're motivated to get rid of so many possessions. That's usually a person in your age bracket—perhaps someone who has already gone through a decluttering of his/her own.

Or if you need help with the physical work, consider hiring a neighborhood teenager or student who might be eager for the $5 to $10 an hour that you would typically pay.

• **Hire a professional organizer who can help you decide what needs to be discarded.** You probably wouldn't need a professional if it were just a matter of discarding a few items. But for a serious uncluttering, it's often helpful to get a pro to keep you on track.

The easiest way to find one is by contacting the nonprofit National Association of Professional Organizers at 856-380-6828, or at *www.napo.net*.

From each organizer you consider, ask for names of two or three former clients with whom you can speak. Then ask each reference how the organizer works—does he just give instructions on what to throw out or does he work in a more collaborative way to help you decide what to keep and what to discard?

Be sure that you're comfortable with the professional's style because the organizer will be taking part in emotion-laden decisions about very personal possessions.

Cost: From $40 to $250 an hour, depending on the region where a professional organizer works, the amount of experience and the type of clients. Highly experienced organizers who work with wealthy customers in big cities are likely, of course, to charge the highest rates.

It's hard to predict how many hours it will take a professional organizer to help you with a major disposal of possessions. The time required depends on the number of belongings you have and on how quickly you can make decisions.

If you have a small house and are truly motivated to unclutter, for instance, several hours of professional help may be ample. On the other hand, several days of help could be necessary if you agonize over every item in an attic full of old possessions.

Professional organizers can also help you decide how to dispose of possessions that you no longer want—whether to put them in the trash or give them to a charity, relative or friend. They may also spot items of monetary value that you may have overlooked.

In that case, you may want to hire an appraiser. Professional appraisers can evaluate about 10 items in an hour, for which they typically charge $150 to $350. To find an appraiser, ask your bank, attorney or insurance agent.

MOTIVATION STRATEGIES

How do you motivate yourself to get rid of all but a few treasured possessions and important documents? *Motivation tactics that work...*

• **Visualize a new phase in your life that can occur only if you're not tied down—physically or emotionally—to reminders of the past.** Getting rid of unneeded possessions will make it easier for you to travel, entertain, start a new career or move into a new residence. It might even make it possible for you to move to a smaller place that you'll like better.

• **Realize that a cluttered house can be hazardous if possessions block walking space or are precariously stacked.**

• **Think about the joy that your possessions can bring to friends, family members or a charitable organization.** Old photos, for instance, might be invaluable to a relative who is researching family history. Or an unused bookcase could be a terrific gift to a neighbor's child who is in college.

Many charities will pick up your old belongings at your door.

Examples: Goodwill Industries (800-741-0186, *www.goodwill.org*) and the Salvation Army (check local listings for phone numbers, *www.salvationarmyusa.org*).

9

Healing Relationships

Get People to Really Listen to You

One of the biggest frustrations for seniors is feeling marginalized. Your adult children are very busy living their own lives… the grandkids would rather spend their time staring at little screens and moving their thumbs…everyone from young coworkers to store salespeople treats you as though you're a bit out of touch. I used to accept the cliché that older people are ignored by society because their minds are slowing down—until I hit my 60s.

Perhaps my mental processing is not as speedy as it used to be, but I'm just as smart, insightful and prepared to make intelligent decisions as ever.

My conclusion: It is not a physical aging problem that can make seniors feel pushed aside—it is actually a communication problem. *And only we can solve it…*

THE COMMUNICATION GAP

Younger people interact with the world differently than seniors. They like to multitask constantly, putting premium value on processing large amounts of information from a variety of sources and communicating in rapid bursts. Rather than speak to someone for 30 minutes over their phone, they prefer to send 30 cell-phone text messages back and forth as they rush about their day. Speed and quantity are more important than the quality of conversations and interactions.

At the same time, older folks are also dealing with unique issues on a daily basis that younger people may not understand or value but that have a powerful effect on the way we act.

Solution: Improve your communication style. I'm not suggesting you change your personality or act in ways you do not believe

Don Gabor, founder of Conversation Arts Media, a communications coaching firm in Brooklyn, New York, *www.dongabor.com*. He is author of *How to Start a Conversation and Make Friends* (Fireside) and *Turn Small Talk into Big Deals* (McGraw-Hill Professional).

199

in. Just a few tweaks in how you behave can make a significant difference in being heard. *My secrets…*

• **Present yourself as physically alert and interested.** Body language is powerful, but it is especially important for seniors who must fight the general perception that they're "out of it." *Strategies…*

•When someone smiles at you, smile back and make eye contact. If it's uncomfortable for you to look into someone's eyes, there is a six-inch diameter surrounding the eyes, including the hair, nose, lips and earlobes, where you can rest your gaze and still appear attentive.

•Keep your arms open when you talk with others. Crossing them may feel more comfortable or warmer, but it also makes you look judgmental and skeptical.

•Lean forward slightly when you are seated. Leaning back can give off a strong sense of disengagement.

•Avoid starting your conversations with negative words. There is no bigger turnoff to people who phone you than launching into a harangue about how they haven't called you in such a long time…or responding to the question, "How are you?" with "My back is killing me." All you do with such responses is make people perceive you as cantankerous.

Much better: In any conversation, engage in some interesting, positive chat before you express any discontent. And if you want to discuss someone's failure to pay attention to you, broach it in positive terms. Instead of saying, "Would it kill you to pick up the phone more often?" try "It makes me so happy to hear your voice that I wish we could talk more often."

• **Make your point right at the beginning.** Younger people need to move through the world as quickly and efficiently as possible. Instead of processing information from start to finish, they jump right to the end and fill in details later.

Situation: Your gutters are clogging, and you want to take your young neighbor up on his earlier offer to clean them. It may feel natural and friendly for you to build up to your request by mentioning details such as the GI loan you got after WWII to buy the house or how the neighborhood has changed, but this makes your neighbor want to roll his eyes at what he considers minutiae.

Solution: Think of your conversations as newspaper headlines. Even though it may feel abrupt or awkward, present the most important information up front—"I need my gutters cleaned." Then you can fill in any supporting background material (including expressions of thanks).

• **Recognize the negative effect you have when you refuse to make decisions.**

Situation: An adult child is worried about whether it's safe for you to keep driving. You make excuses to avoid talking about it. You're being evasive because you're afraid that your car will be taken from you and you're insulted that your child thinks you could be a danger to yourself and others. A discussion may lead to restrictions on your lifestyle and a compromise of your independence. So, you simply ignore the issue, hoping it will go away.

Your child may interpret your evasiveness as an inability to face reality. This colors his/her overall opinion of you. Since you will not give him any constructive input, his conclusion is that decisions must be made for you.

Solution: Be aware of when you evade difficult decisions and instead make an effort to work toward a real solution. For instance, you can acknowledge to your child that many older people should give up their cars. But you are not yet one of them. Offer to take a driving test or a defensive driving course to demonstrate your competence. Or reach a compromise, such as not driving at night or in bad weather. Making an effort to engage in difficult choices increases your chances of getting your own way on the issues most important to you.

• **Avoid condemning people when you disagree with them.** Aging imparts a certain wisdom that you derive from experience, but many older folks take that as a right to speak what's on their minds whenever and however they want.

Making statements such as, "That's the most ridiculous thing I ever heard," may make you feel as if you've won the argument, but it insults other people. What's more, when family or friends are exposed to a steady stream of your opinions and criticism, it undermines their trust and confidence in you and interferes with their ability to take you seriously.

Much better: Show a desire to understand the other person's point of view. Say, "Well, that may be a great movie, but I didn't particularly care for it." You might even use humor to defuse a tense disagreement. Say, "I don't agree with you, but will forgive you anyway" (with a smile).

Who Gets Grandma's Ring?

Marlene Stum, PhD, a professor in the department of family social science at University of Minnesota, St. Paul. She is lead researcher for Who Gets Grandma's Yellow Pie Plate?—a Web site created by University of Minnesota Extension educators that deals with the inheritance of personal possessions. *www.yellowpie plate.umn.edu*

Leaving money, investments and other financial assets to multiple heirs can be straightforward—just divvy it all up.

Splitting nonfinancial assets, however, can be complicated, both practically and emotionally.

Which one of your kids or grandkids will get the antique ring that has been in the family for generations? Who should receive the Christmas ornaments or Chanukah menorah that everyone remembers from the holidays?

If you fail to address this issue, you might be sowing the seeds of family disharmony. Heirs have been known to battle over even the smallest and least valuable items in estates.

Here's how to help heirs cherish, rather than be churlish about, the property you leave them...

FIND OUT WHO WANTS WHAT

Arbitrarily parceling out your possessions among your heirs might not make anyone happy—the antique sideboard that's adored by one might be considered an eyesore by another.

What to do: Stroll through your home with your adult heirs—either separately or all at once, depending on how well they get along and how far apart they live. Open the cabinets and closets, and go through the boxes in the basement. Ask your heirs which items they would like to inherit and why. Also, ask them which items they think might have special meaning for one or more of the other heirs—they might know about emotional attachments that you aren't aware of.

While you're at it, share stories about the possessions that have meaning to you. Once your heirs hear how their great-grandfather earned his war medals or who that man is standing with Dad in the old photo, items they might have ignored will acquire new meaning.

Expect to get some resistance when you raise the subject of property inheritance—adult children don't like to think about their parents or grandparents dying. Tell them that it is not easy for you to talk about either and that you don't plan to die anytime soon, but that you still would like to get this squared away and would appreciate their input. You could point out that it will help put your mind at ease.

If the topic is very difficult to raise in your family, take advantage of natural opportunities to do so, such as when someone close to the family dies...or when you move to a different house.

BE FAIR

In many cases, being "fair" in dividing personal possessions means being "equitable," which is not necessarily the same as being "equal." Perhaps you want the daughter who has been taking care of you in recent years to get a special gift. Or maybe a certain item was a gift from one of your kids, so that one deserves to get it back. Make sure each of your heirs gets at least one item that's important to him/her so that no one feels left out.

Consider that your adult children might have different goals when it comes to inheriting your possessions. One might want your jewelry because of its sentimental value. Another might want to sell it to help pay college bills.

Perhaps the heir who needs money could receive items worth a bit more, while the well-off heir could get the items with the most family history.

MAKE IT LEGAL

Write up your list of who gets what, and update it from time to time. Include important items specifically desired by one or more of your heirs. Sign and date your list…store it with your financial papers…and make sure that the executor of your estate knows where it is. Mention in your will that you have drawn up a separate list covering some of your personal possessions. (This is legally binding in most states, but check with your estate-planning attorney.)

Important: Don't try to include all your possessions in your will, or you will have to update it each time you acquire or dispose of something.

Be careful not to leave more than one heir thinking that they were promised the same item. And don't stick labels on your possessions to identify who gets what. Labels can fall off, and it's depressingly common for one heir to accuse another of switching the labels while no one was watching.

HELP HEIRS SORT IT OUT

If you would rather not worry about who gets what, at least help your heirs come up with a fair and fight-free way to do the dividing themselves. The actual dividing can be done while you are still alive or after you pass away. Some families have the adult children draw straws to decide an order, then take turns picking items. Others assign each heir a specific amount of play money, then auction off the items.

Beware: Problems are likely to develop when an allocation system seems to play favorites.

Examples: The oldest adult child is allowed to select first simply because of age…or all the jewelry is given to the daughters and none to the sons.

The New and Better Way to Solve Family Disputes

Attorney and mediator Carolyn Rodis, Esq., board member and director of training, Senior Mediation and Decision-Making, Inc., a nonprofit organization that promotes mediation to assist seniors and their families, *http://senior-mediation.com.*

Family disputes involving an older person aren't just unnerving. They often drag on for months and years and cause serious harm to the senior involved and to family relationships, not to mention the legal and travel expenses that are frequently incurred in attempting to resolve family disputes.

Good news: Today, many of these quarrels can be resolved through elder mediation, an increasingly popular process used to settle disputes over a wide range of issues, such as discussions about guardianship, housing arrangements, inheritance, medical care, sale of property and limitations on driving a car.

Elder mediation differs from other types of dispute resolution in that mediators are specifically trained to help solve problems involving senior citizens.

Big advantage: Elder mediation can help you resolve problems before they become serious, such as by getting better medical treatment for an aging parent. Mediation can also be a way for families to avoid expensive and prolonged legal action.

The process is voluntary from beginning to end. Participants usually sign an agreement to submit a dispute to mediation. But mediators do not impose any agreement on the participants. Agreements that are arrived at during the course of mediation may or may not be put in writing.

Mediators keep everything they hear confidential. Their role is not to make decisions for the family…in fact, elder mediators don't even suggest decisions that participants should make. Instead, they help participants identify the areas where they need or want to make decisions.

Problem: When you see the need for mediation, how do you get other family members on board?

Answer: Have the mediator do the inviting. Even the most reluctant family members often trust a neutral party when he/she explains the advantages of mediation.

Smart move: Using elder mediation as a planning tool—not just after a crisis occurs. Mediation, for example, can be a very effective way for families to make plans for a time when an elder member might no longer be able to live on his own. During mediation, an older person might choose one relative to make financial decisions and another to handle medical matters.

HOW IT WORKS

The elder mediation process typically begins when the mediator asks all participants to describe the events that led to the dispute. Unlike court proceedings, where witnesses are limited to answering questions posed, participants in mediation can fully explore their feelings in a safe environment.

The mediator rephrases remarks in a way that defuses hostility and encourages a constructive dialogue.

Example: A participant might say, "Dad shouldn't be driving anymore. He's dangerous!" At that point, the mediator may step in and say, "What I'm hearing is that you love your father and are worried about his safety." Rephrasing the remark takes out the sting, encourages the father to participate and directs the discussion toward everyone's concern—his safety.

With the issue defined as safety, the mediator can then help the family brainstorm ways to get the father safely where he wants to go. That could lead to him agreeing to drive only during the day…hiring taxis…or asking a willing friend or neighbor to drive him. The father might like the idea of being chauffeured around—a solution that would have been impossible to find if the family were arguing instead of focusing on the problem.

CHOOSING A MEDIATOR

To find a mediator, contact the department of aging or the equivalent agency in your state and/or local government. Many have information on mediators who specialize in disputes involving senior citizens. Senior Mediation and Decision-Making, an organization of which I am director of training, has a wide variety of information about elder mediation on its Web site, *http://senior-mediation.com*.

Other groups can also be helpful, including EldercareMediators.com (260-483-7660) and the Association for Conflict Resolution (703-234-4141, *www.acrnet.org*). Some lawyers, especially those who are members of the National Academy of Elder Law Attorneys, can also recommend mediators (703-942-5711, *www.naela.org/Public/*).

Choose a mediator who can give you credentials showing that he has been trained in elder mediation and references that show experience in actual cases. Then contact those references.

HOW LONG WILL IT TAKE?

Disputes such as arguments over the ability to drive may require only one two-hour session of mediation, while inheritance and other complex issues can take several sessions to resolve.

It's best for sessions to last no longer than two hours—or shorter to suit the needs of the participants.

Reason: Discussions are often intense and exhausting. In that environment, many older people—as well as some younger participants—have trouble concentrating for longer periods of time.

WHAT IT COSTS

Mediators usually charge $100 to $300 an hour. That's very low compared with the cost of resolving disputes in court or paying for medical treatment that can result from a car accident and/or living in unsafe conditions. Community mediation centers offer free services in many parts of the country, and some local courts also offer free or low-cost mediation. To find these services, contact a state or county court or the local government agency that handles senior citizen services.

When Adult Children Don't Get Along

Peter Goldenthal, PhD, a psychologist and family therapist in Wayne, Pennsylvania. He is author of several books, including *Why Can't We Get Along? Healing Adult Sibling Relationships* (Wiley).

Many adults don't get along with their siblings—and sometimes it's not even clear where the bad blood began. Rivalries and hostilities among adult siblings can often be traced back deep into childhood, obscuring their origins. It's likely that your parents could be a significant contributing factor.

You're likely to have trouble getting along with your adult siblings if...

• **Your parents paid more attention to one child than another.**

Examples: A father shows more interest in the son who is active in sports than the one who prefers acting. A mother devotes more time to her son who has a serious health problem than to her healthy daughter.

• **Your parents implied that one sibling was better than the other.** There are few surer ways for parents to sabotage intersibling relations than to say things like, "Why can't you be more like your sister?" Even subtler, well-intentioned comments can drive a wedge between siblings.

Examples: "I'm proud of you. It's okay that you're not as successful as your brother." Or, "We should talk about money management," followed 20 minutes later by, "Your sister is saving a lot of money."

• **One sibling persistently bullied, taunted or threatened the other,** and your parents did nothing to stop it.

Sometimes these troublesome parental behaviors continue during the siblings' adult lives, sometimes they don't. Either way, the seeds of sibling rivalry have been planted.

WHAT PARENTS CAN DO

Most parents don't believe that they're to blame for problems between their grown children, but if one or more of the kids hold you responsible, citing perceived favoritism or some other reason, you might be able to help heal the situation with an apology. Say something like, "I know we made some mistakes, and we're sorry for them. It's too late to change the past, but understand that we do love you every bit as much as your sibling."

If the issue is favoritism, you might also point out that any unequal treatment that did exist was your fault, not the sibling's, so there's no reason why it should keep siblings from getting along.

It's worth noting that people who believe they were the victims of parental favoritism as children often see evidence of ongoing parental favoritism during their adult lives. Parents can keep the strained family relations from getting even worse by balancing their visits to their grown kids' homes...treating their grandchildren exactly the same (adults who feel they received less parental attention or praise growing up tend to believe that their children now get the short end of the stick from their grandparents)...and never telling a child who feels he doesn't measure up how well his siblings are doing.

WHAT ADULT CHILDREN CAN DO

If you or your sibling thinks, "My brother/sister needs to change before we can get along," your relationship is doomed. There's hope only if you can ask, "What do I need to do to make this relationship work?"

Call your sibling and say you would like your relationship to be closer. Suggest that the two of you get together and try to work through your problems. If you think your parents have poisoned the waters between you, share this idea with your sibling, but don't be shocked if the sibling doesn't agree. Siblings often remember childhood very differently.

Example: Your sibling might think that you were the golden child. While your parents were comparing you unfavorably with your sibling, they might have been doing the same to him/her.

Whatever your sibling has to say, listen without interrupting. Then, before responding, summarize what he said to make sure you understand. Discuss what you can do to improve the relationship before suggesting things your sibling can do.

Helpful: If your relationship with your sibling is so strained that you can't even call him to try to reconcile, start by seeing a family therapist. Let the therapist decide when and how to involve the sibling in the healing process.

Important: Be careful to treat your own kids as equitably as possible. People who feel that their parents treated one kid better than another often unintentionally repeat this behavior with their own children.

When Grown Kids Move Back Home—Living (Happily) Together

John L. Graham, PhD, professor of marketing and international business, University of California, Irvine. He is coauthor of *Together Again: A Creative Guide to Successful Multigenerational Living* (M. Evans). *www.togetheragainbook.com*

In these economic times, more grown children are moving back home. The arrangement can work well for you and your child if you discuss expectations and ground rules upfront.

• **Set a deadline.** If you do not want your child to stay indefinitely, say so. You may want to extend the offer only until the child meets a goal.

Examples: Earning a degree…saving for a down payment on a home…recovering from an illness…or finding a job.

• **Decide if your adult child will pay rent and what expenses he/she will cover.** Many parents don't charge rent as long as the child is pursuing mature goals, such as saving money or getting an education. However, if your money is tight and your child is working, it's not unreasonable to expect him to contribute a fixed sum monthly. Adult children usually pay for any extras they need, such as a separate phone/computer line.

• **Limit babysitting.** Be explicit about your limits in caring for grandchildren who come to live or visit. You may want to limit it to, say, two mornings or one night a week. If you want the overall experience to be a good one, you will need to respect your child's choices in child-rearing and avoid critical remarks.

• **Knock before entering.** Agree on the appropriate rules for entry into one another's private spaces. Do not open your adult child's mail, read his e-mail or answer his cell phone without his okay. He should extend the same courtesy to you.

• **Talk about whether it's acceptable to discuss each other's health, finances and relationships with other people, and with whom.** Also, make specific agreements about visitors, boyfriends/girlfriends and parties.

• **Split the chores.** Adult children typically clean their own living spaces, do their own laundry and take care of their own pets.

Shared chores that tend to cause stress: Moving heavy trash cans…sorting and picking up the mail from shared mailboxes…and moving the car when parking is an issue. Perhaps alternate these tasks or assign them to the person who doesn't mind doing them.

• **Use a headset.** Families often find it desirable to use headsets for listening to radio, television and music so that they don't need to adjust to one another's taste and preferred volume.

• **Meet regularly.** After your child moves in, meet regularly—monthly is usually about right—with the specific purpose of discussing how the current rules are working. I know a mother, father and grown son who have their meeting on a weekend walk. For larger families, meetings may need to be more businesslike. Keep the meeting short, agreeing in advance on the ending time. The organizer begins by asking everyone what is working well before turning to problems. Encourage compromise and creative thinking on all sides.

Social Networking on The Internet—Make Friends and Have Fun

Susan Ayers Walker, technology journalist and consultant who advises companies on technology applications for older adults. Her company, SmartSilvers, is located in Menlo Park, California, *http://smartsilvers. com.*

Want to know which South Florida nightclubs have a senior-friendly reputation? A member of the social networking site Eons recently put together a list. Meanwhile, several AARP networkers shared opinions about dentists in Los Angeles. And would you like to meet some nearby singles in your age group? Members of the Gather social networking site regularly swap information on the subject.

These are a few of the thousands of ways that seniors are exchanging information, making new friends and keeping up with older friends on the Internet's social networking sites.

Networking sites, such as Facebook and MySpace, sprang up several years ago, largely for Web-savvy young people. Today, there's a growing number of social networks specifically for adults who are interested in travel, health, dating, politics, second careers, movies and hundreds of other subjects.

How they work: Social networking sites typically ask you to create a profile about yourself that includes basic information, such as the city where you live, your hobbies and other interests, as well as a network nickname by which members can refer to you. Members usually include pictures in their profiles. There's rarely a charge to join a network, but most sites have lots of advertising.

Once you register on a social networking site, you can search for people with similar interests, location or hobbies. You can get in touch with other members by posting a message on a person's profile, or by joining a discussion group. Only the site has your real e-mail address unless you give it to another member—which you may want to do after developing a trusting relationship. Social networking sites usually have blogs that let users post comments, exchange views and ask for advice on a wide variety of subjects.

Examples: One member of a networking site recently asked for information on jobs for seniors in the Chicago area.

SOCIAL NETWORKING SITES

Some of the best social networking sites for adults…

• **Eons** *(www.eons.com)* is a social network for older adults interested in leading healthy and fulfilling lives. One of the most popular features of the site is the Longevity Calculator, which asks a series of health-related questions and then estimates your life expectancy. Among the popular social groups at Eons are those that discuss spirituality, pop music and saving money.

• **AARP Online Community** (*www.aarp. org/online_community/people*) is a feature of the country's largest organization for seniors. As it does, the social network will connect more and more adults interested in such subjects as entertainment, education, health, careers, sports and volunteering. The network is also expected to offer important information, such as where to find hospitals in your area that specialize in treating particular ailments. You don't have to be an AARP member to take part in its social networking.

• **Gather** (*www.gather.com*) is a social network with an especially large number of interest groups, including those for adults interested in horror movies, baking bread or writing poetry. When members use Gather, they build up credits that can be redeemed at retailers such as Amazon.com, the Gap, Starbucks and Target.

SPECIAL INTERESTS

Many social networking sites are now aimed at people with specific interests…

• **Literature.** At Goodreads (*www.goodreads. com*), you can network with people who love to read books and want to exchange information about authors, best sellers and publishing industry events.

- **Women's issues.** iVillage Connect (*www. ivillage.com/messageboards*) is one of the few social networking sites devoted solely to women, covering a wide range of topics from health, careers and relationships to shopping and style.
- **Careers.** Of the many sites for career-minded networkers, LinkedIn (*www.linkedin. com*) is one of the most popular. Members exchange information about career interests and skill sets, post their résumés and invite people they have met in business to join their online network of business colleagues. Your network expands as you are introduced to other businesspeople—a bit like exchanging business cards, except it is done online in this network.
- **Personal finance.** ValueForum (*www.val ueforum.com*) is one of a growing number of specialized networking sites that charge for membership. For $84.99 for a three-month pass, members exchange information about their personal experiences with a wide variety of timely investments, including municipal bonds, energy-related stocks, real estate, foreign equities and gold.
- **Language learners.** LiveMocha (*www. livemocha.com*) is a network for language learners, allowing them to connect with native speakers throughout the world. LiveMocha supports learners of English, French, German, Hindi, Mandarin Chinese and Spanish and is expected to add more languages.

To find other social networks on the Web, enter "social networking" into Google or another search engine. To find a site for people with a specific interest, add the name of that interest in the search box.

Example: "Social networking cooking."

SMART NETWORKING

With so many social networking sites available, it's difficult to choose the ones that are right for you...and then to use them to your best advantage.

Visit one or two networks frequently for about a month to decide whether you're connecting with like-minded people. If the site is not for you, remove your profile by deleting all the information you provided, including pictures.

But if you do like the site, be sure your profile includes a picture, either of yourself or something that represents your hobby. If you don't, the profile won't attract many interested networkers.

Be cautious about giving out your phone number, street address, real e-mail address or other personal information. Though the majority of networkers are honest, a few disreputable people always sneak in, sometimes to sell you a product or lobby a point of view that doesn't interest you.

It's usually best to remain online friends with a fellow networker unless the person can provide references that you can check (mutual friend, church or club affiliations).

How to Find Old Friends

Troy Dunn, a former private investigator who now hosts *The Locator*, a television show about reuniting lost loved ones, on WeTV. He has helped thousands of people find former friends and relatives through his Web site and TV show. *www.troythelocator.com*

Friends slip from our lives. Relatives can drift away, too. Branches break off the family tree, and adoptions separate family members.

Most people know to do a Google search or to check Facebook to find people. *Here, other ways...*

SEARCH THE OBITS FOR LIVE PEOPLE

Search the obituaries for relatives of the person you are looking for. Obituaries typically include a list of the deceased's surviving relatives complete with their current hometowns. If you know where your missing person's family lived, find out if that town's local newspaper has a searchable archive on its Web site. If not, contact the newspaper or the town's library and ask if there's some other way to search the newspaper's archive. If so, search the archive for obits featuring your missing person's last name (or maiden name, if appropriate), then check whether these obituaries mention your friend's name and hometown in the list of surviving relatives.

If the local newspaper doesn't have a searchable database—or you're not sure where the missing person's family lived and died—use the Social Security Death Index (SSDI) to locate times and places of death for relatives. (This also can help you determine if the person you are looking for has died.) Then scan the obituary section of relevant newspapers, focusing on the papers that came out in the day or two following these deaths. Limited free access to the SSDI is available through *www.RootsWeb.com* (click on "Social Security Death Index") and *www.GenealogyBank. com* (click on "Social Security Death Index"), among other Web sites.

SOLICIT FREE HELP

You may be able to get free help from amateur genealogists. Genealogy is among the fastest-growing hobbies in the US. Many amateur genealogists love solving mysteries involving heritage, missing family members and other long-lost individuals.

To start, visit the free Web site RootsWeb. com and post a note on the message board explaining your search and asking for guidance or assistance. Provide the name of the person you are trying to find, where and approximately when this person was born and any additional details that you have about this person's relatives and places of residence. An amateur genealogist might take up the search for fun.

You will have to register with RootsWeb. com to post a message, but registration is free. This Web site is international and is particularly useful when missing people live outside the US.

CHECK ORGANIZATIONS

Reach out to relevant organizations. If you know where the person you're trying to find once worked, perhaps he/she still works there. Check whether his name is listed on the company's Web site...or call the company's switchboard, and ask for the person.

You also can contact organizations related to this person's line of work and ask if this person is a member...and contact the alumni association of schools he attended. If any organization is unwilling to share contact information for privacy reasons, ask if it can forward a note to this person for you.

SPECIAL SEARCH SITUATIONS

•**Adoptees/birth parents.** Locating birth parents or children given up for adoption is especially difficult because neither parent nor child is likely to know the other's name. Laws usually bar adoption agencies and government officials from supplying this information. Without a name, conventional search techniques are useless.

It is best to sign up for free adoptee registries, such as my TroysList.org and International Soundex Reunion Registry (*http://isrr.net*), a nonprofit organization. These Web sites match birth parent and adoptee if both sign up.

Warning: Be wary of adoptee registries that charge fees. Most deliver less than promised—some are scams.

Helpful: The US Department of Health and Human Services provides details about each state's adoption records access laws on its Web site, *www.ChildWelfare.gov* (select "State Statutes Search," then choose the state where the adoption occurred and "Access to Adoption Records"). Many states let adoptees and birth parents petition in court for the disclosure of "identifying information" about their parents or children—but this information usually is supplied only if the birth parent or adoptee already has filed a written consent form with the state to allow disclosure. (Adoptees generally are allowed to file consent forms only after they reach age 18 or 21.) In some states, the court also is allowed to select an intermediary to contact the birth parents or adoptee and request their permission to share the information if a consent form has not been filed.

•**Military buddies.** Military service records are not open to the general public, which can make it difficult to track military acquaintances. The best way to find former friends from the armed forces—if other methods, including a Facebook search, fail—is through private military registries and reunion associations started by former servicemen. Google the division or unit's name along with the word "association" or "registry." (If you served during wartime, also check the SSDI, in case your friend died in battle.)

•**Women who might have married or divorced.** It can be difficult to track down women when their last names change. One way is to search for one of the woman's male relatives, then ask this relative how you can reach her. Another option is to Google "vital records" and the name of the state where the woman lives or once lived. Among the listings should be a state government Web site with a Web address ending ".gov". This Web site should let you search for any marriages and divorces involving this woman that occurred in that state.

•**People with very common names.** There are too many Jennifer Smiths and Robert Millers to find the one you want through the usual techniques—especially if you don't know the middle name or hometown. Search for a less conventionally named relative instead.

Example: You remember that your friend John Smith had a brother named Caleb...or that his mother's maiden name was Hefferman. If you locate a relative, this person probably knows where to find John or where to find another family member who does.

MAKING CONTACT

Handle the initial contact wisely. *What you say or write will have a significant effect on whether this person is happy to hear from you...*

•**Calmly explain who you are and how you know each other.** Do not assume that this person remembers you—it often takes time for people to rewind through the years and recall past relationships, even relationships that once were quite close. If first contact is made on the phone, continue explaining how you know each other until you receive a strong signal of recollection.

Example: "Oh, sure. Wow. How are you?"

Do not immediately press for an in-person meeting. Explain that you were wondering what became of this person...or if it's a relative, that you are putting together a family tree.

•**If the person you are reconnecting with is a former flame**—or anyone else of the opposite gender who is not a relative—consider asking a friend of that gender to make the initial contact. This reduces the risk that tracking this person down will be seen as creepy...and it avoids creating trouble if this person is married and his/her spouse answers the phone or sees your e-mail.

The Benefits of Family Rituals

Meg Cox, Princeton, New Jersey–based author of *The Book of New Family Traditions* (Running Press).

Many families have built their own rituals around holidays and other significant occasions, but traditions can develop for ordinary days, too. Parents and grandparents have found that rituals have many benefits. *Among them...*

•**Highlighting milestones or other special days.** Grandchildren moving up a grade can cross a "threshold"—a doorway covered with streamers or a balloon tunnel extending up a staircase.

•**Solving problems.** If your grandchild is afraid of monsters under the bed at night, give him a spritz bottle of "monster spray" to send the monster packing. If a child hates getting his hair cut, have him pose for "before" and "after" photos.

•**Coping with loss or celebrating the memory of a loved one.** On Father's Day, one family arranges photos of fathers, grandfathers and great-grandfathers on a special table.

•**Celebrating successes**—even small ones. Keep brownie mix and a star-shaped cookie cutter on hand so that achievements can be acknowledged.

Rituals don't have to be complicated. Just about any activity—Saturday morning pancakes, saying grace before dinner—can develop into a successful ritual if presented with flourish and repeated several times.

Am I Boring You?

Signs that you may be boring your conversation partner: The person fidgets or turns slightly away from you instead of being still, sitting upright and looking at you. He/she changes the subject abruptly...stays silent and doesn't interrupt you to ask questions or to remark on something you said...asks simple questions just to seem polite, such as "Where did you go?"...gives short responses, such as "really" and "wow"...and doesn't ask you to elaborate or explain anything.

Gretchen Rubin, New York City–based founder and author of *The Happiness Project* (Harper). *www. happinessproject.com.*

Divorce Can Age You

Divorce adds 1.7 years to your face...smoking tacks on 2.5 years for every decade you smoke...30 extra hours of sun exposure per week can make you appear two years older by age 40.

Surprising: A widow or widower appears about two years younger.

Bahman Guyuron, MD, chair, department of plastic surgery, University Hospitals, Case Western Reserve University, Cleveland, and leader of a study of 186 pairs of identical twins, published in *Plastic and Reconstructive Surgery.*

Loneliness Raises Blood Pressure

A study of 229 men and women found that those who rated themselves as feeling the loneliest had an average blood pressure increase, over four years, of 14 millimeters more than those who reported feeling the most socially content.

Theory: Loneliness alters physiological functioning, including blood pressure.

Self-defense: Expand the number of friends and relatives with whom you connect...and have contact at least twice a month.

Louise Hawkley, PhD, senior research scientist, Center for Cognitive and Social Neuroscience, University of Chicago.

Testosterone May Boost Mood

In two recent studies that looked at a total of 1,050 men with low levels of the hormone testosterone, those who received testosterone replacement therapy for three years, on average, had a 70% improvement in scores on a standard test used to diagnose depression.

Theory: Hypogonadism (low testosterone) can affect mood and result in depression—as well as fatigue, joint and muscle aches, and erectile dysfunction, conditions that can, in turn, lead to depression.

Self-defense: If you're a man who experiences any or all of these symptoms, ask your doctor to assess your symptoms and check your testosterone level via blood tests. If you are diagnosed with hypogonadism, ask if testosterone replacement therapy is appropriate.

Caution: Men with prostate cancer, liver disease or high hematocrit (the volume of red cells in the blood) should not receive testosterone replacement therapy.

Lawrence Komer, MD, medical director, Masters Men's Clinic, Burlington, Ontario.

Don't Repress Anger

Husbands and wives who repress their anger tend to die earlier than spouses who express it, according to a recent study. Conflict in marriage is inevitable—but couples who air their differences and try to solve them stay healthier and live longer than ones who hold in their resentments.

Possible reason: Repressing anger leads to increased stress, which can shorten life.

Ernest Harburg, PhD, research scientist emeritus, department of psychology, University of Michigan School of Public Health, Ann Arbor, and leader of a study of 192 married couples, published in *Journal of Family Communication.*

How to Handle Your Hard-of-Hearing Husband

Adrienne Rubinstein, PhD, professor and codirector of the clinical doctoral program in audiology, Brooklyn College, New York.

You feel annoyed as you beseech your partner to turn down the TV…frustrated at constantly having to repeat yourself… isolated when he skips social events because he can't follow the conversation. The obvious solution is for him to wear a hearing aid—but he's likely to refuse.

Three-quarters of adults with impaired hearing don't even own a hearing aid. Hearing loss is an emotional issue, and your husband may not be aware of his true concerns. To help him overcome reluctance, be sensitive to his real objections. *What you should know and do if he believes…*

"I can hear just fine." Gradual hearing loss often goes unnoticed. In private, gently point out instances in which he misunderstood someone's words and express concern for his safety—for instance, if he can't hear a car honk. Suggest an exam with an audiologist (his doctor can provide a referral)…or download the at-home test uHear to an iPhone (visit *www.unitron.com*, and click on "Your Hearing," then "Hearing Loss," then "Take a Hearing Test."

"If people didn't mutter, I wouldn't have a problem." Acknowledge that people sometimes mutter, but say that a person with good hearing generally understands mutterings. Tell him you'll speak clearly yourself, but note that he can't control every situation and that speaking loudly can be taxing to others.

"A hearing aid will make me look old." While some people view hearing aids as signs of age-related decline, the inability to follow a conversation is more conspicuous and may be mistaken for mental decline. Besides, some new aids are not noticeable.

"It's too expensive." Features that minimize feedback (annoying whistling) and voice distortion—formerly available only in top models—are now included in aids that cost only about $1,500. Some insurance policies provide partial coverage (Medicare does not). "Your Guide to Financial Assistance for Hearing Aids," contact the Better Hearing Institute (202-499-1100, *www.BetterHearing.org*).

"It's uncomfortable." If he owns an older hearing aid, explain that new models are much more comfortable. Any new aid should be custom-fitted by an audiologist…and he should return for adjustments, if needed.

"Those things don't work." If he has a hearing aid but says it doesn't help, try replacing the battery and brushing earwax out of the mold and tubing. If he has hearing loss in both ears, he'll hear best with two aids.

"Hearing aids aren't worth the trouble." He may not realize the full consequences of his hearing loss. Gently explain that other people may avoid speaking to him…that he no longer enjoys music or parties…and that you miss his company and conversation.

Love the Spouse You Have

Mark O'Connell, PhD, clinical instructor of psychology at Harvard Medical School in Boston. He is author of *The Marriage Benefit: The Surprising Rewards of Staying Together* (Springboard). *www.markoconnell phd.com*

When a marriage becomes contentious, cold or boring, too many couples point fingers or pack bags, lamenting lost dreams of marital bliss. Yet the disappointments behind today's dismal divorce rate often result not from truly unacceptable situations (serial affairs, spousal abuse)—but instead stem from couples' seriously unrealistic expectations of what a marriage can and should be.

The fix: By recognizing that relationships evolve over time and adapting to those inevitable changes, we can come to understand ourselves better...love our spouses better... and experience a deeply satisfying partnership that will last the rest of our lives.

MONEY MATTERS

One way we measure happiness is by comparing ourselves with people around us—and in that regard, the most tangible factor is wealth. When your neighbor's house is nicer or your brother's paycheck is bigger, whom are you likely to resent? Your spouse.

Be realistic: More money is not the key to permanent peace, because there always will be people who are richer. Instead, resolve the underlying conflict by figuring out what money means to each of you...

Is money a sign of self-worth—because you were ashamed of growing up poor or for another reason? If so, remind yourself of nonmaterial achievements—the way you raised wonderful children together or serve as community leaders.

Is money a safeguard against insecurity—because you were horrified when a cousin lost her home or you experienced some other financial trauma? Work with a financial planner to set up a long-term budget.

Is money an expression of love—because your father lavished your mother with jewelry? Appreciate the way your husband shows his love by bringing you breakfast in bed.

Helpful: Make a list of your top five financial goals, and have your husband do the same. Together, compare the lists...agree on several goals you both share...and brainstorm ways to achieve them. When you know what truly matters, money becomes merely a means to an end, not the end goal itself.

BEDROOM BATTLES

He wants more sex...she want more cuddling. She craves variety...he's happy on top.

Toss in the influence of Hollywood—gorgeous couples who are eternally lusty and lip-locked—and unrealistic expectations about sex can run wild.

Be realistic: Take a compassionate look at the underlying reasons why lovemaking has become disappointing. Maybe she avoids sex because she thinks her body is not as beautiful as it once was. Maybe he sticks with one position not because he's indifferent to your preferences, but because he's worried about losing his erection. The key is to talk specifically about what you need or want—and encourage your spouse to do the same. When you both share honestly and listen with open minds, you can reach a satisfying compromise.

Try this: Agree to share a kiss (a real kiss, not a peck) at least once a day—not necessarily with the goal of having it lead to intercourse, but simply to enhance the bond between you. Research shows that kissing sparks sexual desire and reduces levels of the stress hormone cortisol. Less stress is always a good thing—in or out of the bedroom.

AGE PREJUDICE

Have you ever caught sight of yourself in a mirror and thought, "Who is that old person?" Looking at your spouse can be like looking in that mirror. In those wrinkles, you see evidence of your own advancing age—and wish you didn't have to be reminded.

Be realistic: Growing old actually can improve a marriage—once you give up the fantasy that starting over with someone else will automatically make you feel young again.

The trick: Face up to whatever bothers you about aging. Perhaps you're disappointed that your bad shoulder has put an end to your tennis games together...or you're afraid that your spouse's couch potato habits will lead to a heart attack. If so, try new activities together that can accommodate your not-as-young body, such as bicycling...or gently suggest going for walks because you want your spouse to be with you for years to come.

IDEALIZATION OF LOVE

If only we could bottle that passion of the first year of a relationship, when romance made life dreamy. But it's biologically impossible to sustain that intensity of feeling day in and day out for years on end.

Reason: The early stages of romance are associated with big physiological changes—in fact, the brain pathways that govern falling in love appear to be the same as those involved in addiction. However, studies using magnetic resonance imaging (MRI) suggest that about 18 months into a relationship, brain chemistry again begins to alter—this time in ways that promote a change from romance and lust to long-term attachment and contentment.

Be realistic: If love stayed at a fevered pitch, we would never get anything else done…and we would never move past the starry-eyed stage and really get to know each other.

What to do: Make a list of everything your spouse does that pleases you. Does she listen to your mother's endless complaints with a kind ear? Is he a thoughtful planner—for fun activities as well as important life issues? Does he keep his word? Look for the qualities you value in any long-term friendship. You both share a commitment to family and support each other in times of crisis—that kind of partnership provides a path to lifelong marital happiness.

How to Have Good Sex At Any Age…Live Longer, Too!

The late Robert N. Butler, MD, professor of geriatrics at Mount Sinai School of Medicine in New York City and the president and CEO of the International Longevity Center, *www.ilcusa.org*. He is the founding director of the National Institute on Aging and the co-author of *The New Love and Sex After 60* (Ballantine).

Despite what Hollywood would have us believe, sex isn't limited to people under age 40. In fact, recent research shows that a sizable percentage of Americans are remaining sexually active into their 70s, 80s and beyond. But let's be honest—there are obstacles, both physical and psychological, to maintaining a healthy sex life as we age.

Very good news: After years of research and clinical practice as a specialist in longevity, I have found six key principles that, taken together, can help the vast majority of couples—no matter what age—have a good sex life. And when a couple has a satisfying sex life, their feelings of fondness and intimacy can grow stronger—and that improves every aspect of their lives. *For a great sex life at any age…*

•**Realize that sex and intimacy can literally add years to your life.** Numerous studies have shown that close relationships are a key to maintaining good mental and physical health as we get older. Of course, emotional closeness can exist without sexual intimacy—but to the degree that sexuality helps enrich our closest relationships, it can be an important contributor to a long, healthy life.

Bottom line: If you give up on a good sex life, you may die sooner.

•**Ignore what society tells us about aging and sex.** The idea of older people having sex is thought of as a rarity. This stereotype couldn't be further from the truth. A recent study of sexual activity among older Americans, published in the *New England Journal of Medicine*, showed that more than one-half of men and women between the ages of 65 and 74 and more than one-quarter of those between 75 and 85 had been sexually active within the previous 12 months. And among those who reported that they were in good or excellent health, these figures were considerably higher.

Bottom line: Don't let society's false stereotype keep you from one of the great joys of life.

•**Take care of your health.** A healthy blood flow to the sexual organs is essential for sexual response. That's why maintaining good cardiovascular health—including managing cholesterol levels and blood pressure as well as exercising—is key to a good sex life. *Also vital…*

•If you have diabetes, control it. Diabetes is a killer of sexuality because it damages the cardiovascular system and the body's peripheral nerves.

• Discuss with your doctor whether any medications you take might be affecting your sexual desire or response.

Examples: Antidepressants can significantly reduce libido, while diuretics and beta-blockers used for high blood pressure can cause erectile dysfunction. Ask about alternative drugs and/or drugs that might counter the sexual side effects.

• **Steer clear of alcohol.** A character in Macbeth famously said of alcohol, "It provokes the desire, but it takes away the performance." He was right. Alcohol can make us want sex more—and some women, in particular, say that their sexual pleasure is increased after drinking, most likely because alcohol reduces psychological inhibition. But even one drink can reduce a woman's vaginal blood flow and lubrication and intensity of orgasm. For men, intoxication can severely reduce the ability to achieve an erection and the intensity of orgasm—and regular alcohol consumption (even without intoxication) lowers testosterone levels, affecting quality of erection and orgasm.

Bottom line: A little alcohol might help—or at least not hurt your sex life. But it's best to save any imbibing for after sex.

• **Take advantage of medications and sex-related personal-care products.** For older people, the introduction of the oral medications *sildenafil citrate* (Viagra), *vardenafil* (Levitra) and *tadalafil* (Cialis), which help men maintain erections, has been an important development.

Reason: Erectile dysfunction is one of the most frequently cited reasons that older couples are no longer sexually active. While they are safe and effective for most men, talk with your doctor about potential side effects before trying any of these drugs.

What many couples don't realize: It is normal for an older man to need to have his penis physically stimulated to achieve an erection—just thinking about sex, or even kissing and other foreplay, often isn't enough. Ladies, this is not an indication of diminished desire.

As we all know, hormones play a great role in sex…

For men: If you are unhappy with your sexual response after following the advice throughout this article, see an endocrinologist for a check on your levels of testosterone and thyroid hormones. A low level of either can dampen sexual desire and ability. Hormone supplements can be prescribed.

For women: Older women often experience vaginal dryness, which can make intercourse far less enjoyable or sometimes impossible. This problem can be solved by applying an over-the-counter, non-oil-based lubricant, such as K-Y Jelly, Astroglide, or Slip, just before sex…or, to allow for more spontaneity, by using a moisturizing insert such as Lubrin (which lasts several hours) or Replens gel, which lasts several days. (Avoid oil-based lubricants, such as petroleum jelly and baby oil, which tend to remain in the vagina and create a breeding ground for infections.)

Alternative: If a lubricant isn't enough to make sex comfortable, ask your doctor about a topical form of the hormone estrogen, which can be applied to the vagina to increase your body's ability to lubricate itself.

• **Keep all the flames burning.** If you're in a long-term relationship and you want a satisfying sex life, it's important to purposely set aside time for nonsexual intimacy on a regular basis.

Perfect example: Years ago, I lived next door to a couple who had a weekly candlelight dinner in their backyard. This kind of intimate encounter may not always lead to sex—but it creates a psychological closeness that encourages physical intimacy.

More from Dr. Robert Butler…

If You Are Single, Divorced, Widowed…

For older unmarried people, finding an appropriate sexual (and life) partner is a challenge. This is especially true for older women, whose longer life span means they outnumber older men by about two to one.

But remember: The loss of a sexual partner wouldn't stop a 30-year-old from seeking a new relationship, so why should it stop you at age 60, 70, 80 or older?

To find a wonderful partner: The key is to frequently participate in activities that will expose you to potential partners, especially activities in which you have a strong interest, such as dancing, politics or art. This will give you the best chance of meeting someone you're attracted to and who shares your interests, an ideal starting place for developing a more intimate bond.

Living with a Partner... Better for Your Health

People ages 30 to 69 who live alone are almost twice as likely to develop angina, over 50. Living alone itself is not the reason for the increased risk. People who live by themselves eat more fat, are more likely to smoke and are less likely to exercise.

Kirsten Melgaard Nielsen, MD, internist, Aarhus Sygehus University Hospital, Aarhus, Denmark.

Help for the Caregiver

Charles B. Inlander is a health-care consultant and founding president of People's Medical Society, a consumer advocacy group active in the 1980s and 1990s. He is the author of 20 books, including *Take This Book to the Hospital with You* (St. Martin's).

Most of us have never planned on becoming the caregiver for an older family member or disabled spouse or child. There are no courses in high school or college that teach us to care for a loved one in need. However, during any given year, more than 50 million people provide care for a chronically ill, disabled or older family member or friend, according to the National Family Caregivers Association.

No matter how dedicated you are, you quickly discover that caregiving is a difficult task. If you want to spend up to $200 for an eight-hour day, there are several options, including in-home care from a home-care aide or private-duty nurse. But this can present a financial hardship. Few people realize that there also are programs available for minimal fees or free of charge that can help ease the burden of the caregiver. *Best resources...*

- **Adult day care.** Designed primarily for older persons who need supervision, including those with Alzheimer's disease and other types of dementia, adult day care is much more than a "drop-off" center. Most adult day-care programs include daily exercise regimens, social interaction with other participants and staff, along with other activities, such as arts and crafts, that keep the individual occupied and engaged. Many adult day-care programs are sponsored by municipal or county governments, so they can operate free of charge or for minimal fees averaging about $40 per day. To find out about programs in your area, contact your local Area Agency on Aging office, listed in the local government section of your phone book.

- **In-home respite care.** Under this program, paid workers or volunteers come to your home one or two times a week, usually for four hours or less per visit. The helper (a social worker, nurse or agency-trained volunteer) typically sits and visits with your loved one while you rest or run errands. The cost of such services varies according to your need and ability to pay. Find out more by contacting your state welfare department or your local Area Agency on Aging office. In most states, these agencies maintain a list of in-home respite care services or can refer you to an agency that does. There also are a number of Web sites that can help you locate respite services in your local area. I recommend *www.archrespite.org*, a national directory operated by the Chapel Hill Training Outreach Project at the University of North Carolina in Chapel Hill.

Support Groups: The Well Spouse Association (800-838-0879, *www.wellspouse.org*) and the Family Caregiver Alliance (800-445-8106, *www. caregiver.org*) can provide support groups...advice...workshops and/or respite weekends for caregivers...and the reassurance that you are not alone.

How to Talk to Those With Dementia So They Can Hear You

Kristine N. Williams, RN, PhD, associate professor, University of Kansas School of Nursing, Kansas City, Kansas.

Have you noticed how loudly some people talk when attempting to communicate with a person who doesn't speak English? They seem to think turning up the volume will bridge the language gap. Similarly it is common for many, including trained professional caregivers, to use "elderspeak" with people who are old and infirm. It sounds a lot like baby talk, with simplified grammar and vocabulary and liberal use of terms of endearment, such as honey, sweetie and dearie. Though it may be done with the best intentions, a recent study, led by researcher Kristine N. Williams, RN, PhD, an associate professor at the University of Kansas School of Nursing, finds that when elderly patients are spoken to in this way, they often become angry, less responsive and harder to care for. The researchers hypothesized that this "elderspeak" sends a negative message of incompetence, which ends up irritating rather than soothing listeners.

RESPECT YOUR ELDERS

The National Institute on Aging and Dr. Williams offer these tips for communicating with those who have Alzheimer's disease or dementia…

• **Before speaking, gain the person's full attention.** Use his/her name.

• **While interacting, turn off distractions such as the TV or radio.**

• **Speak in a tone that is calm and gentle,** without infantilizing. Dr. Williams also points out that nonverbal cues such as establishing eye contact convey your focus and willingness to communicate.

• **Use simple words and short, clear sentences**—but not baby talk.

• **If someone is having trouble finding the right words,** it's fine to help him/her out by gently making suggestions.

• **Be patient, providing ample time to think and respond.** It is important to give people with dementia time to compose and communicate their thoughts, says Dr. Williams. When you are patient, it shows you believe that what they have to say is important and that you are paying attention to them.

• **Do not talk about a person with AD or dementia in front of him/her as if he/she were not present.**

All it really comes down to is using the same good manners we should be using anyway.

For the Alzheimer's Caregiver: How to Cope With Behavior Problems

Victor A. Molinari, PhD, a psychologist and professor in the department of aging and mental health disparities at Florida Mental Health Institute of the University of South Florida in Tampa. He is coeditor of *Supporting the Caregiver in Dementia* (Johns Hopkins University Press).

Alzheimer's disease robs its victims not only of memories and mental skills, but also of the ability to control their behavior. This leaves family caregivers struggling to cope with their loved ones' behavioral problems—and even can provoke regrettable behavior from frustrated caregivers themselves.

Recent study: 52% of people caring for a relative with dementia admit to screaming at, swearing at or threatening their loved ones. Caregivers then feel guilty—which adds to their stress. *What helps…*

WORKING WITH THE DOCTOR

The more effectively you can communicate with your loved one's doctor, the more likely the patient is to receive treatment that minimizes behavioral difficulties. *Ask the doctor about…*

• **Cholinesterase inhibitors.** These prescription drugs, such as *donepezil* (Aricept) and *rivastigmine* (Exelon), generally are used to treat cognitive symptoms of Alzheimer's.

New finding: These drugs also reduce behavioral and psychological symptoms, such as aggression, wandering and paranoia.

How: Alzheimer's patients have depleted levels of *acetylcholine*, a brain chemical that helps with cognition, memory and judgment. By raising *acetylcholine*, cholinesterase inhibitors promote communication between nerve cells, stabilizing or even improving symptoms. If your loved one experiences digestive upset with one drug, consider trying a different one.

• **Sleep disorders.** Up to 80% of Alzheimer's patients have sleep apnea (frequent halts in breathing during sleep). Apnea reduces oxygen in the brain, impairs cognition and causes sleep deprivation—all of which can negatively impact behavior.

New hope: Patients showed cognitive improvement after three weeks of continuous positive airway pressure (CPAP) treatment. The CPAP machine provides pressurized air via a face mask worn during sleep.

HANDLING PROBLEM BEHAVIORS

Practical strategies help reduce negative behaviors. *Here's how to deal with your loved one's...*

• **Agitation.** Alzheimer's patients often get upset, act restless or pace around. Keep a log to help you identify circumstances that provoke these reactions, then develop a plan to work around such triggers.

Example: If your loved one gets upset when you try to bathe him in the morning, try it in the afternoon instead. Once you find a routine that is comfortable for your loved one, stick with it. Isolation and understimulation also can provoke agitation, so try to keep your loved one active and engaged during the day—for instance, by listening to music or going for a walk together.

• **Aggression.** Shouting, shoving and hitting can be signs of frustration or pain.

To avoid triggers: Protect your loved one from overstimulation (from clutter or noise)...

confusion (from being given too many instructions)...and physical discomfort (from medication side effects or an unnoticed injury).

Soothing: Try to maintain a calm and reassuring demeanor, refrain from arguing or lecturing—and don't take your loved one's behavior personally.

• **Wandering.** Place a large, solid-colored, dark, rubber-backed mat in front of each door to the outside. Your loved one probably won't remember if you say not to go past that point—but mats act as visual deterrents, discouraging an Alzheimer's patient from leaving home unattended.

Also: Install sliding bolts high enough on each door that a person must reach up to unlock them (but not so high as to impede the family's departure in an emergency, such as a fire). Chances are that a person with advanced Alzheimer's will not figure out how to open them.

New technology: The Alzheimer's Association Comfort Zone program includes a GPS-like service that alerts you (via telephone or the Internet) to your loved one's location.

Information: 877-259-4850, *www.alz.org/ComfortZone.*

• **Nighttime restlessness.** Many Alzheimer's patients suffer disturbances in circadian rhythms that affect sleep cycles and alertness. Keep the house brightly lit between 7 pm and 9 pm each evening...then help your loved one get ready for bed, following a consistent routine. This helps normalize his/her body clock, improving sleep and decreasing nocturnal disturbances.

FINDING SUPPORT

Compared with caregivers who get little support from others, those who get the most support keep their loved ones at home longer...feel healthier...and find caregiving more rewarding. *Best...*

• **Ask family and friends for help.** Be specific. Instead of saying, "Can you help me out sometime?" say, "Can you watch Mom for three hours on Monday?" Having even a few hours off a week helps significantly.

• **Contact support organizations.** The Alzheimer's Association (800-272-3900, *www. alz.org*) offers a toll-free helpline, guidance on financial and legal matters, online message boards, information on local support groups and more.

Also helpful: Alzheimer's Disease Education and Referral Center (800-438-4380, *www. nia.nih.gov/Alzheimers*).

• **Consider professional aid.** Your local Alzheimer's Association office can connect you with geriatric health professionals, meal-delivery programs, adult day-care centers and respite-care providers (who come to your home so you can have time off).

• **Recognize the rewards.** Many family caregivers report that they receive significant emotional benefits from taking care of their loved ones. You can, too, if you allow yourself to take pride in your ability to help and to find joy in your deepened sense of devotion.

Caregiving May Lengthen Life

Previous research suggested that caregiving took a toll on health.

Recent study: Spouses who provided more than 14 hours of care weekly were about 35% as likely as non-caregivers of similar health and age to die within seven years.

Theory: Helping others releases the stress-buffering hormone oxytocin.

Stephanie Brown, PhD, assistant professor of internal medicine, University of Michigan, Ann Arbor, and lead author of a study of 1,688 couples, published in *Psychological Science*.

Caregiver Contracts

Caregiver contracts pay adult children or other relatives to take care of elderly or disabled family members. The arrangements can prevent ill will in the family that might arise if the caregivers work without pay but then are left extra money in a will to compensate.

What to do: Set salaries at reasonable levels—no more than it would cost to get needed assistance from nonrelatives. Discuss the agreements with other relatives so that they know about the arrangement to minimize family tensions later.

Study by AARP, *www.aarp.org*, and National Alliance for Caregiving, *www.caregiving.org*.

Grandparent Visitation Rights

Grandparents have visitation rights in all 50 states. But the provisions of state laws vary widely, and you may have to go to court to have them enforced. The US Supreme Court says that parents have priority in resolving visitation disputes unless they have been alleged to be unfit. Grandparents should try to develop and maintain strong relationships with grandchildren that will last even if parents divorce or a parent dies. Negotiate visitation if possible. Otherwise, consider mediation (for information, contact the American Association for Marriage and Family Therapy at 703-838-9808 or visit *www.aamft.org*). Seek court intervention only if absolutely necessary.

Andrew H. Hook, CELA, member, National Academy of Elder Law Attorneys, Vienna, Virginia, *www.naela.org*.

Fun and Easy Travel With Your Grandchildren

Joan Rattner Heilman is an award-winning travel writer based in New York. She is author of *Unbelievably Good Deals and Great Adventures That You Absolutely Can't Get Unless You're Over 50* (McGraw-Hill).

Traveling with your grandchildren—without their parents—is a wonderful way to grow closer to them, especially if you live far away and seldom have a chance to get together. It's a rare opportunity to get better acquainted, strengthen your relationships and have a very good time. You may even find that your grandchildren are the best travel companions you've ever had.

Whether it's a one-day tour of a nearby city, an overnight camping trip, a weekend at a farm, a week at the beach or a dude ranch, or a 10-day tour of the national parks or Europe, this is the kind of togetherness that really counts.

It needn't cost a lot of money, either, especially if you go somewhere near home and do your own driving.

Super money saver: Choose hotels that offer a good senior discount and a children-stay-free policy—or maybe an inexpensive "suite" hotel with a kitchenette, so that you can prepare some of your own meals. Cooking together can be part of the fun.

Even easier: If you don't want the responsibilities of traveling on your own with children, you can go with a tour company that specializes in intergenerational vacations. Everything is planned for you from morning till night, with most activities for the two generations together but some just for the adults alone, so you'll get an occasional breather.

Some tours are designed for children in a certain age range, while others accept all youngsters ages seven or older, up to 17 or 18. Available in all price ranges, these tours are almost always scheduled in the summer, or sometimes during winter breaks, when the kids are out of school.

Some of the tour companies that will take you and your grandchildren on a fun, well-planned vacation...

• **Road Scholar (formerly Elderhostel).** For an educational, low-cost vacation, sign up for one of Road Scholar's intergenerational programs in the US or Canada. For example, next summer, you and your grandchildren ages eight to 12 could enjoy a five-night stay in Minnesota's north woods, hiking to spectacular overlooks, paddling a canoe under tall cliffs, looking for native animals or learning to climb rocks. Or choose a city, perhaps spending five nights in a hotel in San Francisco, riding cable cars, visiting all of its neighborhoods from Chinatown to Fisherman's Wharf, seeing a fortune-cookie factory, and visiting the Gold Rush Museum and the Exploratorium.

Cost: For Minnesota, $542 per adult, $467 per child ages eight to 12. For San Francisco, $1,176 per adult, $842 per child ages 11 to 14.*

Information: Road Scholar, 877-426-8056, *www.roadscholar.org.*

• **Sierra Club.** The largest environmental group in the country, the Sierra Club plans many affordable "outings." Among them is an annual six-day stay at the club's Clair Tappaan Lodge at Donner Pass in Tahoe National Forest, California, for grandparents and kids at least six years old. The activities include short hikes, fishing, swimming, picnics and a tram ride at Squaw Valley.

Cost: $575 per adult, $475 per child ages six and older.

Information: Sierra Club Outing Dept., 415-977-5522, *www.sierraclub.org/outings.*

• **Generations Touring Company.** Another deluxe tour operator, this one offers tours in the US and other parts of the world from Costa Rica to Vietnam. Some of its trips are classified as "journeys" and aren't too physically demanding. Others are "adventures," for grandparents and children who especially enjoy physical activities.

One of the company's more relaxing journeys: Eight nights in Costa Rica takes you to San Jose, the capital, and then to Tortuguero by bus and covered boat to view birds and sea turtles in this wildlife preserve. Fly to Arenal Volcano National Park and walk across the forest canopy on a suspended bridge. Visit the Cloud Forest Reserve in Monteverde, where you can see a butterfly farm and a local school to learn about Costa Rica's way of life.

Cost: For Costa Rica, $2,599 per adult, $2,099 per child ages 11 and under.

Information: Generations Touring Company, 888-415-9100, *www.generationstouring company.com.*

*All prices are double occupancy and exclude airfare. Prices are subject to change.

Animal Lovers Can Volunteer

You don't need to own a pet to spend time with animals. Volunteer to walk dogs and help clean cages at your local animal shelter. Also, spend a few hours a week at the shelter providing the animals with human interaction—grooming and playing with the animals so that they are better socialized and more likely to be adopted. Volunteer your home as a foster home for dogs or cats.

Consensus of veterinarians and shelter managers, reported in Catnip, *Box 8517, Big Sandy, Texas 75755.*

How to Make End of Life Easier For Your Loved Ones

Alexi A. Wright, MD, a hematologist-oncologist, Dana-Farber Cancer Institute, and instructor in medicine, Harvard Medical School, both in Boston, Massachusetts.

Talking about death can be difficult. Yet research demonstrates that end-of-life discussions can improve quality of life in the last weeks for the patient and ease the loss somewhat for family and loved ones.

In particular, patients who are able to clarify their wishes concerning final medical care are more likely to have a peaceful and dignified death, confirms researcher Alexi A. Wright, MD, a hematologist-oncologist at the Dana-Farber Cancer Institute in Boston. End-of-life discussions were not associated with higher rates of worry or depression in patients and family members. And patients who had end-of-life discussions often began hospice care earlier.

SOONER RATHER THAN LATER

According to Dr. Wright, the ideal time to think and talk about the medical care you'd like at the end of your life is well before it is in sight. It's best to create advance directives, including a DNR (Do Not Resuscitate) order and Medical Power of Attorney, so they are in place

ahead of time. "Patients' health can deteriorate precipitously, leaving the family responsible for difficult decisions that may result in treatment patients didn't want," says Dr. Wright. Don't put off talking about this because you aren't sure now how you will feel in the future...you can always change your mind, though evidence suggests you probably won't. New research from the University of Pennsylvania found great consistency in how people anticipated they'd feel about end-of-life care several years in advance and how they actually did feel. Among those who did experience a shift, most changed in the direction of wanting less aggressive care at the end than they'd predicted. Questions to consider include what sort of medical care (pain relief or aggressive treatment) you want at the end of your life, and whether or not you want to undergo heroic measures such as resuscitation and ventilation. If you do, under what circumstances?

End-of-life discussions offer an opportunity to increase patients' control over their own deaths and to reduce their suffering. They bring peace of mind to both patients and their families. In acknowledging that death is near, patients, family members and physicians can focus on comfort, rather than resorting to painful and often fruitless interventions.

To learn more about end-of-life medical care and discussions and options such as advance directives, visit Web sites such as the following...

• **The American Academy of Family Physicians,** at *http://familydoctor.org/online/famdocen/home.html.*

• **The American Hospital Association,** at *http://www.putitinwriting.org/putitinwriting/content/piiwbrochure.pdf.*

• **The Mayo Clinic,** at *http://www.mayoclinic.com/print/living-wills/HA00014/METHOD=print.*

• **The National Cancer Institute,** at *http://www.cancer.gov/cancertopics/factsheet/support/advance-directives.*

• **Caring Connections,** The National Hospice and Palliative Care Organization, at *http://www.caringinfo.org,* then click on "Planning Ahead."

Living Will, Health Care Proxy and Other Critical Paperwork

Martin M. Shenkman, CPA, MBA, JD, an attorney who concentrates on estate and tax planning and estate administration, in New Jersey and New York. Shenkman has published 34 books, including *Living Wills & Health Care Proxies* (Law Made Easy Press, LLC).

The unexpected can happen at any age, and every adult would be doing their families a favor by putting some thought and effort into creating a living will, as well as a health care proxy. A living will is a set of written instructions that communicates in detail your wishes regarding care and treatment in the event you are ill or injured and become unable to make critical health care decisions on your own. A health care proxy appoints a trusted person, called an agent, to implement those decisions. These documents are especially important if you already have an illness and know that different care options are likely to someday present difficult decisions.

CLARIFY YOUR WISHES

Health care "advance directives" (or legal documents that outline health care instructions in case you become unable to communicate them) are critical and can even extend beyond living wills for some people, says Martin M. Shenkman, Esq., an attorney in New Jersey and New York and author of *Living Wills & Health Care Proxies: Assuring That Your End-of-Life Decisions Are Respected.* Shenkman says that every adult needs four important documents. As you grow older or your perspective or life situation changes, you can always revisit advanced directives to make necessary changes, so don't worry about "what if your attitudes change."

• **Living will.** *A living will addresses such considerations as…*

• Life-support measures such as mechanical ventilation…nutritional and hydration assistance (e.g., a feeding tube)…and dialysis. Many people affirm they want such medical interventions in temporary situations from which one can be expected to recover.

• Quality of life issues, such as mental or physical disability, should be addressed. People can have very different feelings on what treatment they'd want. You might feel certain that if you have significant dementia you want no steps taken to preserve life. Others might feel the opposite and want life prolonged in case there is hope of a cure.

• Also, in the event of a terminal illness, you may wish to express whether you want hospice care. Be clear in stating this in your living will and authorize your agent in your health care proxy to implement it.

• The document should outline whether you want aggressive life support to continue or prefer only pain-relieving comfort or palliative care when death appears imminent. In the hospital or not, in case your heart stops beating or you cease breathing, you may want a "do not resuscitate" (DNR) order placed in your chart so no "heroic measures" (such as electric shock to stimulate the heart) are taken. You might want to expressly state that if you are terminally ill and have life expectancy of, say, less than 30 days, that you should not be intubated and attached to a ventilator. Your agent should request and authorize your attending physician to place a DNR order in your patient chart.

• Philosophical issues (such as organ donation), religious issues (for example, do you want last rites?), and even directions for funeral and burial arrangements can free your family to focus on the emotional aspects of their loss, without having to struggle to guess what you might have wanted. Shenkman points out that these important concerns are often overlooked or neglected in standardized forms for living wills.

• **Health care proxy.** Not all states accept living wills, and general statements such as "no heroic measures" are subject to different interpretations by different people, including doctors and family members. As a result, Shenkman strongly advises that you fill out a form known as a health care proxy—or Durable Power of Attorney for Health Care or Medical Directive or Medical Power of Attorney (POA)—in which you designate one particular person to make health care decisions for you when you are no longer able to do so yourself. Choose someone whom you trust and who understands your values, philosophy and wishes. Don't act out of guilt or obligation. For example, you may find it in your best interest to choose a friend rather than a family member.

• **HIPAA release.** HIPAA stands for the Health Insurance Portability and Accountability Act of 1996. HIPAA provides that no one other than you or a medical provider concerned with your care can access your medical records without express authorization. Therefore it is a good idea to authorize a person, called your HIPAA representative, to have access to your medical records (you should indicate which types of records, etc.). This should be included in your health care proxy, but in Mr. Shenkman's view an independent document is helpful as well. This can be useful, for example, if you have surgery and want a trusted person to monitor your care, but don't need to assign decision-making to him/her as under a living will. The HIPPA rep should be the same person you've designated as your health care proxy agent.

• **Emergency child medical form.** This useful form was created by Shenkman, and is available for free on his Web site at *www.laweasy.com*. It covers the above issues (and others) for minor children. For example, if you are traveling abroad and your child is at home with a caretaker and suddenly becomes ill or is hospitalized, this document designates who has the right to make key decisions about medical care. Just as importantly, it is a way to communicate insurance, health and other information to the caretakers (even if it's a grandparent). The designee should also have access to health records and health coverage. It's best to have such a form for every minor child.

State by state considerations: Every state has its own laws regarding advance directives, and requirements vary widely. Your health care provider or hospital may be able to provide the appropriate forms for your state, or you can download forms for free online at Web sites such as *www.laweasy.com*. You can also get further information from most state departments of health.

DOCUMENT SAFETY

Make three originals of the three documents above—power of attorney, health proxy and HIPPA and give one set of originals to a trusted person who is serving as agent…keep an original set at your home…and the third set of originals to your attorney. While you may have heard you should never sign more than one original will, this is a distinctly different scenario, says Shenkman. Though laws vary by state, and it's not always required, it's advisable to have these documents witnessed and notarized as well.

While these documents can be drafted on your own using standard forms it's often best to consult a lawyer who can draw up a more customized document. The more carefully you spell out your wishes and address the many possible scenarios that can develop, the more apt you are to receive the care you want, whether life-sustaining or end-of-life care, and the less likely you will be to leave a legacy of dissension among surviving family members.

10

Stay Safe &
Self Reliant

How Not to Turn into
An "Old Driver"

As you buckle yourself into a two-ton metal machine and rocket down the road at 60 miles per hour or faster, you may ask yourself, "Am I as safe a driver as I used to be?" This can be a legitimate concern even if you're in robust health and still a long way from being a senior. For instance, you may no longer be able to turn your head far enough to look behind you.

Safety concerns become increasingly relevant as the years pass.

Consider: Compared with drivers age 55 to 64, those over the age of 65 are almost twice as likely to die in a car crash...drivers age 80 and older have higher crash-fatality rates than all other age groups except teens.

Aging affects driving ability in several vital ways...

• **Vision and hearing become less acute.**

• **Cognition slows,** impairing the ability to recognize and react appropriately to a hazard (such as a child dashing into the street).

• **The physical ability to operate a car may be impaired by stiff joints, muscle pain, nerve damage and other maladies.**

Advancing age also brings increased frailty. This means that, even if driving skills remain sharp, the ability to recover from accidents decreases.

The modern world also presents hazards that older drivers may not be accustomed to. More than ever, drivers around you are likely to be distracted by cell-phone calls, text messages and GPS devices. These distractions greatly increase the risk for accidents.

NEW RULES OF THE ROAD

Avoid dangerous situations...

Richard A. Marottoli, MD, associate professor of medicine at Yale School of Medicine and medical director of the Dorothy Adler Geriatric Assessment Center at Yale-New Haven Hospital, both in New Haven, Connecticut.

• **Use routes that minimize left turns—** they are more dangerous than right turns. When waiting to turn left, keep your wheels straight so you won't be pushed into oncoming traffic if hit from behind.

• **On the highway, stay in the right lane whenever possible.** There's less risk of being tailgated, and you probably won't need to change lanes to exit.

• **Minimize travel on congested or poorly lit roads.**

• **Do not drive in rain or snow or when you feel tired or stressed.** Stay home or call a taxi.

See and be seen…

• **To determine if you're tailgating,** pick a spot that the car in front of you passes, then count the seconds until you reach that spot. If it's less than three seconds—or six seconds in rain or fog—back off.

• **Use your window defroster on high heat to clear window fog quickly…then switch to cool air (not cold) to keep fog from coming back.** This works in all weather.

• **Keep your windows clean inside and outside.**

• **Be on the watch for distracted drivers.** Stay focused yourself, too—don't talk on the phone or eat or fiddle with the CD player or have emotional conversations with your passengers.

• **Keep headlights on, even during the day—it makes you more visible to others.** Clean headlights often.

• **If you have poor night vision, drive only in daylight.**

Master new car technology…

• **Put your seat as far back as you comfortably can to avoid being injured by the air bag if it deploys.**

• **Tilt the steering wheel so that the air bag points toward your chest, not your head.** If your steering wheel telescopes, move it closer to the dashboard to lessen air bag impact.

• **If you skid, do not "pump" anti-lock brakes—just brake steadily.**

HEALTH CHECKS

Work with a health-care team…

• **Ask your doctor if any of the medications you take can cause drowsiness or light-headedness.** If you start a new drug, avoid driving for a few days until you see how it affects you.

• **Have your vision checked every year or two.**

• **Get a hearing test every three years.** If you have hearing loss, watch dashboard indicators because you may not notice strange engine noises.

Also: Be vigilant about watching for emergency vehicles.

SHOULD YOU TAKE A CLASS?

The more of the following factors that apply to you, the more advisable it is to take a refresher course in driving. *Take it as a clue if you…*

• **Often are honked at by other drivers.**

• **Sometimes have trouble staying in your lane.**

• **Occasionally think that vehicles or pedestrians have appeared out of nowhere.**

• **Caused a recent accident.**

Many insurance companies offer discounts to drivers who pass a refresher course. Contact your insurance agent for more information.

Some classes can be completed in one or two days…some you do at your own pace.

Bonus: Classes review your state's laws, which may have changed—for example, many older drivers are unaware of certain states' requirements to signal at least 100 feet before turning.

Refresher courses are given online and in classroom settings. A course that includes several hours of behind-the-wheel training is most beneficial, though this can add significantly to the cost. For schedules and pricing, contact AARP (888-227-7669, *www.aarp.org/drive*) or your local AAA club (*www.aaa.com*).

PUTTING DOWN THE KEYS

It's time to consider leaving the driving to others if you have taken a refresher course and yet still experience any of the following…

• **Often feel lost or confused on familiar roads.**

• **Occasionally hit the gas when you mean to hit the brake.**

• **Hear that other people worry about your driving or are scared to ride with you.**

• **Have been advised by your doctor to stop driving.**

If you stop driving…

• **Find out about public transportation options,** including discounted fares for seniors.

• **For referrals to civic groups that provide rides,** contact your local council on aging (800-677-1116, *www.eldercare.gov*).

• **Ask nearby friends for rides (and offer to pay for gas). Many people are happy to help out.**

Best Cars for Seniors

Best cars for senior drivers have easy access, good visibility, comfortable seats and a roomy driving position.

Consider: Subaru Forester XT Limited small SUV ($27,720)…Hyundai Azera sedan ($26,270)…Honda Accord family sedan ($22,730)…Honda Odyssey minivan ($28,580).

Consumer Reports, 101 Truman Ave., Yonkers, New York 10703. *www.consumerreports.org*

Alzheimer's and Driving

Early Alzheimer's harms driving skills. Warning signs include loss of memory and cognitive abilities, such as needing more help than before with directions or a new route…getting lost on once-familiar roads…having trouble making turns, especially left turns…becoming confused when exiting a highway…being honked at frequently by other drivers…drifting in and out of the proper lane.

What to do: If you notice these signs in yourself or a family member, talk to a doctor.

Also: Consider consulting a driver-rehabilitation specialist who can provide a comprehensive evaluation to determine one's ability to drive and/or provide rehabilitation to strengthen driving skills—find one through the American Occupational Therapy Association, 301-652-2682, *www.aota.org/olderdriver*.

Jeffrey Dawson, ScD, departments of biostatistics and neurology, University of Iowa, Iowa City, and leader of a study of 155 older people, including 40 with early-stage Alzheimer's, funded by the National Institute on Aging and published in *Neurology*.

What to Do If You're Stuck in a Blizzard

If you can drive no further during a blizzard, pull off the highway, turn on your hazard lights and hang a distress flag from your window or antenna. Remain in your car, where authorities can most easily find you, unless there is shelter nearby. To conserve fuel, run the engine and heater for only 10 minutes an hour to keep warm. Open a downwind window slightly for ventilation, and periodically clear snow from the exhaust pipe to protect against carbon monoxide poisoning. Drink fluids to avoid dehydration. Huddle together, or insulate yourself with maps and blankets. Turn on the inside light at night so that rescue crews can locate your car.

Federal Emergency Management Agency, Washington, DC, *www.fema.gov*.

Easier Travel for The Disabled

Updates to the Air Carrier Access Act require domestic airlines and foreign ones whose flights originate or land in the US to make accommodations for people with disabilities. They must make arrangements for travelers who use personal oxygen or other respiratory equipment…fly with service animals…or have vision or hearing loss. Accommodation must begin on the ground—for example, a passenger who is unable to use automated kiosks to check in or print boarding passes must be given help or be taken to the front of the check-in line.

Helpful: When making reservations, tell the airline what type of accommodations you need.

Eric Lipp, executive director, Open Doors Organization, a nonprofit group improving access for travelers with disabilities, Chicago. *www.opendoorsnfp.org*

Hotel Sites Help Those With Special Needs

The Internet can provide better travel for people with disabilities. Web sites Expedia.com and Hotels.com have added features to their online reservation systems to make it easier to find hotel rooms with appropriate accommodations for people who are disabled. Accessibility information on the Web sites will allow travelers to search for rooms based on their special needs—and book rooms that have the right accessibility options.

Bonnie Lewkowicz, member of AXIS Dance Company, Oakland, California, and plaintiff in a lawsuit against Expedia.com and Hotels.com that resulted in the sites' changes to their features.

How to Stay Safe When Disaster Strikes

Charles B. Inlander, health-care consultant and founding president of People's Medical Society, a consumer advocacy organization active in the 1980s and 1990s. He is the author of 20 books, including *Take This Book to the Hospital with You* (St. Martin's).

It's human nature to tell ourselves that disasters strike other people—not us. But a personal plan of action is essential, especially if you or a loved one has a medical condition that requires daily care. *Steps you should take to develop your own disaster survival plan…*

• **Put it in writing.** Write out a plan of what you will do in case of a disaster and use it for planning purposes and as a checklist to review in the event of an emergency. Note all the ways that you and anyone you might be caring for can get out of the house quickly or to a safe location (such as the basement).

Smart idea: Place emergency phone numbers (including those for public utilities, friends and relatives) in several rooms of your house in case you are trapped in one area.

• **Get a cell phone.** Keep a fully charged cell phone in an easily accessible location in case your land-line phone doesn't work or you need to leave your home.

Smart idea: If you don't already have a cell phone, buy an inexpensive one but do not sign up for cell-phone service. All cell-phone users are able to call 911 without subscribing to a provider's wireless service.

• **Keep the right equipment and supplies on hand.** If you or a loved one uses an oxygen machine, make sure you have several large tanks of portable oxygen in the house in case of a power failure. Keep flashlights, a portable commode, extra blankets, bottled water and anything else you might need if you lose lights and heat or air conditioning.

Smart idea: Keep your daily medication in sealed plastic bags to prevent water damage. If your medication requires refrigeration, make sure you have a portable cooler in the house and keep ice packs in your freezer. Check in advance with your pharmacist on the best way to store refrigerated medication during an extended power outage.

• **Stay in touch.** Make sure family and friends are aware of your medical status. If your medical condition limits your ability to evacuate your home, family or friends can alert authorities.

Smart idea: Contact your local police department today to alert them that you need to be checked on if a power failure or disaster hits your area. Ask for the officer who serves as the community liaison.

•**Act early.** Don't assume that you can weather a predicted blizzard or any other threatening event. Call a family member or friend to help you or a loved one evacuate at the first warning (if there is one).

Smart idea: If no family member or friend is available, call the police or fire department or your local Red Cross or county government and ask for help.

If a disaster strikes, you'll be glad you followed these steps.

Why You Should Always Have a Baby Photo in Your Wallet...

A baby picture can protect your wallet. In a recent study, 88% of people who found wallets with photos of a smiling baby returned them...compared with 53% of people who found wallets with a photo of a cute puppy...48%, a happy family...and 28%, a contented elderly couple.

Richard Wiseman, PhD, professor, psychology department, University of Hertfordshire, UK, and leader of a study in which 240 wallets were planted on the streets of Edinburgh.

Don't Believe These Myths About Crime

Dale Yeager, a criminal analyst who is CEO of SERAPH Corporation, a security consulting and training company based in Phoenixville, Pennsylvania. *www.seraph.net*

Some of the things that people do to avoid crime actually increase their odds of becoming victims. *Here, the truth about common misconceptions about crime—plus important safety strategies...*

Myth: If you're mugged, throw your wallet or purse at the assailant and run. The mugger will stop to pick up your valuables rather than pursue you.

Reality: Many street criminals value respect above all else. Throwing your valuables could be taken as a form of disrespect. The mugger might use violence against you for this.

Better: Politely hand over your valuables without making eye contact. Follow the mugger's directions, and do not say anything beyond, "Take my money...it's all yours."

Exception: If you hand over your valuables and the mugger continues issuing instructions, such as "get down on your knees" or "walk into that alley," it is time to run away. Muggers who do not leave quickly after obtaining a victim's possessions often intend to commit murder or sexual assault.

Myth: The best way to fight back against a male assailant is with a kick to the groin.

Reality: Attempts to disable assailants with kicks or punches to the groin almost always fail. Men usually experience an adrenaline rush when they commit assaults or muggings. One consequence of this adrenaline rush is that their testicles retreat up close to their bodies, making the testicles a very difficult target to hit. Most men also are quite adept at protecting their groin area when they realize that an attack might be coming. Even if an assailant's testicles are struck, the onset of pain is not instantaneous. An assailant might have enough time to seriously injure or kill you before feeling the full effects.

Better: If you do attempt a physical attack on an assailant, go for a kidney. The kidneys are located on our sides, just above the waist—roughly where the thumbs rest when we stand with our hands on our hips. Kidneys are extremely sensitive. If an attacker comes at you, hit or slap the kidney or stab a pen in the area.

Myth: If you act confident, you are less likely to be targeted by criminals.

Reality: Criminals could mistake your show of confidence for arrogance and target you to take you down a peg. When a man acts very confidently, a male criminal might target him for assault to prove that the criminal is the top dog. When Americans abroad act confidently, they sometimes are targeted by criminals who consider the US their enemy. Rape-prevention

227

groups often recommend that women walk and act with exaggerated confidence when they feel threatened, but this can increase the risk for sexual assault.

Better: It is fine to feel confident, but don't act cocky. Arrogance can make you a target. Also, feigned confidence often seems unnatural and makes us stand out from crowds. Acting the way we actually feel helps us blend in, a far better way to avoid unwanted criminal attention.

Myth: The least safe areas are "bad neighborhoods" at night.

Reality: In my experience, the highest-risk areas for physical attacks by strangers are not bad neighborhoods but near nightclubs. The perpetrators typically are nightclub patrons who have had too much to drink.

Better: Avoid parking near nightclubs if you will be returning to your car after midnight. Stay out of nightclubs completely and advise your adult children to do the same.

Myth: Burglars won't come in if they know you're home.

Reality: Most break-ins happen between 2 pm and 9 pm, partly because this is when people are likely to have their doors unlocked. Burglars target homes that appear easy to break into and move on to other homes if the first one selected proves challenging.

Better: Determine what your neighbors do for home security, then do that and a little more in your own home. Dogs, motion-detecting lights, deadbolts and alarm systems all can be effective deterrents. And be sure to lock doors.

Myth: College campuses are safe.

Reality: Unfortunately, our colleges and universities are very unsafe. Security is extremely lax on most campuses, and burglary, assault and rape are distressingly common. Even prestigious colleges have crime problems.

Better: Impress upon your children that college campuses are not safe havens and that attention must be paid to personal and property security.

Don't Be the Victim of a Health-Care Crook

Charles B. Inlander, health-care consultant and founding president of People's Medical Society, a consumer advocacy organization active in the 1980s and 1990s. He is the author of 20 books, including *Take This Book to the Hospital with You* (St. Martin's).

Even though national health-care reform is now a hot topic of discussion, one aspect that is not getting enough attention is the rampant fraud that involves doctors, hospitals, home-care agencies and non-health-care con artists who deliberately try to fleece the government, private insurers and you. One striking example was brought to light recently when federal authorities indicted the owners of two companies and their associates for allegedly billing Medicare nearly $155,000 to send home-health nurses to administer twice-daily insulin shots to an elderly diabetic man. The problem was that the man was neither homebound nor diabetic, and the nurses did not exist. The eight individuals are now charged with running a fraud scheme that bilked Medicare for a total of $22 million. But that's only the tip of the iceberg. At least 3%—or $68 billion—of all health-care spending each year is fraudulent. Consumers pay for these fraudulent claims through higher insurance premiums and out-of-pocket expenses as well as through taxpayer-funded Medicare costs. *What to do…*

• **Carefully read bills and statements.** Doctors, hospitals and other health-service businesses that commit fraud often charge for services and medical equipment that was never received. For example, a doctor might bill your insurer or you for an injection you never had or charge Medicare for two bunion removals when only one was performed. Hospitals may bill for treatment or medication that was never administered. That's why it's so important to go over your bills and insurance statements very carefully. Ask the doctor or hospital for an itemized bill and question anything you don't understand or believe is a charge for a service you didn't receive. If your bill or insurance statement lists medications, tests or treatments that you did not receive and you suspect intentional "misbilling," call your insurance company and ask for the anti-fraud section. If your insurer gives you the runaround, call your state's attorney general's office and report the suspected fraud. If you are on Medicare, call 800-447-8477 and say that you want to report suspected fraud.

•**Beware of the phone.** In recent years, medical identity theft has become a serious problem. Often, these scam artists call unsuspecting individuals claiming to be from the federal government or an insurance company and ask for the person's Social Security number or the number on his/her insurance card. This information is then used to bill the insurer for bogus services. Never give your Social Security number or your insurance ID number over the phone to anyone who has called you. Give this information only if you made the call.

Also important: Follow the same advice if you pay with a credit card over the phone for a medical service. Con artists can run up thousands of dollars in bills in minutes. If you pay for a doctor's visit or hospital stay on a credit card, make sure that the billed amount matches your credit card statement. If it differs, call the health-care provider and ask for a correction. If such billing problems continue, report them to the card company (anti-fraud section) and your state's attorney general.

Medicare Rip-Offs Facing Seniors Today

Sheryl Garrett, CFP, founder of Garrett Planning Network, an international network of fee-only planners, Shawnee Mission, Kansas, *www.garrettplanningnetwork.com*. She is author of *Just Give Me the Answer$: Expert Advisors Address Your Most Pressing Financial Questions* (Kaplan Business).

Seniors are prime targets for scammers. Many have amassed impressive financial resources, while many others are struggling with the challenges of living on a fixed income. Scammers often exploit the most vulnerable areas, such as Medicare.

Rip-off: Unscrupulous insurance agents misrepresent Medicare policies.

Medicare beneficiaries have a bewildering array of health insurance options now. They can choose from dozens of "Part D" prescription drug plans to supplement Medicare, and they can opt out of traditional Medicare and enroll in private Medicare Advantage Plans for their medical and drug coverage. *This is fertile territory for scam artists…*

•**Medicare Advantage.** To reap hefty commissions, some insurance agents push seniors into buying a type of private policy called a Medicare Advantage Plan without explaining the limitations of the plans.

Examples: You may use only doctors and hospitals in the plan's network…you may lose supplemental coverage from a former employer's plan. They've even been known to sign up people without their knowledge.

How: The agent says that he/she needs the senior's Social Security number, and the senior gives it to him. The agent then uses the number to enroll the senior.

•**Part D.** Posing as "Medicare representatives," unscrupulous insurance agents call and ask you about the Part D plan that you have already signed up for. Since you know that you do have Part D, you can be tricked into thinking that it's safe to give personal information to the caller, such as your Social Security number, which the scammer then uses for identity theft.

•**Drug discount cards.** An individual may be offered a plan from a licensed insurance agent that costs less than Medicare Part D, but the agent does not disclose that the plan provides much less coverage than Medicare.

Self-defense: Before buying any Medicare-related plan, card or policy, contact your state insurance department. Ask if the agent is licensed, if the product is legitimate and whether there have been any complaints against the agent or the company. If you have been fraudulently enrolled in a Medicare Advantage Plan, contact State Health Insurance Assistance Programs (SHIP) at *www.shiptalk.org*. (Click on

"Find a Counselor.") Also contact your state insurance department and attorney general's office, which can take action against agents for sales abuses.

Use Technology to Monitor Health and Safety

Jeffrey Kaye, professor of neurology and biomedical engineering, director, National Institute of Aging—Layton Aging & Alzheimer's Disease Center.

Susan Ayers Walker, managing director, SmartSilvers, *www.smartsilvers.com.*

Technology can improve the quality of life for people with chronic health problems—and most particularly for elderly men and women who want to continue to live independently.

Here are some of the technologies currently in use or being developed…

•**Home monitoring.** Grandcare systems (*www.grandcare.com*) offers a customizable combination of motion sensors, weight monitoring, prescription reminders, general messages from family and more.

•**Prescription monitoring.** For patients taking several medications but who are not sick enough to require full-time care, MedSignals (*www.medsignals.com*) monitors up to four prescriptions at a time, records when the pills are taken, and sends information to a designated party (a family member, doctor or other caregiver) to monitor use.

•**GlowCaps** (*www.rxvitality.com*) are special prescription bottle tops that flash and play music when it's time to take a pill…order refills for you…and send a weekly report on use (caps can monitor when and how often they are opened) to physicians and family members.

•**Assisted living.** Elite Care (*www.elitecare. com*), an assisted-living facility in Oregon, uses monitoring technology to help care for its residents, assuming that the patient has granted permission to be monitored. Behavior and cognitive function are monitored unobtrusively

to track changes that can signal decline or the onset of disease.

WE'RE NOT THERE YET…

These products are available but expensive, and at present, few are covered by insurance. Also, industry standards have not been set. Concerns about privacy (who gets to see this electronic medical information and what can be done with it)…liability (if the system makes a mistake, who is to blame?)…and physician participation (do doctors have the capability to handle all this data?) are all kinks that need to be worked out.

But keep an eye out for future developments. Major companies, such as Microsoft (*www.healthvault.com*), GE, Philips and Intel, are already hard at work on their own plans and products. Product standards and design guidelines are being developed (*www.continua alliance.org*).

Love Your Home? Want To Stay There Forever?

Judith G. Willett, MSW, executive director of Boston's Beacon Hill Village, which helps members remain in their homes by arranging for services similar to those of high-end retirement communities. *www. beaconhillvillage.org.*

The secret of staying at home as you grow older is planning ahead. Don't wait until a health crisis forces you to make hasty decisions. With smart planning, you may be able to stay in your home indefinitely. *Here's how…*

SMARTEN UP YOUR HOUSE

Minor renovations, such as increased lighting, extra handrails and decluttering of scatter rugs, electrical cords and other trip hazards, may be all that's needed to keep you safe at home. If major renovations are in order—such as making bathrooms accessible and widening doorways— look for general contractors with experience in home modifications for seniors. The National Association of Homebuilders (800-368-5242, *www.nahb.org/aginginplace*) has a directory of Certified Aging-in-Place Specialists. The National Resource Center on Supportive Housing and Home Modification (213-740-1364, *www. homemods.org*) also has a directory of qualified contractors and remodelers.

Strategy: If you're planning to build or renovate a home, consider adding a first-floor master bedroom and bath and an accessible kitchen and entryway—key features that make a home safe for all ages.

GETTING AROUND

While good public transportation is scarce outside major cities, many communities offer free or reduced-fare vans and buses for seniors. Some services pick up groups of people to visit a shopping center. Others provide door-to-door service for appointments and errands. Of course, there are taxis and limo services, even private or volunteer drivers to help.

Resources: The Edercare Locator (800-677-1116, *www.eldercare.gov*), run by the US Administration on Aging, is a good place to find local transportation help. Most likely you'll be sent to the nearest Area Agency on Aging or the state office of elder affairs, which are often good sources of information on services for older adults.

HOME SWEET HOME

Housekeeping, cooking and laundry can become more than pesky, time-consuming tasks later in life. Reputable home-care companies can provide part-time housekeepers and home health aides. Look for a company that is licensed, bonded and insured and that does background checks on employees. In Boston, the hourly rate for people to perform these services is about $20. Geriatric care managers, specialists in eldercare issues, can also arrange in-home care. The Web site for the National Association of Professional Geriatric Care Managers (*www.caremanager.org*) includes a directory. Personal concierge services are growing quickly and can help with such errands as picking up dry-cleaning or walking the dog.

Resources: Online grocers, such as Peapod (800-573-2763, *www.peapod.com*), that serve customers with free or low-cost delivery of goods. Meals On Wheels (703-548-5558, *www. mowaa.org*), which provides free or low-cost meals to low-income seniors age 60 and older, is another option. These days, many senior centers offer dining options, such as Mather LifeWays' More Than a Café in the Chicago area, which offers breakfast, lunch and take-out, along with fitness classes, speakers and learning programs. Call your local area agency on aging to see if there's a similar senior center near you.

DON'T DO IT YOURSELF

One day, minor household repairs, such as fixing a leaky sink or climbing a ladder to clear gutters, may become difficult, even dangerous. If you can't do it yourself or get a friend or family member to help, your regular carpenter, plumber or electrician may know of a trustworthy person who does minor repairs. Large franchises, such as Rent-a-Husband (877-994-8229, *www.rentahusband.com*), run background checks and insure employees. Local nonprofits, such as senior centers or religious organizations, sometimes will do odd jobs and minor repairs for low-to-moderate-income elders.

Resources: Some Area Agencies on Aging have a fix-it program for older adults or those with disabilities and/or on limited incomes. Volunteers provide minor carpentry, plumbing or electrical work with a fixed cost for materials. Again, contact the Eldercare Locator.

MOVE IT OR LOSE IT

Exercise is a critical part of being able to remain independent. Studies show that walking three or more times a week and exercising with light weights are key to remaining mobile in later years. Your local YMCA, community center, senior center or even the hospital may have age-appropriate classes to improve strength, flexibility and heart health.

What to do: Some fitness clubs offer discounts for age-50-plus adults. Hotels may open up their pools for community water aerobics. If the weather's fine, why not invite a friend for a walk?

STAY CONNECTED

As we age, social support and connection to community become important parts of staying in our own homes. As friends move away or leave us, we must find new people to add excitement to this phase of life. Your community may have many free or low-cost cultural and social events for 50-plus adults, transportation included. Check your local library, senior center or "lifelong learning" programs at community colleges. Ask a friend to join you.

What to do: My employer, Beacon Hill Village, runs a Neighbor-to-Neighbor program of members who volunteer to run quick errands, offer short car rides, water plants and feed pets for other neighbors. Perhaps you could organize a group of friends and neighbors to provide similar help for each other.

---

10 Low-Cost Ways to Make Your Home Easier And Safer to Live In

Tom Kraeutler, a former professional home inspector and contractor in New York City. He is host of *The Money Pit*, a nationally syndicated radio show on home improvement broadcast to more than three million listeners. He is also the home improvement editor for AOL. *www.moneypit.com.*

Remodeling a house to make it safer and more user-friendly can run tens of thousands of dollars. *Here are some clever ways to improve and update your home without spending much...*

THROUGHOUT THE HOME

• **Replace round doorknobs,** which are difficult to grasp and turn, with lever-style handles that you push down to open. Most of the time, the lever handles can be attached to the existing latch mechanism already on the door. You can do the job yourself with just a screwdriver. Also, consider replacing cabinet door and drawer knobs with easy-to-grasp C- or D-shaped handles.

Cost: About $30/lever and $10/handle. Available at home-improvement centers.

• **Switch to rocker light switches.** They are on/off switches that rock back and forth when pressed. They are larger and easier to operate, and many people find them more attractive than the standard, small flip switches used in most homes. Rocker switches let you turn on a light with your elbow or fist if you're entering a room when your hands are full, and they're easier to find in the dark.

Cost: About $5 per light switch. Available at home-improvement centers.

• **Raise the position of some electrical outlets.** Wall outlets that are close to the floor can be hard to reach and inconvenient for plugging in appliances that you use intermittently, such as vacuums, heating pads and chargers for phones and laptops. Use those low outlets for lamps and other devices that you rarely unplug. Hire an electrician to raise other outlets at least 27 inches off the floor. They'll still be inconspicuous but much more accessible.

Cost: Typically $250 and up to move about half a dozen outlets.

• **Use remote controls for more than TVs.** They can operate window coverings, such as drapes and blinds, so you avoid stretching and straining, and let you control interior and exterior lights from your car or from within the home to prevent you from tripping in the dark.

My favorite: Lutron AuroRa (888-588-7661, *www.lutron.com*).

Cost: The AuroRa entry system starts at around $800 and provides wireless house lighting control for up to five dimmers that can be operated from the car or the bedside. Online retailers, such as Amazon.com offer it.

• **Create "wider" doorways.** Residential building codes and home builders don't consider the needs of older people who may need more than the standard 32-inch doorway, especially if they use a wheelchair or walker. Actually widening a doorway can be expensive and impractical, especially if it's along a weight-bearing wall.

Instead: Replace your standard door hinges with expandable "offset" hinges. These special hinges allow the door to close normally. But upon opening, they swing the door clear of the door frame by an extra two inches. This lets you use the entire width of the doorway when you enter or exit.

Cost: About $20 for a set of two door hinges. Available at home-improvement stores. A handy person can install these hinges because they fit in the existing holes in your door frame. Otherwise, a carpenter may charge about $100/hour.

●**Add a second handrail to staircases.** It's easier and safer to climb and descend when you can use both hands. Adding an extra handrail is an inexpensive and easy way to increase safety. Make sure both handrails are at the same height and between 30 and 34 inches above the front edge of the step. Also, for maximum safety, handrails should extend about six inches beyond the top and bottom steps if possible.

Cost: About $60 to $400 for each new handrail plus carpenter installation. Available at home-improvement stores.

KITCHEN

●**Lower your microwave.** Many home builders, contractors and home owners like to save space by mounting microwave ovens above the stove or high on a wall. This position is hazardous because it requires you to reach above your head to get hot foods or forces you to balance on a stool.

Better: If your existing microwave is on the wall, build a shelf under it where you can rest hot foods after they finish cooking. Or choose a new model with a tray feature that slides out and is easier to reach.

Example: The Sharp Insight Pro Microwave Drawer Oven installs just beneath your countertop. The entire oven slides open, drawer-style, giving you access to the cooking compartment from above.

Cost: About $620 for the microwave and $150 and up for carpenter installation.

●**Install a pullout kitchen faucet.** Lugging heavy pots of water to the stove can be difficult and even dangerous. Many plumbing manufacturers now offer kitchen faucets featuring high-arc, pullout spouts. You can remove the spout and use it as a sprayer hose to fill pots within three to five feet of the stove.

Cost: Starts at about $150 plus plumber installation. Available at home-improvement stores.

●**Install a pull-down shelving system inside your kitchen wall cabinets.** Top shelves in cabinets are difficult to reach. This simple device rests in your upper cabinet until you grab a handle on the shelf frame. A set of three or four shelves swings out of the cabinet and down toward you. The shelves lock in place so you can get the item you need.

Afterward, the whole unit swings back into place.

My favorite: Rev-A-Shelf's chrome pull-down shelving system for 24- and 36-inch cabinets. You can do the installation yourself.

Cost: $300 (800-626-1126, *www.rev-a-shelf. com*).

BATHROOM

●**Add upscale grab bars near toilets and tubs.** Some people have avoided installing grab bars in their bathrooms because they look too institutional. Now, there are much more attractive versions. Brushed nickel or oil-rubbed bronze grab bars by Moen are designed to match other Moen bath accessories and faucets for a coordinated look. The grab bars meet all federal government guidelines. They have a stainless steel core and are 1¼ inches in diameter, making them easy to hold.

Cost: About $25 to $70 for the bar. Available at home-improvement stores. You can install them yourself, but it requires drilling holes in the wall.

Practical Ways to Prevent Accidents at Home

Ella Chadwell, home-safety consultant based in Brentwood, Tennessee.

Most of us try to make our houses as safe as possible, but what appears to be a hazard to one person may not be clear to someone else. For example, we all know that loose bannisters and slippery floors can cause accidents, but handling food in the kitchen can create many less obvious risks. *To spot not-so-apparent hazards...*

• **Ask friends or relatives to walk through your house looking for hazards that you may have overlooked.** A friend might spot a loose doorknob that you've neglected to fix. Though you may be accustomed to the defective doorknob, one day when you pull on the knob, it could come off in your hand and trigger a fall, especially if you're carrying something in the other hand.

• **Keep track of close calls.** When you barely avoid an accident, jot it down.

Example: When you nearly trip over a bump in your carpet, don't just consider yourself lucky—write yourself a note to fix the situation.

Potential hazards that are often overlooked...

• **Kitchen tasks.** As we grow older, we often lose strength and agility, making it riskier to use knives and handle hot food.

For cutting food, consider semicircular cutting tools, such as the Rocking T Knife, that let you slice meat, bread and other foods by rocking the blade back and forth. Semicircular knives require less strength and are usually considered safer than standard butcher knives.

Cost: About $30 from kitchen appliance stores.

To make handling hot food easier, consider a "push-pull stick." These devices grip the oven rack so you can easily slide it in or out from a safe distance.

Cost: About $13 at kitchen speciality stores.

• **Poorly lit porches and entryways.** It's easy to trip over a kid's baseball or other unexpected object, such as a windblown branch, that winds up on a walkway or porch step—especially at night.

Solution: Install bright, exterior motion-sensor lights that go on when they detect motion within about 25 feet. These lights have the added advantage of deterring intruders.

Cost: About $40 to $75, plus installation by an electrician.

Also helpful: A remote-controlled light switch that lets you turn on an interior or exterior light from your car or as you approach your house on foot. These pocket-sized switches work at a maximum distance of about 50 feet.

Cost: About $20 to $40 at home appliance stores.

• **Getting up from the couch.** Even young, healthy people can easily lose their balance when they stand up after being in a sitting position for a long time.

Solutions: Stand up slowly while grabbing on to the arm of the couch or chair before taking a step. If the arm isn't high enough to be of help, consider a CouchCane, a stabilizing device that adjusts in height from 29 to 32 inches.

Cost: About $100 at stores that sell wheelchairs, canes and other products for the physically impaired.

• **Carpets.** Many people believe that carpeting is safer than wood flooring because if you fall, a carpet may cushion the impact. In fact, any fall from a standing position can be serious.

Natural wood usually creates the safest floor as long as it's not coated with a slippery finish.

Reason: Unlike carpeting, wood floors are flat surfaces.

Low-pile carpeting is generally safe as long as there are no bulges. If you want an area rug, put a slip-resistant mat underneath, and secure the rug and mat to the floor with carpet tacks. Vinyl flooring is also safe, and so is tile, unless the indentations between individual tiles are deep enough to create an uneven surface.

• **Getting out of bed.** Even though you might have a lamp on your nightstand, turning it on might be tricky when it's dark.

Alternative: A low-wattage light that will stay on in the bedroom during the night. Most people who are accustomed to sleeping in the dark quickly get used to a dim light, but if you have persistent problems, lower the wattage.

• **Medication and nutrition.** We shouldn't drive a car when medicine makes us drowsy or dizzy, but few of us think about the fact that these side-effects can also cause accidents around the house. When you get up from the couch, for example, a stumble can be serious if medication makes you unsteady on your feet.

The problem is compounded if we become accustomed to the slight drowsiness or dizziness that drugs can cause.

Solution: Ask your doctor about the combined effects of all the medication you're taking, including over-the-counter drugs. If they cause drowsiness or dizziness, don't rush when you move around the house, especially when getting up from a chair or bed. And don't try to carry heavy objects, particularly pans of hot food in the kitchen.

Stay Strong For Life

Timothy Doherty, MD, PhD, associate professor of clinical neurological sciences and rehabilitation medicine at the University of Western Ontario in London, Ontario.

Most people have never heard of *sarcopenia*, but risk for it increases dramatically for those in their 40s, 50s and 60s—and an estimated 50% of adults age 75 and older have the condition.

What is this common—but little-known—health problem?

It's age-related muscle loss, also known as muscle atrophy. Sarcopenia can have several causes, including a lack of physical activity, insufficient dietary protein, diminishing levels of hormones that affect muscles and the decline in muscle mass that naturally occurs with aging.

Because sarcopenia progresses very gradually—it's common to lose approximately 1% of muscle mass per year from about age 40 to age 65 and about 2% per year thereafter—you're unlikely to notice it until you discover that you can't do something you've always done, whether it's lift your grandchild, swing a golf club or get out of a chair.

Good news: While you can't entirely prevent sarcopenia, you can substantially control the rate of muscle decline—and even reverse previous losses—with strengthening exercises and an appropriate diet. Numerous studies have shown that as little as two months of proper training can boost muscle strength by as much as 40%—and it's never too late to start. Even men and women in their 90s can improve muscle mass and strength with strength training.

WHY YOU NEED STRONG MUSCLES

If you think bodybuilders are the only ones who need strong muscles, consider this—healthy muscles have been shown to help us…

• **Maintain independence into old age.** Muscle strength enables us to perform the tasks of daily living, including getting dressed, bathing and climbing stairs.

• **Avoid falls.** Strong muscles are essential for balance and help safeguard us against hip fractures and other debilitating or life-threatening injuries.

• **Boost metabolism.** Muscle burns more blood sugar (glucose) than fat does, helping us to keep off unwanted pounds and protecting us against diabetes and obesity.

GETTING STARTED

Aerobic exercise is essential for cardiovascular fitness, but it's typically not enough to maintain the strength of all your major muscles. Even if you regularly walk or run, you're susceptible to sarcopenia.

That's because walking or running does not prevent you from losing muscle mass (the amount of muscle you have) and muscle strength (what you can do with that muscle) from your core and upper-body muscles. Your core muscles (abdomen, low back, hip and buttocks) and upper-body muscles (arm, chest, shoulder, upper back and neck) are crucial—they allow you to pick up heavy packages, rise from a low chair and perform most everyday activities.

My advice: Aim to do two or three strength-training workouts weekly, consisting of six to eight exercises.* Appropriate exercises can be

* Consult your doctor before beginning any exercise program.

performed on weight-training machines, with hand weights (dumbbells) or by using the resistance created by your own body weight. Ideally, your workout will include two sets of 12 to 15 repetitions of each exercise.

Examples: To target your pectoral (chest) muscles, try push-ups…for your back muscles, try a rowing machine…to work your lower body, try leg lifts, squats and lunges (taking long steps forward or backward from an upright position).

 If you're using hand weights, you'll need to experiment to find the right weight. Select a weight you can lift 12—but no more than 15—times using perfect form. By the last repetition, it should be difficult—but possible—for you to lift the weight without jerking it up or dropping it.

Best: Work with a trainer at your local gym, who can help you devise a routine and demonstrate proper technique. You often can accomplish this in a single training session, which typically costs $50 to $100.

UP YOUR PROTEIN INTAKE

Studies show that up to 27% of older Americans are not getting the recommended daily intake of protein (56 g daily for men…46 g daily for women). Yet we appear to need even more protein in later life, as our bodies become less efficient at converting it into muscle.

My advice: To get a better estimate of your protein requirement, divide your body weight in half, and aim for that number daily in grams of protein.

Example: If you weigh 150 pounds, consume about 75 g of protein daily.

Beef, pork, chicken, turkey, tuna and salmon are highly concentrated sources of protein, generally offering more than 20 g of protein per 3.5-ounce serving.

Other good protein sources: Eggs, low-fat milk and yogurt, tofu and legumes (such as black beans, lentils and kidney beans).

Caution: If you want to try protein supplements or shakes (which typically contain high levels of protein per serving), talk to your doctor—especially if you have kidney or liver disease, which can affect your body's ability to break down and excrete large amounts of protein. In addition, high intakes of protein (more than 150 g daily) from food can tax the kidneys and liver.

Preliminary evidence suggests that *creatine,* a substance that is produced naturally in the liver and helps to fuel muscle cells, may boost the beneficial effects of strength training.

Recent finding: Older adults who took a 5-g supplement of creatine daily—and did strength training twice weekly for 60 minutes per session—had 10% to 15% greater gains in muscle mass and strength after six months than those who relied on exercise alone.

If you want to maximize the benefits of your strength training, ask your doctor about taking creatine as an adjunct to a strength-training regimen. Known side effects include muscle cramps and gastrointestinal upset. More studies are needed before creatine can be definitively recommended as a muscle-enhancing supplement for all older adults.

Illustrations by Shawn Banner.

Most People Don't Think About Falling Until It Happens

Mary Tinetti, MD, director of the Program on Aging and the Claude D. Pepper Older Americans Independence Center at the Yale School of Medicine in New Haven, Connecticut.

Every year in the US, about one-third of people age 65 and older fall, with 1.6 million treated in emergency rooms and 12,800 killed. But falling is not an inevitable result of aging.

Falling is associated with impairments (such as from stroke, gait or vision problems, or dementia) that are more common with age. But risk for falling is also increased by poor balance and muscle strength and by side effects of certain drugs, especially those prescribed for sleep and depression.

TRAINING THAT WORKS

Balance training and strength training are often underutilized ways to prevent falls.

With some types of balance training, you move continuously while simultaneously "perturbing" your center of gravity—that is, you intentionally become off-balance during movement, and your body learns how to respond, building your sense of balance. Do not try this on your own. Balance training is taught by physical therapists at many rehabilitation centers.

Another type of balance training is tai chi. This meditative martial art combines gentle, flowing movements with breathing and improves balance with moves that shift weight and increase awareness of body alignment. Teachers don't have to be licensed, so look for one with at least five years' experience.

Surprising: Dancing is a form of balance training. Any type will do, including ballroom, polka or salsa. Take lessons—and go out dancing!

In strength training, you build lean muscle mass by using your body weight (in squats, push-ups and ab crunches), free weights or elastic bands, all of which provide resistance to muscular effort. Stronger muscles and good balance often make the difference between a stumble and a fall.

You can safely learn strength training at a health club with a certified instructor who can correct your form and modify moves as needed. To do these exercises at home, use a book or DVD by a certified instructor, but check with your doctor first.

Caution: If you've had two or more falls in the past year, or feel unsteady on your feet, see a doctor for a referral to a physical therapist, who can create a safe balance- and strength-training program for you.

RISKY MEDICATIONS

Several types of widely prescribed drugs have been linked to an increased risk for falls, including....

• **Sleep medications**, such as the new generation of drugs heavily advertised on TV, including *eszopiclone* (Lunesta) and *zolpidem* (Ambien).

• **Antidepressants,** including selective serotonin reuptake inhibitors, such as *citalopram* (Celexa)...selective serotonin-norepinephrine reuptake inhibitors, such as *duloxetine* (Cymbalta)...and tricyclic antidepressants, such as *amitriptyline*.

• **Benzodiazepines** (antianxiety medications), such as *alprazolam* (Xanax).

• **Anticonvulsants,** such as *pregabalin* (Lyrica), a class of drugs that is prescribed not only for epilepsy but also for chronic pain problems, such as from nerve damage.

• **Atypical antipsychotics,** such as *quetiapine* (Seroquel), which are used to treat bipolar disorder...schizophrenia...and psychotic episodes (such as hallucinations) in people with dementia.

• **Blood pressure medications,** including diuretics, such as *furosamide* (Lasix)...and calcium channel blockers, such as *nifedipine* (Procardia).

Important: Taking five or more medications also is linked to an increased risk for falls.

LOW BLOOD PRESSURE

Side effects of several medications (including drugs for Parkinson's disease, diuretics and heart drugs such as beta-blockers) may increase the risk of falling by causing *postural hypotension* (blood pressure drops when you stand up from lying down or sitting). Not enough blood flows to the heart to keep you alert and stable, and the body's normal mechanism to counteract this fails.

What to do: Ask your doctor to test you if you have symptoms, including feeling lightheaded or dizzy after standing. He/she will have you lie flat for five minutes, and then check your blood pressure immediately when you stand up. You will remain standing and have your pressure checked one or two minutes later. If systolic (top number) blood pressure drops at least 20 mmHg from lying to standing, you have postural hypotension.

If this is the case, ask about reducing your dosage of hypertensive, antidepressive and/or antipsychotic medications—the three drug types most likely to cause this condition.

Also: Drink more water—at least eight eight-ounce glasses a day. Dehydration can cause postural hypotension and is common among older people, who have a decreased sense of thirst.

Helpful: When you wake up in the morning, take your time getting out of bed. Sit on the edge of the bed for a few minutes while gently kicking forward with your lower legs and pumping your arms. This will move more blood to your heart and brain. Then stand up while holding on to a nearby stable object, such as a bedside table.

VITAMIN D

Vitamin D promotes good muscle strength, so people with low blood levels of vitamin D may be at increased risk for falls. If your level is below 30 ng/mL, ask your doctor about taking a daily vitamin D supplement.

More from Dr. Tinetti

"Fall-Proof" Your Home

To prevent falls at home…

•**Maintain bright lighting throughout the house.**

•**Eliminate throw rugs** that could cause you to trip or slip, or use strong double-sided tape to secure them.

•**Have handrails** mounted on both sides of stairs (the most common spot for falls)… and clearly mark the bottom stair with a contrasting color, such as a light-color paint on dark wood.

For more information: Go to the CDC's Web site, *www.cdc.gov*, and type "Home Fall Prevention Checklist" in the search field.

Boost Balance with Ankle Exercise

Ankle exercises boost stability, according to Fernando Ribeiro, PT.

Background: The lower limbs weaken with age, leading to an increased risk for falls.

Recent research: When 48 men and women (average age 78) did no exercise or three 15-minute sessions of ankle exercises (including flexing and extending with elastic bands) weekly for six weeks, only the exercisers significantly improved ankle strength, balance and mobility.

To increase stability: Ask your doctor to recommend ankle-strengthening exercises that you can do at home. You can also consult an exercise guide from the National Institute on Aging at *www.weboflife.nasa.gov/exerciseand aging/toc.html*. Click on "balance exercises."

Fernando Ribeiro, PT, Research Centre in Physical Activity, Health and Leisure, Faculty of Sport, University of Porto, Portugal.

Stay Active to Stay Out Of Nursing Home

High risks for nursing-home admittance include an early diagnosis of type 2 diabetes, smoking, inactivity and high blood pressure. Staying active and maintaining a healthful weight can help reduce blood pressure and lower diabetes risk. Stopping smoking is a must.

Louise Russell, PhD, research professor, Institute for Health, Rutgers University, New Brunswick, New Jersey.

Falls More Likely for Sleep-Deprived Women

A recent study shows that women over age 70 who get five hours of sleep or less on a regular basis are 47% more likely to fall than those women who get seven to eight hours of sleep. Talk to your doctor if you have trouble getting enough sleep—there are several treatment options, including medication and environmental changes, such as darkening the room, eliminating noise, etc.

Katie L. Stone, principal investigator, California Pacific Medical Center Research Institute, San Francisco.

6 Steps to Stay Out Of The Hospital

Mary D. Naylor, PhD, RN, the Marian S. Ware Professor in Gerontology and director of the New Courtland Center for Transitions and Health at the University of Pennsylvania School of Nursing in Philadelphia. She is cofounder of Living Independently for Elders. *www. lifeupenn.org*

More than half of general hospital admissions involve adults age 65 and older—many of whom are hospitalized repeatedly for complications from chronic conditions, such as heart disease, high blood pressure and diabetes.

Problem: Even a short hospitalization of two or three days often precipitates a serious health decline—primarily due to the high rate of hospital-acquired infections and medication errors.

Solution: As many as one-third of repeat hospitalizations among older adults are preventable.

Mary D. Naylor, PhD, RN, a leading researcher at the University of Pennsylvania who has studied the problem of frequent hospitalizations among older adults for nearly two decades gives important advice below…

Step 1: Be aware of your warning signs

Patients who know what symptoms to watch for are far more likely to seek prompt medical attention at a doctor's office. This often can remedy a potential problem without emergency room or hospital care.

Example: Fluid retention (in the feet, legs or abdomen) is one of the first signs of heart failure (inadequate pumping action of the heart) that is poorly controlled. This usually can be reversed by changing a drug or adjusting a prescribed dosage.

Self-defense: Ask your health-care provider to list early symptoms of any chronic conditions you may have and the best ways to watch for these changes. Write down the symptoms and keep them in a conspicuous location, such as on your refrigerator.

Step 2: Don't settle for a standard discharge

When a patient is discharged from a hospital, he/she is given basic instructions for ongoing care. But this process is rarely adequate.

Self-defense: Don't leave the hospital until you and/or a family member completely understand your next steps. Before discharge, find out which medications you received that day, when the next dose is due, and any changes that require filling a new prescription or increasing or decreasing the dosage taken before you were admitted.

You also need to know how soon you should see your doctor after discharge. Insist on getting the name and phone number of someone you can contact—including after-hours—if you have questions. Ideally, this will be one of the doctors or nurses who is most familiar with your medical history.

Step 3: Do medication checks

Medication errors (such as being given the wrong medication or no dosage instructions) are a main cause of repeat hospital admissions. Potentially dangerous drugs, such as *warfarin* (Coumadin) or other types of blood-thinning medication, are among the drugs most commonly involved in repeat hospitalizations.

When researchers at the University of Pennsylvania tracked patients after their discharge from the hospital, they found a 70% error rate in medication use. For example, some patients were given inaccurate information about medication types or doses…or necessary drugs that were discontinued when patients entered the hospital weren't always restarted once they left.

Self-defense: Keep an up-to-date list of your medications (including over-the-counter drugs) and supplements where family members can find it if you go to the hospital unexpectedly. In the hospital, post a list of your medications beside your bed in the hospital. Every time you see a new doctor, ask him to review the list.

Helpful: Don't throw away your older lists. Compare older medication lists with the newest one. If there's been a change in a drug or dose, ask your doctor about it to ensure that it's not a mistake.

Step 4: Prevent falls

Falls account for about 1.8 million emergency room visits and 16,000 deaths annually in the US. People who fall, especially older adults, often experience a cascade of complications—for example, a bone fracture can lead to extended periods of immobility that increases risk for pneumonia, which often requires hospitalization.

Self-defense: If you're age 70 or older, get a comprehensive assessment from a geriatrician once a year.* He will look at fall risk factors, such as muscle strength, balance and vision changes.

Helpful: Improve your muscle strength with regular exercise such as walking or swimming. Specific exercises that improve balance include one-legged stands, in which you stand on each leg (near a counter so you can catch yourself if you lose your balance) for 30 seconds several times a day.

Step 5: Ask for a mental assessment

Most doctors don't routinely check for mental changes.

Recent study: When University of Pennsylvania research assistants went to a number of hospitals to conduct rigorous cognitive assessments, they found that more than one-third of

*To find a geriatrician in your area, contact the American Geriatrics Society's Foundation for Health in Aging, 800-563-4916, *www.healthinaging.org.*

older patients admitted for complications from chronic diseases had some degree of cognitive impairment (primarily memory loss). Of those patients, 65% had never been identified as having memory problems, which increases a person's risk for making the kinds of mistakes (such as forgetting to take medication) that can lead to hospitalization.

Self-defense: Ask your primary care provider whether you should see a geriatrician or neurologist to have your cognitive functioning evaluated. Testing, which takes about 10 to 20 minutes, typically involves measuring your ability to complete simple memory and/or motor tasks.

Step 6: Eat well

Malnutrition and dehydration are common in older adults and can result in gradual declines in mental and physical functioning.

Self-defense: Get a nutritional assessment from your health-care team. Also, keep a diary in which you write down everything you eat and drink, as well as your eating patterns (for example, time of day) and settings, for one to two weeks.

People who do nothing more than eat nutritiously and drink enough fluids are far less likely to require hospitalization—or to suffer complications from underlying chronic diseases.

11

Get a Good Night's Sleep

Have Trouble Sleeping? These Solutions Can Help

Consistently getting a good night's sleep isn't a luxury—it's essential to your health. Insufficient sleep not only leaves you feeling tired and irritable but also weakens your immune system and puts you at risk for depression, weight gain and chronic headaches. To get the full health benefits of sleep, most adults should aim for at least seven hours of uninterrupted sleep a night.

Many of my patients have trouble sleeping. I often help them determine the nature of their sleep problem—and what might help.

Choose your specific sleep problem below—and try one solution at a time for up to two weeks. If the problem persists, try a second solution in combination with the first. (Don't try three solutions at once.) Once you find the remedies that work for you, you can use them indefinitely. Before starting, check

to make sure that your sleep problem is not caused by any prescription medication you might be taking.

TROUBLE FALLING ASLEEP

For any reason when you first go to bed, try…

•**Sublingual melatonin.** Melatonin, the hormone produced in the pineal gland in the brain, helps to control sleep and wake cycles. Sublingual melatonin supplements (lozenges placed under the tongue) generally work better than either capsules or tablets. Start with 1.5 milligrams (mg) of sublingual melatonin, 30 to 45 minutes before bedtime. (If this doesn't help within three nights, try 3 mg.) Do not take melatonin if you are pregnant, breast-feeding or taking oral contraceptives.

Mark A. Stengler, NMD, licensed naturopathic medical doctor and leading authority on the practice of alternative and integrated medicine. He is founder and medical director of the Stengler Center for Integrative Medicine, Encinitas, California, and associate clinical professor at the National College of Natural Medicine, Portland, Oregon. He is author of *The Natural Physician's Healing Therapies* (Bottom Line Books).

If you have feelings of anxiety, depression or stress, start with…

•**5-Hydroxytryptophan (5-HTP).** The body uses this amino acid to manufacture the "good mood" neurotransmitter serotonin. Taking a 5-HTP supplement increases the body's serotonin production, promoting a sense of well-being and better resistance to stress. Start with 100 mg one hour before bedtime. (If symptoms don't improve within three nights, try 200 mg.) Don't take 5-HTP if you are pregnant, breast-feeding or taking an antidepressant or antianxiety medication.

If 5-HTP (above) doesn't help and you need a more aggressive approach to anxiety and depression, add…

•**SedaLin.** This formula, manufactured by Xymogen (health-care professionals can order it at 800-647-6100, *www.xymogen.com*), can help relax the nervous system. It contains *Magnolia officinali extract*, from the bark of a type of magnolia tree, to relieve anxiety…and *Ziziphus spinosa extract* from a shrub to treat irritability and insomnia. Take one capsule at bedtime for a minimum of two weeks to allow your hormone levels to adjust. (SedaLin also can be used on its own to relieve anxiety and nervousness during waking hours. Since its main role is to calm the nervous system, it won't make you drowsy.) It is not recommended for women who are pregnant or breast-feeding.

If you are over age 60, try…

•**Calcium and/or magnesium.** These supplements can help seniors, who are most likely to be deficient in these minerals, fall asleep by relaxing the nervous system. Take 500 mg of calcium with 250 mg of magnesium one hour before bedtime. Some people are helped by taking either the calcium or the magnesium alone. Find what works best for you.

If you are menopausal, try…

•**Natural progesterone.** This bioidentical hormone (not to be confused with the pharmaceutical progestin) has a natural sedating effect for women with sleep problems related to low progesterone.

Best: Have your hormone levels tested. If progesterone is low, apply a total of one-quarter to one-half teaspoon of progesterone cream to the inner forearm and wrist or the inner thighs 30 minutes before bedtime.

One over-the-counter brand to try: Emerita Pro-Gest (800-648-8211, *www.emerita. com*). For a stronger effect, take a progesterone capsule (100 mg to 150 mg), available by prescription.

WAKING IN THE NIGHT

If you have trouble getting back to sleep…

Eat a light snack before bedtime. Some people wake up in the night because their blood sugar dips, triggering the adrenal glands to produce adrenaline—exactly what you don't want while sleeping.

Solution: Eat a small snack before bedtime, such as six ounces of organic yogurt.

If you consistently wake up between midnight and 2 am, try…

•**Balancing stress hormones.** Many people wake up in the wee hours and are unable to fall back to sleep quickly because of an imbalance in stress hormones. Melatonin (see page 241) can help. *In addition, try…*

•**Walking after dinner.** Exercise of any kind decreases the production of stress hormones. Exercise as early as possible in the evening, at least three hours before bedtime.

•**Listening to relaxing music.** One study showed that listening to relaxing music (such as classical) for 45 minutes before bedtime resulted in better-quality and longer sleep.

If you consistently wake up between 2 am and 4 am, try…

•**Balancing other hormones.** Waking between 2 am and 4 am can be related to hormone imbalances, including estrogen deficiency in menopausal women (note that this is a different sleep problem than that caused by progesterone deficiency described above)… testosterone deficiency in men age 50 and older…and/or growth hormone deficiency in people age 60 or older. Have your hormone levels tested—and if they are low, get a prescription for a bioidentical hormone.

NATURAL STRESS BUSTERS FOR THE HOLIDAYS AND BEYOND

When it comes to your health, getting a good night's sleep is just part of the equation. It's also important to maintain a calm, relaxed state during the day. This is not always so easy, especially during the holidays, when people's stress levels can soar because of overloaded schedules. Stress is bad for your health. It can cause gastrointestinal problems...increase risk for cardiovascular disease...and weaken immune response. To stay on an even, upbeat course through the holidays and beyond, I recommend several remedies. Use only one daytime remedy at a time—in conjunction with the sleep remedies listed above.

For ongoing stress or anxiety...

• **Calm Natural Mind.** Created by natural physician Hyla Cass, MD, this remedy contains *gamma aminobutyric acid* (GABA), which increases levels of the calming neurotransmitters serotonin and dopamine, and L-theanine, a substance in tea leaves that has been shown to increase brain waves associated with a relaxed state. Take as recommended on the label during stressful or anxious periods. It helps some people within a day or two. Try for at least five days, and see if you have any improvement. There are no side effects, and it is safe for everyone except those on antipsychotic medications. To order, call 866-778-2646, or visit *www. drcass.com* (and click on "Health Store").

For quick relief of bouts of anxiety...

• **Bach Flower Rescue Remedy.** If you find yourself in a stressful situation during the day, this homeopathic formula, available in health-food stores, can provide relief in about 10 seconds to a few minutes. (It is not as strong or long-lasting as Calm Natural Mind, mentioned above.) Take four drops in a glass of water. It also can be a "back to sleep" aid when you wake up in the middle of the night.

For compulsive or extreme worrying or mind-racing...

• **Coffea cruda.** This is an excellent homeopathic calming therapy. Take two pellets of a 30C potency when your mind goes into overdrive. It's also a sleep aid when you can't sleep because of mind-racing.

The Best Position For Sleeping

When sleeping avoid lying on your stomach, which arches and strains the lower back and stretches the neck asymmetrically.

Better: Sleep on your side or back, using a contoured pillow (sold at bedding stores) that is thicker along one or two edges than in the center—it supports your neck while keeping the head and spine aligned.

Side sleepers: Place a pillow between your knees so your pelvis doesn't twist.

Back sleepers: Put a bolster under your knees to relax leg and hip muscles.

Karen Erickson, DC, chiropractor in private practice in New York City and spokesperson for the American Chiropractic Association.

Pacemakers Are Linked To Sleep Disorder

In a study of 98 people who had pacemakers (implanted devices that regulate heartbeat), 59% of participants were found to have undiagnosed sleep apnea (temporary cessation of breathing while sleeping), a disorder that raises risk for cardiovascular disease.

Theory: Sleep apnea can lower blood oxygen levels, leading to cardiac disorders.

Self-defense: If your doctor has recommended that you have a pacemaker implanted, ask him/her to screen you for sleep apnea and recommend lifestyle changes, such as weight loss, and/or treatment, such as continuous positive airway pressure (CPAP), to prevent upper airway collapse.

Patrick Levy, MD, PhD, professor of physiology, University of Grenoble, Grenoble, France.

New and Natural Sleep Aids

Chris D. Meletis, ND, executive director and officer of Academic Affairs for the Institute of Healthy Aging, Beaverton, Oregon.

Oh for a sweet sleep—and, goodness, how Americans are clamoring to get one.

Naturopathic physician Chris D. Meletis, ND says that if this is a new situation, first consider what may be causing it. Is there something in your life that has increased stress—perhaps conflicts at work or a problem with your child—anything, in fact, causing anxiety that might interfere with sleep? Maybe the problem is something less apparent, for instance, your sleep environment. A mattress that has become uncomfortable or a pillow that is too hard or soft can be just enough of an irritant to intrude on good sleep. Is the bedroom dark enough and the temperature just right for you? Also consider—have you started any new medications (or changed dosages) that might impact the quality of your sleep?

Dr. Meletis also reminds people that food and drink can impact sleep. Caffeine, of course, is often a culprit. Some people must avoid having caffeine after 2:00 pm, but super-sensitive types should stay away from caffeine completely. Only by eliminating or vastly reducing it for a few weeks will you know if you are in that group. Remember, too, that caffeine lurks in chocolate, colas and tea as well as coffee. As to food, Dr. Meletis recommends having the last meal of the day provide a balance of protein and complex carbs—vegetables (except tomatoes and peppers)...whole grains and the like. This will fill you enough that hunger won't wake you up. Avoid spicy, fried and fatty foods and mint, all of which may increase acid reflux, and don't eat or drink liquids for two or three hours before bed to avoid middle-of-the-night treks to the bathroom. The ban includes alcohol, which also interferes with the quality of sleep.

Anyone who is taking sleeping pills may need to be careful when weaning off of them, he says.

The reason: You can become dependent on the drug and need time to recover. Under supervision of the prescriber, gradually decrease dosage until you are off the medication completely. This process often takes several weeks. Dr. Meletis says that drinking green tea (during the day since it also has caffeine) will help in this process because it has L-theanine, an amino acid that potentially helps induce relaxation. He adds that B-complex vitamins also combat stress and, as a bonus, often make dreams more vivid. (Although necessary to take at least twice daily, unduly high B vitamin supplementations can contribute to sleeplessness because they can be energizing.) Certain herbs are also calming and can help produce a more restful sleep, including valerian, Passion Flower and chamomile tea.

Dr. Meletis says there are also herbal formulas that some people find helpful for occasional sleeplessness.

He likes Herbal Sleep by Vitamin Research Products (*www.vrp.com*) that contains the following...

- **L-theanine** (150 mg)
- **Hops (133 mg)**—Humulus lupulus extract, (strobiles)
- **Lemon Balm** (133 mg)—(Melissa officinalis extract, leaf)
- **Valerian** (100 mg)—(Valeriana officinalis extract, root with 0.8% valerianic acid)
- **Passion Flower** (133 mg)—(Passiflora incarnata, arial)

Consult a knowledgeable physician before you take any of the herbs or supplements above, as all botanicals can have side effects or interact with other pharmaceuticals or supplements.

OTHER IDEAS

Some nights, though, you may need other ways to quiet a mind that continues to churn. Dr. Meletis suggests keeping a note pad and pen next to your bed so that you can jot down a few words that capture the worry or great idea so that you can relax knowing you have a reminder for the morning. He also suggests the following self-healing techniques, based in part on existing sleep-inducing methods. Studies show a stressful experience during the day can inhibit sleep at night and so it is important to combat one with relaxation techniques right away.

Try this for a brief mid-day meditation: Sitting up, close your eyes and observe your breathing without changing the way you breathe in any way. How much time do you spend breathing in and how much time breathing out? Pay attention to where the breath goes inside of you and what parts of you don't participate in the breath process. Again, don't change the way you breathe, merely observe it until you feel completely relaxed.

For soothing yourself into sleep, try these techniques, both of which you should do slowly, gently and in bed…

• **On your back, rest your palms on either side of your belly.** As you breathe in, notice how your fingers go along for the ride as your belly gently swells on breathing in and recedes as you exhale. After many breaths, begin to gently, minimally lift one set of fingers, such as your thumbs, then switch to index fingers, just slightly so that ultimately the tips are barely off your skin as you finish breathing in. Allow them to return to the belly as you exhale and your belly recedes. The idea is not to breathe bigger or differently in any way, which is enough to induce stress. Instead simply observe what you do and repeat as necessary.

• **On your back, rest your arms at your sides and bend your elbows so that one forearm is now perpendicular to the bed with your hands in a soft-fist position.** Keeping your forearm upright, gently bend your wrist so that the palm faces the bed. Do this slowly enough that you can feel that pull of gravity on your hand. (Your forearm position does not change.) You will see that your fist gradually and naturally unfolds as you do this. Gently, slowly, return your hand to its original position where it will return to a soft fist, again, naturally. Repeat as necessary.

Fall Asleep Faster… Without Drugs

John Hibbs, ND, senior clinical faculty member at Bastyr University in Kenmore, Washington, and family practitioner at Bastyr Center for Natural Health, in Seattle.

If you often toss and turn for 30 to 60 minutes or more before finally falling asleep, you may be tempted to use prescription sleeping pills.

The problem is, these make it even harder to reconnect with your normal sleep cycle, robbing you of the most restorative type of sleep.

Try natural strategies that support normal sleep patterns…

• **Go to bed earlier.** This may seem counterintuitive, as if you would only lie awake even longer than you already do. But for many people, the body's biochemically preprogrammed bedtime falls between 9:00 pm and 10:00 pm. If you stay up until midnight, your body may secrete stress hormones to cope with the demands of being awake when it wants to be asleep—and this interferes with your body clock.

Best: Move up your bedtime by an hour… give yourself several weeks to adjust…then advance your bedtime again until you're regularly hitting the hay before 10:00 pm.

• **Exercise at the right time.** Don't try to exhaust yourself with strenuous workouts, especially in the evening—this raises adrenaline levels and makes sleep more elusive.

Instead: Exercise for at least 30 minutes every morning. This reduces the stress hormone cortisol, helping to reset your biochemical clock.

• **Get wet.** Hydrotherapy—especially close to bedtime—calms the nervous system by acting on sensory receptors in the skin. Typically it is most effective to take a half-hour bath in water that's the same temperature as the skin. However, some people respond better to a hot bath…others feel more relaxed after a "contrast shower," first using hot water, then cold.

• **Adopt a pro-sleep diet.** Eliminate all stimulant foods (caffeine, sweets, monosodium glutamate) from your diet. Magnesium calms the nervous system, so eat more magnesium-rich foods (black beans, pumpkin seeds, salmon, spinach)…and/or take 200 mg to 300 mg of supplemental magnesium twice daily. Do not skip meals—when hungry, the body secretes stress hormones that can interfere with sleep. Avoid eating too close to bedtime—a full stomach distracts the body from normal sleep physiology.

• **Try nutraceuticals.** Certain supplements help balance brain chemicals.

Recommended: At bedtime, take 500 milligrams (mg) to 1,000 mg of gamma-aminobutyric acid (GABA), a calming brain chemical. Another option is to take a bedtime dose of 50 mg to 100 mg of 5-hydroxytryptophan (5-HTP), a natural compound that relaxes by balancing levels of the brain chemical serotonin. GABA and 5-HTP can be used separately or together for as long as needed. Both are sold in health-food stores and rarely have side effects at these doses.

Less Sleep and Aging

As we age, we need almost as much sleep as we did during our midlife years. Most adults need 7.5 to 8.5 hours of sleep to be fully alert during the day. However, changes in the brain due to aging (such as hardening of the arteries) and side effects from medications we might be taking for other medical problems (such as heart disease, hypertension, type 2 diabetes or arthritis) often make it difficult to sustain adequate sleep. If you can't get to sleep, or you wake up during the night or very early in the morning, you are probably among the 75% of the adult population who have insomnia at least one night a week.

What to do: Avoid caffeine after 2 pm… avoid alcohol within three hours of bedtime… get plenty of exercise and mental stimulation (do not exercise vigorously within two hours of bedtime)…and don't nap during the day.

Caution: If you have a problem getting adequate sleep for more than three weeks, ask your doctor whether you should make an appointment at an accredited sleep disorders center.

James B. Maas, PhD, Weiss presidential fellow and professor of psychology, Cornell University, Ithaca, New York.

A Nap Is Not Enough

A mid afternoon nap does not make up for a poor night's sleep, and it may make it more difficult to sleep the next night.

To determine if afternoon naps affect your nighttime sleep: Take a nap every day for a week. Each morning, document how well you slept the night before. For the next week, don't nap any day, and document how well you slept each night. Compare each week's sleep patterns. If you find that napping does help your energy level and alertness without hurting your nighttime sleep, nap for only 20 to 30 minutes in the late morning or midafternoon.

Mayo Clinic Health Letter, 200 First St. SW, Rochester, Minnesota 55905. *http://healthletter.mayoclinic.com*

Too Little Sleep Increases Risk of Hypertension

People who slept an average of five or less hours per night were more than twice as likely to be diagnosed with hypertension over a 10-year follow-up period as people who averaged more than five hours a night. Blood pressure drops an average of 10% to 20% during sleep, so less sleep exposes the cardiovascular system to additional stress, which over time can raise blood pressure and lead to hypertension.

Best: Try to get seven to nine hours of sleep per night by allowing adequate time in bed… maintaining bedtimes…having a comfortable sleep environment…avoiding alcohol and caffeine before sleep…and exercising regularly but not too close to bedtime.

James Gangwisch, PhD, assistant professor, department of psychiatry, Columbia University, New York City, and lead author of a study of 4,810 people, published in *Hypertension*.

The Natural Way to a Good Night's Sleep

Carl E. Hunt, MD, sleep specialist and director of National Center on Sleep Disorders Research and professor of pediatrics at Uniformed Services University, both in Bethesda, Maryland.

N o one should underestimate the importance of a good night's sleep. Sleep deprivation has been linked to an increased risk of depression, weight gain, diabetes and cardiovascular disease.

Nearly half of American adults experience insomnia at some point in their lives. About 15% of the adult population experiences chronic insomnia lasting at least a month. Many sufferers are unwilling to take sleeping pills on a regular basis because they're afraid that they'll get "hooked"…find that the pills don't work effectively…and/or experience side effects, such as daytime drowsiness or dizziness.

Recent finding: Cognitive behavioral therapy (CBT)—a behavior/ lifestyle modification and sleep education intervention—was found to be more effective than zolpidem (Ambien), a popular sleeping pill, at helping patients fall and stay asleep. The study, published in *Archives of Internal Medicine*, looked at 63 young and middle-aged adults with chronic insomnia. About half of those who received CBT, alone or in combination with drugs, were able to fall asleep sooner, compared with about 30% of the drug-only group.

HOW IT WORKS

The goal of CBT is to teach people to alter their behavior and thought patterns to break the insomnia cycle. In some cases, the therapy is initially combined with sleep restriction.

Example: Patients who usually go to bed at 10 pm might be asked to stay up until midnight or later, then get up at 5 or 6 in the morning. They are then more tired when they go to bed on subsequent nights, which helps them sleep better.

A patient typically meets with a therapist for 30 to 60 minutes. One session is adequate in some cases—other patients may require four or more sessions. Not all therapists who practice CBT are trained to treat insomnia, so ask your doctor for a referral to a therapist who is.

STEPS TO TAKE

To get a good night's sleep…

• **De-stress before bed.** Don't do anything stressful or stimulating, such as balancing the checkbook or playing computer games, within one hour of bedtime. Insomnia sufferers should give themselves time to unwind and separate from the day's pressures.

Some patients write down all the things that are worrying them or making them anxious before they go to bed. This can help prevent negative thoughts from intruding when they're trying to fall asleep.

• **Get up if you can't sleep.** People with insomnia often get trapped in a worry cycle. They associate going to bed with not sleeping. If they don't fall asleep right away, they watch the clock…worry about how tired they'll be in the morning…and get increasingly stressed, which makes it harder to get to sleep.

The solution is to get out of bed if you don't fall asleep within 30 minutes or if you wake in the night and can't get back to sleep. Do something quiet and relaxing—watch television, read a magazine, etc. Don't go back to bed until you feel like you're ready to sleep.

• **Exercise regularly.** Daytime exercise reduces insomnia and improves both the quantity and quality of sleep. Vigorous exercise isn't required. Take a long walk…ride a bike …or go to the gym. Exercise at least three days a week—but don't exercise within two hours of going to bed. It's stimulating and can make insomnia worse.

• **Avoid coffee for six hours before bedtime.** Everyone knows that the caffeine in coffee, tea or soft drinks can keep you awake.

Most people don't realize that caffeine can stay active in the body for up to six hours.

• **Don't drink alcohol late.** Even though alcohol is a sedative that can help you fall asleep, it interferes with sleep quality and increases nighttime awakenings. Refrain from drinking alcohol for at least one to two hours before going to bed.

• **Avoid over-the-counter sleep aids that contain antihistamines.** These actually can disturb sleep and make it less refreshing.

The Hidden Risks of Sleep Problems

Lawrence J. Epstein, MD, instructor in medicine at Harvard Medical School in Boston, medical director of Sleep Health Centers, based in Brighton, Massachusetts and author of *The Harvard Medical School Guide to a Good Night's Sleep* (McGraw-Hill).

Most people assume that lack of sleep is more of an annoyance than a legitimate threat to their health. But that's a mistake. Lack of sleep—even if it's only occasional—is directly linked to poor health. If ignored, sleep problems can increase your risk for diabetes and heart disease.

About two out of every three Americans ages 55 to 84 have insomnia, but it is one of the most underdiagnosed health problems in the US. Even when insomnia is diagnosed, many doctors recommend a one-size-fits-all treatment approach (often including long-term use of sleep medication) that does not correct the underlying problem.

Everyone should have a comfortable mattress...keep the bedroom cool (about 68°F to 72°F)...and dim or turn out the lights (production of the sleep hormone melatonin can be inhibited in the presence of light). Keep TVs and computers out of the bedroom—both can be stimulating, rather than relaxing. But these basic steps may not be enough.

To treat specific sleep problems...

IF YOU WAKE UP TOO EARLY IN THE MORNING

Early risers often have advanced sleep phase syndrome (ASPS), which is seen most commonly in older adults. With this condition, a person's internal body clock that regulates the sleep-wake cycle (circadian rhythm) is not functioning properly. ASPS sufferers sleep best from 8 pm to 4 am.

My solutions: To reset your circadian rhythm, try a light box (a device that uses lightbulbs to simulate natural light). Light boxes don't require a doctor's prescription and are available for $100 to $500 online or from retailers, such as Amazon.com. Most people use a light box for 30 minutes to an hour daily at sundown. (Those with ASPS may need long-term light therapy.) If you have cataracts or glaucoma or a mood disorder (such as bipolar disorder), consult your doctor before trying light therapy. Patients with retinopathy (a disorder of the retina) should avoid light therapy.

Also helpful: To help regulate your internal clock so that you can go to bed (and get up) later, take a 3-mg to 5-mg melatonin supplement each day. A sleep specialist can advise you on when to use light therapy and melatonin for ASPS.*

IF YOU CAN'T STAY ASLEEP

Everyone wakes up several times a night, but most people fall back to sleep within seconds, so they don't remember waking up.

Trouble staying asleep is often related to sleep apnea, a breathing disorder that causes the sufferer to awaken repeatedly during the night and gasp for air. Another common problem among those who can't stay asleep is *periodic limb movement disorder* (PLMD), a neurological condition that causes frequent involuntary kicking or jerking movements during sleep. (Restless legs syndrome, which is similar to PLMD, causes an uncontrollable urge to move the legs and also can occur at night.)

My solutions: If you are unable to improve your sleep throughout the night by following the strategies already described, consult

*To find a sleep center near you, consult the American Academy of Sleep Medicine (630-737-9700), *www.sleepcenters.org*.

a sleep specialist to determine whether you have sleep apnea or PLMD.

Sleep apnea patients usually get relief by losing weight, if necessary…elevating the head of the bed to reduce snoring…using an oral device that positions the jaw so that the tongue cannot block the throat during sleep… or wearing a face mask that delivers oxygen to keep their airways open. PLMD is usually treated with medication.

IF YOU CAN'T GET TO SLEEP

Most people take about 20 minutes to fall asleep, but this varies with the individual. If your mind is racing due to stress (from marital strife or financial worries, for example) or if you've adopted bad habits (such as drinking caffeine late in the day), you may end up tossing and turning.

My solutions: Limit yourself to one cup of caffeinated coffee or tea daily, and do not consume any caffeine-containing beverage or food (such as chocolate) after 2 pm. If you take a caffeine-containing drug, such as Excedrin or some cold remedies, ask your doctor if it can be taken earlier in the day.

Helpful: If something is bothering you, write it down and tell yourself that you will deal with it tomorrow—this way, you can stop worrying so you can get to sleep.

Also helpful: When you go to bed, turn the clock face away from you so you don't watch the minutes pass. If you can't sleep after 20 to 30 minutes, get up and do something relaxing, such as meditating, until you begin to feel drowsy.

IF YOU CAN'T GET UP
IN THE MORNING

If you can't drag your head off the pillow, sleep apnea or a delayed sleep phase (DSP) disorder might be to blame. DSP disorder makes it hard to fall asleep early, so you stay up late at night and then struggle to get out of bed in the morning.

My solutions: To treat DSP disorder, progressively stay up for three hours later nightly for one week until you reach your desired bedtime. By staying up even later than is usual for you, you'll eventually shift your circadian rhythm. Once you find your ideal bedtime,

stick to it. Also consider trying light-box therapy each morning upon arising. Light helps advance your body clock so that your bedtime should come earlier. Taking 3 mg to 5 mg of melatonin one hour before bedtime should also make you sleepy at an earlier hour.

IF YOU CAN'T STAY AWAKE
DURING THE DAY

If you're getting ample rest—most people need seven and one-half to eight hours a night—and still are tired, you may have narcolepsy. This neurological disorder occurs when the brain sends out sleep-inducing signals at inappropriate times, causing you to fall asleep and even temporarily lose muscle function. Sleep apnea or periodic limb movements also can leave people feeling exhausted.

My solutions: Figure out how much sleep you need by sleeping as long as you can nightly (perhaps while on vacation) for one to two weeks. At the end of that period, you should be sleeping the number of hours you need. Give yourself that much sleep time nightly. If you remain sluggish, ask your doctor about tests for sleep apnea, PLMD—or narcolepsy, which is treated with stimulants, such as *modafinil* (Provigil), that promote wakefulness.

Dangers of Sleep Apnea

Ralph Downey III, PhD, DABSM, past chief, sleep medicine, Loma Linda University Medical Center, Loma Linda University Children's Hospital, former associate professor of medicine, pediatrics, and neurology, Loma Linda University School of Medicine, Loma Linda, California, former adjunct associate professor of psychology, University of California, Riverside, California.

Doctors have long known that obstructive sleep apnea (repeated interruptions in breathing during sleep) can harm the overall health of men and women who suffer from the condition.

Now: Research shows that sleep apnea is even more dangerous than experts had previously realized, increasing the sufferer's risk for heart attack, stroke, diabetes and fatal car crashes.

What you need to know...

NO ROOM TO BREATHE

Sleep apnea occurs about twice as often in men as in women, but it is overlooked more often in women. An estimated 70% of people with sleep apnea are overweight. Fat deposited around the neck (men with sleep apnea often wear a size 17 or larger collar, while women with the disorder often have a neck circumference of 16 inches or more) compresses the upper airway, reducing air flow and causing the passage to narrow or close. Your brain senses this inability to breathe and briefly awakens you so that you can reopen the airway.

The exact cause of obstructive sleep apnea in people of normal weight is unknown, but it may involve various anatomical characteristics, such as having a narrow throat and upper airway.

Red flag 1: About half of all people who snore loudly have sleep apnea. One telling sign is a gasping, choking kind of snore, during which the sleeper seems to stop breathing. (If you live alone and don't know whether you snore, ask your doctor about recording yourself while you are sleeping to check for snoring and other signs of sleep apnea.)

Red flag 2: Daytime sleepiness is the other most common symptom. Less common symptoms include headache, sore throat and/or dry mouth in the morning, sexual dysfunction and memory problems.

DANGERS OF SLEEP APNEA

New scientific evidence shows that sleep apnea increases risk for...

• **Cardiovascular disease.** Sleep apnea's repeated episodes of interrupted breathing—and the accompanying drop in oxygen levels—takes a toll on the heart and arteries.

Recent finding: Heart attack risk in sleep apnea sufferers is 30% higher than normal over a four- to five-year period, and stroke risk is twice as high in people with sleep apnea.

• **Diabetes.** Sleep apnea (regardless of the sufferer's weight) is linked to increased insulin resistance—a potentially dangerous condition in which the body is resistant to the effects of insulin.

Recent finding: A Yale study of 593 patients found that over a six-year period, people diagnosed with sleep apnea were more than two-and-a-half times more likely to develop diabetes than those without the sleep disorder.

• **Accidents.** Sleep apnea dramatically increases the risk for a deadly mishap due to sleepiness and impaired alertness.

Recent finding: A study of 1,600 people, presented at an American Thoracic Society meeting, found that the 800 sleep apnea sufferers were twice as likely to have a car crash over a three-year period. Surprisingly, those who were unaware of being sleepy were just as likely to crash as those who were aware of being sleepy.

DO YOU HAVE SLEEP APNEA?

If you think you may have sleep apnea, see a specialist at an accredited sleep center, where a thorough medical history will be taken and you may be asked to undergo a sleep study.* This involves spending the night in a sleep laboratory where your breathing, oxygen level, movements and brain wave activity are measured while you sleep.

BEST TREATMENT OPTIONS

The treatment typically prescribed first for sleep apnea is *continuous positive airway pressure* (CPAP). A stream of air is pumped onto the back of the throat during sleep to keep the airway open. The air is supplied through a mask, most often worn over the nose, which is connected by tubing to a small box that contains a fan.

In recent years, a larger variety of masks have become available, and fan units have become smaller and nearly silent. A number of adjustments may be needed, which may require trying several different devices and more than one visit to a sleep lab.

Other treatments for sleep apnea are usually prescribed to make CPAP more effective, or for people with milder degrees of the disorder who have tried CPAP but were unable or unwilling to use it.

*To find a sleep center near you, consult the American Academy of Sleep Medicine (630-737-9700), *www. sleepcenters.org*.

These treatments include…

•**Mouthpieces.** Generally fitted by a dentist and worn at night, these oral appliances adjust the lower jaw and tongue to help keep the airway open.

•**Surgery.** This may be recommended for people who have an anatomical abnormality that narrows the airway and for whom CPAP doesn't work. The most common operation for sleep apnea is *uvulopalatopharyngoplasty* (UPPP), in which excess tissue is removed from the back of the throat. It works about 50% of the time.

HELPING YOURSELF

Several measures can make sleep apnea treatment more effective and, in some cases, eliminate the condition altogether. *What to do…*

•**Lose weight, if you are overweight.** For every 10% of body weight lost, the number of apnea episodes drops by 25%.

•**Change your sleep position.** Sleeping on your side—rather than on your back—typically means fewer apnea episodes. Sleeping on your stomach is even better. Some obese people who have sleep apnea do best if they sleep while sitting up.

•**Avoid alcohol.** It relaxes the muscles around the airway, aggravating sleep apnea.

•**Use medication carefully.** Sleep medications can worsen sleep apnea by making it harder for your body to rouse itself when breathing stops. If you have sleep apnea, make sure a doctor oversees your use of sleep medications (including over-the-counter drugs).

Natural Remedies For Snoring

Jamison Starbuck, ND, naturopathic physician in family practice in Missoula, Montana. She is past president of the American Association of Naturopathic Physicians and a contributing editor to The Alternative Advisor: The Complete Guide to Natural Therapies and Alternative Treatments *(Time Life).*

Snoring is a problem that many of my patients suffer from but few admit to. For many of them, snoring is embarrassing. For example, Bill, a 44-year-old father of three,

recently told me, "I'm just a heavy breather." However, based on the description from Bill's sleep-deprived wife, snoring was a definite problem in their household.

Snoring regularly affects 37 million Americans (about 25% female). It is defined as noisy breathing during sleep caused by air passing through a constricted airway. Mild snoring can be remedied by awakening the snorer or by changing his/her position…heavy snoring lasts most of the night, regardless of the person's position or how often he/she wakes. Snoring is not the same as sleep apnea. Sleep apnea is a breathing disorder. The sleeper (who may or may not be snoring) stops breathing and must awaken in order to start breathing again.

Chief causes of the airway constriction that triggers snoring are lack of fitness, being overweight, drinking alcohol before bed, smoking and nasal congestion. Men are more likely to snore than women, and if a first-degree relative (parent, sibling or child) snores, that also may make you more likely to suffer from snoring.

•**Food allergies are an often-overlooked cause of snoring.** They lead to nasal congestion, allergic sinusitis and swelling in the upper respiratory tract. In Bill's case, a simple blood test revealed that eggs were a problem for him. Eliminating eggs from his diet cured his nighttime "heavy breathing" and brought peace to the household. For people who snore, dairy, wheat, eggs and soy are the most common food allergens. I've seen all of them trigger snoring in my patients. If you snore, try eliminating these foods for 10 days, one at a time, to see if your snoring is reduced. For quicker answers, ask your doctor for an allergy test. Be sure to get a blood test, which checks for IgG-mediated antibodies to common foods. Skin scratch allergy testing will not adequately determine snore-inducing food allergens.

Other helpful steps for people who snore…

•**Get fit and lose weight.** Strengthening and tightening the muscles of the throat and losing weight will open airways and diminish snoring.

•**If you smoke, quit.** Smoke irritates the tissue of the upper respiratory tract, causing the congestion and swelling that can lead to snoring.

• **Don't drink alcohol within two hours of bedtime.** Drinking alcohol relaxes muscle tension. If you drink just before going to sleep, the muscles of your tongue and throat will be too lax and your airway will be narrowed—a perfect trigger for snoring.

• **Review your medications.** Drugs that relax the body—sleeping pills, antihistamines, tranquilizers and muscle relaxants—can cause snoring. Talk to your doctor about taking the smallest dose possible. Ask your pharmacist and/or doctor whether you can take the medication several hours before bedtime to help reduce the incidence of snoring.

Hidden Dangers Of Snoring

Samuel Krachman, DO, professor of medicine and director of the Sleep Disorders Center in the division of pulmonary and critical care medicine at Temple University School of Medicine in Philadelphia.

S noring may not strike you as a serious health problem. But that belief could cause you to unwittingly increase your risk for a variety of medical conditions, including some that are life threatening.

It's been known for some time that the sleep disorder sleep apnea—commonly marked by snoring—is associated with an increased risk for cardiovascular disease, heart failure and stroke. Recent scientific evidence now links sleep apnea to erectile dysfunction and even eye disorders, such as glaucoma.

Recent news: There are treatments that are relieving sleep apnea symptoms at an unprecedented rate.

ARE YOU AT RISK?

Up to 20 million Americans—including one in every five adults over age 60—have sleep apnea, a condition in which breathing intermittently stops and starts during sleep. Most people who have sleep apnea snore—but not all snorers have sleep apnea.

And contrary to popular belief, sleep apnea also can affect women. About 9% of middle-aged women have the disorder and 24% of middle-aged men.

EVEN MILD CASES ARE DANGEROUS

Doctors once thought that only severe forms of sleep apnea posed cardiovascular risks. Now, research shows that patients who stop breathing more than five times an hour have double or even triple the rate of hypertension as those who breathe normally. With sleep apnea, breathing may stop several dozen or even hundreds of times during the night compared with one to four times an hour during sleep in a healthy adult. The frequent interruptions in breathing that characterize sleep apnea can lead to a potentially harmful decrease in oxygen levels.

WHAT CAUSES SLEEP APNEA

It's not widely known, but there are two forms of sleep apnea...

• *Obstructive sleep apnea* **(OSA),** the most common form, occurs when the muscles of the throat relax and collapse during sleep, interrupting the flow of air.

• **Obesity is a main cause of OSA.** Fatty deposits surrounding the airways may interfere with breathing, and the weight of excess tissue makes it harder for muscles to retain their normal position during sleep. People with large neck sizes (17 inches or more for men, 16 inches or more for women) are at increased risk.

• **Central apnea,** in which the brain doesn't send the appropriate signals to the respiratory muscles, is relatively rare. It is not associated with obesity and sometimes occurs in the presence of a stroke, which affects brain function.

BEST TREATMENT OPTIONS

Patients who are slightly overweight and suffer from mild OSA (defined as five to 15 interruptions in breathing per hour) may improve if they lose just a few pounds. Most patients, however, need medical help. *Best approaches for both types of apnea...*

• **Change sleep position.** Up to 50% of patients with mild OSA and 20% of those with a moderate form of the disease (16 to 30 interruptions in breathing per hour) stop breathing only when they sleep on their backs. This form of OSA, positional sleep apnea, can be completely eliminated if the sufferer sleeps on his/her side or stomach.

Recent development: A product called Zzoma, which is worn around the chest like a belt, has a padded back that prevents people from sleeping on their backs. Developed by researchers at Temple University School of Medicine, Zzoma has been approved by the FDA for patients diagnosed with "positional snoring." It is available at *www.zzomaosa.com*.

Cost: $99.95.

Other treatments (all are available at medical-supply stores)…*

• **Continuous positive airway pressure (CPAP).** This is the standard treatment for OSA and central apnea.

How it works: CPAP delivers room air under pressure through a mask to a patient's nose and/or mouth. The slightly pressurized flow of air helps keep the airways open and helps prevent snoring as well as apnea.

CPAP can be uncomfortable because patients must wear a mask all night. For this reason, the device is used as prescribed—for example, worn all night, every night—only about half of the time.

Helpful: Before choosing a CPAP device, try on different masks until you find one that's comfortable enough to wear all night.

Typical cost: Starting at about $200.

Alternative: Some people with mild OSA prefer to wear a nighttime oral device, such

---

*You should undergo a sleep evaluation at a sleep disorders clinic before buying one of these devices. Insurance won't pay for the device unless you've been diagnosed with sleep apnea by a doctor. To find a sleep disorders clinic near you, consult the American Academy of Sleep Medicine (630-737-9700, *www.aasmnet.org*).

as the Thornton Adjustable Positioner (TAP), which moves the lower jaw forward so that the tongue and throat tissue don't block the airway. The TAP is available online for about $1,800.

• *Bi-level positive airway pressure* (**Bi-PAP**) is similar to CPAP, except the machine delivers more air pressure when patients inhale and less when they exhale. This is helpful for OSA patients who find it uncomfortable to exhale "against" air pressure—and for obese patients who tend to breathe too shallowly.

Cost: Starting at about $800.

• *Adaptive servo-ventilation* (**ASV**) **is an air-flow approach that also involves wearing a mask.** An ASV unit, which is used for central apnea, analyzes normal breathing patterns and stores the data in a computer. If a patient stops breathing, the machine automatically delivers pressurized air—and then stops when the patient's normal breathing resumes.

Cost: About $7,000.

IF YOU STILL NEED HELP

For most sleep apnea patients, surgery is a last resort. It makes a significant difference in only 20% to 30% of cases.

Common procedures…

• **Uvulopalatopharyngoplasty (UPPP)** involves removing tissue from the back of the mouth and the top of the throat. This procedure often stops snoring, but is less effective at eliminating frequent interruptions in breathing during sleep.

• **The Pillar,** a relatively new procedure, involves the placement of small synthetic rods in the soft palate in the mouth. The rods stiffen the tissue and reduce sagging during sleep. Like UPPP, it's effective primarily for snoring.

PART 2

Treating Everyday Ailments

12

Aches & Pains

Five Solutions for Your Aching Back

Who hasn't suffered a backache—particularly as the years tick by? Back pain is one of the most common medical complaints, with four out of five of us experiencing it at some point in our lives. Often people with back pain do need to see a doctor, but if you know your twinges and creaks are the result of overdoing it—perhaps a more vigorous than usual game of racquetball, an overzealous day of yard work, toting around a growing grandchild or simply the aches and pains of age—there are some safe and effective measures that can provide soothing relief.

For advice, we went to Thomas H. Reece, DO, ND, one of just a few practitioners who holds dual degrees in Naturopathic and Osteopathic Medicine. Former medical director of the Southwest Naturopathic Medical Center in Scottsdale, Arizona, Dr. Reece now practices at the Preventive Medical Center of Marin in California. He told us that serious back problems usually involve pain that travels down the leg, producing numbness and a decrease in muscle strength (this may show up as a drop foot or you may simply notice that you are tripping on one foot). This kind of problem requires appropriate diagnosis and care and Dr. Reece strongly advises against any attempts at self-treatment. He reiterated that relatively simple or straightforward backaches respond well to simple, straightforward home care.

EASY FIXES FOR A COMMON PROBLEM

• **Lay around a while.** In the initial stages of back pain from a strained muscle, nothing is quite as simple and effective as ice and rest. It may be beneficial to stay in bed (or at least

Thomas H. Reece, DO, ND, one of only a few practitioners with dual degrees in Naturopathic and Osteopathic Medicine. Former medical director of the Southwest Naturopathic Medical Center in Scottsdale, Arizona, Dr. Reece now practices at the Preventive Medical Center of Marin in California. He is a specialist in Osteopathic Manipulative Medicine.

rest from normal activity) for a day or two after such a strain, but longer bed rest may do more harm than good, leading to further stiffness and weakness. It's best to return to some activity, such as walking on level ground, as soon as possible. Taking magnesium malate, enzymes and homeopathic arnica may help ease the pain of a strain.

Dr. Reece recommends: If back pain is severe (you can't move or you experience the serious symptoms noted above) or a seemingly simple strain persists for more than three days, see your physician for diagnosis and treatment.

•**Bend and stretch.** A study at the University of Oxford in the UK demonstrated that a three-week rehabilitation program was nearly as effective as spinal fusion surgery in overcoming certain types of back pain. Daily exercises were carefully tailored to suit individual ability, and consisted of muscle stretching and strengthening, endurance, low-impact aerobic exercise (e.g., walking or swimming), and spine stabilization exercises for deep abdominal muscles. Specific activities included walking on a treadmill, stationary cycling, step-ups and abdominal-strengthening exercises using a gym ball.

Dr. Reece recommends: A lack of exercise lies at the root of many back problems, with muscle weakness and stiffness opening the door to injury. If you suffer from chronic or periodic back pain, Dr. Reece advises that you begin any new workout under the watchful eye of a physical therapist. He said that a toning exercise program may be more appropriate for this purpose than a stretching program.

Dr. Reece recommends: Perform Qigong over Tai Chi...yoga or Pilates could also be beneficial if the instructor tailors the program to your specific needs.

•**Water works wonders.** Daily sessions of hydrotherapy were part of the rehabilitation program at the University of Oxford. Hot compresses relax muscles and increase blood flow to painful areas, while cold compresses reduce inflammation. With back strains, always use cold only during the first 48 to 72 hours, then alternate cold with hot.

Dr. Reece recommends: Apply alternate cold and hot packs to strained or sore areas of the back, using cold first. Use each for two to five minutes, for a total of 20 to 30 minutes, ending with cold. Instant cold and hot packs are widely available in drugstores or you can use moistened towels.

•**Supplemental solutions.** Conventional drugs for back pain have many possible side effects. NSAIDs (nonsteroidal anti-inflammatory drugs) such as ibuprofen and naproxen can lead to gastrointestinal problems or bleeding problems for some individuals...pain-relieving opioids are potentially addictive...and muscle relaxants are associated with dizziness and drowsiness.

There are some natural solutions, however. Enzymes such as bromelain and herbs such as curcumin are known to have a natural anti-inflammatory impact. Also, supplements such as fish oil may help reduce inflammation and soothe back discomfort. A study published in *Surgical Neurology* suggested that fish oil supplements are as effective as certain NSAIDs in relieving back and neck pain, with fewer side effects, though the study authors acknowledge that further research needs to be done.

Dr. Reece recommends: Magnesium supplements, in the form of magnesium malate. This natural muscle relaxant doesn't provide the powerful pain relief of a pharmaceutical agent, but it certainly has fewer side effects.

•**Basics of body mechanics.** Many back problems stem from poor body mechanics or posture—for example, lifting objects incorrectly or sitting hunched over a computer all day. Good body mechanics mean that you are standing, sitting and moving without putting undue stress on any muscles or joints.

Dr. Reece recommends: To lift an object properly, hold it close to you...bend your knees, squat...and lift it straight up, without twisting. Always use proper posture.

BACK TO NORMAL

Before resorting to complicated, high-tech solutions for back pain, consider going the natural route. The truth is that most episodes of acute pain from back strain resolve on their own and low-tech, side-effect-free options work for many people.

Vitamin D—Helps Reduce Your Chronic Back Pain

Stewart B. Leavitt, PhD, editor of *Pain Treatment Topics* (*www.pain-topics.org*). Pain Treatment Topics provides access to news, information, research and education for a better understanding of evidence-based pain-management practices. It is funded by an unrestricted educational grant from Covidien/Mallinckrodt Inc., a manufacturer of generic opioid analgesic products. Neither the author nor sponsor has a vested interest in nutritional supplements or offers vitamin D prescribing advice for individual patients.

D o you have back pain that is not linked to a specific injury or nerve problem? According to research, the root cause may be as simple as a deficiency of vitamin D and, if so, the solution may be equally simple—a daily dose of this effective and inexpensive nutrient.

HOW VITAMIN D HELPS BACK PAIN

Stewart B. Leavitt, PhD, editor of the Web site Pain Treatment Topics (*http://pain-topics. org/*), believes that most people are functionally deficient in vitamin D. As we know, the body manufactures vitamin D from sunlight exposure or gets it from food sources such as salmon, tuna, eggs and fortified dairy foods. Often though, this is not enough for optimal health. Insufficient levels of this nutrient affect the body's ability to absorb calcium from foods. This, in turn, can negatively affect bones, muscles and nerve function, leading to back pain among other problems.

In reviewing 22 clinical investigations for his peer-reviewed report, "Vitamin D—A Neglected 'Analgesic' for Chronic Musculoskeletal Pain," Dr. Leavitt found that people with chronic body aches and back pain usually had low levels of vitamin D. The good news is that once they began getting enough of this nutrient, aches and pains diminished or even

disappeared. By restoring calcium balance throughout the body, extra vitamin D helps maintain healthier bones and muscle strength. Vitamin D also acts as a hormone, necessary for the health of many tissues and organs in the body. Because it addresses the underlying cause of pain rather than the pain itself, it may take weeks or even months before there is noticeable improvement.

ABC'S OF VITAMIN D

Generally speaking, Dr. Leavitt says that the amount of vitamin D (400 to 800 IU) in regular multivitamins is insufficient. Experts believe the body requires at least 1,000 IU of vitamin D daily and that people with chronic musculoskeletal pain need even more—2,000 or more IU daily. (Note: Supplemental vitamin D should only be taken under physician oversight.) Vitamin D comes in two forms—D-2 and D-3. Dr. Leavitt favors D-3, which is also known as *cholecalciferol*.

More good news: Vitamin D is inexpensive—typically no more than 10 cents a day.

Vitamin D should be viewed as a helping hand, not a miracle worker. It may not replace other medications for people suffering from chronic pain, but it may decrease your discomfort and reduce your need for pain medications. That said, if you suffer from an aching back, it's worth taking a second look at this "neglected analgesic." Consult your doctor for further advice about your specific level of need.

Back Attack

Lee Hunter Riley III, MD, director of the orthopaedic spine division and associate professor of orthopaedic surgery and neurosurgery at Johns Hopkins University in Baltimore. He is coauthor of *The Back Book* (Johns Hopkins).

B ack pain accounts for almost as many doctor visits as the common cold. Despite its prevalence, misconceptions about back pain abound. *Common misleading beliefs…*

Myth: If you throw out your back, you should stay in bed until the pain is gone.

Fact: Although a day or two of rest may be necessary, one of the keys to healing is getting out of bed and moving around as soon as possible.

Myth: When your back hurts so much, it means something is seriously wrong.

Fact: People are shocked to find that getting out of bed or any kind of movement is excruciatingly painful. They worry that something may be terribly wrong. But these are typical symptoms and usually not cause for worry.

Myth: For recurrent or chronic back pain, surgery is the best solution.

Fact: Only a few types of back pain respond well to surgery. In many cases, surgery can worsen chronic back pain.

Back problems are a normal part of aging, as is gray hair. Sitting and walking put a great deal of stress on the back over time. Joints enlarge and stiffen with age, but this doesn't mean you are doomed to suffer or have to limit activities.

Good news: In the vast majority of cases, back pain can be treated with very simple measures. Approximately 95% of the time, acute back pain gets better within two months.

WHEN TO SEE A DOCTOR

Although most cases of routine back pain don't require a doctor's care, back problems can signal a serious condition, such as a fracture, infection or tumor...or a condition that may be helped by surgery, such as spinal stenosis.

See a doctor right away for back pain if you have a history of cancer...if you had a recent infection or are running a fever...if the pain is unremitting...if you also have pain or weakness in your legs...if your bowel or bladder habits or sensations have changed.

You also should see a doctor if incapacitating pain lasts more than one to two days or if milder pain lasts longer than two months.

SIMPLE TREATMENT

Most garden-variety episodes of acute back pain respond to simple, at-home steps...

Immediately begin taking an over-the-counter anti-inflammatory medication, such as *ibuprofen* (Motrin), *naproxen* (Aleve) or aspirin. Choose whatever medication you usually take for minor pain, such as headache, as long as it is an anti-inflammatory and not merely a pain reliever (such as Tylenol)—follow instructions on the label.

Important: Take the anti-inflammatory for a full 12 to 14 days, even if you begin to feel better before that. Most people with back pain mistakenly stop taking medication after a day or two, the way they would for minor aches and pains. However, for back pain, the anti-inflammatory activity is cumulative and takes as long as two weeks to have its full effect. Do not increase the dose or take the drug more often than recommended without a doctor's okay.

If you don't notice any improvement within a few days, ask your doctor for a prescription-strength anti-inflammatory.

Avoid narcotic pain relievers, such as Vicodin. The pain relief is temporary, not cumulative. Also, these drugs make you lethargic, which could discourage you from moving.

• **Gradually increase your activity.** You can rest for a day or two, but studies show that when people with back pain get up and move around as soon as they can, they feel better more quickly.

This does not mean that you should immediately jump back into your everyday lifestyle and force yourself to endure intense pain. Strike a balance—don't be afraid of a little pain, push yourself a bit, but don't overdo it.

• **Reduce stress and tension.** Stress magnifies pain signals and can overwhelm your ability to cope emotionally. Use whatever stress relievers you previously have found to be helpful—such as gentle massage, a heating pad, warm baths, walking, deep breathing or spending time with close friends or family.

PREVENTING FURTHER PAIN

Once the acute phase has passed, take the following steps to avoid future problems. If you have not yet experienced severe back pain, these measures can help you prevent it—and to recover more quickly if it does occur.

• **Don't smoke.** Nicotine compromises blood supply and nutrition to the spinal discs.

• **Get plenty of calcium and vitamin D.** To keep the bones of the spine strong and guard against osteoporosis-related fractures, consume 1,200 grams (g) to 1,500 g of calcium a day, from food and supplements combined… and 400 international units (IU) to 800 IU of vitamin D from supplements.

• **Get and stay physically fit.** Talk to your doctor before starting an exercise program, but the following helps…

Aerobic exercise, such as walking or swimming, maintains joint flexibility and improves overall conditioning so that you can continue to move easily.

Strengthening and stabilizing exercises tone the muscles of the back, as well as the supporting muscles, such as the abdominals.

Your doctor or physical therapist can recommend exercises tailored to your ability level. *Or consider specialized exercise programs, such as…*

• **Pilates,** which uses controlled movements on spring-operated machinery to increase abdominal strength and improve alignment and flexibility. For information, go to *http://pilates methodalliance.org.*

• **The McKenzie Method,** which takes a comprehensive approach to spinal health based on individualized extension and flexion exercises. For information, go to *www.mcken ziemdt.org.*

• **Manage your activities.** You probably won't have to—and shouldn't—give up your favorite activities, but you may need to practice new ways of sitting and moving that reduce strain on your back, including…

When sitting, use a lumbar support and keep your ears, shoulders and hips aligned. Place feet flat on the floor—don't cross your legs.

When you lift, hold whatever you are picking up as close to your body as possible. Bend your knees, and keep your back straight. Slowly straighten your knees using your leg muscles rather than your back to bear the weight of the object.

When lifting something out of your car trunk, put your foot on the bumper for support.

If you know that certain activities—such as gardening, raking or painting—make your back sore, plan ahead. Take an over-the-counter anti-inflammatory an hour or two before you start the activity, and keep taking the drug for a day or two afterward. Also, take a break from the activity every 20 minutes. Brainstorm modifications that minimize strain on your back.

Example: If you are clearing the garage, don't move boxes by hand—use a dolly.

Fish Oil Helps Neck And Back Pain

In a recent finding, when neck and back pain sufferers took a fish-oil supplement (1,200 mg daily) for 75 days, 60% reported significant pain relief that allowed them to decrease or discontinue use of painkillers.

Theory: The omega-3 fatty acids found in fish oil block the inflammation that can lead to neck and back pain. Fish oil also may help relieve joint pain.

If you have neck or back pain: Ask your doctor about taking fish oil. Do not use fish oil if you take *warfarin* (Coumadin) or another blood thinner.

Joseph Maroon, MD, vice chairman of neurological surgery, University of Pittsburgh.

Relieve the Pain of a Pinched Nerve

David Borenstein, MD, clinical professor of medicine at George Washington University Medical Center, Washington, DC. He maintains a private practice at Arthritis and Rheumatism Associates in Washington, DC, and is author of *Back In Control: Your Complete Prescription for Preventing, Treating, and Eliminating Back Pain from Your Life* (M. Evans and Company).

Nerve pain is one of the worst kinds of pain. People with a pinched nerve (sometimes called a "stinger") may experience sharp, burning pain for anywhere from a few seconds to a few days or longer. The pain usually comes on suddenly and may disappear just as fast—only to return. There also might be temporary numbness or slight weakness.

A nerve gets "pinched" when surrounding tissue presses against it and causes inflammation of the nerve. Causes include repetitive motions, traumatic injuries and joint diseases, such as rheumatoid arthritis. The most common pinched nerves occur in the wrist, elbow, shoulder and foot. Nerve roots in the spinal canal also are vulnerable.

Red flag: Nerve pain that is accompanied by significant weakness or that doesn't improve within a few days needs to be checked by a physician. Excessive pressure on—or inflammation of—a nerve can result in loss of function and permanent damage.

SELF-HELP

To reduce the pain…

• **Stop repetitive movements.** A pinched nerve that's caused by performing the same movements over and over again usually will improve once the offending activity—leaning with your elbows on a counter, typing, working a cash register, etc.—is stopped for a few days. Avoiding these activities is also the best way to prevent a pinched nerve.

However, patients with job-related pain can't always afford to take time off. In that case, they should attempt to change their body position when doing the activity. Example: Raising the back of a computer keyboard (most are adjustable) will enlarge the carpal tunnel in the wrist and reduce pressure on the nerve.

• **Ice the area.** Applying cold in the first 24 to 48 hours after nerve pain starts can reduce tissue swelling and nerve pressure. Use a cold pack or ice cubes wrapped in a towel. Hold cold against the affected area for about 15 minutes. Repeat every hour or two for a day or two.

• **Take an anti-inflammatory.** Over-the-counter analgesics that have anti-inflammatory properties, such as aspirin, ibuprofen and naproxen, reduce the body's production of chemicals that cause inflammation and swelling. Don't use acetaminophen. It will reduce pain but has little effect on inflammation.

• **Wear looser clothes.** It's fairly common for women to experience a pinched nerve in the outer thigh (meralgia paresthetica) from too-tight jeans or skirts…or foot pain (tarsal tunnel syndrome) from tight shoes.

MEDICAL CARE

Nerve pain that's severe or keeps coming back—or that's accompanied by other symptoms, such as a loss of bowel or bladder control—requires immediate medical care. Customized splints or braces can be used to minimize pressure on a nerve from repetitive movements. *Also helpful…*

• **An injection of a corticosteroid into the painful area**—or a short course of oral steroid therapy. These drugs reduce inflammation very quickly and provide short-term relief. The pain may disappear after a single treatment, but most patients need repeated courses. Sometimes, if pain is not relieved, acupuncture may be used in addition to medication and physical therapy.

• **Surgery is recommended when the pain is severe or keeps coming back.** The procedures vary depending on the part of the body affected.

Best Ways to Repair That Aching Hip

William Macaulay, MD, professor of clinical orthopedic surgery, director of the Center for Hip and Knee Replacement and advisory dean of students at the College of Physicians and Surgeons, NewYork-Presbyterian Hospital at Columbia University, all in New York City.

For decades, people whose severe hip pain did not improve with painkillers and/or physical therapy had only one option—a hip replacement.

Now: A procedure that "resurfaces" worn-out hip joints rather than replacing them is available in the US. Known as hip resurfacing, the technique can be as durable as hip replacement with less pain during recovery and greater long-term mobility. Originally introduced in England in 1997, the Birmingham Hip System (one of the products used for hip resurfacing) was approved by the FDA.

DO YOU NEED A BETTER HIP?

Osteoarthritis of the hip is the most common reason for hip pain. This disease occurs when the cartilage covering joint surfaces begins to wear out, causing pain and stiffness that can be so severe that sufferers limp and have difficulty climbing stairs, walking, standing and even sitting. Other causes of hip pain include rheumatoid arthritis and serious hip injury.

If you suffer from hip pain that does not improve with pain medication and physical therapy…interferes with activities that you enjoy, such as gardening or brisk walking…and/or disturbs your sleep, you may want to consider one of several surgical options.

A BREAKTHROUGH APPROACH

For several years, Americans who wanted to try an alternative to hip replacement have traveled to England, India or one of the other countries that have offered hip resurfacing. Now this procedure is available at more than 100 medical centers throughout the US.

With hip resurfacing, the round head of the femur (thighbone) is reshaped and covered with a metal cap about the same size as the natural femoral head. The reshaped head moves within a smooth metal socket that is implanted into the pelvic bone. Enough bone is left in place to allow for a future hip replacement, if necessary.

Hip resurfacing is a good option for patients age 55 and younger…people of any age who have relatively healthy bones or who are highly active.

Hip resurfacing may take slightly longer than the hour to hour-and-a-half required for a standard hip replacement surgery. The incision is often two to three inches longer than the six- to 12-inch incision required for conventional hip replacement, due in part to the limited maneuverability the surgeon has with most of the thighbone left in place. As with traditional hip replacement, a two- to three-day hospital stay is usually required following

hip resurfacing, and healing is more than 90% complete within six to eight weeks. The procedure typically costs about $25,000 and is usually covered by insurance.

HIP REPLACEMENT OPTIONS

If you are not a candidate for hip resurfacing (due to age, osteoporosis or bone weakness), total hip replacement is an option. During this procedure, the surgeon makes an incision, removes the femoral head and replaces the ball-and-socket mechanism with an artificial implant that functions much like a natural joint.

A significant amount of bone is removed with hip replacement in order to insert a metal stem that attaches the synthetic ball-and-socket mechanism to the femur. If any part of the implant loosens in the future, this loss of bone makes a follow-up surgery more difficult.

Traditional hip replacement (as described above) is usually recommended for patients who are obese or very muscular. Recovery time is the same as that for hip resurfacing.

With a newer minimally invasive approach, the surgeon uses specially designed surgical instruments to place the hip implant. Minimally invasive hip replacement generally takes one-and-a-half hours, uses one-and-a-half- to three-inch incisions and requires a one- to two-day hospital stay. It is usually recommended for people who are thin. The recovery period is comparable to that for hip resurfacing and a traditional hip replacement. However, the minimally invasive procedure is controversial, because it has been associated with significant complications in some studies.

The same type of artificial implant is used with both procedures. Each procedure costs about $25,000, which usually is covered by health insurance.

INSTALLING HIP IMPLANTS

More than 300 types of hip implants are now available, as well as dozens of different techniques for installing them. *Main choices…*

•**Cemented.** The implant is attached to bone of the thigh with an acrylic cement. The cement gives immediate strength and is extremely durable.

Recommended for: Patients with less-than-healthy bone, such as those with osteoporosis or osteoarthritis.

• **Uncemented.** The joint implants have a porous surface that allows the patient's natural bone to surround and grow into the implant.

Recommended for: Active patients with normal bone metabolism.

• **Metal/ceramic-on-plastic.** A metal or ceramic femoral ball (prosthetic head) is mated with a hard plastic (polyethylene) socket. It's one of the older configurations—proven to be durable and reliable.

Recommended for: Any patient.

RISKS AND RECOVERY

The main cause of hip-replacement failure is aseptic loosening (when normal bone loss occurs around the implant, causing the joint to separate). In this case, the hip replacement must be repeated. *Other risks...*

• **Deep vein thrombosis.** Blood clots can form in the leg veins—a life-threatening complication if a clot travels to the lungs. After the procedure, most patients are treated with blood thinners, such as *warfarin* (Coumadin), and advised to move their ankles up and down frequently (about 10 times at least three times daily), which helps prevent clots.

• **Uneven leg lengths.** In some cases, the leg on the side that was operated on will be slightly longer than the other leg. When this happens, a patient may need to wear a shoe with a slightly raised heel.

Important: Postsurgical exercise, including low-impact activities, such as walking or using an elliptical trainer, are among the best ways to stabilize the joint and maintain hip strength and/or flexibility.

Sciatica Pain

Sciatica pain often gets better on its own. There is no evidence that spinal decompression does any good. Anti-inflammatory drugs, cortisone shots and exercises that strengthen abdominal and back muscles may speed healing.

Also useful: Place a pillow behind your lower back while driving. Place a pillow under your knees when sleeping on your back—or between your knees when you sleep on your side.

Joel M. Press, MD, medical director, Spine and Sports Rehabilitation Center, Rehabilitation Institute of Chicago, and assistant professor of clinical physical medicine and rehabilitation, Northwestern University Medical School, Chicago.

Treatments for Sciatica

Mark A. Stengler, NMD, licensed naturopathic medical doctor and leading authority on the practice of alternative and integrated medicine. He is founder and medical director of the Stengler Center for Integrative Medicine, Encinitas, California. He is author of *The Natural Physician's Healing Therapies* (Bottom Line Books).

There are several ways to treat sciatica, pain caused by injury or compression of the sciatic nerve, which runs from the hip and down the leg. One therapy I recommend is *low level laser therapy* (LLLT), a safe laser therapy that has many applications. For patients with sciatica, LLLT reduces tissue inflammation and pain by stimulating cell growth and enhancing circulation in the area. Disc or spinal decompression therapy can be effective when sciatica is caused by compressed discs of the low back. Offered by chiropractors and medical doctors, spinal decompression is a noninvasive procedure in which a computer-controlled device gently stretches the lower back, relieving pressure. My patients are helped when they understand that their sciatica is not a medical condition but a symptom of another problem, such as tight buttocks or low-back muscles or misalignment of low back and hips. Sciatica also can be caused by constipation, specifically the internal pressure of the bowels and straining.

My Aching Feet!

Crystal M. Holmes, DPM, clinical instructor in podiatry, University of Michigan Medical School, Ann Arbor. Dr. Holmes is a member of the American Podiatric Medical Association and its Public Education & Information Committee, *www.apma.org*.

Foot problems grow more common with advancing age, as a lifetime of wear and tear takes its toll.

But three very common problems—bunions, fungal nail and a painful heel—won't slow you down or keep you from activities you enjoy if you know how to deal with them.

BUNIONS

If the big toe goes awry where it joins the foot and angles back toward the smaller toes, it is a bunion. The characteristic bump—actually the out-of-place head of the first metatarsal bone—typically starts decades before increasing pain brings the bunion to a doctor's attention.

Many people believe that bunions are caused by years of ill-chosen shoes, high heels in particular. The truth is that heredity is the prime culprit—if you have pronounced bunions, it is likely that other family members do, too. Shoes may speed up a bunion's progress and make it more painful by rubbing against and irritating the bump, or by changing the way you walk. Injury can throw muscles and tendons out of alignment (a likely explanation if you have a bunion on just one foot). Arthritis can worsen bunion pain and cause the toe joint to degenerate.

Whether due to injury or heredity, bunions are the result of a flaw in the structure and mechanics of the foot—a muscle imbalance pulls the big toe out of line.

You might keep a bunion from getting worse by avoiding aggravating factors—don't wear shoes that are too tight, narrow or short for your foot, or that have excessively high heels. If you have arthritis, get appropriate care.

Bunions need treatment when they are painful, particularly if the pain makes it difficult to wear normal shoes or participate in your usual activities, or when other toes start pushing up or down or get jammed together by the big toe.

- **Nonsurgical treatment.** An orthopedist or podiatrist will usually evaluate a bunion with X-rays to clarify the structure of the foot, and use this information along with the size of the bunion, its history and the pain it causes in choosing a treatment.

Nonsurgical options are preferable. These include orthotics—shoe inserts to correct the imbalance and change the forces exerted on your feet as you stand and walk—and possibly anti-inflammatory medications.

- **Surgery.** When nonsurgical measures don't work, it's best to consider surgery. There are a number of different procedures—most of which usually involve cutting one or both of the bones at the joint where the toe meets the foot, and holding the bone or bones in place with a pin or other implanted device. In severe cases, the joint must be fused—the space between the two bones is closed and the bones are held together with screws, plates or both. The right procedure for you depends on the severity of the bunion and the structure of your foot, and whether arthritis is present, among other factors.

- **Recovery is generally lengthy.** Bone takes four to six weeks to heal, so you must keep weight off the foot altogether for at least some of this time, and restrict your activity for longer. After more extensive procedures, healing can take months.

What about laser? Laser surgery is sometimes advertised as a simple, comfortable way to correct bunions, with a quick recovery. This procedure will remove the bump by shaving away bone that sticks out. It will not correct the underlying problem, which is the misalignment of the toe, but it may help—depending on the structure of your foot and the extent of the problem.

Don't expect your toes to be absolutely straight after bunion surgery. The achievable goal is restoring normal function, not appearance.

FUNGAL NAIL

When infected by fungus, toenails get thick, yellow and hard to cut. They may be raised from the toe and even fall off. The big toe is most commonly affected, but all are vulnerable. The infection is most common after the age of 50.

Fungi are everywhere and only need a breach in the body's defense to take hold. Even a minor injury can do it—such as you drop a can on your toe or someone steps on your foot. Ill-fitting shoes damage the nail and provide a damp, dark environment where fungi flourish.

If you think you have a fungal nail, see a doctor. *Medical attention is important for two reasons...*

• **Diagnosis.** Although fungus is the most common cause of thick, discolored nails, they can also result from psoriasis and other skin diseases or even illness elsewhere in the body, such as cancer or lung disease. To make the diagnosis, the doctor may need to back up his/her clinical judgment by culturing material from under the nail.

• **Treatment.** Because the fungus is entrenched deep within the root of the nail, it almost always needs more powerful treatment than is available over the counter.

Strong medicine: In recent years, antifungal medications of proven effectiveness have been developed.

Some, such as *ciclopirox* (Penlac), are applied directly to the nail—painted on like nail polish or massaged in as a cream. At prescription strength, they often are enough to do the job.

Important: To be effective, the medication must be applied religiously, every day for four months or more.

Oral medication with drugs such as *terbinafine* (Lamisil) and *itraconazole* (Sporanox) may be preferable or necessary, particularly when several nails are affected or the infection is severe and has been going on for years.

Advantages: Oral treatment is usually briefer. Also, it is preferable for people who have difficulty bending all the way over to apply the cream.

Drawbacks: These drugs may impair liver function. They require blood tests to ensure that the liver continues to function properly,

and they cannot be used by those with existing liver problems. They can interact with other medications, particularly cholesterol-lowering drugs, antidepressants and blood thinners.

Whether you treat fungal nail with topical or oral medication, be patient. It may take months before the damaged nail grows out and is replaced by healthy tissue.

To prevent fungal nail...

• **Don't go barefoot, especially outside and in athletic facilities, such as health clubs.**

• **Avoid prolonged contact with sweat by changing socks frequently.**

• **If excessive perspiration is a problem, seek medical help for it.**

CHRONIC HEEL PAIN

Heel pain is often caused by plantar fasciitis, an inflammation of the fascia, a fibrous band of connective tissue that stretches across the bottom of the foot from heel to toes. Plantar fasciitis is typically a deep ache that feels like a bruise in your heel, most severe when you first get out of bed. The foot may feel better during the day, but become sore again after your foot has been resting—such as if you sit for a long period or when you first wake up.

People often attribute the pain to a heel spur—a spiky protuberance of the bone on the bottom of the heel. But plantar fasciitis is usually involved here as well—the heel spur causes pain by rubbing against and inflaming the fascia.

• **Self-care.** If heel pain is unusual for you and hasn't lasted long, you might try treating it yourself with rest, ice and elevation. To the extent you can, stay off your feet and keep your foot raised to the level of your heart. Apply ice with an ice pack or cold towel to the heel and arch region for 10- to 15-minute periods, three to four times a day. If the pain persists for 48 hours, seek medical care. If the problem began with an injury, don't wait more than a day.

• **Medical care.** If pain is truly due to plantar fasciitis (arthritis or Achilles tendinitis might actually be responsible instead), the treatment may be simply a program of stretching exercises to be done at home or with a physical therapist. If a muscle imbalance is involved, the doctor may prescribe an orthotic to change the mechanics of your foot.

Since plantar fasciitis is an inflammation, treatment often includes an anti-inflammatory drug like *fenoprofen* (Nalfon). In severe cases, for those who don't get better with oral medication, a cortisone injection may be necessary.

WHAT KIND OF DOCTOR?

Most foot problems that a family doctor can't treat should be seen by a podiatrist or orthopedist. Skin conditions such as fungal nail may need to be treated by a dermatologist.

Say Good-Bye to Your Chronic Headaches

Alexander Mauskop, MD, director of the New York Headache Center in New York City (*www.nyheadache. com*). He is author of *What Your Doctor May Not Tell You About Migraines* (Grand Central Publishing).

O f all the medical conditions that send patients to their doctors, chronic headaches (including migraines) are among the least likely to be treated effectively.*

Problem: Most chronic headache sufferers would like to simply pop a pill to relieve their pain. Although there are many helpful medications, each can have side effects and is designed to reduce headache pain rather than prevent it.

Solution: After treating thousands of headache patients, Alexander Mauskop, MD, director of the New York Headache Center in New York City, devised a natural "triple therapy" that helps prevent migraines from developing in the first place.

What you need to know…

WHEN THE PAIN WON'T GO AWAY

Approximately 15 million Americans have chronic headaches (occurring on at least 15 days a month).

*To find a headache specialist or headache support group near you, contact the National Headache Foundation (888-643-5552, *www.headaches.org*).

The most common forms, in order of prevalence, are tension-type headaches (head pain caused by tight muscles—for example, in the neck—often due to stress)…and migraines (throbbing head pain accompanied by other symptoms, such as nausea or dizziness, and sometimes preceded by light sensitivity and visual disturbance known as an aura).

NATURAL THERAPY

Doctors don't know the exact cause of migraines, but the most popular theory focuses on disturbances in the release of pain-modulating brain chemicals, including the neurotransmitter serotonin.

In reviewing the medical literature, Dr. Mauskop found several references to the mineral magnesium, which has been shown to prevent migraines by helping open up blood vessels in the brain. Studies indicate that half of all migraine sufferers are deficient in this mineral.

Within a short time, Dr. Mauskop also discovered several references that supported the use of riboflavin (vitamin B-2), which plays a role in energy production in brain cells…and the herb feverfew, which promotes the health of blood vessels.

Advice: Each day, take a total of 400 mg of magnesium (as magnesium oxide or in a chelated form—if one form causes diarrhea, try the other)…400 mg of riboflavin…and a total of 100 mg of feverfew, divided in two doses with meals. Many people take this therapy indefinitely. Ask your doctor about the appropriate duration of treatment for you.

Caution: Feverfew may interfere with your blood's ability to clot, so consult your doctor before taking this herb. Riboflavin may turn your urine bright yellow, but the change is harmless.

FOR EVEN MORE PAIN RELIEF

Coenzyme Q10 (CoQ10) is a substance that, like riboflavin, is believed to fight migraines by boosting energy production in brain cells. Research has shown that 100 mg of CoQ10 three times a day reduces migraine frequency.

Advice: Take a total of 300 mg of CoQ10 daily, in one or two doses.

An extract from the root of the butterbur plant is another supplement that has shown promise as a remedy for migraines. In one study, 75 mg of butterbur taken twice daily for four months helped reduce the frequency of migraine attacks.

Although the exact mechanism of action is unclear, the herb might help reduce inflammatory substances in the body that can trigger headaches. Butterbur is sold in the US under the brand name Petadolex (888-301-1084, *www.petadolex.com*).

Advice: Take a total of 150 mg of butterbur daily, in one or two doses.

OTHER HELPFUL STRATEGIES

All the natural therapies described earlier help prevent migraines, but you're likely to achieve even better results if you adopt a holistic approach that includes the following steps. These strategies also help guard against chronic tension headaches but are overlooked by many doctors. *My advice…*

•**Get regular aerobic exercise.** Exercise supplies more blood to the brain and boosts levels of feel-good hormones known as endorphins, which help fight migraines. Physical activity also helps release muscle tension that contributes to tension-type headaches.

Scientific evidence: In data collected from 43,770 Swedes, men and women who regularly worked out were less likely to have migraines and recurring headaches than those who did not exercise.

Helpful: Do some type of moderate-intensity aerobic activity for at least 30 minutes five times a week.

•**Use relaxation techniques.** A mind-body approach, such as progressive muscle relaxation (deliberately tensing then releasing muscles from toe to head)…guided imagery (in which you create calm, peaceful images in your mind)…or breathing exercises (a method of slow inhalation and exhalation), can ease muscle tension and relax blood vessels to help prevent migraines and tension headaches.

Also helpful: Biofeedback, which involves learning to control such involuntary functions as skin temperature, heart rate or muscle tension while sensors are attached to the body,

helps prevent migraines and tension headaches. Biofeedback usually can be learned in about eight sessions and should be practiced daily by migraine and tension headache sufferers. To find a biofeedback practitioner near you, consult the Biofeedback Certification International Alliance (866-908-8713, *www.bcia. org*).

•**Try acupuncture.** There's good evidence that this centuries-old needling technique can reduce the severity and frequency of migraines and tension headaches.** It typically requires at least 10 sessions to see benefits. Ask your health insurer whether acupuncture is covered. If not, each session, typically an hour long, will cost $50 to $100, depending on your location.

If you feel that you are developing a migraine or tension headache: Perform a simple acupressure treatment on yourself to help relieve headache pain.

What to do: Place your right thumb on the webbing at the base of your left thumb and index finger, and your right index finger on the palm side of this point. Gently squeeze and massage this area, using small circular motions, for one to two minutes. Repeat on the right hand.

**To find an acupuncturist near you, go to the National Certification Commission for Acupuncture and Oriental Medicine Web site (*www.nccaom.org*) and click on "Find a Practitioner."

Illustration by Shawn Banner.

Excess Weight Associated With Headaches

Excess weight increases headache frequency. People whose body mass indexes were higher than 30 were 30% more likely to have daily headaches than those of normal weight.

Marcelo E. Bigal, MD, PhD, associate clinical professor of neurology, Albert Einstein College of Medicine, New York City, and leader of a study of 30,000 people, presented at the annual meeting of the American Academy of *Neurology.*

Heal Your Headache Without Drugs

David W. Buchholz, MD, associate clinical of neurology at Johns Hopkins University School of Medicine and former director of the Neurological Consultation Clinic at Johns Hopkins, both in Baltimore. He is author of *Heal Your Headache* (Workman).

Most doctors traditionally distinguish minor "tension" headaches from migraine headaches. Until recently, it had been thought that tension in the head and neck muscles produced tension headaches.

Electromyograms—tests that record the electrical currents caused by muscle activity—of patients with so-called tension headaches reveal no abnormal muscle activity in the head or neck.

It now appears that the vast majority of headaches have the same underlying cause—and that they all should be considered forms of migraine.

Why it matters: Many of the medications for so-called tension headaches actually make the problem worse. Instead, the same steps that prevent migraine, such as avoiding "trigger foods," should be followed for virtually all headaches.

We talked with headache expert David W. Buchholz, MD, of Johns Hopkins University School of Medicine explained that most patients can substantially decrease both the frequency and severity of headaches within one to two months. This often can be done without relying on drugs. *Here's how...*

TRIGGERS

The brain contains a headache-generating mechanism that causes swelling and inflammation of blood vessels in and around the head. When this mechanism is fully activated, patients experience the most severe symptoms—pain, as well as nausea, vomiting, sensitivity to light and other classic migraine symptoms.

The same mechanism also can be partially activated. When this happens, patients are likely to experience only mild-to-moderate discomfort.

Two factors determine whether—and how severely—the mechanism is activated...

• **Triggers.** There are dozens of potential triggers—including hormones, foods, sleep deprivation and even weather changes—that can set off a headache. Each person responds individually to different triggers.

• **Trigger threshold.** Exposure to one or more triggers doesn't necessarily activate a headache. Patients first have to exceed their personal, built-in trigger threshold—a genetically determined level at which a headache is activated. People who get few headaches have high thresholds—whereas those who get frequent and severe headaches have lower thresholds.

Example: You might be sensitive to chocolate, along with changes in barometric pressure and high amounts of stress. A headache won't occur as long as the sum of the triggers doesn't push you past the threshold. But if you're exposed to all of these factors and the threshold is crossed, you might develop a splitting headache.

STEPS TO PREVENTION

One way to prevent headaches is to do aerobic exercise (biking, swimming, brisk walking, etc.) most days of the week. No matter what your particular triggers are, aerobic exercise raises the migraine threshold.

Also, take these measures to control headaches...

Step 1: Avoid quick fixes. It's understandable that people reach for analgesics (painkilling drugs) at the first hint of a headache—but beware. Many of these drugs cause rebound headaches by lowering the migraine threshold, which makes subsequent headaches more likely and eventually more frequent and severe.

What happens: Many headache drugs contain ingredients that relieve pain by temporarily constricting blood vessels. After the initial relief, the drugs lead to rebound vasodilation—the blood vessels tend to swell even more than they did before.

Drugs that cause rebound headaches include those that contain caffeine (Excedrin and Anacin)...as well as decongestants (Sudafed)...

triptans (Imitrex, Relpax and others)...and narcotics, among others. Don't use these drugs more than twice a month.

Single-ingredient analgesics, such as ibuprofen, aspirin or acetaminophen, don't constrict blood vessels—but they aren't as effective for most patients. However, they're a better choice for occasional use—up to two days per week at the most—because they don't cause the rebound effect.

The best way out of the rebound cycle is to stop taking rebound-causing analgesics altogether. Headaches may temporarily worsen for one to two weeks—the time it takes to recover from the rebound. You must escape from rebound in order for steps two and three to be effective.

Step 2: Reduce the trigger load. There are dozens of migraine triggers. Foods and food additives are among the most common and the most avoidable. Some people react to inadequate sleep, strong smells (perfume, tobacco, etc.), humidity or high altitudes.

Some triggers cause a headache almost immediately. More often, there's a delay of hours or even a day or two. *The most common dietary triggers...*

• **Caffeinated beverages**—such as coffee, tea and colas. Caffeine is one of the most potent dietary triggers. Decaffeinated coffee and tea aren't completely safe, because they contain other chemicals besides caffeine that can act as triggers. Herbal teas are fine.

• **Processed meats,** such as bacon and salami, that contain nitrites.

• **Chocolate and cocoa.**

• **Monosodium glutamate** (MSG), a flavor enhancer.

• **Alcohol**—particularly red wine.

• **Citrus fruits and juices.**

• **Onions, sauerkraut, lentils and certain beans** (broad Italian, lima, fava and navy).

• **Soy foods,** particularly those that are fermented, such as tempeh and miso.

I advise my patients to avoid these foods as best they can for four months. After that, you can reintroduce individual items, no more than one item per week, to see if it leads to a headache. If it doesn't, it's probably safe, at least for the time being, and you can reintroduce the next item.

Other potentially avoidable triggers include medications, such as birth control pills, estrogen-replacement pills and proton pump inhibitors (Nexium, etc.) for reflux. Certain antidepressants are triggers, too, including *selective serotonin reuptake inhibitors* (SSRIs), such as Prozac...*serotonin and norepinephrine reuptake inhibitors* (SNRIs), such as Effexor and Cymbalta...and *norepinephrine and dopamine reuptake inhibitors* (NDRIs), such as Wellbutrin.

Step 3: Take preventive medicine. Most people can control their headaches with steps one and two. If not, you may need to add preventive medication to raise your migraine threshold.

Some medications used for preventing headaches are not approved by the Food and Drug Administration (FDA) for this use, but they have been found to be safe and effective, including tricyclic antidepressants, calcium channel blockers and beta-blockers. FDA-approved medications include Depakote and Topamax. Talk to your doctor about what might work best for you.

Surprising Foods That Trigger Migraines

Alexander Mauskop, , MD, director of the New York Headache Center in New York City (*www.nyheadache. com*). He is author of *What Your Doctor May Not Tell You About Migraines* (Grand Central Publishing).

Did you know that many seemingly benign foods—including citrus fruits, onions and yogurt—may make your head throb?

Neurologist Alexander Mauskop, MD, director of the New York Headache Center, states that almost any food can trigger a migraine in certain individuals, though what sets off a headache in one person may not affect another at all. Figuring out which foods to avoid can be an exercise in frustration.

Reasons: You may react to a single bite (for instance, just one almond)…or you may get a headache only when you eat at least a full serving of that food. Also, a certain food may set off a cascade of pain every time…or you may react to that food only when some other factor comes into play—for instance, when you're sleep-deprived or stressed.

To identify your problem foods, Dr. Mauskop recommends keeping a food diary and looking for patterns.

Simplest: Make a list of everything that you consumed in the eight hours before a migraine began…and/or use the worksheet from the American Headache Society (*www. achenet.org/resources/trigger_avoidance_in formation/*).

More revealing: Keep a daily journal that tracks what and when you eat…exercise and sleep patterns…stress levels…menstrual cycle…weather…and anything else that you suspect might be linked to your migraines. Continue for two to three months if you typically get six or more headaches per month. For less frequent headaches, you may need to keep the journal longer to detect patterns.

High-tech help: Download the free app Headache Relief Diary (for iPhone, iPad or iPod Touch), developed by Dr. Mauskop, through the iTunes store.

Researchers do not know the exact mechanism behind all dietary migraine triggers. But foods containing naturally occurring substances called amines, which dilate blood vessels, often play a part—because for migraine-prone people, even tiny changes in blood vessel dilation can induce a headache. Particularly suspect are *tyramine*, *phenylethylamine* and *histamine*. Certain categories of amine-containing foods cause problems for many migraine sufferers. *Here are some of the most common culprits…*

•**Nuts.** Though Dr. Mauskop often prescribes magnesium supplements as a preventive measure for migraine patients (and nuts are chock-full of this mineral), he nonetheless cautions against nuts and nut butters because they can trigger headaches—perhaps due to their tyramine content. Almonds and peanuts

are particularly problematic. Your food diary can help you determine which nuts, if any, are safe for you.

•**Fruits and fruit juices.** The most likely offenders are citrus fruits, such as grapefruits, lemons, limes, oranges and tangerines…and tropical fruits, including avocados, mangoes, papayas, passion fruits and pineapples. These all contain tyramine and phenylethylamine… citrus fruits also release histamine.

•**Dried fruits.** Raisins, prunes and dried apricots (as well as red wine) all contain amines.

Additional problem: Dried fruits also contain sulfites, a type of preservative known to provoke headaches in some people. Even organic versions of these foods can trigger headaches, Dr. Mauskop cautioned, because some sulfites occur naturally.

•**Vegetables.** Onions, snow peas and certain beans (broad, fava, lima) all contain tyramine.

•**Fermented, aged or overripe foods.** Fermented foods, such as yogurt, beer and breads made with yeast, contain histamine. Also, tyramine levels rise when food is aged (as with certain cheeses) or no longer fresh (which is why an overripe banana or avocado, for instance, can set off a migraine).

•**Coffee and tea.** These do have amines—but that is only part of the problem. The other factor to consider is caffeine. Dr. Mauskop explained that many nonprescription and prescription headache medicines contain caffeine…and when used no more than twice weekly, caffeine often can relieve headaches.

But: For some people, caffeine—especially when consumed daily—actually can make migraines more frequent, severe and difficult to treat.

Whatever foods you end up needing to avoid, one thing to get plenty of is water. Dr. Mauskop said, "Dehydration is a known migraine inducer, so patients often get better when they drink more fluids. We call this the water cure."

Heal Your Pain without Drugs or Surgery

Ming Chew, PT, a physical therapist with a private practice in New York City, *www.mingmethod.net*. He is author of *The Permanent Pain Cure* (McGraw-Hill).

Most conventional doctors' approach to orthopedic pain and injuries is "medicate or cut." But there are alternatives.

Before resorting to powerful drugs or surgery, people who suffer from aching knees, backs, shoulders, hips or necks owe it to themselves to first try physical therapy.

Secret to permanent pain relief: A specialized form of physical therapy that focuses on *fascia* (the tough sheet of connective tissue found in all parts of your body) is one of the most effective—yet underused—cures for joint pain.

WHY DOES IT WORK?

Over time, the fascia (pronounced *fash-ee-uh*) throughout your body can become less flexible from lack of exercise. Repetitive movements, such as typing, knitting, golfing or tennis playing...bad posture...or trauma, including bruising or surgery, also affect the fascia. When the fascia tightens, your muscles no longer contract properly. This results in muscle weakness that can lead to aches and pains in other parts of the body.

Important: If the fascia is injured, it won't show up on a magnetic resonance imaging (MRI) scan, which doctors routinely use to diagnose orthopedic problems. But unhealthy fascia often is the underlying cause of joint and muscle pain.

THE KEY TO HEALTHY FASCIA

To check the resilience of your fascia, place your palm flat on a table and spread your fingers as wide as possible. Using the thumb and index finger of your other hand, pinch a fold of skin on the back of your flattened hand. Pull it up and hold it for five seconds. Then let go. If the skin snaps back and becomes completely flat instantaneously, your fascia is highly elastic and healthy. If it takes longer than two seconds, your fascia has lost some elasticity.

For the health of your fascia...

• **Stay hydrated.** The fascia in your body is 70% water. For proper hydration, drink *at least* 64 ounces of filtered water or purified bottled water per day if you're male or 48 ounces daily if you're female.

• **Eat an anti-inflammatory diet** by limiting sugar consumption (including fruit juices and sweets), trans fats ("partially hydrogenated oils" found in many packaged and fast foods) and fried foods.

• **Take supplements** to further reduce inflammation. For example, ask your doctor about taking 1.5 g to 2.5 g of fish oil per day (taken with meals)...and a daily joint-support supplement that combines glucosamine and chondroitin (components of joint tissue and cartilage, respectively)—consult a naturopathic or integrative medicine physician for advice on specific dosages and any precautions that should be taken when using these supplements.

STRETCHING TIGHT FASCIA

The following three fascial stretches address some especially common problem areas.

Important: Always warm up with two minutes of continuous movement, such as jogging in place or performing arm circles, before stretching.*

• **Hip flexor stretch.** This stretch affects the *psoas*, a muscle that runs down either side of the pelvis, connecting the base of the spine to the hip bones. Tight psoas muscles are a major—and under-recognized—cause of low-back pain as well as hip and knee pain.

What to do: Place a chair on each side of your body. Kneel on your right knee and place your left leg in front of you with your left foot flat on the ground and your left knee bent 90 degrees. Place the palm of each hand on the seat of each chair.

*These stretches should not be performed by pregnant women or people with bone cancer, acute pain or recent muscle tears or strains.

Next, tilt your entire torso to the left. While maintaining this tilt, rotate your torso to the right.

Lift your chest and tuck your chin to your chest. Clench your buttocks to press your right hip forward. To avoid arching your back, contract your abdominal muscles.

Finally, while pressing your right foot downward, imagine that you're dragging your right knee forward and contract the muscles you would use to do this. You should feel a deep stretch in the front of your right hip. Hold for 20 seconds, keeping your buttocks firmly contracted. Relax for 10 seconds, then hold for 30 seconds more. Switch legs and repeat on the other side.

• **Shrug muscle stretch.** This stretch affects the *trapezius* muscle, which runs from the lower back to the outer shoulder and base of the skull. The stretch can help relieve neck stiffness, which is often due to a tight trapezius.

What to do: While seated or standing, hold your right arm five inches out from your  hip, elbow straight. Bend your wrist slightly behind your body and drop your chin to your chest. Rotate your chin to the right about 30 degrees, and hold it there while you tilt the upper part of your head to the left. Press your right shoulder down hard, away from your ear and hold for 20 seconds. You should feel a stretch from the back of your head to the outer edge of your right shoulder. Rest for 10 seconds, then hold for 30 seconds more. Repeat on the left side.

• **Biceps stretch.** This stretch helps with a range of problems, including shoulder pain, tennis elbow and golfer's elbow. It also strengthens muscles in the mid-back, which helps improve posture. For this stretch, you'll need a chair and a low table.

What to do: Place the chair back against the table and sit with your feet flat on the floor. Put both arms on the table behind you with the backs of your hands facing down. Pull both shoulders backward and lift your chest. Next, walk both feet slightly

leftward so your torso is rotated to the left. Straighten your right elbow and bend your right wrist up, touching the fingers and thumb of your right hand together in a point (your left hand should remain flat on the table).

Next, tilt your head to the left, and rotate it to the left so that the right side of your neck feels a stretch. Then drop your chin to your left collarbone. It should feel like a strap is being pulled from the top front of your shoulder to your elbow. Hold for 20 seconds. Rest for 10 seconds, then hold for 30 seconds more. Switch sides and repeat.

Illustrations by Shawn Banner.

Relieve Chronic Pain Without Drugs

Ingrid Bacci, PhD, *www.ingridbacci.com*, certified craniosacral therapist (a manual therapy that treats chronic pain and other conditions) and a licensed teacher of the Alexander Technique (a movement therapy). She develops and teaches seminars on chronic pain management, is a guest lecturer at the Columbia College of Physicians and Surgeons in New York City, and is the author of *Effortless Pain Relief* (Free Press).

Contrary to popular belief, an injury or accident is hardly ever the only cause of chronic pain—be it a backache, throbbing knee, or stiff neck or shoulder.

Surprising: Chronic pain generally results from lifestyle habits, such as the way we breathe, stand, move or hold tension in our bodies. These habits involve patterns of physical stress—expressed as muscle tension—that either can be the cause of pain or can turn injuries into long-standing problems.

For example, someone with a back injury may find that it's more comfortable to stoop forward slightly or lean to one side. Even when the original injury is healed, the body position can become a habit—and cause excessive muscle stress and pain.

KNOW YOUR BODY

If you suffer any type of chronic pain, it's essential for you to develop a heightened awareness of how your body feels…recognize physical habits that cause muscle tension…

and move in ways that enhance flexibility and comfort. Even if you have severe chronic pain that requires other treatment, such as medication, the strategies described in this article also may be used to promote healing.

My advice…

STEP 1: "Scan" your body. Yoga, meditation and many other relaxation techniques recognize that simply observing your body's sensations without judgment can often encourage your body to spontaneously relax. When we worry about pain, we unconsciously tighten our muscles. The key is to accept whatever you feel.

Solution: When you are in bed at night, or relaxing on a sofa during the day, start by observing the sensations in your feet, then gradually travel up your entire body. Just observe your sensations. While you may feel momentary discomfort as you become aware of areas of tension, this tension will gradually dissipate, leaving you feeling more relaxed both physically and emotionally.

STEP 2: Practice breathing deeply. The diaphragm, located just below the lungs and heart, is a large muscle responsible for about 75% of the work involved in breathing.

Interesting fact: Because the diaphragm is attached via connective tissue and muscles to the low back and hips, tension in the diaphragm can contribute to low back pain. In addition, when the diaphragm does not work optimally—contracting and releasing fully—secondary respiratory muscles in the upper torso must kick in to improve breathing. This contributes to upper torso fatigue and pain. People whose diaphragms are contracted and rigid tend to breathe shallowly. They are known as "chest breathers."

Solution: To relieve muscle tension, practice diaphragmatic breathing. As you breathe in this way, you will notice your breath becoming softer, deeper and slower. *What to do…*

•**While sitting or lying on your back,** put one hand on your chest and the other on your stomach.

•**Slowly inhale through your nose**—or keep your lips slightly parted and breathe slowly through your mouth.

•**If you notice that your chest is expanding, focus more on breathing "into the belly."** Your stomach should rise more than your chest with each breath.

Practice diaphragmatic breathing as often and for as long as you like. The more you practice, the more it will become your preferred way of breathing.

Helpful: If you're not sure that you are breathing in a relaxed, fully diaphragmatic way, count the number of breaths you take in one minute. If you're breathing more shallowly than you're capable of doing, you may take as many as 11 to 20 breaths a minute. If you're breathing deeply and diaphragmatically, you will take as few as four to 10 breaths a minute.

STEP 3: Work on body alignment. As a result of years of sedentary living, most adults have poor body alignment. Since we stand and sit a great deal of the time, it is particularly important to improve alignment in these postures.

Interesting fact: Improving alignment isn't about squaring back your shoulders and being stiff. It's about using your body in more comfortable ways.

Solution: A few simple steps can help improve the way that you stand and sit, reducing pain and fatigue. *Examples…*

•**Bend your knees slightly when standing.** It reduces stress on the low back.

•**Keep your weight distributed evenly over both legs when standing**—and keep both feet pointed in the same direction, instead of turning them in or out.

•**When walking,** roll from heel to toe, pushing off through the ball of the foot and keeping the weight evenly distributed between the inside and outside of the foot.

•**When you get in and out of a chair,** bend fully at the knees and hips, keeping your torso relaxed and straight.

STEP 4: Stretch your body. Few adults move enough of their muscles regularly to stay limber.

Interesting fact: Certain animals, such as cats, stretch their whole bodies each time they get up, which helps keep them limber.

Solution: Spend 15 to 30 minutes daily fully stretching your body. You can do this through a formal discipline, such as yoga, or through an activity such as free-form dancing. Put on some music you enjoy, close your eyes and move to the beat, freeing up every stiff muscle. Or simply lie on the floor and stretch in any way that feels good.

STEP 5: Release body tension. To reduce chronic pain, it is important not only to pay close attention to your body and recognize muscle tension as it occurs, but also to let it go whenever you can.

Interesting fact: Once people learn how their bodies should feel, they're better able to make other physical changes that reduce muscle tension.

Solution: Don't ignore muscle tension. Learn how to move more "intelligently"—using minimum effort to achieve maximum results.

Examples: Grip your car steering wheel less tightly...notice whether you tense your muscles when having a stressful conversation or work long hours at a desk. Then try to relax a little bit. The more you relax, the less pain you will have.

You Can Conquer Nagging Pain Once and for All

Bonnie Prudden, who helped create the President's Council on Youth Fitness in 1956 and has been one of the country's leading authorities on exercise therapy for more than five decades. In 2007, she received the Lifetime Achievement Award from the President's Council on Physical Fitness and Sports. Based in Tucson, Arizona, she is the author of 18 books, including *Pain Erasure* (M. Evans).

Can you imagine living well into your 90s and being able to eliminate virtually all of the aches and pains that you may develop from time to time?

Ninety-seven-year-old Bonnie Prudden, a longtime physical fitness advocate, stays pain free—even though she has arthritis that led to two hip replacements—by using a form of *myotherapy* ("myo" is Greek for muscle) that she developed more than 30 years ago.

Now: Tens of thousands of patients have successfully used this special form of myotherapy, which is designed to relieve "trigger points" (highly irritable spots in muscles) that develop throughout life due to a number of causes, such as falls, strains or disease.

By applying pressure to these sensitive areas and then slowly releasing it, it's possible to relax muscles that have gone into painful spasms, often in response to physical and/or emotional stress.

A simple process: Ask a partner (a spouse or friend, for example) to locate painful trigger points by applying his/her fingertips to parts of your body experiencing discomfort—or consult a practitioner trained in myotherapy.*

If you're working with a partner, let him know when a particular spot for each body area described in this article is tender.

Pressure should be applied for seven seconds (the optimal time determined by Prudden's research to release muscle tension) each time that your partner locates such a spot.

On a scale of one to 10, the pressure should be kept in the five- to seven-point range—uncomfortable but not intolerable.

The relaxed muscles are then gently stretched to help prevent new spasms.

If you prefer to treat yourself: Use a "bodo," a wooden dowel attached to a handle, and a lightweight, metal "shepherd's crook" to locate trigger points and apply pressure. Both tools are available at 800-221-4634, *www.bonnieprudden.com*, for $8 and $30.95, respectively.

For areas that are easy to reach, use the bodo to locate trigger points and then apply pressure to erase them. For spots that are difficult to

*To find a practitioner of Bonnie Prudden's myotherapy techniques, go to *www.bonnieprudden.com* or call 800-221-4634. If you are unable to find a practitioner near you, call local massage therapists and ask whether they are familiar with the techniques.

reach, use the shepherd's crook to find and apply pressure to trigger points.

As an alternative to the specially designed tools, you can use your fingers, knuckles or elbows on areas of the body that can be reached easily. *Common types of pain that can be relieved by this method...***

SHOULDER PAIN

Finding the trigger point: Lie face down while your partner uses his elbow to gently apply pressure to trigger points that can hide along the top of the shoulders and in the upper back. If you are very small or slender, your partner can use his fingers instead of his elbow.

Place one of your arms across your back at the waist while your partner slides his fingers under your shoulder blade to search for and apply pressure to additional trigger points. Repeat the process on the opposite side.

While still lying face down, bend your elbows and rest your forehead on the backs of your hands. With his hands overlapped, your partner can gently move all 10 of his fingers along the top of the shoulder to locate additional trigger points.

Pain-erasing stretch: The "shrug" is a sequence of shoulder exercises performed four times after myotherapy and whenever shoulder tension builds.

From a standing or sitting position, round your back by dropping your head forward while bringing the backs of your arms together as close as possible in front of your body. Extend both arms back (with your thumbs leading) behind your body while tipping your head back and looking toward the ceiling.

Next, with both arms at your sides, raise your shoulders up to your earlobes, then press your shoulders down hard.

LOW-BACK PAIN

Finding the trigger point: Lie face down while your partner stands to your right and

reaches across your body to place his elbow on your buttocks in the area where the left back pocket would appear on a pair of pants. For seven seconds, your partner should slowly apply pressure to each trigger point—not straight down but angled back toward himself.

Repeat on the other side. If the pressure causes slight discomfort, your partner has found the right spot! If not, your partner should move his elbow slightly and try the steps again. Two to three trigger points can typically be found on each buttock.

Pain-erasing stretch: Lie on your left side on a flat surface (such as a bed, table or the floor). Bend your right knee and pull it as close to your chest as possible.

Next, extend your right leg, keeping it aligned with the left leg and about eight inches above it.

Finally, lower the raised leg onto the resting one and relax for three seconds. Perform these steps four times on each leg.

HIP PAIN

Finding the trigger point: The trigger points for hip pain are often found in the gluteus medius, the muscle that runs along either side of the pelvis.

Lie on your side with your knees slightly bent. Using one elbow, your partner should scan for trigger points along the gluteus medius (in the hip area, roughly between the waist and the bottom seam of your underpants) and apply pressure straight down at each sensitive spot for seven seconds.

The same process should be repeated on the opposite side of your body.

Pain-erasing stretch: Lie on your left side on a table with your right leg hanging off the side and positioned forward. Your partner should place one hand on top of your waist and the other hand on the knee of the dangling right leg.

This knee should be gently pressed down eight times. The stretch should be repeated on the opposite side.

**Check with your doctor before trying this therapy if you have a chronic medical condition or have suffered a recent injury.

Best Pain Relievers For Headache, Arthritis, Backache and More

Jacob Teitelbaum, MD, director of The Annapolis Center for Effective CFS/Fibromyalgia Therapies, in Maryland. For 25 years, he has researched ways to relieve pain. He is author of *Pain Free 1-2-3!* (Deva) and *From Fatigued to Fantastic!* (Avery). *www.endfatigue.com*

Most of us turn to *acetaminophen* (Tylenol) and *ibuprofen* (Advil, Motrin) for pain relief—but there can be more effective approaches, including combining conventional and natural pain relievers.

Caution: Check with your doctor before taking any new medication or supplement.

ARTHRITIS

There are two types of arthritis—osteoarthritis, in which cartilage between bones wears away…and rheumatoid arthritis, an autoimmune disease that inflames joints. For relief, people with either type often take nonsteroidal anti-inflammatory drugs (NSAIDs), such as aspirin, *ibuprofen* and *naproxen* (Aleve, Naprosyn)—but 16,000 Americans die annually from side effects of these drugs. Another estimated 55,000 died from taking the recalled Vioxx, Bextra and other COX-2 inhibitors (a class of NSAIDs). *Instead, try…*

FOR OSTEOARTHRITIS

• **Glucosamine sulfate.** Take 1,500 milligrams (mg) of this supplement—made from chitin, which is derived from shellfish—with 3 grams (g) a day of *methylsulfonylmethane* (MSM), a natural substance in the human body. These nutrients repair cartilage, reducing arthritis pain within six weeks. For maximum tissue repair, take these supplements for two to five months. For chronic arthritis, you may continue for up to a year.

• **Lidoderm.** Put a patch, available by prescription, on the joint. It contains the anesthetics Novocain and Lidocaine. Wear it for about 12 hours a day (one lasts that long) for two to six weeks. For a large area, some people may use as many as four patches (the package says three). Many patients experience a 30% to 50% decrease in pain within two weeks.

• **Willow bark and Boswellia.** These herbs are as effective as Vioxx and Motrin. Take 240 milligrams (mg) of willow bark and 1,000 mg of Boswellia daily. It can take six weeks to work. For chronic arthritis, you may need to take these for up to a year to feel the full effect.

FOR RHEUMATOID ARTHRITIS

• **Fish oil.** Studies show that fish oil (one to two tablespoons a day for at least three months) can reduce inflammation and pain. Eskimo-3, available at health-food stores, and Enzymatic Therapy (800-783-2286, *www.enzymatictherapy.com*) don't have the high levels of mercury that may be present in other brands. Keep taking the fish oil after the pain is gone as a preventive measure.

BACK PAIN

Back pain can occur for no apparent reason and at any point on your spine.

• **Lidoderm.** For low back pain, apply a Lidoderm patch in the morning and remove it in the evening. Expect relief in two to six weeks.

• **Colchicine.** About 70% of back pain can be eliminated without surgery, with six intravenous injections of the gout medicine colchicine. It enters the space between the discs of the vertebrae and reduces inflammation. Colchicine's main risk is a rare but severe allergic reaction (similar to that caused by penicillin).

CARPAL TUNNEL SYNDROME

When a nerve passing under a ligament through two bones in the wrist becomes swollen and pinched, it causes pain, numbness and tingling in the hand or forearm. *For relief…*

• **Vitamin B6 and thyroid hormone.** Take 250 mg a day of B6. Also ask your doctor about a prescription for natural thyroid hormone. The combination of B6 and thyroid hormone decreases swelling and usually clears up the problem after six to 12 weeks. You can stay on this treatment for six months to prevent recurrence. During treatment, wear a wrist splint at night and, if possible, during the day.

HEADACHES

Tension headaches begin and end gradually. They can last for minutes or sometimes hours. The pain comes from tightened muscles across the forehead and/or at the base of the skull.

Ultram (tramadol hydrochloride) is an often-overlooked but effective prescription pain reliever. Take up to 100 mg as many as four times a day.

Migraines—severe headaches that may be preceded by lights flashing before your eyes and accompanied by nausea, vomiting, sweating and dizziness—can last for hours, even days. *Natural remedies are more effective than prescription drugs at preventing migraines...*

Butterbur, from the butterbur plant, can prevent—and even eliminate—migraines. Take 50 mg three times a day for one month, then one 50-mg dose twice a day to prevent attacks. Take 100 mg every three hours to eliminate an acute migraine. Use only high-quality brands, such as Enzymatic Therapy (800-783-2286, *www.enzymatictherapy.com*) and Integrative Therapeutics' Petadolex (800-931-1709, *www. integrativeinc.com*).

• **Sumatriptan** (Imitrex). When a migraine is developing, 75% of patients experience tenderness and pain around the eyes. Sumatriptan knocks out 93% of migraines when taken before the pain around the eyes occurs. When it is taken later, it helps in only 13% of cases. Therefore, if you have a migraine, it is best to take sumatriptan within the first five to 20 minutes.

• **Magnesium.** In the doctor's office or the hospital emergency room, intravenous magnesium can eliminate a migraine in five minutes.

IRRITABLE BOWEL SYNDROME

Irritable bowel syndrome (IBS), also known as spastic colon, is a digestive disorder characterized by bloating, abdominal cramps and diarrhea and/or constipation. *Consider...*

• **Peppermint oil.** For symptomatic relief, take one or two enteric-coated peppermint oil capsules three times a day. Peppermint oil decreases spasms of the bowel muscles. Effective brands include Enzymatic Therapy (800-783-2286, *www.*

enzymatictherapy.com) and Mentharil, available at most health-food stores.

• *Hyoscyamine* (Anaspaz, Levsin). Take this prescription antispasmodic as needed. It relaxes the muscular contractions of the stomach and intestines. Dosages range from 0.125 mg to 0.375 mg, taken 30 to 60 minutes before a meal.

SHINGLES

This itchy, blistering rash—from herpes zoster, the virus associated with chicken pox—strikes in middle or old age and usually afflicts one side of the upper body. The virus affects the nerves, so it can leave victims in chronic pain, a condition called *postherpetic neuralgia* (PHN). *Discuss these options with your doctor...*

• **Ketamine.** This prescription anesthetic can decrease shingles pain within days in 65% of cases. Apply a gel of 5% ketamine two to three times daily to the painful area.

• **Lidoderm.** Place a patch over the area of maximum pain.

• **Neurontin.** This prescription medication also can reduce pain. To avoid side effects, start with 100 mg to 300 mg, one to four times a day.

• **Tricyclic antidepressant.** A prescription tricyclic such as *amitriptyline* can relieve nerve pain. To avoid side effects, use a low dose of 10 mg to 50 mg.

Rub Out the Ache!

Beth E. Shubin Stein, MD, sports medicine and shoulder surgeon with the Women's Sports Medicine Center at the Hospital for Special Surgery in New York City.

If you suffer from chronic arthritis pain or have aching muscle strains or spasms after exercising, chances are you regularly take aspirin or another nonsteroidal anti-inflammatory drug (NSAID), such as *ibuprofen* (Advil) or *naproxen* (Aleve).

There is another option. Over-the-counter (OTC) topical pain relievers can be very effective without causing the stomach upset or gastrointestinal bleeding that may accompany oral pain medication.

Latest development: A topical form of the oral prescription NSAID *diclofenac* (Voltaren Gel) is available in the United States.

Meanwhile, a variety of OTC topical pain relievers are available now. The products below relieve arthritis, backache and muscle strain. Most are used three to four times daily. Follow label instructions.

Helpful: If one type of topical pain reliever doesn't work for you, try one from another class until you find a product that provides relief.

Caution: Keep these products away from your eyes, nose and other mucous membranes.

SALICYLATES

These aspirin-based products dull pain and curb the inflammation that often accompanies and worsens pain.

How they work: Topical salicylates inhibit the production of prostaglandins, substances in the body that cause pain and swelling when they are released in response to strains, sprains and other injuries. *Salicylates include…*

•**Bengay Ultra Strength Pain Relieving Cream.**

•**Aspercreme Analgesic Creme Rub with Aloe.**

•**Sportscreme Deep Penetrating Pain Relieving Rub.**

•**Flexall Maximum Strength Pain Relieving Gel.**

Warning: Do not use salicylates if you are sensitive or allergic to aspirin or take blood-thinning medication that might interact with them. Consult a doctor before applying a salicylate to a large area several times a day.

COUNTERIRRITANTS

These pain relievers give the sensation of warmth or coolness to mask pain.

How they work: Creating a secondary stimulus to diminish the feeling of pain reduces physical discomfort. It's what you do instinctively when you stub your toe, then grab it to apply pressure. Both competing sensations travel to your brain at the same time—but because only a limited number of messages can be processed at one time, the initial feeling of pain is diminished. *Counterirritants include…*

•**Icy Hot Pain Relieving Balm, Extra Strength.**

•**Tiger Balm Extra Strength Pain Relieving Ointment.**

•**Therapeutic Mineral Ice.**

In most cases, coolness is beneficial for acute injuries, such as sprains, while warmth eases stiffness.

Caution: People sensitive to heat or cold should avoid counterirritants.

CAPSAICINS

These products, which are a type of counterirritant, contain capsaicin, an extract of hot peppers that causes a burning sensation.

How they work: Unlike most other counterirritants, capsaicin inhibits the production of substance P, a chemical that sends pain messages to the brain via the nervous system. *Capsaicins include…*

•**Zostrix Arthritis Pain Relief Cream.**

•**Capzasin HP Arthritis Pain Relief Creme.**

LIDOCAINE

Lidoderm is a prescription-only patch that contains lidocaine, a topical anesthetic similar to the novocaine that dentists often use to numb the gums.

How it works: Lidocaine blocks signals at the skin's nerve endings. The Lidoderm patch (lidocaine 5%) is worn for 12 hours a day over a period of days. It slowly releases medication, so it has longer-lasting effects than other pain relievers and helps with pain that emanates from nerves near the surface of your skin, such as that caused by shingles or diabetic neuropathy.

Caution: Side effects include dizziness, headache and nausea. Allergic reactions are rare but may occur.

Are Massage Chairs Helpful?

Mark A. Stengler, NMD, licensed naturopathic medical doctor and leading authority on the practice of alternative and integrated medicine. He is founder and medical director of the Stengler Center for Integrative Medicine, Encinitas, California, and associate clinical professor at the National College of Natural Medicine, Portland, Oregon. He is author of *The Natural Physician's Healing Therapies* (Bottom Line Books).

Getting a massage not only feels great, it is good for our health. Studies have shown that massage therapy can reduce stress...relieve pain and swelling...improve circulation of blood and movement of lymph fluids...strengthen the immune system...and help postoperative rehabilitation. But what about massage chairs, those large, recliner-type seats that can give you a massage with the touch of a button any time you want? Do they improve health?

Chances are you have seen these massage chairs—and even have been tempted to try one out. They can be purchased for home use at prices ranging from $900 to $8,000. They're sold at Brookstone and stores that sell therapeutic medical products. Nail salons and day spas often offer the opportunity to enjoy a chair massage. And coin-operated chairs are ready to relax you at malls and airports.

TAKE A SEAT

Manufacturers of massage chairs for home use claim that their products can deliver a full-body massage that mimics one given by a trained massage therapist. With the push of a button, you can select rolling, which replicates a massage therapist's hands pressing firmly on one side of the spine and then the other... kneading, which feels like thumbs pressing in a circular motion on both sides of your spine, going deep into your muscles...and percussion, which feels like fists rapidly tapping on your back. Most chairs massage the back and neck. More expensive models massage the shoulders, arms, calves and even the feet. You also can customize the pressure at which you are massaged, and some massage chairs even have heating units and play music.

FEELING RELAXED?

There have not been many studies on the effectiveness of chair massage, but in one small study published in *The Journal of Alternative and Complementary Medicine*, researchers found that a 15-minute back massage applied by a massage chair was effective in inducing mental relaxation and reducing muscle tension. In the study, skin tests showed less muscle tension in areas that were directly massaged as well as in areas that were distant from the massage area. Participants determined their mental relaxation with a self-assessment tool.

My view: This study shows that massage chairs can provide some general muscle relaxation. But when you use a massage chair, you are missing out on the benefit of being touched by another person—whether it's a massage therapist or a loved one who likes to give massages. Studies have shown that human touch provides many benefits, including a sense of well-being and feeling nurtured. However, regular massages from a professional therapist can be expensive. So if you find a massage chair that makes you feel relaxed, it can be cost-effective and worthwhile. You might benefit from a chair massage if you are prone to stress...tight back and neck muscles...headaches...or low back pain.

Massage of any kind is not recommended for those with acute injuries, such as a fracture or bleeding...skin infection...blood clots...an unhealed wound...uncontrolled high blood pressure...or undiagnosed aches and pains. If you have heart disease, cancer, or liver or kidney disease, speak to your doctor before having any kind of massage.

Water Massage Can Melt Away Aches and Pains

Joyce Reim, director of The Watsu Institute School of Shiatsu and Massage in Middletown, California (*www.watsucenter.com*).

Watsu massage is an intriguing form of bodywork, which incorporates numerous types of therapy, including the gentle Japanese finger-pressure technique called shiatsu...muscle stretching...joint mobilization...and massage, performed by a trained practitioner (or therapist) while the client soaks in warm water. It provides not only pain relief, but also emotional release that people really, really rave about. I have one friend who now schedules a Watsu massage for herself every other week—she says nothing else has been as helpful at soothing her arthritis, plus it's the most pleasant and relaxing experience she has ever had.

The concept of Watsu massage was developed about 30 years ago, when a Shiatsu practitioner named Harold Dull first combined Zen shiatsu stretches and movements as he worked with his students in the naturally therapeutic pools at Harbin Hot Springs in Northern California. Today, trained Watsu practitioners and therapists around the country treat patients for a variety of complaints, including stress, chronic back pain, arthritis, fibromyalgia and orthopedic problems.

To find out more about it, we spoke with Joyce Reim, director of the Watsu Institute at the School of Shiatsu and Massage in Middletown, California. Reim told us that she was a patient suffering from crippling arthritis pain when she herself first experienced Watsu. "Painkillers were all that traditional medicine had to offer me," she says. "After my first Watsu session, I felt invigorated and free of pain." Typically the pain is relieved while the patient is floating in the warm water, but does come back later, says Reim, noting that after regular Watsu sessions arthritis flare-ups are farther apart and the pain is less severe.

WHAT IS IT?

Watsu massage is given in a warm-water therapeutic pool about four feet deep, heated to body temperature (about 98 degrees). The massage therapist is in the water with you. You float on your back while he/she gently holds you, stretches and massages your tight muscles. Flotation devices are often used. The experience has been described to me as feeling like you are melting effortlessly into the warm water, blurring the boundaries between your body and the environment.

According to Reim, warm water is an ideal medium for this kind of passive stretching. It provides support while also taking weight off the vertebrae, allowing the spine to be moved in ways that aren't possible on a solid horizontal surface. "Recipients feel profound physical release and a release from pain and tension," Reim said. Some describe the experience as intense and almost spiritual, as the practitioner cradles the client in his/her arms in the water, delivering physical and often emotional support. Reim told me that practitioners have a specific term for the profound connection that many givers and receivers report experiencing—it's called "heart wrap," and it delivers "a sense of oneness and peace."

WHAT'S WATSU GOOD FOR?

Research shows that the physical benefits are meaningful as well...

• **According to one study,** in the *Journal of Bodywork and Movement Therapies*, Watsu massage patients suffering from fibromyalgia experienced significant improvements in physical and social function, vitality and reduced pain.

• **A study found that after 18 months of twice-monthly,** 30-minute Watsu sessions, residents of a retirement community suffering a range of maladies, including knee replacement, cancer, Parkinson's disease and mild anxiety, reported substantial improvements in self-assessments of emotional stress, along with a reduction of aches and pains and improvements in flexibility, as well as in their ability to relax.

Watsu is generally considered a viable treatment for most people when given by a well-trained practitioner. To find a trained Watsu practitioner, go to the Web site of the Worldwide Aquatic Bodywork Association, *www.watsu.com/waba.html*. It maintains a worldwide registry of therapists who have met requirements to practice and teach Watsu.

13

Save Your Senses

Natural Ways to Save Your Sight

Family history is an uncontrollable risk factor for certain eye diseases. But there are other risk factors for such eye problems as cataracts and macular degeneration that can be minimized with the right nutrition and life-style strategies.*

FOLLOW A "VISION CARE" DIET

The most common eye diseases share a common link—oxidation, a chemical process in which disease-causing free radicals damage cells in the body, in this case, eye tissues.

A natural by-product of metabolism, these oxygen-based molecules are also produced in large amounts because of smoking and exposure to air pollution or excessive sunlight.

*Consult your doctor before beginning any supplement regimen, including the one in this article.

What helps: An antioxidant-rich diet. A recent study found that women (age 56 to 71) who took supplemental vitamin C for more than 10 years were 77% less likely to develop cataracts than those who didn't take vitamin C.

My advice: Take 250 mg to 500 mg of vitamin C twice daily to protect your eyes, especially against cataracts and macular degeneration (dividing the dose improves absorption).

Caution: If you have hemochromatosis (a disorder marked by excessive absorption and storage of iron in the body), don't take vitamin C supplements—vitamin C increases the amount of iron absorbed from foods. *Also crucial for eye health…*

•**Vitamin A improves night vision and enhances the ability of the eyes to adapt**

Marc Grossman, OD, LAc, optometrist and licensed acupuncturist who cofounded Integral Health Associates, a private practice in New Paltz, New York, *www.naturaleyecare.com*. A holistic eye doctor with training in Chinese medicine and naturopathic medicine, he is coauthor of *Greater Vision* (McGraw-Hill).

to changes in light—when you walk from bright sunlight into a dark room, for example. Vitamin A also improves chronic dry eyes.

My advice: Get at least 15 mg of beta-carotene daily (which is converted to vitamin A in the body). People who take a multivitamin and also eat several daily servings of orange- or yellow-pigmented vegetables, including sweet potatoes, carrots and peppers, will get enough beta-carotene and vitamin A to provide substantial eye protection. Smokers should not take beta-carotene supplements—some evidence suggests that they may increase lung cancer risk.

• **Zinc is an antioxidant mineral that can help prevent night blindness as well as macular degeneration.** Take 30 mg of zinc daily in supplement form.

• **Lutein is an antioxidant that's chemically related to beta-carotene.** It reduces eye inflammation induced by ultraviolet radiation from the sun. A Harvard study found that people who consumed about 6 mg of lutein daily (roughly the amount in one-quarter cup of spinach) were 43% less likely to develop macular degeneration than those who consumed less. People who eat a lot of spinach and other green, leafy vegetables can reduce the risk for cataracts by up to 50%.

My advice: Eat at least one-quarter cup of spinach, kale or collard greens daily.

• **Fish oil contains docosahexaenoic acid (DHA),** an omega-3 fatty acid that repairs damage to cell membranes in the eyes. It improves eye circulation and also seems to help people with chronic dry eyes.

My advice: To ensure adequate intake of DHA, take 1,000 mg of purified fish oil liquid or gels (the most absorbable forms) twice daily. Purified fish oil contains no contaminants such as mercury.

Recommended brands: Nordic Naturals Omega-3, 800-662-2544, *www.nordicnaturals. com*…or J.R. Carlson Laboratories, Inc., Very Finest Fish Oil, 888-234-5656, *www.carlson labs.com.*

GET ENOUGH WATER AND EXERCISE

Drinking a lot of fluids improves the transport of antioxidant nutrients to eye tissues.

My advice: Drink at least eight glasses of water a day to lubricate the eyes.

Regular exercise also is good for eye health—especially in helping to prevent glaucoma. It boosts circulation throughout the body (including the eyes) and can reduce pressure within the eye by about 2.5 mm (normal range is 10 mm to 22 mm). That's about the same reduction you would get from using beta-blocker eyedrops, which are commonly prescribed for glaucoma.

My advice: Take a brisk, 40-minute walk most days of the week.

DON'T FORGET SUNGLASSES

Most people wear sunglasses for comfort or to prevent wrinkles around their eyes. But there's a more important reason—the sun's ultra-violet radiation greatly increases oxidation in eye tissues. Excessive sun exposure is a leading cause of cataracts and macular degeneration.

My advice: Except when it's raining, always wear sunglasses when you go outside during the day, even on cloudy days. Buy sunglasses that block 100% of both UVA and UVB radiation. The wraparound styles are ideal as this design blocks most of the sunlight that would otherwise hit your eyes.

RELAX YOUR EYES

Except when we're asleep, our eyes get virtually no rest.

My advice: At least once daily, rub your palms together briskly until they're warm. Cup your hands and place the base of the palms gently over your closed eyes with the fingers of each hand overlapping and resting gently in the center of the forehead for a few minutes. This helps soothe and relax your eyes.

Cataract Danger

When researchers examined data on about 200,000 adults age 65 and older, those taking selective serotonin reuptake inhibitor (SSRI) antidepressants were 15% more likely to develop cataracts than those not taking SSRIs. Those diagnosed with cataracts had been taking SSRIs for nearly two years, on average.

If you take an SSRI: Discuss cataract risk with your doctor.

Mahyar Etminan, PharmD, assistant professor of medicine, University of British Columbia, Vancouver.

Beware of Cataract Surgery Complications

Even though cataract surgery has a 98% success rate, patients can suffer such post-surgical complications as double vision or an inability to read or drive comfortably if the vision in both eyes becomes unequal for near and far distances.

If you are planning to have cataract surgery: Be sure that your surgeon aims for equal vision acuity in both eyes—or allows you to test "monovision" (one eye sees distance and the other sees at reading distance) beforehand by wearing an eye patch, eyeglasses or contact lenses.

Melvin Schrier, OD, optometrist, Rancho Palos Verdes, California.

Help for Watery Eyes

Common causes of watery eyes—and what to do about them…

• **Age-related changes of the surface of the eye can cause tears to pool in the corners of your eyes.** Artificial tears or resurfacing surgery may help—see an ophthalmologist.

• **A blocked tear duct can cause eyes to water.** An in-office procedure or topical steroid drugs can often relieve the problem.

• **Eye irritation or infection can cause constant watering,** which will clear up when the irritation or infection goes away.

• **Excessively dry eyes, caused by allergies or other factors, can cause reflex tearing—** the underlying cause needs to be treated.

• **Some medical conditions, such as a thyroid disorder, can cause eyes to water—**ask your doctor.

Steven L. Maskin, MD, Dry Eye and Cornea Treatment Center, Tampa, *www.drmaskin.com.*

Improve Your Vision

In a study of 22 adults, participants who played an action video game for 50 hours over nine weeks had a 43% improvement in contrast sensitivity—one of the first visual abilities to decline with age—while those who played a slow-moving video game did not improve. The benefits lasted for several months after the study.

Theory: Action video games fine-tune the visual-processing pathways in the brain for challenging visual tasks, such as night driving.

Daphne Bavelier, PhD, professor of brain and cognitive sciences, University of Rochester, New York.

Twitching Eyelid

James Salz, MD, clinical professor of ophthalmology, University of Southern California, Los Angeles.

These involuntary eyelid spasms are most often caused by excessive fatigue, caffeine, alcohol or stress. Typically, they are painless, occurring every few seconds for several minutes, and can be accompanied by blurry vision and light sensitivity. Eye twitches (blepharospasm) can occur intermittently for several days to months. Twitching usually stops on its own.

To help eliminate eye twitches: Get at least eight hours of sleep nightly…limit alcohol and caffeine…lubricate eyes with artificial tear drops (such as Refresh and TheraTears) every four hours. See your eye doctor if twitching persists for more than one week, your upper eyelid droops, the eyelid completely closes with the twitch or tics start occurring in other parts of the face. In rare cases, twitching may be a side effect from medications, such as *chlorpromazine* and *prochlorperazine*, or may indicate a brain or nerve disorder, such as Bell's palsy (in which facial muscles become temporarily paralyzed) or Tourette's syndrome (marked by unusual movements called tics).

Vitamin Helps Decrease Floaters

Robert Abel, Jr., MD, Delaware Ophthalmology Consultants, Wilmington, Delaware. *www.eyeadvisory.com*

Many adults ages 50 to 75 develop floaters (moving bodies in eye liquid). They can appear as cobwebs or specks in your vision. Floaters are caused by age-related changes, sunlight exposure, infection, sudden retinal detachment (when the jelly in the eye peels away from the retina) or blood spots from hemorrhage into the eye liquid due to eye surgery or injury or a retinal tear through a blood vessel. Before starting any treatment, get a proper diagnosis. If you notice flashing lights, changing patterns or a sudden flood of new floaters—symptoms that could signal a retinal tear and/or detachment—contact an eye specialist immediately. For most floaters, vitamin C remains the best way to reduce, or even eliminate, them by changing the makeup of the eye liquid's collagen (fibrous proteins).

My recommendation: Take two 1,000 mg vitamin C capsules daily for three months... wear ultraviolet-blocking sunglasses (look for 100% UV-blocking on the label)...and, after age 45, have a dilated eye exam every few years, depending on your other risk factors.

Red, Itchy Eyes

Mark A. Stengler, NMD, licensed naturopathic medical doctor and leading authority on the practice of alternative and integrated medicine. He is founder and medical director of the Stengler Center for Integrative Medicine, Encinitas, California. He is author of *The Natural Physician's Healing Therapies* (Bottom Line Books).

Blepharitis is an inflammatory condition of the eyelid that can cause swelling of the eyelid and crusting on the lids during sleep. First, I have patients clean the eye area. Apply a warm, wet cloth to the affected area for five minutes. Then dampen another cloth with warm water and a few drops of baby shampoo and wipe away any crusting. With another clean cloth, pat dry. Along with cleaning, I often recommend that patients take the homeopathic remedy Pulsatilla (two 30C pellets, three times daily, for three days) to clear up blepharitis. If that doesn't help after three days, the next step is to try eyedrops made with colloidal silver.

I recommend that patients mix three drops into a half ounce of saline solution and use three times daily. Consult with a doctor if the condition doesn't go away after five to seven days or gets worse.

Could Your Bifocals Be Dangerous?

Stephen Lord, PhD, senior principal research fellow, Falls and Balance Research Group, Prince of Wales Medical Research Institute, University of New South Wales, Sydney, Australia.

Could it be that the glasses meant to help you see better actually put you in danger of a potentially fatal or disabling accident? It could, according to findings that have linked bifocals and trifocals with an increased likelihood of falls in older adults.

WHAT'S THE PROBLEM?

It's not hard to see the root of the danger. The common vision problem called presbyopia, caused by a hardening of the lens of the eye, typically arises at around age 40. Presbyopia makes it more difficult to see images close at hand, which is why middle-aged people have difficulty reading without glasses. If this is your only vision problem, the solution is easy—to read, you wear glasses that magnify. But for those with additional vision problems that also need correction, the usual solution is multifocal glasses or contact lenses (bifocals, trifocals or progressive lenses)—and this is where people, quite literally, run into trouble.

A growing body of research, much of it originating at the Falls and Balance Research Group at the Prince of Wales Medical Research Institute in Sydney, Australia, has demonstrated that when older folks wear multifocal lenses while walking and also performing a secondary task—like reading a sign—they tend to "contact more obstacles" (as in, trip or bump into something). The glasses focus differently for near and far, which means that the wearer's ability to see obstacles near his/her feet gets compromised. The fact that falls are the leading cause of death from injury among older adults in the US makes this especially worrisome.

A SIMPLE SOLUTION

Stephen Lord, PhD, laboratory director at the Falls and Balance Research Group, University of New South Wales in Australia, told me that there's an easy solution to this problem. People who wear multifocal glasses or contact lenses should also keep with them a pair of single-focal glasses—with a prescription for distance vision only—to wear when walking outside their homes. Easy enough and worth doing, I think—far better to spend the money on an additional pair of glasses than on a ride in an ambulance.

Reduce the Risk Of Glaucoma

Treat eye pressure early to reduce glaucoma risk.

Recent study: Researchers gave 1,636 adults with elevated pressure in the eye, a risk factor for glaucoma, immediate treatment (eye-pressure–lowering drops for an average 13 years) or delayed treatment (no treatment for 7.5 years, on average, followed by an average 5.5 years of treatment).

Result: Those treated early reduced glaucoma risk by 27%.

Michael Kass, MD, professor and chair, ophthalmology and visual sciences, Washington University, St. Louis.

Easy Ways to Protect Your Eyes

Jamison Starbuck, ND, naturopathic physician in family practice in Missoula, Montana. She is past president of the American Association of Naturopathic Physicians and a contributing editor to *The Alternative Advisor: The Complete Guide to Natural Therapies and Alternative Treatments* (Time Life).

Researchers have identified a wide range of foods that help protect the eyes—leafy greens, such as spinach, chard and kale, have received the most attention, but there are plenty of other choices if you don't like those foods. *To optimize your eye health…**

• **Eat enough of the right foods.** The carotenoids lutein and zeaxanthin, found in leafy greens (as well as in green peas, corn, zucchini and eggs), have been rightly touted for their ability to act as disease-preventing antioxidants in the retina of the eye. For example, research has found that women ages 50 to 79 whose diets were rich in lutein and zeaxanthin were 32% less likely to develop cataracts (clouding of the eyes' lenses, resulting in blurred vision) than those whose diets contained less. Other studies have shown that these nutrients may reduce the incidence of macular degeneration (an eye disorder that gradually destroys central vision). To get these benefits, be sure to eat enough of these foods—aim for at least

*If you have a serious eye condition, such as macular degeneration, see an ophthalmologist. I also recommend annual eye examinations.

two servings daily. One serving equals one ear of corn, one egg or one-half cup of leafy greens, peas or zucchini.

•**Take coenzyme Q10 (CoQ10).** This nutrient, widely recognized for its heart-protective properties, also helps prevent and treat cataracts and macular degeneration. If you have either of these eye conditions—or a family history (parent or sibling) of them—take 100 mg of CoQ10 daily.

•**Get your berries, too.** The botanical medicine bilberry has long been used to treat retinal diseases. For my patients with cataracts or macular degeneration, I recommend that they take a daily 400-mg bilberry supplement—and eat one-half cup of blueberries or blackberries. These berries contain antioxidants that help protect the eyes. To help prevent eye disease, eat one-half cup of dark berries (fresh or frozen) daily.

Caution: If you take diabetes medication, do not use bilberry.

•**Use fish oil.** Fish oil, which contains *docosahexaenoic acid* (DHA) and *eicosapentaenoic acid* (EPA), is known to improve heart and immune health. These fatty acids also reduce dry eye symptoms and the risk for macular degeneration. For dry eye, cataracts or macular degeneration, ask your doctor about taking a total of 1,750 mg of EPA and DHA daily.

•**Make an herbal eye compress.** The herb eyebright has been widely used to treat eye ailments, particularly the itchy, watery, red eyes that accompany allergies, colds and sinusitis. For relief from these symptoms, make a cold compress (to be used externally on your eyes) with eyebright tea. Use two teaspoons of dried eyebright leaf (available at health-food stores) per eight ounces of boiling water. Steep covered for five minutes, strain and refrigerate in a closed jar. When cool, pour the tea over a clean cotton cloth and place it over your closed eyes for 10 minutes. For additional relief from symptoms, drink a mixture of 60 drops of eyebright tincture in one ounce of water, three times a day.

Warning: Do not put eyebright tea or extract directly into your eyes.

Eye Problems That Should Not Be Ignored

Robert Maiolo, OD, former guest lecturer at Yale University School of Medicine in New Haven, Connecticut, and an optometrist in private practice in Stamford, Connecticut. He specializes in keratoconus.

Cataracts, glaucoma and macular degeneration are the eye disorders that people tend to fear most, but there are other common conditions—some of them seemingly minor—that can gradually impair your vision. *For example…*

ASTIGMATISM

Most people have heard of astigmatism but don't really know what it means. The term refers to an asymmetrical cornea (the transparent, circular part of the front of the eyeball that bends incoming light rays through the pupil). Instead of being curved like a perfect sphere, it's shaped more like a football. Astigmatism is thought to be hereditary, but in some cases it can result from certain diseases or disorders (such as keratoconus, a gradual change in the shape of the cornea). Astigmatism, which affects about 45 million Americans, is diagnosed during a routine eye exam.*

Primary symptoms: Blurred vision, eyestrain and/or headaches.

Main treatment: Glasses or contacts that sharpen the blurred image caused by the irregularity in the cornea's curvature.

DRY EYE

The lacrimal (tear-producing) glands in the eyelids produce tears to keep the cornea moist. Tears are composed of three basic layers—oil (the outer layer), water (middle) and a protein lubricant known as mucin (inner). Dry eye can occur when the glands at the edges of the eyelids produce an insufficient outer layer, which in normal amounts prevents tears from

*Adults age 21 or older should receive an eye exam from an optometrist (a person who specializes in the examination, diagnosis and treatment of the eyes) or ophthalmologist (a medical doctor who specializes in the diagnosis and treatment of eye disorders) every two years. Those who wear contact lenses or whose occupation requires greater vision needs, such as using a computer, should be examined annually.

evaporating too quickly. Another common cause of dry eye is decreased tear production, which occurs as people age. Dry eye also is common in postmenopausal women and is believed to be caused by hormonal changes in those cases. More than 10 million Americans suffer from one of these forms of dry eye.

Primary symptoms: Dry, itchy, burning, irritated eyes. Symptoms worsen when you blink less—often the case when you watch TV, use a computer or drive. Certain medications, including some hypertension drugs and antihistamines, can also exacerbate dry eye.

Main treatment: Artificial tears (eye drops that moisten the eye) are available over-the-counter (OTC) and, in one case, by prescription (Restasis). Single-use, preservative-free eye drops, such as Allergan Refresh or Bausch & Lomb Advanced Eye Relief, are best for long-term use because preservatives can exacerbate dry eye symptoms. Another option is a product, such as GenTeal, that contains a preservative that dissipates when it hits the tear film in the eye.

Omega-3 fish oil, from eating fish and/or taking supplements, also can help. Omega-3s help to normalize the secretion of lipids (fats or oils), which affect the composition of tears. You'll need to consume fish oil for two to three months for your dry eye to improve, but it does work. I recommend 1,000 mg of fish oil supplements daily or three to five weekly servings of cold-water fish, such as salmon or sardines.

An extreme treatment for dry eye is a procedure that involves inserting silicone plugs in the puncta (corners of the eye) to improve the retention of tears. The procedure, known as punctal occlusion, is performed by an optometrist or ophthalmologist and works best for patients who produce insufficient tears.

FLOATERS AND FLASHERS

Our eyes contain a gel-like material called vitreous that fills most of the eye and gives it shape. The vitreous partially liquefies, or shrinks, as we age. This can cause fibers in the gel to shift about, leading to "floaters." If shrinkage of the vitreous pulls on the retina, it can cause flashes of light known as "flashers."

About 70% of Americans experience floaters and/or flashers—both typically affect only one eye—at some point in their lives. They're common in older adults, especially those over age 50.

Both conditions are usually harmless but, in rare cases, can signal a detached retina, a potentially blinding condition in which the retina is pulled from its normal position at the back of the eye. Possible signs of a detached retina include numerous floaters or floaters that significantly interfere with vision...flashers...or a veil moving across the vision, as if a window shade were opening and closing.

Primary symptoms: Floaters are characterized by floating black spots that may resemble cobwebs, rings, dots or worms. Flashers are brief flashes of light that are episodic...floaters can be episodic or constant.

Main treatment: For either condition, see your optometrist or ophthalmologist to rule out a detached retina, which may be caused by age-related changes in the vitreous. A detached retina also may be caused by head trauma, such as that caused by a car accident or a bump on the head. If your retina is detached, it can be surgically repaired by an ophthalmologist.

Harmless floaters and flashers should disappear over time, although they can return.

KERATOCONUS

Keratoconus is an exaggerated form of astigmatism in which the cornea thins and gradually protrudes, forming a conelike shape. This abnormal shape deflects incoming light, causing blurring and distorted vision.

Some people are genetically predisposed to keratoconus. In other cases, people who have allergies can cause the condition by rubbing their eyes too vigorously over a period of years, unintentionally thinning the corneas. An estimated 25 million Americans have keratoconus.

Primary symptoms: Blurring, ghostlike images, halos or glare.

Main treatment: Wearing specially fitted, hard contact lenses usually helps by reducing the distortion. Some people find hard contact lenses to be uncomfortable, but a new product, called hybrid contact lenses, usually works well. These lenses are hard in the center to effectively treat the condition, but soft around the edges for comfort. To find a doctor who can fit you with hybrid lenses, consult SynergEyes, 877-733-2012, *www.synergeyes.com.*

In about 20% of cases, the cornea thins too much or vision significantly deteriorates due to scarring of the cornea. For these patients, corneal transplant for keratoconus can prevent blindness.

Dry Eye Can Hurt Your Vision

Robert Latkany, MD, an ophthalmologist and founder and director of the Dry Eye Clinic at the New York Eye and Ear Infirmary and the Dry Eye Center of New York, both in New York City. He is actively involved in dry eye research and is the author of *The Dry Eye Remedy* (Hatherleigh), *www.dryeyedoctor.com.*

W hat if you had received six new eyeglass prescriptions over a seven-year period? That was the complaint of a 53-year-old patient who recently consulted me. As it turns out, his vision had become increasingly blurry—a common but little-known complication of dry eye.

Here's what can happen: When a person develops dry eye, irregularities in the production of tears or in their composition can cause a "smudge" on the normally clear surface of the eye, leading to progressive declines in vision. Vision usually is restored when dry eye is treated.

As we age, dry eye becomes more common—partly because tear production often diminishes as we grow older. However, eye dryness also can be associated with a wide range of underlying conditions that may require medical treatment to help prevent potentially dangerous complications of dry eye, such as infection, corneal scarring and, in rare cases, even permanent vision loss.

Most common causes of dry eye...

INFLAMMATION

Inflammation is among the main causes of dry eye. It's often due to allergies, exposure to environmental irritants, such as mold or pollen, or low dietary levels of antioxidant nutrients, such as beta-carotene and other carotenoids, which promote eye health.

Self-defense: Take 1 g of fish oil daily. The fatty acids in fish oil have been shown to reduce inflammation, generate antioxidants and increase tear production. People who eat fish regularly (cold-water fish, such as wild salmon, at least once weekly) may get comparable benefits.

TEAR EVAPORATION

In addition to decreased tear production, dry eye can result from increased evaporation of tears. Because a film of tears is spread over our eyes when we blink, anything that disrupts the normal rate of blinks, or that prevents the eyelid from closing completely, will cause tears to evaporate more rapidly. *Main causes of increased tear evaporation...*

•**Diabetes.** It reduces nerve sensitivity and inhibits the urge to blink. It also diminishes nerve signals that stimulate tear production.

Self-defense: Good control of blood sugar (glucose) levels—with a healthful diet and the use of medications—will help keep the eyes lubricated. People with diabetes should see an eye specialist (ophthalmologist) at least twice the first year that their diabetes is diagnosed and once a year after the diabetes is under control.

•**Shingles.** When this painful viral infection involves the face, it can affect the eyes. Shingles can reduce eye sensations and inhibit tear production.

Self-defense: If you develop shingles, ask your doctor about taking oral antiviral drugs, such as *acyclovir* (Zovirax), *famciclovir* (Famvir) or *valacyclovir* (Valtrex), to treat the condition. The drugs are most effective when started within 24 hours of a shingles outbreak and are usually taken for a week to 10 days.

•**Hormonal changes.** Testosterone and other "male" hormones (androgens), which are found in both sexes, appear to suppress eye inflammation in women as well as in men.

When levels of these hormones begin to decline with age (in men, generally after age 30…in women, after menopause), dry eye can result.

Self-defense: Ask your doctor whether you should have a blood test to measure your testosterone level. If a deficiency is detected, you may want to consider using eyedrops containing testosterone or a testosterone cream or gel, under your doctor's supervision. These medications must be prescribed "off-label"—the FDA has not yet approved their use for treatment of dry eye.

Caution: Supplemental testosterone may not be appropriate for men or women with a family or personal history of prostate or breast cancer.

• **Eye surgery.** Laser-assisted in situ *keratomileusis* (LASIK), the most popular form of laser eye surgery for correcting nearsightedness and farsightedness, requires severing many of the corneal nerves (sensory nerves on the eye's surface). Patients who have had the procedure blink less than they should. The nerves eventually regenerate, but this can take months to years.

Self-defense: Two alternative procedures—*photorefractive keratectomy* (PRK) and laser epithelial *keratomileusis* (LASEK)—are often as effective as LASIK, and the eye nerves recover more quickly. PRK and LASEK are less invasive—the surgeon scrapes the top layer of cells in the eye…with LASIK, however, the surgeon cuts the cornea to create a "flap" that is raised to allow the laser therapy.

• **Medications.** The use of certain medications, including antihistamines, decongestants, diuretics, sleeping pills, antidepressants, antipsychotic drugs and urinary bladder control medicines, can lead to dry eye.

Self-defense: Ask your doctor whether a different drug can be substituted.

• **Partial blinking.** Some people have a normal blink frequency (about 15 blinks per minute) but don't completely close their eyes when they blink—another cause of dryness.

Examples: Patients with Parkinson's disease or thyroid disease may have muscular disorders that prevent them from completely closing one or both eyes.

More common: Chronic staring. People who drive long distances, watch a lot of television or use computers get in the habit of keeping their eyes open.

Result: The blink muscles atrophy and become less effective.

Self-defense: Take a "blink break" at least twice an hour. Shut your eyes for 10 seconds, and move your eyeballs around under the closed lids to bathe and lubricate them. If this isn't possible—when driving, for example—at least shift your vision frequently. Look up, down and to the sides, rather than always looking straight ahead.

• **"Rabbit eyes."** About 10% of Americans sleep with their eyes partially open. It's called lagophthalmos (the Greek word for "rabbit eyes"). Tears evaporate more quickly even if the eyes are open just a slit.

Self-defense: Try Tranquileyes hydrating goggles. Available online for $30 to $60, they have a small sponge inside that can be soaked in water—this creates a moist eye environment that helps prevent evaporation during sleep.

BEST TREATMENT OPTIONS

Regardless of what's causing your dry eyes, artificial tears and other eye lubricants (such as Tears Naturale and GenTeal Gel) are useful for occasional relief (up to three or four times daily). But the relief doesn't last very long, and they do nothing to correct the underlying problem, which requires specific treatment (as described earlier).

Better: A prescription eyedrop, *cyclosporine* (Restasis), is the only FDA-approved medication that increases tear production.

Don't Rely on Mouth Rinse for Gum Health

The Food and Drug Administration (FDA) has demanded that three companies that make mouth rinses stop claiming that their products prevent gum disease. The products Listerine Total Care Anticavity Mouthwash, CVS Complete Care Anticavity Mouthwash and

Walgreens Mouth Rinse Full Action do not stop the buildup of plaque above or below the gum line. There's no substitute for daily brushing and flossing.

Mark A. Stengler, NMD, licensed naturopathic medical doctor and leading authority on the practice of alternative and integrated medicine. He is founder and medical director of the Stengler Center for Integrative Medicine, Encinitas, California. He is author of *The Natural Physician's Healing Therapies* (Bottom Line Books).

Cosmetic Mouth Rinses

Cosmetic mouth rinses don't kill germs or protect teeth. These rinses can help to temporarily diminish bad breath but do not treat the underlying cause.

Better: Choose a therapeutic mouthwash approved by the American Dental Association (ADA), with the ADA logo on the label. An ADA-approved mouthwash kills germs, helps reduce plaque and gingivitis and/or protects teeth against cavities.

Marvin A. Fier, DDS, executive vice president, adjunct professor and guest lecturer, American Society for Dental Aesthetics, Pomona, New York. *www.rocklandny dentist.com*

Is Your Bad Breath Caused by Tonsil Stones?

Jordan S. Josephson, MD, director, New York Nasal & Sinus Center, New York City, ear, nose and throat specialist at Lenox Hill Hospital, and author of *Sinus Relief Now* (Perigee Trade). *www.sinusreliefnow.com*

You've heard of kidney stones and gallstones...but tonsil stones? Yes, they exist—and until now, they were a common problem that few had heard of. Public awareness is growing, however, since bloggers began sharing solutions amongst themselves online. Formally known as tonsilloliths, these hard, pea-sized (or smaller) masses form on the tonsils and can cause discomfort, pain and very bad breath, though they're not really dangerous.

We spoke with Dr. Jordan Josephson, director of the New York Nasal & Sinus Center in New York City and author of *Sinus Relief Now*, who told us that tonsils aren't smooth, but rather have a bumpy surface with lots of nooks and crevices—this makes it easy for bacteria, dead cells and food particles to get trapped. This debris can concentrate and harden into whitish pellets over time, most especially in people with large tonsils and/or who suffer from chronic inflammation of the tonsils or repeated bouts of tonsillitis. Chronic sinusitis and gastroesophageal reflux (GERD) make tonsil stones more common as well—and when those conditions flare up, so do the tonsil stones. The resulting bad breath can be horrible.

WHAT'S THE PROBLEM WITH TONSIL STONES?

Small tonsil stones are completely unnoticeable, with no symptoms at all. Some people are unaware they have them until their dentist or doctor points them out, while others may have large stones that can be seen if you peer down your own throat. *These can be bothersome in a number of ways...*

• **Bad breath.** Tonsil stones often are accompanied by the kind of rancid breath that makes others back away from you (think spoiled deviled eggs). This is caused by the buildup of sulfur-producing bacteria and decaying food fragments.

• **Sore throat.** Tonsil stones can feel like something is caught in your throat. They can be especially painful if they occur with tonsillitis.

• **Coughing.** Large stones can dislodge and cause irritation that makes you cough them up.

• **Ear pain.** The tonsils and ears share the same nerve pathway, which means that some people with tonsil stones suffer referred pain that makes it seem like it is coming from the ear.

• **Other nasty symptoms can occur simultaneously.** For instance, your sinuses may flare up at the same time, causing postnasal drip and worsening your tonsil stones. GERD can cause burning of your esophagus, heartburn and indigestion which worsens your bad breath as well.

GETTING RID OF TONSIL STONES

What can you do to rid yourself of these offensive little stones? Some bloggers report using moistened cotton swabs to dislocate the stones, but Dr. Josephson says that is not a good idea, since dislodged cotton fibers can add to the irritation and there also is the danger of aspiration.

Instead, he suggests, focus on oral hygiene techniques that minimize the odds you'll even get them lodged in your tonsils. *These include...*

• **Brush your teeth after every meal and floss daily.** This is basic oral hygiene, which reduces the likelihood stones will develop.

• **Gargle twice a day.** This helps prevent the accumulation of debris. Use a mixture of eight ounces of warm water to one-quarter teaspoon of salt.

• **Avoid eating after your evening brush-and-gargle.** If you have GERD (or a hiatal hernia, which also can cause reflux), Dr. Josephson recommends that you not eat for three or four hours before bedtime. This helps keep you from refluxing when you lie down, which Dr. Josephson believes can worsen tonsil stones.

If you get tonsil stones over and over, you may find it worthwhile to invest in a tool that helps you remove them safely at home. A good one is the Grossan Hydro Pulse Nasal & Sinus System ($97, available online at *http://hydromed online.com* or by calling 800-560-9007). Also, Waterpik makes two versions, the Ultra Water Flosser (about $60) and the Classic Water Flosser (about $40)—both available online at *www. waterpik-store.com* or by calling 800-290-1568.

Chronic Bad Breath?

Andrew Spielman, DMD, PhD, associate dean, academic affairs, and professor, basic science and craniofacial biology, NYU College of Dentistry.

In addition to brushing your teeth at least twice daily, also brush your tongue and floss at least twice daily, in the morning and before bed. Use a tongue cleaner (also called a tongue brush or scraper), available at drugstores, to remove food debris trapped on the back of the tongue near the tonsils. Ask your dentist about prescription mouthwashes containing zinc chloride and sodium chlorite or chlorine dioxide. Some blue-colored generic mouthwashes also contain zinc chloride.

Good brands: SmartMouth and ProFresh. If bad breath persists, ask your dentist to check for gum disease, sinus infection, chronic nasal drip or mouth breathing (which dries the oral cavity, making oral smells airborne). Rarely, bad breath can signal acid reflux or a more serious condition such as diabetes or chronic lung infection.

Burning Mouth Syndrome

Mark A. Stengler, NMD, licensed naturopathic medical doctor and leading authority on the practice of alternative and integrated medicine. He is founder and medical director of the Stengler Center for Integrative Medicine, Encinitas, California. He is author of *The Natural Physician's Healing Therapies* (Bottom Line Books).

Burning mouth syndrome is a painful condition with symptoms described as the sensation of having scalded your lips, tongue, gums, the inside of your cheeks or roof of your mouth. The cause is not known, but the condition is most common in women between the ages of 50 and 70. Triggers that might predispose someone to this problem include upper respiratory tract infections, dental procedures, stress and allergies to food or medications, such as angiotensin-converting enzyme (ACE) inhibitors for blood pressure.

There also are many medical conditions associated with this condition, such as dry mouth, acid reflux, nutritional deficiencies (of many of the B vitamins, iron and zinc), menopause, diabetes, hypothyroidism and habits such as grinding teeth. Since there are many potential root causes of burning mouth syndrome, work with a holistic doctor and a holistic dentist. In the meantime, it can be helpful to take a multi-vitamin daily, along with an additional 50 mg of a B complex vitamin. Reducing stress also can help to ease symptoms.

Cracked Tongue

Vertical cracks or breaks in the surface of the tongue usually reflect an internal imbalance in the body. This can be due to digestive problems or it can reflect an imbalance in body fluids, such as dehydration, hormone imbalance or B-vitamin deficiency. Although tongue cracks alone won't tell a holistic practitioner what is going on inside your body, this symptom, along with any others, could help a practitioner make a diagnosis. Consult a naturopathic doctor or acupuncturist.

Mark A. Stengler, NMD, licensed naturopathic medical doctor and leading authority on the practice of alternative and integrated medicine. He is founder and medical director of the Stengler Center for Integrative Medicine, Encinitas, California. He is author of *The Natural Physician's Healing Therapies* (Bottom Line Books).

Bleeding Gums

Minor bleeding after brushing and flossing is probably nothing to worry about, especially if you see your dentist regularly. Make note of the area that bleeds, and mention it the next time you go in for a cleaning.

However, bleeding that recurs or does not stop after a few days could indicate inflammation caused by bacteria. It also could be related to medication use—for example, people who are taking blood thinners may experience bleeding gums. Avoiding the area when brushing is not an answer. Neither is avoiding medical care—see your dentist and talk to your physician.

Sheldon Nadler, DMD, dentist in private practice in New York City.

Gum Disease Treatment Eases Arthritis

In a study of 40 patients with gum disease and moderate or severe rheumatoid arthritis (RA), those who received periodontal treatment had improvement in arthritis symptoms (such as pain and swollen joints) with the greatest improvement seen in patients who also took arthritis medications known as anti-TNF (tumor necrosis factor) drugs, such as *etanercept* (Enbrel) or *infliximab* (Remicade).

If you have RA or are at risk (due to family history): Be sure to brush your teeth twice daily, floss once daily and see your dentist at least twice a year.

Nabil Bissada, DDS, chairman, department of periodontics, Case Western Reserve University School of Dental Medicine, Cleveland.

Receding Gums

Gums recede when tissue covering the teeth's supportive structure (roots and bone) is lost. When this occurs, more of your teeth's surfaces become visible and/or increasingly sensitive to extreme temperatures. This can be a response to chronic inflammation, infection, irritation or trauma. Using dental products, such as hard toothbrushes that brush away the gums or overly abrasive toothpastes that erode tooth structure, often leads to receding gums.

To protect your gums: Use a soft-bristle toothbrush and a nonabrasive traditional fluoride toothpaste without harsh additives (I recommend Colgate or Crest without whitening).

Even better: An electric toothbrush (which has been shown to clean more effectively and apply less force to teeth than manual toothbrushes). Brush two to three times daily, floss regularly and have a checkup with your dentist every six months.

Timothy Chase, DMD, dentist in private practice, SmilesNY, New York City.

Canker Sores

Canker sores may be caused by vitamin B-12 deficiency.

Recent finding: After taking 1,000 micrograms (mcg) of vitamin B-12 orally every day for six months, 74% of people who regularly had canker sores—painful open sores in the mouth—no longer got them. If you suffer from canker sores, talk to your doctor about supplementing your diet with vitamin B-12.

Study by researchers at Ben-Gurion University of the Negev, Beer-Sheva, Israel, published in *The Journal of the American Board of Family Medicine*.

Tooth Knocked Out? What to Do

Michael Apa, DDS, partner in The Rosenthal-Apa Group, a private aesthetic dentistry practice in New York City, and instructor at New York University College of Dentistry.

An occupational hazard in our line of work is that we are always primed for terrible health news, so when a friend started to tell us that her mother had fallen in the driveway the day before, we expected to hear that she'd broken her hip. We were happy to learn that she'd merely knocked out her tooth! But "merely" wasn't how it felt to her...fortunately, our friend knew what to do and where to go, so the tooth is now back in place and looks like it might heal just fine.

The incident motivated us to check in with Michael Apa, DDS, restorative and aesthetic dentist and instructor at NYU College of Dentistry, to learn about the right things to do in such a situation. His advice was surprising and practical. (Who knew dental first aid involved tea bags and cottage cheese?)

FIRST AID FOR TEETH

According to Dr. Apa, most intact teeth (ones that remain connected, even by just a bit of tissue) and many that have been knocked out altogether can be saved if you follow the right steps. First of all, be aware that this is a dental emergency and that it is important to act fast, because the longer a tooth is out of the socket, the less likely it is to be "re-established." In that case, you'd need an implant.

Here's what to do if you get a tooth knocked out:

If the tooth is loose but hasn't left the socket...

• **Gently try to move the loose tooth back into place beside the tooth next to it,** placing it very close so the edges touch one another smoothly. This doesn't usually hurt.

• **Do not put anything other than your clean fingers in your mouth**...it's important to avoid introducing additional nonresident bacteria.

• **See your dentist immediately. If it's after office hours,** call the emergency number... or, if that's not an option, go to the nearest urgent-care clinic or hospital emergency department.

If the tooth is out of the socket...

The goal is to try to put the tooth back into place in the gum, if it can be done. Time is of the essence—you'll have the best chance of saving the tooth if you get to the dentist (or an urgent-care clinic or the hospital emergency room) within 30 minutes. *Meanwhile...*

• **If the tooth fell onto the ground,** pick it up and clean it in your own saliva, saline solution, milk (any kind), baby formula or water (in this order of preference). Do not scrape off dirt or clean the tooth with alcohol.

• **Take care to handle the tooth by the crown (the biting end),** avoiding contact with the roots and nerve endings so you don't injure or contaminate them.

• **Try to insert the tooth back into place in your gum.** Push it in by gently biting or using your fingers to approximate its normal position. Hold a wet (warm or cool, not hot) tea bag in your mouth, biting down softly on it to keep the tooth in place.

• **If you can't put the tooth in place yourself (or if it makes you too nervous),** tuck the tooth in your mouth firmly against your cheek, your lower lip or under your tongue and keep it there until you can get to the dentist. Saliva protects it and keeps it from drying out. Though it may sound bizarre, another adult (if willing) can hold the tooth for you in this way as well.

•**Another option is to put the tooth in milk (whole is best, but low-fat and skim are fine, too).** If that is not available, use any sugarless, soft dairy product, such as yogurt or cottage cheese—the milk proteins will help keep the nerves and blood vessels alive. Do not put the tooth in a plastic bag or tissue even to transport it, as the nerves and blood vessels will dry out and die.

•**If you need to clean your mouth, rinse gently with water**—your dentist will clean it more thoroughly.

•**Do not eat or drink anything.**

Your dentist will clean your gum and stop the bleeding before trying to permanently re-implant your tooth. This is typically done by inserting and then splinting the tooth (with wires, a metal arch bar or plastic bond) for 10 to 14 days, which is how long it takes to fully reattach. Most people will not need stitches nor antibiotics, though a tetanus booster may be necessary if the tooth fell on the ground.

You'll need to continue to monitor the tooth for some time afterward, with regular follow-up visits. Sometimes root canal becomes necessary down the road, as the nerves may have suffered irreparable damage.

A suggestion: The American Dental Association has endorsed an FDA-approved emergency kit, Save-A-Tooth ($16), containing a storage case and special saline solution for one tooth. It is available from Amazon.com. One final note—this advice is meant for coherent adults, not children or adults who are groggy from injury and likely to swallow or inhale a loose tooth.

Flavored Waters Weaken Teeth

Acid levels in flavored waters, such as Propel Fit Water, SoBe LifeWater and VitaminWater,
can soften tooth enamel, leading to erosion, enamel loss and increased sensitivity.

If you drink flavored waters: Wait at least 30 minutes to brush your teeth so that tooth enamel has time to reharden.

Better: Drink plain water.

Mark Wolff, DDS, PhD, professor and chair, associate dean for predoctoral clinical education, department of cardiology and comprehensive care, New York University College of Dentistry, New York City.

Natural Ways to Keep Your Teeth Healthy

Jamison Starbuck, ND, naturopathic physician in family practice in Missoula, Montana. She is a past president of the American Association of Naturopathic Physicians and a contributing editor to *The Alternative Advisor: The Complete Guide to Natural Therapies and Alternative Treatments* (Time-Life).

Dental health may seem, at first glance, to have little to do with your overall physical health. But that's not true. For example, an increasing body of scientific evidence links dental conditions to heart disease, diabetes and even certain types of cancer. *Areas of dental health that my patients ask about most often…*

•**Periodontal disease.** According to the National Institutes of Health, 25% of Americans over age 65 have lost all of their natural teeth. Much of this is due to periodontal disease—including inflammation of gums (gingivitis) and/or bones around the teeth (periodontitis). For the most part, periodontal disease is preventable, but you may have to do more than just brush and floss.

To fight periodontal disease, you need a strong immune system, a limited amount of harmful bacteria in the mouth and healthy gum tissue. Avoid tobacco as well as sugary foods and beverages—and brush two to three times daily and floss once daily. You will have even greater success if you also use a daily regimen of 1,500 mg of vitamin C…20,000 international units (IU) of vitamin A*…60 mg of

*Pregnant women and people with liver disease should not exceed 5,000 IU daily.

the antioxidant CoQ10…and one-half cup of antioxidant-rich berries, such as blueberries and blackberries (fresh or frozen), or purple grapes. These nutrients help you maintain a strong immune system and healthy gums.

● **Fluoride.** For years, we've been told that fluoride hardens tooth enamel, thereby reducing tooth decay that can lead to cavities. However, some research indicates that this mineral may not reduce cavities or fight harmful bacteria in the mouth and actually may increase the risk for hip fracture. Fluoride also has been linked to osteosarcoma (bone cancer) in teenage boys who were exposed to the mineral during childhood.

Instead of using fluoride in toothpaste and other dental products, I recommend a regimen that includes good dental hygiene (as described above)…and the use of xylitol, a safe, plant-derived sugar product. Xylitol is available in toothpastes and chewing gums that are sold at health-food stores and pharmacies.

A study published in the *Journal of the American Dental Association* found that *xylitol* reduces levels of harmful bacteria in the mouth and discourages the formation of cavities. While cavity risk is greatest in children (whose teeth are still forming), some adults are also in jeopardy—especially smokers, older adults, people with dry mouth syndrome, which often results from Sjogren's syndrome (an autoimmune disease)…radiation therapy to the head or neck…or medication side effects.

● **Mercury fillings. This is a controversial issue. While the American Dental Association has stated that amalgam (mercury-containing) fillings are not dangerous,** mercury toxicity may lead to neurologic problems, such as memory loss, and autoimmune disease, such as lupus. My approach is to test mercury levels (via a urine sample) in patients who have many of these fillings as well as symptoms, such as chronic fatigue and pain. If levels are high, I recommend removing amalgam fillings and replacing them with non-mercury material, such as composite resin.

Whiter Teeth

Mark A. Stengler, NMD, licensed naturopathic medical doctor and leading authority on the practice of alternative and integrated medicine. He is founder and medical director of the Stengler Center for Integrative Medicine, Encinitas, California. He is author of *The Natural Physician's Healing Therapies* (Bottom Line Books).

There are several natural options when it comes to whitening teeth. David Banks, DDS, a holistic dentist in San Marcos, California, explains that most darkening of teeth is due to the accumulation of stains over time.

First: Brush with a quality low-abrasion toothpaste.

His favorites: PerioPaste by Bio-Pro, which contains antibacterial herbs and essential oils, such as peppermint, calendula flower and olive leaf (800-650-9060, *www.docharrison.com*) and PowerSmile Enzyme Brightening Oral Pre-Rinse by Jason Naturals, with papaya and pineapple enzymes (877-527-6601, *www.jason-natural.com*). Both contain calcium carbonate, sodium bicarbonate and colloidal silica—low-abrasion tooth-cleaning compounds that help with stains. Beyond that, if you want still whiter teeth, a bleaching process may be necessary.

Best: Have your dentist perform an in-office procedure, which limits the duration of exposure to the bleaching chemicals.

Dental Detectives: Holistic Dentistry for Whole-Body Health

Mark A. Breiner, DDS, holistic dentist and founder of Breiner Whole-Body Health Centre, in Trumbull, Connecticut. He is a Fellow of the International Academy of Oral Medicine and Toxicology and a member of The National Center for Homeopathy. He is author of *Whole-Body Dentistry* (Quantum Health). *www.wholebodydentistry.com*

Dentists have always been considered health professionals, but some take the concept further than others. As a growing body of medical research affirms the strong connection between poor oral health and chronic disease, including cancer, diabetes and heart disease, some dentists now dedicate their practices to improving and protecting overall health, not just what happens in your mouth. To learn more about the connection between your mouth and the rest of your body, we called Mark A. Breiner, DDS, founder of the Breiner Whole-Body Health Centre (Trumbull, Connecticut) and author of *Whole-Body Dentistry*.

Dr. Breiner explains that holistic dentists work in an entirely different paradigm. He likens standard dentistry to carpentry, calling it "a restorative profession, taking care of cavities and making crowns." The holistic approach looks at how the state of your mouth affects and reflects everything about your health. "Everything I do is with that in mind," he says. He asks patients to fill out extensive health forms and then spends a half-hour or so going over those at the first appointment, discussing their health in general. "I am playing detective, working to learn how their health may have been impacted by current or past dentistry that, with an additional stressor, has caused their health to take a turn for the worse."

WHAT'S DIFFERENT?

Dr. Breiner offered some examples of how the two approaches differ...

Gum check: Conventional dentists check for periodontal (gum) disease, associated with heart disease and stroke, by evaluating how red patients' gums are and if they are bleeding... whereas even if gums seem healthy on examination, in Dr. Breiner's office they investigate further by taking a plaque sample from under the gums, which is viewed under a microscope to determine whether there are destructive microbes and/or parasites.

Heavy metals: Perhaps the most controversial difference relates to the material used for fillings. The American Dental Association continues to support use of mercury-containing amalgam fillings, which some conventional dentists still use. But how can it be, asks Dr. Breiner, that mercury is considered toxic everywhere in the world but not in the mouth?

He points out that after removing amalgam fillings from the mouth, the law requires him to treat them as toxic waste.

Beyond the obvious concerns about the toxicity of mercury that is in your mouth, Dr. Breiner says there are other potential health problems, too. He explains that placing dissimilar metals (mercury fillings contain 50% mercury and 50% copper, tin, zinc and silver) in a salt solution (such as saliva) creates a battery-like electrical current. If a nearby tooth then gets a gold filling, the current gets even stronger. "Every tooth is on an acupuncture meridian, so these currents can interfere with the meridian's energy flow," says Dr. Breiner.

Beware: Only have your mercury fillings removed by a professional who is experienced and knowledgeable in this area. He/she must know how to evaluate if your health can tolerate such removal. Unfortunately, Dr. Breiner says, he has seen too many people who are now very sick because they had their mercury removed by a practitioner ignorant on this topic.

Energy meridians: Dr. Breiner uses EAV (Electro-Acupuncture according to Voll) to test the energy of acupuncture meridians, emphasizing that this technique uses no needles. "Think of it as an energy stress test of the acupuncture points," he says. According to Dr. Breiner, "each tooth energetically relates to a specific organ, vertebrae and/or muscle. Since this is a two-way street, with teeth affecting other parts of the body and vice versa, a root canal may be unnecessarily performed due to a problem elsewhere in the body." EAV helps in this discovery, he believes.

Tooth extractions: Most dental anesthetics contain epinephrine, which reduces bleeding, and dentists often advise use of ice to minimize swelling. (Dr. Breiner uses an epinephrine-free alternative.) Both of these practices, however, slow blood flow and increase the likelihood of a cavitation (a hole in the bone where a tooth has been extracted and never properly healed). Such cavitations are potential reservoirs for toxins and can cause facial pain and trigeminal neuralgia (inflammation of the primary nerve going to the face). Dr. Breiner uses both X-rays and EAV to locate areas on their way to becoming cavitations and to determine if they're likely to become problematic.

Some holistic dentists also believe that all teeth with root canals should be removed because they are breeding grounds for toxicity. Dr. Breiner does not find that to be the case, however. He says numerous factors determine whether a root canal is the cause of other problems, including the health of the associated meridian and the health of the patient.

Forecast: More Holistic Dentistry

Saying that "it is not enough to be a molar mechanic any more," Dr. Breiner told me he believes more dentists are moving in the direction of holistic dentistry—and that a more informed public will be the catalyst that eventually transforms the dental profession. In the meantime, he reminds people that what is good for the heart is good for the mouth including coenzyme Q10, magnesium, vitamin C and other antioxidants—preferably from food and supplements that are whole-food derived.

If you are interested in finding a holistic dentist, you can contact the International Academy of Biological Dentistry and Medicine, *www.iabdm.org*.

Protect Your Sense Of Smell

Alan Hirsch, MD, founder and neurological director of the Smell & Taste Treatment and Research Foundation in Chicago. He is a neurologist and psychiatrist, and author of *Life's a Smelling Success* (Authors of Unity) and *What Your Doctor May Not Tell You About Sinusitis* (Grand Central). *www.smellandtaste.org*

Up to 15 million Americans suffer from a severe-to-total loss of sense of smell. By age 65, up to half of adults have a reduced sense of smell. *What to do...*

CAUSES

It's estimated that the average adult can detect between 10,000 and 30,000 distinct odors. The nasal membranes are lined with cellular receptors that match the shape of different scent molecules. These molecules bind to cell walls at the top of the nose, where they trigger the release of neurochemicals. These, in turn, generate nerve signals that stimulate the parts of the brain that identify different scents.

Cigarette smokers are far more likely to experience a loss of smell than nonsmokers. Damage to the sense of smell also can be caused by brain injury, nasal polyps, a brain tumor or nervous system diseases, such as Parkinson's.

Other causes: Diabetes, a deficiency of some B vitamins and sometimes the use of cholesterol-lowering statins or antihypertensive drugs.

Many patients with a diminished sense of smell also suffer from chronic depression or anxiety disorders. It's possible that the air contains yet-to-be-identified molecules with druglike, antianxiety effects—benefits that don't occur in those with smelling disorders.

SMELL TEST

To test for a diminished sense of smell, most doctors take an alcohol pad and hold it beneath the patient's chin. (You can do this at home with an alcohol pad from a first-aid kit.) If you can smell alcohol at that distance, your sense of smell is fine. If you can smell the alcohol only when the pad is raised closer to your nose, you have a problem.

Self-test: Put vanilla ice cream in one bowl and chocolate ice cream in another. Close your eyes, and move the bowls around so that you don't know which is which. Take a taste from each bowl. Because taste is largely determined by smell, an inability to tell them apart indicates that there's a problem somewhere in your olfactory system.

WHAT TO DO

Often, when the underlying problem is corrected, the sense of smell returns. People who quit smoking usually regain all or most of their sense of smell, but this can take years. *Also...*

•**The nutrients thiamine (100 milligrams daily) and phosphatidylcholine (9 grams daily)** can elevate levels of neurotransmitters that improve the sense of smell. In one study, about 40% of patients improved significantly after taking phosphatidylcholine for three months. The success rate with thiamine is somewhat lower.

• **Sniff therapy.** People who expose themselves to the same scent 20 to 50 times a day for several weeks will have an increase in scent receptors and will sometimes regain their ability to smell that particular scent.

Trouble Smelling? It May Signal Serious Illness

Richard L. Doty, PhD, professor of otorhinolaryngology (ear, nose and throat disorders) at the University of Pennsylvania School of Medicine and director of the school's Smell and Taste Center, both in Philadelphia. He is the author of *The Neurology of Olfaction* (Cambridge University) and has published more than 200 peer-reviewed scientific papers in major medical journals.

Most of us take our sense of smell for granted. But for the surprising number of people for whom this vital sense is dulled, the consequences can be more serious than you might imagine. Smell disorders affect half of people age 65 and older, with more cases occurring in men than in women.

Danger: When a person's sense of smell is not functioning properly, it can lead to related health problems, such as loss of appetite, high blood pressure (due to the use of too much salt) and/or weight gain (due to excessive sugar intake). Gas leaks and fires also may endanger people with an impaired sense of smell.

Why your sense of smell is so important...

WHEN OUR SENSE OF SMELL FALTERS

We all know that allergies, colds and nasal congestion interfere with our sense of smell. These conditions cause nasal obstruction that prevents odors from reaching olfactory receptors (sensory nerve cells) in the nasal lining.

A blunted sense of smell is common with this type of obstruction, but the sense usually returns within a few days or weeks. When the damage is severe or repeated enough times, the cells can be permanently disabled. The persistent state of inflammation that occurs with chronic sinusitis also can permanently impair olfactory cells.

Other causes of impaired smell...

• **Aging.** As we grow older, the nerves involved in smell weaken, and membranes lining the nose become thin and dry.

• **Head injury.** When the brain is jarred within the skull, olfactory nerve fibers may be damaged. Smell loss from traumatic head injury is usually more severe than that caused by infection. Even a relatively mild impact—not enough to cause a concussion—can lead to permanent loss of smell.

• **Medications.** Heart drugs, such as the cholesterol-lowering medication *atorvastatin* (Lipitor), the calcium channel blocker *verapamil* (Covera) and the blood pressure–lowering agent *doxazosin* (Cardura), are among the medications most likely to impair one's sense of smell or taste. Other blood pressure drugs, such as angiotensin-converting enzyme (ACE) inhibitors, including *enalapril* (Vasotec) and enalapril and hydrochlorothiazide (Vaseretic), also may lead to loss of smell or taste.

• **Environmental toxins.** The precise effect of environmental toxins, such as pesticides, is uncertain, but they can clearly damage one's sense of smell. In a study published in *Experimental and Toxicologic Pathology*, a group of residents of Mexico City—notorious for its air pollution—scored significantly lower on a smell identification test than residents of cleaner environments. Upon closer examination, signs of damage in the nasal lining and in the olfactory bulb (which processes smell signals) within the brain were found in the study subjects.

A WARNING SIGN

The olfactory system is highly vulnerable to brain disorders, and a noticeable decline in the sense of smell occurs in 85% to 90% of people in the early stages of Alzheimer's and Parkinson's disease. In fact, the American Academy of Neurology recommends the use of smell tests as an aid to help diagnose Parkinson's disease.

There's even increasing evidence that smell loss begins in the so-called "preclinical" period—preceding classic symptoms of Alzheimer's (such as memory loss) and Parkinson's (such as movement problems) by several years.

Low thyroid function (hypothyroidism) also can lead to loss of smell. Distorted or phantom smells (smelling an odor, such as a chemical or floral scent, that is not present) may point to epilepsy or a brain tumor or Alzheimer's disease.

HOW WELL DO YOU SMELL?

If you think that your ability to distinguish odors has gotten significantly worse, it may be worth having it tested by your doctor. Few physicians routinely provide smell testing, so you will probably need to ask for it.

Or you can take a self-administered smell test that was developed by myself and other researchers at the University of Pennsylvania. Known as the Smell Identification Test (SIT), it is a scratch-and-sniff–type test and is available from the manufacturer (800-547-8838, *www.sensonics.com*)—cost: $27 for the test and $3.50 for the scoring key. For the most accurate results, take the test in your doctor's office and ask him/her to help you interpret the results.

PROTECT YOUR SENSE OF SMELL

Once seriously damaged, one's sense of smell may improve but is unlikely to recover fully.

Smell loss due to nasal inflammation can be treated with steroid drugs, such as *prednisolone* (Prelone), in nasal spray or pill form. But long-term use of the pill form of prednisolone and overuse of the nasal spray are not recommended because damage to the liver, kidney or bones may result.

Meanwhile, research using stem cells is under way at several universities to explore whether damaged olfactory receptor cells could be replaced with healthy cells in the future.

Prevention is the best defense against loss of smell. Exposure to tobacco smoke—both through smoking and exposure to secondhand smoke—dulls the sense of smell but is generally less devastating than one might expect. If you smoke, quitting cigarettes generally will restore any loss of your sense of smell—but that recovery can take years.

Other prevention strategies…

• **Avoid infection.** While occasional colds and the flu are inescapable, good hygiene practices (including frequent hand-washing) will make them less frequent.

• **Protect your head.** Wear seat belts in the car and a helmet when riding a bike, rollerblading, skiing or participating in any sport or activity that could lead to a head injury. Don't participate in sports, such as boxing or football, that may involve frequent blows to the head.

• **Breathe clean.** Take precautions around toxic chemicals at work, and herbicides and pesticides at home. Use these substances only in well-ventilated areas and wear a mask. Instead of using toxic household cleansers, detergents and other such products, choose safer alternatives, such as vinegar and baking soda.

What to Do If You Lose Your Sense of Smell and Taste

Alan R. Hirsch, MD, founder and neurological director of the Smell & Taste Treatment and Research Foundation in Chicago. He is a neurologist and psychiatrist, and author of *Life's a Smelling Success* (Authors of Unity) and *What Your Doctor May Not Tell You About Sinusitis* (Grand Central). *www.smellandtaste.org*

The loss of the sense of smell as one ages (*presbyosmia*) is quite common. Approximately one-half of people ages 65 to 79 and about three-quarters of those age 80 or older have a reduced ability to smell. However, this loss is not always a normal consequence of aging. It can be caused by a wide variety of conditions, from something as simple as a vitamin B-12 or folate deficiency to more complex disorders, such as diabetes, hypothyroidism (low thyroid function) or Parkinson's disease. Certain medications also can cause or contribute to a diminished sense of smell.

In addition, the sense of taste diminishes with age, and because taste and smell are closely linked, taste loss may be due to a loss of smell. Since there is such a wide range of causes for these sensory losses, many of which are easily treated, it is best to consult a neurologist or otolaryngologist (ear, nose and throat doctor), who can evaluate the origin of the smell and taste loss.

How to Stop a Nosebleed

To stop a nosebleed, sit upright, lean forward and pinch the soft part of your nose with your thumb and forefinger for five to 15 minutes.

To prevent recurrent nosebleeds: Humidify your living space…lubricate your nose with saline spray or a thin film of petroleum jelly. Also, talk to your doctor—the blood vessel causing nosebleeds may need to be cauterized.

Caution: If a nosebleed doesn't stop after 30 minutes, go to the hospital. A doctor may have to insert packing material into the nostril or surgery may be needed.

Mayo Clinic Health Letter, 200 First St. SW, Rochester, Minnesota 55905.

Think Your Nose Is Growing?

With age, your nose can thicken, getting wider and bulkier as nasal pores plug with oil that solidifies. To prevent this, cleanse oily skin on the nose twice daily. Cleansing facials also help.

Also: Fatty tissue under the skin of the nose thins with age and can no longer support the nose's heavy tip. The tip then starts to droop, moving closer to the upper lip and possibly blocking breathing at night. If you experience this, use one-half-inch-wide medical tape to hold the tip up while you sleep. Start the tape between the nostrils, then gently lift the tip by pulling the tape up along the main nasal bridge, stopping between the eyes.

Murray Grossan, MD, otolaryngologist, Cedars Sinai Medical Center, Los Angeles.

Cholesterol in the Ear?

In animal studies, researchers found that cholesterol levels in the inner ears' outer hair-cell membranes affect hearing. This finding could open the way to new defenses against hearing loss.

The Journal of Biological Chemistry.

Pain Relievers Linked To Hearing Loss

Among 27,000 men who were tracked for 18 years, those age 60 and older who used *acetaminophen* (Tylenol) or nonsteroidal anti-inflammatory drugs (NSAIDs), such as *ibuprofen* (Advil) or *naproxen* (Aleve), two or more times weekly were 16% more likely to develop hearing loss than those who did not. Regular aspirin users had no increased risk.

Theory: Acetaminophen depletes glutathione, an antioxidant that protects the ears, and NSAIDs reduce blood flow to them.

Sharon Curhan, MD, clinical researcher, department of medicine, Harvard Medical School, Boston.

Slow Hearing Loss Naturally

Folic acid may help slow hearing loss. A three-year Dutch study found that people who took 800 micrograms of folic acid daily had less low-frequency hearing loss than people who took a placebo. Ginkgo biloba may help as well. Take 120 milligrams of a 24% extract twice daily—but check with your doctor first if you are using a blood-thinning medicine, such as *warfarin* (Coumadin).

Mark A. Stengler, NMD, licensed naturopathic medical doctor and leading authority on the practice of alternative and integrated medicine. He is founder and medical director of the Stengler Center for Integrative Medicine, Encinitas, California. He is author of *The Natural Physician's Healing Therapies* (Bottom Line Books).

301

The Surprising Connection Between Diabetes and Your Hearing

Older people who have diabetes have poorer hearing than people the same age who don't have diabetes.

In people age 60 and older with type 2 diabetes, high blood sugar may cause tiny blood vessels in the inner ear to break, disrupting sound reception.

Self-defense: If you have type 2 diabetes, have your hearing tested regularly and wear hearing protection (earplugs, earmuffs, etc.) in all noisy situations—mowing the lawn, using power tools, attending concerts.

Nancy E. Vaughan, PhD, investigator, Department of Veterans Affairs' National Center for Rehabilitative Auditory Research, Portland, Oregon.

Your Hearing Loss And Dementia

When researchers tested 313 people (average age 80) to gauge their central auditory processing—ability to screen out competing sounds, such as background conversations, in a noisy environment—average test scores were significantly lower for patients with dementia or mild memory impairment than for those without either condition.

Theory: Because normal hearing involves both the ears and brain, a decrease in brain cells, which typically occurs with dementia, may impair hearing ability.

George A. Gates, MD, professor of otolaryngology, department of head and neck surgery, University of Washington, Seattle.

Listen Up! These Vitamins Can Prevent Hearing Loss

Josef M. Miller, PhD, professor of otolaryngology at University of Michigan Medical School, Ann Arbor, and Karolinska Institute in Stockholm. He is director of the Cochlear Signaling and Tissue Engineering Laboratory at Kresge Hearing Research Institute, also in Ann Arbor.

If you're middle-aged or older, you've probably heard about—or experienced for yourself—"age-related" hearing loss. Many people do lose some of their hearing with advancing age. That's the bad news.

The good news is that recent research has shown that much of this hearing loss can be prevented with certain nutrients. The right foods and supplements actually can help you hear better.

SILENT DAMAGE

Exposure to loud noises over a lifetime is a major cause of presbycusis, hearing loss that is associated with age and heredity. A structure in the inner ear called the cochlea is lined with thousands of tiny hairs that translate sound vibrations into electrical signals. Noise can damage these hairs and, over time, may result in hearing loss.

Why this happens: Loud noises trigger the production of free radicals, molecules produced in the inner ear that damage the cochlear hairs. Prolonged exposure to noise also causes a constriction of blood vessels and reduces circulation to the inner ear. In laboratory studies at the University of Michigan, animals were exposed to sounds measuring 120 decibels, about the volume of a rock concert.

In the studies, some animals were given the antioxidant-rich nutrients magnesium, beta-carotene (the body converts beta-carotene to vitamin A) and vitamins C and E one hour prior to the noise exposure and then once daily for five days. The test animals had 75% to 80% less hearing loss than animals given their normal food.

WHY NUTRITION HELPS

The antioxidants in fruits, vegetables, whole grains and other plant foods help fight free radicals and inflammation throughout the body, including in the inner ear. People who consume a lot of these nutrients on a regular basis get the most protection because free radical damage persists even when the noise is gone.

The largest spike in free radicals occurs while the noise is present. After that, free radicals intermittently decline and spike again. This cycle continues for five to seven days after the initial exposure, probably because free radicals are produced by the body as it attempts to heal noise-related damage within the inner ear. *Recommended nutrients...*

•Best Combo

Taken together, the combination of nutrients beta-carotene, magnesium and vitamins C and E seems to be most effective at preventing cell damage. Each one inhibits the formation of free radicals in cells in different parts of the body. Vitamin E and beta-carotene reduce free radicals that are formed in the lipid (fatty) portions of cells, while vitamin C acts in the watery compartments. Magnesium dilates blood vessels, improves inner-ear circulation and prevents a noise-induced reduction in blood flow followed by a rebound increase (which would lead to an additional increase in free radicals).

Recommended doses: 18 milligrams (mg) beta-carotene...500 mg vitamin C...267 mg vitamin E (in the form of alpha-tocopherol)... and 312 mg magnesium. These doses are the equivalents of those used in the studies and are only slightly different from the minimum recommended levels.

Studies have shown that the best time to take nutritional supplements to protect your hearing is about 24 hours before an anticipated noise exposure, such as a concert or a car race.

When you're exposed to loud noises that you didn't anticipate, you can gain protection by increasing your antioxidant intake afterward. Antioxidants have been shown to reduce noise damage in animals when taken as much as three days following noise exposure—although protection was greater when taken one day after the noise.

•Folate

The Blue Mountains Hearing Study (a survey of age-related hearing loss) collected data on dietary habits and measured levels of hearing loss in nearly 3,000 participants. Those with the lowest blood levels of folate were 39% more likely to experience hearing loss than those with the highest levels. Folate—the supplemental form is folic acid—is an antioxidant that also lowers levels of homocysteine, an amino acid that indicates the presence of inflammation in the body. Reducing homocysteine with folate or folic acid may reduce inflammatory damage and possibly improve circulation to the inner ear.

Recommended dose: I advise patients to get 400 micrograms (mcg) daily. You can get this much in one or two servings of many fortified breakfast cereals. Most multinutrient supplements also include folic acid. Foods rich in folate include spinach (100 mcg in one-half cup cooked) and asparagus (85 mcg in four spears).

•Omega-3 fatty acids

In the Blue Mountains Hearing Study, those who ate fish two or more times a week were 42% less likely to suffer from age-related hearing loss than those who ate less than one weekly serving of fish.

Recommended: The omega-3 fatty acids in fish are among the healthiest nutrients you can eat. Two or more fish servings a week are probably ideal.

•Zinc

This mineral is a chelator that binds to iron and helps remove it from the body. This process is important for hearing because iron plays a role in the formation of free radicals.

Recommended dose: The recommended daily allowance (RDA) is 11 mg zinc for men and 8 mg for women. A serving of beef can supply nearly 9 mg of zinc. Oysters, the richest source, provide 76.7 mg in a half-dozen.

Hearing Loss

Barbara McLay, MA, clinical associate professor of communication science and disorders and head of the hearing conservation program, University of Missouri, Columbia.

Whether hearing loss can be reversed depends on where in the ear it occurs and what causes it.

Inner ear: Damage to the inner ear from aging, hereditary factors, disease (such as meningitis) and exposure to a sudden loud sound can be irreversible. Some medications (for example, certain antibiotics and chemotherapy drugs) also can cause irreversible hearing loss.

Middle ear: Upper respiratory infections can lead to fluid buildup and difficulty hearing. Treating the infection will restore hearing. Abnormal bone growth around the tiny bones in the middle ear also can cause hearing loss and can be corrected with surgery.

Outer ear: The most common reason for outer-ear hearing loss is wax buildup. Have earwax removed at the doctor's office or try an over-the-counter wax-removal product to help restore hearing.

To prevent hearing loss...

• **Maintain your general health by eating right, not smoking, etc.**

• **Protect ears from loud noises.**

• **Do not put cotton-tipped swabs or other objects in your ears.**

See your doctor immediately if you experience sudden hearing loss in one or both ears.

Hearing Aid Dilemma

Debbie Abel, AuD, doctor of audiology and director of reimbursement at the American Academy of Audiology, Reston, Virginia, *www.audiology.org*, and a practicing audiologist for more than 30 years.

Do friends and family continually push you to get a hearing aid? Or even if you have one and wear it, do you feel isolated—that you're still missing out on what's going on around you at family functions, meetings or having lunch with a friend?

Or do you know someone with a hearing aid who still doesn't seem to hear well?

According to the trade group Better Hearing Institute, about one-quarter of the people who own hearing aids don't wear them regularly. As a result, people who can't hear as well as they would be able to with a hearing aid are missing out on all that life has to offer.

WHAT TO DO

Consider these steps to make your hearing aid more useful...

• **See a doctor of audiology (AuD)** for a yearly audiogram to measure your hearing level and make sure that the programming on your digital aid is up-to-date (analog aids are very rare these days—if you have one, seriously consider upgrading to a digital). Because hearing loss usually progresses gradually, it's easy to miss changes. A digital hearing aid is programmed to correct for your hearing loss precisely and requires adjustments as your hearing deteriorates.

Signs that your hearing aid needs reprogramming: Background noise seems too loud with the hearing aid on, or people seem to be slurring or mumbling their words. Most hearing loss caused by aging occurs in the upper pitch range. In English, this range tends to include the consonants, which makes it easy to confuse, say, "sat" with "cat."

A properly programmed digital hearing aid suppresses background noise and amplifies the pitch ranges where you need help.

Helpful: Get a new audiogram if you are exposed to loud noise (prolonged exposure, or even one very loud sound, can damage hearing) or are taking certain chemotherapy drugs, such as *cisplatin* (Platinol) and *carboplatin* (Paraplatin), since these drugs may damage your hearing.

• **Have your hearing aid checked out with an audiologist at least once a year**—it may need repairs, which the audiologist can perform. If the sound is distorted or weak, it's easy to put the hearing aid aside and forget about it, but a simple repair could make it useful again.

Check whether the ear "mold" (the custom-made part of a hearing aid that fits in the ear) or the hearing aid (if it sits within your ear) still fits. The ear may stretch in response to a hearing aid and aging, and after 18 months, the mold or hearing aid may fit too loosely.

Losing as little as five pounds can also make your hearing aid fit too loosely. A loose aid feels unsecured—which may make you reluctant to wear it—and the looseness could result in feedback noises or ineffective amplification.

• **Clean the hearing aid ear mold once a week.** Earwax in the mold or tubing will block sound, so make sure that the opening is clear. Wiping the aid at least once a week with a tissue or alcohol-free moist wipe may also help prevent infections.

• **Store the hearing aid properly.** Moisture can decrease the efficiency of a hearing aid. If you live in or frequently visit a humid climate, store your aid in a container designed to keep it dry (available from your audiologist) in order to prevent breakdowns. There are also electrical devices currently on the market that can both dry and sanitize the aid. I recommend the Dry & Store brand, found online at *www.dryandstore.com* or through your audiologist.

Cost: $82 to $173.

• **Consider wearing the device every day to build up comfort.** Some wearers get into the habit of using their hearing aids only on special occasions. This means that their ears never have a chance to completely adjust to how the devices fit or sound. Most people eventually find their aids comfortable for all-day use if they give them a chance.

Best: If you are an occasional wearer, allow yourself to grow fully comfortable with your hearing aid by wearing it two hours a day, every day, to start and then gradually wear it for longer and longer periods. After three or four days, you should be able to wear the device with little or no discomfort.

• **Upgrade to a better aid.** The clarity of the sound produced by a good-quality hearing aid has improved much in the last three years. Especially if your hearing aid is not digital, it will have poorer sound quality and inability

to cancel out background noise, among other drawbacks. You may do much better with one of the newer digital aids.

Note: The more sophisticated the technology, the higher the cost—$1,500 is the minimum you should spend. Anything less will be of poorer quality. A financing plan from the audiologist may be available. Some charities and service clubs offer assistance.

A proposed Hearing Aid Tax Credit has been reintroduced in Congress. It would offer up to a $500 tax credit for the purchase of one hearing aid every five years (*www.hearingaidtaxcredit.org*).

• **Consider buying a second aid if you own only one hearing aid and have hearing loss in both ears.** Most types of hearing loss affect both ears about equally. While you can make do with one hearing aid, having an aid in each ear helps you locate the source of a sound and helps you better understand speech in a noisy environment. Some people find that they are more likely to wear any aid when they have the benefits of two.

JOYS OF HEARING

If your hearing aid works and feels fine, but you still don't like to wear it, consider…

• **Hearing well keeps you young.** Some seniors view a hearing aid as a sign of decline. In fact, hearing badly will call more attention to a senior's age because it may mimic mental deterioration and make observers question a senior's attention span or memory.

• **Relationships improve when you hear as well as possible.** Hearing loss leads to miscommunication, which not only makes everyday tasks more difficult, but can easily lead to misunderstandings and arguments. Family members may be stressed by the volume of the radio or television or the need for constant repetition in conversation…the hearing-impaired person may isolate himself/herself rather than struggle to hear. In contrast, families of hearing-aid users report that the resulting better communication improves their relationships.

Ringing in the Ears?

Debara Tucci, MD, professor of surgery in the division of otolaryngology–head and neck surgery at Duke University Medical Center in Durham, North Carolina, and a specialist in ear-related problems. Dr. Tucci is a member of the American Academy of Otolaryngology–Head and Neck Surgery and the Association for Research in Otolaryngology.

I f you have tinnitus, you know how annoying it is to be the only person in the room who "hears" an unwanted sound, such as ringing, buzzing, hissing or roaring. Up to 50 million Americans are bothered by this condition.

Latest thinking: Even though tinnitus is often associated with age-related hearing loss, researchers are now discovering that the telltale "ringing in the ears" and other sounds are probably generated by abnormal activity in the brain regions that are responsible for perceiving auditory sound.

What role does the brain play in tinnitus? It is now thought that because of hearing loss, the brain's auditory system does not receive the sensory input it expects, so the brain compensates by activating brain cells (neurons) to create a perception of sound.

Another reason: Tinnitus is also commonly linked to long-term exposure to very loud noises, which may alter brain function in a way that leads to the unwanted sounds that characterize the condition.

Good news: Fortunately, a number of recent therapies now offer new hope to tinnitus sufferers.

WHAT WILL WORK BEST FOR YOU?

What works for one tinnitus sufferer won't help everyone with the disorder. *Simple steps you can try on your own...*

•**Review all medications you're taking.** More than 200 medications can cause temporary tinnitus in some people—even aspirin or other nonsteroidal anti-inflammatory drugs (NSAIDs), such as *ibuprofen* (Motrin). Prescription drugs that have been linked to tinnitus include diuretics (water pills) and certain antibiotics and cancer medications. If medication is the culprit, stopping or changing the drug usually eliminates symptoms.

Important: If you believe a prescription drug may be causing tinnitus, consult your doctor before decreasing the dose or discontinuing it.

•**Eliminate caffeine.** Caffeine in all forms (including coffee, many teas, some sodas and chocolate) makes tinnitus significantly worse for many people.

•**Try vitamin B-12.** Although the research is mixed, some people have found relief by increasing their intake of certain minerals (such as magnesium or zinc) or B vitamins (especially vitamin B-12) according to the American Tinnitus Association. If you would like to try this approach, talk to your doctor for advice on the supplement (and dosage) that would be best for you.

•**Get checked for earwax.** Ask your doctor to check your ears for earwax—wax buildup commonly causes tinnitus.

Override the sounds. Besides masking the sounds, this can also reduce the brain activity believed to trigger tinnitus. *For example...*

•**Background noise,** such as music, a humidifier, a fan or a white-noise device, can be especially helpful at night if your tinnitus makes it hard to fall asleep.

•**A hearing aid or cochlear implant** (an implanted electrode and external electronic receiver for people with too much hearing loss to benefit from a hearing aid) may help reduce tinnitus symptoms in people with significant hearing loss.

TREATMENTS

If the strategies described above don't relieve your tinnitus symptoms within three to six months...or if your tinnitus is in only one ear (possibly indicating an underlying condition such as a benign tumor) or symptoms are bothersome enough to interfere with daily activities and/or sleep, consult your primary care doctor or an otolaryngologist (ear, nose and throat specialist) for an evaluation.

The physician may refer you to an audiologist (a health-care professional who specializes in hearing loss, tinnitus and balance disorders) for advice.

If you would like to try one of the break-through therapies described below, consider consulting an otolaryngologist or audiologist at a tinnitus treatment program at a university-based medical center (these therapies are typically not covered by health insurance)…

- **Tinnitus retraining therapy (TRT).** Counseling and sound therapy (whereby patients hear steady, low-level background sound, often from in-ear sound generators) help make people unaware of tinnitus.

This therapy is currently being studied in a large clinical trial. Several smaller studies have reported success rates of about 80%. To find an audiologist trained in TRT, contact the American Tinnitus Association (800-634-8978, *www.ata.org*).

- **Music therapy.** Music is used in at least two tinnitus treatments…

- **Neuromonics Tinnitus Treatment** involves the use of an FDA-approved prescription device that plays music (through earphones) embedded with sound that is customized to the person's tinnitus sound frequency. The device can be worn during most activities and is designed to help "retrain" the brain so it filters out the disturbing sounds associated with tinnitus.

There is no independent research on this treatment, but a study conducted by the device manufacturer found that 91% of tinnitus sufferers experienced an improvement of at least 40% in symptoms after six months. To find a provider, contact Neuromonics, Inc. (866-606-3876, *www.neuromonics.com*).

- **"Notched" music therapy** uses a form of tailor-made music modified to remove the sound frequency of the individual's tinnitus. This targets the part of the brain associated with tinnitus. In a recent German study, notched music was found to reduce tinnitus symptoms after 12 months.

- **Acupuncture.** In a Brazilian study conducted on 76 tinnitus patients, acupuncture was found to provide immediate reduction in tinnitus symptoms, but the research is mixed on the long-term efficacy of this therapy.

- **Hypnosis.** Among 49 tinnitus patients who were introduced to hypnosis and taught basic methods of self-hypnosis, 35 completed the therapy and experienced relief from tinnitus symptoms after five to 10 sessions, according to research conducted at the University of Liège in Belgium.

- **Biofeedback.** Some patients have benefited from this therapy, in which monitoring devices are used to give immediate feedback on involuntary bodily responses, such as breathing. This helps patients have some control over negative physical reactions that often accompany tinnitus, such as increased heart rate.

- **Medication.** The drugs below, which are now being evaluated to reduce tinnitus symptoms, are designed to treat other conditions but can be prescribed by doctors "off label" for tinnitus treatment.

- **Acamprosate (Campral)** is used to treat alcohol addiction but has been shown to help some tinnitus patients.

- **Tricyclic and selective serotonin reuptake inhibitor (SSRI)** antidepressants may help relieve severe tinnitus, with possible side effects including dry mouth and constipation.

- **Alprazolam (Xanax)** is an anti-anxiety medication that appears to improve symptoms temporarily in some patients but hasn't been shown to offer long-term benefits. Possible side effects include nausea and drowsiness.

ON THE HORIZON

Another potentially promising treatment is transcranial magnetic stimulation, in which a weak electric current is sent through the brain. A small magnetic coil is placed on the scalp—in this case, near the brain's auditory cortex. Current from the coil stimulates neurons in the targeted area. Studies have shown significant reduction in some patients' tinnitus symptoms, and this therapy is now regularly used in Europe.

Transcranial magnetic stimulation was recently approved by the FDA as a treatment for depression. At this point, it's available to tinnitus sufferers only through clinical trials. To learn more, consult the National Institutes of Health Web site, *www.clinicaltrials.gov*.

14

Looking Your Best

The Most Important Skin Products

Often women compliment dermatologist Karen Burke, MD, PhD, on her smooth, spotless, glowing skin—and assume that she's had "work done" on her face. But that's not the case. "Instead of resorting to lasers, Botox or surgery, it's often possible to achieve wonderful results with just the following four products," Dr. Burke explained.

● **Mild, moisturizing cleanser.** The goal is to remove oil, dirt and bacteria—without leaving skin overly dry.

New technology: Dove Sensitive Skin Nourishing Body Wash with Nutrium Moisture contains a blend of soybean oil, fatty acids and glycerin to penetrate deep into skin (about $9 for 24 ounces). Use it all over.

To minimize facial sagging: Wash twice a day, gently moving fingertips back and forth across vertical lines by your mouth…and up and out over horizontal forehead, cheek and eye wrinkles.

● **Sunscreen.** To guard against wrinkles, spots and skin cancer, use a sunscreen every day with an SPF of at least 30 (better yet, 40 or more) that protects against both UVA and UVB rays.

Transparent: Sunscreens with the new micronized zinc oxide provide excellent UVA/UVB protection with no telltale white film.

Long-lasting: Anthelios face and body sunscreens contain mexoryl, which degrades much more slowly than other UVA filters do (*www.anthelios.com*).

● **Antioxidant serum.** This helps reverse sun damage by stimulating production of collagen

Karen Burke, MD, PhD, assistant clinical professor of dermatology at Mount Sinai Medical Center, and a dermatologist and research scientist in private practice, both in New York City. She is author of *Great Skin for Life* (Hamlyn).

(the protein that gives skin its structure) and neutralizing harmful free radicals.

Transforming: Apply six to eight drops of SkinCeuticals C E Ferulic to your face daily (about $142 for one ounce, *www.skinceuticals. com*).

- **Topical *retinoic acid* (tretinoin).** Ask your dermatologist to prescribe this vitamin-A derivative to rejuvenate skin and help prevent skin cancer.

Thrifty: Generic tretinoin 0.01% gel costs less than brand-name (about $90 for 1.6 ounces, approximately a four-month supply). Apply at bedtime to the face and back of your hands. To minimize flaking, use it every other day to start, working up to daily use.

Note: Nonprescription products are far less effective because they break down quickly.

Red Skin...Blushing... Irritated Eyes...

Mark V. Dahl, MD, professor of dermatology at the Mayo College School of Medicine at the Mayo Clinic in Scottsdale, Arizona, and past president of the American Academy of Dermatology. He has published approximately 300 professional articles on skin disorders and serves on the medical advisory board of the National Rosacea Society, www.rosacea.org.

Rosacea is commonly associated with former President Bill Clinton's red face and W.C. Fields's bumpy nose. Both men are known rosacea sufferers.

What most people don't realize: Rosacea has a complex set of other symptoms that often are mistaken for such conditions as eczema and skin allergies.

An estimated 14 million Americans, including perhaps as many as one in 10 women, are affected by this incurable—but treatable—skin disorder.

ARE YOU AT RISK?

People who are at greatest risk for rosacea have fair skin...a family history of the disorder...and/or are of Irish, Scottish or English ancestry. Women are more likely than men to develop rosacea, but a specific form of rosacea, rhinophyma, which affects the skin on and around the nose, is much more common in men.

No one knows what causes rosacea. Some scientists believe that the disorder results from an overactive immune system. Others theorize that it's a vascular problem due to a defect in the way the rosacea patient's body transfers blood between the face and the brain. Another theory suggests that the condition may be due to noninfectious, ordinary bacteria living on the skin surface that may become inflamed.

SORTING OUT THE SYMPTOMS

Even though facial redness is rosacea's best-known symptom, the disorder actually is a syndrome with many different symptoms that can be broken into four subtypes. *You can have one of the following subtypes—or a combination of all of them—at varying times...*

- **Flushing or blushing** (not every person who blushes has rosacea, but it can be a symptom) and blood vessels becoming apparent just beneath the surface of the skin.

- **Acnelike bumps (pustules)** and inflammation, which typically appear in the center of the face rather than at the edges.

- **Thickened skin,** usually on the nose, which in severe cases can become swollen and bumpy and develop into rhinophyma. Skin thickening also can occur on the forehead, chin or cheeks.

- **Irritated, burning eyes.** With ocular rosacea, loss of vision may occur in severe cases and sties or cysts called chalazions may form on the eyelid...dilated blood vessels may appear in the whites of the eyes...and the corneas can become thinned or eroded.

A TRICKY DIAGNOSIS

Diagnosing rosacea can be difficult because the symptoms can easily be confused with those of other conditions. For example, older adults who have blood vessels that are visible near the surface of facial skin are often misdiagnosed with rosacea when, in fact, they merely have sun damage.

One distinguishing characteristic: With rosacea, the blood vessel damage is more centered in the middle of the face, while sun damage may occur on other areas of the face.

BEST TREATMENT OPTIONS

All types of rosacea can be treated—and some recent therapies are highly effective. *For example…*

• **Rosacea marked by pustules is the most easily treated type.** Topical antibiotic gels and creams, such as *metronidazole* (MetroGel) and *sodium sulfacetamide* (Sulfacet-R), are used.

Recent development: A relatively new prescription oral tetracycline drug, Oracea, is a sustained-release, low-dose antibiotic that has an anti-inflammatory effect. This medication reduces risk for common side effects, such as vaginal yeast infections, which may occur when using other oral antibiotics.

• **Red-skin type of rosacea.** Topical medications, such as metronidazole, are used, as well as pulsed light therapy—a series of brief (10 to 20 milliseconds), intense flashes of light—to remove unsightly blood vessels near the skin's surface.

• **Rosacea that causes skin thickness.** Lasers can be used to remove tissue buildup or smoothe the skin around the nose.

• **Ocular rosacea.** Oral doxycycline antibiotics are prescribed. To further protect your vision, you should have an ophthalmologist monitor your condition.

DON'T FORGET SELF-CARE

There are several additional steps that rosacea sufferers can take to help manage their symptoms.

For example…

• **Identify and avoid triggers.** Common triggers include sun, heat or wind exposure… strenuous exercise…alcohol…hot beverages… and spicy foods. Sufferers need to be aware of their own triggers, which are multiple and varied—physicians rely on these observations to prescribe appropriate treatment.

Anger and embarrassment also can trigger rosacea symptoms—blood vessels dilate as directed by blood-vessel–flow control centers in the brain.

Also: Discuss with your physician all the medications that you are taking. Several could trigger symptoms, especially niacin (vitamin B-3), as well as vasodilators, such as *sildenifil* (Viagra) and *hydralazine* (Hydra-Zide)… nitrates, such as amyl nitrite and isosorbide mononitrate (the anti-estrogen drug tamoxifen…and the antibiotic *rifampin* (Rifamate).

• **Keep your self-confidence in mind.** According to a recent survey, 76% of rosacea sufferers reported having lower self-confidence and self-esteem as a result of their condition…69% said they felt embarrassment…and 63% said it affected their ability to form new relationships. The numbers were even higher for those who said their symptoms were very severe.

If you believe that rosacea is affecting your self-confidence and/or relationships with others, consider seeking help from anonline support group, such as the National Rosacea Society (*www.rosacea.org*).

To find a dermatologist in your area who treats rosacea, contact the American Academy of Dermatology (888-462-3376, *www.aad.org*).

Four Steps to Beautiful Skin

Neal B. Schultz, MD, assistant clinical professor at Mount Sinai School of Medicine, assistant adjunct physician at Lenox Hill Hospital and owner of Park Avenue Skin Care, all in New York City. He is coauthor, with Laura Morton, of It's Not Just About Wrinkles (Stewart, Tabori & Chang).

Getting enough sleep, eating a healthy diet and finding time to relax all contribute to younger-looking skin.

In addition, everyone can have smoother, more lustrous skin with this simple, twice-a-day program, done in the morning and evening. The first three steps are the same for both times of day…the fourth is different in the morning and evening.

Step 1: Cleanse the skin to remove oils and debris. Doing this also allows the active ingredients in other products to penetrate the skin. Never scrub with a washcloth. Use your fingertips to massage a small amount of cleanser onto the face for 10 to 15 seconds, then rinse with warm water.

Step 2: Apply a toner to a soft, thin cotton makeup pad, and gently wipe. Toner removes leftover debris, along with any cleanser that wasn't removed by rinsing.

Step 3: Use the right active ingredient for your skin-care issues—glycolic acid for brown spots, sulfur for reds, etc.

Step 4 (morning): Apply sunscreen after completing the first three steps but before applying makeup. A sunscreen with an SPF of about 30 is right for most people.

Step 4 (evening): Apply a moisturizer that is right for your skin. An oil-based moisturizer is good for extremely dry skin…a water-and-oil moisturizer is good for "normal" skin…and an oil-free, water-based moisturizer is best for oily skin.

Skin Care from The Inside Out

Joy Bauer, MS, RD, CDN, nutritionist/dietitian in private practice in New York City. She is the nutrition expert for the *Today* show and nutritionist for the New York City Ballet, the American Ballet Theatre and several Olympic athletes. She is author of several books, including *Joy Bauer's Food Cures: Treat Common Health Concerns, Look Younger & Live Longer* (Rodale). *www.joybauer.com*

To take care of their skin, most people reach for sunscreen, lotions and creams to protect, smooth and moisturize. These products can help, but beautiful, healthy skin starts with what goes into your body, not what you rub on it. Research shows that good nutrition may reduce the effects of sun damage…minimize redness and wrinkling…and even protect against some skin cancers.

FIRST STEP: HYDRATE

The single most important nutritional factor for keeping skin healthy is water. Staying hydrated keeps cells plump, making skin look firmer and clearer. When cells are dehydrated, they shrivel and can make your skin look wrinkled. Think of it this way—when you dehydrate a juicy grape, you get a raisin. In addition, water transports nutrients into skin cells and helps flush toxins out of the body.

To stay hydrated, drink whenever you feel thirsty.

Helpful sign: If your urine is pale yellow, you are adequately hydrated—but if it is bright or dark yellow, you may need to boost your fluid intake.

Good news: Drinking unsweetened tea helps keep you hydrated, plus you get the benefit of antioxidant nutrients called polyphenols, which may help prevent sun-related skin cancers. Green, white, black and oolong teas provide more polyphenols than herbal teas. It is your choice whether to drink caffeinated or decaffeinated tea. Although caffeine is a mild diuretic (increasing the amount of urine that is passed from the body), the relatively small amount in tea doesn't affect its ability to keep skin hydrated and healthy.

Avoid: Teas sweetened with a lot of sugar—excess sugar can make skin dull and wrinkled.

For extra hydration: Eat "juicy foods" that are at least 75% water by weight—fruits such as apples, berries, cherries, grapes, grapefruit, mangoes, melons, oranges, peaches, plums… and vegetables such as asparagus, beets, carrots, celery, cucumbers and tomatoes.

SKIN-HEALTHY FOODS

Everything we eat is reflected in the health of our skin—for better or for worse. *Among the best nutrients for the skin…*

• **Beta-carotene,** a powerful antioxidant which, once ingested, is converted to vitamin A, a nutrient necessary for skin tissue growth and repair.

Skin-smart: Have at least one serving per day of beta-carotene–rich foods—for instance, orange carrots, sweet potatoes and tomatoes…

green arugula, asparagus and spinach…and fruits such as cherries, grapefruit, mangoes and watermelon.

•**Omega-3 fatty acids,** healthful fats that are important building blocks of the membranes that make up cell walls, allowing water and nutrients to enter and keeping out waste and toxins.

Skin-smart: Eat at least three servings of omega-3–rich foods each week—such as wild salmon (farm-raised salmon may have higher levels of potentially dangerous contaminants) …mackerel (not king mackerel, which has too much mercury)…anchovies, herring and sardines. Good fats also are found in smaller amounts in flaxseed, soybeans and walnuts. If you don't eat enough of these omega-3 foods, consider taking daily supplements of fish oil providing 1,000 mg of combined *eicosapentaenoic acid* (EPA) and *docosahexaenoic acid* (DHA), the most biologically active and beneficial components. Look for brands that have been tested for purity, such as VitalOils 1000 (877-342-3721, *www.myvitalremedymd.com*) and Ultimate Omega by Nordic Naturals (800-662-2544, *www.nordicnaturals.com*).

•**Selenium,** a mineral with antioxidant activity thought to help skin elasticity (which means you'll look younger longer) and prevent sun-related skin damage and cancers.

Skin-smart: Eat at least one serving a day of a selenium-rich food—canned light tuna (which has less mercury than canned albacore or white tuna), crab, tilapia…whole-wheat breads and pasta…lean beef…chicken and turkey (breast meat is lowest in fat).

Caution: Taking selenium in supplement form may increase the risk for squamous cell skin cancer in people with a personal or family history of the disease. Selenium in food is safe and healthful.

•**Vitamin C,** an antioxidant that helps build collagen and elastin (proteins that comprise the skin's underlying structure)…and also protects against free radicals (molecules in the body that damage cells) when the skin is exposed to sunlight.

Skin-smart: Eat at least one serving a day of any of these vitamin C-rich foods—cantaloupe, citrus fruits, kiwifruit, papaya, pineapple, strawberries, watermelon…and bell peppers, broccoli, brussels sprouts, cabbage, cauliflower, kale and kidney beans.

•**Zinc,** a mineral that helps maintain collagen. People with zinc deficiencies often develop skin redness and lesions.

Skin-smart: Eat at least one serving of a zinc-rich food daily—chicken or turkey breast, crab, lean beef, pork tenderloin (lower in fat than other cuts)…peanuts and peanut butter…fat-free dairy products (cheese, milk and yogurt).

Wise for everyone: A daily multivitamin that contains 100% of the daily value for vitamins A, C, E and zinc and no more than 70 mcg of selenium.

WHAT TO AVOID

•**Sugar.** Research suggests that sugary foods (such as soda and cookies) may contribute to skin blemishes. These "bad carbs" may promote harmful inflammation throughout the body, which can trigger breakouts. Limit your indulgence in sweet treats to no more than one small serving per day.

•**White flour.** Minimize white-flour foods (such as white bread and pasta) in your diet by choosing whole-grain breads and rolls, cereals, crackers and pasta.

•**Dairy foods.** Milk may contain hormones (especially if cows are pregnant) and iodine from iodine-fortified feed. Although uncommon, both of these components can cause pimples. If you are prone to acne, try going off dairy for a while to see if your skin improves.

•**Cigarette smoke, including secondhand smoke.** It fills your body with toxins, inflammation causing irritants and free radicals that damage every cell they touch…and also limits blood flow, so skin cells don't receive the oxygen and nutrients they need.

What Your Skin Is Trying to Tell You

Andrew Bronin, MD, associate clinical professor of dermatology at Yale School of Medicine in New Haven, Connecticut. A dermatologist in private practice in Rye Brook, New York, he also is editor-in-chief of *Derm-Clips*, an American Academy of Dermatology (AAD) continuing medical education publication, and a recipient of AAD's Presidential Citation award, given to major contributors in the field of dermatology.

A rash here and an itch there may seem minor—and usually they are. Yet sometimes symptoms that appear to be "only skin deep" actually are warning signs of serious health problems.

This is one reason why it is important to get regular skin checkups, typically yearly. Of course your dermatologist looks for skin cancer, including the potentially deadly malignant melanoma...but during a full body exam, the doctor may spot subtle signs indicating a problem inside the body.

Below are symptoms that your dermatologist should look for during a checkup—and that you should report promptly if you notice them first. Your dermatologist may treat the problem if he/she feels that it is primarily a skin disorder...or, if an underlying condition is suspected, you may be sent to a specialist or back to your primary care doctor for a full diagnosis and treatment.

Referrals to a dermatologist: The American Academy of Dermatology, 866-503-7546, *www.aad.org.*

RED NOSE AND CHEEKS

Skin problem: Often the cause is rosacea, a chronic inflammatory skin disorder sometimes characterized just by facial redness... and sometimes by small red bumps on the face. Though it cannot be cured, rosacea is not dangerous. Usually it can be controlled with topical and/or oral antibiotics.

Below-the-skin problem: Systemic lupus erythematosus sometimes causes a butterfly-shaped red rash that goes across the bridge of the nose and onto the cheeks. Lupus is a chronic autoimmune disorder that affects nine times as many women as men. The rash does not respond to acne drugs and may be exacerbated by certain antibiotics, such as sulfa drugs or tetracycline. Untreated, lupus can damage the joints, kidneys, heart, lungs, digestive tract and nervous system.

Action: If lupus is suspected, a rheumatologist orders diagnostic blood and urine tests. There is no cure, but prompt treatment with medication (such as steroids) and lifestyle changes (including avoiding alcohol and excessive sunlight) minimizes symptoms and reduces risk for complications.

BREAST RASH

Skin problem: A patch of itchy, bumpy redness on the breast could be atopic dermatitis (also called eczema), an inflammatory skin condition common in allergic individuals. Atopic dermatitis frequently affects other areas, too—especially the crooks of the elbows and the backs of the knees. Symptoms often can be controlled with topical medication, such as steroid cream.

Below-the-skin problems: If a scaly rash appears on or around the nipple, it may be Paget's disease of the breast, a rash that can signify underlying breast cancer or intraductal carcinoma (abnormal cells in the breast duct that may become invasive cancer). If the breast is swollen and warm and its skin is discolored or pitted (like an orange peel), this may signal inflammatory breast cancer, most often diagnosed in women in their 50s. A breast rash caused by cancer may not respond to topical creams, though sometimes symptoms spontaneously abate briefly.

Action: A biopsy is needed to confirm the diagnosis. An oncologist provides guidance on treatment options, including surgery, radiation and/or chemotherapy.

UNDER-EYE CIRCLES

Skin problems: Dark circles worsen with age as skin thins and loses elasticity, making veins more visible. Excess sun darkens the area further by increasing production of the skin pigment melanin.

Recommended: Daily use of sunscreen helps prevent sun-related changes.

Below-the-skin problem: Darkening of the skin around the eyes could be "atopic shiners," which sometimes occur in people who have allergies. One theory suggests that atopic shiners result from chronic rubbing of itchy skin in the eye area. Additional allergy-related skin symptoms include rough, dry skin...cracked skin on the hands and feet...and tiny, hard red or white bumps called keratosis pilaris on the upper arms, thighs, buttocks and face.

Action: An allergist can perform skin tests to determine what you are allergic to and then recommend avoidance strategies, medication and/or immunotherapy injections to minimize allergic symptoms, such as asthma or hay fever.

But: Often the skin signs of allergy, such as atopic shiners, persist even when other symptoms respond to treatment.

ITCHING

Skin problem: Common causes include dry skin, sunburn, allergic reactions, insect bites, scabies infestation, poison ivy, bacterial or fungal infections, psoriasis or stress. Treatment depends on the specific condition. For quick temporary relief, it helps to run cool water or place a cold compress on the area...soak in an oatmeal bath...use an over-the-counter cream with camphor, menthol, calamine, benzocaine, hydrocortisone or triamcinolone... and/or take an oral antihistamine.

Below-the-skin problems: Persistent itchiness could signal any of the following...

• **Hodgkin's lymphoma.** Intractable itchiness that does not respond to treatment can be an early sign of this cancer, which starts in the cells of the immune system. Other symptoms include swollen lymph nodes, cough, fever, night sweats, fatigue and/or unintended weight loss.

Action: An oncologist confirms the diagnosis with blood tests, imaging tests and lymph node biopsy. Treatment generally includes chemotherapy and radiation.

• **Liver disease.** A number of liver problems—including a viral disease, such as hepatitis, or the metastasis (spread) of cancer to the liver—can produce intense itching.

Action: A gastroenterologist does tests, such as blood work, imaging studies and/or biopsy, to determine the exact nature of the problem. Treatment depends on the specific diagnosis.

• **Thyroid disorder.** Thyroid hormones regulate metabolism. Both hyperthyroidism (overactive thyroid gland) and hypothyroidism (underactive thyroid) can produce generalized itching. Other symptoms of hyperthyroidism include a rash and swelling on the shins, sudden weight loss despite an increased appetite, rapid or irregular heartbeat, hand tremors, fatigue and/or increased sensitivity to heat. Untreated hyperthyroidism can cause severe heart problems and osteoporosis. Hypothyroidism often is accompanied by dry skin, weight gain, muscle aches and fatigue. Untreated hypothyroidism may lead to infertility and heart disease.

Action: An endocrinologist orders blood tests to measure hormone levels. With medication to regulate thyroid hormones and sometimes with surgery, symptoms generally subside and complications are prevented.

Antioxidant Creams That Smooth Aging Skin

Mark A. Stengler, NMD, licensed naturopathic medical doctor and leading authority on the practice of alternative and integrated medicine. He is founder and medical director of the Stengler Center for Integrative Medicine, Encinitas, California, and associate clinical professor at the National College of Natural Medicine, Portland, Oregon. He is author of *The Natural Physician's Healing Therapies* (Bottom Line Books).

Anti-aging creams are big business in both the cosmetic and natural-health industries. Everyone wants healthy, youthful-looking skin.

ANTIOXIDANTS FOR DAMAGE CONTROL

When it comes to anti-aging products, some of the most popular natural creams contain antioxidants, nutrients that neutralize harmful molecules called free radicals. We associate antioxidants with foods, particularly fruits and vegetables, that can reduce oxidative stress (an increase in cell-damaging free radicals caused by stress, eating fried and processed foods, and breathing pollutants) and subsequent inflammation.

The same idea applies when these nutrients are in topical form—what is good inside the body also is good outside. Our skin incurs oxidative damage from excessive sun exposure and through glycation, a process in which dietary sugar alters the molecular structure of collagen and other skin components. Eventually, in the course of normal aging, these factors overwhelm the skin's natural antioxidant capability.

Contrary to moisturizers that provide on-the-surface fixes (such as mineral oil, which slows evaporation of water from the skin), antioxidant creams work at the cellular level, making lasting changes to the skin and reducing wrinkles and blemishes. As with many products on the market, the potency of antioxidant creams varies.

Give the product a chance to work. Don't expect any changes in a week. Instead, use it for six to 10 weeks. Then check to see whether there is a noticeable improvement in the quality of your skin. Look to see if blemishes have diminished and if your skin is softer, clearer or more radiant. If there is no improvement, try a different anti-aging cream formulation.

Bonus: These natural skin ingredients are all considered very safe. If any product causes skin irritation or redness, stop using it and try another.

TO ENHANCE MOISTURE CONTENT

•**Vitamin C.** This well-known antioxidant was one of the first to be used in anti-aging creams. A Brazilian study showed that vitamin C (ascorbic acid) and several of its derivatives enhanced skin moisture content when it was applied daily for four weeks. A review of studies conducted by a US researcher concluded that vitamin C is effective for treating photoaging (sun damage) and that combining it with other vitamins (A, B-3 and E) is more effective than using individual compounds.

Good brands: Avalon Organics Vitamin C Renewal Facial Cream (888-659-7730, *www. avalonorganics.com*, $20.95 for two ounces)…

or MyChelle Dermaceuticals, The Perfect C Serum, All Skin Types (800-447-2076, *www.my chelle.com*, $41.79 for 0.5 ounce). These products may seem expensive, but they last for a long time because you apply just a pea-size dab at a time.

Best for: Dry, sun-damaged skin.

TO RESTORE ELASTICITY

•**Green tea.** When ingested, green tea protects us against illness, including cardiovascular disease, diabetes and even some cancers. So it isn't surprising to find out that it also can help the skin.

A study conducted at Emory University found that an eight-week regimen of a topical cream containing 10% green-tea extract and a 300-mg twice-daily green-tea oral supplement resulted in tissue improvements that could be seen under a microscope, although the improvements were not visible to the naked eye. Researchers noted that it may take longer than eight weeks to see visible improvements.

Good brands: Green Tea Skin Natural Anti-Aging Cream (781-326-1700, *www. greenteaskin.com*, $19.95 for 1.7 ounces)…or OriginBioMed Green Tea Skin Cream (888-234-7256, *www.originbiomed.com*, $34.95 for 0.7 ounce).

Plus: Take 600 mg daily of an oral green-tea supplement.

Best for: Wrinkles, age-related loss of skin elasticity.

TO SMOOTH WRINKLES AND IMPROVE SKIN HEALTH

•**Coenzyme Q10 (CoQ10).** This natural substance exists in every cell of the body and is a popular ingredient in anti-aging creams. Several studies indicate that it may be able to enhance the skin's ability to combat signs of aging at the cellular level—for example, making skin cells look younger. At an American Academy of Dermatology meeting, researchers reported that CoQ10 cream seemed to reduce fine wrinkles around the eyes without harmful side effects, such as itching.

Good brands: Avalon Organics CoQ10 Wrinkle Defense Night Creme (888-659-7730, *www. avalonorganics.com*, $24.95 for 1.75 ounces)…

or Botanic Spa CoQ-10 Wrinkle Cream (800-644-8327, *www.botanicchoice.com*, $14.99 for two ounces).

Bleach Baths Ease Eczema

Twice weekly, eczema patients soaked for five to 10 minutes in a tub of water mixed with very diluted bleach. After three months, 67% showed improvement, compared with 15% of patients who bathed in plain water.

Theory: Bleach kills the staph bacteria that often accompany eczema and cause painful lesions.

Safety: Use no more than one-half cup of bleach per 40 gallons of water...do not let bleach bathwater enter the eyes or mouth... never apply undiluted bleach to skin.

Amy Paller, MD, chair, dermatology department, Northwestern University Feinberg School of Medicine, Chicago, and leader of a study of 31 eczema patients.

Retinol Helps Your Skin

Retinol reduces wrinkles in aging skin and in skin damaged by the sun.

Recent finding: People 80 years old and older who applied a retinol-containing lotion to their upper inner arm up to three times a week had significantly fewer wrinkles and less roughness and aged appearance after 24 weeks than people using similar lotions not containing retinol.

Reason: Retinol (vitamin A) increases collagen production and boosts water-retaining molecules. Available over-the-counter and by prescription. Prices vary widely.

Sewon Kang, MD, professor and chair, department of dermatology, Johns Hopkins Medicine, Baltimore, Maryland, and leader of a study published in *Archives of Dermatology*.

3 Wrinkle Removers That Work

Gary J. Fisher, PhD, the Harry Helfman Professor of Molecular Dermatology in the department of dermatology at the University of Michigan Health System in Ann Arbor. He is associate editor of *Journal for Investigative Dermatology* and lead author of the review *"Looking Older: Fibroblast Collapse and Therapeutic Implication"* that appeared in *Archives of Dermatology*.

The vast majority of antiwrinkle products and procedures don't work. But some do. A review published in *Archives of Dermatology* identified three approaches—prescription-strength topical retinoids...injections of hyaluronic acid...and carbon dioxide laser resurfacing—that have been proven to reduce facial wrinkles. All three treatments are available from a dermatologist. Ask him/her which is best for you.

HOW SKIN AGES

Collagen is a connective tissue that makes young, healthy skin firm and elastic. It provides the structural support for blood vessels and maintains the skin's shape. In youthful skin, the collagen surrounding skin cells is firm and abundant.

As people age, collagen-producing cells known as fibroblasts become less active. The body produces less collagen, and the skin loses some of its tautness and elasticity. At the same time, collagen fibers that already are present in the skin gradually break down. Both processes are a natural consequence of aging, although they're accelerated by lifestyle factors, such as smoking or excessive sun exposure.

Once collagen starts to break down, or fragment, fewer fibroblasts are able to attach to the remaining collagen fibers. Without these attachments, fibroblasts don't receive the mechanical "stretch" signals that trigger collagen production and reduce the body's output of collagen-degrading enzymes. This is why older adults tend to develop more (and deeper) wrinkles. They have a higher amount of collagen fragmentation...fewer stretch signals between fibroblasts and collagen fibers...a lower rate of collagen replacement...and a greater rate of collagen destruction.

Effective wrinkle treatments influence each stage of this process. They promote new collagen formation, promote the attachment of fibroblasts to collagen fibers and allow the mechanical stretching that both increases collagen and reduces collagen breakdown.

TOPICAL RETINOL

Retinoid-based creams and ointments are derived from vitamin A. Used in prescription-strength doses, products such as *tretinoin* (Renova) and *tazarotene* (Avage) reduce skin roughness as well as wrinkles. A double-blind, placebo-controlled study published in *Archives of Dermatology* looked at two groups of elderly patients. Those in one group were treated with a cream containing 0.4% vitamin A (retinol). Those in a second group were given a placebo cream. Study personnel applied the creams to people in both groups three times a week for 24 weeks.

Results: People treated with retinol had an increase in glycosaminoglycans, molecular chains that absorb water and increase collagen—and an approximately 23% reduction in fine wrinkles.

It's unlikely that most over-the-counter retinoid products contain enough retinoids to have noticeable effects. There's no way to be sure, because few of these products list retinoid concentrations on the label.

The prescription creams are applied once or twice a day. People may see results in as little as eight weeks. Because retinol increases collagen, it probably increases the stretch between fibroblasts and collagen fibers. This potentially could give long-lasting results even when the products are discontinued—but this hasn't been proven.

Side effects: People who use the stronger preparations sometimes develop a minor rash (retinoid dermatitis). The rash clears up once the treatment is discontinued. You're less likely to experience skin irritation if you start with a low-dose product and gradually increase the concentration.

Important: Treatment with a topical retinoid increases the skin's sensitivity to sunlight. People who use it should always apply sunscreen before going outdoors, even when the weather is cool.

Cost: About $150 for 40 grams (g) of 0.02% concentration, which lasts four months or even longer.

HYALURONIC ACID INJECTIONS

Dermatologists once thought that injections of hyaluronic acid derivatives, which are substances with collagen-like properties, mainly worked by plumping the skin and "filling out" wrinkles. Hyaluronic acid does make the skin plumper, but now we know that it also promotes the tissue stretching that increases collagen production and inhibits its breakdown.

Patients usually are given a local anesthetic, and the dermatologist injects a hyaluronic acid derivative (such as a product called Restylane) into the wrinkle. Most people will notice a reduction in wrinkles almost immediately. In studies, an increase in skin collagen occurs after about one month.

Patients can repeat the treatments as often as desired. The improvement from a single injection usually lasts between nine and 12 months.

Side effects: Temporary swelling, redness and bruising in the treated area.

Cost: $550 to $650 per syringe. The average patient requires one to two syringes per treatment.

CARBON DIOXIDE LASER RESURFACING

The patient is given a local anesthetic. Then a laser is used to generate heat that removes the upper skin layer, called the epidermis. New collagen is produced by the body as the skin heals.

It takes two to three weeks for the skin to heal, and skin redness may last for six to 12 weeks. Patients need to keep the raw areas clean. They also should apply wound-care ointments, such as Catrix 10 or Aquaphor, to keep the skin moist and prevent scarring.

The results typically last for several years. Most people get only a single treatment.

Other types of skin resurfacing, such as the use of alpha or beta-hydroxy acids, or the use of less intense lasers, allow patients to heal more quickly after the procedures. However, these approaches haven't been proven to be as effective as carbon dioxide laser resurfacing.

Side effects: Temporary discomfort, swelling and redness. Uncommon complications include infection, changes in skin color and scarring. Patients with darker skin tones have a greater risk of healing with darker pigmentation.

Cost: $1,800 to $4,000.

Secrets to Younger-Looking Skin

Neal B. Schultz, MD, assistant clinical professor at Mount Sinai School of Medicine, assistant adjunct physician at Lenox Hill Hospital and owner of Park Avenue Skin Care, all in New York City. He is coauthor, with Laura Morton, of *It's Not Just About Wrinkles* (Stewart, Tabori & Chang).

When people complain about looking older, they usually talk about lines and wrinkles. However, most people who are dissatisfied with their appearance have color or texture problems as well that make them look older than they should.

Well-known treatments, such as Botox and collagen, are very effective for lines and wrinkles, but they don't affect color and texture issues. About three-quarters of patients will notice a dramatic improvement when they treat these two important factors, too.

COLOR

Color problems are among the easiest skin defects to correct. They basically fall into two categories—browns (such as age spots and freckles) and reds (usually due to engorged or broken capillaries).

•**Browns.** Brown spots go by many different names—sunspots, liver spots, age spots, etc. They're almost always caused by sun exposure, which triggers excessive activity in some of the skin's pigment-producing cells. Most brown spots appear on exposed areas of the skin, such as the face, arms and back of the hands.

On the other hand, blotchy brown areas that don't have a clear border are usually caused by an imbalance of female hormones, such as during pregnancy or in women taking birth control pills.

Virtually all brown defects can be removed with laser treatments, which cost $400 to $1,200 per treatment. A less expensive but more time-consuming approach is to lighten the brown areas with exfoliation.

Best home treatment: A product with 8% glycolic acid used daily. Glycolic acid is one of the alpha hydroxy acids (AHAs). It dissolves keratin, the uppermost layer of dead skin. Over-the-counter products, such as Aqua Glycolic Face Cream, Glytone Day Cream for Dry Skin and Kinerase Cream, lighten brown spots and stop the formation of new pigment cells.

Glycolic acid begins to work within two weeks—and will significantly reduce brownness in four to six weeks.

Important: Continue to apply a sunscreen whenever you are going outdoors. Repeated sun exposure will cause the brownness to return.

Also helpful: Twice-daily applications of over-the-counter topical vitamin C, such as Stallex C Complex Rescue Serum or Skin-Medica Vitamin C Complex. Topical vitamin C lightens brown spots and blocks cell-damaging free radicals. It can be used in addition to glycolic acid.

Skin cancer warning: If there is a change in a brown spot's or a mole's size, shape or color (other than lightening from treatment) or if it bleeds, itches or becomes painful, contact your dermatologist immediately.

•**Reds.** Most people have one or more red spots or lines on their faces. They're often present on the cheeks or alongside the nose and usually are due to dilated or broken capillaries.

Common types: Telangiectasias, which appear as tiny straight or curved red lines…spider hemangiomas, which are raised red bumps with red lines emanating from the center…or cherry hemangiomas, flat or dome-shaped spots. Another type of redness is caused by rosacea—an acnelike condition that's characterized by red blotches (telangiectasias) that appear intermittently on the cheeks and nose.

Best home treatment: An over-the-counter topical sulfur preparation—such as Rezamid Acne Treatment Lotion or Sulforcin Acne Treatment Lotion. Sulfur shrinks blood vessels and helps reduce redness. This can work for rosacea, too, but test an area the size of a dime first to see how your skin reacts.

Because it's difficult to eliminate skin redness entirely, I usually advise patients to conceal it by using color-correcting makeup—a green-tinted foundation works best. Neutrogena makes a good one.

Diet: Certain foods have dilating effects on blood vessels, causing them to temporarily increase in diameter. The most common perpetrators are alcohol and spicy foods. Also, certain medications and vitamins (the most common of which is any form of niacin, one of the B vitamins) are known to cause dilation of facial blood vessels and thus to increase their conspicuousness.

TEXTURE

Young skin is smooth, with a noticeable "slip factor" when you run a finger across the face. Older "dull" skin feels rough, or there are "bumps" when the finger passes over enlarged pores.

Both of the main texture problems—enlarged pores and dull, flaky skin—are caused by the retention of dead skin cells. Skin cells are supposed to shed every 28 days—but not all cells do this. This results in an uneven accumulation of dead cells.

Best home treatment: Exfoliation with glycolic acid. People should start with a product that has 8% glycolic acid. The concentration can be increased to 10% or 15% if needed.

Bonus: Exfoliating can remove early precancerous cells along with the dead skin cells.

In-office exfoliation treatments: There are two types of in-office exfoliation—chemical, with a prescription glycolic acid treatment… and mechanical with microdermabrasion. The latter involves the use of a machine by a properly trained doctor, nurse or esthetician that bombards the skin with sterilized aluminum-oxide crystals. It immediately strips away dead cells and leaves the skin looking uniform and fresh.

In-office treatments cost $100 to $200 per treatment. You will need six to 10 treatments done at one- to two-week intervals.

• **Marionette lines run from the nose down to the corner of the mouth.** They're caused mainly by the age-related loss of fat and skin elasticity. Botox can't be used for these lines because it can paralyze the entire cheek muscle and prevent smiling. A better approach is to inject collagen or another filler, such as Restylane. These products add volume to the skin and fill out the hollow contours.

• **Crow's feet,** the lines that radiate from the corners of the eyes, often can be improved or eliminated with Botox. In about 20% of cases, patients require a combination of Botox plus collagen.

• **Smoker's lines on the lips** (also called "lipstick lines" because lipstick can "bleed" into the tiny crevices) will disappear when injected with a very fine form of collagen. Most patients also are given injections of Botox to reduce muscle contractions that cause the lines.

Vitamin C Fights Wrinkles

Mark A. Stengler, NMD, licensed naturopathic medical doctor and leading authority on the practice of alternative and integrated medicine. He is founder and medical director of the Stengler Center for Integrative Medicine, Encinitas, California. He is author of *The Natural Physician's Healing Therapies* (Bottom Line Books).

British researchers examined the link between nutrient intake and signs of skin aging, such as wrinkling, dryness and thinning (thin skin cuts and bruises easily). Among 4,025 women ages 40 to 74, those with diets high in vitamin C were 11% less likely to have prevalent wrinkles and 7% less likely to have dry skin, compared with those whose diets were low in vitamin C. Higher intake of linoleic acid (a polyunsaturated fatty acid in many vegetable oils) was associated with 25% less dryness and 22% less skin thinning.

My view: Premature aging of skin and other tissues is largely due to poor diet. Foods rich in vitamin C protect skin cells' DNA and promote production of collagen (a fibrous protein that holds skin together). Fatty acids, such as linoleic acid, are important components of skin—so deficiencies contribute to dryness and thinning. Also, the body converts linoleic acid into gamma linolenic acid (GLA), an anti-inflammatory essential fatty acid.

Advised: Supplement daily with 500 mg of vitamin C as part of a bioflavonoid complex...1,000 mg of GLA-rich evening primrose oil...and 1,000 mg of fish oil to balance fatty acids.

Help Hide Scars, Spider Veins, More

Cathy Highland, celebrity makeup artist with Aim Artists Agency in Los Angeles and one of the women profiled in the best seller *The Girls from Ames* (Gotham). *www.aimartist.com*

Everyday makeup can turn pale cheeks rosy or disguise occasional under-eye circles.

But: To camouflage birthmarks, spider veins, vitiligo (unpigmented patches), age spots, tattoos, scars and pimples, you'll have more success with these techniques used by celebrity makeup artists...

• **Use specially formulated cosmetics.** Unlike regular facial foundation, body cosmetics are designed to cover larger areas without rubbing off onto clothing. Facial products for deeply pigmented spots, such as port-wine stains, are concentrated to minimize the amount of product needed. Use concealer when you want maximum coverage...use foundation for medium coverage...use tinted moisturizer for lighter coverage.

Good brands (sold at department or cosmetics stores and/or online): ColorTration (888-350-4505, *www.colortration.com*)...

Dermablend (800-662-8011, *www.dermablend. com*)...DuWop (866-613-8967, *www.duwop. com*).

• **Choose the right color.** With concealer, use a shade one or two shades lighter than your natural skin tone. To counteract redness, such as from the skin disorder rosacea, opt for yellow-to-green undertones.

• **Apply thin layers.** Thick, caked-on makeup only draws attention to the problem area.

Better: With a makeup brush (not fingers, as their heat can cause smearing), apply several very thin layers of foundation or tinted moisturizer, allowing each to dry before applying the next. To finish, apply a dusting of powder using a makeup brush and small circular strokes.

• **Smooth and protect.** For a scar or flaw that's textured or raised, or for a pimple that should be protected from bacteria, apply a thin layer of liquid bandage (sold at drugstores). Let it dry, then apply foundation.

Treating Varicose Veins Is Easier Than You May Think

Neil M. Khilnani, MD, phlebologist at Weill Cornell Vascular and associate professor of clinical radiology at Weill Cornell Medical College and New York-Presbyterian Hospital/Weill Cornell Medical Center, all in New York City.

Up to 25% of all women in the US and about half of women age 55 and older have varicose veins. Men also get them but much less often.

What goes wrong: Veins, unlike arteries, are not simply hollow. They're lined with a series of one-way valves. Pressure—from the movement of muscles, for example—pushes blood upward through the valves. The valves intermittently open and close, allowing blood to move upward without being pulled back down by gravity.

In people with varicose veins, the vein walls dilate and lose elasticity, causing the valves to weaken.

Result: Blood flows backward, rather than circulating to the heart. The veins may appear blue from deoxygenated blood. If enough blood accumulates, the veins enlarge, causing unsightly bulges and twists. "Spider veins" are similar to varicose veins, but they are smaller and closer to the skin's surface.

Most varicose veins occur in the legs because gravity exerts more pressure on those rising columns of blood.

WHO GETS THEM?

People with a family history of varicose veins are more likely to get them. These veins often occur during pregnancy. The surge in progesterone that occurs during the first trimester causes blood vessels and valves to weaken. Obesity and prolonged standing also increase the risk.

For many people, varicose veins are primarily a cosmetic concern and unlikely to cause discomfort.

Exceptions: Large varicose veins are more likely than spider veins to cause leg fatigue, itching, sensations of heaviness and cramping. Even small veins, however, may cause these symptoms.

Caution: In rare cases, pools of stagnant blood in varicose veins can damage the overlying skin and cause ulcers, usually on the ankles. There's also a small risk of thrombophlebitis, which causes a potentially dangerous blood clot.

People who aren't bothered by their varicose veins usually can manage them with exercise, weight loss and compression stockings, which are worn all day and steadily squeeze the legs, helping veins and leg muscles move blood more efficiently. Veins that cause symptoms, however, should be checked by a doctor.

EASY TO TREAT

Many varicose veins are caused by weakness or leaks in the saphenous vein, a blood vessel that runs through the leg and thigh. Blood from this vein can cause multiple varicose veins to form "downstream."

Most varicose veins can be treated with laser and/or chemical therapy. A vascular surgeon or a phlebologist, a physician who specializes in the treatment of veins, makes small nicks in the skin (about 3 millimeters long) to insert a tiny laser fiber into the saphenous vein. Heat from the laser seals the vein shut (laser ablation). That section of the saphenous vein eventually fades and disappears over six months to a year. The visible varicose veins may seem smaller almost right away.

The laser procedure takes about an hour and requires only a local anesthetic.

Any remaining varicose veins are then treated with a sclerotherapy or a microphlebectomy…

• **Sclerotherapy.** This procedure is usually done about one month after the laser procedure. The varicose veins are injected with sodium tetradecyl sulfate, a chemical that shuts down the veins and causes blood to seek an alternate route. Injections of this chemical also are effective in patients who have only spider veins and don't require laser ablation.

• **Microphlebectomy.** During this procedure, small skin nicks are used to remove the vein. This often is done with larger varicose veins at the same time as the laser ablation.

Insurance doesn't usually cover the expense of elective cosmetic surgery for varicose veins. But if you have symptoms such as swelling and bleeding that are affecting your quality of life, insurance often will cover the procedures. The insurance company may require that you try other measures first, such as wearing compression stockings.

PREVENTION

Improving circulation and muscle tone can reduce your risk for developing varicose veins…

• **Exercise.** People who walk regularly or do other leg-strengthening exercises are less likely to get varicose veins.

Reason: Muscle contractions help move the blood upward.

• **Maintain a healthy weight.** Excess body weight exerts pressure on the leg veins and makes it harder for blood to circulate.

Myth: Doctors used to tell patients with varicose veins not to cross their legs. It was thought that this might constrict the veins and reduce circulation. Not true. There's no evidence that crossing the legs has any effect on varicose veins.

Do You Have Liver Spots?

Mark A. Stengler, NMD, licensed naturopathic medical doctor and leading authority on the practice of alternative and integrated medicine. He is founder and medical director of the Stengler Center for Integrative Medicine, Encinitas, California. He is author of *The Natural Physician's Healing Therapies* (Bottom Line Books).

Many patients ask me about the efficacy of cleaners for the skin condition "liver spots"—which have nothing to do with your liver.

This is a confusing term that refers to the flat, dark spots that sometimes show up on sun-exposed parts of the body—the hands, lower arms, shoulders and face.

They also are called age spots, because they become more common after age 40, as you accumulate more sun damage and your skin is less able to heal.

The spots are painless and harmless…and, most important, noncancerous.

If they bother you for cosmetic reasons, you can reduce their appearance with bleaching, cryotherapy (freezing) or laser therapy.

Consult a dermatologist for a diagnosis and treatment plan.

To prevent additional spots, do the same things you would normally do to prevent sunburn—wear sunscreen, a broad-rimmed hat and light-colored clothing with a tight weave.

When "Age Spots" Are Dangerous

Audrey Kunin, MD, board-certified practicing dermatologist with a specialty in nonsurgical cosmetic dermatology. Dr. Kunin is a diplomate of the American Board of Dermatology and is an assistant clinical instructor of dermatology at the University of Kansas School of Medicine. She is founder and president of DERMAdoctor.com, an award-winning Web site considered to be one of the best dermatology Web sites for consumers on the Internet.

One unfortunate result of years of sun exposure is age spots—also known, for no good reason, as liver spots (they have absolutely nothing to do with the liver). Generally small and flat, these are usually brown, all of one shade, which may be anywhere from the color of dark coffee to light tan. They tend to appear in people over the age of 40, most commonly on skin that's been most exposed to sun—the face, arms, backs of the hands and shoulders.

CAUSE AND CURES

Though many consider them unattractive, age spots are generally harmless. Dermatologists report that requests for removal are quite common, if not medically necessary. "These are simply what happens when melanocytes, the cells that create melanin, get busy and make too much pigment in one spot," Audrey Kunin, MD, dermatologist and founder of DERMAdoctor.com, explained. Melanin is the dark pigment that skin cells produce in response to sunlight, causing your skin to tan.

Short of removal, the most common treatment is a topical medication called hydroquinone, the only active ingredient that can legally be marketed for over-the-counter use for bleaching the skin. For topical use, many over-the-counter creams are available at a strength of 2%, while stronger concentrations of 3% to 4% are available by prescription. Some patients find that skin-rejuvenation products, especially the topical retinoids like Retin A, are also helpful, Dr. Kunin said. The most potent ones are available only by prescription.

Also, a variety of simple procedures can be used to help diminish these unattractive spots.

For instance, exfoliating procedures such as microdermabrasion or chemical peels can lift away pigment that has been deposited high up in the epidermis. The use of home glycolic acid-based skin treatments and microdermabrasion creams can also be useful. And certain types of lasers can literally blast the pigment deposits into less visible fragments.

WHEN TO WORRY ABOUT AGE SPOTS

While age spots are of no concern most of the time, very infrequently they can develop into skin cancer. This can be a particular challenge since it can be hard to distinguish which ones are precancerous or actually cancer. Age or liver spots can be difficult to differentiate from actinic keratoses (though these tend to be flatter, scaly and more often reddish-brown than true brown), which turn into squamous cell carcinoma (a kind of skin cancer) 10% to 25% of the time. Another concern is melanoma, which 1% of the population is at risk for developing in their lifetime. Sometimes a melanoma in its earliest stages can look like an age spot. If you feel unsure or are concerned, visit your dermatologist. "It's far better to be safe than sorry," says Dr. Kunin.

Dr. Kunin recommends that all adults receive a complete skin exam by age 25 and then annually or more often if anything is concerning or changing…and then make decisions on follow-up together with your physician.

Age spots are…

- **Smooth and flat**
- **Light brown to dark brown**
- **Larger than a freckle**
- **Appear on sun-exposed areas**
- **Not flaky or scaly**

MELANOMA

See a dermatologist if any spot exhibits any of these signs…

- **Change in size**
- **Irregular border**
- **Unusual color or varying colors within the spot, including black, brown or tan shades**
- **Asymmetry**

ACTINIC KERATOSES

These should always be removed, typically by freezing or burning with electrical current or a laser. *They are…*

- **Rough and wart-like**
- **Brown, pink, red or flesh-colored**
- **Flat and scaly, or hard and slightly elevated**

To view what melanoma and actinic keratoses look like, go to the American Academy of Dermatology's consumer site, *www.skincare physicians.com.*

How to Keep Hands Looking Young

Neal B. Schultz, MD, assistant clinical professor at Mount Sinai School of Medicine, assistant adjunct physician at Lenox Hill Hospital and owner of Park Avenue Skin Care, all in New York City. He is coauthor, with Laura Morton, of *It's Not Just About Wrinkles* (Stewart, Tabori & Chang).

You work hard to keep the skin on your face young and smooth, so don't let your hands give away your age…

- **Apply sunscreen of SPF 30 or higher on hands every day.** Use products with Z-Cote, a microfine zinc oxide. Reapply after washing, swimming or perspiring.

- **Use a bleaching product to fade brown spots (age, sun or liver spots).** Your dermatologist can give you a prescription for one, or you can try one of the milder over-the-counter products, such as Porcelana.

- **Wear gloves whenever possible.**

- **Have bulging blue veins removed by a dermatologist with a laser,** or have a dermatologist inject a sclerosing agent, which causes veins to collapse and fade.

Approximate cost: $300 or more.

- **Remove fine lines** and improve the paperlike quality of aging skin with laser treatments that generate collagen—also available from a dermatologist.

Approximate cost: $2,000 to $4,000.

Help for Ropy Veins On Hands

Hands have thin, delicate skin and little subcutaneous fat. That's why cosmetic procedures, such as chemical peels and injections that minimize the appearance of veins elsewhere on the body, don't work for hands.

Better: A prescription tretinoin cream, such as Renova, that stimulates collagen production, making skin plumper and smoother…or nonprescription Olay Regenerist Targeted Tone Enhancer.

Marianne O'Donoghue, MD, associate professor of dermatology at Rush University Medical Center in Chicago, and past president of the Women's Dermatologic Society.

A Younger-Looking Neck—Without Surgery

Nelson Lee Novick, MD, clinical professor of dermatology at Mount Sinai School of Medicine and a cosmetic dermatologist in private practice, both in New York City. He is author of *Super Skin* (iUniverse) and winner of the American Academy of Dermatology's Leadership Circle Award. *www.youngerlookingwithoutsurgery.com*

Nonsurgical techniques improve the appearance of "necklace lines" (bands of wrinkles encircling the neck) and "turkey wattle" (saggy chin skin and ropey vertical cords at the front of the neck)—without the pain, risks, recuperation or expense of cosmetic surgery. *Fixes for…*

• **Necklace lines.** Microdroplets of muscle-relaxing Botox* (a purified form of a protein produced by the Clostridium botulinum bacterium) are injected at half-inch intervals along, above and/or below each band (except where covered by hair at the back of the neck). Within 14 days, as the sheetlike platysma muscle

*The FDA now requires Botox and other similar anti-wrinkle drugs to carry warning labels explaining that the material has the potential to spread from the injection site to other parts of the body, with risk of causing serious complications.

relaxes in the treated areas, the muscle in the nontreated areas pulls the skin taut so wrinkles smooth out.

Cost: About $500 to $750 per treatment.

• **Turkey wattle.** Botox injections down the length of each ropey cord make the platysma muscle drape more smoothly…Botox under the jawline allows the muscles above to pull the neck skin upward. Then injections of Radiesse (a synthetic gel of tiny calcium-based spheres) along the jawline and under the chin give added volume where needed to make the neck skin more taut. Radiesse also helps stimulate the body's own production of skin-firming collagen.

Cost: About $1,500 per treatment.

With either procedure: There is minor discomfort as local anesthesia is injected. Only tiny amounts of Botox are given at each site, so swallowing and breathing muscles are not affected. No recovery time or activity restrictions are needed. Minor redness, swelling and bruising disappear within two days. Botox lasts about six months…Radiesse lasts nine to 18 months.

Safer Shampoos And More

Mark A. Stengler, NMD, licensed naturopathic medical doctor and leading authority on the practice of alternative and integrated medicine. He is founder and medical director of the Stengler Center for Integrative Medicine, Encinitas, California, and associate clinical professor at the National College of Natural Medicine, Portland, Oregon. He is author of *The Natural Physician's Healing Therapies* (Bottom Line Books).

Many of the health and beauty products we use every day contain trace amounts of toxic substances. Nearly 90% of the 10,000+ chemicals used in these products have not been evaluated for safety by a publicly accountable institution. *Examples…*

• **Coal Tar is the anti-itch,** antiflake ingredient in some shampoos for dandruff and psoriasis, and a color agent in many hair dyes.

In 1994, the FDA warned that coal tar was a possible carcinogen. Further study revealed that low concentrations are not cancerous, but a California law requires that products containing more than 0.5% coal tar must include a warning label. Check hair-color ingredient lists for FD&C Blue 1, Green 3 or Yellow 5 & 6, as well as D&C Red 33.

• **Phthalates are chemicals used as softening agents in perfumes, nail polish, shampoos, conditioners, baby lotions and wipes.** A study published in *Environmental Health Perspectives* linked phthalates to genital abnormalities developed in utero, and animal studies have shown phthalates to be cancerous. Avoid products with "fragrance," because there is no way to tell if this includes phthalates, which help scents to last longer. Look for natural fragrance agents, such as essential oils of mint or lavender.

• **Parabens are chemicals used as preservatives in lotions, shampoos, shaving creams, toothpastes and more.** Animal studies have shown that parabens mimic estrogen in the body and can disrupt hormone balance. Watch for methyl-, propyl-, ethyl- and butyl- on labels, and opt for products marked "paraben-free."

Healthy alternative: Many brands sold in natural-food stores are free of these additives. Good choices include Aubrey Organics, Avalon Organics, Burt's Bees and Light Mountain. Consider that one in four women uses at least 15 personal-care products daily, according to the Environmental Working Group, and it makes sense to consider nature-based varieties.

Dry Scalp Treatment

Put two tablespoons of olive oil in a small zippered plastic bag, then place the bag in a bowl or basin of warm water for several minutes. Dip your fingertips into the warm oil, then gently rub your scalp, continuing to apply the oil until the entire scalp is treated.

Finger-comb the oil through your hair. Wrap your head in a towel…leave it on for 20 minutes…then shampoo as usual. Repeat weekly or as needed.

Dorie Byers, RN, intensive care nurse and herbalist in Bargersville, Indiana, and author of *Natural Beauty Basics: Create Your Own Cosmetics and Body Care Products* (Vital Health).

Hair Care from The Inside Out

Joy Bauer, MS, RD, CDN, nutritionist/dietitian in private practice in New York City. She is the nutrition expert for the *Today* show and nutritionist for the New York City Ballet, the American Ballet Theatre and several Olympic athletes. She is author of several books, including *Joy Bauer's Food Cures: Treat Common Health Concerns, Look Younger & Live Longer* (Rodale). *www.joybauer.com*

Foods that are healthy for your skin also are healthy for your hair. *In addition, hair requires…*

• **Iron-rich protein.** Hair is made primarily of protein. Without enough of it, hair can weaken, grow more slowly or fall out. Iron helps red blood cells carry oxygen throughout the body, including to hair-growth cells. Eat at least one serving per day of protein foods high in iron, such as clams, oysters, shrimp…duck, lamb, lean beef, pork, turkey…eggs…fortified whole-grain breads and cereals…tofu and legumes (beans, peas, etc.).

• **B vitamins.** Folate, biotin, vitamin B-6 and vitamin B-12 are needed to make red blood cells. Without enough of these vitamins, hair follicles can become starved for nutrients and oxygen, and your hair can fall out. Eat two servings a day of foods that contain one or more of these nutrients.

Good choices: Fortified whole-grain breads and cereals…broccoli, leafy dark green vegetables and legumes…eggs and fat-free dairy products…peanut butter…and wild salmon.

How to Have Healthy Hair

For healthy hair, consume protein-rich foods, such as fish, meat, cheese and cereals. Protein helps build strong keratin, which makes up the outer layers of hair.

Also: Silica, commonly found in cucumbers, oats and rice, can boost hair growth. Vitamin C, found in citrus foods, such as oranges, lemons, limes, melons and berries, supports the body's effort to absorb protein and will keep hair follicles and blood vessels in the scalp healthy. Finally, eat salmon, carrots, egg yolks and sardines—the high amounts of vitamin B in these foods promote hair's growth and improve its texture.

Natural Health, 1000 American Media Way, Boca Raton, Florida 33464.

Mask Thinning Hair

Consumers Union, nonprofit publisher of *Consumer Reports*, 110 Truman Ave., Yonkers, New York 10703.

Couvre masking lotion, applied to the scalp and the base of the hair, eliminates the contrast between hair and scalp that makes thinning hair obvious. Comes in a tube with a special applicator…eight colors…washes out with shampoo but holds through wind, sweating and swimming. One tube lasts three to four months. Spencer Forest Labs, 800-416-3325, *www.couvre.com*. DermMatch is a hard-packed powder that coats thin hairs, thickens them and helps them to stand up and spread out for better coverage.

It also colors the scalp, causing bald spots to disappear. It is available in eight colors. It withstands sweat, wind and swimming. DermMatch, Inc., 800-826-2824, *www.dermmatch.com*. Toppik consists of thousands of microfibers of keratin, the protein that hair is made of.

Shaken over the thinning area, the microfibers bond via static electricity with the hair and stay in place through wind and rain—but not swimming. Spencer Forest Labs, 800-416-3325, *www.toppik.com*.

Omega-3s Keep Hair Healthy

Your hair follicles need nutrient-rich blood to look healthy. This requires consuming enough essential fatty acids, especially the omega-3s found in flaxseeds and wild-caught, cold-water fish, such as salmon and trout.

Best: Try to ingest four to six tablespoons of ground flaxseeds per day, along with plenty of water. You can use flaxseed in yogurt, cereal, smoothies and salads. Also, cold water fish at least three times a week.

Susan M. Lark, MD, editor, *Women's Wellness Today,* 7811 Montrose Rd., Potomac, Maryland 20854.

Fight Hair Loss by Getting More Iron

You normally shed about 100 hairs a day, but if hair comes out in clumps, get screened for iron deficiency. Getting more iron (through diet or supplements) may limit shedding and promote regrowth.

Caution: Do not take supplements without consulting a physician—too much iron can lead to heart disease, liver disease and diabetes.

Leonid Trost, MD, associate physician in dermatology at Cleveland Clinic Foundation, Cleveland, and co-author of a research review published in *Journal of the American Academy of Dermatology*.

Aging Gracefully (Not for Women Only)

Valerie Ramsey, coauthor with her daughter Heather Hummel of *Gracefully: Looking and Being Your Best at Any Age* (McGraw-Hill). She was public relations manager for the Pebble Beach Golf Resort, Pebble Beach, California, and is currently a fashion model represented by agencies in San Francisco and New York, and has two national television shows in development. *www.valerieramsey.com*

Looking young is a $60 billion a year industry—that's $1,600 worth of hormone treatments, plastic surgery, skin creams and supplements for every retiree in the US. But you don't need to spend a lot of money to age gracefully—looking and feeling your best.

Here, 70-year-old Valerie Ramsey, one of the most sought-after cover models in the country, tells her secrets. This grandmother of eight is the "centerpiece" for print ad campaigns for fashion and beauty magazines and has graced the runways at numerous fashion shows. Ramsey is also a motivational speaker and has made regular appearances on the *Today* show, *Fox Business News with Neil Cavuto* and *Extra*. She's never hidden her age or tried to pretend her hair wasn't gray. *Her "grace" is as much about feeling great and staying healthy as it is about maintaining her looks...*

MY STORY

My life has unfolded in a reverse direction. Until my 50s, I was a stay-at-home mom raising six children. Then, my husband and I moved cross-country to California, where I learned how to use a BlackBerry and a computer and got a job in public relations. Not long afterward, I discovered that I had uterine cancer as well as a severe case of cardiomyopathy (a weak heart muscle).

I wasn't ready to retire and become an old lady with medical problems. I've always had a sweet tooth and rarely exercised when I was younger. In fact, I was famous in my family for doing "vertical laps" in the pool—bobbing up and down. But in the 1990s, I decided that I had to and would live a healthier lifestyle. I began nutritional and workout regimens and

was able to beat the cancer and control my heart problem.

At age 63, a television producer I met liked my look and recommended me to a modeling agency. Out of the blue, the agency booked me to do a runway show in the Fairmont Hotel Grand Ballroom in San Francisco!

Standing backstage surrounded by 18-year-old waiflike models, I felt like Grandma Moses. What was I doing here?

But I also had a revelation—aging gracefully isn't just about looking younger. That's a losing battle with diminishing returns. It's about feeling younger, making the most of the time you have by becoming happier and more content with who you are. It's about choosing behaviors and attitudes that promote robust health. When you feel young inside, it creates a potent energy that bubbles out of you. Everyone notices it, and heads turn when you walk into a room. *My secrets...*

EATING WELL

Many of us fall into the trap of eating the same foods the majority of the time. So it's easy to slip into eating habits you aren't even aware of. *Rules that I follow every day...*

•**I drink an eight-ounce glass of water first thing in the morning,** which helps me to rehydrate and wake up. (I drink a total of at least 64 ounces of water daily to hydrate my body and skin.)

•**At every meal I sit down—and eat slowly.** Not only do I enjoy the food more this way, but I consume less.

•**I eat a big breakfast (half a grapefruit, one slice of whole-grain toast with butter and two scrambled eggs)** or, at the very least, a snack within 45 minutes of waking, a balanced lunch (turkey or chicken with a complex carbohydrate, such as sweet potatoes, and veggies or half a tuna sandwich on whole-grain bread) and a light dinner (salmon, tomatoes and vegetables) by 7 pm. I also snack on fruit, especially apples, and protein drinks made with whey.

•**I never go longer than four hours without eating.** Otherwise, I get too hungry and tend to overeat at the next meal.

●**I always opt for natural carbohydrates,** the ones that come from the ground, such as rice, yams, sweet potatoes and beans...and whole-grain breads and cereals in moderation. And when eating carbohydrates, I add some fat or protein. When you eat a carbohydrate by itself, you get a bloated-belly feeling.

EXERCISE

I think of working out as the secret weapon that provides me with the stamina for everything else I want to do in life. I have a 30- to 45-minute routine every day that my daughter, who's a personal trainer, prepared for me. This includes 30 minutes on a treadmill or elliptical trainer followed by 15 minutes of weights for my shoulders, biceps and upper body.

To find an exercise regimen that works for you: Do something you like enough to stick with. Try daily power-walking, join a class at your gym, play tennis, do Pilates. Or go back to what was fun when you were a kid, such as bicycling and/or swimming.

SLEEP

I try to get at least seven hours of uninterrupted sleep a night. Sleep is how your body repairs itself from the day's activity. Our bodies are a chemistry lab, not a bank account. When you shortchange your sleep patterns, you're not only tired the next day—you've also lost out on critical healing.

COMMUNICATION

I look people in the eyes and smile when I talk to them. When you greet someone, focus on sending out positive energy, and this energy will translate through your own eyes. People will experience you as radiating warmth—and, yes, youth.

ATTITUDE

Think positively all the time. According to the National Science Foundation, we have more than 65,000 thoughts per day, nearly 95% of which are the same thoughts we had the day before. We have the ability to create and shape our life experiences through our thoughts. This is essential for older people because it's downright rejuvenating to believe that there is still plenty of time left to create positive experiences in life.

As you go through your daily exercise routine, practice turning every negative or fearful thought into a positive one. *Examples...*

●**You're taking the car to the shop because you need new tires.** Rather than dwell on how much they will cost, focus on how much easier and safer it will be to drive through snow and rain.

●**You are waiting for your spouse to come home so that you can go to a dinner party.** You think, "I don't want him to be late."

Better: Turn the thought around and think, "I want him to be on time." That small twist can alleviate a lot of tension when your spouse does arrive.

OTHER STRATEGIES

●**Make a list of your best qualities and stick it on your mirror to read while you brush your teeth.**

●**When someone compliments you, thank him and believe what he said.**

●**Turn confrontations into positive experiences.**

Example: If a situation erupts during a conversation, you can calm the other person down without speaking a word.

How: Imagine a band of gold light beaming down on the other person's head. Keep the imagined stream of light steady as you listen when the other person speaks (or yells). The person will feel you relax, and that will diffuse his own tension.

ON COSMETIC PROCEDURES

I favor only minimally invasive, outpatient procedures with board-certified doctors. This prevents you from spending enormous amounts of money and from winding up with an unnatural, plastic look.

I personally have had treatment on my face to remove skin cancer and sun damage...photorejuvenation, a treatment performed with a cool-tip laser that reduces fine lines and age spots and stimulates collagen production... and copper bromide laser treatments to repair broken blood vessels and sun damage.

Love Your Looks...No Matter What Your Age

Pamela D. Blair, PhD, holistic psychotherapist in private practice, life coach and motivational speaker in Hawthorne, New York. She coordinated the Institute for Spiritual Development at Wainwright House, a learning center in Rye, New York. She is the author of *The Next Fifty Years: A Guide for Women at Midlife and Beyond* (Hampton Roads). *www.pamblair.com*

Do you catch your reflection in a mirror and feel shock when you see an "old woman" gazing back, because inside you still feel so young?

Coping with our changing appearance requires looking inward. Coming to rely on who we are rather than what we look like yields profound confidence, strength and self-assurance that often elude younger people. Paradoxically, that self-knowledge creates a magnetism that also is deeply attractive. *To nourish healthy self-acceptance...*

• **Savor each day.** Perhaps more than any other quality, being able to take pleasure in life makes a woman beautiful.

• **Pay attention to your senses.** Really taste the food you eat. Feel the fresh air on your skin as you walk outdoors. Relish the touch of a loved one. Some attractive qualities we tend to associate with youth—eagerness, curiosity, openness—can become stronger with age if we take time to appreciate the world around us.

• **Reexamine your goals.** Does your life now reflect your true values? Or are you investing time in relationships that are no longer fulfilling...activities that are no longer interesting...surroundings that no longer meet your needs?

Each morning, try this affirmation exercise. Say, "I am a woman who..." 10 times, and finish the sentence with a different ending each time, specifying goals you are striving for.

Examples: "I am a woman who is free of back pain...likes a gentle, relaxed pace to her life...has all the financial rewards she wants and needs...takes pleasure in her work."

After several weeks, notice what has shifted in your life. Even if these dreams have not yet come true for you, the power of positive thought can help bring about profound changes in the choices you make and in the way you live.

Example: If I am a woman who is free of back pain, I will choose not to lift that heavy box, and I will ask for help instead. I will choose not to skip yoga class. I will take actions that support who I want to be.

• **Reclaim beauty.** We all know that the media promotes an impossible standard of beauty. A recent study at the University of Missouri-Columbia found that women felt worse about their bodies after viewing photos of models in ads.

We do not need to accept the media's definition of beauty. I've stopped reading magazines that show only young, implausibly perfect models in their articles and ads. These pictures are not real. My former husband was an art director for a major fashion magazine, so I often saw the "before" photos of models with wrinkles, crooked noses and large hips—all of which were airbrushed away.

I am learning to be proud of my wrinkles. They represent laughter, conversation, concern for others and the hard work to become a good writer, mother, therapist, gardener. They are symbols of a beautiful life.

Find role models who exemplify a more enlightened beauty. My idol is the actress Tyne Daly—a little overweight, gray-haired, strong-willed, absolutely beautiful and unapologetically not "young." Many European actresses, such as Helen Mirren and Judi Dench, proudly look their age and remain elegant and desirable. I enjoy watching their films and reading about their personal and professional successes. If they can pursue their dreams and not be ashamed of their aging faces, then so can I.

• **Revisit your beauty rituals.** Valuing inner beauty doesn't mean ignoring your appearance. Decide which maintenance routines are worth keeping and which ones you can let go. By fighting the aging process a little less, you gain time and energy that you can put into other fulfilling pursuits. You also will become more relaxed, which is an attractive quality.

Example: I get manicures and pedicures because they make me feel pampered and cared for. They are a source of energy for me, rather than an energy drain. On the other hand, this past year I chose to stop dying my hair. I have gained many hours, and my skin looks better, too—the natural gray provides a softer contrast than the dyed color did. My choice wouldn't work for everyone. Someone who loves dying her hair should keep doing it.

Also experiment with new styles and products that acknowledge your changing body.

Helpful: Make an appointment with an image consultant to find out which clothing styles and colors complement your skin, hair and body shape now. Find a consultant through the Association of Image Consultants International (515-282-5500, *www.aici.org*).

Cost: $75 to $350 per hour, depending on your location and the extent of services that are provided.

Alternative: Get a free makeover at a department store cosmetics counter.

Example: I learned to switch to a lighter-consistency foundation and to stop using powder, which can emphasize imperfections in skin. My image consultant also suggested V-necklines to draw attention away from my filled-out chin…and pants that drop gently from my wider hips. I look and feel much more elegant.

• **Pace yourself to allow for physical changes.** Your strength may be slightly less, your reaction time a bit longer. I have been doing Pilates exercises, which have increased my muscle strength, bone density and energy as well as decreased my arthritis pain.

• **Increase your serenity by taking a meditative approach.** Before you start your day, sit quietly and visualize what you need to accomplish that day. Pick no more than three major tasks, and go about them with full attention.

Once you've completed those tasks, you can add one or two more. Notice how much calmer and more graceful you feel than when you race around trying to cross 20 items off your to-do list yet give them all short shrift. Enjoy the alertness that comes from being fully present with one task at a time. Your increasing serenity will radiate outward, assuredly making you feel and look more beautiful.

Look Great for Less

Kathryn "The Budget Fashionista" Finney, author of *How to Be a Budget Fashionista* (Ballantine). She served as a fashion and shopping expert for CNN, NBC's *Today* show and FOX Television Network. *www.thebudgetfashionista.com*

Shopping at off-price and discount retail stores, such as Target, TJ Maxx and Marshalls, is a great way to save money on clothing, but you can't count on fashion-savvy salespeople to help you find what looks good on you. *Here's how men and women can look their best for less…*

• **Emphasize quality over price.** Cheap clothes almost always look cheap. If you care about looking good, find quality garments that have been marked down, rather than cheaply made pieces.

Clues: If a garment has patterns, make sure they're matched up throughout the garment… look for lining in slacks and jackets…buy natural fabrics, such as wool/gabardine and cotton—it's hard to find high-quality synthetics unless you pay top dollar.

• **Dress monochromatically.** Wearing one color from head to toe is an easy way to impart a classy look with inexpensive clothing, and it's slimming. It also makes it much easier to dress—just look for matching colors.

• **Add a high-end accessory.** Adding a high-end accessory from a major designer is a surefire way to upgrade an outfit, especially if the accessory has a visible logo. Wear Calvin Klein loafers with your affordable Levi's Dockers pants…put on your high-end watch with your Old Navy shirt.

15

Allergies, Immune System & Respiratory Health

Best Natural Remedies For Allergies

I n the spring, I treat a lot of people who are miserable because of seasonal allergies—they suffer from itchy eyes and throat, sneezing and a runny nose. Seasonal allergies typically result from exposure to allergens, such as pollen from grass, trees and ragweed. But there's another type of allergy that can affect people year-round. Dust, feathers and animal dander are the most common causes of these so-called "perennial" allergies.

Regardless of the trigger, an allergy is an immune disorder. When an airborne irritant, such as pollen or dust, is inhaled, the body recognizes it as a harmful substance. This activates the body's defensive response, which leads not only to sneezing and a runny nose but also to watery eyes, sinus congestion and/or ear pain. When the body is under assault from allergens, the immune system works

hard. That's why for some people, the only sign of seasonal allergies is lethargy (extreme physical and mental sluggishness).

When allergies are treated with medication (such as antihistamines and corticosteroids), symptoms are temporarily relieved. Allergy shots can reduce allergic reactions in some people but, like medication, they do not cure the problem. *To address the root cause of allergies, try my natural allergy-fighting regimen (products are available at most health-food stores)...*

•**Get more flavonoids.** These powerful antioxidants strengthen the cells in your upper respiratory tract (particularly the membranes of your nose), which helps protect your body

*Check with your doctor before taking any of these supplements.

Jamison Starbuck, ND, naturopathic physician in family practice in Missoula, Montana. She is past president of the American Association of Naturopathic Physicians and a contributing editor to *The Alternative Advisor: The Complete Guide to Natural Therapies and Alternative Treatments* (Time-Life).

from the ill effects of inhaled irritants. Take 300 mg each of supplements containing the flavonoids quercetin and hesperidin four times daily during allergy season. Fruits—particularly citrus and berries—are rich in flavonoids. Eat them daily. Organic fresh fruits are best.

•**Reduce stress.** Researchers at the University of Texas Medical School in Houston have linked worsening allergy symptoms to anxiety, depression and psychological stress. That's because chronic stress triggers immune dysfunction, weakening the body's ability to defend against irritants. If you have allergies, review what causes stress in your life and take steps to remedy these situations, especially during allergy season.

•**Take herbs.** Adaptogen herbs help the body "adapt" to stress, generally by supporting adrenal gland health. I recommend astragalus and borage for allergy season. Mix one-eighth teaspoon each of a tincture of astragalus and a tincture of borage in two ounces of water and take 15 minutes before or after meals, twice daily throughout allergy season.

•**Drink tea.** To safely relieve allergy symptoms, try flavonoid-rich elderflower tea, which reduces nasal and sinus congestion, fights sneezing and relieves watery eyes. Pour one cup of boiling water over two teaspoons of dried elderflower blossoms (or an elderflower teabag) and steep for 10 minutes. Strain and drink hot (add lemon and/or honey, if you like) three times daily until symptoms improve.

Homeopathic Nasal Sprays as Good as the Conventional Ones?

Richard Mann, ND, chair of the homeopathy department at Bastyr Center for Natural Health in Seattle.

Ah, the joys of spring! The birds, the flowers, the greening trees, the warming weather. But for about 40 million Americans, the joy of the season is diminished by seasonal allergies, mainly hay fever. In the arsenal of conventional hay fever remedies, the over-the-counter nasal sprays have been around for a while…and they have been effective in symptom suppression. What about natural alternatives?

It turns out that at least one homeopathic nasal spray, *Luffeel*, has been proven as equally effective as an over-the-counter conventional nasal spray called *cromolyn* nasal spray (Nasalcrom). In a trial comparing the two, 146 participants (all of whom were hay fever sufferers), were either given Luffeel or Nasalcrom. The results? Both Luffeel and Nasalcrom worked equally well in reducing symptoms. Hay fever symptoms typically include sneezing, watery eyes and congestion.

We spoke with Richard Mann, ND, chair of the homeopathy department at Bastyr Center for Natural Health, for his take on homeopathic nasal sprays. He said that the over-the-counter homeopathic nasal sprays can certainly be effective. They are usually comprised of several homeopathic substances that have been known by homeopaths to have the effect of allergy symptom relief—temporary relief or modification of symptoms without permanently removing that symptom. Because the homeopathic nasal sprays are typically a combination of substances, it makes sense that patients will have a good chance of a response to one or more of these.

As for risk? As long as the elements in the homeopathic sprays are low potency (30X or less) and are used occasionally when symptoms occur, there is minimal, if any, side effect risk to the homeopathic sprays. Similarly, Nasalcrom provides minimal side effects, if any, for short-term and occasional usage. According to Dr. Mann, "If one uses these products, he should use them for short-term management of symptoms only, and then be sure to follow up for deeper treatment, that will get to the cause of the symptoms."

In spite of the seeming success of Luffeel, Dr. Mann offered some caveats on using homeopathic products.

HOMEOPATHIC CAVEATS

At the core of homeopathy is that homeopathic treatments for a "medical problem" have subtle differences, depending on the way the symptoms display in one person or another. The trained practitioner creates a personalized prescriptive plan for the treatment that best fits the patient's specific symptom pattern. The aim is not simply symptom suppression as an end in itself, but rather the discovery of the underlying causes of symptoms. In the homeopathic medical paradigm, symptoms represent the state of the whole organism, and not the cause of a medical problem. While a one-size-fits-all nasal spray sounds good, seeing a practitioner for a personalized perspective may be even more effective at eliminating the underlying cause.

In his practice, Dr. Mann has successfully treated people who presented with hay fever with homeopathic remedies tailored to that individual's unique physical condition. In people with hay fever, symptoms did indeed disappear—permanently—along with other symptoms, but it usually took a while, sometimes months or even a year or two, for the body to completely rebalance itself.

Allergies and Vitamin B

Allergies are linked to low levels of a B vitamin, reports Elizabeth Matsui, MD.

Recent study: People who had low blood levels of the vitamin folate were 31% more likely to have allergies...and 16% more likely to have asthma.

Possible explanation: Folate may "silence" genes that are involved in allergic responses. More research is needed to determine whether taking folic acid—the synthetic form of folate—can help relieve allergy and asthma symptoms. Dietary sources of folate include leafy green vegetables, peas, beans and fortified cereals.

Elizabeth Matsui, MD, associate professor of pediatrics and epidemiology, Johns Hopkins School of Medicine, Baltimore, and coleader of a study of 8,083 people, published in *The Journal of Allergy & Clinical Immunology.*

Cure Allergies the Natural Way

Richard Firshein, DO, director of the New York City–based Firshein Center for Comprehensive Medicine, *www.drfirshein.com.* Board certified in family medicine and a certified medical acupuncturist, he is the author of *Reversing Asthma* (Grand Central) and *The Vitamin Prescription* (Xlibris). Dr. Firshein is also founder of the social-networking health site *www.healeos.com.*

Seasonal allergies are most commonly associated with springtime. But the flare-ups that occur in the summer can be just as bad—if not worse—due to the added discomfort caused by unpleasant climate conditions, such as heat and humidity.

Interesting new fact: Allergy symptoms may be lasting even longer due to extended pollen seasons brought on by climate change, according to a recent analysis. And this year's heavy snow and rain are predicted to cause one of the worst tree pollen seasons the US has seen.

That's why it's more important than ever for the 40 million Americans who suffer from seasonal allergies to use the most effective therapies—with the fewest side effects.

Good news: You don't have to fill your medicine cabinet with powerful drugs that simply temporarily relieve your allergy symptoms and potentially lead to side effects ranging from headache and drowsiness to difficulty breathing. Instead, you can get relief from the natural remedies described in this article.

THE ROOT OF THE PROBLEM

Most doctors treat allergies with a regimen that includes oral antihistamines, such as *loratadine* (Claritin) or *cetirizine* (Zyrtec), to block the release of histamine so that runny noses and itchy eyes will be reduced...and/or inhaled steroids, such as *triamcinolone acetonide* (Nasacort) or *flunisolide*, to reduce inflammation, mucus production and nasal congestion.

Problem: Aside from the side effects these drugs can cause, many allergy sufferers experience a "rebound effect"—that is, when the drug wears off, the histamine that has been

333

suppressed by the medication explodes, causing an even bigger allergic reaction.

Important: To transition from medication to the natural regimen described here, first take the natural remedy with the medication, then slowly wean yourself off the medication over a few weeks.

Try these three simple natural approaches…*

STEP 1—SUPPLEMENTS

Mother Nature has tools that work with your body to stop allergy symptoms. The following naturally occurring substances have few side effects and often are just as effective as over-the-counter and prescription allergy medications.

My advice: Try quercetin, then add others in severe cases.

• **Quercetin is a bioflavonoid,** a type of plant pigment that inhibits histamine-producing cells. It's found in citrus fruits, apples and onions but not in amounts that are sufficient to relieve allergy symptoms. For optimal relief, try quercetin tablets.

Typical dose: Up to 600 mg daily depending on the severity of your symptoms. Quercetin also can be taken as a preventive during allergy season. Discuss the dose with your doctor. Quercetin is generally safe. Rare side effects may include headache and upset stomach. People with kidney disease should not take quercetin—it may worsen the condition.

Good brands: Quercetin 300, 800-545-9960, *www.allergyresearchgroup.com*…or Quercetone, 800-228-1966, *www.thorne.com.*

• **Stinging nettle is a flowering plant that,** when ingested, reduces the amount of histamine that the body produces in response to an allergen. Look for a product that contains 1% silicic acid (the key ingredient).

Typical dose: 500 mg to 1,000 mg once or twice a day depending on the severity of symptoms.

Caution: Some people are allergic to stinging nettle. In rare cases, oral stinging nettle may cause mild gastrointestinal upset.

Good brands: Nature's Way Nettle Herb, 800-962-8873, *www.naturesway.com*…or Solgar Stinging Nettle Leaf Extract, 877-765-4274, *www.solgar.com.*

• **Fish oil.** The same potent source of omega-3 fatty acids that is so popular for preventing the inflammation that leads to heart disease also helps with allergies. Look for the words "pharmaceutical grade" and "purified" or "mercury-free" on the label. This ensures that the product is potent enough to have a therapeutic effect and has undergone a manufacturing process that removes potential toxins. Choose a brand that provides at least 500 mg of *eicosapentaenoic acid* (EPA) and 250 mg of *docosahexaenoic acid* (DHA) per capsule.

Typical dose: Take 2,000 mg of fish oil per day. Consult your doctor if you take a blood thinner.

Good brands: Nordic Naturals Arctic Omega, 800-662-2544, *www.nordicnaturals.com*… or Vital-Choice fish oils, 800-608-4825, *www.vitalchoice.com.*

STEP 2—NASAL CLEANSING

Inflammation in the nasal passages due to allergies prevents the sinuses from draining and can lead to sinus infection.

Self-defense: Nasal cleansing once daily during allergy season reduces the amount of pollen exposure and can prevent the allergic reaction in the first place.*

One option: Flush your nasal passages with a neti pot. A neti pot looks like a miniature teapot with an elongated spout (available at drugstores for $8 to $30). Add one tablespoon of aloe vera gel and a pinch of salt to the warm distilled water you place in the pot.

What to do: While standing over a sink, tilt your head horizontally, left ear to ceiling, and gently insert the spout into your left nostril. As you slowly pour the mixture into the nostril, it will circulate through the nasal passages and out the right nostril. Continue for 10 seconds, breathing through your mouth, then let the excess water drain. Repeat on the other nostril. Be sure to run your neti pot through the

---

*Consult a doctor before trying this regimen if you are pregnant or have a medical condition.

*Nasal cleansing may be irritating for some people. If irritation occurs, discontinue it immediately.

dishwasher or clean with soap and hot water to disinfect it after every use.

Alternative: If using a neti pot feels uncomfortable, try using a syringe bulb...or cup warm water (mixed with salt and aloe) in your hand and breathe it in slowly.

Even better: Use a nasal irrigator, which is more thorough and takes less effort than a neti pot. This instrument forcibly expels water —and uses the same aloe/salt/water mixture as you would in a neti pot.

Recommended: The Grossan Nasal Irrigator, developed by ENT doctor Murray Grossan, 800-560-9007, *www.hydromedonline.com*, $97...or SinuPulse Elite Advanced Nasal Irrigation System, 800-305-4095, *www.sinupulse. com*, $97.

STEP 3—ACUPRESSURE OR ACUPUNCTURE

Acupuncture and acupressure can relieve allergies by stimulating certain pressure points to encourage blood flow, reduce inflammation and release natural painkilling chemical compounds known as endorphins.

• **Acupressure.** For 30 to 60 seconds, push (with enough pressure to hold your head on your thumbs) each thumb into the area where each brow meets the nose. Then, press your thumbs just below your eyebrows and slide along the ridges. Finally, press beneath both cheekbones, moving outward with both thumbs toward the ears. Do this sequence three times daily.

• **Acupuncture.** While acupressure helps relieve allergy symptoms, acupuncture is generally more effective. I recommend six to 10 sessions with a licensed acupuncturist during allergy season.

OTHER REMEDIES

• **Allergy shots and drops.** These traditional approaches are in many ways quite natural. Small amounts of an allergen extract are injected. After a number of treatments, you build up a natural resistance to the allergen. Allergy drops (placed under the tongue) are an alternative to allergy shots and work in much the same way.

• **Speleotherapy and halotherapy.** Used for centuries in Europe, these treatments are gaining popularity in the US. With speleotherapy, patients spend time in salt caves. Halotherapy uses man-made salt rooms that simulate caves. The salt ions combined with unpolluted air seem to improve lung function in those with respiratory and sinus ailments as well as allergies.

Salt mines and salt rooms are not always easy to find. Search online under "salt therapy."

Recommended: During allergy season, four to 12 speleotherapy or halotherapy sessions may be helpful. A 45- to 60-minute session typically costs $10 to $15.

"Allergies" May Really Be Food Sensitivities

Andrew L. Rubman, ND, director, Southbury Clinic for Traditional Medicines, Southbury, Connecticut.

When you think about controlling allergies or hay fever, you probably think about avoiding things like pollen or freshly mown grass or your friend's cat or a moldy basement. In many cases, this avoidance strategy is effective at controlling uncomfortable allergy symptoms. However, often the allergy triggers remain elusive and there's a possibility you may be overlooking an important one—what you eat and drink.

EAT, DRINK AND BE MISERABLE?

Since allergic sensitivities may be, in effect, cumulative, certain foods and beverages can make you more vulnerable to allergy symptoms such as sneezing, sniffling, congestion, skin irritations and red, watery eyes, confirms *Daily Health News* contributing editor Andrew L. Rubman, ND. In his opinion, it's simplistic to just suppress these symptoms with medication. Instead, he advises looking deeper into dietary connections to potentially "cure" the problem rather than simply mask it. *Dr. Rubman shared more of his thoughts on so-called food allergies, along with advice on what you can do about them...*

In most cases, what we commonly refer to as food "allergies" would be more accurately described as food "sensitivities." On occasion, a person may experience a true food allergy —in the worst case, a life-threatening allergic reaction (anaphylaxis) to foods such as shellfish or peanuts. Far more commonly, however, a runny nose, sneezing, hives and other sorts of allergy symptoms reflect a sensitivity to certain foods that are difficult for the body to process, notes Dr. Rubman. The foods that typically are hardest to digest—cow's milk and gluten grains (wheat, barley, rye)—are the most likely to cause problems.

We asked Dr. Rubman how a glass of milk and a sandwich on whole-wheat bread—a meal you digest in the gut—can cause symptoms in the nose. The body has several mechanisms to deal with digestive challenges, he explains. Normally, food residues are effectively contained within the intestine, through which nutrients are absorbed while the remainder pass efficiently and completely from the body. However, when factors such as disease, stress, excessive alcohol, medication or foods containing dairy proteins/sugars or gluten cause inflammation, the intestinal wall may "leak," permitting tiny partially digested food particles to escape, causing the body to produce antibodies to attack the unknown particles (called antigens).

One surprising manifestation of these microscopic food particles is rhinitis, due to the body's powerful immune-modulating system. While nasal defenses normally handle airborne challenges, deftly filtering out and destroying millions of irritating pollutants, particles and chemicals in the air you breathe, at these times they also react to immune system responses due to intestinal permeability (or what's called leaky gut). This is asking a lot of the mucous membranes in the sinuses, which react by producing extra mucus (hence, the sniffles) to attempt, often ineffectively, to respond to antigens in the body.

STRATEGY TO REDUCE THE SYMPTOMS

While mainstream medicine generally treats allergy symptoms with antihistamines, decongestants or immunotherapy, far better, says Dr. Rubman, is to examine and change your diet as necessary. In general, he advises consumption of more whole foods—such as fresh vegetables and fruits and legumes, deep-water fish like salmon and tuna, and poultry without skin—and fewer processed foods laden with additives, saturated fats and sugar, all of which can worsen allergy symptoms and leaky gut. In particular, limit your intake of cow's milk, milk products and products with gluten because these have the greatest capacity to disrupt the gut lining, particularly the large intestine.

Specifically, Dr. Rubman recommends...

•**Leave cow's milk to baby cows.** This seemingly "healthy" drink has absolutely no place in the human diet, stresses Dr. Rubman. Every species of mammalian mother produces milk specially designed to be consumed by their young. Given that, it is not surprising that some people are allergic to the specific milk whey and casein proteins, since they are immunologically different from what humans naturally digest. Many people are also sensitive to lactose, a milk sugar. Among the unappealing symptoms cow's milk can cause are digestive disturbances, mucus build-up in the sinuses, immune system reactions and more. (Note: Cheese and yogurt are more easily tolerated in the lactose sensitive or intolerant. Start by cutting out cow's milk, and see whether you feel better.)

Because calcium is essential for healthy bones and teeth, not to mention numerous vital body functions, many people worry about giving up their daily glass of milk. However, there are many other rich—and more readily digestible—sources of calcium, including broccoli, kale, spinach, turnip greens, salmon and sardines canned with bones.

•**Cut back on gluten grain products.** Gluten—the complex protein in wheat, barley and rye, to name a few—causes disturbances in the structural and functional performance of the intestine, explains Dr. Rubman. This can result in both intestinal (gas, bloating, diarrhea, for example) and non-intestinal symptoms (e.g., fatigue, irritability, and bone and joint pain in addition to the allergy symptoms), ranging from mild to severe.

Opt for gluten-free alternatives such as quinoa, amaranth, buckwheat or brown rice. Look for gluten-free labels on processed foods (such as soy sauce, ketchup and salad dressings, which are among the surprising products that often contain gluten). Or, better yet, forego the processed foods altogether.

NOT SUCH AN "EXTREME" MAKEOVER

When you've explored the obvious causes —such as pollen and mold—and your allergy symptoms remain bothersome and unexplained, it's time to wonder whether your diet might be the real problem. Since dairy and gluten products are naturally challenging to the human digestive tract, it is likely that everyone is affected to varying degrees by a dairy and/or gluten sensitivity, says Dr. Rubman.

So the question is not "if", but "how much" milk or cereal it will take to trigger symptoms in you. Often, the answer depends on your overall health. *Dr. Rubman advises taking these factors into account...*

• **How pumped is your immune system?** The healthier you are, the better prepared your body will be to meet the challenge of processing hard-to-digest food and drink.

• **How old are you?** It's not always the case, but usually the older you get, the less robust immune protection you have, compared with younger counterparts.

• **Is your body busy meeting intermittent challenges such as seasonal airborne irritants (pollen, ragweed, etc.)?** If so, on occasion, this will leave you especially vulnerable to the ill effects of digestive challenges, due to systemic inflammation that can affect intestinal permeability.

Dr. Rubman says that even in the absence of obvious allergy symptoms, everyone can benefit from eating more whole foods and fewer processed ones, cutting out cow's milk, and limiting gluten. If you just can't live without the pasta or milk on your cereal, have it as a treat one or two times a week. This allows your body to rid itself of the antigens before the next "attack". The more closely our diet resembles what we were meant to eat, back in the days before processing and manufacturing, the healthier we will be and the better we will feel.

Help for Chronic Sinus Infections

Jordan S. Josephson, MD, ear, nose and throat specialist in private practice in New York City. He is director of the New York Nasal and Sinus Center and an attending physician at Manhattan Eye, Ear and Throat Hospital, both in New York City. He is author of *Sinus Relief Now* (Perigee). His Web site is *www.drjjny.com.*

Chronic sinusitis is the most common long-term disease in the US. Even though more than half of all cases of sinusitis clear up on their own within two weeks, about 40 million Americans develop the chronic variety.

What happens: The sinuses, four pairs of cavities in the skull that filter and warm air as it passes through the nose on its way to the lungs, are lined with mucus-producing tissue. The tissue typically produces more than a quart of mucus a day, which drains through tiny holes into the back of the throat. When these holes are blocked, mucus can't drain properly. The holes often become blocked when the tissues swell during an allergy flare-up or an upper-respiratory infection.

Result: Facial pain, headache, fatigue, nasal and ear congestion, postnasal drip, cough, snoring, nosebleeds and a reduced sense of smell or taste, along with other coldlike symptoms. As mucus accumulates, it provides an optimal environment for bacterial or fungal growth. The resulting infection can further irritate and inflame sinus tissues.

DO ANTIBIOTICS WORK?

Sinusitis is defined as "chronic" when it lasts for more than four weeks or keeps coming back. For many patients, sinusitis is a lifelong disease. The symptoms may come and go, but the underlying problems persist. Patients need to manage it daily just as they would any other chronic disease, such as diabetes or arthritis. A total cure is unlikely—but with the right medical treatment, patients can expect a significant improvement in quality of life.

A short-term course of antibiotics usually will eliminate a case of acute sinusitis (assuming that the infection is bacterial), but this rarely works for chronic sinusitis.

Reason: Most cases are multifactorial. Patients with a bacterial infection might simultaneously harbor viruses or mold, organisms that aren't affected by antibiotics. A Mayo Clinic study found that 93% of all chronic sinus disease cases are caused by fungus (mold) found in the nasal passages. The mold can cause persistent infection. Even in the absence of infection, mold spores can stimulate an allergic reaction that causes persistent congestion.

Antibiotics can make a difference in patients with chronic sinusitis, but only when they are used for three to eight weeks. The same is true of anti-fungal sprays or oral drugs. Long-term therapy (up to three months) usually is required.

Recommended: Regardless of the underlying cause, most patients can get some relief with prescription steroid nasal sprays. Decongestants (oral or spray) also can be helpful but should not be used for more than 48 hours without your doctor's approval. Nasal irrigation (see below) is among the best ways to promote mucus drainage and relieve sinusitis symptoms.

DAILY CARE

Every patient with a history of chronic sinusitis needs to be alert to lifestyle factors that increase congestion and symptom flare-ups. *Important...*

• **Track your diet.** Even patients without clear-cut food allergies may find that they produce more mucus when they eat certain foods, such as dairy or foods with gluten or certain sugars, including high-fructose corn syrup. I advise them to keep a food diary for a month or more. Write down everything that you eat and drink, and make a note when your sinuses feel worse. When you suspect that a certain food is causing problems, give it up for a few weeks and see if you feel better.

• **Take control of allergies.** They are among the main triggers for sinusitis. When you have an allergy flare-up—whether from pollen, animal dander or anything else—treat it promptly with an antihistamine to keep mucus from building up.

• **Blow your nose gently.** Blow one nostril at a time. This is more effective than blowing both at once.

• **Clean your house and car.** Any area that's moist, such as the bathroom or under the refrigerator, can harbor mold spores that irritate sinus tissues. Clean these areas well with soap and water or a commercial mold-killing solution. Don't neglect your car. Cars trap humidity as well as heat, both of which encourage mold growth. Keep the seats and dashboard clean.

SINUS SURGERY

Some patients may require surgery to restore normal drainage. Endoscopic sinus surgery (sinoscopy) is now the standard approach. A thin tube is inserted through the nostrils. Surgical instruments are used to remove blockages and sometimes to remove bone to enlarge the sinus openings. The procedure is done in an operating-room setting. Typically, you are home that night and back to work the next day with minimal discomfort that rarely requires more than Tylenol.

Recently, surgeons have added balloon sinuplasty to the procedure. A guide wire is used to position a deflated balloon inside the sinus openings. Then the balloon is inflated, which enlarges the openings and promotes better drainage, without removing tissue. It is appropriate in only about 10% or fewer of total cases—usually those involving a less severe condition.

Important: Most patients improve significantly after surgery, but few achieve a total remission of symptoms. Most still will need occasional help from steroid nasal sprays, decongestants, etc.

More from Dr. Jordan Josephson...

Nasal Cleanse

Irrigating the nose once or twice daily is among the best ways to improve sinus drainage. This helps relieve symptoms, and it also can prevent sinusitis from getting started.

A neti pot (available at most pharmacies and health-food stores) is an effective irrigation tool. It's an ancient Indian device that has a tapered conical tip at the spout end. You also will need saline solution. You can buy prepared sterile saline from most pharmacies, but large quantities may require a prescription from your doctor (some insurance companies will cover this). Or you can make your own saline. Bring eight ounces of distilled water to a boil, add one-quarter teaspoon of salt to the water, and let the mixture cool to room temperature.

Fill the pot with the cooled saline. Tilt your head to one side, and gently insert the spout of the neti pot into the raised upper nostril. Continue to breathe through your mouth, and slowly pour the saline into your upper nostril. The saline should pour through the upper nostril and out the other lower nostril into the sink (you also can try this in the shower).

When you're done, compress one nostril at a time by placing pressure on it with your finger and then blow your other nostril by exhaling firmly several times.

Then reverse the tilt of your head and repeat the process on the other side by pouring saline into the other nostril.

Boost Your Immunity— Proven Ways to Stay Healthy

Michael F. Roizen, MD, chief wellness officer at The Cleveland Clinic. He created the RealAge concept and wrote the best-selling *RealAge: Are You As Young As You Can Be?* (Collins). He is author, with Tracy Hafen and Lawrence A. Armour, of *The RealAge Workout* (Collins). *www.realage.com*

It's amazing that we're not sick all the time. We are attacked more than 100 million times a day by viruses, bacteria and other disease-causing organisms. Our hands alone harbor up to two million germs. The only reason we're not continually sick is that the immune system is remarkably effective at recognizing and fighting threats.

Many harmful organisms are blocked by barriers, such as skin and mucous membranes, that prevent harmful organisms from getting into the body.

Those that get past the initial barriers are spotted by antibodies and attacked by a barrage of immune cells. The antibodies "remember" individual pathogens and attack and neutralize them during subsequent exposures.

FLAWS IN THE SYSTEM

The immune system isn't perfect, however. Immune cells aren't always effective—due to nutritional deficiencies, emotional stress and aging.

If the immune system has never been exposed to a particular virus or bacterium, it may not be able to mount an effective defense. Also, viruses and bacteria can develop their own defenses, which make them harder to detect and eliminate. In addition, the immune system can mistake healthy tissues for foreign invaders and launch an attack. This is what happens in autoimmune diseases, such as lupus.

Almost half of all deaths are due to infection or other immune-related problems. Even some cancers are caused by infectious organisms that break down the immune system.

Here's how to build up your immune system...

IMMUNITY BOOSTERS

Limiting exposure to harmful organisms is one of the best preventive measures. Wash your hands after you shake hands or touch surfaces that others have touched. Avoid people who are sneezing or coughing. These measures alone can significantly cut infection from colds or flu.

Also helpful...

• **Stay social.** People with active social lives and those who participate in religious or community groups are less likely to experience depression than those without social ties. Depression reduces immune response, mainly by inhibiting the activity of "attack" immune cells called T cells and B cells.

• **Get professional help if you're experiencing depression.** The majority of depressed patients who receive medication or therapy improve within three months—and nearly all of them improve within six months.

• **Exercise daily—but don't overdo it.** People who get regular exercise and take care of themselves in other ways—eating nutritious meals, not smoking, etc.—can improve immune response. Symptoms of depression also can be reduced by exercise. Thirty minutes a day is optimal for most people.

Caution: Exercising more than two hours daily actually causes immunity to decline.

• **Manage stress.** Stress itself doesn't weaken immunity, but poor responses to stress—such as smoking, not eating healthfully and not exercising—are linked to infection. Not getting enough sleep is both a cause and a result of stress and can impair the activity of infection-fighting T cells and B cells.

Stress reducers: Set aside 20 minutes to listen to music or meditate...breathe deeply for a few minutes...go for a walk or engage in other exercise.

• **Get enough omega-3s.** The omega-3 fatty acids in nuts and fish have been shown to reduce depression and improve immunity. Have one-quarter cup of walnuts daily...three servings of fish weekly...or take two grams of a fish oil supplement daily.

• **Boost vitamin C.** Studies indicate that vitamin C may prevent infection by boosting levels of T cells and B cells. The optimal dosage is 500 milligrams (mg) twice daily. You can get this much vitamin C with several daily servings of vitamin C–rich foods, such as tomatoes, bell peppers and citrus fruits—or you can take a supplement.

• **Favor flavonoids.** These vitamin-like substances in fruits, vegetables and whole grains minimize age-related declines in immune function. You need about 31 mg of flavonoids daily.

Best sources: Cranberry juice (13 mg per eight-ounce glass)...tomato juice (7.2 mg per eight-ounce glass)...apples (4.2 mg per medium apple)...strawberries (4.2 mg per cup)...broccoli (4.2 mg per cup)...onions (3 mg per small onion)...red wine (3 mg per five-ounce glass).

• **Avoid sugar.** Sugary foods, such as candy, cakes, cookies, etc., can drive blood glucose levels above 250 milli-moles per liter of blood (a normal level is between 65 and 140). Elevated blood sugar impairs the ability of immune cells to destroy bacteria.

Herbs That May Fight Flu

Kathy Abascal, RH, registered herbalist with the American Herbalists Guild who practices herbal medicine in Vashon, Washington. She is the author of *Herbs & Influenza: How Herbs Used in the 1918 Flu Pandemic Can Be Effective Today* (Tigana).

While scientists are furiously working to develop a vaccine and/or drug treatment to help protect us against the world's next major influenza outbreak, many herbalists believe that potentially effective natural medicines already exist.

Within the last century, three influenza pandemics—in 1918, 1957 and 1968—killed millions of people worldwide. Medical science has changed dramatically since the outbreaks, but a little-known yet highly effective approach to treating the flu of 1918 may prevent people from contracting the illness during a future outbreak—or help aid in recovery if they do become sick.

NEW LESSONS FROM OLD RESEARCH

In 1918 and 1919, a strain of influenza dubbed "the Spanish flu" (in part because it received the most press coverage in Spain, which was not preoccupied with World War I) circled the globe and resulted in not just one, but two (and in some places three) waves of deadly illness. The Spanish flu and its associated complications, including pneumonia and pleurisy (inflammation of the covering of the lungs), killed as many as 50 million people worldwide.

Some people received what were then believed to be the most progressive and scientific conventional treatments available—mercury, strong laxatives, aspirin, arsenic, quinine and a mixture of ipecac and opium called Dover's powder. According to the Centers for Disease Control and Prevention, more than 2.5%, or 25 out of every 1,000 people treated conventionally, died.

Surveys from the period show that patients given herbal remedies used by a nationwide group of physicians who called themselves the

"Eclectics"—because they practiced "eclectic" medicine (what we today might call herbal or alternative medicine)—died at a rate of 0.6%, meaning that six out of every 1,000 who received these botanical treatments died.

Who documented this huge disparity? At the onset of the Spanish flu outbreak, John Lloyd was a respected pharmacist, plant extract researcher, past president of the American Pharmaceutical Association and owner, with his brothers, of Lloyd Brothers, a Cincinnati, Ohio–based distributor of pharmaceutical botanicals.

In 1919—when the Spanish flu pandemic was on the wane—Lloyd conducted a survey of 222 physicians who had purchased his company's herbal products, asking which ones they had used to treat influenza and pneumonia, how the products were administered and which of the treatments they considered to be the most effective.

Respondents listed more than 40 botanical treatments, including gelsemium (the dried root and rhizome of the yellow jasmine plant native to the Southeastern US), echinacea (purple coneflowers that are native to Midwestern North America), aconite (a bluish flowered herb of the buttercup family) and boneset (a white-flowered plant native to Eastern North America).

Most of the Eclectics practiced "specific medication," treating the flu by addressing each individual patient's specific symptoms —respiratory illness, fever, coughs, vomiting, fatigue, etc. This approach differed from that of conventional doctors, who treated every influenza patient basically the same with purgatives, quinine, aspirin and Dover's powder, regardless of the individual's symptoms.

INCREASE YOUR IMMUNITY

A number of herbal medicines can be used to strengthen the immune system.

The herbs listed below are generally safe and are widely available at health-food stores.*

*Check with your health-care provider before using these herbs, especially if you are taking prescription medications, such as blood thinners or drugs to treat high blood pressure or diabetes. Pregnant and nursing women, in particular, should be especially careful to consult a professional before using herbs.

Good manufacturers that offer these herbs include Herbalist & Alchemist (*www.herbalist-alchemist.com*) and HerbPharm (*www.herbpharm.com*).

Adaptogens are herbs used to balance the immune system. They work slowly, so they should be started six to eight weeks before the flu season (typically November to April) and continued throughout that period. Also, adaptogens can be used as needed for general immunity strengthening to help fight colds and other respiratory ailments.

Take one of the following...

• **Ginseng.** Chinese or Asian ginseng (Panax ginseng) and American ginseng (Panax quinquefolium) have been used for centuries to fight fatigue and increase immunity. Siberian ginseng, or eleuthero (Eleutherococcus senticosus), has similar properties but is not a member of the ginseng family.

Immune-boosting dosage: Chinese or Asian ginseng: 5 ml to 10 ml of tincture daily...American ginseng: 3 ml to 5 ml of tincture three times daily...Siberian ginseng: 3 ml of tincture three times daily.

• **Ashwagandha (Withania somnifera).** Ashwagandha has been used for more than 4,000 years in India to treat and fight infectious diseases and immune system disorders.

Immune-boosting dosage: 3 ml of tincture three times daily.

• **Astragalus (Astragalus membranaceus and related plants).** Though little research has been conducted on this herb in the West, it has been used here since the 1800s to strengthen the immune and respiratory systems.

Immune-boosting dosage: 4 ml to 8 ml of tincture three times daily.

THE ECLECTICS' FLU TREATMENT

Herbs used by the Eclectics to treat influenza included echinacea (Echinacea purpurea, Echinacea angustifolia and Echinacea pallida) and boneset (Eupatorium perfoliatum). Echinacea traditionally is used to boost immune functioning at the onset of a cold or flu, while boneset is used to reduce fever and relieve aches and pains caused by the flu.

Dosage: For echinacea, mix one ounce of tincture in four ounces of water and take one teaspoon every waking half hour for up to 14 days. For boneset, mix 1 ml to 2 ml in one ounce of warm water and take every one to two waking hours.

USING HERBS SAFELY

The American Herbalists Guild (203-272-6731, *www.americanherbalistsguild.com*) and the American Association of Naturopathic Physicians (866-538-2267, *www.naturopathic. org*) can help you find a qualified practitioner of herbal medicine in your area. Like all medicines, some herbs can be harmful if taken in the wrong quantities or combinations.

The Powerful Herb Echinacea

The herb echinacea does boost the immune system and helps to fight upper-respiratory tract infections, despite a recent study indicating the contrary, says Mark A. Stengler, ND. The study dosage (1 gram daily) was too low. During acute illnesses, such as colds, flu, bronchitis and ear infections, echinacea should be taken in high doses of 2 milliliters of liquid extract or two 300-mg capsules every two waking hours for the first 24 hours and every three hours after that. It is helpful as a skin ointment for wounds, eczema and burns. It also may be effective for sore throats and as a cream for rheumatoid arthritis. Check with your doctor before starting treatment.

Mark A. Stengler, NMD, licensed naturopathic medical doctor and leading authority on the practice of alternative and integrated medicine. He is founder and medical director of the Stengler Center for Integrative Medicine, Encinitas, California, and associate clinical professor at the National College of Natural Medicine, Portland, Oregon. He is author of The Natural Physician's Healing Therapies (Bottom Line Books).

Natural Ways to Boost Your Immunity

Mark A. Stengler, NMD, licensed naturopathic medical doctor and leading authority on the practice of alternative and integrated medicine. He is founder and medical director of the Stengler Center for Integrative Medicine, Encinitas, California, and associate clinical professor at the National College of Natural Medicine, Portland, Oregon. He is author of The Natural Physician's Healing Therapies (Bottom Line Books).

You can boost your immunity. With the right preparation, quick intervention and a lineup of powerful, natural virus fighters, there's a good chance that you can enjoy fall and winter without a cold or flu. This is especially important as we face the prospect of a deadly avian flu pandemic.

KNOW YOUR ENEMY

Colds and flu are both caused by viruses. They are spread through the air by coughs and sneezes and through contact with contaminated objects, such as a doorknob or a hand that has been used to cover a cough.

Flu viruses are a lot more powerful than typical cold viruses. Cold symptoms are mainly confined to the head, neck and chest. Flu causes more generalized symptoms—fever, body aches, nausea, cramping, vomiting and severe fatigue. Flu also can develop into bronchitis. In the worst cases, it can lead to pneumonia and other severe respiratory diseases that are sometimes fatal, especially in the elderly or others with weakened immune systems.

START WITH PREVENTION

• **Avoid spending time around people who already are sick,** particularly if they're coughing or sneezing. If you live with someone who is sick, sleep in separate rooms. Wash your hands frequently during cold-and-flu season, and don't share towels—assign one to each family member or use paper towels. Keep your hands away from your face, especially your nose, mouth and eyes.

• **Take a multivitamin/mineral supplement that provides a base of nutrients to support a healthy immune system.** A formula that I recommend in my practice as a preventive against viral infections is Wellness Formula by Source Naturals (to find a retailer near you, call 800-815-2333 or go to *www.sourcenaturals.com*). It contains vitamins A and C, which are involved in the formation of antibodies...the minerals zinc and selenium ...and immune-supportive herbs, such as garlic, echinacea and astragalus, which increase the activity of virus-fighting white blood cells. The dosage used to prevent infection is two capsules daily during cold-and-flu season, taken in conjunction with your year-round multisupplement.

• **Reduce exposure to toxins.** You are more vulnerable to viral infection when your body is "distracted" by having to deal with toxins that can damage or suppress the immune system. Toxins aren't necessarily exotic—they could include sugar and alcohol consumed to excess, fast food and other unhealthy food laced with artificial preservatives and/or pesticides. Toxins also include small but significant amounts of metals—mercury, arsenic and lead—that you can get from food, water and air pollution.

It is even more vital to eat healthfully during cold-and-flu season. Go easy on holiday sweets and other treats, and you will be less likely to get sick.

Many people cut back their exercise regimens in winter months—a big mistake because exercise strengthens your immune system. Also consider sitting in a dry sauna once or twice a week for 20 to 30 minutes... or a wet sauna for 10 to 15 minutes. Saunas increase sweating, which excretes toxins. Be sure to check with your doctor first if you have diabetes or heart disease.

• **Be positive.** Toxic emotions can have a negative impact on your immune system. Anger, anxiety, resentment, loneliness and other chronic emotional difficulties trigger the release of hormones that suppress immune function. Seek support to overcome these problems if they linger.

RELY ON NATURE'S VIRUS KILLERS

If you start to come down with a cold or the flu, eat lightly so that your body can focus on healing. For the first 24 hours, consume filtered water, broths and soups with lots of garlic, onions and spices, such as turmeric and cayenne, which relieve congestion, promote circulation and have a natural anti-inflammatory effect. Herbal teas (especially ginger, cinnamon and peppermint) and steamed vegetables also are good choices. When you're feeling better, move toward a more normal diet.

I have found several supplements to be effective for treating colds and flu. Consider taking these when people around you are sick or when you first feel symptoms. You can use one or any combination until you feel better. These are safe for children when given in dosages of one-quarter to one-half of what I recommend for adults. The bigger the child, the higher the dose.

• **Lomatium dissectum** is a plant once used by Native Americans to fight Spanish flu. Preliminary research shows that lomatium has the ability to prevent viruses from replicating and to stimulate white blood cell activity. With colds and flu, I often see improvement within 24 hours. In my experience, the only side effect has been an allergic reaction in the form of a measles-like rash in a small percentage of users. This rash disappears a few days after lomatium is discontinued.

Eclectic Institute makes a potent product called Lomatium-Osha (800-332-4372, *www.eclecticherb.com*), which soothes the respiratory tract. This product is 50% alcohol, so take only the dosage recommended on the label. For children, add one-quarter to one-half of the adult dosage to hot water and let it sit for five minutes so that the alcohol evaporates. Women who are pregnant or nursing should not use lomatium.

• **Elderberry** can stimulate the immune system, enhance white blood cell activity and inhibit viral replication. Flu patients have reported significant improvement within 48 hours of taking elderberry. It also helps with colds. The elderberry used in research studies is Sambucus Original Syrup from Nature's Way (to find a retailer, call 800-962-8873 or go to *www.naturesway.com*). Adults should take two teaspoons four times daily...children, one teaspoon four times daily.

• **Echinacea.** Contrary to recent media reports, extracts from this plant can be effective for treating colds and flu. Echinacea makes the body's own immune cells more efficient in attacking viruses. The key is using a product that has been processed to contain a high level of active constituents. Two potent, well-researched products are Echinamide Anti-Cold Alcohol-Free Herb Tincture, Natural Berry Flavor, and Echinamide Anti-Viral Potent Fresh Herbal Extract, both from Natural Factors (to find a retailer, call 800-322-8704 or go to *www. naturalfactors.com*).

If you feel a cold or the flu coming on, take 20 drops of liquid extract or two capsules every two waking hours for 24 hours, then cut back to every three waking hours until the illness has passed.

The same company makes a liquid preparation called Echinamide Anti-Viral Potent Fresh Herbal Extract, which contains Echinamide, lomatium and other virus fighters. It is the most aggressive product for colds and flu from the Natural Factors line and can be used instead of the other supplements. Take 1.5 ml every two waking hours for the first 48 hours and then every three waking hours until the illness is gone.

• **N-acetylcysteine (NAC).** This nutrient thins the mucus that comes with colds and the flu. In addition to making you feel better, NAC helps to prevent sinus and more serious chest infections. It increases levels of the powerful antioxidant glutathione in the body, which, in turn, improves immune function. NAC is available at any health-food store and many pharmacies. If you tend to get the flu every year, take 600 mg twice daily when you are around people who have the flu or if you start feeling sick yourself.

• **Vitamin C fights viral infections.** Start with 5,000 mg daily in divided doses. If loose stools occur, cut back to 3,000 mg (or less).

HOMEOPATHIC REMEDIES

Homeopathy is based on the idea that "like cures like"—substances that cause certain symptoms in a healthy person can cure those same symptoms in someone who is sick. *For the flu, I recommend the following homeopathic treatments...*

• **Homeopathic influenzinum.** Made from active flu strains, this stimulates the body's own defense system to resist infection. It can be used for prevention or treatment of flu and has no side effects.

Take two 30C-potency pellets twice daily for two weeks at the beginning of flu season (in early November). Take two pellets four times daily when exposed to flu sufferers or if you start to have symptoms. It is available from health-food stores and The Vitamin Shoppe (866-293-3367, *www.vitaminshoppe.com*).

• **Oscillococcinum** is another great homeopathic remedy for flu, which is also available from The Vitamin Shoppe, health-food stores and pharmacies or by calling 800-672-4556 or visiting *www.oscillo.com*. It can be taken at the first sign of flu and is the number-one–selling homeopathic flu remedy in the US.

Health Benefits Of Massage

The health benefits of massage may be greater than were previously realized, say researchers from Cedars-Sinai Medical Center in Los Angeles. Researchers found significant improvements in the body's immune and endocrine responses following Swedish massage (a type of deep muscle massage), including an increase in the number of white blood cells (cells that defend the body) and a decrease in levels of the stress hormone cortisol. Schedule a massage as often as you can—it will do more than make you feel good.

Mark A. Stengler, NMD, licensed naturopathic medical doctor and leading authority on the practice of alternative and integrated medicine. He is founder and medical director of the Stengler Center for Integrative Medicine, Encinitas, California. He is author of *The Natural Physician's Healing Therapies* (Bottom Line Books).

Mushroom Power: Maitake Is a Leader in The World of Medicinal Mushrooms

Mark Blumenthal, founder and executive director, American Botanical Council, Austin, Texas, and editor, *HerbalGram* and *HerbClip. www.herbalgram.org*

For some people, mushrooms are such an odd food. They are both ugly and fabulous at the same time. Many mushrooms have strong healing powers. Compounds in various mushrooms have been shown to enhance immunity, fight off infections and cancer, and lower blood sugar and blood pressure. Among the most popular "medicinal mushrooms" is the maitake (Grifola frondosa), which is not only tasty but prized—particularly in Asian cultures—for its healing abilities.

To learn more about this versatile fungus, we consulted Mark Blumenthal, founder and executive director of the American Botanical Council in Austin, Texas. He told me that maitake can be used by healthy people as well as those with health issues such as a compromised immune system, with no significant risk of adverse side effects. While incorporating mushrooms into the diet is always a good idea, maitake in the form of dietary supplements packs considerably more punch.

IMMUNE ENHANCEMENT AND MORE

The number-one use for maitake lies in boosting immune system function, though it has also been used for certain specific ailments. According to Blumenthal, some cancer patients use maitake-based preparations as part of their natural treatment regimens in order to reduce the adverse effects of chemotherapy drugs. Additionally, maitake has demonstrated the ability to increase apoptosis, the natural programmed death of old, worn-out cells that acts as a check against their becoming cancerous. (Cancer cells proliferate instead of undergoing apoptosis.) Maitake also has been shown to improve cardiovascular-related parameters such as blood pressure, cholesterol and glucose (blood sugar) levels.

HOW TO TAKE MAITAKE MUSHROOMS

Maitake preparations can be taken with vitamins and certain other dietary supplements, usually in the morning and evening or with meals. They are typically sold as liquid extracts, capsules or tablets containing dried maitake extract powder, says Blumenthal. Blumenthal recommends taking the "D-fraction standardized maitake" because it has the most powerful immune-stimulating activity, according to much of the published research. The package label will indicate if it is D-fraction standardized.

Dosage usually depends on the intended use and the form of the product, notes Blumenthal. Given the power of maitake and the potentially severe conditions that it can be used for, it is best to work with a naturopathic physician or other trained professional when taking maitake. *Blumenthal notes that research shows that maitake can be used as an adjunct therapy for...*

- **High blood pressure and/or cholesterol levels.**

- **High blood sugar levels associated with diabetes or metabolic syndrome.**

- **Increased immune function to help prevent colds and flu.**

- **Adjunct supplementation to chemotherapy.**

To Blumenthal's knowledge, there are no significant adverse side effects or drug interactions associated with the use of maitake mushroom preparations when used as directed. Still, as noted above, with serious diseases such as diabetes or cancer or high blood pressure, it is always best to add a trained naturopathic or conventional physician to your treatment team before taking dietary supplements. This is especially important if you are taking prescription medications for any of the above conditions.

Breathe Easier

Ronald G. Crystal, MD, professor and chairman of the department of genetic medicine of the Weill Cornell Medical College, where he is also the Bruce Webster Professor of Internal Medicine, director of the Belfer Gene Therapy Core Facility and chief of the division of pulmonary and critical care medicine at the New York-Presbyterian Hospital/Weill Cornell Medical Center in New York City. He has published more than 700 scientific articles.

The lung disorder chronic obstructive pulmonary disease (COPD) kills about 125,000 Americans every year—more than accidents, diabetes, Alzheimer's disease or influenza. But treatment can be a challenge because half of the 24 million Americans with COPD don't know they have the disease, often assuming that their symptoms are due to smoking, poor physical fitness and/or aging.

Good news: With proper testing, COPD can be diagnosed early—when treatment is most effective. And even though COPD cannot be cured, you still can lead an active, healthier life and slow the progress of the disease.

HOW THE LUNGS WORK

To visualize the airways, think of an upside-down tree—the trunk is the windpipe...the large branches are tubes called bronchi...and the twigs, bronchioles. At the tip of the bronchioles are about 300 million tiny air sacs called alveoli, where microscopic blood vessels (capillaries) help remove carbon dioxide from the bloodstream and replace it with oxygen.

In emphysema, the airways and air sacs lose their elasticity, like old hoses and balloons...in chronic bronchitis, inflamed airway walls thicken, while their cells pump out airway-clogging mucus (sputum)...and the walls of air sacs collapse. Chronic bronchitis (marked by a chronic cough that may produce sputum) involves the bronchi...emphysema (characterized by severe breathlessness) involves the bronchioles and alveoli. Most people with COPD have chronic bronchitis and emphysema.

The earliest symptom of COPD might be a chronic cough with or without sputum. Later, you may find yourself unexpectedly short of breath while carrying groceries or climbing stairs. As the disease advances, you may wheeze, have difficulty taking a deep breath or sometimes feel like you can't breathe at all.

DIAGNOSE THE PROBLEM EARLY

Because the lungs have so much capacity and strength, the early stages of COPD are often symptom-free—but a medical test known as spirometry can detect the disease.

Spirometry uses a breathing device to measure lung capacity (the amount of air lungs can hold) and strength (exhalation speed after taking a deep breath). During the test, the patient blows into a large tube connected to a spirometer (a recording device). The test, which takes about five minutes, can be done in a doctor's office—usually by a pulmonologist (lung specialist)—or at a hospital.

Problem: Many primary care physicians don't use spirometry.

Solution: If you are a current or former smoker...have early symptoms of COPD (as previously described)...have asthma...or were exposed for years to secondhand smoke or occupational dust and fumes (other common causes of COPD), ask your doctor for spirometry and a chest X-ray, which can detect signs of lung cancer and emphysema. Both tests should be done annually—more often if you have COPD symptoms.

THE RIGHT EXERCISE

Exercise and lung rehabilitation help reduce and control breathing difficulties, improve quality of life, and decrease the use of medical care and the length of hospital stays. *Best choices...*

• **Lower-body training.** Walking or riding a stationary bicycle.

Benefit: Strengthens leg muscles to help you move about more easily and for longer periods of time.

• **Upper-body training.** Strength-training exercises (using hand weights or exercise machines) for the arm and shoulder muscles.

*These exercises should be performed as part of a pulmonary rehabilitation program near you, contact the American Association of Cardiovascular and Pulmonary Rehabilitation (*www.aacvpr.org*).

Benefit: Stronger muscles support the rib cage and improve breathing. Ask your doctor how often and how long you should perform such exercises.

STRENGTHEN YOUR BREATHING

Strengthening the muscles used for breathing is also important.

Recent study: When researchers studied 40 people with COPD, those who learned "pursed-lip breathing" (designed primarily for patients with severe COPD) had sustained improvement in overall physical functioning. *To perform pursed-lip breathing...*

Step 1: Relax your neck and shoulder muscles. Inhale slowly through your nose and count to two in your head.

Step 2: Pucker your lips as if you are whistling. Exhale slowly and gently through your lips while you count to four or more in your head. Use this breathing technique often throughout the day—not only during exercise (including walking) but also while engaged in daily activities, such as climbing stairs.

COPD PREVENTION

Quitting smoking is the most important step to prevent COPD as well as to slow and reduce its severity. Smoking causes about nine out of 10 cases of COPD—with the remaining cases probably due to long-term exposure to secondhand smoke, fumes and/or dust. If you are a smoker, talk to your doctor about a smoking-cessation plan. Don't give up—you may have to try two to three times before quitting for good.

Diet also may play a role in COPD prevention.

Recent finding: When researchers analyzed diet and health data from more than 70,000 women, those who ate a diet rich in fruit, vegetables, fish and whole grains had a 25% lower risk of developing COPD, while those eating refined grains, cured and red meats, desserts and french fries had a 31% higher risk. Similar results were found in men.

CHOOSING MEDICATION

The newest, most effective drug treatment for COPD combines two medication stalwarts in one inhaler—a bronchodilator that opens the airways and a corticosteroid that decreases inflammation.

Two of these combination-drug inhalers are now available—Advair combines the bronchodilator salmeterol and the corticosteroid fluticasone...Symbicort combines the bronchodilator formoterol and the corticosteroid budesonide. Studies have shown that people with COPD who use either of these inhalers have improved lung function, better overall health and less breathlessness, compared with those who use either a corticosteroid or a bronchodilator alone.

Asthma Attacks— Now You Really Can Prevent Them

Francis V. Adams, MD, pulmonologist in private practice and an assistant professor of clinical medicine at New York University School of Medicine, both in New York City. He is author of *The Asthma Sourcebook* (McGraw-Hill).

Six to 10 percent of Americans age 65 and older suffer from asthma—a chronic condition marked by a sudden narrowing of the airways that leads to an "attack," characterized by uncontrollable coughing or gasping for air.

Asthma sufferers are all too aware that when an attack occurs, it's important to reopen the airways immediately, which is why they typically carry a fast-acting "rescue" inhaler at all times. These inhalers contain a bronchodilator, a type of medication known as a short-acting beta-2 agonist, such as *albuterol* (Ventolin, Proventil) or *pirbuterol* (Maxair), that quickly opens the bronchial tubes and allows air to flow through.

While asthma can't be cured, it can be controlled. The goal is to reach a point where a bronchodilator needs to be used no more than twice a week.

Good news: A number of new long-term medications help control asthma and prevent attacks.

People with mild asthma (two attacks a week or fewer) may be able to work with an allergist or board-certified internist to develop a treatment plan. Those with moderate to severe asthma, however, should see a lung specialist.

LONG-TERM MEDICATIONS

These drugs are all available by prescription only...

•**Inhaled corticosteroids.** For persistent asthma, which causes frequent symptoms (daily or several times a week), inhaled corticosteroids are the first line of treatment. These drugs reduce inflammation in the airways, decrease swelling and mucus production and make breathing easier. They should be used daily even if symptoms have subsided.

Until recently, the only inhaled corticosteroids approved for use in the US—*fluticasone* (Flovent), *budesonide* (Pulmicort), *triamcinolone* (Azmacort), *flunisolide* (AeroBid) and *beclomethasone* (Qvar)—had to be taken two or more times a day. But the newer medications are taken just once a day. The first of these to become available in the US was *mometasone* (Asmanex), in 2005. Another, *ciclesonide* (Alvesco), is widely used in Canada and many other countries, and has recently been approved by the US Food and Drug Administration (FDA).

Big advantage: Corticosteroids are known, in general, to have unpleasant or even serious side effects. However, when inhaled rather than taken orally, they carry a much lower risk for these side effects because they are mainly absorbed into the airways with little passing into the rest of the body. While all corticosteroids carry some risks, the most severe—including weakening of the bones, glaucoma and cataract formation—generally occur only when the drugs are injected or swallowed. Still, inhaled corticosteroids may cause local side effects—most often dry mouth, throat irritation or hoarseness. These can be minimized by using a spacer (an attachment that protects the inside of the mouth) with your metered-dose inhaler (a pressurized container that propels the drug directly into the lungs). Both are available by prescription from a doctor. Alvesco is the safest of the inhaled corticosteroids because it is activated only when it enters the lungs.

•**Long-acting beta-2 agonists (LABAs).** For people with moderate to severe asthma that can't be fully controlled (based on frequency of symptoms, breathing function, how often patients are using their rescue spray) by inhaled corticosteroids, the next step is to combine a corticosteroid with an LABA. Like the short-acting beta-2 agonists used to treat acute asthma attacks, LABAs also dilate the airways when inhaled. They require about 20 minutes to take effect, but continue to work for 12 hours. This is why they help prevent asthma attacks but are not useful for treating attacks in progress. Two common LABAs are *salmeterol* (Serevent) and *formoterol* (Foradil Aerolizer).

Two more medications—Advair Diskus and Symbicort—combine a corticosteroid and an LABA in a single inhaler, allowing patients to take both drugs at once. The FDA has issued a warning on LABAs—in a large clinical study, more patients with asthma who used an LABA alone without a corticosteroid died of asthma problems than did asthma patients who did not use that drug. But, based on their many years of use without problems—especially when combined with a corticosteroid—most pulmonologists, in my experience, consider LABAs safe.

•**Leukotriene antagonists.** This type of medication, taken in pill form, neutralizes the effects of leukotrienes, which are immune system chemicals the body releases as part of its inflammatory response. These are taken either on their own instead of an inhaler, or as maintenance with an inhaler. The most popular leukotriene antagonist is *montelukast* (Singulair). Others include *zafirlukast* (Accolate) and *zileuton* (Zyflo). These drugs are especially helpful for treating anyone who has difficulty using an inhaler. They carry no risks of steroid-related side effects, though they sometimes cause gastrointestinal distress. And studies have found that leuko-triene antagonists are less effective than corticosteroids, which is why they generally aren't strong enough for severe asthmatics.

Note: A possible association between Singulair use and suicidal thoughts is being investigated by the FDA, but most doctors consider it safe.

•**Immunoglobulin E antagonists.** These drugs are used for treating moderate or severe asthma that does not respond to other medications. The only version available in the US is the recently approved omalizumab (Xolair). Injected by a doctor once a month, it blocks the body's receptors for immunoglobulin E, a protein that attacks cells in the airways, causing an asthma attack in people with allergies.

Xolair costs about $1,000 per injection (covered by health insurance) and is recommended only for severely allergic asthma patients. For these people, it represents an exciting breakthrough, since it can often replace a laundry list of other drugs.

HOME MONITORING

In addition to working with your doctor, it's important to have a peak flow meter at home and to use it once a day. This is a plastic device that you blow into as hard as possible so it can measure your breathing capacity—and identify an incipient asthma attack before any symptoms are noticeable.

Most meters have green, yellow and red levels. Green means your breathing is normal. Yellow indicates a 20% to 50% reduction in breath flow, indicating an attack is imminent, and that you should administer a bronchodilator and contact your doctor. Red indicates a 50% or more reduction in breath flow, in which case you should go directly to an emergency room.

ENVIRONMENTAL TRIGGERS

Studies show that people who are chronically exposed to environmental asthma triggers, such as cigarette smoke, dust mites, cockroaches, pet dander and ozone, have significantly higher asthma rates with more frequent attacks. Work with your doctor to figure out what your triggers are and how to avoid them or minimize exposure. *Steps to take include...*

•**Stay indoors** with the air conditioner running on days when the news media reports high levels of pollen or ozone. You can also sign up to receive free daily pollen count E-mail alerts at Pollen.com (*www.pollen.com*).

•**Avoid cigarette smoke.**

•**Allergy-proof your home** by running a high-efficiency particulate air (HEPA) filter 24 hours a day.

•**Replace thick-pile rugs** with bare floor or thin-pile rugs.

•**Put dust-mite-proof covers** on mattresses and pillows.

•**Remove any mold in your home.**

•**Keep your home cockroach-free,** because they leave saliva and urine trails that can trigger asthma and allergy symptoms.

•**Dust and vacuum often** using a vacuum with a built-in HEPA filter.

In addition, because obesity is a risk factor for asthma, lose weight if you need to...exercise regularly to increase lung capacity...and eat a diet rich in fruits and vegetables—they contain antioxidants, which reduce asthma risk.

16

Digestive Disorders

Best Supplements for A Healthy Diet

Of all the changes that occur with aging, one of the most under-recognized is the body's reduced ability to absorb nutrients. As we grow older, our bodies become less efficient at secreting the digestive enzymes that are necessary for the absorption of essential vitamins. Because of this absorption problem, I advise my older patients to follow the nutritious and heart-healthy Mediterranean diet—rich in fresh greens (such as chard, kale and spinach), fresh fruit, whole grains, nuts, seeds, beans, healthful oils (olive, for example) and lean protein, such as turkey and fish. For more on the Mediterranean diet, visit the Web site of the American Heart Association, *www. americanheart.org.*

But it's not always easy to stick to a nutritious eating plan. What's more, many older adults suffer conditions that interfere with appetite—for example, dry mouth, nausea or constipation caused by common medications, such as pain relievers and hypertension drugs. Dentures and waning senses of smell and taste also can interfere with the consumption of healthful meals. In my opinion, all people over age 50 should consider taking certain supplements—in addition to a daily multivitamin—to compensate for nutrients that might be lacking in their diets. *My favorite "healthy aging" supplements (all available at health-food stores)...*

• **Vitamin B-12**—800 micrograms (mcg) to 1,000 mcg daily, in sublingual (dissolved under the tongue) form. It helps with poor memory, a lack of energy, depression and neuralgia (nerve pain).

Jamison Starbuck, ND, naturopathic physician in family practice Missoula, Montana. She is past president of the American Association of Naturopathic Physicians and a contributing editor to *The Alternative Advisor: The Complete Guide to Natural Therapies and Alternative Treatments* (Time-Life).

• **Vitamin A**—10,000 international units (IU) daily. It helps promote health of the eyes and skin and general immunity. If you also take a multivitamin containing vitamin A, do not exceed 10,000 IU daily unless recommended by your doctor.

• **Vitamin E**—400 IU daily. It protects nerve and muscle cells, reduces leg cramps and helps prevent heart disease.*

• **Vitamin D**—1,000 IU daily. Recent research shows that many older adults are deficient in vitamin D, a nutrient that is essential for calcium absorption and osteoporosis prevention and may protect against certain malignancies, including cancers of the breast and colon.

• **Essential fatty acids,** in the form of fish oil, containing 1,800 mg daily of combined eicosapentaenoic acid (EPA) and docosahexaenoic acid (DHA). Fish oil acts as a natural antidepressant for patients of all ages and improves brain function.

• **Digestive enzymes.** Typically derived from papaya or pineapple, digestive enzyme supplements promote digestion—and, in turn, the absorption of nutrients from foods and other supplements. Follow the manufacturer's directions for dosages. If you have a gastrointestinal disease, such as an ulcer or diverticulitis, consult your physician before taking plant enzymes, which can irritate an inflamed gastrointestinal tract.

*If you take a blood-thinning drug, such as warfarin (Coumadin), check with your doctor before taking vitamin E supplements.

Acupuncture for Irritable Bowel Syndrome (IBS)

People who received six acupuncture treatments over a three-week period experienced less abdominal pain, bloating, diarrhea, constipation and other IBS symptoms than those who received no treatment. Needles were inserted at various points, including near the stomach, liver, spleen and large intestine.

Researchers believe acupuncture may help by balancing hormones and triggering a relaxation response. To find a board-certified acupuncturist, go to *www.nccaom.org*—the Web site for the National Certification Commission for Acupuncture and Oriental Medicine.

Anthony Lembo, MD, associate professor of medicine, Harvard Medical School, Boston, and leader of a study of 230 adult IBS patients, published in *The American Journal of Gastroenterology*.

Foods That Explode In Your Bowel

Elizabeth Lipski, PhD, CCN, who has been working in the field of holistic and complementary medicine for more than 25 years. She is director of doctoral studies at Hawthorn University in Whitethorn, California, which offers online holistic health education and nutrition programs. A member of the board of directors for the National Association of Nutrition Professionals, she is author of *Digestive Wellness* (McGraw-Hill)...*Digestive Wellness for Children* (Basic Health) and *Leaky Gut Syndrome* (McGraw-Hill). *www.lizlipski.com*

Your abdomen bloats and cramps. You pass so much gas that you think you might be contributing to global warming. You have diarrhea or constipation or an alternating assault of both.

Your problem: Irritable Bowel Syndrome (IBS), the most common gastrointestinal complaint, accounting for 10% of doctor's visits and about 50% of referrals to gastroenterologists. But the fact that doctors see a lot of IBS doesn't mean that they understand the condition or treat it effectively.

IBS is a well-recognized but unexplained set of symptoms—medical science knows what is happening but not exactly why. A diagnosis isn't made by detecting telltale biochemical or structural changes unique to IBS—it's made after other digestive disorders, such as colorectal cancer and inflammatory bowel disease, have been ruled out.

At that point, the typical doctor offers a predictable prescription—eat more fiber, drink more water, get more exercise, reduce stress.

While that regimen may work for some, it fails many because it overlooks a common but often ignored trigger of IBS—food hypersensitivity.

TRIGGER FOODS

To understand food hypersensitivity, you first need to understand what it is not—a food allergy. Food allergies are relatively rare, affecting 1% to 2% of the adult population. The ingested food attracts the immune system's immunoglobulin E (IgE) antibodies, which identify the food as "foreign" and attack it, sparking the release of histamine and cytokines, inflammatory chemicals that cause tissue to swell, eyes to tear, skin to itch and other allergic symptoms. Eggs, milk, nuts, shellfish, soy and wheat are common allergy-causing foods.

Food hypersensitivity involves other antibodies, such as IgA, IgG and IgM. Their attack isn't immediate—it can occur hours or days after eating an offending food and cause bloating, cramping, constipation and/or diarrhea.

What to do: For one week, eat an "elimination diet" consisting solely of foods that almost never cause hypersensitivity—fruits (except citrus), vegetables (except tomatoes, eggplant, white potatoes and peppers), white rice, fish and chicken. You can use olive and safflower oils. If after seven days you are symptom-free, food hypersensitivity is triggering your IBS. *Follow these steps…*

Step 1: Reintroduce one category of food every two to three days. Start with one of the foods that together account for 80% of food hypersensitivity—beef, citrus, dairy products, eggs, pork and wheat. For two days, stay on the elimination diet and eat as much of the reintroduced food as you like.

If IBS symptoms return, you have detected a hypersensitivity. Stop eating the offending food, and wait until symptoms disappear to reintroduce another food.

If you don't get symptoms, try the next food after the two days of eating the previous one. Repeat this process, reintroducing foods one by one.

Step 2: For the next six months, avoid all foods that caused IBS during the elimination testing. This will help your bowel heal.

Step 3: After the six months, you can try a "rotation diet"—reintroduce the offending foods (as long as they don't cause symptoms), but eat any offending food no more than once every four days. Now that your digestive tract is healed, you may be able to handle small amounts of the offending foods.

Also helpful: Digestive enzyme supplements can help reduce gas and bloating. Effective products include Tyler Enterogenics…Transformation Enzymes DigestZyme and TPP Digest…Enzymedica Digest and Digest Gold…and Enzymatic Therapy Mega-Zyme. These products are available at most health-food stores and many drugstores.

INFECTIONS

Food hypersensitivity triggers 50% to 75% of all cases of IBS. Another 25% or so is caused by infections.

Research: Israeli doctors studied 564 travelers. While traveling, people are more likely to be exposed to new microbes that can cause diarrhea. Those who developed traveler's diarrhea were five times more likely to later develop IBS. In reviewing eight studies, American scientists found a seven times higher risk of IBS among those who had infections in the gastrointestinal tract.

What to do: See your doctor—he/she can perform tests to detect abnormal bacteria, fungi and parasites, and prescribe the appropriate treatment.

NATURAL REMEDIES

Supplements to help relieve IBS symptoms…

• **For diarrhea.** Probiotic supplements provide friendly intestinal bacteria that can help restore normal bowel function. Saccharomyces boulardii is an unusual probiotic—it's yeast, not bacteria—but doctors have used it for decades to control diarrhea effectively.

Look for a product called Florastor or other probiotic brands containing the yeast. Take 250 milligrams (mg), three times a day. If that works, try twice a day and then once a day, finding the lowest dosage that works for you.

• **For constipation.** You've probably tried fiber supplements—and found that they didn't work. Instead, take a magnesium supplement, which naturally loosens bowels.

Use magnesium glycinate, starting with 300 mg a day. If that dosage doesn't work, increase the dose by 100 mg per day, until you develop diarrhea. Then cut back by 100 mg—to produce regular bowel movements.

Probiotic supplements can help as well (see above).

THE PROBLEM WITH MEDICATIONS

Doctors have tried a range of drugs for IBS—bulking agents for constipation, antidepressants to affect brain chemicals that play a role in digestion, spasmolytics to decrease cramping. A review by Dutch doctors of 40 studies on medications for IBS concluded, "The evidence of efficacy of drug therapies for IBS is weak."

The drugs also can be dangerous. In March 2007, the FDA pulled the IBS drug Zelnorm (tegaserod maleate) from the market when studies showed that it increased the risk for heart attack and stroke 10-fold.

Drug-Free Relief For Heartburn

Elaine Magee, MPH, RD, author of more than 26 books on nutrition and healthy cooking, including Tell Me What to Eat If I Have Acid Reflux (New Page). She is based in Northern California and writes the syndicated newspaper column "The Recipe Doctor." She serves as a nutrition expert for the WebMD Weight Loss Clinic. Her DVD, The Heartburn-Friendly Kitchen, is available on her Web site, www.recipedoctor.com.

Millions of Americans suffer from gastroesophageal reflux disease (GERD), the chronic backsplash of acid into the esophagus, more commonly known as acid reflux disease. Acid reflux can injure the lining of the esophagus and lead to complications, including a condition called Barrett's esophagus, which may lead to cancer.

Symptoms include a burning sensation behind the breastbone, hoarseness, cough, asthma, belching and bloating. Medication can soothe symptoms, but it doesn't cure reflux. *Here's what to do to prevent the condition in the first place...*

FOODS TO AVOID

It's essential to limit foods that promote stomach acid, but keep in mind that what bothers one person may not bother another and that a cup of coffee may be fine in the morning but risky in the afternoon. *Most common offenders...*

- **Fried or fatty foods**
- **Chocolate**
- **Peppermint and spearmint**
- **Garlic and onions**
- **Coffee and nonherbal tea, caffeinated and decaffeinated**
- **Carbonated beverages**
- **Tomatoes and citrus fruits**
- **Hot peppers and chili powder**

OTHER TRICKS

- **Chew gum for one hour after a meal.** A study from the Veteran Affairs Medical Center in New Mexico found that this reduced the time that acid was in contact with the esophagus.

- **Suck on lozenges.** This stimulates production of saliva, which bathes the esophageal lining. Some people find that eating sweet pickles also increases saliva.

- **Drink water regularly** to dilute stomach acid and wash acid from the esophagus.

- **Reduce fat content.** Steam, bake or broil instead of frying. Replace whole milk with 1% or skim.

- **Use caution with alcohol.** Small amounts— one drink a day or less—may aid digestion, speeding up the movement of acidic stomach contents into the intestines. Too much alcohol has the opposite effect—and some people report a particular problem with red wine.

- **Keep portions small.** A full stomach is more likely to cause heartburn.

- **Eat dinner early.** Don't have anything to eat within three hours of bedtime, so there will be nothing to splash up into the esophagus when you lie down.

- **Lose weight.** Extra pounds put pressure on stomach contents and push acid up toward the esophagus.

- **Raise the head of your bed by at least six inches**—you can put wood blocks under the top two legs of your bed—or try a wedge-shaped pillow.

• **Sleep on your left side.** Doctors at Philadelphia's Graduate Hospital found that people who sleep on their left sides experienced acid reflux less frequently than those who sleep on their right sides or backs.

Warning: See your doctor if you have heartburn more than twice a week.

Natural Therapies For Ulcers

James N. Dillard, MD, DC, in private practice, New York City and East Hampton, New York. He is a former assistant clinical professor at Columbia University College of Physicians and Surgeons and clinical director of Columbia's Rosenthal Center for Complementary and Alternative Medicine, both in New York City. *www.drdillard.com*

If you've got an ulcer, chances are you're taking an over-the-counter (OTC) antacid and/or prescription medication to neutralize gastric acid or inhibit its production. These medications include proton pump inhibitors (PPIs), such as *esomeprazole* (Nexium) and *lansoprazole* (Prevacid), and H2-blocking drugs, such as *cimetidine* (Tagamet) and *ranitidine* (Zantac).

What most people don't realize: There are several natural, complementary remedies that help reduce ulcer symptoms and promote healing while conventional treatment is under way. Some of these treatments also can help prevent ulcers in some patients.

WHAT CAUSES ULCERS

It's been more than 20 years since doctors learned that an infectious disease—rather than emotional stress—was the primary cause of most ulcers.

A screw-shaped bacterium, Helicobacter pylori, or H. pylori, burrows through the protective mucous lining in the small intestine and/or stomach, allowing harsh digestive fluids to accumulate and ulcerate the lining. About 50% of Americans over age 60 are infected with H. pylori. The bacterium doesn't always cause ulcers—but about 60% of patients with ulcers harbor H. pylori.

The remainder of ulcers are caused by regular use of stomach-damaging nonsteroidal anti-inflammatory drugs (NSAIDs), such as aspirin, *ibuprofen* (Advil) and *naproxen* (Aleve)…alcohol…and/or smoking. Excessive alcohol wears down the lining of the stomach and intestines. Nicotine causes the stomach to produce more acid.

Best complementary treatments…*

NONDRUG THERAPIES

• **Probiotics.** The intestine contains up to four pounds of "friendly" bacteria, which aid digestion. There's some evidence that maintaining adequate levels of beneficial bacteria helps create an inhospitable environment for H. pylori and makes it harder for this ulcer-causing bacterium to thrive.

Self-defense: Take a probiotic supplement that contains Lactobacillus acidophilus and Bifidobacterium bifidus. These organisms create a healthful mix of bacteria and can inhibit the growth of harmful organisms. Probiotics are helpful if you've taken antibiotics, which can kill off some beneficial bacteria.

The optimal dose for probiotics hasn't been determined. Preliminary research cites a daily dose of up to 10 billion organisms—the amount usually included in one to two capsules. Probiotics are available at health-food stores.

• **Cabbage juice.** This folk remedy has some evidence to support it. Cabbage is high in vitamin C, which seems to inhibit growth of H. pylori. It also contains glutamine, an amino acid that may strengthen the protective lining in the stomach.

A small Stanford University School of Medicine study found that ulcer patients who drank about a quart of cabbage juice daily healed significantly faster than those who didn't drink it.

Self-defense: If you have an active ulcer, consider drinking a quart of cabbage juice (about the amount in half a head of cabbage) once daily for up to two weeks.

*Check with your doctor before taking supplements. They can interact with prescription medications.

• **Deglycyrrhizinated licorice (DGL).** Herbalists often recommend fresh licorice root to heal ulcers. Licorice contains mucin, a substance that protects the stomach lining, and antioxidants that may inhibit H. pylori growth.

However, natural licorice can increase the effects of aldosterone, a hormone that promotes water retention and can increase blood pressure in some people. DGL supplements (available at health-food stores) are a better option, because the substances that increase blood pressure have been removed.

Self-defense: Take one DGL tablet before meals, and another before bed. DGL may be effective for people with ulcers whose H. pylori has been successfully treated with antibiotics but who still have some stomach irritation.

• **Vitamin A.** Vitamin A helps repair damaged mucous membranes. A report in the British medical journal *The Lancet* suggests that ulcers heal more quickly in patients given supplemental vitamin A.C

Caution: High-dose vitamin A therapy can be toxic, so get your vitamin A from dietary sources along with a daily multivitamin—not from a separate vitamin A supplement.

Self-defense: Get 10,000 international units (IU) of vitamin A daily if you're undergoing ulcer treatment. (A multivitamin typically contains 3,500 IU to 5,000 IU of vitamin A.)

Good food sources: Beef liver (one-and-one-half ounces contains 13,593 IU)…carrots (one raw carrot contains 8,666 IU)…and spinach (one cup of raw spinach contains 2,813 IU).

• **Zinc.** Like vitamin A, zinc is involved in tissue healing. In Europe, a drug compound made with zinc plus an anti-inflammatory is often used for treating ulcers. Early studies indicate that zinc alone can speed ulcer healing and possibly even help prevent some ulcers.

Self-defense: Don't exceed the recommended daily intake (15 mg) of zinc. Take a daily multivitamin that includes zinc…and get adequate intake from dietary sources (five medium fried oysters, 13 mg…3/4 cup fortified breakfast cereal, 15 mg…three-ounces lean beef tenderloin, 5 mg).

ANOTHER WAY TO FIGHT ULCERS

NSAIDs alleviate pain by inhibiting the production of pain-causing chemicals called prostaglandins. However, the body produces several kinds of prostaglandins, including some that protect the stomach lining. That's why NSAIDs, which block the production of pain-causing and stomach-protecting prostaglandins, make people who regularly use the drugs more susceptible to ulcers.

Self-defense: If you require regular pain relief, start with acetaminophen (Tylenol). It relieves pain without depleting stomach-protecting prostaglandins.

Caution: Taking more than the recommended dosage or drinking alcohol with acetaminophen can cause liver damage.

Also helpful: Ask your doctor about taking Arthrotec, a prescription drug combination that includes the NSAID diclofenac along with misoprostol, which protects the stomach and intestinal lining. One study found that patients taking Arthrotec experienced up to 80% fewer ulcers than those taking an NSAID alone.

Remedy for Gas

Mark A. Stengler, NMD, licensed naturopathic medical doctor and leading authority on the practice of alternative and integrated medicine. He is founder and medical director of the Stengler Center for Integrative Medicine, Encinitas, California. He is author of *The Natural Physician's Healing Therapies* (Bottom Line Books).

If you are using antacids and still having gas, ask your doctor if any of the drugs you take commonly cause flatulence or digestive upset. Gas may result when digestive bacteria fail to break down foods sufficiently. To fix this, stimulate stomach acid secretion with the herb gentian root. Take 10 to 20 drops of liquid extract (in one ounce of water) or 300 mg in capsule form about 10 minutes before meals. (Do not use gentian if you have an active ulcer.) Also take an equal dose of gingerroot, which acts as a carminative (gas-reducer) and improves stomach function.

For improved digestion, restore friendly bacteria to your digestive tract by eating sauerkraut, kefir and/or yogurt, or by taking a probiotic supplement that contains at least 5 billion colony-forming units (CFU) of lactobacillus acidophilus and/or bifidobacterium. If gassiness persists after three weeks, consult a holistic doctor for food-intolerance testing—you may have a sensitivity to dairy, grains or other foods.

Self-Defense For Flatulence

Anil Minocha, MD, professor of medicine and director of division of digestive diseases, University of Mississippi Medical Center, Jackson.

Diseases such as irritable bowel syndrome, Crohn's disease, ulcerative colitis and cancer can lead to excess gas and bloating. Certain medications, including calcium channel blockers, tricyclic antidepressants and narcotic-based painkillers, slow digestion and lead to excess gas. Diet changes, such as adding fiber to ease constipation, can create gas. Lactose intolerance leads to flatulence because lactose-laden foods are improperly digested. Loss of muscle tone around the anal sphincter and loss of elasticity of the valve itself can weaken control.

Self-defense: Limit intake of milk products, except for yogurt with active cultures, which consume much of the lactose during fermentation. Avoid carbonated beverages and foods that are heavy in carbohydrates, such as beans, brussels sprouts, broccoli and cauliflower. Also avoid foods that contain sugars such as fructose (including onions, artichokes, pears and wheat) and sorbitol (apples, peaches and prunes). Sorbitol also is used as an artificial sweetener, as is mannitol—both should be avoided. Eat slowly and chew food thoroughly. Consider taking Gas-X, sold over the counter.

What You May Not Know About Diarrhea

Douglas L. Seidner, MD, Center for Human Nutrition, Vanderbilt University Medical Center, Nashville, Tennessee.

Diarrhea—bowel movements that are looser and more frequent than usual—is the second most common medical complaint (after respiratory infections) in the US.

Most people associate a bout of diarrhea with a viral infection or food poisoning.

Now: Researchers are identifying new—and sometimes surprising—triggers, including the use of some medications.

Development: *The Journal of the American Medical Association* published a study that links the use of acid-lowering heartburn drugs, such as *omeprazole* (Prilosec), *lansoprazole* (Prevacid) and *ranitidine* (Zantac), to increased infection with the bacterium Clostridium difficile—a cause of severe and persistent diarrhea.

In an unexpected finding, the same researchers identified an association between diarrhea and regular use of nonsteroidal anti-inflammatory drugs (NSAIDs). More study is needed to confirm this NSAID-diarrhea link.

HOW DIARRHEA DEVELOPS

What's left of food after most of it has been digested reaches the large intestine as a sort of slurry. There, the body absorbs water from this material, creating a solid mass to be excreted. Normal stool is 60% to 90% water. Diarrhea occurs when stool is more than 90% water.

When stool does not remain in the large intestine long enough, it is excreted in a watery form. This "rapid transit" diarrhea can be caused by stress, overactive thyroid (hyperthyroidism) and certain drugs, such as antacids and laxatives that contain magnesium, and chemotherapy for cancer.

Other types of diarrhea...

• **Osmotic diarrhea** occurs when too much food remains undigested or unabsorbed. Water is drawn into the colon to dilute unabsorbed chemicals, which makes the stool looser.

Large amounts of certain fruits and beans as well as sugar substitutes (sorbitol and xylitol) that are used in some brands of fruit juice, chewing gum and candy are common causes of osmotic diarrhea. When the diarrhea sufferer stops eating the offending food, the condition stops.

Lactase deficiency—a lack of the enzyme needed to break down milk sugar (lactose)—is another cause of osmotic diarrhea. Most people know if they have this deficiency and avoid milk products.

Osmotic diarrhea also may develop in people taking antibiotics. That's because the drug eliminates beneficial bacteria that live in the intestinal tract, allowing harmful bacteria to proliferate. These microorganisms normally help the body process and absorb the small amount of food that hasn't been digested yet. Diarrhea usually develops within a few days of treatment. If it's bothersome enough, your doctor may prescribe a different antibiotic.

More rarely, diarrhea develops toward the end of antibiotic treatment—or even up to a month later. This may be caused by C. difficile or another bacterium that can flourish and cause inflammation of the large intestine when beneficial bacteria are eliminated.

Helpful: This infection is usually treated with the antibiotics vancomycin (Vancocin) or metronidazole (Flagyl).

• **Secretory diarrhea** occurs when an excessive amount of water, salt and digestive fluids are secreted into the stool. Viral infections, bacterial toxins that cause some types of food poisoning and rare tumors of the small intestine and pancreas can trigger the secretions that lead to secretory diarrhea.

With food poisoning, excess secretions are stimulated by chemicals produced by bacteria that have contaminated something you ate. This diarrhea usually lasts for 12 to 24 hours and stops without treatment. If it persists, your doctor may order tests, such as stool cultures, to determine whether a virulent bacterium, such as Salmonella, Shigella or Campylobacter, is involved and will require medication.

Travelers' diarrhea has a similar cause. The culprit is generally a mild strain of a toxin-producing bacterium, such as Escherichia coli, that is present in food and/or water. Natives of the region you're visiting have been exposed to the microorganism for years and usually are immune to it. You're not. Traveler's diarrhea typically goes away within one to two days.

Exudative diarrhea occurs when the large intestine's lining becomes inflamed. This triggers the release of blood, mucus, proteins and other fluids. Infection with the bacterium Shigella can cause this type of diarrhea. Crohn's disease (chronic inflammation of the small bowel or colon) and ulcerative colitis (chronic inflammation and ulceration of the colon) can also cause exudative diarrhea.

An antibiotic is sometimes used to treat a bacterial infection. Medication, such as the corticosteroid prednisone, and sometimes surgery are used to treat the inflammatory conditions.

BEST RELIEF STRATEGIES

In some cases, diarrhea can be a sign of a serious infection and should be treated by a doctor. *Even though most types of diarrhea run their course within a few days, the following steps can hasten the process and ease your discomfort...*

• **Eat right.** If food poisoning is the problem, you should abstain from all food until symptoms resolve, usually one to two days.

For other acute diarrhea, follow the "BRAT" diet: bananas, rice, applesauce and toast. Bananas and applesauce contain pectin, a water-soluble substance that helps firm up the stool...the carbohydrates in white rice and white toast are easy to digest. If you eat other foods, stick to small portions and avoid dairy products.

Yogurt is an exception. If it's made from live and active cultures, such as Lactobacillus bulgaricus and Streptococcus thermophilus, yogurt may replace beneficial bacteria in the colon, helping to relieve antibiotic-related diarrhea.

When the diarrhea subsides, return to your normal diet cautiously. For the first few days, avoid fatty foods (they're harder to digest).

357

Important: Drink 64 ounces of fluids daily to replace what you're losing. Choose weak tea, water and/or small amounts of clear juice or soda, such as apple juice or ginger ale.

If diarrhea is severe: Drink "replacement fluids," such as CeraLyte, Pedialyte or Enfalyte. These contain salt and simple sugars that help the body retain water. Diarrhea-related dehydration isn't a danger for most adults, but it is a danger for children and many adults over age 65. Young children do not have as large of a reserve of water in the body as healthy adults. Older adults may have heart disease or kidney disease, which can be exacerbated by dehydration.

• **Medication.** Several over-the-counter preparations can help relieve diarrhea…

• *Loperamide* (Imodium) is a semi-synthetic narcotic that slows food as it passes through the bowel, allowing more time for water to be absorbed. Try loperamide if diarrhea is mild and hasn't been resolved in one to two days. It should not be taken if you have a fever or the stools are bloody.

• *Bismuth subsalicylate* (Pepto-Bismol, Kaopectate) absorbs toxins—it's quite effective for traveler's diarrhea. It should not be taken with aspirin. Do not take it if you have a fever or bloody stools. Children should not take this product.

Constipation: Get the Whole Story

Norton J. Greenberger, MD, clinical professor of medicine at Harvard Medical School and a senior physician at Brigham and Women's Hospital, both in Boston. He is a former president of the American Gastroenterological Association and coauthor, with Roanne Weisman, of *Four Weeks to Healthy Digestion* (McGraw-Hill).

Constipation is one of those ailments that most people think they know how to treat—the majority believe that simply eating more fiber is the answer. But this often doesn't work.

What few people realize: Chronic constipation can have some very surprising causes… and dietary changes alone help only about one-third of those with the condition. What's more, if overused, some of the same laxatives that relieve constipation initially can exacerbate it in the long run, so most people need additional help to really get rid of their constipation.

WHAT'S NORMAL?

Most people have one to three bowel movements daily, while others have as few as three a week. This variability is normal.

What's more important are changes in bowel habits, particularly if you're having fewer bowel movements than usual and also are experiencing other symptoms that could indicate a more serious problem—such as blood in stool (colon cancer)…unexplained weight loss (diabetes or colon cancer)…or weight gain (low thyroid function).

The first step: Even though not all people with constipation will improve by eating a fiber-rich diet, it's still wise to start by eating more fruits, vegetables, legumes and whole grains that are high in fiber. In general, people who consume 20 g to 35 g of dietary fiber daily—and who exercise regularly—are less likely to suffer from constipation than those who mainly eat a meat-and-potatoes diet.

Examples of fiber sources: One cup of oatmeal or a bran muffin provides 4 g to 5 g of fiber.

Helpful: Be sure to eat the vegetables and fruits that are most likely to draw water into the stool to facilitate soft, bulky bowel movements.

Best vegetables to ease constipation: Those in the Brassica family, such as broccoli, asparagus, Brussels sprouts, cauliflower and cabbage.

Best fruits to ease constipation: Peaches, pears, cherries and apples (or apple juice).

If your constipation doesn't improve within a few weeks, then…

1. Check your medications. Many prescription and over-the-counter medications slow intestinal movements and cause constipation. Narcotic painkillers, such as *oxycodone*

(OxyContin) and the combination of *acet-aminophen* and *oxycodone* (Percocet), are among the worst offenders. Tricyclic antidepressants, such as *amitriptyline*, also can cause it. So can medications that treat high blood pressure (calcium channel blockers) and Parkinson's disease.

Helpful: Constipation also can be triggered by the antihistamines used in allergy medications, such as *cetirizine* (Zyrtec) and *diphenhydramine* (Benadryl), if used daily. Lowering the dose of an antihistamine drug or taking it less often may reduce constipation.

2. Get your magnesium and potassium levels tested. Most people get sufficient amounts of both minerals in their diets. But if you take a daily diuretic or laxative or have an intolerance to gluten (a protein found in wheat, barley and rye), you may be deficient. Low magnesium or potassium decreases the strength of intestinal contractions—this may contribute to diarrhea or constipation.

Important: If constipation doesn't improve within a month of boosting your fiber intake, see your doctor. The problem could be due to a deficiency of either or both minerals. If a blood test shows that you have low magnesium and/or potassium, supplements can restore normal levels within a week or two (ask your doctor for the appropriate dosage).

3. Be cautious with calcium. High-dose calcium often causes constipation, particularly in people who take antihistamines or other drugs that slow intestinal transit time (how long it takes food to pass through the bowel).

My advice: Get most of your calcium from calcium-rich foods. If your constipation is related to high-dose calcium supplements, talk to your doctor about limiting the supplement dose to 500 mg to 1,000 mg daily—and be sure to eat plenty of high-fiber foods and drink lots of fluids.

4. Drink at least two quarts of fluids daily—more if you exercise or engage in activities that cause you to perspire heavily. Drinking this much fluid increases lubrication and makes stools larger, which helps them pass more easily (and frequently). Water is best—it has no calories and usually is the most readily available fluid.

5. Avoid laxatives. Some of the most popular products actually can increase constipation. So-called stimulant laxatives, such as Dulcolax and castor oil, cause the intestinal muscles to stretch and weaken with continued use. People who use these products frequently may become dependent—they can't have a bowel movement without them.

Important: It's fine to use these products occasionally—when, for example, you haven't had a bowel movement for several days and are feeling uncomfortable. But if you use them more than once or twice a week, it's too much. Talk to your doctor about healthier methods such as those described in this article.

6. Relax and reregulate. If you get enough fiber and drink enough fluids but still are constipated, see your doctor. You may have a type of constipation known as dyssynergic defecation (different parts of the anorectal area—pertaining to the anus and rectum—contract and relax at the wrong time).

This type of constipation can be diagnosed by giving patients oral radiopaque markers that allow the doctor to view intestinal movements on an abdominal X-ray. Normally, people initiate a bowel movement by instinctively contracting the upper part of the rectum while relaxing the lower part. People with dyssynergic defecation constipation often do the opposite. Stools aren't propelled through the colon, or they get "hung up" due to inappropriate muscle movements.

People with this type of constipation usually are referred to a gastroenterologist, who often uses biofeedback, along with exercises such as Kegels (a type of pelvic-muscle exercise), to help them learn to relax and contract different parts of the anorectal area. They're also taught not to strain during bowel movements—this decreases the force of intestinal contractions and impairs one's ability to have a bowel movement.

When You Should Worry About Constipation And Diarrhea

Andrew L. Rubman, ND, medical director, Southbury Clinic for Traditional Medicines, Southbury, Connecticut. *www.naturopath.org*

Bowel movements are hardly the stuff of polite dinner table conversation, so it's not surprising that many people don't know exactly what healthy, normal bowel habits are. The reality is that "normal" varies from person to person.

And whatever normal is, it needs to stay that way in order for you to avoid other health challenges down the road. What changes might be worrisome?

NORMAL OR NOT?

Bowel movements vary in their degree of regularity, color, texture, odor and difficulty. It can be normal to have three a day or as few as three a week. The normal, healthy stool color is dark butterscotch, says Andrew L. Rubman, ND, but that can be affected by what you eat—especially if you had spinach or beets, for instance. The shape should be something like a sausage—soft but solid…relatively easy to pass…and emerging in one nearly continuous movement, as the different segments of the colon consecutively empty.

CONSTIPATION AND DIARRHEA— WHEN TO WORRY

Constipation and diarrhea are the most common complaints, affecting most people from time to time, and not particularly worrisome on an occasional basis. You qualify as constipated if you have fewer than three bowel movements a week, with stools that are hard, dry and difficult to pass. There's often related abdominal discomfort and bloating as well. Dehydration, inadequate dietary fiber and a lack of exercise are the usual causes, according to Dr. Rubman.

As many people already know, you can help move matters along by eating more fiber-rich foods (e.g., whole grains, vegetables and fruits) and fewer processed foods. Various fiber supplements may also be helpful. Discuss with your doctor what type you should take. Exercising about 30 minutes most days of the week will also help ease constipation.

Diarrhea refers to loose, watery stools more than three times in a day. It's usually temporary—perhaps caused by food, antibiotics or the stomach flu—and typically clears on its own without treatment. In the meantime, good foods to eat include bananas, rice, applesauce and toast (called the BRAT diet) and Dr. Rubman also recommends egg drop soup, since diarrhea depletes not only water but salt and albumin (protein) as well. Consult your doctor if diarrhea persists longer than three days…if you become dehydrated…or you see blood, frothiness or large amounts of mucus.

WHAT CHANGES DO YOU NEED TO REPORT?

Occasional digestive disturbances are part of life, but if you notice significant changes in regularity, color, texture or experience difficulty in passing stool for longer than a few weeks, it's time to take notice. Dr. Rubman suggests keeping a journal to help you identify what is different, including dietary factors, and advises seeing your doctor. Such changes may signal any of a number of digestive challenges—e.g., hemorrhoids, irritable bowel syndrome, ulcerative colitis or colorectal cancer (especially if you're 50 or older). In particular, always call your doctor if you see blood in the stool. Any abnormal color that lasts more than a few days and can't be traced to something you ate is a reason to call your doctor—most especially if it is accompanied by other symptoms, such as abdominal pain or unexplained weight loss. The earlier you diagnose and address any gastrointestinal disorder, the more successful the treatment.

KEEP YOUR DIGESTIVE TRACT ON TRACK

To keep digestion on the right track, Dr. Rubman advises that you watch your diet and get regular exercise…avoid prolonged use of antacids or anti-inflammatory drugs such as ibuprofen, naproxen or aspirin…refrain from alcohol or tobacco use…chew food thoroughly …and limit water with meals. If you notice changes or are concerned about any symptoms, a naturopathic physician, specially trained and attuned to digestive issues, will be able to examine the state of your digestive function by ordering diagnostic tests, recommending diet and lifestyle changes and prescribing medicines, such as nutrients in which you are deficient. If necessary, he/she will refer you to a gastroenterologist for further treatment.

Constipation Solution?

Leo M. Galland, MD, founder and director, Foundation of Integrated Medicine, New York City. His Web site, *www.pilladvised.com*, has a free online database of information about drug/supplement/food interactions.

If you don't know much (or anything) about prebiotics—with an "e"—you are far from alone. Many people don't know the difference between prebiotics and their better known cousins, probiotics…so we decided to explain more about how both can be used to optimize digestive health and boost immunity. We placed a call to a medical doctor who also is highly active and respected in the world of natural medicine, Leo M. Galland, MD.

PREBIOTICS—WHAT PROBIOTICS EAT

Your high school Latin provides an easy and obvious way to differentiate prebiotics from probiotics—focus on the "pre." Prebiotics are the predecessor. Their primary purpose is to provide nourishment to probiotics, thus helping to sustain a healthy level of these good bacteria in the gut.

Research has shown prebiotics to be beneficial for people with Crohn's disease and ulcerative colitis. Prebiotics can serve as a natural remedy to ease constipation, and they can be helpful for a number of other digestive complaints, including constipation-associated irritable bowel syndrome (IBS) and some cases of inflammatory bowel disease. Prebiotics also help absorption of calcium and magnesium in people who have low mineral levels in their diets, and there's some evidence that they might help prevent colon cancer as well.

Unlike probiotics, prebiotics are not bacteria—they're a form of soluble fiber that can be found in a few complex carbohydrates. What makes them unique is their ability to pass unabsorbed through the small intestine, which makes them available to feed tissue and probiotics in the large intestine. One of the most common prebiotics is a kind of complex fructose polymer found in some plant foods called inulin (which, in spite of the similarity in names, has nothing to do with insulin). There are other kinds, too, including non-inulin prebiotics and a type called fructo-oligo-saccharides (or FOS).

ARE DIETARY SOURCES SUFFICIENT?

Some foods are rich sources of prebiotics. For instance, inulin can be found in generous amounts in Jerusalem artichokes (a potato-like tuber)…chicory…jicama…and dandelion. And many common foods contain lesser amounts of inulin and/or FOS, such as onions, garlic, leeks, bananas, tomatoes, spinach and whole wheat.

Since prebiotics aren't abundant in these foods, it can be useful to take prebiotic supplements if you have certain types of problems.

Dr. Galland prescribes prebiotic supplements for many of his patients, he told me, noting that a typical dose can range from 4 grams to 8 grams. They come in various forms, including powders and capsules. *He often prescribes…*

- **Extracts of Jerusalem artichokes or extracts of chicory,** best for chronic constipation.
- **FOS extracted from fruits and grains,** which can be helpful for constipation and colitis.
- **Non-inulin prebiotics, which include oat beta-glucan**—a soluble fiber that is separated from oats to make supplements. These have the additional benefit of lowering cholesterol. Oat beta-glucan is less likely to cause gas or bloating than inulin and can be excellent for boosting immune function, Dr. Galland said.

START SLOWLY AND
TALK TO YOUR DOCTOR

Since this is all fairly complex, it is important to consult with a physician who has expertise in treating patients with prebiotic supplements. If you and your doctor agree that prebiotics may be helpful to you, plan to start slowly and increase the dosage gradually, or your body may overrespond to added prebiotics, Dr. Galland cautions. "Let your GI tract get used to the prebiotics and shift the bacteria slowly," he said. Stop taking them if you notice an upset stomach, gas, diarrhea, bloating and other uncomfortable digestive symptoms that don't dissipate within a few days.

A group that is especially likely to experience such difficulties, Dr. Galland said, is people with inflammatory bowel disease—as well as some folks with other types of digestive problems. Why? While the prebiotics are not themselves irritating, they may increase production of irritants by stimulating the growth of beneficial intestinal bacteria, Dr. Galland explained.

Note: Unpleasant as it may be, this actually may be a sign that the prebiotics are beginning to do their job.

Some people should avoid prebiotics altogether, including people who have fructose malabsorption, a limited ability to absorb fructose (including that found in inulin-based prebiotic supplements and inulin-containing foods such as Jerusalem artichokes). If you have this problem, you may experience gastrointestinal problems (gassiness, bloating, diarrhea) that get worse and worse if you take prebiotics. Don't know whether this might apply to you? Here's a clue. People with fructose malabsorption are very likely to get gassy and/or bloated or have diarrhea if they consume the sweeteners sorbitol or xylitol, because these are fermented by the same bacteria that ferment inulin.

Suffering from Constipation? How to Keep Things Moving

Brian Lacy, MD, PhD, director of the gastrointestinal motility lab, Dartmouth-Hitchcock Medical Center, Lebanon, New Hampshire, and associate professor of medicine, Dartmouth Medical School, Hanover, New Hampshire.

The word "constipation" comes from the Latin meaning "to press or crowd together." And that's just what happens in this common digestive disorder—stool becomes hard and compressed...and/or difficult to expel from the body. There are traditional remedies—some of which can work in the right circumstances—and there's also a new drug that has been created to help with chronic constipation.

We all get constipation sometimes. *Here's what you need to know to remedy constipation and keep it from becoming chronic...*

WHAT'S NORMAL?

While most people think of constipation as the inability to have a daily bowel movement, the definition is broader than that. Studies show that the "normal" frequency of bowel movements varies. Some people may have more than one bowel movement per day, while others may routinely have a bowel movement every couple of days. I generally consider someone constipated if he/she typically goes three or four days between bowel movements. On the other hand, you may have a daily bowel movement that involves lengthy straining—which also qualifies as constipation.

While constipation can cause discomfort and may affect your quality of life, it doesn't pose a health threat in and of itself. Until recently, it had been thought that infrequent bowel movements could increase the risk for colorectal cancer. But a recent large-scale study in Japan found that only very infrequent bowel movements (every 10 to 14 days) could increase the risk. Some of the main health risks associated with constipation arise from the physical stress of passing hard stools—which may cause hemorrhoids and, in some cases, a fissure or tearing of the rectum.

CAUSES OF CONSTIPATION

Most people experience constipation as a temporary condition brought on by a change in diet...medication (constipation can be caused by narcotic pain relievers, high-dose iron supplements and some blood-pressure drugs)...or travel (when you are thrown off your routine, not following your normal diet or not able to make regular bathroom visits). For this group, self-treatment with an over-the-counter laxative will usually restore regular bowel function.

For others, constipation is chronic—it does not go away. *The two main causes of chronic constipation are...*

• **Irritable bowel syndrome (IBS).** This occurs when the nerves and muscles of the colon fail to function properly. It accounts for 30% to 40% of all chronic constipation and is usually associated with bloating and pain in the lower abdomen.

• **Pelvic floor dysfunction.** This condition accounts for another 30% to 40% of chronic constipation. More common in women than men, it occurs when the muscles and nerves in the pelvic floor (the muscles under the pelvis) aren't coordinating properly. Constipation due to pelvic floor dysfunction won't respond to laxatives but can usually be cured through physical therapy.

Chronic constipation also can result from other disorders including neurological disorders (such as Parkinson's, multiple sclerosis and stroke)...metabolic and endocrine conditions (such as diabetes and an underactive thyroid)...and systemic disorders (such as lupus or scleroderma). A problem in the colon, such as diverticulosis or cancer, can also cause constipation, although this is not common.

Whatever the cause, constipation becomes much more prevalent over age 65, and women are more likely than men to become constipated.

TREATMENTS THAT WORK

For occasional constipation or constipation due to IBS, the first line of treatment involves establishing a regular bathroom schedule, dietary changes and over-the-counter medications. *What to do...*

• **Establish a regular bathroom schedule.** A wave of motility goes through everyone's GI tract around 5 am, which is why many people feel the urge to have a bowel movement in the morning. A similar wave occurs after eating. I encourage my patients to listen to their bodies and to arrange for scheduled bathroom times that coincide with their urges to have bowel movements. Give yourself three to four weeks to adjust to this schedule.

• **Add fiber to your diet.** Dietary fiber speeds movement of food through the GI tract and binds with water, causing stools to become bulkier and pass out of the colon more easily. Optimal fiber intake is 25 to 30 grams a day, but the average American consumes less than half this amount.

Solution: Eat more high-fiber foods, such as legumes (split peas, lentils, black beans, lima beans, baked beans, etc.), fresh fruits and vegetables (artichokes, raspberries, pears, broccoli), whole-wheat pasta and cereals and other foods containing whole bran or oats. You can also boost fiber intake with supplements, such as *psyllium husk powder* (Metamucil, Serutan) or *methylcellulose* (Citrucel). It may take three or four days to notice positive effects.

• **Try an over-the-counter laxative.** If regular bathroom visits and additional fiber don't solve the problem, add an over-the-counter laxative. There are different types—for example, osmotic, which draw water into the area, or lubricant, which help stools move more easily. Milk of magnesia is a safe, effective and inexpensive choice. To avoid elevated magnesium levels, however, it shouldn't be taken for longer than two weeks—and should be avoided by anyone with kidney disease. Miralax, another laxative, also is safe and effective for seven days, but some people don't like mixing the powder. Stimulant laxatives, such as *bisacodyl* (Dulcolax), have been shown to improve constipation with short-term use, though they may cause cramping. After two weeks, however, the body develops a tolerance to them. If your constipation is not improved within two weeks, consult your doctor.

Not recommended: Stool softeners. These popular laxatives are a waste of money. They are supposed to work by drawing water into the stool, making it softer and easier to pass. But they bulk up stool by only 3%—not enough to make any difference in your bowel movements.

Also not helpful: Exercise. While regular physical activity is beneficial in many ways, studies have shown conclusively that it has no effect on chronic constipation.

WHEN TO SEEK MEDICAL HELP

Most people are helped by the steps above. But if you see no improvement after several weeks, ask your primary care doctor for a prescription-strength laxative. An osmotic agent called *lactulose* (Chronulac, Constilac)—which is made of sugar molecules that make the gut more acidic and causes more water to be drawn in—makes bowel movements easier. Although side effects can include gas and bloating, people can take lactulose indefinitely. There is also a new medication for chronic constipation called *lubiprostone* (Amitiza) that has been found to be safe and effective. It is the first medication for constipation that works by stimulating intestinal fluid secretions that help the bowels move. Most patients prefer lubiprostone because it comes in a pill, not a sugary drink (like lactulose) and because there is no bloating.

If these prescriptions drugs still don't help, there may be an underlying condition that is causing the problem and you may need to see your primary care provider or a gastroenterologist for testing. This may include a *complete blood count* (CBC) test to make sure that you are not anemic and a *thyroid-stimulating hormone* (TSH) test to make sure that you do not have an underactive thyroid gland. This visit should also include a physical exam to check for pelvic floor dysfunction or any neuromuscular disorder. Since constipation can sometimes be a sign of colon cancer, a colonoscopy may be recommended.

Lastly, some patients with severe constipation swallow a capsule with markers to determine how quickly the markers pass through the gastrointestinal tract.

If pelvic floor dysfunction is detected, the patient will be referred to a physical therapist for a series of specific exercises for the pelvic floor and surrounding muscles.

If the constipation still doesn't improve and is seriously affecting quality of life, the last resort is a surgical procedure, called a colectomy, in which the colon is removed and the small intestine connected directly to the rectum. While this relieves constipation, it also results in frequent bowel movements—up to four per day.

Natural Ways to Improve Digestive Health

Jamison Starbuck, ND, naturopathic physician in family practice Montana, Missoula. She is past president of the American Association of Naturopathic Physicians and a contributing editor to *The Alternative Advisor: The Complete Guide to Natural Therapies and Alternative Treatments* (Time-Life).

Though sometimes overlooked by doctors, gastrointestinal (GI) health is fundamental to overall wellness. The GI tract, also known as the "gut," allows us to draw nourishment from our food and eliminate toxins. A variety of medications claim to promote intestinal health, but I prefer my own eight-step natural approach, which is both inexpensive and easy to follow. Add one new step each day. If you're like most people, your GI tract will be healthier within two weeks. *My advice...*

1. Avoid foods that cause indigestion. Indigestion is your body's way of telling you that a certain food is not readily digestible. Instead of trying to make a food digestible by taking drugs, choose foods that you can easily digest, such as fish, brown rice and steamed vegetables.

2. Shortly after awakening in the morning, drink an eight-ounce glass of room-temperature water. This "wakes up" the GI tract, preparing you for both digestion and elimination. Repeat this step five to 10 minutes before each meal. Avoid iced beverages, including water, with meals and 15 minutes before and afterward. Some research suggests that cold beverages decrease the secretion of digestive enzymes.

3. Squeeze fresh lemon or sprinkle vinegar on your food. For most people, one-half teaspoon of lemon or vinegar per meal fights indigestion by increasing stomach acidity and improving the digestion of fats.

4. Take a 15-minute walk after meals. Doing so will improve your digestion and elimination. If you can't do this after every meal, do so following the largest meal of the day.

5. Practice simple home hydrotherapy. This practice increases blood flow to your intestines, which helps them function properly.

What to do: Finish your daily shower or bath with a 30-second spray of cool or cold water to your entire abdomen. Towel dry with brisk strokes immediately after the cool water spray.

Caution: If you have a history of stroke, check with your doctor before trying hydrotherapy.

6. Drink chamomile or peppermint tea after dinner. These herbs soothe the lining of the stomach and intestines. Add one tea bag or two teaspoons of loose herb to eight ounces of water.

7. Use foot reflexology to relieve intestinal pain. Massaging reflexology points on the feet is thought to help increase blood flow to and improve the function of corresponding organs or body parts.

What to do: Whenever you have GI discomfort, firmly massage (for five to seven minutes) with your thumb and forefinger the outside portion of the middle one-third of the soles of the feet. According to reflexologists, this area corresponds to the colon. Your strokes should move toward the heel.

8. Never eat when you are stressed. Our bodies are not designed to simultaneously manage both stress and digestion. Studies show that just a few moments of relaxation, such as deep breathing or prayer, before a meal will improve the digestive process.

How to Prevent and Treat Transient Nausea

Sonja Pettersen, NMD, licensed in Arizona and Oregon to practice primary care medicine specializing in natural therapeutics. Her practice exemplifies a holistic approach to patient care through a variety of modalities, including clinical nutrition, botanical medicine and IV therapy, homeopathy, functional medicine and mind-body techniques.

I t is hardly uncommon to get a little queasy once in a while. We asked Sonja Pettersen, NMD, why transient nausea happens and what we can do about it.

"Almost anything—from a headache to an antibiotic—can make you temporarily nauseated," she told us. "But when there is no obvious cause, it frequently comes down to low stomach acid." According to Dr. Pettersen, when you have chronically low stomach acid you can get almost any symptom in the body, from a headache to poor skin...and of course, transient nausea. Low stomach acid can occur for a number of reasons, but the worst offenders are a high sugar (refined carbohydrate) diet...stress...and the use of acid-suppressing and/or neutralizing medications. When a meal enters your acid-impaired stomach you experience incomplete digestion of your food...ingested organisms that would otherwise be killed by stomach acid are able to survive...and fermentation of slowly digesting food results in an inflammatory response. Any and all of these processes are instigators of nausea.

Dr. Pettersen also pointed out that frequent nausea is highly related to sluggish or inadequate function of the gall bladder, which in turn is usually related to chronic stomach problems (impaired digestion, feeling overly full) and/or age and poor diet. She told me that in elderly people, constipation and dehydration are also common causes of nausea since they, too, are connected to the digestive process...and when that is out of whack anywhere along the line, nausea can develop.

NAUSEA SELF-DEFENSE

What to do? Prepare the stomach for the meal to come. "This used to be the purpose of an *aperitif* or an appetizer. By having the diner relax, think about and smell food, the system has a chance to anticipate what's coming," Dr. Pettersen said, "but we don't prepare for eating anymore. We just pull up to a drive-in window. That could be part of the problem."

Dr. Pettersen often prescribes HCl (hydrochloric acid) in pill form, usually bound to a common material called *betaine*, derived from the common beet, to be taken with meals as a way to ensure thorough digestion. She also likes ginger root in fresh, dried or capsule form, taken before the meal, as a way to get digestive juices flowing. "You can cut up fresh ginger and steep it in warm water and sip it," she told me. "Lemon juice squeezed fresh into warm water also does the job very well." Sip the ginger or lemon beverage, or her favorite—apple cider vinegar (1 tablespoon with a little warm water)—about 15 minutes before a meal. "It's not fully understood how it works, but I suspect it helps prepare the digestive tract and gets digestive juices as well as blood flowing," she told me.

NAUSEA FIRST AID

While these strategies are helpful for preventing nausea, we asked *Daily Health News* consulting medical editor, Andrew L. Rubman, ND, what to do when nausea strikes.

His response: "It depends on when it occurs."

If nausea occurs between meals, the fiber supplement *glucomannan* with a glass of sparkling water often works. If nausea occurs during a meal, digestive enzymes, particularly the betaine HCl described above, can help. If, however, nausea occurs an hour or more after a meal, it can be a sign of gall bladder disease or duodenitis. These conditions should always be addressed with a physician.

Of course, especially for frequent sufferers, it is important to have gastric pathology ruled out—and as always to have all interventions overseen by someone knowledgeable, such as your naturopathic physician. Read drug inserts of any medications you are taking, because it is a common drug side effect. It's fascinating to me that low stomach acid is at the root of so many common complaints and yet acid-suppressing medications continue to be top sellers. Maybe it's time to start doing something about it.

What Makes Us Burp—Surprising Reasons Why Certain Foods Cause It

Andrew L. Rubman, ND, director, Southbury Clinic for Traditional Medicines, Southbury, Connecticut.
National Digestive Diseases Information Clearinghouse, *http://digestive.niddk.nih.gov.*

The curious thing about burping is that certain foods seem to have a tendency to produce more gas than others. Which are the worst culprits? What causes excess gas? And, how can you avoid it? *Daily Health News* consulting medical editor Andrew L. Rubman, ND, director of the Southbury Clinic for Traditional Medicines in Connecticut, told us that burping has many causes, from difficult-to-digest foods, to eating too fast, to our favorite culprit for anything and everything—plain, old-fashioned stress. *Dr. Rubman offered a number of common-sense suggestions on how to prevent burping, before it becomes a problem...*

A NORMAL (IF EMBARRASSING) BODY FUNCTION

Everyone has gas, so everyone occasionally burps, since it is one of only two ways to get gas out. It's a normal body function. While we all swallow small amounts of air when eating or drinking, when we eat or drink too quickly, we take in too much air...and we burp (or belch). Chewing gum, talking while eating, smoking and loose dentures can also be at the root of troublesome burping, since all can result in excess air entering the stomach.

IT'S ALL ABOUT FOOD CHOICES

However, when that lasagna with meat comes back to visit an hour after you eat it, it is often not because you swallowed air, but due to gas and fermentation from what you ate—particularly in combination, explains Dr. Rubman. The most troublesome kind of food combination, says Dr. Rubman, is simple carbohydrates eaten with dense fats—think garlic bread and a well-marbled steak, or a bacon cheeseburger on a white bun...or lasagna with meat. Similarly, dessert (even fruit) eaten immediately following a fat-filled meal can cause fermentation, as the fat in the meal slows down digestion of the simple sugars in the dessert or refined carbohydrates, causing them to begin to react in your stomach. Not surprisingly, fried, fatty and processed foods present more of a challenge to the digestion than whole foods (e.g., fresh fish, steamed veggies and ripe fruits).

WHAT YOU CAN DO

An occasional burp is no big deal. Still, it's hardly the impression you want to make at a business dinner or on a date. The single most important thing you can do to avoid burping? Think about what you eat and drink, advises Dr. Rubman. If you eat fried clams followed by a hot fudge sundae, understand in advance that your body may make you pay a price for that choice, whether in burping, intestinal gas or a bellyache.

Other helpful strategies include…

• **Take it slow.** Try to eat at a leisurely pace, and chew food thoroughly. And, as mom always said, chew with your mouth closed.

• **Limit liquids with meals.** These dilute stomach acid, inhibiting digestion. The result is that the food ferments in your stomach, producing the CO2 that comes back up as a burp.

• **Monitor food combinations.** Don't combine simple carbs with high saturated fatty foods…eat fruits at least one half hour before meals…and skip dessert.

• **Forego the antacids.** Although they may help you feel better in the short run, insufficient stomach acid leads to insufficient digestion. You may be replacing a burp today with even more troublesome intestinal gas tomorrow.

• **No carbonated beverages.** They're made with CO_2, and therefore sure to generate a good belch.

• **Avoid chewing gum, hard candy, straws and smoking, all of which permit more air to enter the stomach.** If you smoke, here's yet one more good reason to quit.

• **If you wear dentures, check with your dentist to make certain they fit properly.** Poorly fitting dentures may cause you to take in air as you chew, which gets in the way of good digestion.

Gingerroot—Not Just For Cookies

Mark A. Stengler, NMD, licensed naturopathic medical doctor and leading authority on the practice of alternative and integrated medicine. He is founder and medical director of the Stengler Center for Integrative Medicine, Encinitas, California. He is author of *The Natural Physician's Healing Therapies* (Bottom Line Books).

For centuries, ginger (*Zingiber officinale*) has been widely valued as a medicinal herb. It is one of the most widely prescribed herbs by practitioners of Ayurvedic and Chinese traditional medicines. The botanical name for ginger is zingiber, which, in Sanskrit, means "shaped like a horn." Technically speaking, the root is actually a *rhizome*, a stem that runs underneath the surface of the ground.

It's most commonly used to treat digestive disorders and arthritis in all the healing traditions. It is known as a warming herb, especially suited to people with "cold constitutions," and it's said to enhance circulation. Chinese herbalists use fresh ginger to "warm the lung and stomach."

Ginger is prescribed in Chinese medicine for the common cold, flu, coughs, vomiting, nausea and general digestive upset and bleeding. It also reduces the toxicity of other herbs, so it's essentially an antidote to plants that might have side effects. Also, ginger can help protect an intestinal tract that has been ravaged by tainted or toxic food.

To practitioners of traditional Chinese medicine, every form of gingerroot has certain distinct properties. Fresh ginger has a warming effect on the exterior of the body, while the dried ginger is apt to be recommended for warming the middle of the body.

One of the more intriguing Chinese medicine cures is quick-fried ginger, which is made by frying ginger until the surface is slightly blackened. Practitioners say this is the type that's effective for stopping bleeding and treating conditions that affect the lower abdomen.

Today, ginger is used by herbalists and physicians to treat colds, arthritis, digestive conditions, respiratory-tract infections, headaches, motion sickness and cardiovascular disease.

As with many herbs, ginger has many different active constituents. Dried gingerroot contains between 1% and 4% volatile oils, which account for the strong taste and aroma. (The volatile oils include bisabolene, zingiberene and zingiberol.) Two of the pungent principles—gingerol and shogaol—are believed to be responsible for a lot of the medicinal effects.

Ginger also contains proteolytic enzymes that help to digest proteins and reduce inflammation. Many commercial products are standardized to the constituent gingerol.

DIGESTIVE POWER

Ginger has the unique ability to improve many organs that are involved with digestion. Known as an "aromatic bitter," it tonifies the intestinal muscles and stimulates the digestive organs. It also stimulates secretion of bile from the liver and gallbladder, which helps digest fats. Ginger is also a well-known carminative, meaning that it can reduce gas and bloating.

ANTI-INFLAMMATORY

Ginger acts as a natural anti-inflammatory by inhibiting the release of prostaglandins and other chemicals in the body that promote inflammation and pain. Unlike nonsteroidal medications such as aspirin, it does not have the potential to damage the stomach, liver and kidneys. For centuries, people used ginger as an anti-inflammatory without knowing how or why it worked. Modern tests have now proven the herb's anti-inflammatory powers.

CIRCULATION AND CARDIOVASCULAR HEALTH

Ginger promotes cardiovascular health by making platelets (cells responsible for blood clots) less likely to clump together. This preventive action allows the blood to keep flowing smoothly and helps prevent hardening of the arteries.

Studies have shown that this protective effect is achieved by inhibiting the formation of thromboxanes, substances that promote blood clotting. Other substances in ginger promote the synthesis of prostacyclin, a component that helps prevent platelets from "aggregating" or clumping together.

Animal studies have also shown that ginger improves the pumping ability of the heart.

Dosage: Fresh gingerroot can be made into tea. It's also sold in capsules, tablets, and tinctures. I have found all these forms to work with patients and myself.

The tea is relaxing and works well for digestive upset, as do the capsule and tincture forms. For the treatment of inflammatory conditions, I recommend a standardized capsule to get high levels of the active constituents that reduce inflammation.

The typical capsule dosage is 500 milligrams two to four times daily. If you're taking the tincture, I recommend 20 to 30 drops two to three times daily.

What are the side effects?: Side effects are rare with ginger, though some people (my wife among them!) report heartburn after taking it. In the short term, pregnant women can take ginger for nausea and vomiting related to morning sickness. One to two grams appear to be safe and effective.

Ginger stimulates bile production, so some herbal experts recommend that you should avoid this herb if you have gallstones.

Although I have seen no human studies on drug interactions and ginger, it theoretically may cause a problem with blood-thinning medications such as Coumadin. So check with your physician before using high doses of ginger if you are on a blood-thinning medication.

One last piece of advice you may not find in many books is that gingerroot by itself may aggravate those who are very warm-blooded. If you are the type of person who gets warm and sweats easily, then long-term use of ginger is not recommended just because it can cause discomfort by making you even warmer.

Recommendations for...

• **Arthritis.** Many herbal medicine experts mention that ginger is effective in treating arthritis, but in day-to-day treatment of patients, I have not found this to be true. Ginger by itself does not usually provide substantial relief. That said, however, it can be helpful to some people as part of a comprehensive herbal formula, such as practitioners of Chinese herbal formulas have created for patients with a "cold constitution."

• **Bloating and flatulence.** Ginger is the remedy par excellence for relieving bloating and flatulence, which is the common result of what I call SAD (Standard American Diet). It reminds me of one lady who came up to me after a talk, looked around to make sure no one else was listening, and asked if there was anything I could recommend for her 36-year-old son who was having trouble with a lot of gas. It turns out this son was newly married, and his mother was worried that his flatulence would cause marital problems.

I recommended she give her son a bottle of ginger capsules to use with meals. Hopefully it rescued the young groom from some embarrassment—or possibly saved the marriage!

●**Cardiovascular disease.** Since ginger is a natural blood thinner, it promotes good circulation and therefore improves cardiovascular health. Animal studies show that it helps with the pumping action of the heart. To me, it is most beneficial as a synergistic herb—one that makes other herbs more effective rather than working by itself.

●**Diarrhea.** There's a specific type of diarrhea, called "cold diarrhea" in Chinese medicine, that ginger seems to help significantly. This is the kind that gives you a case of the chills as well as loose stools. (What's called "hot diarrhea," as you might expect, is the kind where loose stools are accompanied by a feeling of feverishness.)

●**High cholesterol.** In animal studies, ginger has been found to lower cholesterol levels in rats. Unfortunately, it doesn't show exactly the same effect in humans. But if you're taking ginger for other conditions, there is a possibility that it could also help lower your cholesterol.

●**Morning sickness.** Ginger has actually been studied as a relief for severe morning sickness. In 19 of the 27 women who took ginger for nausea and vomiting, both symptoms became less frequent within four days of treatment. The dosage of gingerroot capsules was 250 milligrams taken 4 times daily.

Since publication of the earliest studies, which were done in 1990, many conventional doctors have started to recommend gingerroot for morning sickness. (My wife's obstetrician, for instance, recommends it to her patients.) However, I don't advise that women take more than one gram daily during pregnancy, and there's no reason to continue taking it after the morning sickness passes.

●**Motion sickness.** Ginger has received a lot of attention for its ability to prevent and treat motion sickness. A study in 1982 revealed that ginger was superior to the drug Dramamine for reducing motion sickness. Not every study, since then, has supported this finding, but some excellent research done in 1994—involving 1,741 people—confirmed that ginger was indeed very effective in treating motion sickness.

The 1994 study was done with a group of people who were taking a whale-watching trip. Before boarding the boat, people were asked to take various kinds of motion-sickness remedies, ginger among them. (None of the passengers knew which remedy they were being given.) The study showed that 250 milligrams of ginger was just as powerful as the pharmaceutical medications, but without side effects such as drowsiness.

●**Nausea and vomiting.** Bad food, flu, chemotherapy and surgical treatments are just a few of the possible causes of nausea and vomiting. No matter what the cause, however, ginger has been shown to be an effective remedy.

In two studies, ginger helped reduce nausea and vomiting in patients who had just undergone surgery where they received anesthesia. (Anesthesia makes some people very nauseated.) If you are scheduled to have surgery, talk with your surgeon about taking one gram of ginger before and after surgery.

The Right Way to Chew— It's Not as Simple as You Think

Karyn Kahn, DDS, staff member of the Head and Neck Institute in the dentistry department and consultant for craniofacial pain and jaw dysfunction at Cleveland Clinic, and associate professor at Case Western Reserve University School of Dentistry, both in Cleveland.

Mastication, or chewing, begins the digestive process and prepares food for swallowing. Front teeth cut and tear the food...back teeth crush and grind it, increasing its surface area so that digestion of carbohydrates can begin. *Be careful about chewing...*

●**Too little.** Often the result of eating too fast, this can cause choking or pain upon swallowing. Additionally, heartburn or stomach pain can occur because saliva's digestive enzymes don't have time to work. And because gobbling food inhibits the release of hormones that tell you when you're full, you may overeat.

Solution: Start with smaller bites, and use your molars more—you should barely feel food going down when you swallow.

To slow down: Put your fork down between bites, and take a deep breath after each swallow.

•**Too long.** Once a bite is ready to be swallowed, teeth should separate and not touch. Chewing past the point when the normal swallowing reflex occurs can overload jaw muscles, resulting in muscle pain and/or dysfunction. This is one reason why gum chewing—in which teeth touch during chewing—can lead to disorders of the temporomandibular joint (TMJ), or jaw joint.

•**On just one side of your mouth.** If you have a full set of teeth and a normal diet, having a favorite side on which to chew—as many people do—is not a problem.

But: If you wear full dentures, food must be distributed during the chewing process from one side of the mouth to the other to maintain the dentures' stability.

Important: If you avoid chewing on one side because it is painful, see your dentist.

Eight Simple Ways To Eat Better

Jamison Starbuck, ND, naturopathic physician in family practice in Missoula, Montana. She is past president of the American Association of Naturopathic Physicians and a contributing editor to *The Alternative Advisor: The Complete Guide to Natural Therapies and Alternative Treatments* (Time-Life).

If improving your diet has ever been a personal goal for you—or perhaps a New Year's resolution—I have good news. There are some very practical and simple steps you can take to reach this goal—and you don't have to make radical changes that are next to impossible to sustain.

Several years ago, a patient named Eugene asked me how he could improve his eating habits. As I told Eugene, the key is substituting a few healthful foods for some of the less nutritious items that most people eat. *My advice...*

1. Use plain, low-fat yogurt instead of milk, ice cream or sour cream. Yogurt offers all of the nutrition of milk plus the addition of beneficial bacteria that help improve digestion and nutrient absorption and fight overgrowth of yeast. Yogurt is an excellent choice for breakfast or a snack. It can be used on vegetables, in soup or as a healthful dessert. If you don't like the taste of plain yogurt, add your own honey, maple syrup, fresh fruit and/or nuts.

2. Replace iceberg lettuce with chopped red chard leaves. Iceberg lettuce provides few nutrients. By replacing it with red chard, you can add vitamin A, iron and fiber to your salads.

3. Try romaine lettuce leaves in place of bread. Romaine lettuce is firm enough to be filled with spreads or something more substantial, such as tuna or turkey. Simply roll up the leaf as you would a sandwich wrap. Romaine "sandwiches" will help you reduce calories, contribute to your daily fiber intake and improve your digestion.

4. Use sesame butter instead of peanut butter. Sesame butter is a richer source of calcium and healthful omega-3 fatty acids.

5. Substitute ground flaxseed for flour. Ground flaxseed is more nutritious than wheat flour and is a great source of fiber and a form of heart- and brain-healthy omega-3s. Add ground flaxseed to oatmeal or cereal or substitute ground flaxseed for one-third of the flour in recipes for muffins and breads.

6. Add a few bok choy leaves to soup. Like chard, bok choy is high in folic acid (needed for red blood cell formation) and iron—and the compounds that give the leafy, green vegetable its bitter quality aid digestion. To improve the nutritional value of even canned soup, sprinkle several coarsely chopped bok choy leaves on top when it's steaming hot and almost ready to eat. Cover and let simmer for four minutes.

7. Eat parsley regularly. It's rich in vitamin C, helps freshen your breath and reduces intestinal gas. Chop it up raw and add it to green salads or tuna. Or make a batch of parsley pesto (substitute parsley for some or all of the basil in a pesto recipe).

8. Go vegetarian one day a week. Use crumbled tempeh (fermented soy) instead of ground beef in chili or soups. Also, scramble tofu, instead of eggs, with onions and veggies for breakfast. Avoiding meat for just one day a week will help reduce your cholesterol levels.

Fabulous Flaxseeds

Mark A. Stengler, NMD, licensed naturopathic medical doctor and leading authority on the practice of alternative and integrated medicine. He is founder and medical director of the Stengler Center for Integrative Medicine, Encinitas, California, and associate clinical professor at the National College of Natural Medicine, Portland, Oregon. He is author of *The Natural Physician's Healing Therapies* (Bottom Line Books).

Flaxseeds are very healthy for you. There are three very important benefits that they provide…

• **Fiber,** which prevents and treats constipation and reduces blood glucose and cholesterol levels.

• **Lignans,** compounds that convert during digestion into hormonelike substances that may protect against breast and prostate cancers by preventing the cancer-promoting effects of estrogen.

• **Omega-3s,** fatty acids that reduce inflammation and promote heart, brain, joint and skin health.

Flaxseeds also provide copper to protect connective tissues…folate for normal cell division…magnesium to help the heart contract…manganese for joint health…phosphorous to strengthen bones…and vitamin B-6 to aid in liver detoxification. Flaxseed oil offers some but not all of the benefits of the seeds.

How to eat flaxseeds: To be digested properly, flaxseeds must be ground before being eaten. Grind seeds in a coffee grinder until flaky—about five seconds for the recommended daily serving of one to two tablespoons—or buy preground flaxseeds called flax meal.

To prevent cramps and constipation, always drink eight to 10 ounces of water when eating flaxseeds. (If you have the digestive disorder diverticulitis, ask your doctor before eating seeds.)

Choose a product in a vacuum-packed, resealable bag to prevent spoilage. Once opened, keep the bag in the refrigerator. Ground flaxseeds are delicious when added to cereals, salads and shakes. When cooking, substitute three tablespoons of ground flaxseeds for one tablespoon of butter…or replace each egg with one tablespoon of ground flaxseeds soaked in three tablespoons of water. Recipes for chicken, rice, baked goods and more can be found at *www.ameriflax.com.*

For a light, nutritious snack, try Golden Flax Crackers from Foods Alive (*www.foodsalive. com*), sold at health-food stores. They come in seven flavors, including onion/garlic and Mexican harvest.

My favorite: Maple and cinnamon.

The Healing Power of Herbal Teas

Brigitte Mars, adjunct professor of herbal medicine at Naropa University in Boulder, Colorado. She is the author of 12 books, including *Healing Herbal Teas* (Basic Health) and a professional member of the American Herbalist Guild (AHG).

Herbal teas, which are generally rich in vitamins, minerals and other healthful compounds, have been used as healing agents for thousands of years.

However, because of the prevalence of over-the-counter and prescription medications, most Americans don't think of drinking tea to treat common ailments. That's a mistake.

Dozens of scientific studies have supported the use of herbals for a wide variety of health problems.* Herbal teas have the same active ingredients as herbs sold in capsules, powders

*Check with your heath-care practitioner before drinking herbal tea, especially if you are a pregnant woman, nursing mother or have a chronic medical condition. Some herbal teas should not be combined with other drugs.

and extracts. Herbal teas also have fewer side effects than medication and can be much less expensive.

Loose tea herbs, which are available at health-food stores, tend to be more potent than tea bags. To prepare tea with loose herbs, use one heaping tablespoon of dried herb or three tablespoons of fresh herb in eight ounces of boiling water. Steep for 10 minutes.

For best results, drink four eight- ounce cups of herbal tea per day until the problem subsides. If you are age 65 or older, do not exceed three cups daily...or two cups daily if you are age 70 or older.

Best teas for treating some common health conditions...

COLDS AND FLU

Echinacea, which has an aromatic, earthy flavor, promotes white blood cell production...acts as an anti-infection agent...and stimulates the immune system.

How to use: Echinacea should be used for no more than 10 consecutive days, because it loses its effectiveness when taken continually. Drink echinacea tea at the onset of cold or flu symptoms, such as sore throat, sneezing and/or nasal congestion.

Caution: Echinacea stimulates the immune system, so people with autoimmune diseases, such as lupus, should consult a doctor before using this herb. People who are allergic to plants in the daisy family, such as ragweed, are more likely to have an allergic reaction to echinacea.

Other teas that fight colds and flu: Elderflower and elderberry.

DIGESTIVE DISORDERS

Peppermint, which has a zesty, fresh taste, calms muscle spasms...eases intestinal cramping...contains antibacterial compounds...soothes ulcers...and freshens breath after a meal.

Caution: Do not drink peppermint tea if you are suffering from an acute episode of a digestive disorder, such as a gallstone attack. Seek immediate medical attention.

Other teas that fight digestive disorders: Cardamom, ginger and cinnamon.

HEADACHE

Lemon balm, which has a gentle lemon flavor and aroma, acts as an anti-inflammatory and antispasmodic...and contains magnesium, which acts as a muscle relaxant.

Caution: This herb may inhibit thyroid function. If you have low thyroid function (hypothyroidism), avoid lemon balm tea.

Other teas that fight headache: Feverfew and rosemary.

INSOMNIA

Linden flower, which has a sweet flavor and jasminelike aroma, is rich in vitamin C...calms nerves...and promotes rest. In Europe, linden flower tea often is given to patients before surgery to help them relax.

Other teas that fight insomnia: Chamomile and passionflower.

LOW LIBIDO

Oat seed, which has a slightly sweet, milky flavor, relaxes the nerves...and is often used as an aphrodisiac.

Caution: Oat seed contains gluten, so this herb should be avoided by people with gluten intolerance.

Other teas that fight low libido: Cinnamon and raspberry leaf.

Choose a More Healthful Yogurt

Mark A. Stengler, NMD, licensed naturopathic medical doctor and leading authority on the practice of alternative and integrated medicine. He is founder and medical director of the Stengler Center for Integrative Medicine, Encinitas, California, and associate clinical professor at the National College of Natural Medicine, Portland, Oregon. He is author of *The Natural Physician's Healing Therapies* (Bottom Line Books).

Yogurt is a true health food. Live microorganisms in yogurt—known as probiotics ("good bacteria")—can promote digestion and strengthen immunity. Yogurt also is a source of protein, calcium and potassium. But not all yogurts are created equal. *Choose the most healthful yogurts...*

Avoid: Yogurts that have artificial flavors and sweeteners…and those with "fruit on the bottom" because they are loaded with sugar.

Look for: Low-fat yogurts. Opt for organic, whenever possible, or yogurt that uses milk produced without added growth hormones. Choose products with the National Yogurt Association's "Live and Active Cultures" (LAC) seal. This designation can be found on labels of yogurt products that contain significant levels (at least 100 million cultures per gram) of live and active cultures.

Here are some brands that I recommend to patients. Several have lots of protein, which make them good snacks or mini-meals.

- **Brown Cow Plain,** cream top, 6 oz

Number of different strains of active (live) cultures:	4
Calories:	130
Calories from fat:	60
Sugar:	9 g
Protein:	6 g

- **Fage Greek-Style Plain,** 2%, 8 oz

Number of different strains of active (live) cultures:	At least 2
Calories:	150
Calories from fat:	40
Sugar:	9g
Protein:	20g

- **Siggi's Icelandic-Style Plain,** nonfat, 6 oz

Number of different strains of active (live) cultures:	7
Calories:	100
Calories from fat:	0
Sugar:	4g
Protein:	17g

- **Stonyfield Plain,** certified organic, lowfat, 6 oz

Number of different strains of active (live) cultures:	6
Calories:	90
Calories from fat:	15
Sugar:	11g
Protein:	7g

Quick Recovery From Food Poisoning

Sonja Pettersen, NMD, licensed in Arizona and Oregon to practice primary care medicine specializing in natural therapeutics. Her practice exemplifies a holistic approach to patient care through a variety of modalities, including clinical nutrition, botanical medicine and IV therapy, homeopathy, functional medicine, and mind-body techniques.

Although headlines sometimes describe food poisoning as the killer that lurks in your dinner, the problem rarely causes death. But food poisoning does create extreme discomfort in as many as 76 million Americans every year with vomiting, diarrhea and abdominal pain that can last from a few hours to more than a week. Sometimes food poisoning is also accompanied by fever, severe dehydration and even shock—which can be life-threatening, so it's very important to take symptoms seriously. Though there are ways to decrease the incidence of food poisoning, it's nearly impossible to avoid ever facing it —so it is important to know how to handle the problem. With that in mind, we called naturopathic physician Sonja Pettersen, ND, in private practice in Scottsdale, Arizona, for her treatment recommendations.

She told me that food poisoning in North America mostly comes from assorted naturally occurring bacteria, including *Salmonella, E. coli* and *Campylobacter.* Listeria is not common, but approximately 20% of patients die from it…and botulinum, which causes botulism, is also rare. (Another kind called Shigella is found in tropical climates, especially where poor hygiene is present.) Botulism is far and away the most serious of these. It usually results from poor canning techniques, and fortunately occurs much less often than it once did. Nevertheless, when the live botulism organism is ingested, it can kill quickly, so it is crucial to act immediately. In the case of food poisoning, botulism is a toxin that paralyzes nerves—so it can affect many bodily functions, including breathing, balance, speech and swallowing, notes Dr. Pettersen. The onset is rapid (incubation is six hours to 10 days) and unmistakable, characterized by paralysis in any or all of those functions. Effective anti-toxin treatment is now available, and any sign of botulism requires a 9-1-1 call and a rush trip to the ER.

Fortunately, most other cases of food poisoning can be handled at home. Although the vomiting and diarrhea are often intense and painful, Dr. Pettersen explains that this is the body's way of purging itself of the bacteria. "There is a turf war going on," she says, "between the body's natural immunity and protective intestinal flora, and the invading bacteria." The goal is to eliminate the bad bacteria promptly—if it is allowed to linger, toxins develop that can cause much more serious problems. The violent elimination is your body's natural defense against the organisms and their associated toxins. Therefore, you shouldn't take medications, such as Imodium, to slow or stop the diarrhea. "Better out than in," says Dr. Pettersen. Also, don't take an antacid to quell the upset. Stomach acid is crucial as the first line of defense to diminish the toxins and keep the live bacteria from spreading through the rest of the GI tract.

AT HOME

Even as your digestive system is turning inside out, there are ways to make yourself more comfortable. Dr. Pettersen advises taking a probiotic in the form of a high-quality acidophilus powder in capsules or mixed in a liquid per instructions on the container, and as prescribed by your physician. Often you'll be instructed to take a dose every half hour or so even when vomiting—it can't hurt you and will get more good bacteria into your system when it stays down. Other natural remedies include anti-microbial essential oils, herbs and/or supplements such as cilantro, ginger, tarragon, oregano, garlic, thyme or peppermint. Activated charcoal caps neutralize toxins to help stop symptoms quickly. (It is usually the bacterial toxins and not the bacteria itself that create the symptoms.) A homeopathic remedy often prescribed is Arsenicum album.

POST-ATTACK CARE

Within a few days, the attack begins to ebb and you will start to feel better. But understand that your digestive system has been under siege, and isn't ready for a normal diet. Instead, Dr. Pettersen advises the following…

• **Drink Pedialyte, an electrolyte-replacement drink.** (Avoid Gatorade, though, because it will make you feel worse, according to Dr. Pettersen. The high fructose corn syrup (anything sweet) can easily induce an osmotic diarrhea on top of gut troubles.)

• **Eat simple foods**—remember the acronym BRAT (bananas, rice, apple sauce, dry toast). Do not challenge your system.

• **Avoid sugar completely**—and this includes the 7-Up and ginger ale your mother probably gave you as a child after a bout (disruptive gut organisms tend to thrive on such sugary treats).

EMERGENCY MEASURES

Bleeding from the nose or mouth, or blood in your urine, feces or vomit are signs of an emergency. If this happens, go to an ER right away. Any neurological symptoms such as balance or visual problems, muscle weakening and the like also mean you need to get immediately to the hospital. Barring these symptoms, you'll need to stay in touch with your doctor if the debilitation from food poisoning is prolonged. "How bad this might get depends on your general health, but your recent experiences are a factor," says Dr. Pettersen. For example, if you've just completed a long, dehydrating flight, food poisoning will affect you much worse than it might if you are well rested and hydrated. Your physician will decide if IV fluid replacement is necessary and, in the case of Salmonella, if you need an antibiotic.

Note: Dr. Pettersen says that with many cases of food poisoning, the general prescription of antibiotics without a specific target can make the situation worse because they kill the friendly bacteria in the gut that would otherwise be warriors in the battle.

While much is known about how to avoid food contamination, it's a problem that remains very much with us today—as those scary headlines make all too clear. I wouldn't wish food poisoning on anyone, but most of us get it at one point or another. Knowing how to deal with it can minimize unpleasantness.

Age and Celiac Disease—Going Against the Grain?

Joseph A. Murray, MD, gastroenterologist, professor of medicine, department of gastroenterology, Mayo Clinic, Rochester, Minnesota.

It's a good thing that age brings wisdom, because it brings lots of other less desirable changes, too. One of the more surprising ones we've heard about lately is an increased susceptibility to celiac disease (or gluten intolerance). According to Joseph Murray, MD, a Mayo Clinic gastroenterologist, it was once unusual for a new case of celiac disease to be diagnosed in an older man or woman, but that's no longer the case. "Now it's as common as in younger people, and we're making diagnoses in 70- and even 80-year-olds," he said. This means that seniors should be alert to the possibility that while new digestive difficulties that seem to develop as they get older could be the result of age, they also could be celiac disease.

Celiac disease is a tough diagnosis to pin down, Dr. Murray acknowledged, so it is possible that at least some of those older folks have gone undiagnosed for years. But he emphasized that incidence of the disease is unquestionably rising dramatically, most particularly among older people who are now known to be twice as likely as the general population to develop celiac disease.

WHY IS THIS HAPPENING?

Genetics definitely play a role in susceptibility to celiac disease, but Dr. Murray and others believe that environmental factors are contributing to the problem. Looking for antibodies that accompany celiac disease, he and his team analyzed three sets of blood samples—blood (taken for other reasons) from Air Force recruits that was drawn 50 years earlier and stored in a lab freezer...blood taken recently from young men whose ages matched those of the airmen at the time that their blood had been drawn...and new blood samples taken from elderly men who are contemporaries of the now elderly Air Force recruits. Using modern testing methods, the researchers found evidence of undiagnosed celiac disease in some of those old frozen blood samples.

Their comparisons of the groups showed that the elderly men today have four times the incidence of celiac disease compared with the young recruits of 50 years ago and that the disease is 4.5 times more common among today's young men than the young men of the 1950s. Also, in investigating the health records of the 1950s recruits, Dr. Murray learned that the ones who'd had undiagnosed celiac disease were four times more likely than the other recruits to have died since then.

"These results tell us that whatever happened to increase celiac disease happened after 1950," says Dr. Murray—hence the theory that some change in the environment is responsible.

Two possibilities: Dr. Murray said one reason might be that our "clean" lifestyles have so dramatically reduced the number of germs in our environment that our immune systems have been left with too little to do, so they've turned against us...or that changes in how much wheat we eat as well as how wheat is grown and processed may be partially or fully to blame.

SHOULD YOU GET TESTED?

It's generally thought that the majority of people with celiac disease remain undiagnosed (estimates vary, but some believe that 90% of cases aren't identified), so it makes sense to be highly suspicious if you have certain types of digestive symptoms. These include abdominal bloating and pain, diarrhea, vomiting, gas, constipation and unexplained weight loss. Some folks should be especially on guard, said Dr. Murray, citing those who have a sibling, child, grandchild or indeed any other blood relative with known celiac disease. If any of those symptoms or categories describes you, you may want to ask your doctor to order a blood test for celiac disease. Don't first experiment with a gluten-free diet, since doing so can result in a false-negative result when you do get the test. And, speaking of false-negative results, these occur quite often with celiac disease, so if your test is negative but your symptoms persist, you may want to seek further evaluation.

People with celiac disease need to follow a gluten-free diet. You can obtain a list of foods to eat and foods to avoid by visiting *www.mayoclinic.com* and inserting Celiac Disease into the search box. This is the National Institute of Diabetes, Digestive, and Kidney Disorders (NIDDK) Web site. "The good news is, this diet works," said Dr. Murray. "Most older people with celiac disease do well after diagnosis—in fact, 80% to 90% of patients feel completely better."

17

Penny Cures & Home Remedies

Cures from Your Kitchen

You don't need to go to the pharmacy to find powerful cures for everyday ailments. The answers could be in your kitchen. Joan and Lydia Wilen have been collecting, researching and testing folk remedies for more than two decades—and all their remedies have been reviewed for safety by medical doctors, naturopathic doctors and other experts.

Bonus: You might even save a few pennies in the process—having to turn no further than your own kitchen. If you have an existing health condition, check with your physician before trying any of these remedies.

BAD BREATH, GUM DISEASE AND TOOTHACHE

• **Coconut oil, baking soda.** Coconut oil can soothe ailments of the mouth, such as bad breath, gum disease and toothache. For help with any of these conditions, brush your teeth with a mixture of one-eighth teaspoon of baking soda and one-half teaspoon of organic extra-virgin coconut oil (which you can find at a health-food store). Sore gums also are helped when you rub them with coconut oil.

BUMPS AND BRUISES

• **Lemon.** Most bruises that turn black and blue go away on their own, but you can speed the healing process—and reduce both the swelling and the bruising—with this Mayan remedy. Cut a lemon in half, and rub the pulpy side over the bruise once an hour for several hours. Avoid any cuts or breaks in the skin.

CONSTIPATION

• **Lemon, honey, prune juice, prunes, papaya, apples, dried figs.** Drinking water on an empty stomach can stimulate bowel movements. Before breakfast, drink the juice of

Lydia Wilen and Joan Wilen, folk-remedy experts based in New York City. The sisters are coauthors of many books, including *Bottom Line's Healing Remedies: Over 1,000 Astounding Ways to Heal Arthritis, Asthma, High Blood Pressure, Varicose Veins, Warts and More!* (Bottom Line Books). *www.bottomlinepublications.com*

one-half a lemon in one cup of warm water. If it is too tart, sweeten it with honey. If that doesn't help move your bowels, try one of the following—prune juice (at room temperature, not chilled) or stewed prunes, papaya, two peeled apples or six to eight dried figs. (Soak the figs overnight in water. In the morning, drink the water, then eat the figs.)

DANDRUFF

• **Thyme.** We all have dead cells that fall from our scalp as new cells come in. But some people have a greater number of cells falling that are bigger and easier to see. Dried thyme can help get rid of dandruff. Boil one cup of water, and add two heaping tablespoons of dried thyme to the cup. Let it simmer for seven to 10 minutes. Use a strainer to collect the thyme, and get rid of it. Let the tea cool. Wash your hair with a regular shampoo. While your hair is still damp, gently massage the cooled tea into your scalp. Do not rinse.

DIARRHEA

• **Milk, allspice, cinnamon, powdered cloves.** There are several remedies from other countries that use milk. A West Indian remedy is one cup of milk (or warm water) with a pinch of allspice. The Pennsylvania Dutch recommend one cup of warm milk with two pinches of cinnamon. A Brazilian remedy includes two pinches of cinnamon and one pinch of powdered cloves in one cup of warm milk. (Do not drink milk if you are lactose intolerant. It may cause diarrhea.)

HEADACHE

• **Green tea, mint.** Fatigue, anxiety and stress can trigger headaches. For fast relief, brew one cup of green tea and add sprigs of fresh mint. You can use either spearmint or peppermint. If you don't have fresh mint available, use a peppermint or spearmint tea bag. Combine a bag each of green tea and mint tea to make a powerful brew that will diminish your headache in about 15 minutes.

INDIGESTION

• **Grapefruit, potato.** If you are prone to any of the unpleasant symptoms of indigestion, including stomachache or nausea, you can prepare this remedy in advance to have at the ready. Grate the peel of a grapefruit, and spread the pieces out on a paper towel to dry overnight. Store the dried peel in a lidded jar. When you feel the first signs of indigestion, eat one-half to one teaspoon of the grated peel. Chew thoroughly before swallowing.

Another remedy: Raw potato juice can neutralize stomach acid. Grate a potato, and squeeze the gratings through a piece of cheesecloth or a fine strainer to get the juice. Take one tablespoon of potato juice diluted with one-half cup of warm water. Drink slowly.

INSOMNIA

• **Whole nutmeg, grapefruit juice, yellow onion.** Nutmeg can work as a sedative. Crush a whole nutmeg, and steep it in hot water for 10 minutes. Drink it 30 minutes before bedtime. Or drink a glass of pure, warmed grapefruit juice. If you prefer it sweetened, use a little bit of raw honey. Or cut a yellow onion and put it in a glass jar. Keep it near your bed. When you can't sleep, or if you wake up and can't fall back to sleep, open the jar and inhale deeply. Close the jar. Close your eyes, think lovely thoughts and you'll fall back to sleep.

MEMORY PROBLEMS

• **Carrot juice, milk, fresh ginger, sage tea, cloves.** For mild memory problems, try this memory-improving drink. Mix one-half glass of carrot juice with one-half glass of milk—and drink daily. Or use daily doses of fresh ginger in cooking or in tea. Ginger is known to improve memory. Or brew one cup of sage tea, and add four cloves. Drink daily. Sage and cloves are believed to strengthen memory.

POISON IVY/OAK/SUMAC

• **Banana skin, lemon, garlic, tofu. These remedies can help ease the itching and redness of poison ivy.** Rub the inside of a banana skin directly on the affected skin. Use a fresh banana skin every hour for a day. (Freeze the leftover banana pieces to use in smoothies or to eat on hot days.)

Or slice one or two lemons, and rub them on the area. This helps to stop the itching and clears the skin. Or chop up four cloves of garlic, and boil them in one cup of water. When the mixture is cool, apply it with a clean cloth to the area.

Another remedy: Mash up pieces of tofu directly on the itchy area—and hold them in place with a cloth or bandage. This should cool off the area and help any poison ivy flare-up.

SINUS PROBLEMS

• **Tomato juice, garlic, cayenne pepper, lemon juice.** When your sinuses feel clogged and uncomfortable, this bracing drink can help. Combine one cup of tomato juice, one teaspoon of freshly chopped garlic, one-quarter to one-half teaspoon of cayenne pepper (according to your tolerance for spicy food) and one teaspoon of lemon juice. Heat the mixture until it is warm but not too hot to drink. Drink it slowly, and it should help clear up sinuses quickly.

To learn more about the Wilen sisters and their books, visit *www.bottomlinepublications. com.*

KITCHEN CURES SHOPPING LIST

Keep your kitchen stocked with these ingredients—and you'll have homemade remedies and cures at the ready!

- **Allspice**
- **Apples**
- **Baking soda**
- **Banana (skin)**
- **Carrot juice**
- **Cayenne pepper**
- **Cinnamon**
- **Cloves (whole)**
- **Cloves (powdered)**
- **Coconut oil**
- **Figs (dried)**
- **Garlic**
- **Ginger**
- **Grapefruit**
- **Grapefruit juice**
- **Green tea**
- **Honey**
- **Lemon**
- **Lemon juice**
- **Milk**

- **Nutmeg (whole)**
- **Onion (yellow)**
- **Papaya**
- **Potato**
- **Prune juice**
- **Prunes (stewed)**
- **Sage tea**
- **Spearmint or peppermint**
- **Thyme**
- **Tofu**
- **Tomato juice**

Heal Yourself With Acupressure

Mark A. Stengler, NMD, licensed naturopathic medical doctor and leading authority on the practice of alternative and integrated medicine. He is founder and medical director of the Stengler Center for Integrative Medicine, Encinitas, California. He is author of *The Natural Physician's Healing Therapies* (Bottom Line Books).

Many people are aware of acupuncture as a treatment to relieve pain. However, acupressure has been used long before acupuncture in China, Japan and India. Actually, it could be said that most every culture used acupressure to some degree. Simply, it was pushing on "tender" spots to relieve local pain and discomfort. Sometimes, it's what we do naturally—pressing on a sore, aching muscle, for instance. But practitioners in acupressure and acupuncture have identified less obvious, specific points of the body that can contribute to pain relief or healing.

Chinese medicine has relied on acupressure for over 4,000 years. Today, it remains a major treatment at Chinese hospitals. Its popularity has been growing steadily throughout the world.

CHANNELS OF ENERGY...

The traditional Chinese system of medicine focuses on the concept that the life-giving energy called "Qi" (pronounced chee) circulates throughout the body in 12 main channels.

Each channel represents a certain organ system—such as kidney, lung and large intestine. The points that connect to that system are located bilaterally—that is, on both sides of the body. These channels are all interconnected, so they link up to one another.

Along each of the channels, known as meridians, are specific acupressure points that can relieve local pain and inflammation, and also affect pain or tension in other areas of the body. Many of the points can be used to influence the function of internal organs. It is believed that when there is a blockage of Qi circulation in the channels, then disease or illness arises.

To prevent a disease from occurring, or to treat a disease, one must keep the Qi moving. One way to do this is to stimulate the acupressure points where a blockage is occurring. Usually these points are tender to the touch, indicating a blockage. Whether you relieve sore muscles or an internal problem such as digestive upset depends on which points you press. Mental and emotional imbalances can also be helped with acupressure.

CHEMICAL REACTION?...

It is not known exactly how acupressure relieves pain or improves the functioning of internal organs. One theory is that the brain releases certain chemicals that inhibit pain and stimulate the immune system. It is also thought that acupressure relaxes trigger points so muscle tension calms down.

Acupressure may improve blood and lymphatic circulation, as well as improve electrical flow along nerves and between cells. Much research is ongoing in this area, including studies funded by the prestigious National Institutes of Health. Acupressure does work and is a major reason why traditional Chinese medicine is one of the fastest growing medical fields.

While someone trained in acupressure can obtain the best results, there are many easy-to-locate points that you can apply pressure to yourself to alleviate discomfort or improve certain conditions.

ADMINISTERING AN ACUPRESSURE TREATMENT...

Here are four easy steps to follow for self-treatment...

1. Make sure you are relaxed. The room should be free of noise. If possible, you should wear light clothing.

2. Locate the desired point to which you are going to apply pressure. Press on the point using your thumb or fingers. The pressure should be direct, yet not cause great discomfort. Some points may be very tender, indicating a blockage.

Start with very light pressure, see how you feel, and adjust the pressure accordingly. Press the acupressure point and hold for 10 to 15 seconds. This can be repeated 5 to 10 times to see if it helps relieve the symptoms.

Chronic conditions will need more treatments to see if the acupressure is working. Some people prefer rubbing or massaging the acupressure points; this is fine to do as well. As the same channel runs on both sides of the body, try to stimulate the points on both sides simultaneously. For example, massaging Gallbladder 20 on both sides of the back of the head helps to relax tense neck muscles. Or, Stomach 36, located four finger widths below the kneecap and one finger width toward the outside of the leg (outside the shin bone on the muscle), can be stimulated simultaneously to improve digestive function.

3. Make sure to breathe while you stimulate the acupressure point. Slow, deep, relaxed breaths are best.

4. Relax in a quiet atmosphere after a treatment and drink a glass of water to help detoxify your body.

What are the side effects?: Acupressure is a very safe treatment. Temporary soreness of the acupressure point is common and normal. Acupressure should not be applied to open wounds or areas of extreme swelling or inflammation, such as varicose veins.

There are certain points that should not be stimulated on a pregnant woman because of the risk of miscarriage. It is important that pregnant women avoid the use of Gallbladder 21, Large Intestine 4 and Liver 3. Pregnant women should consult with a practitioner of acupressure before self-treating.

Recommendations from the Natural Physician for...

- **Allergies.**
  - Large Intestine 4, located between the webbing of the thumb and index finger, relieves nasal symptoms and head congestion.
  - Large Intestine 20, located on the lower, outer corner of each nostril, reduces sneezing and nasal symptoms.
- **Anxiety.**
  - Pericardium 6, located two-and-one-half finger widths below the wrist crease in the middle of the forearm (palm side), helps relieve anxiety.
- **Cold and flu.**
  - Large Intestine 4, located between the webbing of the thumb and index finger, relieves head congestion and sinus discomfort. Gently push on this spot. You want to work this acupressure point on both hands, so after you've treated your left hand, be sure to do the same to the right.
  - Large Intestine 20, located on the lower, outer corner of each nostril, reduces sneezing and nasal symptoms.
- **Cough.**
  - Lung 1, located in the front of the shoulder area, in the space below where the collarbone and shoulder meet, reduces cough.
- **Constipation.**
  - Large Intestine 4, located between the webbing of the thumb and index finger, relieves constipation. Gently push on this spot on both hands.
- **Headache.**

The following are all helpful. Choose the point or points that provide the most effective relief for you.

  - Gallbladder 20, located below the base of the skull, in the space between the two vertical neck muscles.
  - Large Intestine 4, located between the webbing of the thumb and index finger. Gently push on this spot on both hands.
  - Liver 3, located on top of the foot in the hollow between the big toe and second toe.
  - Yuyao, indentation in the middle of the eyebrow (directly straight up from pupil).
- **Indigestion.**
  - Stomach 36, located four finger widths below the kneecap and one finger width toward the outside of the leg (outside of shin bone on the muscle), improves digestive function.
  - Conception Vessel 6, located two finger widths below the navel, relieves abdominal pain, gas and other digestive problems.
- **Muscle pain.**
  - Find the points that are most tender in the sore muscle and gently press on them and release, or massage these points.
- **Nausea.**
  - Apply pressure on Pericardium 6, which is located two-and-one-half finger widths below the wrist crease in the middle of the inside of your forearm. This point works so well for nausea that special wrist bands can be bought that stimulate this point. They are used for any kind of nausea, including morning sickness and motion sickness.
  - Conception Vessel 6, located two finger widths below the navel, relieves nausea and abdominal symptoms. It is also effective for motion sickness.
- **Neck pain.**
  - Gallbladder 21, located on the highest point of the shoulder (trapezius muscle), relieves stiff neck and shoulder tension. Feel for a tender spot.
  - Gallbladder 20, located below the base of the skull, in the space between the two vertical neck muscles, relieves stiff neck and neck pain.
  - Large Intestine 4, located between the webbing of the thumb and index finger, reduces neck and head discomfort. Gently push on this spot on both hands.
- **Sinusitis.**

The following two points relieve sinus pain and promote drainage.

  - Large Intestine 20, located on the lower, outer corner of each nostril.
  - Large Intestine 4, located between the webbing of the thumb and index finger.

Spice Up Your Health With Everyday Seasonings

Jonny Bowden, certified nutrition specialist, author of The 150 Healthiest Foods on Earth (Fair Winds) and The Most Effective Natural Cures in the World (Fair Winds). His free audio course on 7 Super Foods is available at www.jonnybowden.com.

Cinnamon is so good for you it can almost be considered a health food—simple, ordinary, pumpkin-pie flavoring cinnamon, the same stuff they now have in shakers at Starbucks. It's exciting to see the increasing focus of research on the health benefits of everyday spices like this—capsaicin for prostate cancer...turmeric to reduce inflammation... ginger for nausea, to name just a few. A recent *Wall Street Journal* article reported how several plants abundant in China are being studied as a potential source of medicines by drug company Novartis AG. It's no surprise. Herbs and spices, derived from various plants, have a long history of medicinal use in Chinese medicine. So what else is there in the spice rack that we can use to "healthify" our meals in a delicious way?

"Everyday spices are an amazing source of phytochemicals, which are plant compounds with extraordinary healing properties," explained Jonny Bowden, author of *The 150 Healthiest Foods on Earth* (Fair Winds). "Many of these spices have been used in traditional medicine for hundreds of years, and Western medicine is just beginning to realize their potential." *Here are a few of Bowden's top picks for powering up your foods...*

CINNAMON

Let's take another look at cinnamon, for example. "There are anti-inflammatory compounds in cinnamon that can be helpful in alleviating pain, stiffness and even menstrual discomfort," said Bowden. "Additionally, compounds in cinnamon increase the ability of the cells to take in sugar, which is how it effectively lowers blood sugar and reduces the need for higher levels of insulin." A study published in *Diabetes Care* showed that cinnamon lowered not only blood sugar, but also triglycerides, total cholesterol and LDL ("bad") cholesterol in people with type 2 diabetes. Though it's not always the case with our other plant-based remedies, with cinnamon the inexpensive supermarket variety is basically as good as any of the pricier oils and extracts sold in specialty stores.

GINGER

Then there is ginger, known as the "universal medicine" in Ayurvedic medicine. In one study on ginger root, it was shown to be as effective as Dramamine in holding seasickness at bay. Ginger also packs plenty of powerful antioxidants, Bowden told us. "And animal studies show that ginger has antimicrobial effects and helps boost the immune system as well."

TURMERIC

Turmeric—the spice Bowden waxed most enthusiastic about—is a member of the ginger family, and also a heavy hitter in health benefits. "It's as close to a magical substance as you're likely to find in the kitchen cupboard," he told us. He attributes this spice's anti-inflammatory properties to "curcumin," which is also responsible for making Indian food and curry dishes yellow. In India, turmeric is used to treat arthritis precisely because of its ability to lower inflammation, Bowden said, noting that research indicates that curcumin also may have an anti-tumor effect. If you're not an Indian food eater, you can try it in rice dishes or even on eggs. Do not use medicinal amounts of turmeric during pregnancy, though, because it stimulates contraction of the uterus.

OREGANO

Another spice touted for its health properties is oregano, which Bowden tells us "has been shown by research to have 42 times more antioxidant activity than apples and 12 times more than oranges." Oregano contains a powerful cancer-fighting compound called rosmarinic acid as well, and its anti-inflammatory properties make it useful in supporting joint function. Oregano is also a source of calcium, magnesium, zinc, iron and potassium.

GARLIC

Of course garlic is not always used as a spice, but it does have a well-deserved reputation for adding flavor and boosting health. One of the oldest medicinal foods we know of, it is recognized even by conservative mainstream medical professionals as being helpful in reducing cholesterol. Bowden cited a study that found garlic reduces triglycerides by up to 17%. It has a small but notably positive effect on blood pressure. "In places where the consumption of garlic is high, there's a decreased risk of stomach and colon cancer," Bowden added.

Some other spices that have health-promoting properties include...

•**Cardamom.** Another member of the ginger family, cardamom is in spiced chai tea and used to flavor Turkish coffee, and is added to baked goods in Scandinavia. It stimulates digestion and flow of bile.

•**Mustard seeds.** These are a source of magnesium and selenium, and can be taken orally to stimulate appetite and circulation, and to help neutralize inflammatory materials in the GI tract.

•**Parsley.** A good source of vitamin K and potassium, and also helpful for detoxification.

•**Rosemary.** Contains lots of antioxidants and anti-inflammatory compounds, plus substances that help prevent the premature breakdown of acetylcholine, a neurotransmitter that's vital for memory and healthy brain function.

•**Sage.** Contains rosmarinic acid (like oregano), which is both an antioxidant and an anti-inflammatory, along with thujone, which can be protective against salmonella and candida.

•**Thyme.** Helps relieve chest and respiratory problems, including coughs and bronchitis.

MORE THAN A PINCH?

Since many of the research studies on these items used high doses of them, how much of each is needed to make a difference? The answer varies, Bowden said, but usually more than is typically used for seasoning is required to achieve a notable benefit—though it seems logical that adding a variety of spices, more often and in plentiful amounts, would have a cumulative positive effect. Though some of the dried spices retain their healthful properties, usually fresh herbs are nutritionally superior—not to mention delicious, and fun and easy to grow.

One thing that is especially nice about Bowden's recommendations is the fact that all of these spices are common flavors you can add to all sorts of foods—they're easy to find and don't require a refined palate to enjoy. So go ahead and spice up your menu—your food will taste more interesting and you'll feel better, too.

Spice It Up: Cloves

Mark A. Stengler, NMD, licensed naturopathic medical doctor and leading authority on the practice of alternative and integrated medicine. He is founder and medical director of the Stengler Center for Integrative Medicine, Encinitas, California. He is author of *The Natural Physician's Healing Therapies* (Bottom Line Books).

We tend to think of cloves as a spice used during the winter months. (Think gingerbread, mulled cider, pumpkin pie and holiday ham.) But cloves can add a unique flavor to your dishes year-round—in salads, French toast, even seafood dishes such as crab cakes.

A clove actually is the dried flower bud of the clove tree, a tropical evergreen that once grew wild in China and on the Molucca "Spice" Islands, but today it also is found in Sri Lanka, Brazil and Tanzania. With their strong, floral aroma and slightly bitter but sweet taste, cloves can be used as a sweet or a savory spice in your kitchen—and they are healthful.

Medicinal properties: Cloves contain an oil that is believed to have powerful antibacterial properties. A stimulant, it has been used to relieve digestive problems, such as flatulence and indigestion. Cloves also can help circulation and metabolism, and they regulate temperature.

Nutritional benefits: Cloves contain calcium, manganese, potassium, omega-3 fatty acids and vitamins A and C.

Ways to use: Cloves can be purchased ground or whole. You can add whole cloves to cooked desserts, such as stewed fruits...or sprinkle ground cloves when baking cookies or cakes. Add to chicken, vegetable or fish dishes for a slightly Indian or curry flavor...to rice or quinoa...to sauerkraut recipes, especially slaw containing apples, since cloves and apples make a nice pairing.

Foods That Protect Against Alzheimer's

Columbia University Medical Center researchers found that study participants who followed a Mediterranean-type diet (rich in vegetables, grains and healthful fats) and engaged in the most physical activity had a 35% to 44% reduced risk for Alzheimer's disease compared with those who did not adhere to the diet and engaged in little physical activity. Through diet and exercise, you do have some power to ward off Alzheimer's disease.

Mark A. Stengler, NMD, licensed naturopathic medical doctor and leading authority on the practice of alternative and integrated medicine. He is founder and medical director of the Stengler Center for Integrative Medicine, Encinitas, California. He is author of *The Natural Physician's Healing Therapies* (Bottom Line Books).

Ivy Extract Helps Bronchitis

Mark A. Stengler, NMD, licensed naturopathic medical doctor and leading authority on the practice of alternative and integrated medicine. He is founder and medical director of the Stengler Center for Integrative Medicine, Encinitas, California. He is author of *The Natural Physician's Healing Therapies* (Bottom Line Books).

There's evidence that ivy extract (*Hedera helix*) can help improve symptoms of bronchitis. Results of a recently published study showed that those with bronchitis who took an ivy extract syrup had as much improvement in symptoms as those who took both the syrup and a medication (an antibiotic or an antihistamine).

Study participants—ages nine to 98 years—were given ivy extract at the recommended dose for their age group for an average of seven days. Those who took only the ivy extract syrup had fewer side effects, including diarrhea and/or stomach pain, than those who took ivy extract and medication. Researchers believe that the saponins, plant-based compounds found in ivy extract, are responsible for its ability to reduce lung secretions and improve bronchodilation, or opening of the airways.

Ivy extract products, including those in tablet form, are available at health-food stores and online.

Brands to try: Enzymatic Therapy Ivy Extract (800-783-2286, *www.enzymatictherapy.com*) or Natural Factors Dr. Murray's Lung, Bronchial and Sinus Health (800-322-8704, *www.naturalfactors.com* for a store locator).

Green Tea Lowers Heart Attack Risk by 30%

Patrick M. Fratellone, MD, executive medical director of Fratellone Medical Associates in New York City...attending physician at St. Luke's Hospital, Roosevelt Hospital and Beth Israel Hospital in New York City...former chief of medicine and director of cardiology at Atkins Center for Complementary Medicine...and coauthor of a comprehensive review article on the health benefits of green tea in *Explore*. *www.fratellonemedical.com*

Green tea has remarkable powers to combat disease. I think we all should include green tea in our daily health regimen.

The leaves of the evergreen shrub Camellia sinensis are used to make green, black and oolong tea—but green tea contains the most *epigallocatechin* (EGCG). EGCG (a type of plant compound called a polyphenol, flavonoid or catechin) is a powerful anti-inflammatory and antioxidant. Research shows that chronic low-grade inflammation (produced by an immune system in overdrive) and oxidation (a kind of internal rust that damages cells) are the two processes that trigger and advance most chronic diseases. *Evidence shows that green tea can prevent and treat many of these diseases…*

HEART DISEASE AND STROKE

Researchers studied 14,000 people ages 65 to 84 for six years. They found that men who drank seven or more cups of green tea a day had a 30% lower risk of dying from heart disease or stroke, and women had an 18% lower risk, compared with those who drank less than one cup of green tea a day.

How it works: Green tea can…

• **Lower blood levels of "bad" LDL cholesterol and reduce the oxidation of LDL,** which generates the small, dense particles that can clog arteries and cause a heart attack or stroke.

• **Reduce the activity of platelets,** blood components that clump and form artery-plugging clots.

• **Prevent ventricular arrhythmia,** a spasm of the heart muscle that can trigger or worsen a heart attack.

• **Reduce high blood pressure,** a risk factor for stroke.

• **Improve the flexibility of the endothelium** (the lining of the arteries), boosting blood flow to the heart and brain.

TYPE 2 DIABETES

Type 2 diabetes is a major risk factor for cardiovascular disease and can lead to many other disastrous health problems, including kidney failure, blindness and lower-limb amputation.

In a study of 60 people with diabetes, those who took a daily supplement of green tea extract for two months significantly reduced hemoglobin A1C—a biomarker of blood sugar levels.

How it works: People with diabetes who drank green tea for 12 weeks boosted their levels of insulin (the hormone that helps move sugar out of the blood and into muscle cells)— and decreased their levels of A1C.

OVERWEIGHT

More than 65% of Americans are overweight. Those extra pounds are a risk factor in dozens of health problems, including cardiovascular disease, cancer, osteoarthritis and type 2 diabetes.

Researchers from the Netherlands reviewed 49 studies on green tea and weight loss and analyzed the results of the 11 most scientifically rigorous. They found that drinking green tea "significantly decreased body weight" and "significantly maintained body weight after a period of weight loss."

Why it works: EGCG blocks the action of an enzyme that breaks down noradrenaline (NA). This hormone and neurotransmitter stimulates the sympathetic nervous system, which controls heart rate, muscle tension and the release of energy from fat. By preserving NA, EGCG triggers your metabolism to stay more active and burn more calories.

CANCER

Researchers have conducted more than 1,000 scientific studies on the ability of green tea and EGCG to prevent and reverse cancer, including…

• **Breast cancer.** Researchers at Harvard School of Public Health found a 19% reduction in risk among women who drink more than three cups of green tea a day and a 27% reduction in risk for breast cancer recurrence.

• **Colon cancer.** Japanese researchers studied 136 people with colorectal adenomas (benign tumors that often precede colon cancer). Half of the participants were given a green tea extract. A year later, only 15% of those receiving the extract had developed new adenomas, compared with 31% of those who didn't receive the extract.

• **Prostate cancer.** In a study published in *American Journal of Epidemiology,* Japanese researchers found that men with prostate cancer who drank five or more cups of green tea a day had a 48% lower risk of developing advanced prostate cancer, compared with men who drank less than one cup a day.

• **Lung cancer.** Chinese researchers found a 22% lower risk among those with the highest consumption of green tea, compared with those who did not consume green tea.

Why it works: EGCG interferes with cancer through various mechanisms, including stopping the production of factors that stimulate tumor growth and inhibiting movement of cancer cells.

GUM DISEASE

Research links the chronic bacterial infection of gum (periodontal) disease to many health problems, including heart disease and diabetes. Japanese researchers studied nearly 1,000 men ages 49 to 59 and found that those who regularly drank green tea had fewer cases of, or less severe, periodontal disease. For every additional daily cup of tea the men drank, there was a significant decrease in the depth of periodontal pockets (the grooves around the teeth that deepen as gum disease advances), a decrease in the loss of attachment of the gum to the tooth and a decrease in bleeding.

How it works: The polyphenols in green tea may decrease the inflammatory response to oral bacteria.

THE RIGHT AMOUNT

To guarantee a sufficient intake of EGCG, I recommend one or more of the following strategies. You can safely do all three.

• **Drink green tea.** Five to 10 eight-ounce cups a day of regular or decaf.

Best: For maximum intake of EGCG, use whole-leaf loose tea rather than a teabag, using one teaspoon per cup. Steep the tea for at least five minutes.

• **Take a supplement of green tea extract.**

Minimum: 400 milligrams (mg) a day of a supplement standardized to 90% EGCG.

• **Add a drop of green tea liquid extract to green tea or another beverage.** Look for a product that is standardized to a high level (at least 50%) of EGCG, and follow the dosage recommendation on the label.

Example: HerbaGreen from HerbaSway, at 90% polyphenols, 50% from EGCG.

SAFE USE

Talk to your doctor if you use…

• **An antiplatelet drug** (blood thinner), such as *warfarin* (Coumadin), because green tea also thins the blood.

• **A bronchodilator** for asthma or chronic obstructive pulmonary disease, because green tea can increase its potency.

• **An antacid,** because green tea can decrease the effect.

Fresh Garlic Better Than Bottled

Garlic contains allicin, a pungent compound that may help fight infection, prevent food poisoning, and protect against blood clots and certain cancers. Bottling interferes with enzymes needed to activate allicin.

Best: Stick to fresh cloves to get the most from garlic's immune-boosting properties.

Toyohiko Ariga, PhD, professor, department of applied life sciences, Nihon University Graduate School of Bioresource Sciences, Japan, and leader of a study published in *Journal of Agricultural and Food Chemistry*.

Grapefruit Lowers Cholesterol

Men and women whose elevated cholesterol levels did not respond to cholesterol-lowering drugs ate balanced meals with one red grapefruit, one white grapefruit or no grapefruit daily.

Result: Total cholesterol dropped by 15.5% in those who ate red grapefruit and by 7.6% in the white grapefruit group. Cholesterol did not drop in those who did not eat grapefruit. Grapefruit juice also may confer this benefit.

Theory: Antioxidants found in grapefruit lower cholesterol levels.

Caution: Grapefruit can interact with some drugs. Consult your doctor.

Shela Gorinsten, PhD, chief scientist, Hebrew University of Jerusalem.

Honey Acts As a Natural Antibiotic

How it works: Honey's natural acidity creates an inhospitable environment for germs… and it contains a small amount of germ-killing hydrogen peroxide.

Important: Heat can destroy honey's beneficial properties, so buy the raw and unpasteurized kind. Honey can be used on most wounds. If you have a puncture wound, consult your doctor.

What to do: Work one tablespoon of warmed honey into a four-inch by four-inch gauze pad, then place it on the wound. Change the dressing at least twice daily until the wound heals.

Caution: Infants younger than age one should not eat honey.

Peter Molan, PhD, professor of biological sciences, University of Waikato, Hamilton, New Zealand.

Got a Tickle In Your Throat?

Scratch the inside of your ear canal with your finger. Stimulating the nerves in the ear triggers a muscle spasm in the throat that cures the tickle.

Scott R. Schaffer, MD, president, ENT Specialty Center, PC, ear, nose and throat specialty center, Gibbsboro, New Jersey.

Hiccup Cures

Pour a tall glass of water. While holding your breath and pinching your nostrils, take small sips until you feel you are drowning. Stop, inhale deeply and breathe normally.

Alternative: Ice the nerve fibers responsible for hiccups. Find your Adam's apple—for women, this is about two inches below the chin. Move your finger around your neck to just above your clavicle, the protruding bone at the base of the neck, well below and behind the carotid arteries. Apply ice cubes to each side of the neck at those points until the hiccuping stops. See your doctor if hiccups last more than 48 hours.

John T. Walbaum, Chicago-based freelance writer and author of *The Know-It-All's Guide to Life* (Career).

Sitz Baths: A Water Remedy for Many Ailments

Mark A. Stengler, NMD, licensed naturopathic medical doctor and leading authority on the practice of alternative and integrated medicine. He is founder and medical director of the Stengler Center for Integrative Medicine, Encinitas, California, and associate clinical professor at the National College of Natural Medicine, Portland, Oregon. He is author of *The Natural Physician's Healing Therapies* (Bottom Line Books).

Sitz baths—sitting so that your bottom is in water—can be an easy, at-home way to help many health problems, including urinary tract infections, insomnia, even headaches.

Sitz baths promote healing by changing blood flow to the area, reducing pain and inflammation. Warm water increases blood flow to the area, while cold water helps blood move to other body parts.

What you'll need: Purchase a plastic sitz-bath tub that is placed on the toilet (available at drugstores). These are contoured to focus circulation on the buttocks.

Next best: The bathtub. Fill the tub with water high enough to reach just under the navel while you are seated.

How to do it: Use a thermometer to determine water temperature. To alternate between warm and cold water, have two buckets of water ready or use both the purchased sitz bath and the bathtub.

Conditions: Abdominal or uterine pain, low-back pain, insomnia, hemorrhoids, muscle spasms (add 2 cups of Epsom salts).

Warm treatment: Water 106°F – 110°F, 5 to 8 minutes, one to two times daily.

Conditions: Acute bladder infection, itchy rectum, acute urinary tract infection.

Lukewarm treatment: Water 92°F – 97°F, 15 minutes to one hour (depending on your comfort level), one to two times daily.

Conditions: Constipation, prostate enlargement, uterus or rectum prolapse.

Cold treatment: Water 55°F – 75°F, 5 to 8 minutes, one to two times daily.

Conditions: Vaginal infections, prostatitis, headache, postpartum recovery, chronic urinary tract infection.

Alternating treatment: Warm water for 3 to 5 minutes, followed by 30 to 60 seconds in cold. Repeat three times daily.

If you have diabetes, heart disease or high blood pressure, speak to your doctor before taking a sitz bath because it can cause changes in blood pressure, pulse and glucose levels.

Natural Rx for Arthritis

We have received several letters attesting to the effectiveness of this tea for arthritis pain…

Bring one-half cup of water to a boil. Add fresh ginger, cut into thin slices—you can use as much as you like—and let simmer for five minutes. Remove and discard the ginger. Turn off the heat, and add one-quarter teaspoon of turmeric powder, one tablespoon of unflavored gelatin and one tablespoon of coconut oil. Stir until the gelatin is dissolved, then add one-half to one cup of calcium-enriched orange juice. Drink this tea once or twice a day.

Lydia Wilen and Joan Wilen, folk-remedy experts based in New York City. The sisters are coauthors of many books, including *Bottom Line's Healing Remedies: Over 1,000 Astounding Ways to Heal Arthritis, Asthma, High Blood Pressure, Varicose Veins, Warts and More!* (Bottom Line Books). *www.bottomlinepublications.com*

The Wilen Sisters' Home Remedies That Work Better Than Drugs

Lydia Wilen and Joan Wilen, folk-remedy experts based in New York City. The sisters are coauthors of many books, including *Bottom Line's Healing Remedies: Over 1,000 Astounding Ways to Heal Arthritis, Asthma, High Blood Pressure, Varicose Veins, Warts and More!* (Bottom Line Books). *www.bottomlinepublications.com*

The Wilen sisters have been using home remedies all their lives, and for the last quarter of a century, they've been researching and writing about them as well.

Below, asked the Wilens share the remedies they use most often for a variety of health challenges. The sisters may not always be able to explain why the remedies work—but they work. All use ingredients readily available in most kitchens, supermarkets or health-food stores. Of course, always check with your doctor before taking any dietary supplement or herb.

SORE THROAT

At the first sign of a sore or scratchy throat, mix two teaspoons of apple cider vinegar in six-to-eight ounces of warm water. Take a mouthful, gargle with it and spit it out—then swallow a mouthful. Repeat the gargle/swallow pattern until there's nothing left in the glass. Do this every hour until your throat is better. We usually feel better within two or three hours.

COLDS

We eat chicken soup when we feel a cold coming on. Aside from being a comfort food, it helps prevent a cold from becoming full-blown and/or it shortens the duration of one. We either prepare the soup from scratch, adding lots of veggies (carrots, onions, parsnip, celery, string beans), or we do the next best thing—buy packaged soup found in the supermarket's frozen food section, then add vegetables. In either case, we add the most potent and health-restoring ingredient—garlic. To derive the full healing powers of garlic, add one or two finely minced raw cloves after the warmed soup is in the bowl.

STOP BLEEDING

A simple first-aid procedure to stop a minor cut or gash from bleeding is to cover the cut with cayenne pepper from your spice cabinet. Gently pour on the pepper. Yes, it will sting. And yes, the bleeding will stop quickly.

HEARTBURN

We use our mother's remedy. As soon as the burning starts, eat a palmful of almonds—that's about one ounce—and the heartburn stops immediately. Our mom used dry-roasted almonds. We buy raw almond slivers.

STY

A sty is an inflamed swelling on the eyelid. This classic folk remedy sounds ridiculous but has worked for us many times. The minute you feel as though you're getting a sty, take a 14-carat gold ring (wash it first) and rub it several times across your eyelid every 15 minutes or so, until that "sty-ish" feeling disappears... along with the sty. In our experience, it works right away.

BURNED FINGERTIPS

Ever reach for a pot handle that's surprisingly hot? How about grabbing the wrong side of a plugged-in iron? We have a unique way of treating these minor first-degree burns, where the skin is painful and red but unbroken. It's a form of acupressure. Place your thumb on the back side of your earlobe, and the burned fingertips on the front side of the same earlobe. Press firmly. After a minute, the pain is gone.

Ten Natural Medicines For Every Home

Jamison Starbuck, ND, naturopathic physician in family practice in Missoula, Montana. She is past president of the American Association of Naturopathic Physicians and a contributing editor to *The Alternative Advisor: The Complete Guide to Natural Therapies and Alternative Treatments* (Time Life).

Most Americans make a mad dash to the nearest drugstore if an acute illness, such as sore throat or diarrhea, or a minor injury, such as muscle strain, needs attention. But that's not always necessary. It's easy to keep a few well-chosen natural medicines on hand to treat most minor ailments. At my home, we keep rubbing alcohol, 3% hydrogen peroxide, adhesive bandages, gauze and medical tape for basic first aid. *Here are the natural medicines (available at health-food stores) that I keep at home (unless I've indicated otherwise, follow manufacturers' recommendations for dosing)...*

1. Traumeel.

Use for: Sprain, muscle strain or pain after surgery or dental procedures. This homeopathic anti-inflammatory/analgesic (topical or oral) contains a variety of plant medicines, including arnica.

2. Rescue Remedy.

Use for: Emotional stress, anxiety and worry. This Bach flower remedy contains essences of five plants, including impatiens and clematis. Use four drops on the tongue as needed—up to five times daily.

3. Calendula spray.

Use for: Skin injuries—cuts, abrasions, insect bites and burns. Used topically, tincture of calendula flowers acts as a mild antiseptic and anti-inflammatory.

4. Echinacea tincture.

Use for: Cold, flu or sore throat. At the onset of illness, take 60 drops in one to two ounces of water every four waking hours—continue for two to five days.

5. Cough formula.

Use for: Dry cough and sore throat. Use a tincture formula that contains the herbs elecampane, marshmallow, osha, cherry bark, fennel and licorice mixed in a honey base. This remedy moistens the throat and reduces the frequency of coughs.

6. Charcoal.

Use for: Acute diarrhea. Take two tablets every two to three waking hours.

Caution: Charcoal should not be taken with medication—it can block the drug's absorption.

7. Aloe plant.

Use for: Burns. Immediately after a burn, cut off a small piece from the tip of an aloe leaf (I keep an aloe plant in my kitchen), slice it open and place the moist inner gel directly on your burn to reduce pain. (If you prefer to buy aloe gel, be sure to refrigerate it.)

8. Peppermint leaf.

Use for: Fever, nausea, gas and sore throat. To make peppermint tea, steep loose-leaf peppermint tea or tea bags covered for at least five minutes in boiled water. Drink one to four cups daily.

9. Epsom salts.

Use for: Sore muscles or tension headaches. Rich in magnesium, which helps relax muscles, Epsom salts (two cups) can be used in a bath.

10. Homeopathic flu remedies.

Use for: Flu. Take at the first signs. My favorite homeopathic flu remedies: Mucococcinum by UNDA and Oscillococcinum by Boiron.

For safety and optimal effectiveness, keep all medicines, including natural ones, in a cool, dry place that is out of the reach of children…and check the expiration dates of your products.

Live Longer By Meditating

Transcendental meditation (TM), a technique that produces a state of "restful alertness," has been shown to reduce stress levels and lower blood pressure.

People with hypertension (average age 72) who regularly practiced TM for 20 minutes twice daily were 30% less likely to die from heart disease over an 18-year period than those who did not practice TM.

Theory: TM lowers levels of adrenaline and cortisol, stress-related hormones, in the body.

Helpful: Practice TM for 20 minutes twice daily.

Robert H. Schneider, MD, director, Institute for Natural Medicine and Prevention, Maharishi University of Management, Maharishi Vedic City, Iowa.

Natural Remedies from A Pharmacist's Own Medicine Cabinet

Suzy Cohen, RPh, registered practicing pharmacist for nearly 20 years and author of *The 24-Hour Pharmacist* (Collins). Her syndicated newspaper column, "Dear Pharmacist," reaches more than 24 million readers. Based in Florida, she is a member of the Association of Natural Medicine Pharmacists and the American Holistic Health Association.

As a pharmacist for almost two decades, Suzy Cohen knows the importance of medication—but she also has learned to "think outside the pill" and recommend natural options that often are just as good or better at promoting health without the risk of dangerous side effects.

Here are the remedies she recommends most often. All are free of significant side effects unless otherwise noted, but always talk with your doctor before using any supplements.

TEA TREE OIL FOR WOUNDS

This oil kills germs, reduces pain and helps wounds heal more quickly. You can use it in place of antibiotic ointment for minor cuts, scratches and burns…to treat toenail fungus…and, when diluted, as a gargle to kill the germs that cause sore throat.

How it works: It's a strong antiseptic that kills bacteria as well as fungi.

How to use: Moisten a cotton ball or swab with one or two drops of the oil, and apply it to the area two to three times daily until it heals.

For a gargle for sore throat: Mix a few drops in a cup of water, gargle and spit it out.

Caution: Do not swallow it.

GINGER FOR NAUSEA

Studies have shown that ginger can relieve nausea—due to pregnancy, seasickness, etc.—as well as or better than over-the-counter drugs.

How it works: Ginger increases the pH of stomach acid, reducing its acidity. In one study, published in *The Lancet*, volunteers were given either ginger or Dramamine (a nausea-preventing drug), then were seated in a chair designed to trigger motion sickness. Those given ginger were able to withstand the motion 57% longer than those given the drug.

How to use: Put one teaspoon of peeled, grated fresh gingerroot in a cup of boiling water. Let it steep for 10 minutes, then drink (you can filter out the ginger if you want). Or chew and swallow a piece of crystallized ginger, sold in health-food stores.

Caution: Ginger can increase the risk of bleeding when taken with blood-thinning drugs, such as warfarin (Coumadin).

RHODIOLA ROSEA FOR STRESS

This herb acts like a natural form of Valium by reducing physical and emotional stress. The supplement is made from the root of the Siberian plant.

How it works: Herbalists classify Rhodiola as an adaptogen, a class of herbs that "sense" chemicals in the body and either raise or lower them. It normalizes levels of brain chemicals that affect mood, such as monoamines and beta-endorphins, which help counter the effects of stress. Rhodiola also may increase serotonin, which enhances feelings of well-being.

How to use: During times of stress, take 100 milligrams (mg) of rhodiola rosea in capsule form, two to three times daily. It's best taken on a cyclical basis—two months on, two weeks off.

CALCIUM PLUS MAGNESIUM FOR CRAMPS

People who experience frequent and/or painful menstrual or muscle cramps often have a deficiency of calcium and magnesium.

How it works: Calcium and magnesium regulate the contraction and relaxation of muscles.

How to use: Before going to bed, take 500 mg to 600 mg of calcium, along with 150 mg to 200 mg of magnesium (using the chelate or glycinate forms—check the label). Combination formulas are easy to find and fine to use.

For menstrual problems, start 10 days before you expect your period to begin each month and continue until your period is complete.

GABA FOR INSOMNIA

Gamma-aminobutyric acid (GABA) is a neurotransmitter (mood-related brain chemical) that is naturally present in the body. It's taken in supplement form to reduce insomnia, as well as anxiety and depression.

How it works: GABA is an inhibitory neurotransmitter that slows activity in the brain and makes it easier to fall asleep.

How to use: Take 500 mg to 1,000 mg one hour before bedtime if you have trouble getting to sleep. If your problem is that you wake in the middle of the night and can't get back to sleep, take it then. Don't exceed recommended doses on the package. Do this for two weeks. If it doesn't help, talk to your doctor.

Caution: Combining GABA with prescription or over-the-counter sleep aids can cause excessive sedation.

CAPSAICIN CREAM FOR PAIN

Capsaicin is the chemical compound that puts the "hot" in chili peppers. It is effective for easing muscle aches, back and joint pain and nerve pain caused by the herpes virus (post-herpetic neuralgia).

How it works: When applied as a cream, it causes nerve cells to empty their reservoirs of substance P, a pain-causing chemical. This results in less pain from the underlying disorder.

How to use: Start with a 0.025% concentration. Apply it two to three times daily—the initial burning sensation diminishes with continued use. If needed, you can always buy the stronger 0.075% concentration—but it's best to work your way up to this strength.

Caution: Wear latex gloves when applying capsaicin—and wash your hands thoroughly after using to prevent residual cream from getting into the eyes, nose, etc.

PROBIOTICS FOR DIGESTIVE DISCOMFORT

A healthy digestive tract contains trillions of bacteria, many of which have beneficial effects. These so-called "good" (probiotic) organisms promote digestive health, improve immunity and aid in the synthesis of B vitamins, among many other functions.

How they work: Probiotic supplements replenish beneficial bacteria and crowd out harmful organisms that can cause gas, bloating, diarrhea and other digestive problems.

How to use: Take a daily supplement of a least 10 billion organisms that contains a variety of living organisms, such as L. bulgaricus, L. bifida and B. longum. Some yogurts contain these live active cultures, but avoid those that contain sugar or artificial sweeteners.

BIOTIN FOR CRACKED NAILS

The B vitamin biotin is the only nutrient that has been shown to improve nail health in generally healthy adults. People with a deficiency of biotin often have fragile nails that crack easily.

How it works: Biotin is absorbed by the nail matrix, the part under the fingernail where nail cells are generated.

How to use: Take 2,000 micrograms (mcg) to 4,000 mcg of biotin daily, as well as a B-complex supplement. Most people will notice an improvement in nail strength and thickness in one to two months.

Best-Bet Juices with Surprising Health Benefits

Carol S. Johnston, PhD, RD, professor and nutrition department chair, Arizona State University, Mesa, board member of the Dietary Supplements/Non-Botanicals Expert Committee of the US Pharmacopoeia and board member of the American College of Nutrition.

To boost nutrition, try the unusual juices now sold at health-food stores and juice bars…or use a juicer to create your own blends. Aim for six to 12 ounces of antioxidant-rich unsweetened juice daily. *Choices…*

• **Berries**—açaí, blackberry, blueberry, cranberry, goji, guarana, mangosteen, strawberry—provide prebiotics that improve digestion…beta-sitosterol, an alcohol that inhibits cholesterol absorption…and/or oleic acids, which may reduce blood pressure.

Energizing: Blend berry juice with soymilk for protein.

• **Citrus**—grapefruit, kumquat, orange, lemon, lime, tangelo—supplies vitamin C, which improves iron absorption…and potassium, needed for proper heart and kidney function.

Flavor boost: Squeeze citrus onto salads.

• **Rose family fruits**—apple, apricot, cherry, loquat, peach, pear, plum, quince—**contain chlorogenic acid,** an antioxidant that may combat cancer.

Sweet treat: Fill an ice-pop tray with juice and freeze.

• **Tropical fruits**—guava, kiwifruit, mango, papaya, pineapple—**have enzymes** that aid digestion and reduce inflammation.

Healthful breakfast: Stir juice into plain yogurt and top with whole-grain cereal.

• **Bright vegetables**—beet, carrot, pumpkin, red pepper, tomato—provide carotenoids (plant pigments) that may fight cancer.

Smart soup: Make borscht with beet juice, adding chopped carrots and peppers.

• **Green vegetables**—cabbage, celery, kale, lettuce, spinach—are rich in vitamin K, which improves blood clotting and may help heal ulcers.

For sweetness: Combine green juice with fruit juice.

• **Grasses**—wheat, barley—are loaded with chlorophyll, a pigment that may promote tissue growth and stimulate oxygen-carrying red blood cells.

Best: Mix with other juices to disguise the strong grassy taste.

The Healing Power of Aromatherapy

Mindy Green, practicing aromatherapist for more than 35 years. The Minneapolis-based coauthor of *Aromatherapy: A Complete Guide to the Healing Art* (Ten Speed) is a founding member of the American Herbalists' Guild.

A scented spray or candle may smell good, but true "aromatherapy" does much more. This ancient healing practice involves the therapeutic use of aromatic substances known as essential oils (highly concentrated extracts distilled from plants).

Some people scoff at the idea of using aromatherapy, but ongoing research has shown that essential oils are effective in treating a variety of common health problems, including muscle cramps, cough, fatigue and insomnia.

How does it work? Smelling an essential oil releases neurotransmitters and other chemicals that affect the brain. When used topically, chemical constituents in essential oils are absorbed through the skin and enter the bloodstream, where they affect overall physiology, including hormones and enzymes.

Best way to use topical therapy: Add five to 10 drops of essential oil to one ounce of a "carrier" oil, such as almond oil, which is odorless, and apply it to the affected part of your body. For a bath, add five to eight drops of essential oil mixed with a teaspoon of a carrier oil to a tub full of warm bathwater.

Best way to use inhalation therapy: Add three to six drops of essential oil to a basin of hot water (boil then cool slightly). Bend your head over the bowl and cover your head with a towel, creating a tent to trap the scented steam. Staying at least 12 inches away from the water source, inhale deeply for three to five minutes.

My favorite essential oils and their uses…

MUSCLE CRAMPS

•**Marjoram.** Add a mixture of marjoram and a carrier oil to your bath and soak for 20 minutes. Or massage marjoram oil and a carrier oil into the painful area as needed.

COUGH AND CONGESTION

•**Eucalyptus.** Rub a mixture of eucalyptus and a carrier oil onto your chest and back. The oils work via skin absorption and inhalation to ease coughs and congestion. For congestion, try inhalation therapy three times daily for five minutes each session.

Caution: Do not try this therapy during an asthma attack—it can exacerbate symptoms. If you don't get relief within a few days, see your doctor.

FATIGUE

•**Rosemary.** Add rosemary and a carrier oil to a warm bath and soak for 10 to 15 minutes as needed.

INSOMNIA

•**Lavender.** Add lavender and a carrier oil to warm bathwater and soak for 20 minutes before going to bed.

NAUSEA

•**Ginger and peppermint.** Mix two drops of ginger oil with one drop of peppermint oil and one tablespoon of a carrier oil. While lying on your back, gently massage the mixture onto the abdomen. When rubbing, follow the natural flow of intestinal movement—move your hand up the right side of your stomach, across the middle and down the left side. This is the way food normally moves through the large intestine. For even greater relief, also drink a cup of ginger or peppermint tea after the massage.

ESSENTIAL OIL BASICS

Essential oils are available at most health-food stores and online.

Typical cost: $5 to $15 for a small bottle. High-quality oils can be purchased from Aura Cacia, 800-437-3301, *www.auracacia.com*… The Essential Oil Company, 800-729-5912, *www.essentialoil.com*…or Oshadhi, 888-674-2344, *www.oshadhiusa.com*.

Herbs That Help Treat Arthritis

Devil's claw has an anti-inflammatory component that may relieve pain.

Suggested dose: 750 mg of standardized 3% iridoid glycosides three times a day.

•**Extract of avocado and soybean oil can reduce pain and stiffness—300 mg a day.**

•**Phytodolor, a mixture of ash, aspen and goldenrod,** may also reduce symptoms—30 drops three times a day.

•**Niacinamide can ease pain and swelling—100 mg three to four times a day.**

•**Tart cherry juice.** A daily cup can ease mild arthritis.

Note: Check with your doctor before taking any dietary supplements.

Andrew Heyman, MD, adjunct clinical instructor in family medicine, University of Michigan Medical School, Ann Arbor.

Natural Remedies For Cold Sores

Caused by the herpes simplex virus, cold sores can be brought on by stress, an overtaxed immune system or an imbalance of the amino acids arginine and lysine.

Remedies: Zinc helps sores heal faster when taken as a supplement or applied topically. Propolis, an anti-inflammatory and antiviral, can be applied twice daily…or take a 1,000-mg supplement once a day. Lysine decreases the duration of an outbreak by two-thirds—apply it topically or take a 1,000-mg supplement. Dab the cold sore with a cotton ball saturated with apple cider vinegar to dry out lesions. Licorice root tincture—put 15 to 20 drops into a glass of warm water and drink three times a day during an outbreak. To avoid any possible interactions or side effects, talk to your doctor before taking any supplements.

Melissa Gallagher, ND, founder of Healthy Being, a natural health and wellness business, St. Petersburg, Florida. *www.healthybeingllc.com*

Quick Cure for Dry Skin on Hands

To quickly ease the cracked, dry skin that can irritate hands during the winter, try the homeopathic remedy Petroleum (not to be confused with petroleum jelly). Take two 30C pellets twice daily for seven days, then use as needed. It may seem counterintuitive to take an oral remedy, but it really helps. Petroleum is available in health-food stores and is safe for everyone. This remedy is for the hands only.

Mark A. Stengler, NMD, licensed naturopathic medical doctor and leading authority on the practice of alternative and integrated medicine. He is founder and medical director of the Stengler Center for Integrative Medicine, Encinitas, California. He is author of *The Natural Physician's Healing Therapies* (Bottom Line Books).

Migraine Relief

Eliminate migraine pain with pepper. Capsaicin, an ingredient in cayenne pepper, cuts off neurotransmitters in the brain that cause headache pain.

Best: Dissolve one-quarter teaspoon of cayenne powder in four ounces of warm water. Dip a cotton swab into the solution, and apply the liquid inside your nostrils. It will burn—and by the time the burning stops, the headache pain will be reduced and sometimes gone altogether.

Eric Yarnell, ND, assistant professor, department of botanical medicine, Bastyr University, Kenmore, Washington.

Fruit Therapy

Eating pineapple may relieve arthritic pain. It may also help other inflammation, such as sunburn and joint pain.

Why: Pineapple contains bromelain, an enzyme that new research shows has anti-inflammatory benefits.

Bromelain can also be purchased in supplement form, with a recommended dose of about 100 milligrams a day for sore joints. Check with your own doctor to be sure it is OK for you.

Michael Roizen, MD, chief wellness officer Cleveland Clinic, and Mehmet Oz, MD, vice-chair of surgery and professor of cardiac surgery at Columbia University, coauthors of *You: On a Diet* (Free Press).

Stop Pain Without Drugs

Donna Finando, Roslyn Heights, New York–based licensed acupuncturist (LAc) and massage therapist (LMT). She is the author of the *Trigger Point Self-Care Manual for Pain-Free Movement* (Inner Traditions).

Most over-the-counter and prescription pain relievers temporarily ease aches and pains, but these medications do not address the root cause of the problem. In a surprising number of cases, muscular tightness is responsible for common types of pain.

Here's what happens: When any one of the more than 200 muscles in your body suffers from overuse or an injury, it can develop a trigger point—a tiny knot in which a strand of the muscle becomes constricted, making the muscle stiff and weak.

Left untreated, this condition can persist for years, causing pain to recur repeatedly. Fortunately, you can relieve this type of pain with a simple technique known as trigger-point therapy. It involves locating the associated trigger points and compressing them for 20 to 30 seconds several times a day. Press only hard enough to feel the tightness of the muscle and the soreness of the trigger point. Stretches for each condition also should be repeated several times daily.

Helpful: Whenever possible, also apply 20 minutes of moist heat once or twice a day to the affected muscle. Moist heat brings blood and body fluids to the muscle, increasing circulation. (Moist heating pads by Cara, Sunbeam or Thermophore can be purchased at most drugstores for $20 to $50.)

If you've worked on your muscles for several days and felt little or no relief, check with your doctor to make sure there is no other source of pain, such as arthritis.

Conditions often caused by trigger points—and how to treat them...

STIFF NECK

Stiff neck frequently occurs after sleeping with your head turned all the way to one side, or as a result of holding a phone between your ear and shoulder. The condition is often due to a trigger point in the levator scapulae muscle, which runs from the inner edge of the shoulder blade to the neck.

To find the trigger point: Reach the hand that is on your pain-free side over to touch your shoulder on the painful side. Locate the inside edge of the shoulder blade, then move your hand a bit closer to your spine, feeling for a hard band the size of a pencil running up toward your neck. While bending your neck toward your pain-free side, use your fingers to locate a tender spot along this band, then press it for 20 to 30 seconds.

Helpful stretch: Turn your chin 30 degrees away from the affected side, then drop your chin down slightly toward your chest. Hold for a slow count of 20.

HIP, BUTTOCK AND LEG PAIN

Pain in the hips, buttocks or legs is often diagnosed as sciatica (pain in your back that radiates into your buttocks and legs) when it actually may be caused by trigger points in the muscles of the back and buttocks. One of these muscles, the gluteus medius, lies midway between the top of your pelvis and the top of your thighbone.

To find the trigger point: Lie on the floor on your pain-free side with your knees slightly bent, and use your fingers to massage your hip under the top of your pelvis and down toward the top of your thighbone. If trigger points are present, you'll feel taut bands and tender spots. Once you've located a tender spot, roll onto your painful side and place a tennis ball between this spot and the floor. Then let your weight press the ball into the tender area for 20 to 30 seconds.

Helpful stretch: Stand facing a wall with your arms raised and the backs of your hands pressed against your forehead. Cross your pain-free leg in front of your other leg. Bend the knee of your rear leg into the back of your pain-free leg while shifting your weight onto your painful hip. This should create a stretch between your pelvis and the top of your thighbone. Hold for a slow count of 20.

CALF PAIN

If you're experiencing pain or soreness in your calf or the back of your knee, it may be caused by trigger points in the gastrocnemius muscle (the large muscle that gives the calf its characteristic shape).

To find the trigger point: Sit in a chair and place the sole of the foot of your affected leg on a footstool or coffee table in front of you. Place one hand on the outer side of this leg and the other on the inner side of this leg—in both cases, just above the ankle. Run your fingers along your Achilles tendon (the large tendon at the back of your heel) and work your way to the middle of the calf, feeling for tender spots. Continue upward, toward the back of the knee. When you find a tender spot, compress it with your fingers for 20 to 30 seconds.

Helpful stretch: While standing about 12 inches from a wall, facing the wall, place your hands on the wall at chest level. Keeping your feet hip-width apart and the toes of both feet facing the wall, move your painful leg 18 inches behind the other leg. Bend your front knee, keeping your rear leg straight. Your weight should remain on the front leg. Hold for a slow count of 20.

TENNIS ELBOW

Inflammation of the tendon on the outside of the elbow, known as "tennis elbow," can cause sharp pain down the back of the forearm into the wrist, making it hard to grip objects. However, sometimes the condition may not be an inflammation but a result of trigger points in the extensor muscles of the hand and fingers, which can be caused by repeated or forceful gripping, such as when holding a tennis racket—or even a coffee cup.

To find the trigger point: Rest the elbow and forearm of your sore arm on a table, with your palm facing up. Use your opposite hand to feel along the muscle on the outside (thumb side) of your elbow crease, then follow this muscle down toward your hand. When you find a tender spot, press down and hold for 20 to 30 seconds.

Helpful stretch: Sit on a chair, and keeping your elbow straight, place the back of the hand on the affected arm flat on the seat beside you, palm up, feeling a stretch in your forearm. Hold for a slow count of 20.

Illustrations by Shawn Banner.

18

Arthritis &
Joint Health

Nine Ways to Keep Joints Young

Exciting developments are occurring in the field of arthritis research. In many cases, even among people who are genetically predisposed to arthritis, unless there also is an environmental or lifestyle trigger (being a smoker, for instance) to spur the onset of the disease, chances are good that arthritis will never develop.

What this means: Far from being an inevitable result of aging or an inescapable fate for those with a family history of the disease, arthritis is quite possibly preventable…and many of the same strategies that guard against the development of arthritis also help slow its progress, making the condition more manageable if you do get it.

What it is: Arthritis is an umbrella term for more than 100 conditions that affect the joints. Osteoarthritis, which is by far the most common type, involves the deterioration of the cartilage that covers the ends of bones, leading to pain and loss of movement as bone rubs against bone. Among young adults, osteoarthritis most often is seen in men—but after age 45, women sufferers outnumber men. Second-most common is rheumatoid arthritis, an autoimmune disease in which the immune system attacks and inflames the synovium (membrane lining the joints). One of the most severe types of arthritis, it affects women twice as often as it does men.

What to do: Follow the steps below to help prevent various types of arthritis…

1. Reduce the weight load on your knees. The more you weigh, the more likely you are to get arthritis in the knees.

Helpful: Even if genes place you at increased risk, dropping your excess weight—or

Joanne M. Jordan, MD, MPH, professor and chief of the division of rheumatology, allergy and immunology, University of North Carolina, and director of the Thurston Arthritis Research Center, both in Chapel Hill.

perhaps even as little as 10 to 12 pounds—makes your arthritis risk drop, too.

2. Guard against joint injury. People who have had any type of knee or shoulder injury are more likely to eventually develop arthritis in that joint than people with no such history of injury.

Prudent: To help prevent neuromuscular injuries that can place added stress on joints, warm up for five minutes before you exercise or perform any strenuous activity (shoveling snow, moving furniture)…and stretch afterward. Watch out for hazards that could lead to falls and bone fractures, such as icy sidewalks and cluttered floors.

3. Avoid repetitive motions. Some evidence suggests a link between osteoarthritis and activities that require repetitive use of specific joints, such as continuous typing or cashiering.

Self-defense: Vary your motions as much as possible…and take frequent breaks.

4. Minimize exposure to infection. Arthritis can develop after a person contracts certain infections, such as salmonella, erythema infectiosum ("fifth disease") or hepatitis B.

Theory: These infections trigger cellular damage, especially in people genetically predisposed to arthritis.

Precautions: Wash hands often…avoid contact with people who have infections.

5. Stay away from cigarettes. Toxic chemicals in smoke appear to damage joint fibers—so refrain from smoking and minimize your exposure to secondhand smoke.

To quit smoking: Visit *www.smokefree.gov* for referrals to quit lines and advice on smoking cessation.

6. Exercise for 75 minutes or more each week. In a recent study, women in their 70s who exercised for at least an hour and 15 minutes weekly for three years reported significantly fewer joint problems than women who exercised less. Doubling that workout time was even more beneficial.

Good options: Walking, tai chi, yoga, swimming, weight lifting.

7. Eat the "Big Three" anti-arthritis antioxidants. Antioxidants neutralize tissue-damaging molecules called free radicals. Some observational studies suggest that three in particular may guard against arthritis.

Findings: In a study of more than 25,000 people, researchers found that those who developed arthritis ate, on average, 20% less zeaxanthin and 40% less beta-cryptoxanthine than those who did not get arthritis. Both of these antioxidants are found in yellow-orange fruits and vegetables (apricots, pineapple, peppers, winter squash)…zeaxanthin also is found in leafy green vegetables (arugula, chicory, kale, spinach). Another study of 400 people showed that those with the highest blood levels of lutein—also found in leafy greens—were 70% less likely to have knee arthritis than those with the lowest levels.

Sensible: Boost your intake of foods rich in these three important antioxidants.

8. Get the "Top Two" vitamins. In one study of 556 people, those with the lowest blood levels of vitamin D were three times more likely to have knee osteoarthritis than participants with the highest levels. A larger clinical study is in progress, so it is too early to make specific recommendations—but it probably is wise to include plenty of vitamin D–rich foods (such as fish and low- or nonfat dairy) in your diet.

Observational studies also suggest that vitamin C helps keep arthritis from progressing—perhaps by stimulating the production of collagen, cartilage and other connective tissues in the joints.

Healthful: Foods high in vitamin C include citrus fruits, guava, peppers and sweet potatoes.

9. Do not neglect omega-3 fatty acids. These natural anti-inflammatories appear to reduce the risk of developing arthritis (especially rheumatoid) and to ease symptom severity in people who already have the disease.

Best: Ask your doctor about taking fish oil supplements that provide the omega-3s *eicosapentaenoic acid* (EPA) and *docosahexaenoic acid* (DHA).

Interesting: You have an advantage if you were born, raised and currently live in the western part of the US.

Recent finding: Compared with women in the West, those in other areas of the country have a 37% to 45% higher risk for rheumatoid arthritis.

Possible influences: Regional differences in lifestyle, diet, environmental exposures and/or genetic factors.

What to do: You can't necessarily change where you live, of course—but if your location suggests an increased risk for arthritis, you can be extra conscientious about following the self-defense strategies above.

have RA, but they might not. In addition, a negative RF reading might not rule out RA.

An alternative: A blood test developed several years ago, which is becoming more widely used, serves as a better diagnostic tool. Called the anti-cyclic citrullinated peptide (anti-CCP) test, it is able to identify RA in its earliest stages. It also is able to detect RA in healthy individuals years before symptoms of the disease are noticeable. Those diagnosed with RA in its earliest stages have a better chance of preventing joint deterioration and getting the condition under control with natural treatments.

Best: Have both tests to ensure accuracy.

Diagnostic Joint Test

Mark A. Stengler, NMD, licensed naturopathic medical doctor and leading authority on the practice of alternative and integrated medicine. He is founder and medical director of the Stengler Center for Integrative Medicine, Encinitas, California, and associate clinical professor at the National College of Natural Medicine, Portland, Oregon. He is author of *The Natural Physician's Healing Therapies* (Bottom Line Books).

I see a lot of patients who are suffering from joint pain that has not been properly diagnosed. A blood test that is becoming more popular can help.

Joint pain, including swelling in the hands, knees, shoulders and even neck, develops in many people over age 50. It could be osteoarthritis, the most common form of arthritis, in which the cartilage covering bones deteriorates. Or it could be rheumatoid arthritis (RA), a common type of arthritis that causes inflammation of the joints. RA is an autoimmune disease in which the immune system doesn't recognize healthy tissue and attacks it. About two million Americans have RA, and it affects three times as many women as men.

The problem: The standard test for RA, the rheumatoid factor (RF) blood test, is not the most reliable way to diagnose RA. The test measures blood levels of RF antibody, which is present in 80% of adults with RA. Those with a significant concentration of RF likely

How People with Arthritis Can Avoid Joint Replacement

Kimberly Beauchamp, ND, licensed naturopathic doctor and health and nutrition writer based in North Kingstown, Rhode Island. Her blog, Eat Happy, helps take the drama out of healthy eating. *www.eathappy blog.com*

Arthritis is easily the most common cause of physical disability in America. A newly released report from the National Institutes of Health (NIH) says that nearly 50 million Americans have doctor-diagnosed arthritis (including both osteoarthritis, or OA, and rheumatoid arthritis, or RA) and predicts that that number will soar to 67 million in the next 20 years. That's a lot of stiff, painful knees, hands, shoulders and feet!

While some folks joke that they're headed straight for joint replacement, the truth is that arthritis responds well to many natural therapies, including dietary supplements. The staggering numbers in the recent NIH report motivated us to check in with Kimberly Beauchamp, ND, a licensed naturopathic physician and health and nutrition writer in North Kingstown, Rhode Island, who treats many arthritis patients.

PAIN SOOTHERS FOR ARTHRITIS PATIENTS

Dr. Beauchamp shared some supplements and natural therapies that many arthritis patients find helpful…

• **Zyflamend.** This proprietary blend of supplements contains 10 anti-inflammatory plant extracts that can be helpful for many people with both OA and RA. Dr. Beauchamp has patients take one capsule twice daily with meals. (Available online at *www.newchapter.com* and at many health-food stores.)

• **Red Seaweed Extract.** Red seaweed extract (Lithomanion calcarea) can help people with OA. One study reported in *Nutrition Journal* and funded by Marigot, the company that makes Aquamin (a patented red seaweed extract), found that taking the extract for one month was associated with a 20% reduction in arthritis pain. Patients also reported less stiffness and better range of motion and were able to walk further than those taking a placebo. A typical dose would be 2,400 mg of seaweed extract in capsule form each day, Dr. Beauchamp said. (Note: Seaweed contains iodine in amounts that may be dangerous to thyroid patients.)

• **Vitamin D.** New research indicates that vitamin D may play a key role in slowing the development and progression of both OA and RA. If you have either, it's a good idea to get your blood level of vitamin D checked, said Dr. Beauchamp. If you are deficient, she suggests taking at least 1,000 IU of vitamin D-3 (cholecalciferol) each day.

• **Peat/Peloid Packs (also called balneotherapy).** Commonly used in Europe, this is a form of thermal mud therapy that holds heat particularly well. Peat (or peloid packs that are sheets of peat mud on fabric) is applied to the aching area for about 20 minutes. The treatment can be done at home, but Dr. Beauchamp said it is far better to work with a physical therapist or doctor who is knowledgeable in the technique, as the packs are cumbersome and must be carefully applied to protect the skin from burning. Peat therapy treatments are typically administered over the course of several visits, declining in frequency as the patient's pain begins to ease—the results are long-lasting and you can resume treatment if and when the pain returns.

OLDIES BUT GOODIES

Here are some other remedies that you've likely already heard about but that shouldn't be overlooked if you are searching for relief from arthritis pain…

• **Fish oil (omega-3 fatty acids).** Effective at reducing inflammation for both RA and OA, studies show that omega-3s can be so helpful for RA patients that they sometimes can reduce their medications. OA patients usually see results quickly —Dr. Beauchamp said two grams of fish oil daily is a common dosage, while RA patients may require higher levels to benefit. Ask your doctor about the appropriate amount for you.

• **Glucosamine sulfate/chondroitin sulfate** (or chondroitin sodium sulfate). Dr. Beauchamp often prescribes 1,500 mg of glucosamine and 1,200 mg of chondroitin daily, divided into three doses.

Caution: Glucosamine and chondroitin often are derived from crabs and other hard-shelled sea creatures, so do not take them if you are allergic to shellfish. Glucosamine and chondroitin should also be avoided by people on blood-thinning medications such as *warfarin* (Coumadin).

• **Methylsulfonylmethane (MSM) is** a sulfur derivative that is beneficial for some people with OA. It may help prevent cartilage degeneration, and it's also known to decrease pain and improve physical function. It's thought that MSM works better when combined with glucosamine—take one gram of MSM twice daily with meals.

AND DON'T FORGET ABOUT THESE!

• **Massage and acupuncture.** Many people, including those with RA or OA, find these treatments to be soothing—it makes sense, since both techniques increase blood flow to the muscles and ligaments around the joints (particularly the knees and hips), which are stressed by arthritis.

• **Exercise.** Acknowledging that this often is the last thing people in pain feel like doing, Dr. Beauchamp says exercise is still essential for both OA and RA patients.

The primary benefit: Exercise delivers fresh blood cells to the affected areas, bringing in nutrients and removing waste, including acidic waste products in the muscles that may provoke inflammation. She suggests swimming, walking or perhaps working with a trainer who is knowledgeable about arthritis.

●**Weight control.** Keeping your weight down reduces the pressure on painful joints for both OA and RA patients. The NIH study mentioned earlier in the story found twice as much arthritis in obese people as in people of healthy weight. One study showed that losing just 11 pounds reduced risk for knee OA by half and significantly reduced pain in the knees of those already afflicted.

Dance to Avoid Arthritis

Women in their 70s who reported no stiff or painful joints at the start of a three-year study and who engaged in moderate exercise, such as dancing or brisk walking, for a little more than one hour a week reduced their risk of developing arthritis symptoms by 26%. Women who did at least two hours per week of moderate exercise reduced their risk by 46%.

Other good options: Tai chi, yoga and swimming.

Kristiann Heesch, DrPh, research fellow, School of Human Movement Studies, University of Queensland, Australia, and researcher on a study of 8,750 women, published in *Arthritis Research & Therapy*.

Rheumatoid Arthritis

Mark A. Stengler, NMD, licensed naturopathic medical doctor and leading authority on the practice of alternative and integrated medicine. He is founder and medical director of the Stengler Center for Integrative Medicine, Encinitas, California. He is author of *The Natural Physician's Healing Therapies* (Bottom Line Books).

Rheumatoid arthritis (RA) is an autoimmune condition in which the joints (usually the hands, wrists and knees) become painful, swollen, red and deformed to varying degrees. While the cause is unknown, it is believed that the immune system malfunctions and attacks its own joint tissues, causing cartilage to degenerate. There are a variety of natural remedies that can be used to reduce the symptoms associated with this disease. One of the best is high doses of fish oil, which has been shown in studies to reduce stiffness and the need for nonsteroidal anti-inflammatory drugs. Look for a product that includes *eicosapentaenoic acid* (EPA) and *docosahexaenoic acid* (DHA). Take 6,000 mg daily of combined EPA and DHA. If you are on a blood-thinning medication, such as *warfarin* (Coumadin), check with your doctor before taking this. It takes about 12 weeks to achieve a therapeutic benefit from fish oil.

Arthritis Relief Treatments That Work Very Well

John D. Clough, MD, rheumatologist in the department of rheumatic and immunologic disease at The Cleveland Clinic. He is author of *Arthritis* (The Cleveland Clinic).

More than 21 million Americans suffer from osteoarthritis, a degenerative joint disease. That's the bad news.

The good news—we know more about the disease now than ever before, including how to slow its progression.

CAUSES

There are many different forms of arthritis. Osteoarthritis is the most common form. When you have osteoarthritis, the cartilage that cushions the ends of the bones in your joints deteriorates. Over time, the cartilage may wear down completely, leaving bone rubbing on bone.

Osteoarthritis commonly affects the fingers, neck, lower back, hips and knees. *The exact cause of the disease isn't known, but the following are key risk factors...*

• **Advancing age.** People 45 years and older are at greater risk for the disease. In older people, the joint cartilage contains less fluid and may become brittle, which leads to deterioration.

• **Family history.** Heredity plays a role, especially in osteoarthritis of the hands. This particular type of osteoarthritis, which ultimately gives the fingers a gnarled appearance, is more common in women whose mothers also suffered from the condition.

• **Previous injury.** Not every joint injury causes a problem, but if you have had torn cartilage or a disruption of the ligaments in a major joint, then you are more likely to develop a problem in that area.

• **Obesity.** Being overweight puts unnecessary stress on weight-bearing joints—particularly hips and knees.

EARLY WARNINGS

Osteoarthritis often progresses slowly, but there can be early signs...

• **Joint pain during or after use,** after a period of inactivity or during a change in the weather.

• **Swelling and stiffness in a joint,** particularly after using it.

• **Joint instability,** especially noticeable in the knees, which can even take on a knock-kneed or bowlegged appearance as the cartilage deteriorates.

• **Bony lumps.** With osteoarthritis of the hands, these lumps (called Heberden's nodes and Bouchard's nodes) can appear on the middle or end joints of the fingers or at the base of your thumb.

PROTECT YOURSELF

There is no known cure for osteoarthritis, but lifestyle measures can help. *To prevent or slow progression of the disease...*

• **Lose weight.** While it's obvious that running and jumping can be hard on the joints, if you're overweight, even everyday tasks such as walking and climbing stairs can be problematic. Shed pounds, and you can ease the pressure on your weight-bearing joints.

• **Exercise.** Choose low-impact activities, such as walking, cycling and swimming, so that you don't put too much pressure on your joints.

If you've had a knee injury, it also pays to do quadriceps-strengthening and hamstring-stretching exercises so that those muscles can better stabilize and operate the knee.

Recent finding: A study published in *Arthritis & Rheumatism* shows that people with knee osteoarthritis who exercised regularly for as long as 18 months had less disability and were able to walk much greater distances than people who dropped out of the program.

Check with your doctor before beginning a regular exercise program. He/she may recommend working with a physical therapist who can design an exercise program to meet your specific needs.

MEDICATIONS

Osteoarthritis sufferers have a range of treatment options...

• **Oral medications.** The most commonly used drugs for osteoarthritis are pain relievers, such as acetaminophen (Tylenol) and nonsteroidal anti-inflammatory drugs (NSAIDs), which fall into two categories...

• **Nonselective NSAIDs.** Drugs such as aspirin, *ibuprofen* (Advil), *diclofenac* (Voltaren) and *naproxen* (Aleve) are commonly used to treat the symptoms caused by inflammation (pain, swelling, redness, etc.), and they work very well for some people. However, long-term use of NSAIDs can cause problems ranging from stomach upset to gastrointestinal bleeding.

• **Selective Cox-2 inhibitors.** These drugs were originally touted as being less likely to cause gastrointestinal problems than traditional NSAIDs, but most have been pulled from the shelves because of potentially devastating side effects. *Rofecoxib* (Vioxx), for example, was pulled in September 2004 after a study showed that the drug predisposed people to heart attacks. Currently, there's only one Cox-2 inhibitor, *celecoxib* (Celebrex), still in use. Celebrex does not seem to cause the same heart risks as Vioxx.

In a paper published in *The Journal of the American Medical Association*, three researchers at Harvard University examined 114 clinical trials of Vioxx, Celebrex and other drugs. The researchers found that Celebrex was associated with lower blood pressure readings (unlike Vioxx, which was associated with higher blood pressure readings).

• **Injections.** In cases where a particular joint is acutely inflamed, a physician might opt to inject a corticosteroid preparation into the joint. This can provide rapid relief for up to several months, but long-term use of corticosteroids can be harmful to tissue and bones.

SUPPLEMENTS

Glucosamine and chondroitin sulfate play a role in the structure of cartilage and other connective tissue—and you can get them over-the-counter in supplement form. A massive study, known as the "Glucosamine/Chondroitin Arthritis Intervention Trial (GAIT)," coordinated by the University of Utah School of Medicine, found that in patients with moderate to severe pain, glucosamine and chondroitin provided statistically significant pain relief. However, the combination did not work any better than a placebo for the overall group of patients.

Also, one study suggests that glucosamine could potentially slow the progression of osteoarthritis of the knees, although not all studies of this supplement confirm this finding. More research is needed, but the supplements seem safe to use if you choose to try them.

Exception: People who are allergic to shellfish should steer clear of glucosamine, which is made from shellfish.

JOINT REPLACEMENT

In joint-replacement therapy (arthroplasty), the damaged joint is removed and replaced with a plastic or metal prosthesis. Joint replacement can be very effective, particularly for the major weight-bearing joints, such as the hips and knees, allowing you an active, pain-free life. Shoulder replacement also is effective, and the technology for smaller, more complex joints, such as the wrist and ankle, is improving.

Breakthrough Research On Beating Arthritis Pain Naturally

Peter Bales, MD, board-certified orthopedic surgeon and author of *Osteoarthritis: Preventing and Healing Without Drugs* (Prometheus).

Osteoarthritis has long been considered a "wear-and-tear" disease associated with age-related changes that occur within cartilage and bone.

Now: A growing body of evidence shows that osteoarthritis may have a metabolic basis. Poor diet results in inflammatory changes and damage in cartilage cells, which in turn lead to cartilage breakdown and the development of osteoarthritis.

A recent increase in osteoarthritis cases corresponds to similar increases in diabetes and obesity, other conditions that can be fueled by poor nutrition. Dietary approaches can help prevent—or manage—all three of these conditions.

Key scientific evidence: A number of large studies, including many conducted in Europe as well as the US, suggest that a diet emphasizing plant foods and fish can support cartilage growth and impede its breakdown. People who combine an improved diet with certain supplements can reduce osteoarthritis symptoms—and possibly stop progression of the disease.

A SMARTER DIET

By choosing your foods carefully, you can significantly improve the pain and stiffness caused by osteoarthritis. *How to get started...*

• **Avoid acidic foods.** The typical American diet, with its processed foods, red meat and harmful trans-fatty acids, increases acidity in the body. A high-acid environment within the joints increases free radicals, corrosive molecules that both accelerate cartilage damage and inhibit the activity of cartilage-producing cells known as chondrocytes.

A Mediterranean diet, which includes generous amounts of fruits, vegetables, whole grains, olive oil and fish, is more alkaline.

(The body requires a balance of acidity and alkalinity, as measured on the pH scale.) A predominantly alkaline body chemistry inhibits free radicals and reduces inflammation.

What to do: Eat a Mediterranean-style diet, including six servings daily of vegetables...three servings of fruit...and two tablespoons of olive oil. (The acids in fruits and vegetables included in this diet are easily neutralized in the body.) Other sources of healthful fats include olives, nuts (such as walnuts), canola oil and flaxseed oil or ground flaxseed.

Important: It can take 12 weeks or more to flush out acidic toxins and reduce arthritis symptoms after switching to an alkaline diet.

•**Limit your intake of sugary and processed foods.** Most Americans consume a lot of refined carbohydrates as well as sugar-sweetened foods and soft drinks—all of which damage joints in several ways. For example, sugar causes an increase in *advanced glycation endproducts* (AGEs), protein molecules that bind to collagen (the connective tissue of cartilage and other tissues) and make it stiff and brittle. AGEs also appear to stimulate the production of cartilage-degrading enzymes.

What to do: Avoid processed foods, such as white flour (including cakes, cookies and crackers), white pasta and white rice, as well as soft drinks and fast food. Studies have shown that people who mainly eat foods in their whole, natural forms tend to have lower levels of AGEs and healthier cartilage.

Important: Small amounts of sugar—used to sweeten coffee or cereal, for example—will not significantly increase AGE levels.

•**Get more vitamin C.** More than 10 years ago, the Framingham study found that people who took large doses of vitamin C had a threefold reduction in the risk for osteoarthritis progression.

Vitamin C is an alkalinizing agent due to its anti-inflammatory and antioxidant properties. It blocks the inflammatory effects of free radicals. Vitamin C also decreases the formation of AGEs and reduces the chemical changes that cause cartilage breakdown.

What to do: Take a vitamin C supplement (1,000 mg daily for the prevention of osteoarthritis...2,000 mg daily if you have osteoarthritis).* Also increase your intake of vitamin C–rich foods, such as sweet red peppers, strawberries and broccoli.

•**Drink green tea.** Green tea alone won't relieve osteoarthritis pain, but people who drink green tea and switch to a healthier diet may notice an additional improvement in symptoms. That's because green tea is among the most potent sources of antioxidants, including catechins, substances that inhibit the activity of cartilage-degrading enzymes.

For osteoarthritis, drink one to two cups of green tea daily. (Check with your doctor first if you take any prescription drugs.)

•**Eat fish.** Eat five to six three-ounce servings of omega-3–rich fish (such as salmon, sardines and mackerel) weekly. Omega-3s in such fish help maintain the health of joint cartilage and help curb inflammation. If you would prefer to take a fish oil supplement rather than eat fish, see the recommendation below.

SUPPLEMENTS THAT HELP

Dietary changes are a first step to reducing osteoarthritis symptoms. However, the use of certain supplements also can be helpful.

•**Fish oil.** The two omega-3s in fish—*docosahexaenoic acid* (DHA) and *eicosapentaenoic acid* (EPA)—block chemical reactions in our cells that convert dietary fats into chemical messengers (such as prostaglandins), which affect the inflammatory status of our bodies. This is the same process that's inhibited by nonsteroidal anti-inflammatory drugs (NSAIDs), such as *ibuprofen* (Motrin).

What to do: If you find it difficult to eat the amount of omega-3–rich fish mentioned above, ask your doctor about taking fish oil supplements that supply a total of 1,600 mg of EPA and 800 mg of DHA daily. Look for a "pharmaceutical grade" fish oil product, such as Sealogix, available at FishOilRx.com, 888-966-3423, *www.fishoilrx.com*...or RxOmega-3 Factors at iherb.com, *www.iherb.com*.

*Check with your doctor before taking any dietary supplements.

If, after 12 weeks, you need more pain relief—or have a strong family history of osteoarthritis—add...

•**Glucosamine, chondroitin and MSM.** The most widely used supplements for osteoarthritis are glucosamine and chondroitin, taken singly or in combination. Most studies show that they work.

Better: A triple combination that contains *methylsulfonylmethane* (MSM) as well as glucosamine and chondroitin. MSM is a sulfur-containing compound that provides the raw material for cartilage regrowth. Glucosamine and chondroitin reduce osteoarthritis pain and have anti-inflammatory properties.

What to do: Take daily supplements of glucosamine (1,500 mg)...chondroitin (1,200 mg)...and MSM (1,500 mg).

Instead of—or in addition to—the fish oil and the triple combination, you may want to take...

•**SAMe.** Like MSM, S-adenosylmethionine (SAMe) is a sulfur-containing compound. It reduces the body's production of TNF-alpha, a substance that's involved in cartilage destruction. It also seems to increase cartilage production.

In one study, researchers compared SAMe to the prescription anti-inflammatory drug *celecoxib* (Celebrex). The study was double-blind (neither the patients nor the doctors knew who was getting which drug or supplement), and it continued for four months. Initially, patients taking the celecoxib reported fewer symptoms—but by the second month, there was no difference between the two groups.

Other studies have found similar results. SAMe seems to work as well as over-the-counter and/or prescription drugs for osteoarthritis, but it works more slowly. It usually takes at least three months for patients to see effects.

What to do: Start with 200 mg of SAMe daily and increase to 400 mg daily if necessary after a few weeks

Qigong Eases Arthritis

Kevin W. Chen, PhD, MPH, associate professor, Center for Integrative Medicine, University of Maryland, Baltimore, and coauthor of a study of 106 arthritis patients, published in *Clinical Rheumatology*.

Practitioners of qigong use traditional Chinese medicine techniques—such as mind-body breath work, acupressure, therapeutic touch and focused attention—to stimulate the healing flow of qi (energy).

New study: Among patients with knee osteoarthritis, those who participated in five or six qigong sessions reported 13% to 26% greater reduction in pain and 13% to 28% more improvement in function than patients who got placebo treatments.

Results vary depending on the practitioner—so look for an experienced practitioner when starting out, then take classes to learn to practice qigong on your own.

Resources: National Qigong Association, 888-815-1893, *www.nqa.org*...Qigong Research Society, 856-234-3056, *www.qigongresearchsociety.com*.

The Anti-Arthritis Diet

Harris McIlwain, MD, board-certified specialist in rheumatology and geriatric medicine who practices with the Tampa Medical Group in Florida, *www.tampamedicalgroup.com*. He is coauthor of *Pain-Free Arthritis—A 7-Step Program for Feeling Better Again* (Holt).

In my rheumatology practice I often treat patients suffering from painfully arthritic joints who have been unable to get relief, despite seeing many doctors. I tell them that one of the most important things they can do for their arthritis is to change their diets. After just a few weeks on my pain-free diet plan, I've had many patients cut back on their anti-inflammatory medications and even put off joint-replacement surgery. The diet helps alleviate pain and stiffness in most types of arthritis, including rheumatoid arthritis and osteoarthritis.

How it works: The pain-free diet guides you toward healing foods that are known to reduce inflammation and boost the immune system. It helps you eliminate those foods that promote inflammation and might trigger symptoms. The diet also includes recommendations on nutritional supplements.

Bonus: This nutritional approach makes it easier to maintain a healthy body weight, which is essential for patients who need to take pressure off their joints. Maintaining a healthy body weight also produces metabolic changes that lessen the body's inflammatory response.

Helpful: It's easier to maintain a healthy weight when you eat frequent, smaller meals. Instead of three large meals, eat about six mini-meals throughout the day. In addition to a breakfast, lunch and dinner of about 300 calories each, eat three snacks between meals of about 150 to 200 calories each.

FOODS THAT HEAL

Foods that are high in antioxidants and other inflammation-fighting nutrients can noticeably reduce arthritis pain and stiffness when consumed daily. *The following are especially effective…*

• **High-antioxidant fruits and vegetables.** Antioxidants help reduce inflammation. Several years ago, the US Department of Agriculture ranked the following foods according to their antioxidant activity. Among the top 10 fruits and vegetables from highest to lowest were blueberries, kale, strawberries, spinach, Brussels sprouts, plums, broccoli, beets, oranges and red grapes. Eat a variety of these foods, raw and cooked, to get the greatest benefit.

Also beneficial: Asparagus, cabbage, cauliflower, tomatoes, sweet potatoes, avocados, grapefruit, peaches and watermelon.

• **Oil-rich fish.** Research has shown that the omega-3 fatty acids contained in anchovies, mackerel, salmon, sardines, shad, tuna, whitefish and herring help reduce inflammation—particularly levels of leukotriene B4, a chemical that contributes to many types of arthritis. Researchers have found that women who ate at least three servings of baked or broiled fish weekly had about half the risk of

getting rheumatoid arthritis as those who ate only one serving.

• **Soy.** Studies have found that a diet rich in soy may help reduce inflammation-related pain and swelling. Try tofu, soy milk, soy yogurt, soybeans or miso, a traditional Japanese food consisting of fermented soybeans and made into a thick paste.

• **Green and black tea.** Green tea contains a polyphenol (a chemical found in plants that acts as an antioxidant) called EGCG, which can inhibit a key gene involved in the arthritis inflammation response. Research suggests that the more you drink, the more benefit you'll get. Black tea, while processed differently than green, also provides benefits. It contains anti-inflammatory chemicals of its own called theaflavins. The Iowa Women's Health Study found that women who drank three or more cups of tea (not including herbal tea) reduced their risk of rheumatoid arthritis by 60%.

• **Pineapple.** This tasty fruit contains bromelain, an enzyme that reduces inflammation associated with arthritis. Fresh pineapple is the most beneficial, but canned is also good.

• **Onions and apples.** Both of these foods are especially high in flavonoids, which are also inflammation-fighting compounds. Eat a variety of these foods, both raw and cooked.

FOODS TO AVOID

The only way to know which of the foods below affect your joint pain is to eliminate each one for at least two weeks and assess your symptoms. That way, you'll know which type of food increases your inflammation and pain.

• **Avoid foods that increase inflammation.** There are a variety of foods that trigger the body to produce cytokines—naturally occurring proteins that can promote inflammation, leading to pain and deterioration of cartilage in the joints. These include beef and other red meat…foods cooked at high temperatures, particularly fried foods…and any foods containing man-made trans fats (often called partially hydrogenated fats or oils on food labels), including junk food and commercial baked goods. Eat these types of foods sparingly.

• **Reduce intake of foods from animal products.** I tell my patients to eat turkey and chicken in moderation. But the fact is that all animal products—including poultry, some farm-raised fish, egg yolks and other dairy products—contain arachidonic acid, a fatty acid that is converted by the body into prostaglandins and leukotrienes, two other types of inflammation-causing chemicals. I've had many patients tell me that they reduced arthritis symptoms by adopting a "modified vegetarian" diet.

Key: Decrease your intake of animal protein and increase the amount of protein you get from fish and plant sources, such as beans, nuts, soy, portobello mushrooms (a common meat substitute) and whole grains.

Start by substituting one-fourth of the animal protein you normally eat with plant-based foods, cold-water fish and low-fat dairy. After two or three months, increase the substitution to half—adding more vegetables, fruits, lentils, beans, fish, whole grains and low-fat dairy. After a while, many of my patients choose to give up all animal protein because they enjoy the benefit of reduced pain and inflammation.

Note: A small percentage of people find that certain vegetables—including tomatoes, white potatoes, peppers and eggplant—make their arthritis worse. These nightshade family plants contain solanine, a substance that can be toxic if not sufficiently digested in the intestines. Eliminate all of these foods, then add them back one at a time—as long as you do not have pain or inflammation.

• **Stay away from foods with a high glycemic index.** While high-glycemic foods (foods that quickly raise your blood sugar) should be avoided by people with diabetes or prediabetes, they pose problems for people with arthritis as well.

Reason: They increase insulin production, which promotes accumulation of body fat and causes a rebound sensation of hunger a few hours after eating—making it harder to maintain a healthy weight, which is important for reducing arthritis symptoms.

High-glycemic foods include table sugar, baked white potatoes, French fries, pretzels, white bread and rolls, white and brown rice, potato and corn chips, waffles, doughnuts and corn flakes.

The following supplements may also help reduce arthritis inflammation. Always check with your doctor before taking any dietary supplement—even a "natural" one.

• **Glucosamine (1,500 mg/daily).** While the data on this nutritional supplement are mixed, it's perfectly safe. Some studies suggest that it may slow arthritis progression. It's often combined with chondroitin (1,200 mg), another nutritional supplement that may help relieve arthritis symptoms for some people.

• **Vitamin C (500 mg to 1,000 mg/daily)** plays a key role in building and protecting collagen, an important component of cartilage. Among other things, it contains antioxidants that fight inflammation and help regenerate damaged joint tissue.

• **Bromelain.** This anti-inflammatory enzyme is found in pineapple, but it's also available in pill or capsule form. Include fresh pineapple (two servings daily) in your diet or take capsules (follow directions on label for amounts)—or do both.

• **Fish oil capsules.** For people who aren't eating two or more servings of fish per week, this is a good option. Your dose should provide 600 mg of combined DHA and EPA in a 2:1 ratio—the ratio that occurs naturally in wild salmon. Read your product's label for its DHA/EPA content.

• **Ginger.** Clinical studies have found that this herb reduces arthritis symptoms and inflammation. It can be taken in the form of tincture, capsules, as a spice added to foods or as a tea made from boiling ginger root. You may benefit by drinking ginger juice or extract. Since ginger inhibits blood clotting, don't consume more than four grams a day.

A Consumer Guide to Hip Replacements

Douglas E. Padgett, MD, chief of the Adult Reconstruction and Joint Replacement Division and an associate clinical investigator at the Hospital for Special Surgery in New York City.

A hip replacement operation can be a godsend for the thousands of people each year who have been living in pain from arthritis or other hip problems. Key to the long-term success of the operation is the choice of which type of replacement hip is used, since materials have different advantages for different types of people…and unfortunately, as Douglas E. Padgett, MD, chief of the Adult Reconstruction and Joint Replacement Division and an associate clinical investigator at the Hospital for Special Surgery in New York told us, none of the choices are perfect. "What's best is human cartilage on human cartilage—everything else is second best," he said. Given that, what factors influence which kind of joint is used on you? And, what are the risks involved with each option? *We spoke with Dr. Padgett about it…*

HOW HIP JOINTS WORK

• **Just like a natural hip, an artificial hip joint is composed of a ball (highly polished metal or ceramic) and a socket** (a durable cup of metal, plastic or ceramic, sometimes with an outer metal shell). However, the bones of natural hip joints are sheathed with cartilage that enables them to glide smoothly, whereas in artificial ones the friction is literally hundreds of times greater. As a result, they may wear out in 15 to 20 years depending on how active the patient is and which materials are used. Of greater concern is what's known as "wear debris"—particles that get released when the surfaces rub together, causing inflammation, scar tissue and degradation of surrounding tissue. This can result in the need for additional surgery or even a "redo" hip replacement.

Since all materials have their pros and cons, it makes sense to know as much as you can about the different kinds of implants so you can participate with your surgeon in deciding which is right for you. Factors that affect the decision include age, gender, activity level and the extent of damage to your natural hip.

Dr. Padgett reviewed the options currently available. There are advantages and disadvantages to each type of bearing. "I use all of them for different reasons, for different types of patients," he said.

• **Metal or ceramic ball on polyethylene liner bearings.** In this type of coupling, a polyethylene cup is mated with either metallic (cobalt chromium) or a ceramic (alumina or zirconia) head. "Polyethylene is a medical-grade plastic, much like the material used to make cutting boards," explained Dr. Padgett. "Early versions of polyethylene bearings were highly susceptible to wear, but recent technology has improved its durability. Polyethylene bearings are well tolerated in the body and they almost never fracture." Unfortunately, with wear these bearings erode and they may potentially shed polyethylene debris. The resulting inflammatory response around the bone may lead to resorption (osteolysis) or destruction of bone…and may be associated with implant loosening or even bone fracture.

Dr. Padgett says: "I use metal or ceramic on polyethylene bearings for older adults in their 70s and 80s, whose activities are somewhat less demanding—this type of coupling should last them for the rest of their lives." For younger, more active people, including those who engage in high-impact sports, he uses metal on polyethylene, noting "the newer polyethylene is more forgiving and less likely to lead to catastrophic failure."

• **Metal on metal bearings.** Made of cobalt chromium, metal bearings are "highly polished surfaces associated with low friction and low wear rates," said Dr. Padgett. However, he cautions, there may be problems associated with metal bearings. "At the end of the day, it's still metal in your body, even though new technology has helped reduce the problem by decreasing impurities and improving the hardness and smoothness of the metal bearings."

Also, he noted that some individuals develop a hypersensitivity to the metal, with an abnormal reaction leading to pain, loosening of the joint or implant failure. "There have been several reported cases of metal hypersensitivity leading to bone resorption and soft tissue injury," he said, adding that for anyone, leaving metal in the body for a long time may lead to other problems, including long-term concerns about kidney or liver toxicity that may cause disease or even be possibly carcinogenic.

Active people are at greatest risk for having their hip replacement wear out, with some data showing greater metal ion release with greater activity. However, this type of implant has potential for long-term function. Dr. Padgett uses these implants on young males, but not patients with known kidney or liver disease and not females of childbearing age, due to concerns that the ions have the potential to penetrate the placental barrier and affect a fetus.

• **Ceramic bearings.** Ceramics are composed of metal and non-metal compounds. "Ceramic surfaces are smooth and wettable, and will hold lubrication—factors which dramatically reduce wear rates for these bearings," said Dr. Padgett.

However, as with the other bearings, ceramics have some inherent problems—most significant is that they are brittle, and therefore vulnerable to chipping, cracking and breaking. When this became apparent after numerous adverse incidents in the 80s and 90s, surgeons abandoned ceramics in favor of other bearings, Dr. Padgett told us, adding that "improvements in the materials have made this rare, but not unheard of, today."

Lately there have been reports that some ceramic hips squeak audibly as patients go about their lives. Possible causes include a lack of lubrication of the joint by the body or the deposition of metal debris on the ceramic surface. Orthopedists have had a mixed response to this—some are unconcerned, but Dr. Padgett calls it worrisome. "If you are squeaking I would be concerned that you either have non-lubricated surfaces rubbing against one another, or some abnormality of the ceramic surface which could cause some damage to the bearing," he said.

Dr. Padgett says: "I use a ceramic on ceramic hip for patients who remain active but aren't involved in repetitive high-impact activities." "Patients in their 50s who want to remain actively engaged in less rigorous, low-impact sports such as golf are typically a good fit for this type of implant."

HIP FORECAST

Unfortunately, all bearings (metal, ceramic, polyethylene) have the potential to cause wear debris and elicit an inflammatory response. Scientists continue to work on developing new materials for artificial hips that promise longer wear and fewer potential problems. Possibilities include different types of metallurgy, such as diamond. "Highly compressed carbon would be very hard, very smooth and shatterproof," explained Dr. Padgett. For more information on hip replacement, go to the American Academy of Orthopaedic Surgeons Web site at *www.aaos.org*...or the American Association of Hip and Knee Surgeons at *www.aahks.org*.

19

Osteoporosis &
Bone Health

The Real Secret to Strong Bones

Contrary to popular belief, the degenerative bone disease osteoporosis is not an inevitable result of aging. Recent research shows that an important but overlooked cause of osteoporosis is an acid-forming diet.

We spoke with Susan E. Brown, PhD, author of *Better Bones, Better Body*, to learn more about this important research. *Her insights…*

THE ACID/ALKALI BALANCE

For survival, the body must maintain a balance between acids and alkalis, with good health depending on slight alkalinity. If the body's alkali reserves run low—a condition called chronic low-grade metabolic acidosis— alkaline mineral compounds are drawn from bones to buffer excess acids in the blood. The immediate benefit is that the body's pH (a measure of acidity or alkalinity) is balanced.

But over time, if bone mineral compounds are not replenished, osteoporosis develops.

Bone-depleting metabolic acidosis is easily reversible through diet. Yet the average American diet is woefully deficient in many of the nutrients needed to balance pH.

To protect bones: Follow the dietary suggestions on the next page. It's generally best to get nutrients from food. However, to help ensure adequate intake, take a daily multivitamin/mineral plus the other supplements noted…and consider additional supplements as well.

Before you start: Gauge your pH with a urine test kit, such as those sold in some pharmacies…or use the Better Bones Alkaline for Life pH Test Kit.

Susan E. Brown, PhD, medical anthropologist, certified nutritionist and director, The Center for Better Bones and Better Bones Foundation, both in Syracuse, New York. She is author of *Better Bones, Better Body* (McGraw-Hill) and *The Acid-Alkaline Food Guide* (Square One). *www.betterbones.com*

Cost: $29.95 (*www.betterbones.com*, click on "Visit Our Store," or call 877-207-0232). An ideal first morning urine pH is 6.5 to 7.5. The lower your pH is, the more helpful supplements may be. As with any supplement regimen, talk to your doctor before beginning.

BONE-SUPPORTIVE DIET

For a diet that builds bones...

•**Emphasize vegetables** (particularly dark, leafy greens and root vegetables), fruits, nuts, seeds and spices—these are alkalizing.

Daily targets: Eight servings of vegetables...three to four servings of fruit...two servings of nuts or seeds...and plentiful spices.

•**Consume meat, poultry, fish, dairy, eggs, legumes and whole grains in moderation—** they are acidifying.

Daily targets: One serving of meat, poultry or fish...one serving of eggs or legumes... one to two servings each of dairy and whole grains.

•**Minimize sugar, refined grains and processed foods**...limit coffee to two servings daily...limit alcohol to one serving daily. All these are very acidifying.

•**Fats neither increase nor decrease blood acidity—**but for overall health, keep fat intake moderate and opt for those that protect the heart, such as olive oil.

Important: It's not the acidity of a food itself that matters, but rather its metabolic effects. For instance, citrus fruits taste acidic, yet once metabolized, they are alkalizing.

MINERALS THAT BONES NEED MOST

Bone is composed of a living protein matrix of collagen upon which mineral crystals are deposited in a process called mineralization. *Key minerals, in order of importance...*

•**Potassium** neutralizes metabolic acids and reduces calcium loss.

Daily goal: 4,000 milligrams (mg) to 6,000 mg.

Sources: Avocados, baked potatoes, bananas, beet greens, cantaloupe, lima beans, sweet potatoes.

•**Magnesium** boosts absorption of calcium and production of the bone-preserving hormone calcitonin.

Daily goal: 400 mg to 800 mg.

Sources: Almonds, Brazil nuts, kelp, lentils, pumpkin seeds, soy, split peas, whole wheat, wild rice.

•**Calcium** gives bones strength.

Daily goal: 1,000 mg to 1,500 mg.

Sources: Amaranth flour, broccoli, canned sardines with bones, collards, dairy, kale, mustard greens, sesame seeds, spinach.

Also: Supplement daily, at a two-to-one ratio, with calcium citrate or calcium citrate malate plus magnesium—increasing calcium intake without also increasing magnesium can exacerbate asthma, arthritis and kidney stones.

•**Zinc** aids collagen production and calcium absorption.

Daily goal: 20 mg to 30 mg.

Sources: Alaskan king crab, cashews, kidney beans, meat, oysters, sesame seeds, wheat germ.

•**Manganese** helps form bone cartilage and collagen.

Daily goal: 10 mg to 15 mg.

Sources: Beets, blackberries, brown rice, loganberries, oats, peanuts, pineapple, rye, soy.

•**Copper** blocks bone breakdown and increases collagen formation.

Daily goal: 1 mg to 3 mg.

Sources: Barley, beans, chickpeas, eggplant, liver, molasses, summer squash.

•**Silica** increases collagen strength and bone calcification.

Daily goal: 30 mg to 50 mg.

Sources: Bananas, carrots, green beans, whole grains.

•**Boron** helps the body use calcium, magnesium and vitamin D.

Daily goal: 3 mg to 5 mg.

Sources: Almonds, avocados, black-eyed peas, cherries, grapes, tomatoes.

•**Strontium** promotes mineralization.

Daily goal: 3 mg to 20 mg.

Sources: Brazil nuts, legumes, root vegetables, whole grains.

VITAL VITAMINS

The following vitamins enhance bones' self-repair abilities…

• **Vitamin D** is essential because, without adequate amounts, you cannot absorb enough calcium. Many people do not get adequate vitamin D from sunlight. Vitamin D deficiency accounts for up to 50% of osteoporotic fractures.

Daily goal: 1,000 international units (IU) to 2,000 IU.

Best source: A daily supplement of cholecalciferol (vitamin D-3)—foods that contain vitamin D (fatty fish, fortified milk) do not provide enough and are acidifying.

• **Vitamins K-1 and K-2** boost bone matrix synthesis and bind calcium and phosphorous to bone.

Daily goal: 1,000 micrograms (mcg) of K-1 …and 90 mg to 180 mg of K-2.

Sources: Aged cheese, broccoli, Brussels sprouts, collard greens, kale, spinach, green tea.

If you supplement: For vitamin K-2, choose the MK-7 form.

Caution: Vitamin K can interfere with blood thinners, such as warfarin (Coumadin)—so talk to your doctor before altering vitamin K intake.

• **Vitamin C** aids collagen formation, stimulates bone-building cells and helps synthesize the adrenal hormones vital to postmenopausal bone health.

Daily goal: 500 mg to 2,000 mg.

Sources: Cantaloupe, kiwifruit, oranges, papaya, pink grapefruit, red peppers, strawberries.

• **Vitamins B-6, B-12** and folate help eliminate homocysteine, an amino acid linked to fracture risk.

Daily goal: 25 mg to 50 mg of B-6…200 mcg to 800 mcg of B-12…800 mcg to 1,000 mcg of folate.

Sources: For B-6—avocados, bananas, brown rice, oats, turkey, walnuts. For B-12—beef, salmon, trout. For folate—asparagus, okra, peanuts, pinto beans.

• **Vitamin A** helps develop bone-building osteoblast cells.

Daily goal: 5,000 IU.

Sources: Carrots, collard greens, pumpkin, sweet potatoes.

If you supplement: Choose the beta-carotene form.

Aspirin Can Help Build Bone

Low doses of aspirin—81 milligrams daily—increase production of bone-forming cells. More study is needed before aspirin can be recommended as an osteoporosis preventive.

Songtao Shi, DDS, PhD, associate professor, University of Southern California School of Dentistry, Los Angeles, and leader of an animal study reported in PLoS ONE *2008.*

The Best Bone-Building Exercises

Raymond E. Cole, DO, clinical assistant professor, Department of Internal Medicine, Michigan State University College of Osteopathic Medicine, East Lansing. He is author of Best Body, Best Bones: Your Doctor's Exercise Rx for Lifelong Fitness *(Wellpower). www.drraymondcole.com*

Women whose bones are fragile and porous—due to the severe loss of bone density that characterizes osteoporosis—often avoid exercise for fear that jarring or twisting motions could cause fractures.

Done properly, however, exercise is not only safe for people with osteoporosis or its milder form, osteopenia, it actually can reduce or even reverse bone loss. For people whose bones are still healthy, exercise helps ensure that osteoporosis never develops.

Reason: When a muscle exerts tension on a bone, it stimulates specialized cells that increase new bone formation. Also, when muscles that contribute to balance are strengthened, falls (and resulting fractures) are less likely.

Keys: Doing the types of workouts that build bone most effectively...and modifying techniques as necessary to avoid overstressing already weakened bones.

What to do: Start by exercising for 10 to 20 minutes several times a week, gradually building up to 30 minutes a day six days per week. Alternate between a strength-training workout one day and an aerobic activity the next.

Important: Before beginning the exercise program below, ask your doctor which instructions you should follow—the ones labeled "If you have healthy bones" or the ones labeled "If you already have bone loss."

STRENGTH TRAINING FOR BONES

The only equipment you need are hand weights (dumbbells) and ankle weights (pads that strap around the ankles), $20 and up per pair at sports equipment stores.

For each exercise, begin with one set of eight repetitions ("reps"). If you cannot do eight reps using the suggested starting weights, use lighter weights. Over several weeks, gradually increase to 10, then 12, then 15 reps. Then try two sets of eight reps, resting for one minute between sets...and again gradually increase the reps. When you can do two sets of 15 reps, increase the weight by one to two pounds and start again with one set of eight reps.

Keep your shoulders back and abdominal muscles pulled in. With each rep, exhale during the initial move...hold the position for two seconds...inhale as you return to the starting position. Move slowly, using muscles rather than momentum. Do not lock elbow or knee joints.

• **Upper body.** These exercises build bone density in the shoulders, arms and spine.

If you have healthy bones: Stand during the exercises. Start by holding a five-pound weight in each hand...over time, try to work up to eight, then 10, then 12 pounds.

If you already have bone loss: To guard against falls, sit in a straight-backed chair while exercising. At first, use no weights or use one- or two-pound weights...gradually work up to three-, then five-, then a maximum of eight-pound weights if you can. Avoid heavier weights—they could increase the risk for vertebral compression fractures.

• **Arms forward.**

To start: Bend elbows, arms close to your body, hands at chest-height, palms facing each other.

One rep: Straighten elbows until both arms are extended in front of you, parallel to the floor...hold... return to starting position.

• **Arm overhead.**

To start: Raise right arm straight overhead, palm facing forward.

One rep: Bend right elbow, bringing right hand down behind your head... hold...return to starting position. Do a set with the right arm, then with the left.

• **Arms up-and-down.**

To start: Have arms down at your sides, palms forward.

One rep: Keeping elbows close to your sides, bend arms to raise hands toward shoulders until palms face you...hold...lower to starting position.

• **Midbody.** This strengthens and stabilizes "core" muscles (abdomen, back, pelvic area). By improving body alignment, it helps prevent falls and reduces pressure on the vertebrae, protecting against compression fractures of the spine. No weights are used.

If you have healthy bones: Do this exercise while standing...or try it while lying on your back, with knees bent and feet flat on the floor.

If you already have bone loss: Done while standing, this is a good option for osteoporosis patients who are uncomfortable exercising on the floor. If you have balance problems, hold onto a counter...or sit in a chair.

• **Tummy tuck/pelvic tilt.**

To start: Have arms at sides, feet hip-width apart.

One rep: Simultaneously contract abdominal muscles to draw your tummy toward your spine, tighten buttocks muscles, and tilt the bottom of your pelvis forward to flatten the arch of your back…hold…return to starting position.

• **Lower body.** These moves increase bone density in the legs and feet. For each rep, raise the leg as high as possible without leaning…hold for two seconds…return to starting position.

Advanced option: Try not to touch your foot to the ground between reps.

If you have healthy bones: Start by wearing a two-pound ankle weight on each leg… gradually increase to 10 pounds per ankle.

If you already have bone loss: Hold onto a counter for balance. To begin, use no weights…build up, one pound at a time, to five pounds per ankle.

• **Leg forward-and-back.**

To start: Stand on your right foot.

One rep: Keeping both legs straight, slowly swing left leg forward and up…hold…swing leg down through the starting position and up behind you… hold…return to starting position. After one set, repeat with the other leg.

• **Leg out.**

To start: Stand on your right foot.

One rep: Keeping both legs straight, slowly lift left leg out to the side…hold…return to starting position. After one set, repeat with the other leg.

BONE-BENEFITING AEROBICS

Biking, stationary cycling, swimming and rowing are good for heart health—but they do not protect against osteoporosis.

Better: Weight-bearing aerobic activities in which you're on your feet, bones working against gravity, build bone mass in the hips and legs.

If you have healthy bones: Good choices include jogging, dancing, stair climbing, step aerobics, jumping rope, racket sports and interactive video games, such as Wii Fit and Dance Dance Revolution. If you enjoy walking, you can boost intensity by wearing a two- to 20-pound weighted vest ($50 and up at sports equipment stores).

Warning: Do not wear ankle weights during aerobic workouts—this could stress your joints.

If you already have bone loss: Refrain from high-impact activities (running, jumping) and those that require twisting or bending (racket sports, golf). Do not wear a weighted vest.

Safe low-impact options: Walking, using an elliptical machine (available at most gyms), qigong and tai chi.

Illustrations by Shawn Banner.

Cut Back on Cola

Women who drink one can of cola a day—diet, regular or decaffeinated—have significantly decreased bone mineral density, compared with women who don't drink cola. Low bone density weakens bones and increases osteoporosis risk.

Theory: Cola contains phosphoric acid, which may interfere with calcium absorption, lowering bone mineral density in women. There is no correlation between bone density and other soft drinks, and cola had no similar effect on men.

Katherine Tucker, MD, director, nutritional epidemiology, Tufts University, Boston, and lead author of a study program of 2,538 people, published in *The American Journal of Clinical Nutrition.*

The Benefits Of Potassium

Susan E. Brown, PhD, medical anthropologist, certified nutritionist and director, The Center for Better Bones and Better Bones Foundation, both in Syracuse, New York. She is author of *Better Bones, Better Body* (McGraw-Hill) and *The Acid-Alkaline Food Guide* (Square One). *www.betterbones.com*

Practically everyone knows how important calcium is to bone health, but there's another mineral that is equally critical, albeit in lesser amounts—potassium. A most recent study from the University of Basel, Switzerland, showed that a group of postmenopausal women with low bone density had, on average, a 1% increase in density after a year of taking a particular potassium supplement.

BALANCING THE EQUATION

Susan E. Brown, PhD, director of the Better Bones Foundation in Syracuse, New York (*www.betterbones.com*, explains how potassium relates to bone health.

Potassium is important in helping the body achieve a proper pH balance. In fact, when out of balance, you can die—really fast—so our bodies make this process a high priority. How does it work? As part of its normal metabolic processing, the body creates acids, which exit our systems via the lungs and kidneys. To buffer the harshness of these acids and protect delicate kidney tissue, the body neutralizes them with diet-derived alkali (base) compounds derived from fruits and vegetables. These are stored in our blood, other fluids, in muscle tissue and above all in bones. Our skeleton, in fact, is our largest storehouse of alkali mineral reserves. Just in case we run short, we keep extra alkali stores in our bones.

The severe lack of fruits and vegetables in the modern American diet creates an acidic environment in many. To neutralize excess acid, we need alkali compounds, which the body obtains first from easily available blood reserves, then from muscles, leading to muscle loss, and then by reaching into the bones. When and if that happens, we're left with bone breakdown and mineral loss—in other words, weakened bones.

NATURAL POTASSIUM CITRATE SOURCES

The particular form of potassium that serves to buffer the acids is potassium citrate, generally found in fruits, vegetables and legumes. People who regularly consume enough potassium citrate through a diet rich in those foods assure their body sufficient alkaline compounds to avoid any need to call on emergency supplies for homeostasis. Dr. Brown notes, "If you eat enough potassium-containing foods,

which should not be a problem, you have the proper pH balance." However, people today load their diet with meat, poultry, dairy and grains, which are metabolized as acids, creating a greater need for offsetting alkalids. If the body can't find these in foods, it turns to body tissue, including bones.

Though the US "Adequate Intake" (AI) potassium recommendation for adults is 4,700 mg per day, average consumption by adults in this country is around 2,200 mg for women and 3,200 mg for men.

Our lack of dietary potassium consumption looks to be a health crisis in the making, putting our bodies at risk for "consuming themselves," says Dr. Brown. In addition, potassium serves many other essential functions in the body. It contributes to nerve impulse transmission, muscle contraction and heart function, and also helps protect against stroke, kidney stones and high blood pressure.

GETTING IT RIGHT

Getting the right amount is trickier, however, than just swallowing a potassium citrate supplement each day. Though we know too little potassium is a problem, too much can also be an issue. By law potassium supplements do not exceed 99 mg units to discourage people from taking too much. (Excess potassium can cause heart problems in individuals with weak kidneys). Because potassium can accumulate in the blood, potassium supplements should only be taken with care under proper supervision.

The 1% increase in bone density achieved by the women in the Swiss study is considered significant, especially because it affected the hips and spine—two areas especially vulnerable to fracture. Though the study used potassium citrate supplements, it is possible, as Dr. Brown points out, to get what you need from dietary sources. You can achieve the AI of 4,700 mg per day by including 13 one-half cup servings of fruits, vegetables and legumes in your daily food intake. Admittedly, 13 sounds like a lot, but a large salad, for example, is four to six servings, a large apple is two. Those, plus a banana (440 mg, about one-and-a-half fruit servings) for an afternoon snack, and a baked potato at dinner along with a green vegetable and other vegetables, bring you easily to the goal of 4,700 mg.

Again, if you decide to take potassium citrate supplements, it is important to do so under the direction of a health-care professional who is well-versed in potassium needs and balance, such as a naturopathic physician or nutritionist. Potassium levels can be monitored by a simple blood test to be sure that you are getting neither too little, nor too much.

Fight Osteoporosis The Natural Way

Mark A. Stengler, NMD, licensed naturopathic medical doctor and leading authority on the practice of alternative and integrated medicine. He is founder and medical director of the Stengler Center for Integrative Medicine, Encinitas, California, and associate clinical professor at the National College of Natural Medicine, Portland, Oregon. He is author of *The Natural Physician's Healing Therapies* (Bottom Line Books).

Misconceptions abound when it comes to osteoporosis, a dreaded disease marked by porous, brittle bones and hunched backs. Most people think of osteoporosis as a women's disease, but it's more than that. While 8 million American women have been diagnosed with osteoporosis, more than 2 million men also are affected by it.

OSTEOPOROSIS: A SILENT PROBLEM

Osteoporosis can develop because, starting at about age 35, our bone cells do not make new bone as fast as it is broken down. Our bones become more frail and fracture more easily. Fractures, especially of the hip, spine and wrist, are more likely to occur, even without trauma. Osteoporosis has no symptoms until a bone is fractured. Many people go for decades without a diagnosis of osteoporosis—until they fall and an X-ray reveals porous bones.

Bone density can be measured with a *dual-energy X-ray absorptiometry* (DEXA) scan, but many people don't get this test. I recommend a baseline DEXA scan by age 50, and if

results are normal, follow-ups every three to five years.

The most worrisome risk for a person with osteoporosis is a hip fracture. According to the National Osteoporosis Foundation (*www.nof.org*), an average of 24% of hip-fracture patients age 50 or older die in the year following their fractures, often as a result of long-term immobilization that leads to blood clots or infection. Six months after a hip fracture, only 15% of patients can walk unaided across a room.

Virtually every person with osteoporosis who has come to my clinic is confused about the best way to promote bone health. Conventional doctors typically prescribe osteoporosis medication, such as *alendronate* (Fosamax) and *ibandronate* (Boniva). However, these drugs can cause side effects, such as digestive upset and blood clots, and they don't address the underlying nutritional deficiencies that promote bone loss.

The natural protocol I recommend includes a healthful diet (rich in vegetables, fruit and fish and low in refined-sugar products and red meat)...weight-bearing exercise (such as walking and stair-climbing)...and good hormone balance (deficiencies of some hormones, such as testosterone, accelerate bone loss). I also suggest certain bone-protecting supplements.

Caution: People with kidney disease should not take supplements without consulting a doctor. With kidney disease, the kidneys cannot process high doses of nutrients.

My recommendations for women and men: To help prevent osteoporosis, take the first three supplements listed below. *If you have osteoporosis or osteopenia (mild bone loss that can be diagnosed with a DEXA scan), take the first three supplements listed and as many of the others as you're willing to try, in the dosages recommended...*

SUPER TRIO PREVENTS AND TREATS OSTEOPOROSIS

•**Calcium is the most prevalent mineral in bone tissue.** Taking supplements helps prevent a deficiency. Most studies have found that calcium slows bone loss but does not increase bone density when used alone. Women with osteoporosis should take 500 mg of calcium twice daily with meals. It should be a well-absorbed form, such as citrate, citrate-malate, amino acid chelate or hydroxyapatite. To boost absorption, take no more than 500 mg per dose. Calcium carbonate, which is widely used, is not well-absorbed. For osteoporosis prevention, men and women, as well as boys and girls starting at age 13, should take 500 mg daily.

Calcium supplementation for men with osteoporosis is more complicated. Some recent research has identified a link between high calcium intake (from dairy products) and increased prostate cancer risk. A meta-analysis in the *Journal of the National Cancer Institute* that reviewed 12 studies on this association concluded, "High intake of dairy products and calcium may be associated with an increased risk for prostate cancer, although the increase appears to be small." A recent study found that calcium intake exceeding 1,500 mg a day (from food and supplements) may be associated with a higher risk of advanced, and potentially fatal, prostate cancer. The saturated fat in dairy products may raise prostate cancer risk.

Until there is more definitive information, I recommend that men who have osteoporosis, regardless of whether they have eliminated calcium-rich foods from their diets, take no more than a 500-mg calcium supplement daily. Men with prostate cancer should consult their doctors before using calcium supplements.

●**Vitamin D promotes absorption of calcium.** Deficiencies of this vitamin are more common in Americans over age 50 than in younger adults. Sun exposure prompts the body to produce vitamin D, and the kidneys help convert it to its active form. As we age, our skin cannot synthesize vitamin D as effectively from sunlight, and our kidneys become less efficient. People with darker skin, those with digestive problems (due to malabsorption conditions, such as Crohn's disease) and those with limited exposure to sunlight are also at greater risk for vitamin D deficiency. Preliminary studies indicate that an inadequate intake of vitamin D is associated with an increased risk of fractures.

For the prevention of osteoporosis, I recommend 600 IU to 800 IU of vitamin D daily. People with osteoporosis should take 800 IU to 1,200 IU daily. Vitamin D is fat soluble, meaning it is better absorbed when taken with meals (containing small amounts of fat).

For many patients with low vitamin D levels, I recommend 2,000 IU of vitamin D daily. To ensure that vitamin D levels are optimal, I monitor blood levels once or twice a year. Overdosing can lead to heart arrhythmia, anorexia, nausea and other ill effects.

●**Magnesium,** an important constituent of bone crystals, is crucial for the proper metabolism of calcium. A deficiency of magnesium impairs bone-building cells known as osteoblasts. Like calcium, magnesium requires vitamin D for absorption.

Researchers at Tel Aviv University in Israel looked at the effect of magnesium supplementation on bone density in 31 postmenopausal women with osteoporosis. This two-year, open, controlled trial (both the researchers and patients knew who was receiving the placebo or the supplement) involved giving the participants 250 mg to 750 mg of magnesium daily for six months and 250 mg for another 18 months. Twenty-two patients (71%) experienced a 1% to 8% increase in bone density. The mean bone density of all treated patients increased significantly after one year and remained at that level after two years. Among an additional 23 postmenopausal women not receiving magnesium, mean bone density decreased significantly.

For osteoporosis prevention, take 400 mg to 500 mg of magnesium daily...for osteoporosis, take 500 mg to 750 mg daily. In both cases, take in divided doses.

IF YOU HAVE BONE-LOSS DISEASE

●**Vitamin K** has received attention in recent years for its role in treating osteoporosis. It activates osteocalcin, a bone protein that regulates calcium metabolism in the bones and helps calcium bind to the tissues that make up the bone. It also has been shown to inhibit inflammatory chemicals that cause bone breakdown.

417

Studies have shown that low vitamin K intake and blood levels are associated with reduced bone density and fractures in people who have osteoporosis. A recent meta-analysis published in the *American Medical Association's Archives of Internal Medicine* found that vitamin K supplements were associated with a consistent reduction in all types of fractures. Leafy, green vegetables, such as spinach, kale, collard greens and broccoli, are the best sources of vitamin K, yet many people do not consume these vitamin K–rich foods on a regular basis. High-dose vitamin K (above 2 mg) should be used only under the supervision of a doctor, because excess vitamin K may increase blood clotting. Vitamin K supplements should not be used by people who take blood-thinning medication, such as *warfarin* (Coumadin) or heparin, or by pregnant women or nursing mothers. I typically recommend 2 mg to 10 mg daily of vitamin K for people who have osteoporosis to help increase their bone density.

• **Essential fatty acids** (EFAs) have been shown to improve bone density in older women and are believed also to promote bone health in men. Many researchers theorize that osteoporosis develops because of chronic inflammation of bone tissue (due to stress, toxins, poor diet and infection). EFAs, especially those found in fish oil, reduce inflammation. Some studies show that EFAs also improve calcium absorption. I recommend that people with osteoporosis take fish oil daily (containing about 480 mg of EPA and 320 mg of DHA), along with 3,000 mg of evening primrose oil, which contains inflammation-fighting *gamma-linolenic acid* (GLA). Because EFAs have a blood-thinning effect, check with your doctor if you are taking a blood thinner.

• **Strontium** is a mineral that doesn't get much attention, because it is not regarded as essential for the human body. However, 99% of the total amount of strontium found in the body is located in the teeth and bones. Supplemental strontium is not the radioactive type that you may have heard about in relation to nuclear facilities. Strontium is a valuable mineral for people with osteoporosis, and I often recommend it.

A clinical trial in *The New England Journal of Medicine* found that strontium prevents vertebral fractures and increases bone density. The most common supplemental forms are strontium chloride and strontium citrate. I suggest a supplement that contains 680 mg of elemental strontium daily (similar to the dose used in most studies). Because calcium inhibits strontium absorption, strontium should be taken at least four hours before or after calcium is taken. Strontium should not be taken by pregnant women and nursing mothers. It is not available at most health-food stores, but you can buy it from Vitacost (800-381-0759, *www.vitacost.com*).

• **Soy,** as a supplement and/or food, has been shown in several studies to improve bone density. Soy contains isoflavones, estrogen-like constituents that support bone mass and relieve menopausal symptoms in women. Women and men with osteoporosis or osteopenia should take 125 mg of soy isoflavones daily in soy protein powder or supplement form and consume three to five servings of soy foods weekly. (One serving equals one-half cup of tofu…one-half cup of soy beans…or one cup of soy milk.)

Caution: Soy supplements are not well studied in women who have had breast cancer, so they should avoid supplements and nonfermented soy products.

• **Vitamin C** is required for the production of the protein collagen, a component of bone tissue. I recommend that people with osteoporosis take 1,000 mg twice daily. Reduce the dosage if loose stools develop.

Silicon is a trace mineral required for bone formation. I recommend 2 mg to 5 mg daily.

BEST OSTEOPOROSIS FORMULAS

These products contain all the vitamins and minerals described in this article, in the therapeutic doses used for osteoporosis treatment…

• **Bone Up by Jarrow.** To find an online retailer, call 800-726-0886 or go to *www.jarrow. com*.

- **Osteoprime by Enzymatic Therapy.** To find a retailer, call 800-783-2286 or go to *www. enzymatictherapy.com.*

- **Pro Bone by Ortho Molecular Products** is available from health-care professionals, including naturopaths, holistic MDs, chiropractors, nutritionists and acupuncturists. If you cannot locate a health-care professional in your area who sells the formula, it is available from my clinic at 858-450-7120, *http://mark stengler.com.*

Obesity Raises Osteoporosis Risk

Excessive body fat may be associated with lower bone mass. This contradicts previous studies suggesting that obesity increased bone mass and was therefore good for bone health.

Self-defense: Maintain a healthy weight.

Hong-Wen Deng, PhD, professor, department of basic medical sciences, University of Missouri–Kansas City, and leader of a study of 6,400 people, published in *The Journal of Clinical Endocrinology & Metabolism.*

Secrets to Better Bone Health

Jamison Starbuck, ND, naturopathic physician in family practice in Missoula, Montana. She is past president of the American Association of Naturopathic Physicians and a contributing editor to *The Alternative Advisor: The Complete Guide to Natural Therapies and Alternative Treatments* (Time Life).

If you are among the 44 million American women and men over age 50 who have or are at risk for osteoporosis, you've no doubt heard that it's important to boost your intake of calcium-rich foods. What most people do not realize is that other factors can have a significant impact on whether the nutrients in bone-building foods are actually absorbed so that they can provide the maximum benefit.

Our bones are living parts of our anatomy, as vital and alive as the heart or the brain. What you eat—and how you assimilate what you eat—helps determine your bone health and whether or not you develop osteoporosis.

A recent study published in the *Journal of the American Medical Association* illustrates this point. Researchers examined data linking long-term use (more than one year) of heartburn and ulcer medications known as proton pump inhibitors (PPIs) and the risk for hip fracture in people over age 50.

The unequivocal results: Hip fracture risk increases with long-term PPI use. PPIs, such as omeprazole (Prilosec), lansoprazole (Prevacid) and esomeprazole (Nexium), reduce stomach acid. However, I've never recommended a PPI for a patient of mine, because I believe that a good supply of acid in the stomach improves the absorption of bone-building minerals, such as calcium and magnesium, and fat-soluble vitamins D and K, all of which are necessary for bone growth and maintenance.

For bone health, eat calcium-rich foods and/or take 600 mg of calcium citrate daily, which is readily absorbed, and perform weight-bearing exercise, such as walking, hiking, gardening or dancing. *Also...*

- **Limit mineral-robbing foods.** Eat plenty of mineral-rich whole foods, including whole grains, vegetables, fruits and nuts, but consume only small amounts of foods that steal minerals from your body. These include coffee, hard liquor and carbonated beverages.

- **Use vinegar or fresh lemon.** Add one teaspoon of vinegar or fresh lemon juice to your vegetables or salad at lunch and dinner. Substituting vinegar or lemon juice for fat-laden butter, ranch dressing or sour cream will enhance your body's absorption of essential nutrients.

Caution: Vinegar and lemon juice are not recommended for people with ulcers or gastritis.

- **Don't forget to take vitamin D.** Vitamin D, known as the sunshine vitamin, increases the absorption of calcium from the intestines, eventually increasing calcium deposition in bones. Get 800 international units (IU) of vitamin D through diet and supplementation.

• **Eat foods rich in vitamin K.** Good choices include broccoli, cabbage and spinach—and green tea. Recent studies show that vitamin K is very effective in maintaining and building bone.

Caution: If you take warfarin (Coumadin), consult your doctor before eating vitamin K–rich foods and do not take a vitamin K supplement. Vitamin K can interfere with blood-thinning medication.

Millions of Men Have "Silent" Osteoporosis

Angela J. Shepherd, MD, associate professor, Department of Family Medicine at University of Texas Medical Branch, Galveston. She specializes in osteoporosis screening and prevention.

Virtually every woman knows about osteoporosis, the main cause of weakened bones and fractures as women age. Few men, however, realize that they face similar risks.

Fact: About 30% of men 50 years and older will suffer an osteoporosis-related bone fracture at some time in their lives. Yet only about 10% of men with osteoporosis ever get diagnosed.

According to the National Osteoporosis Foundation, more than two million men have osteoporosis. Nearly 12 million more have osteopenia, a precursor condition that commonly leads to full-fledged osteoporosis.

Few doctors take the time to investigate bone loss in men. They, too, tend to think of osteoporosis as a "woman's disease," even though men are twice as likely as women to die following a hip fracture or hip-replacement procedure due to osteoporosis.

WHO GETS IT?

The strength and density of bones largely depend on the amount of calcium and other minerals that are present. The body is constantly creating and breaking down bone, a process called remodeling. For both men and women, the formation of new bone exceeds bone breakdown until about age 35. After age 35, the reverse happens. Men and women lose more bone than they create, leading to an overall loss of bone strength.

Women experience a precipitous loss of bone mass when estrogen declines after menopause. They also have smaller bones to begin with, which means they have fewer bone reserves. It's not unusual for women in their 70s to have lost up to 50% of their total bone mass.

Men experience a similar process, but without the rapid "bone drain" caused by declining estrogen. They lose bone more slowly than women—and because they start out with more bone mass, it takes them longer to start getting fractures. But once a man reaches his mid-70s, his risk for getting osteoporosis is about the same as a woman's.

Men with osteoporosis often are diagnosed only when they suffer a low-impact fracture. This is when even a minor impact or movement—falling down or bumping into something—causes a bone to break. Most fractures occur in the wrists or hips. Spinal fractures also are common, although they're typically asymptomatic and thus less likely to be diagnosed.

MALE–RISKS

A sedentary lifestyle and nutritional deficiencies—mainly of calcium and vitamin D—are among the main causes of osteoporosis in men as well as women. Also, people who have taken oral steroids for a six-month period over their lifetime (for severe asthma, rheumatoid arthritis or some other condition) are at increased risk. *Additional risk factors for men...*

• **Low body weight.** Older men who weigh less than 154 pounds are more than 20 times more likely to get osteoporosis than heavier men—partly because they have smaller bones and possibly because men with other osteoporosis risk factors, such as smoking and heavy alcohol consumption, tend to be thinner.

• **Prostate cancer.** The disease itself doesn't increase a man's risk of osteoporosis but some of the treatments do. For example, the drug leuprolide (Lupron) reduces levels of androgens, male hormones that play a protective role in bone strength. Men who are given antihormone drugs for prostate cancer—or who have undergone actual castration—are now assumed to be at high risk for osteoporosis.

•**COPD.** Men with chronic obstructive pulmonary disease (COPD) often develop osteoporosis. Smoking, the main cause of COPD, weakens bones. Also, COPD is commonly treated with steroids, drugs that decrease bone strength.

DIAGNOSIS

The dual-energy X-ray absorptiometry (DEXA) test measures bone density at the hip and spine, and sometimes at the wrist. The test gives a T-score—your bone density compared with what normally is expected in a healthy young adult with peak bone mass. *Any reading with a minus sign indicates that bone density is lower than average...*

•**-1 indicates some bone loss.**

•**-2.5 is a borderline reading that indicates a significant problem.**

•**Below -2.5 is diagnosed as osteoporosis.** It's not unusual for older men to have a T-score of –4, which indicates their bones are almost like paper.

Who should get tested? Men over age 60 with low weight and/or COPD should get a bone-density test—as should anyone who has taken steroids for six months.

TREATMENT AND PREVENTION

Recently, The National Osteoporosis Foundation issued official guidelines for treating and preventing osteoporosis in women and men age 50 and older. *These include...*

•**Get regular exercise.** It's among the best ways to increase bone mass during peak bone-building years. It also can increase bone density and strength in men who already have osteoporosis.

Bonus: Exercise increases balance and muscle strength—important for avoiding falls.

Any exercise is beneficial, but weight-bearing aerobic workouts, such as walking or lifting weights, may be superior to swimming or biking for stimulating bone growth.

•**Supplement with calcium and vitamin D.** Both are essential for bone strength. Dietary sources probably aren't enough. The body's ability to absorb calcium declines with age. There's also an age-related decline in vitamin D synthesis from sunshine.

Men need 1,000 milligrams (mg) to 1,200 mg of calcium daily until age 65 and 1,500 mg thereafter. After age 40, men should take 200 international units (IU) of vitamin D daily...400 IU after age 50...and 600 IU at age 71 and older.

•**Ask your doctor about bone-building drugs.** Many drugs that treat osteoporosis in women also are effective in men. These include the bisphosphonates (such as Fosamax and Actonel), calcitonin (Miacalcin) and parathyroid hormone (Forteo). Each of these drugs slows bone loss, and some increase the body's ability to build new bone. Your doctor can tell you if you need drugs and, if so, which one is right for you.

A T-score of –2.5 or worse may warrant drug intervention, and many doctors think a score of –2.0 is reason for a "drug discussion" with patients.

•**Don't smoke.** Nicotine is toxic to bone marrow. Also, men who smoke tend to weigh less than those who don't.

•**Limit alcohol.** Heavy alcohol use in men is one of the main risk factors for osteoporosis. Excessive alcohol inhibits the body's ability to form new bone, and men who are alcoholics often eat poorly.

•**Deal with depression.** People who are depressed tend to have lower-than-normal bone density, possibly because they exercise less and eat less.

Caution: Some research has linked SSRI antidepressants, such as Prozac, Paxil and Zoloft, with lower bone density. People should not stop taking these drugs because of concerns about osteoporosis—but they should ask their doctors if they need to be screened for osteoporosis.

Prunes Prime Bones for Growth and Repair

Bahram H. Arjmandi, PhD, RD, Margaret A. Sitton Professor and Chair, department of nutrition, food and exercise sciences at Florida State University, Tallahassee.

Prunes for fiber... for regularity... and sometimes just because they taste good. But prunes for strong bones? That's not what comes to mind for most people, but perhaps that will change. In a number of studies prunes have shown themselves to be great for your bones, helping to prevent bone loss and repair bone density as well.

The man behind much of this research is Bahram H. Arjmandi, PhD, RD, Margaret A. Sitton Professor and Chair, department of nutrition, food and exercise sciences at Florida State University in Tallahassee. He started this research back in the 1990s, when he was approached by the California Dried Plum Board. "I was skeptical," he says, "but I figured if they wanted to fund a study, I would take a look." To his astonishment, he discovered that prune consumption prevented bone loss in female rats. Still, he says he knew a number of substances did that. The bigger question on his mind was if prunes could rebuild lost bone... and they actually did. In earlier research, Dr. Arjmandi had searched for "bone builders" in growth hormone, growth factors, raisins, dates, blueberries and more. Prunes out-performed all of them, he says.

PROOF THAT PRUNES BUILD BONES

Dr. Arjmandi conducted a clinical study funded by the US Department of Agriculture and the California Dried Plum Board comparing the effects of dried apples versus prunes on bone mineral density in post-menopausal women. He says that 30 women in the prune group have had at least a 6% increase in hip bone (a critical area for maintaining strong bones) and that one woman had a notable 11% increase over her baseline measurement. In earlier preliminary data, all prune-eaters showed at least some improvement in bone mass by six months into the trial, he says.

Research to determine what substance in prunes creates improved bone mineral density has been done in conjunction with a team from Oklahoma State University. It revealed that particular polyphenols in the dried fruit achieve two effects—they up-regulate growth factors linked to bone formation and they counter the activity of tumor necrosis factor-alpha (TNF-alpha), an inhibitor of bone formation. Prunes also contain potassium and boron (a trace mineral), both believed to contribute to bone mineral density.

Interestingly, consumption of fresh plums has not been shown to substitute for prunes in matters of bone benefits, says Dr. Arjmandi.

The reason: Only certain kinds of plums become prunes. Dr. Arjmandi's team used an offshoot of La petite d'Agen, a native of Southwest France, which at maturity has a royal purple outer skin and amber colored flesh. This is the commercially available dried plum/prune. So, while all prunes are dried plums (the preferred name these days), most fresh plums cannot become prunes.

If you want to boost prune consumption, go slow. Dr. Arjmandi advises starting with just three prunes, and increasing to nine or 10 per day as you adjust to the fiber levels. Because prunes are so low on the glycemic scale, they shouldn't be a problem for people with diabetes, he adds.

Build Strong Bones... Naturally

Richard Podell, MD, clinical professor of internal medicine at Robert Wood Johnson Medical School in New Jersey and a leading expert on nutritional and holistic medicine. Dr. Podell is in private practice in Summit, New Jersey. He is the author of five books, including *Patient Power: How to Protect Yourself from Medical Error* (Fireside).

It happens all too often—a woman slips and falls, but instead of suffering a mere bruise, her hip fractures.

Culprit: Osteoporosis, a disease in which bones become porous, brittle and prone to break. Fractures of the hip, spine and wrist are common and can lead to long-term disability or even death.

About 10 million Americans—an estimated 80% of them female—have osteoporosis. Another estimated 34 million are at increased risk due to low bone mass, a condition called osteopenia that often advances to osteoporosis.

A SILENT DISEASE

Our bodies continually build new bone and dissolve older bone. Until about age 30, the skeleton gets stronger because bone is added more quickly than it is lost. But by about age 40, bone loss begins to outpace bone formation. When estrogen production decreases at menopause, bone loss accelerates.

Thinning bones give no warning signs, so periodic screening is key to timely diagnosis and treatment. The most up-to-date imaging test involves dual-energy X-ray absorptiometry (DEXA), a technique that uses two different X-ray beams to measure bone mineral density (BMD).

Self-defense: Have your first BMD screening test at menopause, and repeat it every two years unless your doctor recommends more frequent testing.

The more of the following factors you have, the more important it is to safeguard your bone health…

•**Age.** Because risk rises with age independently of BMD, an older woman's risk for fracture is much greater than a younger woman's.

•**Digestive disorders.** Any condition that decreases the body's absorption of dietary calcium, such as Crohn's disease and celiac disease, can interfere with bone formation.

•**Excessive alcohol use.** Alcohol impairs calcium absorption.

•**Excess soda consumption.** Phosphoric acid in soda, perhaps colas in particular, may contribute to bone loss by altering the balance of acid in the blood.

•**Family history.** Having a parent or sibling with osteoporosis puts you at greater risk.

•**Frame size.** Small-framed women have less bone to begin with.

•**Menstrual history.** Production of bone-strengthening estrogen is greatest in childbearing years. The later you began menstruating and the earlier you reached menopause, the higher your risk.

•**Medication.** When used for many months or years (depending on the drug), certain medications may increase the risk for osteoporosis. These include steroids (such as prednisone and cortisone)…the blood thinner heparin…some cancer drugs…diabetes drugs called thiazolidinediones (such as Actos and Avandia)…some antiseizure medications…aluminum-containing antacids…and possibly antidepressants called selective serotonin reuptake inhibitors, such as fluoxetine (Prozac).

•**Race.** For unknown reasons, Caucasian and Asian women are at higher risk for brittle bones than Black and Hispanic women.

•**Sedentary lifestyle.** The less exercise you've gotten—from childhood on—the greater your risk.

NATURAL THERAPIES

Osteoporosis medications can help, but they have limitations and risks. The most widely used ones, called bisphosphonates, can cause nausea and abdominal pain, and occasionally inflammation or ulceration of the esophagus. They also can damage the jaw—an uncommon side effect most often seen in patients with gum disease.

Other bone-building drugs have side effects, too. Estrogen therapy that eases menopausal symptoms also protects bones but can increase heart disease and breast cancer risk. Teriparatide (Forteo) must be given by daily injection for no longer than two years and may slightly increase risk for bone tumors. The newest drug, zoledronic acid (Reclast), given intravenously once yearly, is convenient and effective but does carry a small risk for severe bone, joint and muscle pain.

Best: Use natural therapies to prevent osteoporosis…or in conjunction with medication to treat the disease. You know you should eat right and exercise regularly—but there is a lot more you can do. *The keys…*

•**Calcium.** Dairy foods and green vegetables, such as broccoli, do provide calcium—

423

but it is not easy to get sufficient calcium from diet alone.

Recommended: Supplement daily with 1,000 mg of calcium before menopause…or 1,200 mg after menopause. For better absorption, take calcium citrate in two divided doses …and take 250 mg to 300 mg of magnesium at the same time.

•**Vitamin D.** Optimizing intake of vitamin D can double or triple calcium absorption. Evidence indicates that the most healthful dose of vitamin D is much higher than the 400 international units (IU) or less often found in multivitamins. I generally recommend that women supplement daily with 800 IU to 1,000 IU of vitamin D3 (cholecalciferol). For most people, it is safe to take 2,000 IU, unless there is a history of kidney stones or hypercalcemia (excess calcium in the blood).

Simple test: To determine your appropriate dose of vitamin D, ask your doctor to measure your blood level of 25 hydroxy vitamin D (a vitamin D derivative). The lower limit of the normal range is officially 16 nanograms per milliliter (ng/ml)—but I think a more appropriate minimum is 32 ng/ml. This test is especially important if you spend most of your time indoors or if you live in the northern third of the US, because you may not get enough sunlight for your body to synthesize sufficient vitamin D.

Caution: Do not take more than 2,000 IU of supplemental vitamin D per day. Excesses cause blood levels of calcium to go too high, which can lead to problems with digestion, heart rhythm, kidney stones and brain function. Get your doctor's approval before taking vitamin D if you have a history of kidney or parathyroid gland problems.

•**Strontium.** Consider supplementing daily with about 750 mg of this mineral if you have severe osteopenia or osteoporosis. Studies suggest that a form called strontium ranalate significantly improves BMD. Efforts are under way to make this an FDA-approved drug, but you can buy a form called strontium citrate at health-food stores. No risks or side effects are known at this time.

A urine test called N-telopeptide (NTx) can quickly reveal changes in bone density. Ask your doctor to do an NTx test before you start osteoporosis treatment and three months later. If improvement is not sufficient, consider adding more treatment strategies.

How Often Should Adults Get a Bone Density Test?

Bone density, measured by a dual-energy X-ray absorptiometry test (referred to as a DEXA scan), indicates whether any bones have weakened. The test should be performed every two years on all women age 65 or older… all postmenopausal women younger than age 65 who have one or more additional risk factors, such as smoking, an inactive lifestyle and excessive alcohol consumption…and women and men of all ages who have sustained a fracture not caused by an injury. While men are less at risk, due to the fact that they don't experience the abrupt and substantial hormonal change that women do after menopause, a decrease in testosterone as part of normal aging may cause bone loss.

Kevin D. Plancher, MD, Plancher Orthopaedics & Sports Medicine, New York City and Cos Cob, Connecticut. www.plancherortho.com

Vitamin C for Healthier Hips

In a four-year study of 606 men and women, researchers found that men with the highest intake of vitamin C (314 mg daily) from food and supplements had the lowest levels of bone loss in the hip. Vitamin C is required for the formation of collagen, the main protein in bone. There was no similar finding in women, possibly because they already had adequate vitamin C levels.

For strong bones: Strive to eat five to nine servings daily of vitamin C–rich fruits and vegetables (such as strawberries and red peppers).

Katherine Tucker, MD, director, nutritional epidemiology, Tufts University, Boston, and lead author of a study program of 2,538 people, published in *The American Journal of Clinical Nutrition*.

How NOT to Die Of a Broken Hip

John E. Morley, MD, Dammert Professor of Gerontology and director of the Division of Geriatric Medicine at Saint Louis University School of Medicine. He is director of geriatric research at St. Louis Veterans Affairs Medical Center and is coauthor, with Sheri R. Colberg, PhD, of *The Science of Staying Young* (McGraw-Hill).

About 25% of hip-fracture patients 65 years and older die within six months of the fracture...two-thirds die within two years.

Surgery is almost always necessary to repair a hip fracture. Generally, the better your health before a hip fracture, the better your chances for a complete recovery. But for elderly patients, especially those with health problems, a hip fracture can be deadly.

How not to die of a broken hip—plus how to prevent one in the first place...

BASICS TO PREVENT AND HEAL

These measures can help prevent a hip fracture and aid in recovery...

Vitamin D. We've seen a significant increase in hip fractures over the last 20 to 30 years. During this same period, people have been increasingly avoiding the sun or using sunscreen to reduce their risk for skin cancer.

What's the connection? The body synthesizes vitamin D from exposure to the sun's ultraviolet radiation. People who get little sun often are deficient in vitamin D. Low vitamin D decreases bone and muscle strength, increasing the risk for falls as well as fractures.

What to do: Have your vitamin D measured now and also if you suffer a hip fracture. The level shouldn't be less than 30 nanograms per milliliter. Many Americans, including younger adults, have a significant vitamin D deficiency. You can supplement with vitamin D—the recommended dose is 400 international units (IU) to 800 IU daily—but I usually advise patients just to get more sun. About 20 to 30 minutes of sun exposure daily without sunscreen—new research shows that noon is best—will provide adequate vitamin D without increasing the risk for skin cancer.

More protein and calcium. Poor nutrition can impair balance, cognitive abilities and bone and muscle strength. It also can delay healing by impairing tissue repair after surgery.

Recommended: Ask your doctor about taking a balanced amino acid (protein) drink one to three times daily after a hip fracture. I also advise patients to eat eight ounces of yogurt a day. Most yogurts supply about 400 mg of calcium. Combined with the calcium in a normal diet, that's usually enough to promote stronger bones.

MORE HEALING HELP

The following can keep a hip fracture from becoming a death sentence...

•***Zoledronic acid.*** It was discovered recently that an intravenous medication called *zoledronic acid* (Zometa, Reclast), typically used to treat cancer, can aid in recovery from a hip fracture. A study in *The New England Journal of Medicine* showed that zoledronic acid reduced hip-fracture mortality by about 28%. Similar to drugs used to treat osteoporosis, it's a bisphosphonate that inhibits bone breakdown and increases bone strength.

Patients who have fractured one hip have a fivefold increased risk of fracturing the other. This means that their mortality risk is doubled. Zoledronic acid helps to prevent future fractures of the hip as well as the spine.

The drug is given as a five-milligram (mg) infusion once a year. Some patients experience fatigue, muscle aches or fever after the first injection. Subsequent injections are unlikely to cause significant side effects.

●**Treatment for depression.** Depression is extremely common after a hip fracture, partly because patients often feel helpless and dependent.

Why it matters: Patients who are depressed are less likely to exercise and follow through with a rehabilitation program. They also are more likely to get a subsequent fracture because depression increases the body's production of cortisol, a substance that depletes bone calcium.

Most patients with depression do best with medication, alone or in combination with talk therapy.

Caution: Drugs in the SSRI class of antidepressants, such as *paroxetine* (Paxil), can impair alertness and coordination and increase the risk for falls. These drugs also pull calcium from the bones. Some of the older antidepressants, such as *nortriptyline* (Pamelor, Aventyl), are a better choice for hip-fracture patients because they are less likely to impair alertness and balance.

●**Pain relief.** Postsurgical pain is normal—chronic pain that lasts months or years after hip surgery is unacceptable. Chronic pain interferes with exercise and rehabilitation. It also is a leading cause of depression. You should never have chronic pain after hip surgery. Some patients do fine with over-the-counter pain relievers, such as ibuprofen, but others need stronger painkillers. If you're hurting, tell your doctor.

Helpful: The Wong-Baker FACES Pain Rating Scale. Patients look at illustrations of facial expressions (which are accompanied by a number) and choose the one that reflects their pain. During rehabilitation, no one should experience pain greater than a three or four. During daily life, pain should be rated no higher than a one or two.

●**Prevention of clots and pneumonia.** Hospital patients have a high risk of developing deep vein thrombosis, a life-threatening condition in which blood clots in the legs travel to the lungs and cause a pulmonary embolism. They also have a higher risk for pneumonia, partly because being sedentary can allow mucus to collect in the lungs, providing a breeding ground for bacteria.

What to do: In the hospital, move as much as you can, even if it is nothing more than regularly flexing your legs or sitting up in bed.

Patients who have had hip surgery are routinely referred to a physical or occupational therapist. After that, they should continue to be active—ideally, by walking or doing other forms of exercise for 20 to 30 minutes most days.

PART 3

Managing Chronic Conditions

20

Diabetes
& Insulin Resistance

How to Prevent Serious Complications of Diabetes

Diabetes is a slow and often "silent" disease. Most people who have it feel fine initially. By the time they develop symptoms, however, years of elevated blood sugar (glucose) have already caused widespread damage and complications, including cardiovascular disease, nerve damage and kidney disease. These complications from diabetes can shorten life expectancy by about a decade.

Good news: Most people can reduce or eliminate these complications by maintaining optimal glucose control.

Here, the dangerous complications of diabetes and how to control them...

PERIPHERAL NEUROPATHY

Excess blood sugar can damage capillaries—tiny blood vessels—in the fingers, legs and/or feet. A lack of circulation to nerves can cause neuropathy, which can be painful and produce sensations of numbness, tingling and burning.

Important finding: One of my colleagues had his patients with neuropathy eat a low-fat, vegan diet (no animal foods or dairy products) and take a daily 30-minute walk. In 17 out of 21 patients, leg pain stopped completely—the remaining four had partial relief.

Many patients with neuropathy eventually lose all sensation in the extremities. This is dangerous because small injuries, such as cuts or an ingrown nail, for example, won't be noticed and can progress to serious infections and tissue damage—and, in some cases, require amputation. *What to do...*

Neal D. Barnard, MD, adjunct associate professor of medicine at George Washington University School of Medicine and president of the nonprofit Physicians Committee for Responsible Medicine, a Washington, DC–based group that promotes preventive medicine and higher standards of effectiveness and ethics in research. He is author of *Dr. Neal Barnard's Program for Reversing Diabetes* (Rodale). *www.nealbarnard.org.*

• **Exercise daily.** It helps with weight loss and glucose control, which help reduce capillary damage and may reduce pain from neuropathy as well.

• **Check your feet every day.** Look for abrasions, cuts and blisters. See a doctor if an injury isn't healing.

Also, ask your doctor to examine your feet two to four times a year. Most doctors don't do this routinely.

Helpful: Take off your shoes and socks while you're waiting in the examination room. This makes it impossible for the doctor to ignore your feet.

EYE DAMAGE

Diabetes is the leading cause of blindness in American adults. High blood sugar can lead to glaucoma, resulting in optic nerve damage, which causes loss of vision. It also can damage the retinas (retinopathy) or the lenses of the eyes (cataracts). *What to do...*

• **Avoid dairy.** Many people lack the enzyme needed to metabolize galactose, a sugar that is released when the lactose in dairy is digested. This can lead to lens damage and cataracts.

• **Eat more produce.** The antioxidants in fresh fruits and vegetables, such as vitamin C, lutein and zeaxanthin, appear to have a stabilizing effect on the retina and can reduce the risk for cataracts and other eye diseases.

I do not recommend supplements for eye health because natural foods provide large amounts of these nutrients. It's likely that the combination of nutrients in foods, rather than in single-source nutrients, offer the most protection.

PERIODONTAL DISEASE

Doctors have known for a long time that patients with diabetes have a high risk for periodontal disease, a chronic bacterial infection of the gums that can lead to tooth loss.

Recent finding: A review of research by the Cochrane Database of Systematic Reviews found that people with diabetes who were treated for periodontal disease achieved better blood sugar control, indicating that periodontal disease is both caused by and causes higher blood sugar. Periodontal treatment includes regular scaling, the removal of bacteria

and inflammatory material from beneath the gums. *What to do...*

• **See your dentist four times a year.** The usual twice-a-year schedule might not be enough for people with diabetes.

• **Eat less sugar.** This is important for everyone, but more so for those with diabetes and periodontal disease. A high-sugar diet makes it easier for bacteria to proliferate.

• **Floss and brush your teeth after every meal**—not just once or twice a day.

HEART DISEASE

Most people in the US have some degree of atherosclerosis, plaque buildup in the arteries that increases the risk for heart attack. The risk for heart disease is much higher in people with diabetes, particularly when atherosclerosis is accompanied by hypertension and kidney disease.

Recent finding: People with diabetes who eat a typical American diet tend to accumulate intramyocellular lipids, tiny bits of fat inside muscle cells. This fat inhibits the ability of cells to respond to insulin, which leads to elevated blood sugar. *What to do...*

• **Avoid animal products and added fats.** Research by Dean Ornish, MD, showed that people who get no more than about 10% of total calories from fat (preferably unsaturated) can reverse blockages in the arteries. (Traditional diabetes diets allow up to 35% of calories from fat.)

• **Reduce cholesterol.** It's one of the best ways to reduce cardiovascular risks.

Helpful: Foods that are high in soluble fiber, such as oatmeal, fruits, whole grains and beans. People who eat beans regularly have average cholesterol readings that are about 7% lower than those who don't eat beans.

• **Reduce blood pressure.** The same strategies that reduce cholesterol and arterial blockages also reduce blood pressure.

KIDNEY DISEASE

The filtering units of the kidneys, or nephrons, consist of millions of small blood vessels that frequently are damaged by diabetes. Extensive damage can lead to kidney failure and the need for a transplant. *What to do...*

●**Give up animal protein.** Amino acids in meats and eggs that contain sulphur are harder for the nephrons to process than the proteins from plant foods. People with diabetes who switch to a vegetarian diet have a lower risk of developing kidney disease.

●**Maintain healthy blood pressure.** Uncontrolled hypertension is a leading cause of kidney failure. The same low-fat, plant-based diet that reduces glucose and cholesterol also is effective for lowering blood pressure.

ALZHEIMER'S DISEASE

A Japanese study reported in *Neurology* found that patients with type 2 diabetes or resistance to insulin were more likely to develop brain plaques, clusters of abnormal proteins that occur in those with Alzheimer's disease.

It's not yet clear whether diabetes increases the risk of getting Alzheimer's or there's an underlying process that causes both conditions. *What to do…*

●**Avoid meat.** Many studies have shown that people who eat diets that are high in meat, fat and cholesterol are more likely to develop Alzheimer's disease than those who eat a healthier diet. It's possible that the heme iron in meats is more likely than the non-heme iron in plant foods to be associated with brain plaques.

Diabetes Raises Irregular Heartbeat Risk in Women

When 34,744 adults were followed for an average of 7.2 years, women with diabetes were 26% more likely to develop atrial fibrillation (irregular heartbeat) than women without diabetes. No such association was found in men, but past research has shown an increased risk for heart disease in general in both men and women with diabetes.

If you have diabetes: Ask your doctor to closely monitor your cardiovascular health.

Gregory A. Nichols, PhD, senior investigator, Kaiser Permanente Center for Health Research, Portland, Oregon.

New Diabetes "App"

If you have a smartphone, staying current on news about your condition just got easier. The Point-of-Care Information Technology Center Diabetes Guide, from Johns Hopkins physicians, provides up-to-date diabetes news. Find it on smartphones and at *www.hopkins-diabetesguide.org.*

Johns Hopkins University School of Medicine.

Considering Bypass Surgery?

For diabetes patients with severe heart disease, bypass surgery is more effective than medication.

Recent finding: Only 22.4% of diabetes patients with severe coronary disease who had immediate bypass surgery died or had a heart attack or stroke within the next five years, versus 30.5% who elected to take medication instead.

Study of 2,368 people by researchers at University of Pittsburgh Graduate School of Public Health, presented at a recent meeting of the American Diabetes Association.

Pycnogenol Helps Diabetic Retinopathy

Mark A. Stengler, NMD, licensed naturopathic medical doctor and leading authority on the practice of alternative and integrated medicine. He is founder and medical director of the Stengler Center for Integrative Medicine, Encinitas, California, and associate clinical professor at the National College of Natural Medicine, Portland, Oregon. He is author of *The Natural Physician's Healing Therapies* (Bottom Line Books).

Pycnogenol (pronounced pic-noj-en-all), an extract from the bark of the French maritime pine, is known to improve circulation, reduce swelling and ease asthma.

431

Now Italian researchers have found another use for it—it helps patients with diabetes who are in the early stages of diabetic retinopathy, a complication of diabetes in which the retina becomes damaged, resulting in vision impairment, including blurred vision, seeing dark spots, impaired night vision and reduced color perception.

All people with diabetes are at risk for diabetic retinopathy—and it's estimated that as many as 80% of people with diabetes for 10 years or more will have this complication.

Participants in the Italian study had been diagnosed with type 2 diabetes for four years, and their diabetes was well-controlled by diet and oral medication. Study participants had early stage retinopathy and moderately impaired vision. After two months of treatment, the patients given Pycnogenol had less retinal swelling as measured by ultrasound testing. Most important, their vision was significantly improved. This was especially noticeable because the vision of those in the control group did not improve.

My view: If you have type 1 or 2 diabetes, undergo a comprehensive eye exam at least once a year. If retinopathy is detected, it would be wise to supplement with Pycnogenol (150 milligrams daily). Because retinopathy among diabetes patients is so prevalent, I recommend this amount to all my patients with diabetes to protect their vision. Pycnogenol is known to have a blood-thinning effect, so people who take blood-thinning medication, such as *warfarin*, should use it only while being monitored by a doctor.

Prevent Diabetes-Related Blindness

After a year of treatment, almost half of patients with diabetic macular edema (diabetes-related swelling of the central part of the retina) treated with lasers and the injectable drug *ranibizumab* (Lucentis) showed substantial visual improvement—versus 28% of patients treated with lasers alone.

Neil M. Bressler, MD, retina division chief and professor of ophthalmology, The Wilmer Eye Institute, Johns Hopkins University School of Medicine, Baltimore, and coauthor of a study of 691 patients with diabetic macular edema, published in *Ophthalmology*.

Shingles Vaccine to Fight Off Lasting Nerve Pain

Mark A. Stengler, NMD, licensed naturopathic medical doctor and leading authority on the practice of alternative and integrated medicine. He is founder and medical director of the Stengler Center for Integrative Medicine, Encinitas, California, and associate clinical professor at the National College of Natural Medicine, Portland, Oregon. He is author of *The Natural Physician's Healing Therapies* (Bottom Line Books).

Shingles is a painful skin condition characterized by blisters that can occur anywhere on the body but most often on the chest and back, where they wrap around one side. It is caused by the *varicella-zoster virus*, the same virus that causes chicken pox. If you have had chicken pox, the virus remains dormant in the nerve tissue near your brain and spinal cord and can be reactivated later in life. I find that stress, poor nutrition and use of medications, including immunosuppressants such as prednisone or chemotherapy, weaken the immune system and make patients more susceptible to a shingles outbreak. About 50% of those who live to age 85 will experience shingles at some point in their lives. If you have diabetes, your immune system is even more susceptible to this virus.

While I don't believe in the benefit and safety of all vaccines, I do think that the shingles vaccine (Zostavax) should be considered by those age 60 and over—especially because shingles is a very painful condition that can last for several weeks. This single one-time injection vaccine does not guarantee that you won't develop shingles, but it does cut your risk in half and significantly reduces the risk for postherpetic neuralgia, lasting nerve pain caused by shingles. Serious side effects from the vaccine are rare.

More from Mark Stengler, NMD...

Help for Frequent Urinary Tract Infections

People with diabetes are more prone to infections than people without the disease because elevated blood sugar (glucose) levels reduce immunity. The first thing to do is to improve glucose control. Work with a nutrition-oriented holistic physician to get started on eating a low-glycemic, high-soluble fiber diet. You'll also want to exercise regularly and take supplements, such as chromium, *gymnema* (an Ayurvedic herb) or Pycnogenol (French maritime pine bark extract) that can help lower glucose levels. Cranberry extract is a great supplement to use to prevent urinary tract infections. It is better than cranberry juice because there is too much sugar in the juice for someone with diabetes.

One brand to try: Cran-Max (available at drugstores and at *www.cranmaxinfo.com*). Also, take a daily probiotic supplement containing at least 3 to 5 billion colony-forming units.

Probiotics to try: BioK+ (800-593-2465, *www.biokplus.com*) or Multiflora ABF (800-422-3371, *www.uaslabs.com*). These friendly bacteria are an important part of the immune system of the urinary tract.

How to Overcome Chronic Illness

Brenda Stockdale, director of mind-body medicine at the RC Cancer Centers in Cumming, Georgia. She completed clinical training at Harvard Medical School's mind-body medicine program and is the author of *You Can Beat the Odds—Surprising Factors Behind Chronic Illness and Cancer* (Sentient).

Scientists have long known that our genes play a role in determining whether we develop various medical conditions ranging from cancer and heart disease to diabetes and dementia.

Researchers are now discovering that certain genes must be "expressed" (activated) in order to trigger their disease-causing effects. One of the most significant findings in the emerging field of epigenetics (the study of gene expression) is the degree to which the environment—including what we eat and how we respond to stress—affects our genetics. The unchecked flow of stress hormones can lead to inflammation and deregulate immune function, increasing the likelihood that inborn genetic vulnerabilities to disease will be activated.

Important finding: People with a 10-year history of workplace stress had five times the incidence of colorectal cancer as people with less job stress. Besides the link to increased cancer risk, stress also has been shown to make cancer patients less responsive to treatment.

If you have any chronic medical condition, here are some important ways to increase your odds of overcoming your illness—or at least keep it in check...

●**Take control.** Researchers who study "survivors"—people who remain healthy after stressful life events that make others sick—have found that one of several traits that they all share is a feeling of being in control of their own lives.

Helpful: To start taking better control of your life, draw a circle and divide it into your various daily activities. Next, identify which activities energize you and which leave you feeling depleted. Then look for ways to spend more time on the former and less on the latter. If certain friends or relatives drain you, modify or limit your time with them. If your job has stressful elements, work on solutions.

●**Commit...to yourself.** Another survivor trait pinpointed by research is a strong commitment to self.

To cultivate this trait, try this exercise: Sit quietly and breathe deeply. Consider all that your lungs, internal organs, muscles, bones and five senses allow you to do.

Then ask yourself: "Is there something extra I can do for my body to help it heal more completely?"

This could include steps to improve your nutrition, exercise or lifestyle—or any action that would make your body's job easier.

• **Don't forget your childhood.** In a large study sponsored by the federal Centers for Disease Control and Prevention, childhood physical, sexual or emotional abuse was the single most predictive factor of chronic illness in adulthood. While you can't undo the past, several studies show that disclosing and working through troubling childhood experiences can lead to health benefits, such as a reduction in harmful levels of stress hormones.

You can talk to a psychotherapist or mental health counselor and/or write about these experiences.

Helpful: Expressive writing (a form of writing that focuses on feelings) has been found to improve both physical and psychological health. For those who have undergone traumatic experiences, this type of writing has been shown to have a number of benefits, including a reduction in post-traumatic stress disorder symptoms.

• **Make sure you have a confidant.** Just as toxic relationships can be damaging, positive relationships benefit your health. In one Harvard study of 56,000 subjects, those without at least one confidant had the worst health. If you feel your social network could be stronger, consider inviting more potential friends into your life…joining a support group (such as one that focuses on a medical condition)…and/or seeing a therapist or counselor (who can provide support and perhaps help improve your relationship skills).

• **Find a bigger purpose.** Research shows that helping people—by doing some form of public service, for example—reduces illness and mortality. Studies also have found that spirituality and belief in something greater than oneself is linked to increased longevity.

• **Embrace stillness.** A regular habit of quieting yourself is important. This can be achieved through meditation, which can take many forms.

Examples: Repeating a calming phrase, such as "In this moment, all is well" or "I am safe and secure"…breathing deeply while sitting quietly…or taking walks in nature can be considered meditation.

A 19-year study found that people who meditated regularly had 30% fewer heart attacks and 49% less risk of dying from cancer over a 7.6-year period than those who didn't meditate regularly—perhaps due to reduced levels of disease-promoting stress hormones.

How to Fudge on Your Doctors' Orders

Julian Seifter, MD, associate professor of medicine at Harvard Medical School in Boston. A nephrologist at Brigham and Women's Hospital, also in Boston, he has practiced medicine for 30 years. He is the author of *After the Diagnosis: Transcending Chronic Illness* (Simon & Schuster).

I f you're one of the more than 90 million Americans who suffer from a chronic illness, such as high blood pressure, diabetes, kidney disease or asthma, chances are your doctor has recommended that you take medication and/or change your lifestyle.

Following your doctors' orders isn't always easy, but a bit of judicious "cheating" is almost always OK.

Julian Seifter, MD, is a Harvard nephrologist (kidney specialist) who has diabetes himself. He shares some advice based on his personal experiences.

MY HEALTH CHALLENGES

As a nephrologist, I'm an expert in the complications of diabetes, but I've sometimes been unable to change my own habits to keep my diabetes under control. At different times, I've been out of shape and overweight and allowed my blood pressure and blood sugar to get too high. *What I've learned…*

WHY WE CHEAT

Being diagnosed with a chronic illness profoundly affects your sense of identity. You may need to give up things that are important to you…forever. And doing what you're told by your doctor means that you're losing some control over your life.

It's only human that we often respond to these losses with denial. That's especially true if you don't feel particularly sick, as with high blood pressure. You can ignore dietary guidelines your doctor has given you or not take your medication—and if you're lucky enough to not suffer ill effects, this cheating lets you tell the world, and yourself, there's nothing wrong with you.

Even if you accept your illness, giving up favorite foods or pleasurable habits can hurt your quality of life. And letting your illness define you—becoming afraid to do things you enjoy and worrying about everything you eat—isn't healthy either. Life has to be worth living, which requires compromise.

FIND THE RIGHT DOCTOR

Doctors shouldn't just be instruction givers…they should be problem solvers. They should meet their patients halfway and help them figure out how to do what's necessary for their health while maintaining their pleasure in life.

If your doctor is rigid and moralistic, this creates a communication barrier that makes matters worse. You will be tempted to lie or simply cancel your appointment if you haven't followed your diet or you stopped taking medication that was causing uncomfortable side effects.

To find out if you can work with your doctor, say something like, "I'm worried that I'll never be able to have corned beef (or a glass of wine…or a piece of pie) again. Is there any way we can compromise on my diet?" You also may want to ask about larger worries, such as how you can continue to travel or participate in your favorite sport.

STRIKE A BALANCE

It's almost always possible to build some flexibility into a diet or medical regimen and still achieve a high level of care.

Example: A pastrami sandwich is not part of a low-fat or low-salt diet. But one every other week won't make much difference to most people's health, and if you love pastrami, it's likely to make you a lot happier with the whole eating plan.

If you're prescribed a low-salt diet for hypertension, can you name three salty foods that you wouldn't mind giving up? And are there three foods that you would truly miss? Talk to your doctor about the foods you will miss most to see whether a compromise can be made. The "special foods" may need to be rotated or scheduled with appropriate portion sizes.

If you feel that you must cheat, work with your doctor to find a creative solution.

Example: When I told one of my patients that alcohol contributed to his high blood pressure, he insisted that he had to have his two martinis nightly. To compromise, I said he could have one martini per night but without the high-sodium olive.

FORGET YOU ARE SICK

With my diabetes, the turning point for me came after I collapsed, due to poorly controlled blood sugar that was compounded by anxiety, while visiting Paris with my wife.

What I realized: Ironically, cheating less could give me what I wanted most—to simply forget about my illness. Thereafter, I made it a habit to check my blood sugar before and after meals, as well as to exercise, take my blood pressure pills and eat the right foods.

I'm not perfect. But I make repeated efforts to get it right, and this has allowed me to live with greater confidence and freedom—and simply have more fun. I aim for the art of the possible and try to help my patients do the same.

If You Have Diabetes, A Joint Replacement or Arthritis...

George Cierny, MD, and Doreen DiPasquale, MD, physician-partners at REOrthopaedics in San Diego. Dr. Cierny is an international lecturer in orthopedic surgery who has published more than 100 scientific papers and book chapters in the field of musculoskeletal pathology and infection. Dr. DiPasquale, an orthopedic surgeon, is former residency program director at George Washington University in Washington, DC, and National Naval Medical Center in Bethesda, Maryland.

When most people think of bone problems, broken bones and osteoporosis (reduced bone density and strength) come to mind. But our bones also can be the site of infections that can sometimes go unrecognized for months or even years.

This is especially the case if the only symptoms of bone infection (a condition known as osteomyelitis) are ones that are commonly mistaken for common health problems, such as ordinary back pain or fatigue. *What you need to know...*

ARE YOU AT RISK?

Older adults (age 70 and older), people with diabetes or arthritis and anyone with a weakened immune system (due to chronic disease, such as cancer, for example) are among those at greatest risk for osteomyelitis.

Anyone who has an artificial joint (such as a total hip replacement or total knee replacement) or metal implants attached to a bone also is at increased risk for osteomyelitis and should discuss the use of antibiotics before any type of surgery, including routine dental and oral surgery. Bacteria in the mouth can enter the bloodstream and cause a bone infection.

TYPES OF BONE INFECTIONS

Before the advent of joint-replacement surgery, most bone infections were caused by injuries that expose the bone to bacteria in the environment (such as those caused by a car accident) or a broken bone...or an infection elsewhere in the body, such as pneumonia or a urinary tract infection, that spreads to the bone through the bloodstream.

Now: About half the cases of osteomyelitis are complications of surgery in which large metal implants are used to stabilize or replace bones and joints (such as in the hip or knee).

Osteomyelitis is divided into three categories, depending on the origin of the infection...

• **Blood-borne osteomyelitis** occurs when bacteria that originate elsewhere in the body migrate to and infect bone. People with osteoarthritis or rheumatoid arthritis are prone to blood-borne infections in their affected joints due to injury to cells in the lining of the joints that normally prevent bacteria from entering the bloodstream.

• **Contiguous-focus osteomyelitis** occurs when organisms—usually bacteria, but sometimes fungi—infect bone tissue. These cases usually occur in people with diabetes, who often develop pressure sores on the soles of their feet or buttocks due to poor circulation and impaired immunity.

• **Post-traumatic osteomyelitis.** Trauma or surgery to a bone and/or surrounding tissue can open the area to bacteria and other microbes. The use of prosthetic joints, surgical screws, pins or plates also makes it easier for bacteria to enter and infect the bone.

Important: Any of the three types of bone infections described above can lead to chronic osteomyelitis, an initially low-grade infection that can persist for months or even years with few or no symptoms. Eventually it gets severe enough to literally destroy bone. Left untreated, the affected bone may have to be amputated.

DIFFICULT TO DIAGNOSE

When osteomyelitis first develops (acute osteomyelitis), the symptoms—such as pain, swelling and tenderness—are usually the same as those caused by other infections.

If the initial infection is subtle (low-grade) or doesn't resolve completely with treatment, it can result in chronic osteomyelitis. In this case, you may have no symptoms or symptoms that are nonspecific. For example, someone who has had surgery might blame discomfort on delayed recovery, not realizing that what they have is a bone infection.

Surprising finding: When we studied the histories of more than 2,000 osteomyelitis patients, we found that most of those with chronic infections had relatively little pain from the infection itself. About 28% of those who required surgery for infection had normal white blood cell counts—suggesting that, over time, the body adjusts to lingering infections.

If a doctor suspects that you may have osteomyelitis because of chronic pain…swelling… possibly fever…fatigue…or other symptoms, he/she will usually order special laboratory tests that detect the formation of antibodies. If the results indicate the presence of infection, he may then order an X-ray or magnetic resonance imaging (MRI) scan. These and other imaging tests can readily detect damaged bone tissue and reveal the presence of infection.

BEST TREATMENT OPTIONS

About 60% to 70% of people with acute osteomyelitis can be cured with antibiotics (or antifungal agents, if a fungal infection is present) if treatment begins early enough to prevent the infection from becoming chronic. In these cases, patients exhibit symptoms…test positive for infection…and readily respond to drug treatments. Most patients can be cured with a four- to six-week course of antibiotics. Fungal infections are more resistant to treatment—antifungal drugs may be needed for several months.

For chronic osteomyelitis, surgical debridement (the removal of damaged tissue and bone using such instruments as a scalpel or scissors) usually is necessary.

Reasons: Damaged bone can lose its blood supply and remain in the body as "dead bone"—without living cells or circulation. Such bone is invulnerable to antibiotics.

After debridement, the surgeon may insert a slow-release antibiotic depot, a small pouch that releases the antibiotic for up to a month. This approach can increase drug concentrations up to 100 times more than oral antibiotic therapy.

Even with these treatments, in people with chronic osteomyelitis who are otherwise healthy, up to 6% may require a second or even a third operation to cure the infection. In people with diabetes or other disorders, the percentage may be as high as 25%.

To improve your chances of a full recovery from chronic osteomyelitis: Eat well, maintain healthy blood sugar levels, stay active after treatment (to promote blood circulation, prevent blood clots and help maintain an appetite) and don't use tobacco products.

Safer Diabetes Medication Is Available

An FDA panel recently voted to keep the diabetes drug *rosiglitazone* (Avandia) on the market but suggested tougher warning labels to reflect research showing that the drug is linked to an increased risk for heart attack and stroke in some people.

If you take rosiglitazone: Ask your doctor about switching to *pioglitazone* (Actos), a similar but safer medication. Both drugs lower blood sugar levels, but pioglitazone also helps improve cholesterol/triglyceride profiles.

If you have heart failure: Don't take either drug—both may worsen this condition.

Frederic Vagnini, MD, cardiovascular surgeon and medical director, Heart, Diabetes and Weight Loss Centers of New York, New York City. He is coauthor of *The Weight Loss Plan for Beating Diabetes* (Fair Winds).

Actos and Avandia Warning

Diabetes medications Actos and Avandia may increase fracture risk in women over age 50. Higher doses are associated with greater risk. Postmenopausal women should be careful to consume adequate amounts of calcium and vitamin D to protect bone health.

William H. Herman, MD, MPH, director of the Michigan Diabetes Research and Training Center, University of Michigan, Ann Arbor, and leader of a study published in *The Journal of Clinical Endocrinology & Metabolism*.

Insulin May Fight Alzheimer's

An insulin nasal spray improved or maintained cognitive abilities in Alzheimer's patients.

Theory: Insulin might regulate the beta-amyloid proteins associated with the disease.

Alzheimer's Association International Conference.

Diabetes Drug Causes Pancreas Problem

The FDA has revised the prescribing information for the diabetes drugs Januvia (*sitagliptin*) and Janumet (*sitagliptin/metformin*). It now includes information about reported cases of acute pancreatitis among users. If you take either of these drugs, have your doctor monitor you for the development of pancreatitis, especially if you are just starting on this drug or if your dosage has increased recently.

Mark A. Stengler, NMD, licensed naturopathic medical doctor and leading authority on the practice of alternative and integrated medicine. He is founder and medical director of the Stengler Center for Integrative Medicine, Encinitas, California, and associate clinical professor at the National College of Natural Medicine, Portland, Oregon. He is author of *The Natural Physician's Healing Therapies* (Bottom Line Books).

More from Mark Stengler, NMD...

Byetta May Cause Kidney Problems

At the FDA's request, the maker of Byetta (*exenatide*) has revised its label to include information about reports of acute renal failure and other kidney problems in people using the product. If you take Byetta, have your doctor monitor you for signs of kidney dysfunction.

Also from Dr. Stengler...

Topical Testosterone Helps Diabetes

Researchers at the University of Sheffield and other research facilities in England gave men with testosterone deficiency and type 2 diabetes and/or metabolic syndrome a daily application of transdermal testosterone gel or a placebo gel. Insulin resistance was reduced by 15% in those who applied the testosterone gel, compared with those who used the placebo gel. If you are a man with diabetes, get tested for testosterone deficiency. Applying a testosterone gel could help to lower your glucose levels.

Arthritis Drug May Help Diabetes

In a clinical trial, *salsalate*, used for arthritis pain, reduced hemoglobin A1c—a marker of overall blood sugar control—in patients with type 2 diabetes. Salsalate is an anti-inflammatory drug related to aspirin but is gentler to the stomach.

Allison B. Goldfine, MD, section head of clinical research, Joslin Diabetes Center, Boston, and coprincipal investigator, TINSAL-T2D (Targeting Inflammation Using Salsalate in Type 2 Diabetes).

Statins May Increase Risk for Diabetes in Older People

Cholesterol-lowering statin medications may raise the risk for type 2 diabetes among people over age 60 by 9%. For people at high risk for heart disease, the benefits of statins significantly outweigh the risks—but doctors should take into account the risk for diabetes and other side effects when prescribing statins for people at low risk for heart disease. Lifestyle changes, such as improved diet and more exercise, should help reduce any increased risk.

Naveed Sattar, PhD, professor, department of metabolic medicine, University of Glasgow, Scotland, and leader of a review of 13 studies with 91,140 participants, published in *The Lancet*.

Must You Give Up Fruit?

Mark A. Stengler, NMD, licensed naturopathic medical doctor and leading authority on the practice of alternative and integrated medicine. He is founder and medical director of the Stengler Center for Integrative Medicine, Encinitas, California, and associate clinical professor at the National College of Natural Medicine, Portland, Oregon. He is author of *The Natural Physician's Healing Therapies* (Bottom Line Books).

Some fruits do, indeed, have a high sugar content, but that doesn't mean that patients with diabetes must give up this healthy habit. Fruits are low in fat and rich in phytonutrients, vitamins, minerals and fiber—and in moderation (two or three servings daily), they can be safely consumed by those with diabetes. One general way to choose fruits is using the Glycemic Index, which measures how slowly a food increases blood sugar (the lower the number, the more healthful). Choose low-to-mid-GI fruits such as cherries (22), plums (24), grapefruit (25) and bananas (47). A high-GI fruit is anything over 70.

Eating fruit with other foods also can prevent a spike in insulin. Combining fruit with low-GI foods, such as a slice of whole-grain bread, can prevent the insulin spike that comes with eating a high-GI fruit. To find the GI of specific fruits and other foods, go to *www.glycemicindex.com.*

Also helpful: Watch your serving size. One-half cup to one cup of most fruits counts as one serving. Some individuals have food sensitivities to certain fruits—and regardless of their GIs, these fruits (one example is grapefruit) can spike an individual's glucose level. Only by monitoring your diet and glucose levels closely will you truly know which fruits work best for you.

More from Mark Stengler…

Drink Blueberry Smoothies, Improve Blood Sugar Control

Researchers from Louisiana State University have found that drinking two blueberry smoothies daily helped obese, prediabetic adults improve their blood sugar control. The blueberry smoothie contained 22.5 grams of freeze-dried blueberry powder.

Everyone can benefit from eating blueberries year-round. You can buy them frozen in the off-season…and freeze-dried blueberry powder is available online and at health-food stores. Sprinkle a teaspoon of the powder on toast (instead of jam), or stir a half cup of fresh blueberries into yogurt.

Also from Dr. Stengler…

Mediterranean Diet for Type 2 Diabetes

After four years of following a Mediterranean-style diet, 44% of patients who had been diagnosed with type 2 diabetes before initiating the diet required medication for their condition, compared with 70% of patients who followed a low-fat diet after diagnosis, say researchers from Second University of Naples, Italy.

Both diets included about 30% of calories from fat, although the fat in the Mediterranean-style diet was mainly from olive oil, whereas the low-fat diet included all types of fat.

Diet details: www.mayoclinic.com (search for "Mediterranean diet").

A Spoonful of Vinegar Helps the Blood Sugar Go Down

Adding vinegar to a meal slows the glycemic response—the rate at which carbohydrates are absorbed into the bloodstream—by 20%.

Reason: The acetic acid in vinegar seems to slow the emptying of the stomach, which reduces risk for hyperglycemia (high blood sugar), a risk factor for heart disease, and helps people with type 2 diabetes manage their condition.

Ways to add vinegar to meals: Use malt vinegar on thick-cut oven fries...marinate sliced tomatoes and onions in red-wine vinegar before adding the vegetables to a sandwich... mix two parts red wine vinegar with one part olive oil, and use two tablespoons on a green salad.

Carol S. Johnston, PhD, RD, director, nutrition program, Arizona State University, Mesa, and coauthor of a study published in *Diabetes Care*.

Black Tea Helps Treat Diabetes

When researchers compared concentrations of polysaccharides (a type of carbohydrate) in black, green and oolong teas, the polysaccharides in black tea were the best blood sugar (glucose) inhibitors.

Theory: Polysaccharides in black tea block an enzyme that converts starch into glucose.

If you have diabetes or prediabetes: Consider drinking three cups of black tea daily to better control blood sugar.

Haixia Chen, PhD, associate professor, School of Pharmaceutical Science and Technology, Tianjin University, Tianjin, China.

Beans Lower Blood Sugar

Diabetics who ate one-half cup of beans a day—garbanzo, black, white, pinto or kidney beans—had significantly lower fasting glucose, insulin and hemoglobin A1C, a marker of long-term glucose control. When eaten as a regular part of a high-fiber, low-glycemic-index diet, beans lower hemoglobin A1C by an average of 0.48%, which lies at the lower level of effectiveness for medications such as *metformin* (Glucophage).

Cyril Kendall, PhD, research associate, department of nutritional sciences, University of Toronto, and the Clinical Nutrition and Risk Factor Modification Centre, St. Michael's Hospital, Toronto, and leader of research analyzing 41 trials regarding the effects of beans on blood sugar levels, published in *Diabetologia*.

Surprising Symptoms Of Prediabetes

Frederic J. Vagnini, MD, a cardiovascular surgeon and medical director of the Heart, Diabetes & Weight Loss Centers of New York in New York City. He is coauthor of *The Weight Loss Plan for Beating Diabetes* (Fair Winds).

One of the best ways to prevent diabetes is to spot blood sugar (glucose) problems before the full-blown disease develops. But most people don't realize that diabetes—and its precursor, prediabetes—can cause no symptoms at all or a wide range of symptoms that are often misinterpreted.

Common mistake: Because type 2 diabetes is strongly linked to excess body weight, many people who are a normal weight assume that they won't develop the disease. But that's not always true. About 15% of people who are diagnosed with diabetes are not overweight. And paradoxically, even weight loss can be a symptom of this complex disorder in people (normal weight or overweight) who have uncontrolled high glucose levels.

Shocking recent finding: The Centers for Disease Control and Prevention now estimates that 40% of Americans ages 40 to 74 have prediabetes, and nearly two out of three Americans over age 65 have prediabetes or diabetes—most likely due to the increasing numbers of people who are overweight and inactive, both of which boost diabetes risk.

However, most primary care doctors aren't diagnosing and treating prediabetes early enough in their patients—often because they fail to order the necessary screening tests (see below). And because the symptoms of prediabetes can be subtle, especially in its early stages, most people are not reporting potential red flags to their doctors.

Fortunately, prediabetes can virtually always be prevented from progressing to diabetes if the condition is identified and treated in its early stages (by following a healthful diet, exercising regularly and taking nutritional supplements and medications, if necessary).

WHAT IS PREDIABETES?

Prediabetes occurs when the body's cells no longer respond correctly to insulin, a hormone that regulates blood sugar. With prediabetes, blood sugar levels are higher than normal, but they are not high enough to warrant a diagnosis of diabetes.

Prediabetes affects about 57 million Americans—most of whom are unaware that they have the condition.

RED FLAGS FOR DIABETES

Being overweight (defined as having a body mass index, or BMI, of 25 or higher) is perhaps the best-known risk factor for type 2 diabetes.* The more excess body weight you have, the more resistant your cells become to the blood sugar–regulating effects of the hormone insulin, ultimately causing blood glucose levels to rise.

Greatest danger: Abdominal fat, in particular, further boosts diabetes risk. That's because belly (visceral) fat hinders the processing of insulin. The single biggest risk factor for prediabetes is having a waistline of 40 inches

*For a BMI calculator, go to the Web site of the National Heart, Lung and Blood Institute, *www.nhlbisupport.com/bmi.*

or more if you're a man...or 35 inches or more if you're a woman. Lesser-known red flags for prediabetes (and diabetes)—if you have one of these symptoms, see your doctor...

• **Increased thirst and need to urinate.** Because excess blood glucose draws water from the body's tissues, people with elevated blood glucose levels feel thirsty much of the time. Even when they drink fluids, their thirst is rarely quenched. Therefore, they drink even more, causing them to urinate more often than is normal for them.

• **Unexplained weight loss.** While being overweight is a significant risk factor for prediabetes, the condition also can paradoxically lead to unexplained weight loss resulting from a lack of energy supply to the body's cells and a loss of glucose-related calories due to excessive urination.

• **Dry, itchy skin.** Excess blood glucose also draws moisture from the skin, leaving it dry and prone to itching and cracking—especially on the legs, feet and elbows.

• **Blurred vision.** Glucose can change the shape of the eye lens, making it difficult to focus properly.

• **Slow-healing cuts, sores or bruises and frequent infections.** For unknown reasons, excess blood glucose appears to interfere with the body's healing processes and its ability to fight off infection. In particular, women with prediabetes and diabetes are prone to urinary tract and vaginal infections.

• **Red, swollen and tender gums.** Because the body's ability to heal can be compromised by prediabetes, gum inflammation, involving red, swollen, tender and/or bleeding gums, may develop.

• **Persistent feelings of hunger.** When the body's cells don't get enough glucose due to prediabetes, the cells send signals to the brain that are interpreted as hunger, typically about one hour after consuming a meal.

• **Lack of energy.** Because their cells are starved of energy-boosting glucose, people with prediabetes tend to tire quickly after even mild physical effort. Dehydration due to excess blood glucose also can contribute to fatigue.

• **Falling asleep after eating.** An hour or so after eating, our digestive systems convert the food we've eaten into glucose. In people with prediabetes, the process is exaggerated— blood glucose levels spike, triggering a surge of insulin as the body attempts to stabilize high glucose levels. This insulin surge is ineffective in lowering blood glucose, causing the person to become drowsy. If you feel sleepy after meals, it can be a sign that your blood glucose levels are riding this prediabetic roller coaster.

• **Moodiness and irritability.** Lack of energy production in your cells, together with sharp rises and dips in blood glucose levels, can trigger feelings of restlessness, irritability and exaggerated emotional responses to stress.

• **Tingling or numbness in the hands and feet.** Excess blood glucose can damage small blood vessels feeding the body's peripheral nerves, often causing tingling, loss of sensation or burning pain in the hands, arms, legs or feet.

• **Loss of sex drive and erectile dysfunction in men.** Prediabetes is associated with low testosterone in men, which often reduces libido. In addition, glucose-related damage to the body's small blood vessels often impairs the ability of prediabetic men to have an erection.

More from Dr. Frederic Vagnini...

Three Key Diabetes Tests

If you suspect that you may have prediabetes, ask your doctor to order the following tests...

• **Fasting blood glucose.** This traditional blood test for diabetes is usually part of a standard physical. Until recently, a result over 125 milligrams per deciliter (mg/dL) was considered a sign of diabetes, while 100 mg/dL to 125 mg/dL indicated prediabetes.

New finding: Standard guidelines established by the American Diabetes Association have not changed, but recent data suggest that a person who has a fasting blood glucose reading over 90 mg/dL should be evaluated by a physician.

• **Hemoglobin A1C.** This blood test, also included in many annual checkups, measures the average blood glucose level over a two- to three-month period. An A1C result of 4.5% to 5.9% is considered normal...6% to 6.5% indicates prediabetes...and two separate readings of 6.5% or above indicate diabetes.

Danger level: Standard guidelines still use 6% as the lower end of the prediabetes range, but recent data suggest that results as low as 5.6% or 5.7% may signal prediabetes.

• **Oral glucose tolerance test.** Administered over two hours in your doctor's office, this test can spot problems with blood-sugar regulation that may not show up in the other tests. For the oral glucose tolerance test, blood levels of glucose are checked immediately before drinking a premixed glucose formula and two hours afterward.

A result of 140 mg/dL to 159 mg/dL is a sign of increased risk for diabetes...160 mg/dL to 200 mg/dL indicates high risk for diabetes... and over 200 mg/dL signals full-blown diabetes. Also ask your doctor to measure your insulin levels—insulin fluctuations can be an even earlier predictor of prediabetes than the tests described above.

Too Much Sugar in Your Diet Carries More Risk Than Weight Gain

Richard J. Johnson, MD, professor and chief of the division of renal diseases and hypertension at the University of Colorado, Denver, and an adjunct professor in the division of nephrology, hypertension and renal transplantation at the University of Florida in Gainesville. Dr. Johnson's medical research has appeared in *The New England Journal of Medicine,* the *American Journal of Clinical Nutrition,* the *International Journal of Obesity, Diabetes* and many other leading medical journals. He is the author of *The Sugar Fix: The High-Fructose Fallout That Is Making You Sick* (Rodale).

We all know that it's not good for our health to consume too much sugar. Excessive amounts of sugar in the diet are widely known to cause weight gain. But that's only part of the story.

Both table sugar and high fructose corn syrup (HFCS) contain fructose, which recent research has shown can increase the risk for diabetes, fatty liver disease, high blood pressure and chronic kidney disease when consumed in excessive amounts. Currently, most Americans consume way too much added sugar in their daily diets, putting them at risk for all these diseases.

WHAT'S THE TROUBLE WITH FRUCTOSE?

Fructose is a simple sugar. It is found naturally in honey, fruits and some vegetables. But a typical fruit contains only about 8 g of fructose, compared to about 20 g in a sugary soda. Unlike soda, fruits and vegetables contain nutrients and antioxidants that are beneficial to health.

The two main sources of fructose in the American diet are table sugar (which is squeezed from beet and cane plants) and HFCS (which is processed using enzymes that turn corn starch into glucose and fructose). Table sugar and HFCS are almost identical in their chemical composition—and both, consumed in excess, can contribute to health problems.

But few Americans are aware of just how much added sugar they are getting in their diets. That's because many added sugars are often listed as ingredients that are not recognizable as sugar and are found in unexpected food sources (see next page for a list of these terms). For example, added sugar is found in not only obvious places like soft drinks and other sweet beverages, but also in great abundance in many salad dressings, condiments (such as ketchup), cereals, crackers and even bread.

My research and that of other scientists show that Americans' ever-increasing sugar consumption is hurting their health in unexpected—even deadly—ways.

•**High blood pressure (hypertension).** About one in three American adults has hypertension, an underlying risk factor for heart attack, stroke and kidney disease. Historically, high blood pressure has been linked to excessive sodium intake. Now preliminary evidence shows that sugar may play a bigger role than was previously thought.

Important finding #1: In a study published in the journal *Circulation*, researchers found that among 810 overweight adults with stage 1 or borderline hypertension, those who drank one less drink sweetened with sugar or HFCS (such as soft drinks, fruit drinks and lemonade) per day for 18 months lowered their blood pressure. Although more research is needed, this study is a first step in confirming a sugar–blood pressure link.

Important finding #2: A *Journal of the American Society of Nephrology* study found that among 4,528 adults, those whose diets included 74 grams or more of fructose daily had up to 77% higher risk for blood pressure problems than those who consumed less fructose daily.

•**Liver disease.** Traditionally, liver disease was widely linked to excessive alcohol intake. Then doctors began to identify a condition known as nonalcoholic fatty liver disease (NAFLD), in which fat builds up in the liver of a person who drinks little or no alcohol. Now research is showing that sugar may be involved in the development of NAFLD. For example, research at Duke University showed that those who ingested the most fructose had more rapid disease progression (fattening of the liver and formation of fibrous tissue) than those who ingested the least. NAFLD is common among people who have type 2 diabetes or are overweight and can progress to cirrhosis and liver cancer.

EMERGING RESEARCH ON FRUCTOSE

While there are many studies being conducted on different types of added sugars, there is important research that now focuses on various forms of fructose. For example, recent research suggests that fructose is harmful because it increases levels of uric acid, a naturally occurring acid found in the urine. In crystalline form, uric acid can deposit in the joints and lead to gout.

Eating foods rich in a compound called purines (found in foods such as anchovies, beer, brewer's yeast supplements, clams, goose, gravy, herring, lobster, mackerel, meat extract, mincemeat, mussels, organ meats, oysters, sardines, scallops and shrimp) can also produce high levels of uric acid.

SMART WAYS TO LIMIT SUGAR

It's important to remove added sugar from your diet—with a special focus on fructose due to its unique potential risks that are now being discovered in new research.

To minimize the health risks associated with added sugars, try these steps...

• **Beware of "hidden" sugar.** When buying processed foods, remember that added sugars can appear on food labels in various ways. (See list at right.)

• **Avoid any prepared or processed product that does not provide an ingredient list.**

• **Don't eat more than four fruits daily.** Even the naturally occurring fructose found in fruit counts toward your total daily intake of fructose. It's also important to limit your intake of fruit juice, which has been stripped of the nutritious fiber present in whole fruit and often contains added sugar.

• **Limit fructose intake to 25 g to 35 g per day.** Consuming more than that amount could trigger the physiological changes that may lead to disease.

To learn the fructose content of specific foods, go to the USDA Food Database at *www. nal.usda.gov/fnic/foodcomp/search.*

• **Take nutritional supplements.** Limiting fruit in your diet may lower your levels of important nutrients. To replace them, take a multivitamin plus an additional 250 mg of vitamin C daily.

• **Be cautious when eating in restaurants.** Limit restaurant meals and takeout food to items for which you know the ingredients.

• **Be prepared for sugar withdrawal.** In rare cases, you may develop withdrawal symptoms from sugar and fructose, such as headache, fatigue and an intense craving for sweets.

To help ease these symptoms, be sure to drink plenty of water (five to eight cups daily).

SUGAR ALIASES

Take this list to the supermarket with you to help you identify the various terms for added sugars...

• **Beet sugar**
• **Brown sugar**
• **Cane sugar**
• **Corn sweetener**
• **Corn syrup**
• **Demerara sugar**
• **Fruit juice concentrate**
• **Granulated sugar**
• **High-fructose corn syrup**
• **Honey**
• **Invert sugar**
• **Maple syrup**
• **Molasses**
• **Muscovado sugar**
• **Raw sugar**
• **Sucrose**
• **Syrup**
• **Table sugar**
• **Tagatose**
• **Turbinado sugar**

Do Sweets Give You Diabetes?

Steven Edelman, MD, professor of medicine at the University of California, San Diego, and founder and director of Taking Control of Your Diabetes, a not-for-profit diabetes education organization based in Del Mar, California.

Many people believe this myth, but in fact there is no direct link between eating excessive amounts of sugar and developing diabetes. However, if you are already at risk for type 2 diabetes and you become overweight or obese from eating too much sugar—or too much of anything, for that matter—you can bring on diabetes.

The factors that put you at increased risk for diabetes include high cholesterol...high blood pressure...a history of gestational diabetes or giving birth to a baby who weighed more than nine pounds...a family history of type 2 diabetes...or being of African-American, Hispanic, Native American, Pacific Islander or Asian-Indian descent. If you have none of these risk factors, gaining weight from over-indulging in sugar is not likely to lead to diabetes. But it certainly can contribute to many other health problems, such as heart disease and cancer—so it's still best to eat sweets only in moderation.

Melt Away Abdominal Fat

Mark A. Stengler, NMD, licensed naturopathic medical doctor and leading authority on the practice of alternative and integrated medicine. He is founder and medical director of the Stengler Center for Integrative Medicine, Encinitas, California, and associate clinical professor at the National College of Natural Medicine, Portland, Oregon. He is author of *The Natural Physician's Healing Therapies* (Bottom Line Books).

The size of your waist is believed to be a better indicator of health problems than the number on the scale or your body mass index (BMI), a measure of weight relative to height.

It is far more healthful to have a "pear" body shape (fat stored around the hips, buttocks and thighs) than an "apple" shape (fat stored around the middle). Both men and women with apple shapes (men with waists of 40 inches or more and women with waists of 35 inches or more) are more likely to be insulin resistant—a condition in which the cells do not receive insulin properly and which often leads to diabetes—than those with smaller waists. In fact, research shows that having just an extra four inches around your waist increases your risk for heart failure by 15%. Belly fat is associated with a greater risk for stroke, and every additional two inches around the waist in men increases the risk for deep-vein thrombosis and pulmonary embolism (blockage of the main artery of the lungs) by 18%.

Why abdominal fat is so bad: This fat, also known as visceral fat, produces hormones that work against you in the following ways...

- **Releasing free fatty acids** (the breakdown product of fat cells that circulate in the bloodstream)

- **Decreasing insulin sensitivity** (the degree to which your cells recognize insulin and use it properly)

- **Increasing cytokines,** compounds that contribute to inflammation and insulin resistance, including resistin, another chemical that reduces insulin sensitivity.

- **Decreasing hormones** such as leptin that help regulate metabolism and appetite.

HELP IS ON THE WAY

Abdominal fat often is associated with hormonal imbalances, such as high insulin (yes, even insulin is a hormone)...high cortisol...and high estrogen. Once the vicious cycle of abdominal weight gain and hormonal imbalance begins, it is hard to stop—especially because each one causes the other.

I put those who are caught in this cycle on a hormone-balancing protocol that they follow for at least two months and up to six months. The results are impressive.

THE PROTOCOLS

If you are a man with a waist measurement of 40 inches or more or a woman with a waist of 35 inches or more, ask your doctor to test your levels of cortisol, insulin and estrogen.

Note: Excess estrogen is not just a female problem. While high levels most often occur in women younger than 45 and in postmenopausal women, they can appear in men as well, especially when made worse by the presence of environmental estrogens, compounds found in many plastic household products.

If you have excess estrogen...

High levels of estrogen, particularly combined with low levels of progesterone, can cause abdominal fat. When either a male or female patient has excess estrogen, especially in conjunction with low levels of progesterone (a condition called estrogen dominance), I recommend an estrogen detox program. This includes eating two to three daily servings of cruciferous vegetables (such as broccoli, cabbage, brussels sprouts, cauliflower and kale), which contain plant compounds called indoles that help regulate estrogen metabolism and can make estrogen less toxic.

Supplements that help include indole-3-carbinol and diindolymethane (DIM). These phytochemicals in supplement form are similar to those found in cruciferous vegetables. Patients take 300 milligrams (mg) to 400 mg daily of indole-3-carbinol and 200 mg to 400 mg of DIM daily. (I recommend both the food, for the fiber, and the supplements because it's difficult to get enough of these phytochemicals through food.)

For women who are perimenopausal or menopausal (and some men with prostate problems) with this type of hormonal imbalance, I also may prescribe a bioidentical progesterone cream.

If you have insulin resistance...

Abdominal fat and insulin resistance often go together like the proverbial chicken and egg, and it isn't always easy to know which one was there first. Insulin resistance increases the chances of developing type 2 diabetes and cardiovascular disease. It can be effectively treated by eating a diet with high-fiber foods, including vegetables, legumes and grains. Regular exercise also helps keep insulin resistance under control. For my insulin-resistant patients, I also recommend PGX, a form of glucomannan fiber.

Brand to try: Natural Factors PGX Daily (800-322-8704, *www.naturalfactors.com* for a store locator).

Also helpful: Chromium picolinate, a trace mineral (start with 500 mcg daily and increase to 1,000 mcg daily, if needed), which can help balance blood sugar levels...and resveratrol (50 mg to 100 mg daily), which improves insulin resistance.

If you have high levels of cortisol...

Cortisol, the major stress hormone produced by the adrenal glands, can signal the body to store fat around the middle. For my patients whose blood tests reveal high cortisol levels, I prescribe a basic program of aerobic exercise (30 minutes daily of swimming, jogging, bicycling or walking)...strength training...stress

reduction...and deep breathing, all of which have been found to lower cortisol levels. The herb ashwagandha also can help normalize blood cortisol levels.

Brand to try: Sensoril Ashwagandha made by Jarrow Formulas (310-204-6936, *www.jarrow.com* for a store locator). Take one 225-mg capsule daily. Women who are pregnant or breast-feeding should not take this herb.

More from Mark Stengler, NMD...

If You Have Gum Disease, Look for Diabetes

Researchers at New York University College of Nursing found that 93% of Americans with periodontal disease were at high risk for diabetes, while a far smaller proportion of people without gum disease—about 63%—were at risk for diabetes. If you have periodontal disease, get it treated—and be sure that you are tested for diabetes.

Coffee and Tea Lower Diabetes Risk

People who drank three or more cups of coffee daily had a 25% lower risk for type 2 diabetes than people who drank two or fewer cups. Similar results were shown for tea and decaffeinated coffee, indicating that the effect is not entirely due to caffeine but is likely to include other compounds present in these beverages, such as magnesium.

Rachel Huxley, DPhil, director of the nutrition and lifestyle division and associate professor in the faculty of medicine, University of Sydney, Australia, and lead author of a meta-analysis of 18 studies involving more than 450,000 people, published in *Archives of Internal Medicine.*

Magnesium May Fight Diabetes

When researchers studied 4,497 healthy adults' diets for 20 years, those who consumed the most magnesium (about 200 mg per 1,000 calories) were 47% less likely to develop diabetes than those who consumed the least (about 100 milligrams [mg] per 1,000 calories).

Theory: Magnesium enhances enzymes that help the body process blood sugar.

Self-defense: Eat foods that are rich in magnesium, such as almonds (one-quarter cup roasted, 97 mg) and spinach (one-half cup cooked, 77 mg).

Ka He, MD, associate professor, departments of nutrition and epidemiology, University of North Carolina, Chapel Hill.

Strong Muscles Help Ward Off Diabetes

Maintaining a healthy weight helps to fend off diabetes. But now researchers at the University of California, Los Angeles, have found that having strong muscles can prevent diabetes. Sarcopenia (low muscle mass and strength) was associated with insulin resistance, a precursor to diabetes. To maintain muscle mass, consume low-fat protein, such as chicken or tofu, and participate in strength-training exercises. Men and women should have their testosterone levels checked and, if necessary, treated, since low levels can affect muscle mass.

Mark A. Stengler, NMD, licensed naturopathic medical doctor and leading authority on the practice of alternative and integrated medicine. He is founder and medical director of the Stengler Center for Integrative Medicine, Encinitas, California, and associate clinical professor at the National College of Natural Medicine, Portland, Oregon. He is author of *The Natural Physician's Healing Therapies* (Bottom Line Books).

Tai Chi Helps Lower Blood Sugar

In a six-month study of 62 people with diabetes, those who practiced the Chinese martial art tai chi weekly (two supervised sessions and three at home) significantly reduced their blood sugar levels compared with those who did not practice tai chi.

Theory: Tai chi coordinates breathing with slow, gentle movements, which may improve insulin sensitivity.

To find a tai chi class near you: Consult *www.taichiforhealth.com* and click on "How to Find an Instructor."

Beverly Roberts, PhD, RN, professor for teaching and research, University of Florida College of Nursing, Gainesville.

21

Heart Disease

Heart Attack: All About The Hidden Risk Factors

We've all been told how important it is to control major risk factors for heart attack and coronary artery disease. We know, for example, not to smoke…to maintain LDL (bad) cholesterol at safe levels…raise HDL (good) cholesterol as high as possible…keep blood pressure below 120/80…and monitor our blood levels of C-reactive protein and homocysteine—a protein and amino acid that, when elevated, indicate increased heart attack risk.

What you may not know: Cardiovascular risk factors are synergistic, so any one of the risk factors mentioned above increases the effect of other risk factors.

Example: Even slightly elevated cholesterol or blood pressure becomes more dangerous in the presence of smaller, lesser-known risk factors such as…

• **Steroid medications.** Most people now know that nonsteroidal anti-inflammatory drugs, including the prescription medication *celecoxib* (Celebrex) and over-the-counter products such as *ibuprofen* (Advil) and *naproxen* (Aleve), increase heart attack and stroke risk by making blood platelets sticky. However, steroid drugs are perhaps the most dangerous of the "stealth" risk factors for heart attack.

Steroids, which include *cortisone, prednisone* and *prednisolone* (Orapred), are prescribed for inflammatory conditions such as colitis, inflammatory bowel disease, psoriasis, asthma and rheumatoid arthritis.

Besides raising cholesterol levels and blood pressure slightly, steroids also tend to promote

Robert M. Stark, MD, a preventive cardiologist in private practice in Greenwich, Connecticut. He is also a clinical assistant professor of medicine at the Yale University School of Medicine in New Haven, Connecticut, and medical director of the Cardiovascular Prevention Program at Greenwich Hospital (affiliated with the Yale New Haven Heart Institute). Dr. Stark is a Fellow of the American College of Cardiology.

the entry of cholesterol into the artery wall to form atherosclerotic plaque deposits.

Important: Only oral and injectable forms of steroid medications carry these risks—the inhaled form used to treat asthma does not.

Taking steroid medications also raises risk for atrial fibrillation, an irregular heartbeat associated with increased risk for stroke.

Self-defense: Avoid using oral and injectable steroids if at all possible. If you must use them, make sure your cholesterol levels and blood pressure are well-managed…take the lowest possible dose…and, whenever possible, avoid using them for more than a week or two.

Important: Abrupt discontinuation of steroids, without gradually tapering off, may cause serious side effects. Consult your physician before stopping a steroid medication.

•**Stress.** Both chronic and acute stress can be hard on the heart—but in slightly different ways.

Chronic stress, such as from ongoing financial pressures or a strained relationship, raises blood levels of the stress hormones epinephrine (adrenaline), norepinephrine and cortisol, accelerating buildup of dangerous plaque in the coronary arteries much as steroid drugs do.

Self-defense: Address the underlying cause of the chronic stress…engage in daily aerobic exercise, which burns off excess epinephrine in the bloodstream and reduces anxiety…and practice stress-reduction techniques, such as biofeedback and meditation, which have been shown to lower epinephrine and norepinephrine levels.

Acute stress, such as from the sudden death of a spouse, not only increases stress hormones but also causes the coronary arteries to constrict. In addition, acute stress increases the heart's need for, and consumption of, oxygen. If you already have a partially blocked coronary artery due to plaque buildup, this constriction and increased oxygen consumption can contribute to a dangerous shortage of blood flow to the heart.

Self-defense: If you are confronted with acute or chronic stress, ask your doctor to consider prescribing a beta-blocker, such as *propranolol* (Inderal), *atenolol* (Tenormin) or *metoprolol* (Lopressor). These drugs are typically used to treat heart conditions and high blood pressure. However, beta-blockers also protect against the harmful arterial effect that occurs with stress and can be taken as long as stress-related symptoms occur. These drugs are not recommended for those with low blood pressure, asthma or abnormally low heart rate.

•**Sleep apnea.** People who suffer from this condition stop breathing during their sleep for a few seconds at a time many times per night. Sleep apnea not only disrupts sleep but also is associated with an increased risk for heart attack and heart disease.

Self-defense: Half of people with mild sleep apnea (those who stop breathing five to 15 times per hour) and 20% of those with moderate apnea (15 to 30 breathing stoppages per hour) have so-called positional sleep apnea—that is, the disturbed breathing occurs only when the person is sleeping on his/her back.

Good solution: A relatively new strap-on foam device called Zzoma, which forces you to lie on your side, appears to help prevent positional sleep apnea (available for $99.95 from the manufacturer at 877-799-9662 or *www.zzomaosa.com*).

For more serious cases, continuous positive airway pressure (CPAP), a type of therapy in which the sleeper wears a mask that blows air into his nostrils, helps reduce apnea symptoms. For those who find the CPAP mask uncomfortable, oral appliances, prescribed by dentists, also help reduce apnea symptoms.

•**Anemia.** With this condition, the blood's ability to carry oxygen is impaired. This can trigger chest pain (angina) or even a heart attack in people whose coronary arteries are partially blocked. Always seek immediate medical attention if you have chest pain.

Self-defense: Anemia often can be treated with iron, vitamin B-12 or folic acid supplements or medications. After you've sought medical attention for chest pain, be sure that your physician tests you for anemia.

•**Chlamydia infection.** *Chlamydia pneumoniae* is a bacterium found in the respiratory tract of more than two million Americans. Different from the germ that causes the sexually transmitted disease chlamydia, C. pneumoniae is associated with increased risk for coronary artery disease, possibly because it contributes to arterial inflammation.

Self-defense: If you have signs of a respiratory infection, your doctor may want to order a blood test for C. pneumoniae. Antibiotics can effectively treat an infection caused by this bacterium.

• **Vitamin K deficiency.** Vitamin K (found mostly in meats, cheeses and leafy green vegetables) has been shown to reduce cardiovascular risk in people by more than 50% and also has prevented hardening of the arteries in animal studies. Vitamin K is also produced by the bacteria naturally residing in the intestine. Researchers have found, however, that most people don't get enough vitamin K in their diets.

Self-defense: To ensure that you get enough of this crucial vitamin, ask your doctor about taking a high-dose vitamin K supplement (100 micrograms daily for adults). Because vitamin K can reduce the effects of blood-thinning medication, it is never recommended for people taking *warfarin* (Coumadin) or other blood thinners.

• **Horizontal earlobe creases.** Though no one knows why, some research has shown that people who have a horizontal crease in one or both of their earlobes may be at increased risk for coronary artery disease.

Self-defense: While there's nothing that can be done to change this risk factor, anyone with such creases should be especially careful about monitoring other cardiovascular risk factors.

Attitude Counts

Researchers surveyed 396 young, healthy people to determine their attitudes toward older people and aging...then reviewed their medical records 38 years later.

Results: People who had rated aging most negatively when they were young were significantly more likely to have experienced a heart attack or other cardiovascular problems than those who had had the most positive feelings about aging, even after adjusting for health risk factors such as cholesterol, weight and family history.

Implication: Nurturing a positive attitude about the benefits of aging—such as wisdom and maturity—may promote your long-term health.

Becca Levy, PhD, associate professor of epidemiology and psychology, Yale School of Public Health, New Haven, Connecticut, and lead author of a study published in *Psychological Science*.

Aggressive Treatment Best for Heart Failure

Gregg Fonarow, MD, a professor of medicine and director of the Ahmanson-UCLA Cardiomyopathy Center, Los Angeles. He directs the UCLA Cardiology Fellowship Training Program and is codirector of the Preventive Cardiology Program. He has published more than 400 research studies and clinical trials in heart failure management and preventive cardiology.

About five million Americans suffer from heart failure, but this disease can be avoided.

WHAT IS HEART FAILURE?

Any disease that weakens the heart muscle can, over time, result in heart failure. With heart failure, the heart is damaged and becomes unable to supply sufficient amounts of blood to the rest of the body. Symptoms include fatigue, shortness of breath and swelling in the legs, ankles and feet.

Unfortunately, few patients and doctors are aggressive enough in following through on treatment of the risk factors, such as high blood pressure (hypertension), elevated cholesterol and atherosclerosis (fatty buildup in the arteries), that can lead to heart failure.

Without adequate treatment, the heart muscle becomes damaged and weakened to the point that it can no longer adequately pump blood throughout the body.

It sounds obvious and it may be inconvenient, but research shows that about 50% to 80% of all cases of heart failure could be prevented with lifestyle modifications and/or better management of the risk factors.

AN UNDERTREATED DISEASE

Over time, the impaired circulation that marks heart failure can cause "congestion" of blood in the lower legs, lungs, liver orabdomen—often leading to fatigue, weakness and shortness of breath.

When heart failure is inadequately treated, many serious complications can result, including pump failure (when the heart malfunctions and pumps inefficiently)...sudden arrhythmias (abnormal heart rhythms)...kidney failure (due to reduced blood flow)...and heart attack or stroke (from clots triggered by impaired circulation).

There isn't a cure for heart failure. The challenge is to relieve symptoms and restore most of the heart's normal function. When heart failure is severe, pumping devices or even a heart transplant may be considered. *Latest findings on treating heart failure...*

MOST EFFECTIVE TREATMENTS

In addition to controlling the conditions that often accompany heart failure, patients can reduce heart symptoms with a combination of medications...

• **Beta-blockers.** They're among the most effective drugs for heart failure because they slow the heart rate, reduce the heart's workload and protect the heart against harmful neurohormones (chemical messengers that overproduce and cause damage in heart failure).

Patients treated with beta-blockers can experience an improvement in ejection fraction (a measure of the heart's squeezing ability) of seven to 10 percentage points, which is enough to reduce symptoms, such as fatigue. Their risk of dying from heart failure can be reduced by 30% to 40%.

Two drugs, which are often underdosed, have been shown to be effective.

For best results: *Metoprolol* (Lopressor) taken at a dose of 200 milligrams (mg) daily...or *carvedilol* (Coreg) at a dose of 25 mg twice daily.

• **Aldosterone antagonists.** These drugs, which include *spironolactone* (Aldactone), are known as potassium-sparing diuretics because they're less likely than older drugs to deplete potassium from the body. Most people with heart failure require diuretics to remove excess fluids from the body since the heart's inefficient pumping action can lead to fluid buildup.

Troubling research: Researchers at the University of California, Los Angeles, published a study showing that only about one-third of patients who should be taking these drugs are getting them. Many doctors are reluctant to prescribe aldosterone antagonists because these drugs require frequent monitoring and dose adjustments to prevent increased levels of potassium.

However, aldosterone antagonists can reverse scarring of the heart and improve its pumping ability. They improve survival by at least 30% and also reduce the risk for sudden death from heart disease.

For best results: A typical starting dose of spironolactone is 12.5 mg once daily, but your dose may vary depending on your symptoms, renal function and potassium level.

• **Angiotensin receptor blockers.** These drugs, including *losartan* (Cozaar), are designed to relax blood vessels so that it's easier for the heart to pump blood.

For best results: The standard dose for losartan used to be 50 mg, but new research indicates that 150 mg can significantly reduce the need for hospitalization due to uncontrolled heart failure symptoms. Side effects include cough, elevated potassium, dizziness and headache.

WHEN MORE HELP IS NEEDED

If you have made lifestyle changes (such as reducing fat in your diet and getting regular exercise) and have received maximum treatment with medication but still suffer symptoms of heart failure, you may need even more help.

• **Cardiac resynchronization** is a relatively new treatment in which electrodes are placed on the left and right sides of the heart. Electrical impulses delivered to the electrodes from an implanted biventrical pacemaker paces both sides of the lower chambers of the heart, improving the heart's pumping action. A battery pack that is a little smaller than a deck of cards is implanted under the collarbone.

How it helps: Cardiac resynchronization, combined with medication, can reduce hospitalizations from heart failure complications by 50%…and reduce the risk of dying from heart failure by 35% to 40%.

• **Left ventricular assist device (LVAD).** Former vice president Dick Cheney recently had surgery for implantation of an LVAD. This device gives a boost to the heart's main pumping chamber and helps it deliver blood to the rest of the body. The LVAD, which is surgically attached to the left ventricle and connected to a power source (such as batteries) outside the body, is an important breakthrough because the majority of patients who receive the implant may survive long enough to get a heart transplant.

One device, the HeartMate II, was approved by the FDA in April 2008. Research found that patients given this device had one-year survival rates of 68% compared with 55% with earlier-generation LVADs.

ADDITIONAL USEFUL THERAPIES

Other therapies that can help ease heart failure symptoms…

• **Omega-3 fatty acids.** In a study of nearly 7,000 heart failure patients who received either placebos or 1,000 mg of omega-3s daily, those taking omega-3s were about 10% less likely to die.

• **Intravenous iron.** Heart failure patients who are deficient in iron may improve slightly when they receive iron intravenously. This treatment isn't approved by the FDA for this use, and it hasn't been proven to prolong survival times. However, in those who are iron-deficient (even if they don't have anemia), intravenous iron may help ease symptoms. If you have heart failure, ask your doctor about having your iron levels tested.

• **Sodium and fluid restriction.** Since a high-sodium diet can significantly increase blood pressure in many people, individuals with heart failure should limit their sodium intake. The optimal sodium intake for heart failure patients hasn't been established, but they are usually advised not to exceed 1,500 mg daily.

Fluid restriction is also important, particularly for those who have congestion. Patients who struggle with fluid retention should limit the amount they drink to about two liters (about 68 ounces) daily.

Caution: Heart failure patients should never take aspirin or any other nonsteroidal anti-inflammatory drug (NSAID) without consulting a doctor. These drugs have been associated with a worsening of heart failure symptoms. *Acetaminophen* (Tylenol) may be a better option. Certain diabetes drugs, such as *rosiglitazone* (Avandia) and *pioglitazone* (Actos), also should be avoided by people with heart failure.

Do You Take Nitroglycerin Pills?

Most *nitroglycerin* pills sold for heart problems have not been tested for safety or effectiveness. There is only one approved nitroglycerin tablet—Nitrostat from Pfizer. Nitroglycerin is difficult to make in a stable and effective form. Patients who take the unapproved tablets may be fine—or they may not get adequate pain relief and cardiac protection. The FDA has warned two manufacturers of the drug to stop marketing unapproved tablets, but the drugs are still being sold until the FDA order takes effect.

Self-defense: Insist that your doctor prescribe Nitrostat.

Harry M. Lever, MD, cardiologist and medical director, Hypertrophic Cardiomyopathy Clinic, Cleveland Clinic, Ohio.

Don't Ignore This Heart Risk Warning

An electrocardiogram (ECG) measures various heart functions, including *QRS duration* (QRSd), the time it takes an electrical signal to get through the pumping chambers.

Recent finding: An increase in QRSd is linked to elevated risk for sudden cardiac death and suggests the need for additional heart testing and preventive treatment.

Best: ECGs often are done during annual physical exams—so ask your doctor about your QRSd results.

Peter Okin, MD, a cardiologist and professor of medicine at Weill Cornell Medical College in New York City and senior author of an analysis of data from more than 9,000 people.

Better Heart Care For Women

When researchers analyzed past studies comparing how atrial fibrillation (irregular heart rate) affected men and women, women had higher stroke risk and more stroke-related disability and were less often prescribed blood thinners.

Theory: Because some evidence shows that women have a significantly higher risk of bleeding from blood-thinning medication, doctors may be reluctant to prescribe *warfarin* (Coumadin), resulting in more stroke-causing blood clots.

Self-defense: Women with atrial fibrillation should consult their doctors about the risk–benefit ratio of taking blood-thinning medication.

Annabelle Volgman, MD, medical director, Heart Center for Women, Rush University Medical Center, Chicago.

New Treatment for Irregular Heartbeat

Patients with irregular heartbeats may benefit from a new treatment. In the procedure called catheter ablation, a thin, flexible, wire-containing tube is guided through a blood vessel to the heart. High-frequency radio waves are used to burn away heart tissue that is responsible for the irregular rhythm. It can help people who have atrial fibrillation that cannot be controlled with medication.

David J. Wilber, MD, codirector of the Cardiovascular Institute at Loyola University Chicago Stritch School of Medicine, Maywood, Illinois. He was author of a study published in *The Journal of the American Medical Association.*

Depression and Heart Disease

In a study of 1,017 heart disease patients, those who were depressed were 31% more likely to have a heart attack, heart failure (insufficient pumping action of the heart), a stroke or to die over a five-year period.

If you have heart disease: The American Heart Association recommends that you get routinely screened for depression.

Mary Whooley, MD, physician investigator, Veterans Affairs Medical Center, San Francisco.

Heart Attack Symptoms Are the Same in Men And Women

It is commonly believed that men and women experience different heart attack symptoms. Canadian researchers tested this perception in

453

a small study. They found that men and women were equally likely to report chest discomfort, shortness of breath, nausea and clammy skin before a heart attack. Women were more likely also to report pain in the throat, jaw and neck. If you experience any of these symptoms, seek medical attention immediately.

M.H. Mackay, et al., "Gender Differences in Reported Symptoms of Acute Coronary Syndromes," *Canadian Journal of Cardiology*.

Cold Weather Warning— For Your Heart

Researchers analyzed 84,010 hospital admissions for heart attacks over four years.

Result: For every half-degree drop in temperature, relative risk for heart attack increased by 2%. Adults ages 75 to 84 were especially vulnerable.

Theory: Cold temperatures may increase blood pressure, blood thickness and the heart's workload.

Self-defense: In winter, bundle up when going outdoors and closely monitor other heart attack risk factors, including stress and body weight.

Krishnan Bhaskaran, PhD, lecturer, statistical epidemiology, London School of Hygiene & Tropical Medicine, University of London, United Kingdom.

Gout Increases Heart Attack Risk

Researchers compared 9,500 men and women with gout (a common type of arthritis linked to uric acid deposits in joints) with 48,000 people without the disease. After seven years, women with gout were 39% more likely to have had a heart attack than women without gout—a significantly higher increased risk than that for men (11%).

Theory: Excess uric acid (a by-product of purines, compounds found in such foods as beef and pork) may increase inflammation and platelet stickiness (cardiovascular disease markers).

If you have gout or risk factors (such as family history and/or high blood pressure): Be monitored closely for heart disease.

Hyon Choi, MD, professor of medicine, rheumatology section, Boston University School of Medicine, Boston.

Flu Raises Heart Attack Risk

Research has revealed consistent associations between influenza infection and heart attack. Dr. Andrew C. Hayward of University College London, led a review of 39 studies done between 1932 and 2008. Several of the studies showed that, on average, in 35% to 50% of cases in which flu patients died, the cause of death was a heart attack or other cardiovascular event.

Theory: Flu causes inflammation that alters arterial plaque, triggering clots that lead to heart attacks. People vaccinated against flu were at significantly lower risk for death related to cardiac events.

Lesson: If you have heart problems, it is especially important to get a flu shot.

Andrew C. Hayward, MBBS, senior lecturer, the University College London Centre for Infectious Disease Epidemiology in England.

Good Night's Sleep Helps the Heart

Not getting a good night's sleep hurts your heart.

Recent finding: People with no history of sleep disorders whose sleep was disrupted showed the same pattern of increased clot-promoting proteins as patients with sleep apnea, putting them at the same high risk for heart attack as those who suffer from regular sleep disruption.

Joel E. Dimsdale, MD, professor of psychiatry, University of California, San Diego, and lead researcher of a study of 135 people, published in *Chest*.

Ultrasound Helps Cardiac Patients

An ultrasound of the carotid artery can be used to measure the thickness of the artery's wall and look for plaque in the artery. This information provides a more accurate clinical picture of the patient's risk for a heart attack—allowing earlier intervention through lifestyle changes and medication.

Christie M. Ballantyne, MD, director of the Center for Cardiovascular Disease Prevention, Methodist De-Bakey Heart & Vascular Center, and professor of medicine, Baylor College of Medicine, both in Houston. He led a study of 13,145 patients, published in *Journal of the American College of Cardiology*.

The Great American Heart Hoax: Needless Cardiac Surgery

Michael D. Ozner, MD, cardiologist and medical director of Cardiovascular Prevention Institute of South Florida in Miami. He is author of *The Great American Heart Hoax: Lifesaving Advice Your Doctor Should Tell You About Heart Disease Prevention (But Probably Never Will)* (BenBella). *www.drozner.com*.

Americans get more than 1.5 million cardiac bypass surgeries and angioplasty procedures a year, which makes heart surgery among the most commonly performed surgical procedures in the US.

Fact: These procedures have not been proved to extend lives or to prevent future

heart attacks except in a minority of patients. More than one million people get needless cardiac surgery every year. Between 70% and 90% of angioplasties and bypass surgeries are unnecessary in stable patients with coronary artery disease.

While American patients are seven times more likely to undergo coronary angioplasty procedures and bypass surgery than patients in Canada and Sweden, the number of Canadians and Swedes who die from cardiovascular disease is nearly identical (per capita) to the number of people who die from heart disease in this country.

These are not harmless procedures. About 30% of angioplasties fail, requiring patients to repeat the procedure—and eventually, many of these angioplasty patients will undergo bypass surgery. People who have bypass surgery are nearly four times more likely to suffer a stroke at the time of surgery and are vulnerable to postsurgical infections. Between 3% and 5% of patients die from bypass surgery—that's 15,000 to 25,000 lives lost a year.

So why do we keep doing these procedures?

A FLAWED MODEL

Cardiologists used to compare the coronary arteries to simple pipes under a sink. The thinking went that these arteries sometimes accumulated sludge, called plaque (cholesterol deposits within an artery wall), that impeded the flow of blood to the heart. Treating this sludge with angioplasty or shunting blood around it with bypass surgery seemed like an obvious solution.

That approach, however, is flawed. We now know that the arteries are highly dynamic structures. What happens within the artery wall is more significant than blockages that obstruct the lumen (arterial openings).

The majority of heart attacks can be linked to small, yet highly inflamed, plaques. These small plaques have no effect on circulation, because they take up little space within the lumen. Yet they may rupture and cause a sudden heart attack due to a clot that forms at the site of the rupture.

What happens: Cholesterol-carrying particles that enter an artery wall undergo oxidation and modification that trigger an immune response. White blood cells flood the area and engulf the oxidized cholesterol particles and cause plaque to form. Then the white blood cells secrete substances, such as proteinases, that break down the fibrous cap that covers the plaque. When the fibrous cap ruptures, blood enters the plaque and a blood clot forms that can block the artery.

Sudden clots that form following plaque rupture are the cause of most heart attacks. Angioplasties and bypass surgery do nothing to prevent plaque rupture or clot formation.

HEART-SAVING STEPS

The following steps may save lives. Of course, always ask your doctor about the best heart-health strategies for you...

•**Test for high sensitivity (hs)-C-reactive protein (CRP).** It's a "marker" that indicates simmering inflammation in blood vessel walls and can be measured with a simple blood test. Inflammation within arterial plaques contributes to plaque rupture and clot formation and subsequent heart attacks.

The landmark JUPITER study looked at more than 17,000 participants with elevated hs-CRP (above 2 milligrams per deciliter [mg/dL]) and normal cholesterol. Those who were treated with medication to lower hs-CRP were significantly less likely to have a heart attack or stroke or to die than those in the control group. CRP can be lowered with lifestyle changes (diet, exercise, weight loss, smoking cessation) and medical therapy (including statin drugs).

•**Test for *apolipoprotein B* (apoB).** This is a better indicator of heart disease than standard cholesterol levels (including HDL, LDL and triglycerides). Even if your LDL "bad" cholesterol level is normal, you still could have elevated particle numbers, which means that your LDL cholesterol is distributed across a lot of very small, dense particles. These small, dense particles are the most dangerous kind—they are more likely to squeeze through the lining of the artery and more likely to become oxidized once they're there, leading to atherosclerosis (hardening of the arteries). You can check your "bad" particle number by testing for apoB. Blood tests for apoB are performed

routinely in Europe and Canada but not in the US. Ask for this test when you have your usual cholesterol screening.

The optimal level of apoB is less than 90 mg/dL (or even lower for high-risk patients). To lower apoB, follow the recommendations for lowering CRP.

•**Choose an anti-inflammatory diet.** People who follow a Mediterranean-style diet—high in plant foods and cold-water fish (such as salmon) and low in red meat and processed foods—can reduce inflammation.

The Lyon Diet Heart Study compared a Mediterranean diet to a diet resembling the American Heart Association's cholesterol-lowering Step 1 Diet. Participants on the Mediterranean plan were 70% less likely to die from all causes and 73% less likely to have a recurrent cardiac event than those on the standard "healthy" diet.

The Mediterranean diet is effective partly because it limits saturated fat and does not contain trans fat. The fat present in the Mediterranean diet, mainly from olive oil and fish, has anti-inflammatory effects. Also, the antioxidants in fruits and vegetables reduce the oxidation of cholesterol-containing particles within artery walls.

Avoid high-fructose corn syrup, which goes straight to the liver, where it causes an increase in triglycerides, a major risk factor for heart disease.

•**Laugh, pray, get a pet.** Anything that reduces stress can significantly reduce your risk for heart disease. Research at the University of Maryland Medical Center, for example, found that laughing is almost as effective as exercise at improving arterial health.

Laughter relaxes blood vessels and improves circulation to the heart. And like other stress-control strategies, including prayer, loving relationships (with pets as well as people) and yoga, it lowers cortisol, a stress-related hormone.

•**Get moving.** There is a dose-response relationship between exercise and the heart—more exercise gives a greater benefit. Aim for 30 to 45 minutes of exercise most days of the week.

Good news: Walking for as little as 30 minutes five to seven days a week can significantly decrease the risk of dying from heart disease.

More from Michael Ozner...

Who Needs Surgery?

Americans often undergo needless heart surgery, but stents or bypass surgery can be lifesavers for a select group of patients, including those with...

• **Unstable angina** with increasing frequency and intensity of chest pain, often occurring at rest.

• **Disabling chest** pain that does not respond to lifestyle intervention or optimal medical therapy.

• **Significant obstructions** in the left, right or other coronary arteries and a weak heart muscle.

• **Significant blockage** in the main trunk of the left coronary artery.

Better Heart-Surgery Procedure

After any type of cardiovascular surgery, fluid often collects around the heart.

Recent study: When 39 adults underwent a little-known procedure called computed tomography (CT)-guided tube *pericardiostomy* to drain the pooled fluid, they required only local anesthesia and no recovery time. The traditional surgical drainage procedure is invasive, requires general anesthesia and has a higher risk for complications.

If your doctor has recommended heart surgery: Ask him/her whether CT-guided tube pericardiostomy is an option for you, and if so, how to find a radiologist experienced in this interventional procedure.

Suzanne L. Palmer, MD, associate professor of clinical radiology, University of Southern California Keck School of Medicine, Los Angeles.

The Heart Test Women Should Get

Only 44.5% of patients who had nonemergency angioplasty (using a balloon) or stenting to unblock coronary arteries were first given a cardiac stress test. Guidelines from various medical organizations recommend the stress test—which measures heart function while patients walk on a treadmill—to confirm that the artery procedure is warranted.

Note: Stress tests are less reliable in women than in men—but they should still be discussed with your doctor before you consent to angioplasty.

Rita F. Redberg, MD, MSc, professor of medicine, University of California, San Francisco, and coauthor of a study of 23,887 patients.

Heart Supplements That Can Save Your Life

Dennis Goodman, MD, *www.dennisgoodmanmd. com*, a clinical associate professor of medicine at New York University School of Medicine in New York City and at the University of California in San Diego. Dr. Goodman also is director of integrative medicine at New York Medical Associates, a group private practice in New York City. He is board certified in internal medicine, cardiology, interventional cardiology, critical care, clinical lipidology and holistic (integrative) medicine.

One of the most common reasons that people take nutritional supplements is to improve their heart health.

Problem: Very few cardiologists are aware of the ways in which heart supplements work synergistically—that is, by taking carefully selected supplements in combinations, you will heighten the effectiveness of each one. Over the past 22 years, I have treated thousands of heart patients with this approach.

What you need to know to make the most of your nondrug regimen for better heart health...*

THE ESSENTIAL THREE

There are three daily supplements that I recommend to anyone who is concerned about heart health...

• **Fish oil capsules** primarily lower harmful blood fats known as triglycerides but also have a mild blood pressure–lowering effect.

Typical dose: 1 gram (g) total of the omega-3 fatty acids *eicosapentaenoic acid* (EPA) and *docosahexaenoic acid* (DHA) for blood pressure benefits. To reduce triglyceride levels, the typical daily dose is 2 g to 4 g total of EPA and DHA.

Caution: Fish oil can increase bleeding risk, so talk to your doctor if you take a blood thinner, such as *warfarin* (Coumadin).

• **CoQ10** helps enhance energy production in cells and inhibits blood clot formation.

Typical dose: 50 milligrams (mg) to 100 mg per day. CoQ10, which is commonly taken with the classic HDL-boosting treatment niacin (vitamin B-3), also helps minimize side effects, such as muscle weakness, in people taking cholesterol-lowering statin drugs.

• **Red yeast rice** is an extract of red yeast that is fermented on rice and is available in tablet, capsule, powder and liquid form. Long used by the Chinese, it mimics the action of cholesterol-lowering statin drugs.

Typical dose: 600 mg twice daily.

Red yeast rice is often used in combination with plant sterols, naturally occurring chemical compounds found in small amounts in fruits, vegetables and nuts...and added to food products, including butter substitutes, such as Promise activ and Benecol spreads.

Typical dose: About 400 mg daily of plant sterols.

Also important: Low levels of vitamin D (below 15 nanograms per deciliter [ng/mL]) have been linked to a 62% increase, on average, in heart attack risk.

Typical dose: 5,000 international units (IU) of vitamin D-3 per day for those who are deficient in the vitamin...at least 1,000 IU daily for all other adults.

BETTER BLOOD PRESSURE CONTROL

The heart-friendly properties of fish oil are so well-documented that the American Heart Association endorses its use (by eating fatty fish at least twice weekly and/or taking fish oil capsules).

To enhance fish oil's blood pressure–lowering effect, ask your doctor about adding...

• **L-arginine.** This amino acid boosts the body's production of the chemical compound nitric oxide, which causes the blood vessels to dilate, thereby lowering blood pressure.

Typical dose: 150 mg daily.

L-arginine is also used to treat erectile dysfunction and claudication (impeded blood flow in the extremities) and has a mild and beneficial HDL-boosting effect.

Caution: L-arginine should not be taken by children or pregnant or nursing women, or by anyone with genital herpes—it can stimulate activity of the herpes virus. Possible side effects include indigestion, nausea and headache.

• **Lycopene.** This phytochemical is found in tomatoes—especially processed tomato sauce—watermelon, pink grapefruit, red bell peppers and papaya. I usually recommend that patients try L-arginine first, then add lycopene, if necessary, for blood pressure reduction.

Research conducted at Ben-Gurion University in Israel has shown that lycopene lowers systolic (top number) blood pressure by up to 10 points and diastolic (bottom number) by up to four points.

A potent antioxidant, lycopene is also thought to have potential cancer-preventive effects, but this has not been proven.

Typical dose: 10 mg daily.

In rare cases, lycopene supplements can cause diarrhea and/or nausea. Because tomatoes and other acidic foods can aggravate ulcer pain, people with stomach ulcers should consult their doctors before consuming tomatoes and tomato-based products regularly.

---

*To find a doctor to oversee your heart-health supplement regimen, consult the American Board of Intergrative Holistic Medicine, *www.holisticboard.org.*

BOOST HDL CHOLESTEROL

In addition to taking CoQ10 and niacin, ask your doctor about trying…

• **Policosanol.** This plant-wax derivative has been found to boost HDL levels by more than 7%. The research on policosanol is considered controversial by some, but I have found it to be an effective HDL booster in my practice.

Typical dose: 10 mg daily.

There is also some evidence that policosanol may have LDL- and triglyceride-lowering benefits. There are no known side effects associated with policosanol.

Bonus: Used together, CoQ10, niacin and policosanol will allow you to raise your HDL levels while taking much lower doses of niacin (about 20 mg daily). A lower niacin dose reduces the risk for facial flushing, a common side effect in people who take the vitamin.

REDUCE LDL CHOLESTEROL

Red yeast rice extract and plant sterols (both described earlier) are well-known natural methods of lowering LDL cholesterol levels.

To lower your LDL cholesterol further, ask your doctor about adding policosanol (described earlier), along with…

• **Pantethine.** This is a more biologically active form of pantothenic acid (vitamin B-5).

Typical dose: 600 mg daily.

Numerous small studies have found that pantethine significantly lowers LDL cholesterol and triglycerides.

• **Grape seed extract.** This antioxidant-rich substance reduces the blood's tendency to clot and helps lower blood pressure by boosting levels of the chemical compound nitric oxide found in the body. Some research shows that grape seed extract also reduces LDL cholesterol.

Typical dose: 200 mg daily.

In addition, studies suggest that grape seed extract helps protect against Alzheimer's disease.

Caution: Because grape seed extract has a blood-thinning effect, it should not be taken by anyone who uses warfarin or other blood-thinning medications or supplements.

More from Dr. Goodman…

Best Nutrients for Heart Health

Food is our best source of nutrients. That's because food sources offer a variety of minerals, vitamins and antioxidants that work synergistically to boost the nutritional value of each. *I urge all of my patients to get ample amounts of the following heart-healthy nutrients from food…*

• **Antioxidants,** which help prevent plaque formation on the walls of your arteries.

Good sources: Pomegranate, blueberries, and fruits and vegetables in general.

• **Magnesium,** which helps regulate blood pressure and stabilize heart rhythm.

Good sources: Dark green, leafy vegetables…soy beans…almonds…cashews…black-eyed peas…and peanut butter.

• **Potassium,** which helps regulate blood pressure and heart function. Good sources: Apricots, cantaloupe, melons, kiwi, oranges (and orange juice), bananas, lima beans, tomatoes, prunes, avocados…as well as meat, fish and poultry.

Caution: If you have kidney disease, consult your doctor before consuming potassium-rich foods.

The Rise of Vitamin "T": The Amazing Healing Properties of Tocotrienols

Mark A. Stengler, NMD, licensed naturopathic medical doctor and leading authority on the practice of alternative and integrated medicine. He is founder and medical director of the Stengler Center for Integrative Medicine, Encinitas, California, and associate clinical professor at the National College of Natural Medicine, Portland, Oregon. He is author of *The Natural Physician's Healing Therapies* (Bottom Line Books).

Ten years ago, food scientist Barrie Tan, PhD, was on a trip to South America investigating plant pigments when he stumbled across a colorful, lipstick-red plant—and couldn't take his eyes off it. Dr. Tan knew that the annatto plant (*Bixa orellana*) was phototropic, meaning that it moved and turned its blossoms toward the sun. Usually plants with blossoms this color don't follow the sun—if they did, they would be harmed by overexposure to UV rays. What was in this plant that protected it?

Dr. Tan discovered, to his surprise, that the plant's protector was *tocotrienols*, one of two main groups of compounds that constitute vitamin E. It was the first time a plant had been found to be a source of pure tocotrienols—and the discovery called into question everything that was previously known about vitamin E, the vitamin we have been taking for years. Dr. Tan found that the tocotrienols in the annatto plant (the purest form ever found) consisted of 90% delta-tocotrienol and 10% gamma-tocotrienol. And they helped to prevent cardiovascular disease, cancer and certain eye diseases.

Tocopherols, the other main compound that constitutes vitamin E, do not provide these same benefits.

Even today, most vitamin E supplements are made mainly of tocopherols. Alpha-tocopherol is most often used, and most vitamin E research has focused on this subtype. (Tocotrienol and tocopherol include subtypes called alpha, beta, delta and gamma.) Alpha-tocopherol is the most common form of vitamin E in the body and the only form found in blood plasma.

HOW TO BENEFIT

It is estimated that tocotrienolos are 50 times more potent than tocopherols. *How tocotrienols can help you...*

•**Cardiovascular disease protection.** *Tocotrienols seem to protect cardiovascular health by...*

•Lowering LDL cholesterol and triglycerides. Tocotrienols inhibit the same LDL (bad) cholesterol–producing enzyme that is targeted by statin drugs but without statins' side effects, such as fatigue and muscle pain. In one study, people with high cholesterol took 25 milligrams (mg), 50 mg, 100 mg or 200 mg daily of tocotrienols in combination with a heart-healthy diet. The researchers found that 100 mg daily provided optimal benefit, since it lowered LDL cholesterol levels by 25% and triglycerides (blood fats) by 12%. It also raised HDL (good) cholesterol slightly in some studies. More than 100 mg provided no additional benefit.

•Preventing atherosclerosis. This effect stems from the inhibitory effect of tocotrienols on molecules that help plaque adhere to artery walls. In a landmark study at Elmhurst Medical Center in Queens, New York, 50 people with atherosclerosis of the carotid arteries, a major risk factor for stroke, were given 240 mg daily of tocotrienols (along with 60 mg of alpha-tocopherols).

Result: 88% showed either stabilization or regression of arterial plaque, while only 8% in the placebo group had stabilized or improved amounts of plaque. About 60% in the placebo group had plaque buildup during the study. (Alpha-tocopherals on their own do not reduce atherosclerosis.) Tocotrienols also have been found to reduce the formation of blood clots that can lead to heart attack and stroke.

•**Anticancer activity.** Tocotrienols appear to fight cancer in several ways. They neutralize vascular endothelial growth factor (VEGF), the chemical that stimulates development of new blood vessels needed for tumor growth—an effect known as *anti-angiogenesis*. Tocotrienols also interfere with the processes that tumor cells use to multiply. Clinical trials are currently under way to study the safety of delta-tocotrienol for treating breast and pancreatic cancers. Because preliminary studies are promising and there is no toxicity related to tocotrienols, it seems that cancer patients may benefit when taking 300 mg per day of tocotrienols.

•**Eye health.** Tocotrienols' anti-VEGF effects appear to inhibit the sight-damaging growth of blood vessels associated with macular degeneration and diabetes-related retinopathy (damage to the retina).

Dose: 50 mg to 100 mg daily.

For these conditions, a concentrated form of vitamin E is best—namely, a supplement made of "pure" annatto-derived tocotrienols consisting of 90% delta- and 10% gamma-tocotrienols.

Brands to try: A.C. Grace Unique E Tocotrienols, 125 mg (800-833-4368, *www.acgrace. com*)...Doctor's Best.

Tocotrienols, 50 mg (800-333-6977, *www. drbvitamins.com*, for a store locator)...and Nutricology. Delta-Fraction Tocotrienols, 50 mg and 125 mg (800-545-9960, *www.nutricol ogy.com*).

IF YOU ARE HEALTHY

Tocotrienols are found in small amounts in foods such as coconut and wheat germ—but not enough to provide the benefit of supplements. People who are healthy (and don't have one of the conditions described above) are helped by taking a multivitamin or a full-spectrum vitamin E product that contains a blend of tocopherols and tocotrienols (5 mg is a good amount), which is still the best choice for disease prevention.

If you are healthy but have elevated cholesterol, try taking 50 mg to 100 mg of tocotrienols daily in addition to your multivitamin.

Caution: Tocotrienols inhibit blood clotting, so people on blood-thinners should consult their doctors before taking them.

Calcium Supplements Can Raise Heart Attack Risk by as Much as 30%

Calcium from supplements, including antacids such as Tums and Rolaids, elevates blood calcium quickly, which may contribute to artery disease. Calcium in food is absorbed slowly. If you are taking supplements on medical advice, do not stop without speaking with your physician.

One possibility: Spreading the dose throughout the day instead of taking it all at once.

Ian Reid, MD, a professor on the faculty of medical and health sciences, University of Auckland, New Zealand, and leader of an analysis of clinical trials involving about 12,000 people, published in *BMJ Online First*.

Exciting New Health Benefits of CoQ10

Peter H. Langsjoen, MD, a cardiologist in private practice in Tyler, Texas, who specializes in noninvasive treatment. He is an active researcher and world-recognized expert in the biomedical benefits of CoQ10. A fellow of the American College of Cardiology, Dr. Langsjoen was a founding member of the International Coenzyme Q10 Association, *www.icqa.org*.

Until recently, the dietary supplement coenzyme Q10 (CoQ10) was recommended primarily for people who wanted to avoid the side effects of cholesterol-lowering statin drugs, including muscle pain and weakness.

Now: Researchers are discovering that CoQ10 may confer a variety of other health benefits that are unrelated to statin use.

Peter H. Langsjoen, MD, is one of the world's foremost CoQ10 researchers.* He provides insight into the latest developments in this research.

WHAT IS COQ10?

CoQ10 is a vitamin-like substance that plays a key role in the production of energy in every cell in the body. Discovered in 1957, the substance is naturally present in such foods as organ meats (including cow's liver and kidney), and, in smaller amounts, in beef, sardines, mackerel and peanuts. Because CoQ10 appeared to be everywhere in the body—or "ubiquitous"—it was fittingly dubbed *ubiquinone*.

Without adequate levels of CoQ10, the body's organs and systems, including the immune system and nervous system, will not function optimally.

UNEXPECTED HEALTH BENEFITS

Increasing scientific evidence now offers support for the use of CoQ10 supplements to help treat...

•**Heart disease.** CoQ10 is involved in creating 90% of cellular energy in the heart. Research has shown that people with heart failure (inadequate pumping action of the

*Dr. Langsjoen has no financial interest in any company that manufactures or sells CoQ10 supplements.

heart) have lower blood levels of CoQ10, on average, than people without heart failure—and the lower the CoQ10 level, the worse the problem.

Recent research published in the journal *Biofactors* showed that the ejection fraction (the amount of blood pumped with each heartbeat) in heart failure patients who took CoQ10 supplements rose from an average of 22% to an average of 39% after six to 12 months.

Important: Because statin medications deplete the body's supply of CoQ10, ask your doctor about adding CoQ10 supplements (to help protect the heart and counteract statin-related side effects) to your regimen if you take one of these drugs.

• **High blood pressure.** CoQ10 can also help improve high blood pressure (hypertension). Studies have shown that about half of people using one or more drugs for high blood pressure can stop taking at least some of their medications after taking CoQ10 supplements for about five months.

• **Cholesterol.** CoQ10 also acts as a powerful antioxidant. It is transported in the blood (along with cholesterol and other fat-soluble nutrients) and helps protect cholesterol from damaging oxidation, which plays a role in atherosclerosis (fatty buildup in the arteries).

• **Fatigue.** Because CoQ10 is part of the body's energy-producing processes, it is particularly valuable in reducing fatigue—even among people with severe fatigue, including that caused by such conditions as chronic fatigue syndrome.

• **Migraines.** In one study, 32 people who took CoQ10 supplements for three months had only half their usual number of migraines.

• **Neurological disorders.** Some of the most promising recent research involves the ability of CoQ10 to slow the progression of degenerative neurological disorders, including Parkinson's disease, Alzheimer's disease and Huntington's disease (a genetic disorder).

HOW TO USE COQ10 SAFELY

People who eat organ meats at least once or twice weekly usually have healthy CoQ10 levels. But other adults can improve their blood levels of CoQ10 by taking supplements. Work with your doctor to find an optimal dose.

For best absorption, do not take more than 180 milligrams (mg) at one time. CoQ10 is fat-soluble (dissolves in fat), so it is best to take the supplement with meals that contain at least a little bit of fat (any type).

In some people, CoQ10 may cause temporary side effects, such as nausea and other gastrointestinal disorders…dizziness…insomnia…or headache. However, these side effects are rare. If you experience side effects, try a different CoQ10 formulation.

Caution: One case study suggested that CoQ10 may act like vitamin K, lessening the blood-thinning effect of *warfarin* (Coumadin). But a controlled trial subsequently found no such effects.

Nevertheless, people taking warfarin or any other blood-thinning medication should consult a doctor before taking a CoQ10 supplement. After a few weeks of taking CoQ10, anyone who uses a blood thinner should have his/her prothrombin time (a measure of clotting ability) checked.

Also important: Because CoQ10 may cause your blood pressure and/or blood sugar (glucose) level to gradually improve, your doctor may want to adjust the dosage of any medications you may be taking to control elevations of either.

FINDING THE BEST PRODUCT

One reliable producer of CoQ10 is the Japanese company Kaneka, which sells CoQ10 in the US under many different brand names, including Healthy Origins (888-228-6650, *www.healthyorigins.com*) and Jarrow Formulas, available through ProVitaminas (800-510-6444, *www.provitaminas.com*). Kaneka uses a yeast fermentation process with 99.9% pure natural CoQ10.

In addition to CoQ10 supplements, you may see products labeled "ubiquinol." Ubiquinol is a more bioavailable (absorbable)—and more expensive—form of CoQ10. However, if you take CoQ10, your body will naturally convert it to ubiquinol. While most healthy adults readily absorb CoQ10, patients with advanced heart failure absorb ubiquinol about four times better than CoQ10.

If you purchase ubiquinol (not CoQ10), test it for freshness (in case it has deteriorated during storage or shipping).

What to do: Cut one capsule in half, and look at the color of the contents. Cream-colored is good—orange or brown means that the product has become oxidized.

Whichever form you choose, shop around—a month's supply of a high-quality supplement can cost $20 to about $60.

Heart Attack Survivors Live Longer With Omega-3s

Heart attack patients who had the highest intake of omega-3 fatty acids (from food, not supplements) had a 47% lower risk for ventricular ectopy, a type of heart rhythm abnormality that can result in sudden death in these patients, say Duke University researchers. Plant sources of omega-3s (walnuts, kale and brussels sprouts) and fish sources (salmon, herring and mackerel) were of benefit. Whether you have cardiovascular disease or not, have two to three weekly servings of omega-3–rich foods.

Mark A. Stengler, NMD, licensed naturopathic medical doctor and leading authority on the practice of alternative and integrated medicine. He is founder and medical director of the Stengler Center for Integrative Medicine, Encinitas, California...author of many books and the newsletter *Bottom Line Natural Healing. www.drstengler.com.*

Prescription Fish Oil?

JoAnn E. Manson, MD, DrPH, professor of medicine and women's health at Harvard Medical School and chief of the division of preventive medicine at Brigham and Women's Hospital, both in Boston. She and her colleagues are conducting a clinical trial of the health effects of omega-3s and vitamin D.

The most beneficial components in fish oil are the omega-3 fatty acids *eicosapentaenoic acid* (EPA) and *docosahexaenoic acid* (DHA). A prescription formulation provides these in a more concentrated form appropriate for people who need a high dosage of omega-3s.

Many over-the-counter (OTC) fish oil formulations are only about 30% EPA/DHA. So if you had heart disease and wanted 1,000 milligrams (mg) per day of EPA/DHA (a typical recommendation from many doctors), you would take about three 1,000 milligrams (mg) capsules of nonprescription fish oil each day. That's not hard.

But: If you had very high triglycerides (a type of blood fat) and your doctor advised a dosage of 2,000 mg to 4,000 mg of EPA/DHA daily, you might have to take about six to 12 nonprescription capsules each day. That's a lot of pills!

Prescription fish oil supplements provide 840 mg of EPA/DHA per 1,000-mg capsule—so even if you required high doses of omega-3s, you wouldn't need to take many pills. Called Lovaza, the product is typically prescribed at two capsules twice daily for people with triglyceride levels of 500 mg/dL or higher.

Bonus: As an FDA-approved drug, prescription fish oil must meet pharmaceutical-grade standards and is subject to stricter regulatory oversight than OTC supplements are.

Editor's note: Lovaza costs about $180 for a 30-day supply. How that compares to what you would pay for nonprescription fish oil depends on the OTC brand you buy, your dosage of EPA/DHA and whether your insurance covers the prescription product (as many policies do).

Dairy Lowers Hypertension Risk

People who consume more low-fat dairy products (more than one serving per day) were about 20% less likely to develop high blood pressure after two-to-six years than those who consumed less low-fat dairy.

Study of 2,245 healthy people over age 55 by researchers at Wageningen University, the Netherlands, published in *The American Journal of Clinical Nutrition.*

What Women With Heart Disease Need— But Often Fail to Get

Theresa M. Beckie, PhD, RN, a professor at the University of South Florida College of Nursing in Tampa. She has done extensive research on cardiac rehabilitation and was the lead investigator and author of a recent study on a women-only cardiac rehab program.

Suppose you had recently suffered a heart attack. If there were a magic pill that could slash your risk of dying by 25%, wouldn't you take it?

Well, there's no magic pill...but there is a program that provides the same benefit. This evidence-based intervention is called cardiac rehabilitation. Yet among women with heart disease who are eligible for the program, only 15% to 20% actually participate in it, according to Theresa M. Beckie, PhD, RN, of the University of South Florida, who has done extensive research on cardiac rehab.

One reason women don't avail themselves of cardiac rehab is that their doctors often do not refer them to this program. According to Dr. Beckie, "Some doctors are less likely to refer women to cardiac rehab than men. The mistaken perception is that women don't need the program—despite the fact that women are more likely than men to die within the first month following a heart attack."

Docs shouldn't get all the blame...because even when women do get referrals, they often fail to take advantage of the program.

Evidence: In a study from the University of Alabama at Birmingham, among hospitalized female patients who were referred to cardiac rehab, 66% failed to enroll.

Women often say that family responsibilities keep them from participating in cardiac rehab. The flaw in that thinking, of course, is that a woman who doesn't take care of herself cannot take the best possible care of her loved ones. Depression—which often occurs along with heart disease, particularly in women—also interferes with willingness to attend cardiac rehab.

Who needs it: Generally, cardiac rehab is appropriate (and covered by Medicare and health insurance) for a person who has had a heart attack, coronary artery bypass grafting, angioplasty, stenting, angina, valve surgery or heart transplant within the past year.

If you meet any of the criteria above, don't wait for your doctor to bring up the subject— ask him or her whether cardiac rehab is appropriate for you. If the answer is no, ask for an explanation. Should you sense a brush-off ("Oh, you don't need it—just walk more and lose some weight"), get a second opinion, and perhaps select another cardiologist, Dr. Beckie said. If the answer is yes, get a referral. Most hospitals offer outpatient cardiac rehab.

WHAT HAPPENS AT CARDIAC REHAB

A multifaceted outpatient program, cardiac rehab typically includes counseling on heart medication use, nutrition and ways to deal with stress and depression...plus three hour-long exercise sessions per week for 12 weeks. The exercise component is not just like going to a regular gym, Dr. Beckie emphasized. Instead, workouts are specifically designed by an exercise physiologist to meet an individual patient's needs...and a nurse monitors the patient's heart rate and rhythm (using an EKG) throughout the session to ensure safety. The exercises—aerobic activity, resistance training and stretching—get increasingly challenging as the patient improves.

The primary goals of cardiac rehab are to strengthen the heart muscle...reduce the risk for another cardiac event...promote lifelong behavioral changes...and improve quality of life by easing the physical symptoms (such as shortness of breath, dizziness and fatigue) and emotional consequences of heart disease.

GETTING THE MOST OUT OF THE PROGRAM

Dr. Beckie recently led an intriguing study that compared the effects of a mixed-gender cardiac rehab with an all-female program. She found that participants in the women-only group attended more of the exercise and educational sessions and experienced greater improvement in symptoms of depression. She explained, "Depression can interfere with

464

patients' motivation to make the lifestyle changes that could improve their health. A gender-specific program not only provides exercise and education targeted toward women's needs, it also allows for the social support that is crucial to women's recovery."

Frustrating: Currently there are no cardiac rehab programs specifically for women. Even the hospital where Dr. Beckie conducted her study doesn't have a dedicated women-only program.

The fix: To simulate the environment and reap the benefits of a just-for-females cardiac rehab, Dr. Beckie suggested that you get to know the other women in your program and…

Try to arrange your schedules so that you all attend at the same time.

Establish a support group, either at the rehab facility or a nearby coffee shop, where you can talk together before or after workouts.

Continue to exercise together as much as possible after your formal program ends—for instance, by going for group walks. Dr. Beckie said, "Sticking with an exercise routine is a crucial factor in retaining the benefits of cardiac rehab…and working out together helps maintain the beneficial emotional ties, too."

Essential: Schedule time every day for exercise and self-care, Dr. Beckie advised—so that other obligations don't interfere. Even after rehab ends, it's critical that you take care of you.

Red Tea for Your Heart Health and More

Jennifer Zartarian, ND, CNS, coordinator at Long Island College Hospital in Brooklyn. Her private practice, Element Natural Healing Arts in Brooklyn, New York, focuses on botanical medicine, homeopathy, nutrition, lifestyle counseling and community education.

Move over, chamomile. The rising star among healthful herbal "teas" is red tea, says Jennifer Zartarian, ND, CNS.

A growing body of research suggests that red tea—which is not technically tea but an herbal drink made with the leaves of the South African rooibos plant—has potent antioxidants (including flavonoids, such as quercetin and rutin) that may protect against heart attack, stroke, arterial damage, inflammation and cancer. Red tea also is used to ease digestive upset and asthma.

Red tea is sold in health-food stores and online…is prepared like any other herbal tea…is caffeine-free…and has an earthy flavor with hints of vanilla and honey. Try it hot or iced.

Caution: People who have liver problems or hormone-sensitive cancers or who are undergoing chemotherapy should consult their doctors before consuming rooibos.

Mineral Water May Help Lower Blood Pressure

After drinking one liter of mineral water per day for one month, people between the ages of 45 and 64 with borderline hypertension (high blood pressure) experienced a significant decrease in blood pressure.

Theory: Most mineral waters contain significant amounts of magnesium and calcium, both of which help to reduce blood pressure.

Study of 70 people by researchers at Gothenburg University, Gothenburg, Sweden, published in *BMC Public Health*.

Insomnia Linked to High Blood Pressure

When researchers analyzed data for 1,741 adults, those who suffered from chronic insomnia (and slept fewer than five hours nightly, on average) were five times more likely to have high blood pressure than adults who did not have insomnia and slept more than six hours nightly, on average.

Theory: Insomnia, combined with short sleep duration, is associated with increased heart rate—a risk factor for hypertension.

Alexandros N. Vgontzas, MD, director, Sleep Research and Treatment Center, Pennsylvania State College of Medicine, Hershey.

Nighttime Aspirin Lowers Blood Pressure

Previous studies have linked nighttime aspirin use with lower blood pressure, but there was no explanation for the drug's effect.

Recent research: Bedtime aspirin use was found to lower blood and urine levels of naturally occurring chemicals associated with high blood pressure in a study of 16 adults with untreated, mildly elevated blood pressure.

If your doctor has prescribed daily aspirin: Ask about taking the pill at night.

Jaapjan Snoep, MSc, researcher, department of clinical epidemiology, Leiden University Medical Center, the Netherlands.

Be Wary of Cold Remedies

If you have high blood pressure, consult your doctor before using over-the-counter (OTC) cold products. These also can be dangerous for people with diabetes, glaucoma or enlarged prostate. The products generally contain decongestants, such as *pseudoephedrine* and *phenylephrine*, that help clear a stuffy nose by narrowing blood vessels. That also can raise blood pressure and heart rate and alter blood sugar levels. Ask your doctor or pharmacist for details. To safely relieve cold symptoms if you have high blood pressure, consider zinc lozenges, which may help shorten the duration

of a cold, and a saline nasal spray to reduce congestion.

Prevention, 33 E. Minor St., Emmaus, Pennsylvania 18098.

Blood Pressure Drugs Can *Raise* Blood Pressure

Researchers analyzed the medical records of 945 adults who had elevated systolic (top number) blood pressure.

Results: Among those who had low levels of the blood pressure–controlling enzyme renin and were treated with a beta-blocker or an angiotensin-converting enzyme (ACE) inhibitor, 16% had a significant increase in systolic pressure.

When prescribed a blood pressure drug: Ask your doctor to check your renin levels—a diuretic or calcium channel blocker may be a better medication option.

Michael Alderman, MD, professor of medicine, Albert Einstein College of Medicine, Bronx, New York.

Lower Blood Pressure With Even a Small Reduction in Salt

University of London researchers have determined that even a slight reduction—from two teaspoons to about one-and-a-half teaspoons of salt daily—can help lower blood pressure. For those who have moderate-to-high blood pressure, aim to reduce the table salt you add to food to less than one teaspoon—and ideally one-half teaspoon—daily.

Mark A. Stengler, NMD, licensed naturopathic medical doctor and leading authority on the practice of alternative and integrated medicine. He is founder and medical director of the Stengler Center for Integrative Medicine, Encinitas, California, and author of many books, including *The Natural Physician's Healing Therapies* (Bottom Line Books).

Walnuts Lower Blood Pressure

After eating 18 walnut halves and taking one tablespoon of walnut oil daily for six weeks, study participants had lower blood pressure when exposed to stressors than participants who did not consume walnuts and walnut oil. Healthful omega-3 fatty acids in walnuts are likely responsible for lowering the body's stress response.

Sheila G. West, PhD, associate professor of biobehavioral health and nutritional sciences, Pennsylvania State University, University Park, and leader of a study published in *Journal of the American College of Nutrition*.

Cognitive Decline and High Blood Pressure

Several studies have shown that high blood pressure is linked to increased risk for cognitive decline.

Recent finding: In a four-year study of 19,836 adults, those with a diastolic (bottom number) blood pressure of 90 mmHg or higher were more likely to have impaired memory and cognition than those with normal readings.

Theory: Elevated diastolic pressure, in particular, weakens arteries in the brain, which may damage small areas of the brain.

If you have high blood pressure: Ask your doctor to recommend lifestyle changes (such as regular exercise and weight loss) and medication, if necessary.

Georgios Tsivgoulis, MD, adjunct assistant professor of neurology, University of Alabama, Birmingham.

Pressure Cuff Accuracy

Blood pressure is gauged by measuring how much resistance to blood flow there is in the arteries. Both wrist and finger cuffs are not reliable because the arteries in these areas are too small. Blood pressure is best measured using an inflatable arm cuff and a pressure-measuring gauge. But even arm cuffs are not always accurate (for instance, the cuffs may not fit properly), so don't rely on blood pressure machines at supermarkets and drugstores. Get your blood pressure measured only by trained health-care professionals at medical facilities. Even if you've been told to do home blood pressure monitoring, have your doctor also regularly check your blood pressure.

Mark Houston, MD, associate clinical professor of medicine, Vanderbilt University School of Medicine, and director, The Hypertension Institute, both in Nashville.

Stress Busters That Help Beat High Blood Pressure

C. Tissa Kappagoda, MBBS, PhD, a professor of medicine in the Preventive Cardiology Program at the University of California, Davis. Dr. Kappagoda has published more than 200 medical journal articles on matters relating to cardiology and cardiovascular health.

A recent study in the journal *Circulation* found an alarming trend—that rates of uncontrolled hypertension are increasing among women even as rates among men are decreasing.

The Centers for Disease Control and Prevention reports that more than one-third of women age 45 to 54 now have high blood pressure...while among women age 75 and older, 80% do!

A report from the National Center for Health Statistics states that, in the past decade, there has been a 62% increase in the number of visits to the doctor due to high blood pressure.

These days, chronic stress—due to lack of job stability or other factors at home—is a significant contributor to hypertension. As C. Tissa Kappagoda, MBBS, PhD, a professor in the preventive cardiology program at the University of California, Davis, explained,

"Chronic stress raises blood pressure by increasing levels of adrenaline and cortisol, hormones that promote artery spasm and salt retention. It also increases vascular resistance, the resistance to flow that must be overcome to move blood through the blood vessels, which is a primary cause of hypertension." Stress also can impede basic self-care, such as eating healthfully and exercising—which probably explains why stress is such a "massive multiplier of the effects of conventional risk factors," Dr. Kappagoda added.

Though high blood pressure doesn't cause pain or other obvious symptoms, it does damage arteries—increasing the risk for heart attack, diabetes, stroke and kidney problems. How high is too high? Hypertension is diagnosed when blood pressure hits 140/90 mmHg or higher...but doctors now realize that prehypertension (blood pressure between 120/80 and 139/89) also is risky.

Of course, it's important to follow your doctor's advice regarding blood pressure-lowering lifestyle changes, such as limiting salt and alcohol and losing excess weight. But stress reduction should be a priority, too, Dr. Kappagoda said—and may reduce the need for hypertension medication. That's good, because these drugs can have side effects, such as dizziness, chronic cough and muscle cramps, and often are taken for the rest of a person's life.

Research shows that the following stress-lowering techniques help reduce blood pressure. *If you have hypertension or prehypertension, consider...*

• **Breathing control.** When you're relaxed, your breathing naturally slows...and if you slow down your breathing, your body naturally relaxes. This encourages constricted blood vessels to dilate, improving blood flow.

Target: Practice slow breathing for 15 minutes twice daily, aiming to take six breaths per minute.

If you find it difficult (or even stressful!) to count and time your breaths, consider using a biofeedback device instead. One example designed for home use is Resperate (877-988-9388, *www.resperate.com*, from $299.95), which looks like a portable CD player with headphones and uses musical tones to guide you to an optimal breathing pattern. Typically, it's used for 15 minutes three or four times per week, and results are seen within several weeks. In studies, users experienced significant reductions in systolic pressure (the top number of a blood pressure reading) and diastolic pressure (bottom number). There are many similar and effective devices, said Dr. Kappagoda, so ask your doctor about the options. Biofeedback devices are safe and have no side effects.

• **Meditation.** A recent analysis of nine clinical trials, published in *American Journal of Hypertension*, found that regular practice of transcendental meditation reduced blood pressure, on average, by 4.7 mmHg systolic and 3.2 mmHg diastolic. Though these results are for transcendental meditation specifically, many experts believe that any type of meditation works.

Goal: Meditate for 20 minutes daily.

• **Exercise.** Regular physical activity reduces blood pressure not only by alleviating stress, but also by promoting weight loss and improving heart and blood vessel health. Research shows that becoming more active can reduce systolic pressure by 5 mmHg to 10 mmHg, on average. An excellent all-around exercise is walking, Dr. Kappagoda said—so with your doctor's OK, take a 30-minute walk at least three times weekly.

Caution: Weight training can trigger a temporary increase in blood pressure during the exercise, especially when heavy weights are used. To minimize this blood pressure spike, use lighter weights to do more repetitions...and don't hold your breath during the exertion.

When Cholesterol Just Won't Go Down

Anne Carol Goldberg, MD, associate professor of medicine in the division of endocrinology, metabolism and lipid research at Washington University School of Medicine in St. Louis. A former president of the National Lipid Association, she has participated in numerous clinical trials involving the use of lipid-modifying agents, including the Lipid Research Clinic Coronary Primary Prevention Trial, which was one of the first to show that lowering blood cholesterol levels decreases risk for coronary artery disease.

Most of the estimated 42 million Americans with high cholesterol can successfully lower it with diet and exercise—or, when necessary, with statins or other cholesterol-lowering drugs.

But what if your cholesterol levels do not improve substantially with these standard therapies?

About one in every 500 Americans has an inherited (genetic) predisposition to high cholesterol—a condition known as *familial hypercholesterolemia* (FH), which is marked by LDL "bad" cholesterol levels ranging from 150 milligrams per deciliter (mg/dL) to 1,000 mg/dL.

Dietary changes may have some positive effect on people with FH but typically do not lower LDL levels to a normal range. Cholesterol-lowering medication is sometimes sufficient for people with FH—but not always.

What most people don't know: A high-tech treatment that filters LDL from the blood (described later in this article) can reduce LDL levels by as much as 75% in people with FH whose cholesterol is not controlled with standard therapies. The procedure also can be used by others, including people who cannot tolerate statin drugs due to side effects.

SKYROCKETING LDL

On the surfaces of a healthy person's cells, there are LDL receptors that remove LDL from the blood. Lower levels of LDL cholesterol reduce the risk for atherosclerosis (the accumulation of cholesterol and other fatty substances on artery walls). A genetic mutation in people with FH results in a greatly reduced number of LDL receptors—or none at all.

People who inherit a defective gene from one parent (the heterozygous form of FH) typically have cholesterol levels of 250 mg/dL to 500 mg/dL, while those with two defective copies of the gene (the homozygous form) can have cholesterol readings as high as 1,000 mg/dL. Genetic tests are available to detect the defective genes, but most doctors diagnose FH based on such factors as very high LDL levels and the presence of fatty deposits on certain parts of the body.

Important red flag: Cholesterol levels in people with FH may be so high that they develop *xanthomas* (deposits of cholesterol that accumulate). These occur most often in the Achilles tendons (backs of the ankles) but also over the knuckles, elbows, knees and bottom of the feet. They're most commonly seen in people with FH who have LDL levels above 200 mg/dL. If you have any such deposits, see a doctor for an evaluation.

MEDICATION TO TRY

Most people with FH can achieve normal—or nearly normal—cholesterol levels with the use of medication. Typically, more potent statins are prescribed at the upper end of the daily dose range—for example, *simvastatin* (Zocor)—40 mg to 80 mg...*atorvastatin* (Lipitor)—80 mg... or *rosuvastatin* (Crestor)—40 mg.

Good news about side effects: Even though statin-related side effects, such as muscle pain, are more likely to occur when high doses are used, people with FH who take such doses of these drugs don't appear to have more side effects than individuals without FH who take lower doses.

Most patients with FH require combination therapy—treatment with a statin plus one or more additional cholesterol-lowering drugs, such as *ezetimibe* (Zetia)...bile-acid resins, such as *cholestyramine* (Questran)...or high-dose niacin.

"DIALYSIS" FOR LDL

A relatively new procedure, known as *LDL apheresis*, filters LDL from the blood—similar to the way dialysis filters toxins from the blood when the kidneys are unable to do so. LDL apheresis can reduce LDL levels by at least 50% and sometimes by as much as 75%.

How it works: At an outpatient clinic, a needle attached to a catheter is inserted into a vein in the arm. Over a period of about 90 minutes, up to three quarts of blood are withdrawn from the body and passed through a series of filters that remove the LDL. The "cleansed" blood is then returned to the body through another vein.

Who can benefit: LDL apheresis is recommended for people who don't have atherosclerotic cardiovascular disease and whose LDL levels are 300 mg/dL or above and who can't significantly lower their LDL after maximum therapy, including medication. Additionally, if you have been diagnosed with atherosclerotic cardiovascular disease and your LDL level is 200 mg/dL or above after maximum treatment, you may benefit from LDL apheresis. Patients with cardiovascular disease whose LDL levels are above 200 mg/dL and who cannot tolerate the side effects of statins also are eligible.

The results of apheresis are immediate. Cholesterol levels are tested before and after the procedure. It's not uncommon for LDL to drop from levels greater than 300 mg/dL to as low as 35 mg/dL. The procedure also causes a reduction in C-reactive protein and fibrinogen, substances that increase the risk for blood clots.

Not a cure: Because apheresis does not eliminate the underlying genetic defect in people with FH, LDL levels start to rise immediately after the procedure is completed. Patients who opt for LDL apheresis must repeat the treatment every two weeks, possibly for the rest of their lives.

LDL apheresis is very safe. There is a potential risk for unwanted bleeding (both internally or from the needle site) because the blood thinner heparin is used to keep blood flowing during the procedure. However, this type of bleeding rarely occurs because the patient's "bleeding times" (how fast small blood vessels close to stop bleeding) are frequently tested and the dose of heparin is adjusted as needed.

Doctors don't yet know how effective LDL apheresis is at reducing cardiovascular disease, but patients who receive the therapy often report a rapid reduction in cardiovascular

symptoms, such as leg discomfort (caused by insufficient blood flow) and chest pain from angina.

People who are eligible for LDL apheresis should ask their doctors where they need to go for the procedure. It is currently offered at more than 40 medical centers across the US. Each treatment costs, on average, $2,500 to $3,000 and is covered by Medicare and most insurance plans.

Are Statin Drugs Destroying Your Muscles?

Mark A. Stengler, NMD, licensed naturopathic medical doctor and leading authority on the practice of alternative and integrated medicine. He is founder and medical director of the Stengler Center for Integrative Medicine, Encinitas, California, and associate clinical professor at the National College of Natural Medicine, Portland, Oregon. He is author of *The Natural Physician's Healing Therapies* (Bottom Line Books).

I have long warned against the dangers of taking statin drugs to reduce cholesterol—especially for those who can reduce cholesterol with the help of natural substances and lifestyle changes. But now there is even more reason for concern. New research has uncovered disturbing information that muscle damage is much more common among statin users than was previously known. If you take a statin, such as *simvastatin* (Zocor) or *atorvastatin* (Lipitor), you risk the breakdown of the muscles in your arms and legs and suffering myalgia (muscle aches and pain) or myopathy (a disease in which muscle fibers cease to function).

It is estimated that myalgia develops in 10% of statin users. Based on the patients I see, I believe the percentage is much higher. (*Rhabdomyolysis*, a condition in which muscles actually dissolve, is another potential consequence of statins, although this side effect is not as common as myalgia and myopathy.)

Researchers at University of Bern, Switzerland, and Tufts-New England Medical Center,

Boston, reported in *Canadian Medical Association Journal* that 57% of study participants suffered statin-induced muscle damage. Some even had muscle damage after they had stopped taking the drugs. Remember, too, that the heart is your body's most active muscle. It's no surprise that there is a strong relationship between the use of statins and the development of cardiomyopathy, a life-threatening disease of the heart muscle.

NUTRIENTS THAT PROTECT YOUR MUSCLES

Several dietary supplement regimens can help protect muscles.

If you take a statin, then take the first two nutrients for as long as you are on the statin…

• **Coenzyme Q10 (CoQ10).** While reducing the body's production of cholesterol, statins also interfere with the body's manufacture of CoQ10, a vitamin-like nutrient. Many side effects of statins appear to be related to low levels of CoQ10. CoQ10 supplements can significantly reduce statin-induced muscle myopathy. Considerable research supports the use of CoQ10 in treating statin side effects. Take 100 milligrams (mg) to 200 mg of CoQ10 daily.

• **Vitamin D.** Vitamin D is needed for the normal synthesis of muscle tissue. Current medical thinking is that weak muscles, not weak bones, lead to most falls and fractures. Add statins to the picture, and connect the dots. Statins disrupt the biochemical process that makes vitamin D in your body, and it's likely that statins will significantly increase the incidence of sarcopenia and fractures. Take at least 2,000 international units (IU) of vitamin D daily. Have your vitamin D level checked by a physician and take a higher dose if it is necessary.

If you have stopped taking a statin because of muscle pain, try either of the following (in addition to the two nutrients above)…

• If the muscle pain is bearable, try one or two of the supplements below for one month and then evaluate how you feel. If you still feel pain, try different supplements from the group below.

• For severe pain, take a more aggressive approach and use all the supplements below until your muscle pain subsides.

• **Magnesium.** Your body uses this essential mineral to help break down food and make *adenosine triphosphate* (ATP), the chemical form of energy in the body. Take 300 mg to 400 mg daily of magnesium citrate, aspartate or amino acid chelate.

• **Amino acids.** You need these protein building blocks to make muscle.

Best: Take an amino acid supplement that contains eight to 10 amino acids.

Most important amino acids to supplement: The three branched-chain amino acids (BCAA), which are *L-leucine, L-isoleucine* and *L-valine.* Studies have shown that these supplements increase muscle synthesis in seniors. They are made by many companies. Take 5 grams (g) to 10 g daily of a multi–amino acid blend or 3 g daily of BCAAs.

• **Methylsulfonylmethane (MSM).** MSM supplements are rich in the sulfur and chemical methyl groups, both important building blocks of tissue and biochemicals. MSM supplements are a safe, natural anti-inflammatory that can help muscles recover from statin-related damage. Take 3,000 to 4,000 mg daily.

• **Turmeric extract.** Rich in curcumin, turmeric is an anti-inflammatory that aids muscle healing. Curcumin blocks dozens of different inflammatory processes in the body.

Brand to try: Terry Naturally's CuraMed (866-598-5487, *www.europharmausa.com*). Take 750 mg one to two times daily.

If you have muscle pain and continue to take a statin…

I believe that anyone taking a statin who experiences muscle pain should stop taking the statin (under a doctor's supervision)—and I think that most conventional physicians would agree with me. If you do continue to take the statin, you can take all of the remedies described above indefinitely.

Vitamin B-3 Beats Cholesterol Drug

Many cardiovascular disease patients who take cholesterol-lowering statins also take the drug *ezetimibe* (Zetia) to further combat cholesterol.

Recent study: Ezetimibe reduced LDL "bad" cholesterol but also reduced HDL "good" cholesterol and had no effect on artery wall thickness. In comparison, among patients who took 2 grams (g) daily of niacin (vitamin B-3) instead of Zetia, LDL dropped…HDL r*f*ose…arterial wall thickness was reduced (a desirable effect)…and there were significantly fewer adverse cardiac events.

Best: Ask your internist or cardiologist about how to use niacin safely since the various B vitamins are best taken in a balanced combination.

Allen J. Taylor, MD, director of advanced cardiovascular imaging, Washington Hospital Center, Washington, DC, and leader of a study of 208 cardiovascular patients.

Types of Niacin

Mark A. Stengler, NMD, licensed naturopathic medical doctor and leading authority on the practice of alternative and integrated medicine. He is founder and medical director of the Stengler Center for Integrative Medicine, Encinitas, California, and author of many books, including *The Natural Physician's Healing Therapies* (Bottom Line Books).

Several different forms of niacin, also known as vitamin B-3, are available and effective for lowering cholesterol. While conventional medicine doctors will tell you that only the prescription version is effective, it has been my experience that all forms of niacin are effective if taken at the right dose for the individual, which can be between 500 milligrams (mg) and 2,000 mg daily with meals. The prescription drug Niaspan is extended release, which means that it dissolves more slowly than regular-release drugs, providing the body with sustained blood levels of niacin.

Benefit: You usually need to take the extended-release drugs less often, because the effects last longer. There also are nonprescription versions of extended-release niacin available from nutrition-oriented doctors. As you note, regular niacin also is available over the counter. Inositol hexaniacinate is a form of niacin that is less likely to cause the skin redness and itching that often occurs with regular niacin.

Besides skin flushing and itching, all types of niacin can cause vomiting, nausea and coughing, although these side effects are not common. Occasionally liver enzymes, uric acid or glucose can become elevated. This is why blood tests need to be performed on a regular basis to monitor those on niacin therapy, regardless of the form used.

More from Mark Stengler, NMD…

Broccoli Boosts Arterial Health

Research funded by the British Heart Foundation found that the phytochemical sulforaphane in broccoli and other cruciferous vegetables, such as kale, cabbage and cauliflower, can activate a protein in the arteries that prevents inflammation and buildup of fatty plaque, both of which can lead to heart attack and stroke.

Best: Eat one-half cup of a raw or lightly steamed cruciferous vegetable daily.

Also from Dr. Mark Stengler…

Eat More Nuts, Lower More Cholesterol

A survey of 25 clinical trials published in *Archives of Internal Medicine* has found that eating 2.4 ounces (about one-half cup) daily of any kind of nuts can lower both total cholesterol and LDL (bad) cholesterol. Snack on nuts—but since they are high in calories, reduce your intake of other high-calorie foods and snacks.

Salt-Free Seasoning Made Easy

Judith Wylie-Rosett, EdD, RD, professor of epidemiology and population division head for health behavior and nutrition research at Albert Einstein College of Medicine in New York City. She is the author of *The Complete Weight Loss Workbook: Proven Techniques for Controlling Weight-Related Health Problems* (American Diabetes Association) and has published more than 130 journal articles on nutrition and health.

Have you had much luck in getting your loved ones (not to mention yourself) to put down the saltshaker? Most people are more bothered by the taste of bland, boring food than by the increased threat of a heart attack or stroke.

More than half of Americans age 60 and older have hypertension. If you or someone you cook for is among them, you may have tried to fool the taste buds with a commercial salt substitute but found the flavor too bitter.

Well, take heart. Nutrition researcher Judith Wylie-Rosett, EdD, RD, whose book *The Complete Weight Loss Workbook* includes many health-promoting recipes, suggested some much better ways to put zing into low-salt foods. *To get started...*

• **It can take a lot of seasoning to make up for the missing salt**—so when you drop salt from a recipe, try doubling one or more of the other seasonings the recipe calls for.

• **For maximum flavor from herbs and spices,** opt for fresh rather than dried.

• **Choose herb-infused oils and vinegars instead of unflavored ones.**

Tasty, salt-free ways to spice up...

• **Beef.** For seasoning that stands up to red meat's strong flavor, marinate beef for two to three hours in pineapple juice or orange juice mixed with balsamic vinegar, red wine, diced onions and/or chopped garlic.

• **Chicken.** For delicate-flavored lemon chicken, add chopped tarragon, which is subtly aromatic with hints of licorice. Robust chicken Parmesan needs more aggressive seasonings, such as fennel, basil, rosemary, garlic and/or oregano. For stews, add a bay leaf (remove before eating) plus mustard, marjoram and freshly ground black pepper... or use strong spices, such as cumin, turmeric and/or ginger.

• **Fish.** Complement mild-flavored white fish with the tangy taste of yogurt. Mix plain low-fat or nonfat yogurt with dill, ginger, mustard and garlic, then add one tablespoon of mayonnaise per cup of yogurt to keep the yogurt from separating. Use this as a marinade...or serve with the fish as a sauce. Fatty fish (mackerel, bluefish) have a strong flavor that blends well with the hearty taste of curry, lemon pepper and garlic.

• **Pasta.** Don't salt the cooking water. Instead, add a little flavored olive oil to the cooking water, which also helps to keep the pasta from sticking. Drain pasta one minute earlier than you normally would, return it to the pot, stir in whatever sauce you're going to use and cook them together for that final minute—so the pasta absorbs more flavor from the sauce.

• **Soups.** For delicate-flavored soups, such as chicken soup, use chopped sage, parsley and thyme to enhance but not overwhelm the flavor. To give zest to hearty-tasting soups, add a splash of balsamic vinegar and/or wine when the soup is almost done.

• **Vegetables.** Stir together two or more types of cooked veggies before serving—they taste more interesting that way than alone—and boost flavor with a generous amount of fresh-squeezed lemon juice. Simmer root vegetables in reduced-fat coconut milk mixed with curry. Dress salads with herb-infused olive or sunflower oil...champagne vinegar or vinegar made from sweeter fruits (pears, figs, raspberries)...and some flat-leaf parsley, chervil or tarragon.

Salt? Who needs it?

The 15-Minute Heart Cure

John M. Kennedy, MD, medical director of preventive cardiology and wellness at Marina Del Rey Hospital, California. He is a clinical associate professor at Harbor-UCLA Medical Center and is on the board of directors for the American Heart Association. He is author, with Jason Jennings, of *The 15 Minute Heart Cure: The Natural Way to Release Stress and Heal Your Heart in Just Minutes a Day* (Wiley). *www.the 15minuteheartcure.com.*

Most people know that smoking, high cholesterol and high blood pressure are among the main risk factors for heart disease. Few of us realize that daily stress is another key risk factor. It can damage the heart and arteries even in people who are otherwise healthy.

Recent finding: A University of Southern California study that looked at 735 patients for more than 12 years found that chronic stress and anxiety were better predictors of future cardiovascular events (such as a heart attack) than other risk factors. The researchers estimate that those who reduce or stabilize their stress levels are 50% to 60% less likely to have a heart attack than those who experience increasing stress.

TOXIC OVER TIME

Researchers have known for a long time that sudden traumatic events can trigger heart problems. Three years after the 9/11 terrorist attacks, for example, study participants—most of whom watched the attacks on live television—were questioned about their stress levels. Those who still were severely stressed were 53% more likely to have heart problems, and twice as likely to develop high blood pressure, as those with lower stress levels.

It appears that even "normal" stress—financial pressures or an unhappy job situation—is dangerous when it continues for a long time. It's estimated that more than 75% of visits to primary care physicians are linked to stress-related disorders.

What happens: Chronic stress increases vascular resistance, the main cause of high blood pressure. It increases the activity of platelets, cell-like structures in blood that clump together and trigger most heart attacks. It increases levels of cortisol, adrenaline and other stress hormones that promote arterial inflammation.

Doctors have been slow to acknowledge stress as a major cardiovascular risk factor. This is partly because stress (like pain) is subjective and highly individual—it's difficult to quantify, because everyone has different stress triggers and experiences stress differently. One lawyer might thrive on hectic 16-hour days, while another might react with high anxiety.

Stress can't be directly measured, but tests show its toxic effects. When laboratory subjects who are asked to count backward from 100 by eights get increasingly frustrated, there is a corresponding increase in their heart rate, adrenaline and substances linked to inflammation, such as C-reactive protein and *interleukins*.

STRESS REDUCTION WORKS

We can only partly control our emotional environments—stress-causing events can't always be avoided. But we can greatly change the ways in which we react to stress. People who do this can significantly lower their cardiovascular risks.

In one study, patients with heart disease were divided into three groups and followed for up to five years. Those in one group practiced stress reduction. Those in the other groups were treated either with an exercise program or with standard medical care. (The standard-care group maintained their regular medical regimen and did not participate in an exercise or stress-management program.)

Only 10% of those in the stress-control group had a subsequent heart attack or required bypass surgery or angioplasty, compared with 21% in the exercise group and 30% in the medical-care group.

BREATHE

The traditional techniques for reducing stress, such as yoga, are helpful but typically too complicated and time-consuming for most people. My colleagues and I have developed a simpler approach that anyone can do in about 15 minutes a day. It goes by the acronym B-R-E-A-T-H-E, which stands for Begin, Relax, Envision, Apply, Treat, Heal and End.

• **Begin.** Pick a time of day when you won't be interrupted for 15 minutes. Find a comfortable location. Many patients use their bedrooms, but any quiet, private place will work.

• **Relax.** This phase of the exercise is meant to elicit the relaxation response, a physiological process that reduces stress hormones, slows electrical activity in the brain and reduces inflammation.

• **Sit or lie quietly.** Focus so completely on your breathing that there isn't room in your mind for anything else. Inhale slowly and deeply through your nose. Then exhale just as slowly through your mouth. Each inhalation and exhalation should take about seven seconds.

• **Repeat the breathing cycle seven times.** You'll know you're ready to go to the next step when your body is so relaxed that it feels as if all of your weight is supported by the chair or bed rather than by your muscles.

• **Envision.** Spend a few minutes imagining that every part of your heart—the arteries, muscles, valves and the electrical system—is strong and healthy. Form a mental picture (it doesn't have to be anatomically accurate) of the heart pumping blood and sending nourishment throughout your body. Hold the mental image for several minutes.

Studies using PET scans show that people who imagine that they are performing an action activate the same part of the brain that is involved when they actually do that action. Imagining a healthy heart literally can make the heart healthier.

• **Apply.** It's up to you when (and how often) you perform this relaxation exercise. Most people can find 15 minutes a day to take a mental break from stress to keep their hearts healthy. Others also use this technique when they notice that their stress levels are rising.

During a hectic day at work, for example, take a break for 15 minutes to calm down with conscious breathing and visualization.

• **Treat and heal.** I encourage patients to embrace the pleasurable aspects of this exercise. Don't consider it a chore. It's more like a spa treatment than a physical workout.

The healing aspect can be strongly motivating, particularly if you already have a history of heart disease. Every time you do this exercise, you are strengthening the neural networks that connect the heart and brain. This can lead to a decrease in heart arrhythmias (irregularities), an increase in immune-cell activity and even better sleep.

• **End.** Finish each relaxation session by making a mental checklist of what you have achieved. You have imagined that your heart and arteries are healthy. You have reduced stress hormones, and you are feeling more relaxed and energized than you did before.

The results are long-lasting. People who practice this for a few weeks will find themselves dealing with unexpected stressful events productively and in a calm, focused manner.

Hatha Yoga Lowers Risk for Heart Disease

People who practiced yoga regularly had lower blood levels of *interleukin-6*, a component of the body's inflammatory response that contributes to heart disease, stroke, arthritis and type 2 diabetes. People who practiced one to two times a week for at least two years and at least twice a week for the last year also had lower inflammatory responses to stress.

Janice Kiecolt-Glaser, PhD, professor of psychiatry and psychology, The Ohio State University College of Medicine, Columbus, and leader of a study published in *Psychosomatic Medicine*.

Resuming Sexual Activity After a Heart Attack

If it's been at least six weeks since you've had a heart attack, but you—or your spouse— are still worried about the risk of resuming sexual activity despite your doctor's OK, you may benefit from some extra reassurance.

Ask your doctor about a stress test—which involves walking on a treadmill while your heart is electronically monitored. If you can perform mildly strenuous activity (brisk walking or slow jogging at about three to four mph) without the test showing decreased blood flow to your heart muscle, this should give you additional confirmation that it's safe for you to have sex.

Henry G. Stratmann, MD, clinical professor of medicine, St. Louis University, and a cardiologist in private practice in Springfield, Missouri.

Holding in Anger at Work Doubles Heart Attack Risk

In a recent study of employed men in Sweden, those who did not speak up when they felt unfairly treated on the job were five times more likely to have a heart attack than men who vented their frustration.

Constanze Leineweber, PhD, psychologist, Stress Research Institute, Stockholm University, Sweden, and leader of a study of 2,755 employed men, published in *Journal of Epidemiology and Community Health*.

Toe-Touch Test Reveals Heart Health

When 526 men and women (ages 20 to 83) were asked to reach for their toes while seated on the floor with their legs flat and their backs straight against a wall, poor trunk flexibility (reach that was farthest from toes) was linked to high blood pressure and predicted arterial stiffness (a precursor to heart disease).

Theory: Flexibility may delay age-related arterial stiffening.

Self-defense: Improve flexibility through regular stretching, Pilates or yoga.

Kenta Yamamoto, PhD, research fellow, integrative physiology department, University of North Texas, Fort Worth.

Having Sex Good For the Heart?

In a recent finding, men who had sex once a month or less were approximately 50% more likely to suffer cardiovascular events, such as heart attack, stroke or heart failure, than men who had sex at least twice a week. Further research is needed. The frequency of sex may simply indicate a man's overall health. In the meantime, men should discuss with their doctors any sexual problems.

Susan A. Hall, PhD, senior research scientist, department of epidemiology, New England Research Institutes, Watertown, Massachusetts, and lead author of a study of 1,165 men, published in *The American Journal of Cardiology*.

Your Personality Could Be Harming Your Heart

When researchers gave 5,614 adults personality tests, those who were antagonistic (aggressive, competitive, manipulative and/or quick to express anger) were 40% more likely to develop arterial thickening (a risk factor for heart attack and stroke) than those who were least antagonistic. To help control anger and antagonism, consult the American Psychological Association Web site, *www.apa.org/helpcenter/controlling-anger.aspx*. Or consider seeing a therapist for more strategies.

Angelina Sutin, PhD, postdoctoral fellow, National Institute on Aging, Baltimore.

22

Stroke Alerts

Stroke Risk: Little-Known Triggers That May Surprise You

Many risk factors for stroke are well known. For example, high blood pressure (hypertension), elevated cholesterol, diabetes, inactivity, smoking, having a prior stroke or "ministroke" (also called a transient ischemic attack, or TIA) or a family history of stroke all increase your odds of suffering this potentially devastating condition.

STROKE FACTS

Of the nearly 800,000 Americans who suffer a stroke each year, about 87% have an ischemic stroke (a clot blocks blood flow to the brain) and 13% have a hemorrhagic stroke (a blood vessel in the brain ruptures). In the US, stroke is the third leading cause of death and a leading cause of disability—complications can include paralysis...weakness in an arm or leg...and/or speech problems.

What few people realize: There are many little-known risk factors for stroke, which also should be taken seriously, particularly if you have one or more of the risk factors mentioned above. Each additional risk factor increases your chance of having a stroke.

For example...

COLD WEATHER

•**High blood pressure can triple your risk for a stroke.**

Recent development: A study of nearly 9,000 people found that cold weather raises blood pressure levels in people age 65 and older. One-third of those studied had hypertension in

---

Steven R. Messé, MD, assistant professor of neurology and director of the vascular neurology fellowship at the Hospital of the University of Pennsylvania in Philadelphia. Board-certified in neurology and vascular neurology, he has published scientific papers in *Stroke, Neurology* and the *Journal of Neurology, Neurosurgery and Psychiatry.*

the winter, compared with about one-quarter during the summer.

Self-defense: If you have hypertension—a systolic (top number) reading of 140 mmHg or higher and/or diastolic (bottom number) of 90 mmHg or higher—consider taking your blood pressure every day during the winter (at the same time of day) with an at-home device. Follow the same advice if you have prehypertension (the stage before hypertension)—systolic reading of 120 mmHg to 139 mmHg and/or diastolic reading of 80 mmHg to 89 mmHg. If you have hypertension or pre-hypertension and your blood pressure rises in the winter, see your doctor.

SHINGLES

If you had chicken pox as a child, you're at risk for an outbreak of the same virus—a condition known as shingles—years later.

After a bout of chicken pox, the virus (*varicella-zoster*) becomes dormant in sensory nerves along the spinal cord or near the brain. With shingles, the virus re-emerges, typically causing a painful rash that affects one side of the body. For example, the rash may wrap itself around the trunk from mid-back to one side of the chest. The trigger behind this reactivation is thought to be related to stress and suppression of the immune system.

Recent research: In a study of nearly 8,000 adults who had been treated for shingles and 23,000 who had not suffered the disease, the shingles patients were 31% more likely to have had a stroke in the year following the shingles outbreak. It's important to note that shingles often occurs in people who are already ill or have a suppressed immune system—factors that in themselves raise stroke risk.

Self-defense: There is not enough evidence to recommend that the shingles vaccine be given for stroke prevention. However, it's wise for older adults to receive the vaccine, since it's estimated that half of people who live to age 85 will suffer a shingles attack. If you have a history of shingles, follow your doctor's advice on stroke prevention, such as making lifestyle changes and taking medication to prevent or control hypertension, cholesterol levels and/or diabetes.

STRESS AND DEPRESSION

When researchers studied 600 people who had recently had a stroke and 600 people who hadn't, those who had experienced stress for one year or longer had a 3.5 times higher risk for ischemic stroke.

What happens: Unrelieved stress triggers secretion of the hormone cortisol. Ongoing secretion of cortisol can raise blood pressure, destabilize blood sugar levels and increase inflammation—all of which can raise stroke risk.

Self-defense: Chronic stress is often linked to clinical depression. If you suspect that you may be depressed (symptoms include change in weight and/or sleep habits), see your doctor. He/she may prescribe an antidepressant and/or recommend *cognitive behavioral therapy* (CBT), which research shows is as effective as medication in reducing depression. Regular exercise, a healthful diet and sufficient sleep also help fight depression. If you are not depressed but regularly experience stress, follow the lifestyle changes described above.

MIGRAINE

People who suffer migraines with "auras" (visual disturbances such as jagged lines and flashes of light) have twice the risk for ischemic stroke as people without migraines, according to recent research. The increased risk is most apparent in women who smoke and take oral contraceptives.

Self-defense: If you notice auras when you get migraines, discuss your stroke risk with your doctor.

CHIROPRACTIC ADJUSTMENT

Because chiropractic adjustments to the neck often involve physical manipulation of the cervical spine (neck region), neurologists and chiropractors have long debated whether such movements can lead to a rare form of ischemic stroke known as *vertebrobasilar artery* (VBA) stroke, which can be triggered by a tear in the vertebral arteries that run along the neck bones.

Recent research: A study of 818 people found that those under age 45 who had suffered VBA strokes and were hospitalized for that type of stroke were three times more likely to have seen a chiropractor or a primary care physician before the hospitalization than people without VBA strokes. In people over age 45, VBA stroke was associated with visits to primary care practitioners.

The researchers speculated that the visits to both practitioners occurred when people had symptoms of a VBA tear, such as neck pain or stiffness, but had not yet had a VBA stroke.

Self-defense: It is unlikely that a chiropractic adjustment of the neck will greatly increase your risk for a stroke. But since all medical treatments have some risks, you'll need to decide whether the benefits of a chiropractic manipulation of the neck outweigh the likely small risk for stroke.

Warning: You can cause a VBA tear by bending your head backward over a sink while having your hair washed at a hair salon. If you've had a previous stroke or TIA, do not put your head in this position. If you have no history of stroke, make sure your neck is resting comfortably and securely on a towel and not on the sink itself.

FAST FOOD

People living in neighborhoods with the most fast-food restaurants had a 13% higher risk for ischemic stroke, according to a new study. This research doesn't prove that fast food causes stroke but shows a statistical association between the two factors. However, there is proof that high levels of saturated fat and salt—both commonly found in many fast-food meals—increase stroke risk.

Self-defense: Limit your intake of fast foods. If you go to a fast-food restaurant, choose more healthful menu items, such as salads.

Women Have Higher Stroke Risk Than Men

Researchers who analyzed health data on 2,274 adults found that women were nearly three times more likely than men to suffer a stroke.

Theory: Although women generally have healthier blood pressure and cholesterol levels compared with men, women tend to carry more harmful abdominal fat, a known stroke predictor.

Self-defense: Even healthy women should discuss their abdominal waist measurements with their doctors (aim for a waist smaller than 35 inches).

Amytis Towfighi, MD, assistant professor of neurology, Keck School of Medicine, University of Southern California, Los Angeles.

Hidden Cause of Stroke, High Blood Pressure and Aneurysm

Jeffrey W. Olin, DO, professor of cardiology at the Mount Sinai School of Medicine and director of vascular medicine at the Zena and Michael A. Wiener Cardiovascular Institute and the Marie-Josée and Henry R. Kravis Center for Cardiovascular Health at Mount Sinai, all in New York City. He is a recipient of the Founders Award from the Fibromuscular Dysplasia Society of America for outstanding achievements in promoting research and awareness of FMD.

Most people have never heard of the blood vessel disorder known as *fibromuscular dysplasia* (FMD), but doctors now recognize that it can be a hidden cause of high blood pressure (hypertension), strokes and brain aneurysms (due to bulging in the wall of an artery in the brain).

Recent development: Once considered a rare condition, FMD now appears to be more common than previously thought, possibly affecting up to 5 million adults in the US.

What you need to know…

WHAT IS FMD?

In people with FMD, abnormal cell growth occurs on the walls of one or more arteries (blood vessels), typically in the carotid (neck) arteries (leading to the brain) and renal arteries (leading to the kidneys). The normally smooth artery wall develops bumps, often resulting in a "string of beads" that can be seen on imaging tests used to examine blood vessels, such as ultrasound, a *computed tomography angiogram* (CTA) or magnetic resonance angiogram (MRA).

When cell growth becomes extensive, the artery narrows, disrupting blood flow and possibly resulting in hypertension, a stroke or an aneurysm. While atherosclerosis—fatty buildup in the arteries—occurs at the opening of a blood vessel, FMD occurs at the middle and end of a blood vessel.

ARE YOU AT RISK?

Though FMD typically strikes adults under age 50, doctors now are finding more and more previously undiagnosed cases in people age 60 and older—perhaps due to the increasing use of imaging tests. FMD is often diagnosed as a result of an incidental finding on an unrelated radiological test. In many of these cases, the patient has no symptoms of the disorder.

No one knows what causes FMD. Genetics may play a role, but not everyone with FMD has a relative with the disease. FMD occurs more often in women (about 85% of cases) than in men. Researchers suspect that a gene predisposes an individual to the condition and that the gene is expressed due to outside influences, such as hormones.

GETTING A PROPER DIAGNOSIS

FMD often goes undiagnosed because many doctors mistakenly believe that it is very rare. In fact, many medical schools don't even teach their students about FMD.

To complicate matters further, many people with FMD have no symptoms. When symptoms do occur, they are related to the arteries that are affected and the degree of narrowing that has developed.

Example: Since the majority of FMD cases occurs in the arteries leading to the kidneys, high blood pressure may develop (due to narrowing of the renal arteries, which triggers a series of adverse effects). Abnormal kidney function and flank pain (occurring on one side of the body between the upper abdomen and the back) also can occur.

In about 25% to 30% of FMD patients, the disease affects the carotid arteries. In these people, symptoms may include severe and unrelenting headaches…dizziness…ringing in the ears (tinnitus)…and neck pain.

FMD in the carotid artery also may lead to a swishing sound in the ears…temporary or permanent loss of vision in one or both eyes…brain aneurysms…and transient ischemic attacks (TIAs)—or "ministrokes"…as well as full-blown strokes.

Though less likely, FMD can affect the arteries supplying the liver, spleen and intestines, which may cause abdominal pain after eating, unexplained weight loss or gangrene of the bowel. If the arteries to the legs or arms are affected, pain or fatigue when using the affected limb can occur. In very rare cases, FMD may affect the coronary arteries in the heart, leading to angina (chest pain) or a heart attack.

Helpful: Regardless of your age, ask your doctor during all routine physicals to place a stethoscope on your neck and abdomen and listen for a bruit, a noise that indicates a narrowing of a blood vessel. If a bruit is heard, your doctor can follow up with the appropriate test, such as an ultrasound or CTA.

Important: Not all FMD patients have an audible bruit.

BEST TREATMENT OPTIONS

FMD has no cure. The goal is to improve blood flow in the affected artery. Treatment depends on which artery is narrowed and the severity of the symptoms. Medication that alleviates high blood pressure, such as an angiotensin-converting enzyme (ACE) inhibitor, may be prescribed. Many patients take daily aspirin to help prevent clots from forming, thus reducing stroke risk.

FMD patients who have "new-onset" hypertension may require *percutaneous transluminal renal angioplasty* (PTRA). This procedure (usually outpatient) involves inserting a catheter into the affected artery and inflating a small balloon to open the narrowed area.

Important finding: A study published in the *Journal of Vascular Surgery* showed that renal artery angioplasty reduced high blood pressure in 72% of the 29 FMD patients studied—and the reduction was still evident five years after the procedure.

FINDING THE RIGHT DOCTOR

If you have FMD—or suspect that you may—see a vascular specialist or a physician who is experienced in treating the organ affected by the disease.

For example: A nephrologist (kidney doctor) if FMD affects your renal arteries (or you are having kidney problems such as those described above)...or a neurologist if the carotid arteries are affected.

More from Dr. Olin...

Cutting-Edge Research on FMD

Several medical centers in the US, including the Mount Sinai Medical Center in New York City and the Cleveland Clinic, participate in an international registry of FMD patients to help scientists conduct cutting-edge research to unravel some of the mysteries of the disease.

If you or a family member has been diagnosed with FMD, contact the Fibromuscular Dysplasia Society of America (FMDSA), 888-709-7089, *www.fmdsa.org*, which can provide information about the registry closest to you.

Surprising Blood Pressure Danger

When 668 adults over age 65 had three blood pressure readings over six years, people whose blood pressure fluctuated between readings (even within normal range) were more likely to develop cerebrovascular disease, which can lead to stroke, than people with stable or low blood pressure.

Theory: Blood pressure changes interrupt blood flow to the brain.

If your blood pressure fluctuates or is high: Manage it with proper diet, exercise and, when needed, medication.

Adam M. Brickman, PhD, Herbert Irving Assistant Professor of Neuropsychology, Columbia University College of Physicians and Surgeons, New York City.

What's Causing Your High Blood Pressure?

Jamison Starbuck, ND, naturopathic physician in family practice in Missoula, Montana. She is past president of the American Association of Naturopathic Physicians and a contributing editor to *The Alternative Advisor: The Complete Guide to Natural Therapies and Alternative Treatments* (Time Life).

You probably know that about one of every three American adults has high blood pressure (hypertension). But you may not realize that there are two types of hypertension—primary and secondary. The distinction is crucial since primary and secondary hypertension require different treatment. With the wrong treatment, hypertension can go uncontrolled, which can lead to kidney failure, stroke or even death.

The cause of primary hypertension is unknown, but genetics is among the most likely culprits. Primary hypertension often starts in a person's mid-20s, with readings creeping upward as the years go by. It's treated with diet and exercise and/or antihypertensive drugs.

Secondary hypertension, which usually comes on quickly and can occur in people with no family history of high blood pressure, is actually a symptom of a preexisting problem. Underlying health problems can be the trigger for secondary hypertension. The most common include congenital heart defects, kidney disorders (including a tumor on the adrenal gland at the top of the kidney) or hormonal disorders (including overactive thyroid or overproduction of the steroid hormone aldosterone). Secondary hypertension also can result from medications, including steroids, migraine drugs, the antidepressant *bupropion* (Wellbutrin) and nonsteroidal anti-inflammatory medicines, such as *ibuprofen* (Motrin). Or the underlying cause may be lifestyle issues, such as sleep deprivation, obesity, chronic stress or excessive alcohol consumption.

When I see a patient with high blood pressure, I look for an underlying cause. I do a physical exam and order a variety of blood and urine tests. I also inquire about personal habits, including sleep, exercise and diet, and review the patient's prescription and over-the-counter (OTC) medications and supplements (ones with licorice, ephedra or an ingredient to which a person is allergic can raise blood pressure). I also ask about major life shifts, such as a move, divorce or job change—all can affect blood pressure.

When the underlying cause is treated, secondary hypertension usually goes away. A change in prescription or OTC medication may be needed. Psychotherapy or a class in stress management may be the answer. Hormonal problems often are resolved with hormone therapy. Kidney disorders may require the care of a specialist. With some patients, I treat the underlying problem and prescribe antihypertensive medicines.

A healthful diet is essential. My favorite is the so-called DASH diet, Dietary Approaches to Stop Hypertension. To learn more about this diet, which is high in fruits, vegetables, dietary fiber, magnesium and potassium, check *www.dashdiet.org*. Daily yoga and breathing exercises also help hypertension.

Try this: Hold one finger over your right nostril and breathe in and out through the left nostril for 15 breaths, then repeat with the other nostril. Usually, this immediately lowers the blood pressure and can be done as often as you wish. Results may last for an hour or all day, depending on the person.

Insomnia Linked to High Blood Pressure

When researchers analyzed data for 1,741 adults, those who suffered from chronic insomnia (and slept fewer than five hours nightly, on average) were five times more likely to have high blood pressure than adults who did not have insomnia and slept more than six hours nightly, on average.

Theory: Insomnia, combined with short sleep duration, is associated with increased heart rate—a risk factor for hypertension.

Alexandros N. Vgontzas, MD, director, Sleep Research and Treatment Center, Pennsylvania State College of Medicine, Hershey.

Hidden Red Flag for Heart Attack and Stroke

Michael S. Conte, MD, a vascular surgeon and professor and chief of the division of vascular and endovascular surgery and codirector of the Heart and Vascular Center at the University of California, San Francisco. In 2006, he received the Distinguished Achievement Award from the New York Weill Cornell Medical Center Alumni Council.

How serious is peripheral artery disease (PAD)? We all know that plaque in arteries near the heart can lead to heart attack and plaque in the arteries of the neck and brain can lead to stroke.

With PAD, plaque is typically found in arteries that supply blood to the legs—an indication that blood flow also may be inhibited throughout the body, which increases risk for heart attack and stroke, as well as severe disability or loss of a limb.

Doctors have long been aware of PAD, but the disease has received relatively little attention because patients either don't have symptoms or have only mild or moderate ones that are wrongly attributed to normal aging.

What's new: The link between PAD and cardiovascular disease is now so strong that virtually all doctors agree that a diagnosis of PAD warrants a checkup and monitoring by a vascular specialist.

What you need to know to protect yourself or a loved one…

ARE YOU AT RISK?

• **PAD is surprisingly common.** It affects up to 10 million Americans. Because PAD is associated with the same risk factors as heart attack and stroke, the risk for PAD is higher among adults who are over age 50 and/or people who have elevated cholesterol or high blood pressure.

• **Having diabetes doubles the risk of developing PAD.** Prediabetes also increases risk. But the greatest risk comes from smoking. At least 80% of people with PAD are current or former smokers. Statistically, the worst combination is smoking and having diabetes—when combined, they increase the risk of developing PAD fivefold.

SYMPTOMS CAN BE TRICKY

PAD is dangerous. It can creep up on you without causing symptoms. In fact, up to half of people with PAD do not have symptoms.

When symptoms do occur, they start out mild and may be easy to dismiss. Because blood flow is compromised, activities that involve the use of the legs—walking, for example—can become more difficult.

As plaque blockages become more severe, PAD causes *intermittent claudication*—legs become painful or cramp up while walking.

At first, a person with PAD may experience symptoms of intermittent claudication only after walking long distances or up a hill or while climbing stairs. The discomfort usually goes away after sitting down and resting for a few minutes. If the condition is left untreated, even a short stroll will trigger the pain.

What most people don't know: In rare cases, PAD can occur in the hands and arms, leading to symptoms such as aching or cramping in the arms.

GETTING A PROPER DIAGNOSIS

Not all doctors agree on who should be screened for PAD. *However, it's wise to be tested if any of the following risk factors identified by the American College of Cardiology and the American Heart Association apply to you...*

•**Younger than age 50.** If you have diabetes and one additional risk factor (such as smoking or high blood pressure).

•**Age 50 to 69.** If you have a history of smoking or diabetes.

•**Age 70 and older**—even if you have no known risk factors. *Many experts believe that screening also is warranted—regardless of your age—if you have...*

•Leg symptoms, such as aches and cramping with exertion.

•Diagnosis of atherosclerosis, fatty buildup in the walls of the arteries, including those in the heart and neck.

•Numbness, tingling or loss of sensation in the feet or cold feet or areas of color change (bluish or dark color, for example) on your toes—an indication of compromised blood flow.

•High blood levels of C-reactive protein (CRP), an inflammation marker.

THE TESTS YOU NEED

If you meet one of the criteria described above, ask your doctor to test you for PAD. He/she will perform a measurement called an ankle-brachial index to get a sense of whether blood pumps equally through your arms and your legs. Your doctor will measure your blood pressure in your ankle as well as in your arm and compare the two numbers.

BEST TREATMENT OPTIONS

There is no medication that will dissolve PAD plaque, so you should work with your doctor to manage your risk factors. If you're a smoker, stopping smoking is the most important step you can take to help control PAD.

Everyone with PAD should...

•**Get the right kind of exercise.** Surprising as it might sound, walking is the most beneficial form of exercise for PAD sufferers. It won't get rid of the plaque, but it can improve your stamina and make walking less painful.

What to do: Walk on flat ground every day—or try a treadmill if you prefer.

Use your level of leg pain to determine the amount of time you walk. For example, walk until the leg pain reaches a moderate level... stop walking until the pain is relieved...then resume walking. This approach "trains" the muscle to be more efficient in using its blood supply. Try to work your way up to 50 minutes of walking at least five days a week.

Consult your doctor before starting a walking program, especially if you have other conditions, such as heart disease, arthritis or spine disease. Supervised exercise, such as that offered at rehab centers, has been shown to be the most effective for PAD patients—perhaps because people are more likely to stick to a walking program in these settings.

•**Monitor other risk factors.** It is critically important to pay attention to all your other health-related risk factors. For example, if you have diabetes, keep glucose levels under control. If you have elevated cholesterol or high blood pressure, discuss medication with your doctor.

To reduce the risk for blood clots, which could lead to limb damage, heart attack or stroke, your doctor may suggest a daily aspirin (81 mg) or a medication that prevents clotting, such as *clopidogrel* (Plavix). A statin also may be prescribed. Statins not only lower cholesterol, but also lower levels of the inflammation marker CRP.

WHEN ADDITIONAL TREATMENT IS NEEDED

In about 30% of PAD patients, the condition causes severe pain that affects their quality of life or the amount of blockage significantly restricts blood flow. In these cases, your doctor may recommend a more invasive measure, such as angioplasty or bypass surgery, to improve blood flow in the affected artery.

With angioplasty, a tiny balloon and, possibly, stents are inserted via a catheter into the artery to widen the artery as much as possible. Bypass surgery involves creating a blood-flow "detour" around a blockage, allowing the blood to flow more freely.

Important: Treatment for PAD is highly individualized. If you've been diagnosed with the condition, you should see your doctor at least once or twice each year.

For more information on PAD, contact the PAD Coalition at 888-833-4463, *www.padcoalition.org.* To find a vascular specialist near you, contact the Vascular Disease Foundation at 888-833-4463, *www.vdf.org.*

Chocolate May Reduce Stroke Risk

In one study, people who ate one serving of chocolate a week were 22% less likely to have a stroke than those who ate no chocolate. In another study, people who ate 50 grams (1.75 ounces) of chocolate per week were 46% less likely to die following a stroke than those who ate no chocolate.

Possible reason: Chocolate is a rich source of antioxidants that may protect against stroke.

Sarah Sahib, researcher at McMaster University, Hamilton, Ontario, Canada, is lead author of an analysis of studies on chocolate and stroke.

Drinking Doubles Your Stroke Risk

Your risk for ischemic stroke is doubled in the hour after you have a single alcoholic drink. The heightened risk goes away within three hours.

Theory: Alcohol may temporarily raise blood pressure or affect the blood's ability to clot.

Self-defense: Avoid consuming multiple drinks in a short time because this may cause a sharp increase in stroke risk. One drink is defined as 12 ounces of beer, four ounces of wine, 1.5 ounces of 80-proof spirits or one ounce of 100-proof spirits.

Murray A. Mittleman, MD, DrPH, director of the Cardiovascular Epidemiology Research Unit, Beth Israel Deaconess Medical Center, Harvard Medical School, Boston, and leader of a study published in *Stroke.*

Shingles Increases Stroke Risk

Having shingles anywhere on the body increases the risk of having a stroke over the next 12 months by about 30%. Having eye-related (ocular) shingles increases the risk by more than 400%

People who have had shingles should take extra care to reduce stroke risk. Exercise regularly...maintain a healthy, low-salt, low-fat diet...don't smoke...and, if necessary, take medication to control blood pressure and cholesterol.

Daniel T. Lackland, DrPH, professor of epidemiology, department of neurosciences, Medical University of South Carolina, Charleston, and spokesperson for the American Stroke Association. *www.strokeassociation.org*

Overactive Thyroid Linked to Stroke

A diagnosis of hyperthyroidism, or overactive thyroid, before age 45 increases stroke risk by 44%.

Possible connection: Hyperthyroidism is linked to atrial fibrillation, a heart rhythm disorder that is associated with elevated stroke risk.

To cut stroke risk: Follow a low-fat, high-fiber diet, and exercise regularly. Don't smoke. Have blood pressure, blood sugar and cholesterol levels measured at least once a year.

Brian Silver, MD, senior staff neurologist at Henry Ford Hospital and assistant professor of neurology at Wayne State University School of Medicine, both in Detroit.

Screening Test Has Risk of Its Own

Angiograms are riskier than people think, though the test is of great value in patients with coronary artery disease. One in 1,000 patients who have angiograms has a stroke... eight in 1,000 suffer a vascular injury. Patients who have not been diagnosed with coronary artery disease should talk with their doctors about less invasive forms of testing.

Ralph G. Brindis, MD, MPH, president of the American College of Cardiology and clinical professor of medicine at University of California, San Francisco. He led an analysis of angiograms, published in *The New England Journal of Medicine.*

Women with Chest Pain Need a Specific Test

A patient with chest pain or pressure typically gets a stress test and, if that is abnormal, has an angiogram (blood vessel X-ray) to check for arterial plaque, a sign of coronary artery disease.

Troubling new finding: When a woman's angiogram appears normal, she typically receives no treatment—yet she may in fact be at increased risk for heart attack and stroke.

Reason: Women may be more prone than men to endothelial dysfunction, in which cells lining blood vessels do not work properly— an early-stage form of coronary artery disease not detectable with standard testing.

Self-defense: If you have chest pain and an abnormal stress test but your angiogram reveals no coronary disease, ask your doctor about having a cardiac MRI or other test for endothelial dysfunction.

Martha Gulati, MD, associate director, Center for Women's Cardiovascular Health, Northwestern Memorial Hospital, Chicago, and leader of an analysis of studies on 1,540 women.

High Rate of Recurring Vascular Disease

Even with all the advances in vascular disease treatment, patients have a 14.4% rate of recurring heart attack or stroke at one year and a 28.4% rate at three years, say researchers at Northwestern University Feinberg School of Medicine, Chicago. If you have vascular disease, such as atherosclerosis, resolve to stay on a healthful diet and exercise program.

Mark A. Stengler, NMD, licensed naturopathic medical doctor and leading authority on the practice of alternative and integrated medicine. He is founder and medical director of the Stengler Center for Integrative Medicine, Encinitas, California, and author of many books, including *The Natural Physician's Healing Therapies* (Bottom Line Books).

If You Have a Stroke...

Rebecca Shannonhouse, editor, *Bottom Line/Health,* Boardroom Inc., 281 Tresser Blvd., Stamford, Connecticut 06901.

We've long known that you must get to a hospital immediately if you think you or a loved one might be having a stroke.

Now: The American Academy of Neurology has released a new guideline that states the standard use of a computed tomography (CT) scan to diagnose acute ischemic stroke (when an artery to the brain is blocked) should be replaced with a magnetic resonance imaging (MRI) scan.

The change resulted from a study that found MRIs accurately detected stroke in 83% of cases, versus 26% for CT scans. The panel added that the decision on which imaging tool to use is influenced by MRI availability.

Many hospitals do not have MRI machines or they are located far from the emergency room, says Steven R. Messé, MD, a neurologist at the Hospital of the University of Pennsylvania in Philadelphia.

Even though MRIs are more sensitive than CT scans, the tests are equally effective at detecting bleeding in the brain—a condition that will worsen if *tissue plasminogen activator* (tPA), the standard treatment for an ischemic stroke, is given.

The key is to get to the hospital. Once you're there, you can ask to be transferred, if necessary, to a different hospital with an accredited stroke center, where you will have rapid access to an MRI.

Use the FAST test to recognize stroke symptoms: Face (does one side of the face droop?)…Arms (can both be lifted?)…Speech (can the patient speak without slurring words and understand what's being said?)…and Time (if you see any of these signs, call 911 immediately).

Better Stroke Treatment

Researchers analyzed eight studies involving 3,680 stroke patients who received *tissue plasminogen activator* (tPA, a clot-busting drug also called *alteplase*) or a placebo.

Results: Benefits of the drug outweighed the risks if it was administered within 4.5 hours of initial stroke symptoms. Patients treated later were 1.5 times more likely to die within three months.

Theory: Restoring blood flow later increased brain swelling. This finding supports a 2009 recommendation by the American Heart Association and the American Stroke Association extending the window for treating ischemic stroke (caused by a blood clot) with tPA from three to 4.5 hours.

Kennedy Lees, MD, professor of medicine, University of Glasgow, UK.

Know Where the Nearest Stroke Center Is

Fewer than 25% of Americans can get to a stroke center within 30 minutes. These facilities are best-equipped to care for stroke patients when every minute counts. To find the stroke center nearest to you, go to *www.stroke.org* (click on "Emergency Stroke Center Locations").

Brendan G. Carr, MD, assistant professor of emergency medicine and biostatistics and epidemiology, University of Pennsylvania School of Medicine, Philadelphia, and leader of a study of primary stroke centers.

Older People Often Don't Recognize Stroke Signs

Fewer than half of survey respondents age 65 and older could list warning signs of stroke—sudden numbness and/or weakness in the face or extremities…sudden confusion or trouble speaking…sudden vision difficulty…sudden trouble walking…loss of balance or coordination…and/or sudden and severe headache.

Anne Hickey, PhD, Royal College of Surgeons, Dublin, Ireland, and leader of a study of 2,033 people, published in *BMC Geriatrics*.

The "Secret" Organ That Prevents Plaque-Filled Arteries

Mark A. Stengler, NMD, licensed naturopathic medical doctor and leading authority on the practice of alternative and integrated medicine. He is founder and medical director of the Stengler Center for Integrative Medicine, Encinitas, California, and author of many books, including *The Natural Physician's Healing Therapies* (Bottom Line Books).

I find that many patients think they know everything there is to know about veins and circulatory health—until I tell them a little secret about controlling the prevention of deadly plaque and clots. It's all about the endothelium (pronounced en-doe-THEE-lee-um), the thin layer of cells that lines the inside of blood vessels. The endothelium is so vast and involves so many physiological functions that researchers now consider it to be an organ.

To protect yourself from cardiovascular disease, focus on the lining of your blood vessels. The endothelium plays a crucial role in the cardiovascular system—producing chemicals that open blood vessels…influencing the formation and breakdown of dangerous blood clots…and helping to maintain blood flow throughout the body.

Fact: The health of your endothelium is within your control. *Here's what you need to know…*

THE ENDOTHELIUM IS EVERYWHERE

There are miles of blood vessels in your body—and endothelial cells are active participants in keeping them healthy. Healthy blood vessels flex and stretch as they accommodate blood flow throughout your body. Their lining is slick, allowing blood to flow freely and preventing plaque and blood clots from sticking.

Unhealthy arteries are rigid, and their endothelium is sticky, attracting plaque and blood clots and causing diseases such as atherosclerosis and *peripheral artery disease* (PAD), or hardening of the arteries of the legs and the arms.

HOW WELL DOES YOUR ENDOTHELIUM WORK?

Your chances of having endothelial dysfunction are high if you have any risk factors for cardiovascular disease, such as elevated cholesterol or homocysteine…are overweight, sedentary or smoke…or have diabetes. I recommend that everyone over age 40 have a screening test for endothelial function. One common test: Pulse-wave velocity. During this noninvasive test, a sensor placed on the wrist detects electric pulses that pass through the artery in advance of blood flow. The stiffer the artery wall, the faster the wave moves. This test can be provided by any type of physician and costs about $50 to $125.

HOW TO HELP YOUR ENDOTHELIUM

You may be surprised to find out how easy it is to help your endothelium—and how easy it is to harm it. In a landmark study published more than a decade ago, researchers from the State University of New York at Buffalo found that two or three hours after study participants ate a fast-food meal high in saturated fats and trans fats, their endothelial function (measured by blood flow) was reduced by half. This was a stunning finding—your body does know what you eat and knows it fast.

To improve blood vessel tone…

• **Eat a Mediterranean-style diet.** Consume a diet that emphasizes fish, poultry, legumes, whole grains, olive oil, fruits and vegetables—and minimizes intake of saturated fats and trans fats. The Mediterranean diet is high in antioxidants, omega-3 fatty acids and other healthful fats that can keep the endothelium pliant.

• **Exercise.** There is evidence that a sedentary lifestyle increases the risk for endothelial dysfunction. When people with heart disease begin a supervised exercise regimen, their endothelial function and blood flow improve significantly.

Lesson: If you're sedentary, get moving. Start by going for short walks. People who are already active should make sure that they participate in aerobic exercise (walking, jogging, swimming) for at least 20 to 30 minutes most days of the week.

SUPPLEMENTS FOR YOUR BLOOD VESSELS

To prevent or treat endothelial dysfunction, consider taking all of the supplements listed below...

• **L-arginine.** This amino acid is the most important supplement for endothelial dysfunction. It helps the body produce nitric oxide, which relaxes and opens blood vessels. Nuts, soy and legumes contain L-arginine, although not enough to provide the same benefit as a supplement. To prevent endothelial dysfunction, take 500 milligrams (mg) to 1,000 mg of L-arginine daily. Those with atherosclerosis, PAD, high blood pressure or congestive heart failure can take 1,000 mg to 2,000 mg daily.

Brand to try: Perfusia-SR by Thorne Research (800-228-1966, *www.thorne.com*), a time-released supplement that ensures that your body maintains optimum levels of L-arginine throughout the day.

Caution: Don't take L-arginine if you have herpes (either herpes simplex virus-1 or herpes simplex virus-2), since it may trigger outbreaks...are pregnant or nursing...or immediately following a heart attack because it may lower blood pressure too much.

• **Garlic.** The body converts *allicin*, one of the compounds in garlic, to the compound hydrogen sulfide, which has a blood vessel–relaxing effect similar to that of nitric oxide.

Dose: 2.4 grams daily of aged garlic extract.

• **Fish oil.** Omega-3 fish oil has a mild blood-thinning effect and has been shown to improve endothelial function.

Dose: One fish oil supplement daily with 2,000 mg of EPA and DHA combined.

• **Vitamins E and C.** Studies have found that vitamins E and C, individually or in combination, prevented endothelial dysfunction after participants ate a fast-food meal. If you're not already taking them, try 400 international units (IU) daily of vitamin E and 1,000 mg of vitamin C.

• **Niacin.** Niacin, also known as vitamin B-3, increases HDL (good) cholesterol and enhances its ability to protect the endothelium. Look for nonflushing forms of niacin.

Dose: 500 mg twice daily. Niacin may elevate liver enzymes—so have your doctor monitor your levels.

Blood Thinners Are More Dangerous Than You Think

Matthew L. Flaherty, MD, a neurologist at University of Cincinnati Medical Center and associate professor of neurology at University of Cincinnati Academic Health Center. He is lead author of "The Increasing Incidence of Anticoagulant-Associated Intracerebral Hemorrhage," published in *Neurology*.

Millions of Americans take aspirin, *warfarin* (Coumadin) or other medications to reduce the risk for clots, the cause of most heart attacks and strokes. These drugs, known as antithrombotic agents, are very effective, but they have to be used carefully to prevent excessive bleeding, the most serious side effect.

Recent finding: A study that my colleagues and I did found that the incidence of bleeding into the brain (intracerebral hemorrhage) associated with antithrombotic agents increased fivefold between the late 1980s and late 1990s. This rise corresponds to the increased use of warfarin, a commonly used medication.

When antithrombotic medications are used properly, the benefits often outweigh the risks. Yet all of these drugs, including aspirin, are more dangerous than most people think. *Here's how to reduce your risks...*

HOW BLOOD THINNERS WORK

Although antithrombotic medications are sometimes called blood thinners, they don't actually thin the blood. They inhibit the ability of substances in blood to form clots. They also can prevent some clots from getting bigger.

There are two main categories of antithrombotics. Each works at different stages of the clotting process.

• **Antiplatelet drugs** inhibit the ability of cell-like structures in blood (platelets) to form clots. Drugs in this class include aspirin, *clopidogrel* (Plavix), *ticlopidine* and a combination of aspirin plus *dipyridamole* (Aggrenox). Antiplatelet drugs are usually recommended for patients with a vascular disease (such as coronary artery disease) that increases their risk for clots.

• **Anticoagulants** work to inhibit proteins in the blood that trigger clotting. The most commonly used anticoagulant, warfarin, acts on the liver to inhibit the production of substances that cause clotting. Warfarin is more effective than aspirin for patients with atrial fibrillation (irregular heartbeat)...deep-vein thrombosis (a clot in a deep vein, usually in the legs)...or pulmonary embolism (clot in the lungs).

Some anticoagulants, such as *heparin*, are given by intravenous infusion or subcutaneous (under the skin) injection and are mainly used in hospitalized patients who have a high risk for clots.

GENETIC TESTING

The American Medical Association estimates that 21% of patients who take warfarin will experience some degree of bleeding because of the drug.

A genetic test now can identify certain at-risk patients. Studies have shown that people with two genetic variations (in the CYP2C9 and/or VKORC1 genes) metabolize warfarin more slowly and develop a higher blood concentration and so may need to be given a lower initial dose.

Preliminary research indicates that genetic testing can help predict a patient's optimal dose of warfarin when he/she first starts taking the medication. This may help reduce bleeding complications during this period. Genetic testing is not expected to help patients who have been taking warfarin for some time and have already established their optimal dose. Ask your doctor if genetic testing is for you. The test is expensive (up to $500) and may or may not be covered by insurance.

GENERAL SAFETY TIPS

To reduce your risks if you're taking any antithrombotic agent...

• **Watch for warning signs of excessive bleeding,** in particular unexplained bruising. It's a sign of bleeding under the skin. Other warning signs include bleeding gums when flossing or brushing the teeth...small cuts that continue to bleed...excessive fatigue (this could be due to blood loss)...or dark urine or black stools, which can indicate internal bleeding. If you have any of these signs, contact your doctor.

• **Control high blood pressure.** This is among the most important things that patients can do. High blood pressure increases the risk for hemorrhagic (bleeding in or around the brain) strokes—and the risk is higher in patients who also are taking an antithrombotic medication.

• **Ask your doctor about dangerous interactions.** Many common drugs, including some antibiotics, can interact with warfarin and change its effectiveness. Other medications have been reported to interact with antiplatelet drugs such as clopidogrel. If you're getting a prescription from a new doctor, make sure that he/she knows what other drugs you're taking.

Also, let your doctors know about any herbs and supplements you're taking. Some of these products, including fish oil, chamomile and ginger, can increase bleeding when combined with antithrombotic medications. Check with your doctor before taking them—or before you stop taking them.

WARFARIN SAFETY

If you're taking warfarin, be sure to do the following...

• **Know your INR.** The International Normalized Ratio (INR) is a measure of how quickly blood clots. It's used to determine the correct dose of warfarin, which differs widely from patient to patient. For most patients, the INR should be between two and three.

Patients often are advised to have a blood test several times a week after starting warfarin. Once they've achieved good control, they are tested monthly—or more often for patients who are starting (or stopping) other medications that can affect blood clotting.

• **Use aspirin and NSAIDs cautiously.** Patients taking warfarin can experience unwanted bleeding when they combine it with aspirin, *ibuprofen* or other nonsteroidal anti-inflammatory drugs (NSAIDs). Those who need these drugs—for arthritis, for example—should take them under a doctor's supervision.

Helpful: Acetaminophen (Tylenol) is not an NSAID and is less likely than other over-the-counter analgesics to increase bleeding in patients taking warfarin.

• **Don't double up.** Patients who miss a scheduled dose of warfarin by about six hours or more should wait until their next scheduled dose before taking it again. Doubling the amount to make up for a missed dose increases risks.

• **Maintain a stable diet.** Foods that are high in vitamin K, including leafy green vegetables and cruciferous vegetables, such as broccoli, cauliflower and cabbage, can increase the ability of blood to clot. Patients who are taking an antithrombotic medication who suddenly start eating more (or less) of these foods can experience changes in the way the drug works.

You don't have to avoid foods high in vitamin K. However, don't make major dietary changes without checking with your doctor. He might recommend a blood test to determine whether drug doses need to be adjusted.

• **Avoid contact sports, such as hockey and football.** Traumatic injuries can cause internal bleeding that's difficult to control in patients who are taking warfarin.

Minor cuts or scrapes—from shaving or working in the yard, for example—usually aren't a problem unless there's a significant change in your usual bleeding time. This could mean that the medication dose needs to be adjusted.

BLOOD THINNER BREAKTHROUGH

A new anticoagulant, antithrombotic medication, *dabigatran* (Pradaxa)—now approved by the FDA—may be a safer choice than warfarin. Studies indicate that dabigatran is at least as effective as, and possibly more effective than, warfarin at preventing clots. It doesn't require as much blood monitoring…is easier to dose… and interacts with fewer drugs.

Stents vs. Surgery

Stents are as effective as surgery for clearing blocked neck arteries, according to a recent study. And insertion of stents is less invasive than endarterectomy, the surgical treatment of carotid blockages.

Caution: While many hospitals perform the procedure, it is best to have it done at a hospital that specializes in cardiac care.

Wayne M. Clark, MD, director of Oregon Stroke Center and professor of neurology, Oregon Health & Science University, Portland. He is coauthor of a study of 2,502 patients presented at the American Stroke Association's International Stroke Conference.

A New Reason to Be Flexible: Healthier Arteries

Mark A. Stengler, NMD, licensed naturopathic medical doctor and leading authority on the practice of alternative and integrated medicine. He is founder and medical director of the Stengler Center for Integrative Medicine, Encinitas, California, and author of many books, including *The Natural Physician's Healing Therapies* (Bottom Line Books).

There might be a new way to measure the arterial health of older adults—and it's as easy as reaching for your toes from a seated position on the floor.

Researchers from Texas and Japan had 526 healthy volunteers ages 20 to 83 perform a simple stretch. Seated against a wall on the floor, each participant bent forward at the waist, extending the arms over the toes as far as possible. Based on the extent of their reach, researchers assigned each participant to a poor- or high-flexibility group with others matched for age, height and weight.

The investigators also measured other factors, such as the participants' blood pressure, cardiorespiratory fitness and muscle strength.

Findings: For people who were middle age (40 to 59) and older (60 to 83), trunk flexibility was a better predictor of arterial stiffness than any other measure of fitness. In younger people (20 to 39), trunk flexibility was not a better predictor.

Bottom line: This study might present a new way of looking at flexibility in middle-aged and older people—the more flexible they are, the better their arterial health. In the future, a simple flexibility test might determine who is at risk for heart attack or stroke, both of which often are preceded by arterial stiffness. Make flexibility training part of your fitness regimen by including 10 minutes of stretching daily.

More from Mark Stengler, NMD...

Drinking Coffee Aids Arterial Health

University of Athens researchers found that adults with high blood pressure who drank a specific amount of traditional Greek coffee—one to two cups daily—had 25% greater elasticity in their major blood vessels than those who drank less or more coffee. Greek coffee is prepared by boiling finely ground coffee in water.

Better Stroke Protection

In a study of 673 men and women who suffered ischemic strokes (due to impaired blood flow to the brain), those who performed aerobic exercise (such as brisk walking or swimming) at least four times weekly before their strokes were better able to perform daily tasks (such as bathing) and had fewer functional problems (related to driving, for example) than those who were less active.

Theory: Exercise promotes blood flow, building resilience to stroke-related neurological damage.

To help protect against the disabling effects of a stroke: After checking with your doctor, aim to exercise briskly (intensely enough to sweat) for at least 30 minutes most days.

James Meschia, MD, director, cerebrovascular division, Mayo Clinic, Jacksonville, Florida.

Stroke Rehab Made Easier

Yaffa Liebermann, PT, GCS, a physical therapist who is board certified by the American Physical Therapy Association and a geriatric clinical specialist. Founder and CEO of Prime Rehabilitation Services, Inc., in Tarrytown, New York, she has worked with stroke survivors for more than 30 years as a practicing physical therapist. Liebermann is the author of *Stroke Restoration: Functional Movements for Patients and Caregivers* (Prime Rehabilitation Services, Inc.).

Until relatively recently, doctors and physical therapists believed that a person who underwent physical rehabilitation immediately following a stroke would reach his/her maximum recovery within six months.

Now: Researchers have discovered that an intensive program of physical therapy can produce positive results for many stroke survivors far beyond this time frame.

Even though physical rehabilitation ideally begins as soon as possible after a stroke (to stimulate brain-cell function and help prevent joint stiffness and muscle weakness), the following techniques can be used by most people who are trying to regain function and mobility—no matter how long ago the stroke was experienced...*

SURVIVING A STROKE

There are approximately 5.5 million people in the US who have survived a stroke. About two-thirds of stroke survivors lose basic functional abilities, such as movement, speech and balance. Without enough blood, brain cells die and the abilities controlled by the parts of the brain affected by the stroke are lost.

The severity of the disability depends on the size of the stroke. Some who have a stroke may experience weakness in an arm or leg, but more extreme cases can involve paralysis.

Problem: Stroke rehabilitation (typically administered by a physical therapist) is offered at facilities across the US, but many stroke

*Before starting this regimen, discuss the strategies with your doctor and/or a physical therapist.

patients stop exercising when they complete their initial rehabilitation program.**

This is a an important issue since research shows that repetition is the best way to improve neuroplasticity—the brain's ability to "rewire" itself to promote recovery.

Solution: Stroke survivors can incorporate into their daily activities basic techniques that focus on three key areas that are crucial to continued rehabilitation. Because they are so simple and easy to perform, these strategies don't even feel like formal exercise and can be used with or without the help of a physical therapist.

STRATEGY 1
CHALLENGE THE WEAK SIDE

It's tempting, if you've had a stroke, to use the stronger side of your body. For example, you may prefer to put your weight on your stronger leg when you stand or use your stronger arm to perform tasks. However, you must shift weight to your weak side to regain movement.

What to do: To begin, bear your body weight as evenly as possible on both legs when you stand to improve muscle tone and normalize your movements. Use your stronger hand to support yourself and/or ask someone to stand beside you. You can practice this while standing behind a stable chair, holding on to a table or gripping a counter. Whenever possible, try to stand with equal weight on both feet.

Also helpful: If you have leg weakness, tap your feet whenever possible while standing or sitting. If you have weakness in an arm, use both hands to drum your fingers on a tabletop for several minutes each day. While seated, lean on your weak arm (for one to two minutes—but stop if you feel pain) while keeping your elbow straight. Repeat on your other arm. Do this several times daily.

STRATEGY 2
MASTER TRUNK CONTROL

The trunk—or core—of the body provides strength for virtually all movements. But if one side of the body is weakened, the corresponding side of the trunk is not as strong, which forces the other side to do more. Strengthening the trunk creates more stability, which improves posture and helps facilitate easier movement of the arms and legs.

What to do: If you've had a relatively mild stroke, observe yourself in a standing position in front of a full-length mirror. If you lean to one side, that is generally your stronger side. Even though you may think that you would know whether you have weakness in certain parts of your body, you should look in a mirror because it's common to reposition your body to accommodate an injury without even realizing it.

To strengthen your trunk: Do rotation exercises (on your own, if possible, or with the help of a physical therapist or family member). To begin, lie on your back in bed, bend your knees, then slowly move your legs from side to side. Do this for about 10 minutes or until you feel fatigued first thing in the morning and at bedtime.

Also helpful: Once you can stand from a seated position and distribute your weight evenly on both legs, stand near a waist-high surface, such as a desk or counter. In each hand, roll an object, such as a can or bottle, on the surface. Do this for about 10 minutes or until you feel fatigued.

For the lower body: Hold on to the back of a stable chair and lift one leg backward as high as you comfortably can without leaning forward. Hold the position for a few seconds, then repeat on the other side. Do three sets of 10 repetitions on each leg three times weekly. When this becomes easy, ask your doctor or physical therapist about adding a light ankle weight to each leg.

STRATEGY 3
USE THE POWER OF YOUR BREATH

Many people who suffer a stroke are greatly weakened by the experience and, as a result, may suffer from shortness of breath. But correct breathing techniques practiced in rehabilitation prepare patients to cope with stressful situations (such as stair climbing) and overcome shortness of breath.

**To locate a stroke rehabilitation center near you, contact the Commission on Accreditation of Rehabilitation Facilities (888-281-6531, *www.carf.org*).

What to do: To improve breathing skills, exhale twice as long as you inhale.

Example: A few times a day, inhale for a count of three and exhale for a count of six. Since deep inhalations may cause feelings of light-headedness in some stroke survivors, do not repeat the inhalation-exhalation series more than five times in a row.

If someone is able to gently massage your shoulders at the same time, this often helps release tension and promotes good airflow.

Make a game: Whenever you bend your trunk, exhale for a count of six, and inhale for a count of three when you straighten up.

Also, try exhaling when you reach for a cup or when you stoop down to retrieve an object. Then inhale as you sit back to drink or stand.

Better Stroke Recovery

When researchers reviewed 14 studies involving 429 stroke patients, they found that a lower-leg splint supporting the foot and ankle—designed to keep joints properly aligned—immediately helped patients walk faster and improved balance, while an upper-limb splint (such as a wrist splint) did not improve function.

If a loved one has suffered a stroke: Ask his/her physical therapist or podiatrist whether a lower-leg splint might improve your loved one's mobility and balance.

Sarah T. Tyson, PhD, physiotherapist, School of Health, Sport and Rehabilitation, University of Salford, Greater Manchester, England.

Antidepressant Aids Stroke Recovery

Stroke victims' learning and memory skills can be improved by the antidepressant Lexapro.

Recent finding: Stroke patients given a 12-week course of *escitalopram* (Lexapro) after a stroke had higher scores on tests of verbal and visual memory. The drug, a selective serotonin reuptake inhibitor (SSRI), helped stroke recovery even if given as much as three months after the stroke, although it should be administered as soon as possible.

Ricardo E. Jorge, MD, associate professor of psychiatry, Carver College of Medicine, University of Iowa, Iowa City, and leader of a study that tracked 129 nondepressed stroke patients, published in *Archives of General Psychiatry*.

Botox Can Help Stroke Patients

Recently, the FDA approved the use of Botox to treat elbow, wrist and finger spasticity that many stroke patients experience. The injections temporarily block connections between certain nerves and muscles, ending the spasms and improving patients' ability to grasp objects, dress themselves and perform other activities. Botox also may help relax leg and foot muscles in stroke patients.

Ralph L. Sacco, MD, president of the American Heart Association (*www.heart.org*). He is professor and chair of neurology, Miller School of Medicine, University of Miami, Florida, and neurologist-in-chief, Jackson Memorial Hospital, both in Miami, Florida.

23

Cancer Risks & Prevention

Symptoms That Can Be Red Flags for Cancer

If you are one of the estimated 1.5 million people in the US who will be told "you have cancer" this year, much of your medical fate will depend on how advanced the malignancy is when it is diagnosed.

When cancer is caught early—before the abnormal cells multiply and spread—the odds of defeating the disease improve dramatically.

Problem: Because cancer is tricky—early symptoms most often (but not always) are painless, and they often mimic common noncancerous conditions—many people ignore red flags that could help them get an early diagnosis.

For the best possible chance of beating cancer: Be alert for subtle symptoms of the disease. Here are nine such cancer symptoms that you should never ignore—and how to distinguish them from more benign causes.*

1. Difficulty swallowing. When you swallow, you've probably had the uncomfortable or painful experience of food getting "stuck"—for example, high in the esophagus or in the middle of the upper chest.

It may be cancer if: You have this sensation all or most times that you eat, and it's usually not painful. Difficulty swallowing is common in people with esophageal or stomach cancer and may be a sign that a tumor is obstructing the esophagus or that inflammation and scarring have narrowed the opening. Inflammation can be a precursor to cancer and also can indicate that a malignant tumor has irritated surrounding healthy tissue.

*Important: If you have a troubling symptom that is not listed in this article, see your doctor.

Amy P. Abernethy, MD, program director of the Duke Cancer Care Research Program and associate director of the Cancer Control Program at the Duke Comprehensive Cancer Center, both in Durham, North Carolina. Dr. Abernethy is also an associate professor of medicine in the division of medical oncology at the Duke University Medical Center.

Because difficulty swallowing evolves slowly, many people adjust the way they eat, taking smaller bites, chewing longer and perhaps even switching to a diet that is mostly liquid. If eating becomes difficult—for any reason—see a doctor.

2. Excessive bleeding and/or unexplained bruising. Leukemia causes a shortage of blood platelets (cellular elements responsible for clotting), which results in easy and excessive bleeding and unexplained bruising. (Normal bleeding, such as that caused by a cut, should stop after application of direct pressure.)

It may be cancer if: You have an unusual number of unexplained nosebleeds (for example, not due to dry air, a common trigger) and/or develop unexplained bruises (a change in frequency or severity from the norm) that tend to be painful when touched, dark purple and large (the size of a fist or bigger).

Important: Bleeding gums may be a sign of poor dental care or a serious medical problem, such as leukemia. If brushing causes bleeding, see your dentist for an evaluation to determine the cause.

3. Exhaustion. Everyone gets tired, but extreme fatigue due to cancer is quite different. Although all cancers can cause fatigue, this symptom is most common with colon cancer, leukemia and other cancers that may cause anemia.

It may be cancer if: For no apparent reason, you experience overwhelming and debilitating fatigue similar to that caused by the flu.

Important: Fatigue due to cancer is sometimes mistaken for depression.

Key difference: A person with depression often lacks the will and desire to perform daily activities, while a person with cancer-related fatigue wants to stay active but lacks the physical ability to do so.

4. Fever and night sweats. The presence of cancer causes a storm of chemical processes as the body ramps up its immune defenses to fight cancer cells. Fever is one indication that your immune system is fending off an illness, such as a cold or the flu, or even cancer.

It may be cancer if: You have fevers (typically 100°F or higher) that come and go over a period of days or weeks. Cancer-related fevers occur most often at night—often along with drenching night sweats.

Important: Menopausal women often have hot flashes that may lead to night sweats—but sweats due to menopause also occur during the day. Anyone who experiences night sweats—including menopausal women who have night sweats but experience no daytime hot flashes—should see a doctor.

5. Lumps. Any new, firm, painless lump that is growing in size or that is bigger than a nickel should be immediately examined by a doctor. Worrisome lumps typically feel firmer than the tip of your nose, while spongy or painful lumps are less of a concern. Lumps can be caused by several types of cancer, including breast, testicular and throat malignancies, and melanoma (skin cancer).

The immune response launched by your body when it is fighting a serious disease—including cancer—may lead to enlarged lymph nodes (the small filtering structures that help prevent foreign particles from entering the bloodstream). Painful and/or swollen lymph nodes are common signs of infection and usually return to normal size within a few days of the infection resolving.

It may be cancer if: Enlarged lymph nodes do not return to normal size and/or have the characteristics described above.

Helpful: Lymph nodes can be found throughout the body, but enlarged ones are easiest to feel behind the neck (at the base of the skull or behind the ears)…in the armpit… in the groin (at the junction of the torso and leg)…in the hollowed space above the collarbone (clavicle)…in back of the knee…and at the crook of the elbow.

6. Persistent cough. Longtime smokers get used to coughing, so they tend not to notice this important symptom of lung cancer. Nonsmokers can experience persistent cough as well, which also can be a symptom of other cancers, including malignancies of the throat and esophagus.

It may be cancer if: You have a cough—with or without breathlessness—that persists for longer than one month. Coughing up blood also can be a cancer symptom.

7. Skin changes. Most people know that changes in a mole can be a sign of skin cancer. But the moles that are most prone to cancerous changes are the type that are flat (as opposed to raised or bumpy in shape).

It may be cancer if: You have a mole that becomes darker…changes color…changes shape (especially in an asymmetrical pattern)…or grows larger. Guidelines recommend seeing a doctor if you have a mole that grows larger than a pencil eraser, but don't wait to see your doctor if you have a mole that undergoes any of the changes described above.

Important: A sore that doesn't heal also can be skin cancer. (In healthy people, most superficial wounds heal within days.)

8. Stumbles or falls. If you suddenly become "clumsy," it may signal a neurological problem, such as nerve damage from diabetes or multiple sclerosis, or it could be a sign of a brain tumor.

It may be cancer if: Your clumsiness is accompanied by confusion, difficulty concentrating and an inability to move your arms and/or legs. Although paralysis is an obvious sign that something is wrong, it is rarely the first sign of a brain tumor. Check with your doctor immediately if your body's basic functions change in any way.

9. Unexplained weight loss. If you experience significant weight loss (about 10 pounds or more) that is not a result of an intentional weight-loss regimen, it often is a symptom of a potentially serious medical condition, such as cancer or depression.

It may be cancer if: Weight loss is due to a reduced appetite. Always see your doctor promptly if you experience unexplained weight loss.

How to Save Your Life If You Have Cancer

Mark R. Fesen, MD, oncologist, clinical associate professor at University of Kansas Medical School, Kansas City, and a member of the department of oncology at Hutchinson Clinic, Hutchinson, Kansas. He has trained at the National Cancer Institute and is a Fellow of the American College of Physicians. He is author of *Surviving the Cancer System: An Empowering Guide to Taking Control of Your Care* (Amacom). *www.hutchclinic.com.*

Panic typically follows a cancer diagnosis. Few patients can think clearly about their choices. The usual response is to stop thinking and to let their doctors (or their loved ones) make decisions for them.

This is understandable—but it can be harmful to the patient. Even at the best hospitals, cancer care tends to be chaotic. The primary physician might not know what the oncologist is doing. The oncologist might not communicate with, or might disagree with, the surgeon or radiologist.

Here's how to take charge of your care…

UNDERSTAND YOUR PATHOLOGY REPORT

It contains critical information about the type of cancer you have and how advanced it is. These reports are based on the microscopic findings of a biopsy.

It's rare for a biopsy to be completely incorrect, but even slight points of confusion can lead to ineffective treatments.

Example: One of my cousins passed away after he was diagnosed with a spinal tumor. The pathology report said that the tumor originated in the large intestine. Years later, I reexamined the biopsy sample and discovered that what he really had was a lung cancer—which requires totally different treatments.

Get a copy of your report, and talk to your oncologist to find out what everything means. Does the report seem to waffle with words or phrases such as "ranging from" or "possible"? These indicate that there's uncertainty about the findings. You need to understand if the tumor is "aggressive" or "slow-changing," or whether the cells are "poorly differentiated" (which means it might be hard to identify the specific cancer).

Important: You may want to get a second pathology opinion, particularly if the diagnosis seems unusual for someone of your age or lifestyle.

CHOOSE YOUR ONCOLOGIST

The oncologist is the point person who will supervise—and, in many cases, determine—your treatments. You want someone who is more than just an expert. He/she should also be a good listener…understand your concerns about quality of life…and help you cope with the emotional upheaval. *Here's how to find such a person…*

• **Talk to people you know.** A good oncologist will have a reputation in the community for being helpful as well as knowledgeable. A doctor might be a world-class expert, but that won't help if he/she won't return phone calls or always shifts your care to an assistant.

• **Plan a tryout.** Before committing to one oncologist, schedule a tryout visit to decide if you can trust this person with your life.

Helpful: Listen for "we" statements, such as, "We need to treat this" or "We have to get these tests done." The use of "we" instead of "you" is a good clue that the doctor plans to be closely involved with your care.

BOND WITH YOUR DOCTOR

Cancer patients are understandably frightened, which can make them difficult and/or argumentative. Many oncologists avoid or even drop difficult patients. Be respectful and courteous. Try to get to know your oncologist and his/her staff. Whenever possible, meet with your oncologist face-to-face, rather than telephoning or e-mailing your concerns.

Just as you would expect your sister-in-law or trusted uncle to give you the real scoop, when you make the oncologist your friend, you may get a more complete opinion.

BRING A SECOND SET OF EARS

Whenever possible, bring a friend or family member every time you meet with the oncologist. Most patients are too anxious to concentrate on details, including information about follow-up tests, treatment plans, etc. A friend or relative can take notes for you and ask pertinent questions.

DECIDE WHERE YOU'LL GET THE BEST TREATMENT

It's usually advisable to go to a hospital or cancer center close to where you live. This is where you are at your most comfortable and where the emotional support of your family and friends is at its strongest. Also, complications, such as infections and blood clots, are common in cancer patients. You might need emergency care, and it's always preferable to see doctors who know your history.

In general, I advise patients to go to a major cancer center only if they already live near one of these institutions…have a rare cancer… or require specialized treatments or surgery that can be provided only by a leading institution. Patients who are candidates for research studies also may benefit by going to a major center.

LISTEN TO YOUR DOCTOR, NOT THE "BOARD"

In large cancer centers, patient treatments are routinely reviewed, and sometimes guided by, recommendations from a "tumor board." This is a weekly discussion group that may include surgeons, medical oncologists and radiation oncologists, among other specialists. You can and should receive a written copy of the board's opinions. Ask for a transcript.

The problem: A tumor board is a good source of second opinions and specialized knowledge, but most of the doctors who attend have never seen the individual patient and may not be aware of his/her unique circumstances.

Follow the treatment suggestions of the oncologist who has interviewed and examined you directly—even if his conclusions differ from those of the tumor board.

ASK ABOUT RESEARCH STUDIES

This is mainly an issue for patients who are getting treatment at major cancer centers (which focus on research) or those with rare or difficult-to-treat cancers. Clinical trials may offer patients the best treatment, but there's no guarantee of this. No one should delay mainstream treatment in hope of being accepted into a clinical trial.

Patients who are seriously ill can lose valuable time when they wait to be admitted into a study. Patients often think that getting into a study means that they're going to get a better drug or therapy. Not necessarily. I've seen many patients in these studies get worse because the "cutting-edge" treatment turned out to be inferior to the already available treatments.

Caution: If you're a candidate for studies, pick one carefully. Review the study and your circumstances with your doctor (not someone who is involved with the study). Patients who participate in clinical trials may be prohibited from participating in certain other clinical trials. Understand whether this applies to you before you sign up for any clinical trial.

What Do All Those Cancer Stages *Really* Mean?

Sunil M. Patel, MD, a medical oncologist/hematologist and assistant professor in the general oncology department at the University of Texas MD Anderson Cancer Center and MD Anderson Regional Care Center–Katy, both in Houston. He is board certified in internal medicine, hematology and medical oncology. Dr. Patel's clinical interests include solid and hematologic malignancies, with a focus on melanoma and cancers of the lung and breast.

Whenever we hear about someone having cancer, usually included in the news is what particular "stage" cancer he/she has.

In general, cancers with lower stages are easier to treat and have a more promising outlook than those with higher designations. But sometimes the numbers don't tell the whole story. Other factors, such as your overall health and type of cancer, may affect prognosis and treatment.

Important: Cancer staging is merely a guide. It determines how much cancer is in the

body and where it is located to aid prognosis and treatment—but it cannot predict the result of a person's battle with cancer. *What to consider when breaking down the numbers...*

TYPES OF STAGING

When a person is first diagnosed, and before starting treatment, he will have tests to determine the type and the extent of the cancer.

•**Clinical staging.** This battery of tests measures how much cancer is present and helps the oncologist identify the best treatment. Typical tests: Physical exam, imaging tests (such as CT, MRI or PET scans or ultrasound) and tumor biopsies. For some cancers, results of other tests, such as blood tests, are also used in staging.

•**Pathological staging.** This type of staging, also known as surgical staging, is based on tissue obtained during surgery to remove the cancer and nearby lymph nodes. It delivers more precise data that's used to predict responses and outcomes. Pathological staging also occurs after exploratory surgery, which determines how much cancer is present in the body and may remove tissue samples.

Ideally, clinical and pathological staging should complement each other. However, not all cancers are staged by analyzing the size of the original tumor and whether the cancer has spread. For example, it's not used for leukemia, because this cancer affects the blood and bone marrow, or brain cancer, which tends to spread throughout the brain only.

ELEMENTS OF STAGING

The American Joint Committee on Cancer, made up of academic physicians, epidemiologists, nurses and statisticians, developed the TNM classification system for staging most cancers. TNM stands for primary **tumor**, regional lymph **nodes** and distant **metastasis**. The TNM system was first developed in the 1940s and is continuously revised based on new discoveries and treatments for different cancers. *It looks at three main factors...*

•**T** indicates the size of the primary (original) tumor and whether the tumor has penetrated into nearby tissue.

The higher the T number, the more dangerous the tumor with regard to size and whether it has penetrated nearby tissue. A T1 tumor is relatively small...a T2 or T3 tumor will be larger...and a T4 tumor is the largest and/or has penetrated the deepest.

The actual sizes of tumors with different T numbers will vary depending on the type of cancer. A T1 tumor of the breast, for example, will be less than two centimeters (about an inch), whereas T2, T3 and T4 tumors are larger. *Other T values...*

TX means that the tumor can't be measured at the time of diagnosis. For example, tests might indicate that cancer has spread to one or more lymph nodes, but imaging tests that would visualize the tumor haven't yet been done.

T0 means that there's no evidence of a primary tumor. This doesn't mean that the tumor doesn't exist. It just means that it can't be located.

Tis means that a tumor is in situ (precancerous). Cancerlike cells are present, but only growing in the most superficial layer of tissue.

•**N** describes whether the cancer has spread to regional (nearby) lymph nodes. The more lymph nodes with evidence of cancer, and the farther away these nodes are from the original tumor, the greater the extent of the spread.

N1, N2 or N3 describes the size, location and/or number of lymph nodes involved and indicates how the cancer has spread. Higher numbers indicate a greater degree of lymph node involvement—and, in most cases, a poorer prognosis.

The N numbers don't necessarily indicate the exact number of lymph nodes with signs of cancer. A designation of N3 could mean that cancer is present in several lymph nodes...in one very large lymph node...or in bilateral lymph nodes (for example, in both sides of the neck). *Other N values...*

NX means that the regional spread of the cancer cannot be determined because the lymph nodes cannot be evaluated.

N0 means that there's no cancer in nearby lymph nodes, a very promising finding.

•**M** describes the spread (or metastasis) of cancer to distant areas of the body. Cancers that have spread beyond the regional area of the original tumor can sometimes be treated but are rarely cured. The risk for recurrence is high.

However, there are exceptions. With colon cancer, for example, the cancer often spreads to the liver. Between 10% and 20% of these patients can be cured with a combination of surgery, radiation and/or chemotherapy.

M1 indicates that a cancer has spread out of the immediate area to distant organs or tissue. MX means metastasis can't be evaluated. A designation of M0 means that no distant metastases were found.

CRUNCHING THE NUMBERS

Once these TNM system values are determined, they are combined to come up with an overall stage number for the cancer (I to IV for most cancers). *Examples...*

•**A woman might be diagnosed with a T1, N0, M0 breast cancer.** This means that the primary tumor is less than two centimeters in the largest dimension (in any direction)...there's no lymph node involvement...and the cancer hasn't spread to distant areas of the body. This would be considered stage I cancer.

•**Or a woman could have T3, N2, M0 breast cancer.** This would indicate a large tumor that has spread to nearby lymph nodes but not to other parts of the body. This would be designated a stage III cancer.

GRADE: A FOURTH FACTOR

For some cancers, other factors may affect staging. Oncologists might consider a tumor's grade—how abnormal the cancer cells look (usually assigned 1 to 4) under a microscope. *Cancers with more abnormal-looking cells (a higher number) tend to grow and spread faster...*

•**Normal cells.** After a biopsy—or, in some cases, after the removal of the entire tumor—a pathologist examines individual cells. The more the cells resemble normal tissue, the less aggressive the cancer is likely to be.

•**Abnormal cells.** Conversely, the cells might look highly abnormal.

STAGING AND TREATMENTS

People with the same stage and type of cancer tend to have similar survival rates and often respond similarly to treatments. Staging allows oncologists to make an accurate prognosis and helps to identify the best treatments.

Examples: Women with T1, N0 breast cancer (stage I)—small primary tumor and no cancer in lymph nodes—tend to do well. Those with T2, N0 breast cancer (stage II)—larger primary tumor and no cancer in lymph nodes—do almost (but not quite) as well. The slight difference in outcome is reflected in this stage difference.

For most cancers, the treatment options include surgery, radiation or chemotherapy or a combination of the three. The choice of specific treatments depends on both the tumor type and stage.

A CRITICAL STEP

For a person with newly diagnosed cancer, getting clear information regarding the type of cancer and stage is critical. Occasionally, doctors disagree about the diagnosis or stage in a given situation—a second opinion can give you a different perspective.

What Medical Studies Mean for You

Charles B. Inlander is a consumer advocate and health-care consultant based in Fogelsville, Pennsylvania. He was the founding president of the nonprofit People's Medical Society, a consumer advocacy organization credited with key improvements in the quality of US health care in the 1980s and 1990s, and is the author of 20 books, including *Take This Book to the Hospital with You: A Consumer Guide to Surviving Your Hospital Stay* (St. Martin's).

In 1986, when I was 40 years old, my father was diagnosed with prostate cancer. He was successfully treated and lived 13 more years, dying at age 90. His cancer was discovered because his prostate specific antigen (PSA) levels were quite high—a sign of a possible prostate malignancy. Knowing that prostate cancer risk is higher in men whose fathers or broth-

ers have the disease, I went to my doctor and asked for a PSA test. He told me that studies had not found the test to be beneficial for men under age 50 and that my health insurer was unlikely to pay for it. But my doctor agreed that because of my family history, I should be tested annually. I had the PSA test, and the results were normal. My insurer refused to pay because the test was not recommended at that time by any major health organization for men under age 50, but I appealed, had my doctor write a letter to the insurer and, ultimately, I was reimbursed for the test. Today, the PSA test is routinely recommended for men age 50 and older…and for younger men if there is history of prostate cancer in the family. And generally, insurers pay for it.

I was reminded of this situation when the US Preventive Services Task Force (USPSTF) recently issued some controversial recommendations regarding mammography. According to some press reports, the USPSTF had concluded that women under age 50 do not benefit from routine mammograms and should not get them. But that wasn't the full story! What the task force said was that only limited clinical evidence showed that mammography offered a significant benefit for healthy women under age 50 but that women in this age group who have a history of breast cancer in their families or an increased risk for the disease due to such factors as a genetic mutation or a history of chest radiation should discuss the optimal frequency for mammography with their doctors. In other words, women should do what I did in 1986—talk to their doctors and arrive at an appropriate personal decision. *My advice on interpreting recommendations…*

• **Stay current.** Recommendations do change. In the mid-1990s, it was recommended that only men ages 35 to 65 and women ages 45 to 65 get routine cholesterol screening. Those guidelines were in place until 2001 when the USPSTF recommended that all men age 35 and older and all women age 45 and older get routine cholesterol screening.*

*The USPSTF revised its recommendations again in 2008 to state that adult women, regardless of their age, should get routine cholesterol screening only if they have heart disease risk factors.

Helpful: To stay current on medical recommendations related to any condition you may have, consult reliable sources of information, such as the Centers for Disease Control and Prevention (*www.cdc.gov*) and the National Institutes of Health (*www.nih.gov*).

●**Keep the focus on yourself.** Widespread recommendations, such as the ones mentioned above, are meant to help doctors and health insurers decide who should get certain tests and how often.

Helpful: Remember that your situation is unique, and let your doctor be your guide regarding routine screening tests.

Vitamin C—A Natural Form of Chemotherapy

Mark A. Stengler, NMD, licensed naturopathic medical doctor and leading authority on the practice of alternative and integrated medicine. He is founder and medical director of the Stengler Center for Integrative Medicine, Encinitas, California, and associate clinical professor at the National College of Natural Medicine, Portland, Oregon. He is author of *The Natural Physician's Healing Therapies* (Bottom Line Books).

Most people have never heard of intravenous (IV) vitamin C, and yet it is one of the best alternative therapies to fight cancer. As most people know, vitamin C is an antioxidant with an immune-boosting effect. But when I—and a host of other natural physicians—administer it at very high doses, it plays an altogether different role, acting like a type of natural chemotherapy and killing cancer cells. When used in conjunction with regular chemotherapy, IV vitamin C works right alongside it, helping to kill cancer cells while also boosting the immune system and helping the body to rid itself of unwanted waste products.

At my clinic, I use IV vitamin C treatment for patients at all stages of cancer. All of these patients are also under the care of an oncologist. I give IV vitamin C to cancer patients at the outset of their treatment, to those who have tried conventional treatments to no avail and to those in remission who want an immune system boost. For patients with terminal disease, it helps to improve quality of life by increasing their energy and reducing nausea.

The use of vitamins in the treatment of cancer is controversial, extending back 40 years to when Nobel Laureate Linus Pauling, PhD, first proposed the use of high-dose vitamin C in the treatment of cancer. Many oncologists today remain skeptical about using any type of vitamin therapy in the treatment of cancer. Cancer specialists maintain that some types of chemotherapy and radiation kill cancer cells by generating large numbers of destructive free radicals. Because vitamin C is an antioxidant, they believe that it will neutralize these free radicals and reduce the effectiveness of chemotherapy and radiation.

I think this view is simplistic. At low doses (under 25 grams, or 25,000 milligrams), vitamin C's antioxidant properties do help to neutralize disease-causing free radicals. But at doses higher than 25 grams, vitamin C has a pro-oxidant effect that exploits a weakness in the biochemistry of cancer cells and increases production of hydrogen peroxide, an acid that has been shown to kill cancer cells without harming healthy cells.

It's impossible to achieve the required high concentrations of vitamin C through oral supplements alone. The body regulates the amount of vitamin C that can be absorbed through the gut, and very large amounts of the vitamin will cause diarrhea. Intravenous vitamin C bypasses this problem because it goes directly into the bloodstream. I provide my patients with IV vitamin C in the office. They lie comfortably in a reclining chair during a one- to two-hour treatment session, at which time they receive doses of 30 grams to 75 grams of vitamin C.

PROMISING RESEARCH

The benefits of IV vitamin C for cancer patients has been demonstrated in studies, including those by researchers at the National Institutes of Health. Laboratory studies have shown that IV vitamin C kills cancer cells but not normal cells. Other research has shown the benefit of this treatment for terminally ill patients. A Korean study found that a combination of IV and oral vitamin C improved quality of life, reducing nausea and increasing energy in terminally ill patients.

Most researchers agree that data from large clinical trials is needed. Several clinical trials currently are under way to assess the effect of IV vitamin C and other antioxidants on different types of cancers.

WHAT TO DO

Many oncologists will not advocate vitamin therapy in any form.

My advice: While you're undergoing conventional therapy, look for a medical doctor or naturopathic physician experienced in IV therapies to work with your oncologist. You and your doctors can decide whether to administer IV vitamins during or immediately after receiving conventional therapies. Your doctor will determine the number of treatments you need. Some patients get one or two IV vitamin C infusions weekly for the first year after diagnosis and initial treatment for cancer, and then every other week for a few years to help prevent cancer cells from returning and to boost the immune system.

Large amounts of vitamin C are nontoxic and generally safe for everyone except those with kidney failure, who can't tolerate large amounts. In addition, a small percentage of people are deficient in the enzyme *glucose-6-phosphate dehydrogenase* (G6PD), which is needed to maintain normal red blood cells. Without this enzyme, large amounts of vitamin C can cause hemolytic anemia, a type of anemia that involves the abnormal breakdown of red blood cells. Before receiving IV vitamin C, ask your doctor to test you for this deficiency. If you have it, you should not have IV vitamin C.

Note that patients' response to cancer treatment of any kind varies, and no physician can ever know for certain how a tumor will respond to a specific treatment.

Cold Kills Cancer

Doctors can now perform cryotherapy, which freezes and destroys tumor cells, through a nick in the skin. It may be effective for many cancers, including breast and ovarian.

Wayne State University.

Vanishing Cancers

Keith I. Block, MD, director of integrative medical education at University of Illinois College of Medicine and medical director of Block Center for Integrative Cancer Treatment in Evanston, Illinois. He is founder and scientific director of the nonprofit Institute for Cancer Research and Education. He is editor in chief of *Integrative Cancer Therapies* and author of *Life Over Cancer* (Bantam). *www.blockmd.com.*

A common belief about cancer is that it is an irreversible process. Normal cells become malignant and grow uncontrollably. The only way to stop the process is to remove or kill the cancer through surgery, chemotherapy and/or radiation. Cancer doesn't just disappear.

That belief is proving to be untrue. In a recent study in *Archives of Internal Medicine*, researchers from Norway and the US analyzed the six-year incidence of invasive breast cancer in two very similar groups of Norwegian women.

About 119,000 of the women had mammograms every two years. Another 110,000 women in the study had not had mammograms and then had one mammogram.

To the surprise of the researchers, the six-year incidence of breast cancer in the two groups was quite different. The more frequently screened group had a 22% higher incidence of breast cancer.

So, what caused less cancer to be found in the second group? The intriguing theory is that cancer did indeed start in this group at an equal rate…and then spontaneously disappeared without ever being noticed (because the women were not being screened).

Other research has shown that spontaneous regression of cancer occurs in cases of advanced melanoma, advanced kidney cancer and neuroblastoma (a childhood cancer of nerve tissue). Regression also occurs in colonic adenomas (precancerous growths of the colon) and in precancerous lesions of the cervix.

Keith I. Block, MD, one of America's top integrative cancer therapy experts, explains that the number of documented cases of spontaneous cancer remission is quite low. He estimates that only one in 500 cancer tumors regress without surgery, chemotherapy or radiation treatment.

However, he suggests that the unalterable, one-way trajectory of cancer is an outdated paradigm.

Cancer is not only mutagenic—propelled by damage to DNA—it also is mitogenic and the growth (mitogenesis) of cancer cells may be stopped by inhibiting molecular signaling and correcting disruption in the body's internal biochemical environment. This can be influenced by lifestyle factors that are alterable through personal choices.

WHY CANCERS VANISH

There are three main factors that can cause a cancer to regress…

•**Innate biology.** Some people are born with a naturally stronger constitution that is capable of stopping a cancer before it takes firm hold.

•**Transformation of the body's biochemical and molecular environment.** Many lifestyle factors influence the body's inner biochemical and molecular environment, including what you eat, how much you exercise and how much stress you're under.

The latest research shows that positive lifestyle factors can influence genes by turning on the tumor-suppressor genes and turning off the tumor-promoting genes.

•**Better communication.** This includes two types of communication—biochemical communication between cells and emotional communication with yourself and others.

What happens: In a normal biochemical environment, one cell sends a message to another, Don't grow, I'm using this space. One reason tumor cells can divide and grow is that they don't receive this message.

The breakdown in communication is fundamental in the biology of cancer in other ways. Studies show that meditation—one way to communicate with your inner spirit—reduces cancer-causing inflammation.

Close personal relationships also are relevant. A preclinical study from researchers at the University of Chicago suggested that social isolation and its impact on stress resulted in a greater than threefold increase in the onset of breast cancer.

STEPS YOU CAN TAKE

Various lifestyle factors can strengthen you against cancer…

•**Exercise and fitness.** Numerous studies link increased physical activity to lower incidence of cancers of the colon, lung, prostate, testicles, breast, ovaries and uterus.

Exercise counters many cancer-causing biological factors, including cancer-fueling molecules called growth factors…oxidative stress (a kind of internal rust)…a weakened immune system…and poor response to inflammation. Aim for a minimum of 30 minutes of aerobic exercise daily, which can be divided into multiple sessions.

•**Whole-foods diet.** The right diet deprives a tumor of the compounds it most likes to feed on and supplies you with nutrients that help your body keep malignant cells in check.

Example: The Japanese have long had a diet rich in land and sea vegetables and fish—and low in meat, refined sugars and high-fat foods. Japan also has lower cancer rates than the US and better survival rates. For instance, men in Japan and the US are equally likely to have very early prostate cancer—the kind that never causes clinical problems—but American men have much higher rates of the clinical type that can lead to advanced prostate cancer.

Bottom line: If you eat too much dietary fat and refined carbohydrates, you run the risk of increasing body fat and weight while weakening your immune system and increasing oxidative stress, inflammation and blood levels of substances that promote tumors.

•**Power foods.** There are "power foods" rich in phytochemicals that are uniquely anticancer. These include turmeric…grapes (with the phytochemical resveratrol)…green tea…milk thistle…ginger…and pomegranate.

But to get enough turmeric, resveratrol and all the rest, you would have to eat curry and guzzle grape juice until you exploded.

Best: Supplements and concentrates, such as "green drinks," often sold in health-food stores. Talk to your doctor about the best supplements for you.

•**Stress reduction.** Chronic anxiety and stress contribute to cancer's ability to thrive in your body.

What happens: Stress triggers biochemistry that is procancer—high levels of certain growth factors…an excess of oxidation-causing free radicals…high blood sugar…and raging inflammation.

Techniques such as relaxed abdominal breathing, progressive muscle relaxation and calming imagery can help you create emotional ease.

IF YOU HAVE CANCER

The fact that a cancer can vanish without conventional treatments is important knowledge for a person diagnosed with cancer and for his/her doctor. However, a patient should never simply wait for a cancer to disappear. Getting started quickly on a plan of care can be essential for one's survival—losing time can be detrimental, even life-threatening.

Promising Vaccine

An experimental vaccine for *mesothelioma*, a rare cancer primarily associated with asbestos exposure, increases antibodies that can potentially suppress tumor growth. Researchers hope that this finding may one day improve survival rates for people who have mesothelioma.

American Journal of Respiratory and Critical Care Medicine.

Hallucinogen Helps Patients with Advanced Cancer

When given *psilocybin*, patients reported improvements in anxiety and depression.

None experienced harmful psychological changes that can occur with hallucinogens.

Archives of General Psychiatry.

Another Reason to Diet

Excess body fat causes 100,000 cases of cancer in the US every year. It is the underlying cause of 49% of endometrial cancers…35% of esophageal cancers…28% of pancreatic cancers…and 24% of kidney cancers. It also causes some cases of gallbladder, breast and colorectal cancers.

Estimates by American Institute for Cancer Research, reported in *University of California, Berkeley Wellness Letter*, 500 Fifth Avenue, New York City 10110.

Should You Get a "Virtual" Colonoscopy?

David H. Kim, MD, associate professor of radiology and the residency program director at the University of Wisconsin School of Medicine and Public Health in Madison. He is a researcher in computed tomographic colonography and the lead author of multiple studies, including recent analyses published in *The New England Journal of Medicine* and in *Radiology*.

Until recently, most doctors agreed that the "gold standard" for the screening of colorectal cancer was conventional colonoscopy. Also known as optical colonoscopy, this procedure allows the doctor to view the inside of a patient's colon with a camera that is attached to the end of a long, flexible tube that is inserted into the rectum and colon.

Now: A large study recently reported in *The New England Journal of Medicine* found that computed tomographic (CT) colonography—also known as "virtual" colonoscopy—may be just as effective as a colorectal screening tool as conventional colonoscopy—without carrying a risk for colon perforation (damage to the intestinal wall).

What you need to know about your options for colonoscopy...*

A PREVENTABLE CANCER

Cancers arise from growths (polyps) over the course of 10 to 15 years. If every eligible adult had a colonoscopy to detect and remove these growths, the vast majority of cancers could be prevented. However, only about half of American adults who should be screened for colorectal cancer actually undergo any type of testing.

Why are so many people avoiding this potentially lifesaving form of cancer screening?

PROS AND CONS OF SCREENING TESTS

Any pain related to conventional colonoscopy is typically well controlled by sedation, but the exam requires a 24-hour bowel preparation, including a liquid diet and medications that cause diarrhea to cleanse the colon. When receiving conventional colonoscopy, most patients spend about half a day at a hospital or clinic, and they must arrange transportation because they are not allowed to drive after being sedated.

CT colonography also requires a colon cleanse, but the test itself takes only about 15 to 20 minutes. No sedation is given, so people who drive can take themselves home.

For these reasons, many medical experts believe that more Americans will undergo screening for colorectal cancer when CT colonography becomes more widely available—about 17% of US hospitals currently offer CT colonography services. The American Cancer Society now includes CT colonography as one of its recommended tests for colorectal cancer screening.

Key issues that influence the effectiveness of colonoscopy—and how each method stacks up...

• **"Hidden" polyps.** Conventional colonoscopy is very effective, but there are problem

*Men and women at average risk of developing colorectal cancer should start screening for colorectal cancer at age 50, or earlier if they have a personal history of colorectal cancer or polyps, a history of chronic inflammatory bowl disease, a strong family history of colorectal cancer or polyps, or known family history of hereditary colorectal cancer syndromes.

areas that the camera can't see, including the back side of folds and the right side of the colon. Skilled doctors can often minimize these "blind spots" during conventional colonoscopy, but those areas appear to be easier to view with CT colonography.

• **Polyp size.** The high-definition cameras and computer monitors that are often used in conventional colonoscopy allow the doctor to examine the intestinal lining in crisp detail.

Small polyps (less than 5/16 inch) can be more difficult to see on a CT scan compared with conventional colonoscopy. Some experts argue that any missed growth is unacceptable—that conventional colonoscopy, at least for now, is superior because it's more likely to detect small polyps and possibly flat lesions that can lead to colon cancer.

It's important to note, however, that fewer than three in 10,000 growths smaller than 3/16 inch are cancerous. Moreover, the few tiny polyps that could develop into cancer in the future could be removed at a later screening, when they have grown larger and before they change to cancer.

• **Incidental findings.** Conventional colonoscopy examines only the intestinal wall. Since a CT scan has a field of view that encompasses tissues and organs beyond the intestine, 7.4% to 11.4% of people who undergo CT colonography are found to have abnormalities, including life-threatening conditions, such as an aortic aneurysm (an abnormal swelling in the wall of the body's main artery), that might have gone undetected without the test.

However, incidental findings can lead to batteries of expensive tests to investigate abnormalities that usually turn out to be harmless. About 2% of screened people have findings beyond the colon that turn out to be significant and require treatment.

• **Repeat testing.** With CT colonography, people who have growths that need to be biopsied or removed will require a subsequent conventional colonoscopy.

My advice: People with normal colon cancer risk factors are good candidates for CT colonography. Among average-risk people, about 10% will need conventional colonoscopy as well. If you're at high risk for polyps and/or cancer (due to a personal history of an inflammatory bowel disease, for example), it's usually better to have a conventional colonoscopy.

Before scheduling a CT test: Ask the doctor whether a subsequent colonoscopy, if needed, can be performed the same day. This saves you from having to repeat the bowel-prep procedure.

• **Risks.** With conventional colonoscopy, perforation—which typically leads to surgical removal of part of the injured colon and can, in rare cases, cause death—occurs in about one in 1,000 procedures. CT colonography doesn't require the insertion of a lengthy optical tube, although a small tube is inserted a few inches into the rectum to inflate the colon with carbon dioxide gas so that the intestinal wall can be easily viewed. There's virtually no risk for perforation during the CT procedure.

Recent finding: With conventional colonoscopy, research shows that the complication risk (including perforation) rises with age in adults age 65 and older.

• **Radiation.** If you're concerned about radiation exposure, you may choose to avoid CT colonography. Depending on the imaging machine, patients are exposed to 50 to 100 times the radiation that they would get from a single chest X-ray.

To put this into perspective, someone who lives in Denver is exposed to about the same amount of radiation each year—from cosmic rays and radon—as is used in two CT colonographies.

• **Cost and insurance.** Medicare currently does not cover CT colonography (cost: about $400 to $800) as a mass screening procedure, but that may change considering recent data that now supports the use of this technology in older adults. Conventional colonoscopy (cost: about $1,500) is covered by most insurance plans. While conventional colonoscopy is usually repeated every 10 years, CT colonography is typically performed every five years.

CONVENTIONAL VS. "VIRTUAL" COLONOSCOPY

Conventional colonoscopy and "virtual" colonoscopy—known as computed tomographic (CT) colonography—are good tests for detecting polyps that could turn into colon cancer. *Strengths and weaknesses of each...*

	Conventional Colonoscopy	CT Colonography
One procedure to diagnose and remove polyps	X	
Detects large polyps and cancers	X	X
Detects small polyps better	X	
No radiation	X	
Covered by Medicare and most insurance	X	
No sedation/anesthesia		X
Virtually no risk for perforation		X
Better viewing of right side of colon		X
Detects abnormalities outside the colon extra-colonic abnormalities		X

Quick Colon Test Could Save Thousands of Lives

A recent study found that a single flexible sigmoidoscopy test around age 60 can cut colon cancer risk by about one-third. It is cheaper than a colonoscopy (important for people without insurance), takes an average of five minutes and involves no anesthesia. A tiny camera is used to detect any abnormal tissue in the lower-left side of the colon—where about two-thirds of all colon cancers occur—and aid in the removal of precancerous polyps. The test does require a night-before bowel preparation.

Wendy Atkin, PhD, MPH, professor of surgery and cancer, Imperial College London, England, and lead author of an 11-year study of 170,038 people ages 55 to 64, published in The Lancet.

Aspirin Raises Survival Rate In Colon Cancer Patients

In a recent study, patients who started taking aspirin regularly for the first time after their colon cancer diagnoses had a 47% lower risk of dying from the disease than patients who did not take aspirin. Aspirin was most effective against a type of colon cancer that overproduces an enzyme called COX-2.

Andrew T. Chan, MD, MPH, assistant professor of medicine at Harvard Medical School, Boston, and leader of a study of 1,279 colon cancer patients, published in The Journal of the American Medical Association.

Better Colonoscopy

Doctors recently performed a standard colonoscopy on 1,000 adults, followed immediately by a colonoscopy only on the right side of the colon using the newer *retroflexion* technique, which involves turning the tip of the scope around inside the colon for increased visibility. Recent studies have shown colonoscopy to detect cancer less effectively in the right side of the colon—perhaps because colon prep is typically less thorough there.

Results: Retroflexion increased the number of polyps found by 14%.

When having a colonoscopy: Ask your doctor about retroflexion.

Douglas Rex, MD, professor of medicine, Indiana University School of Medicine, Indianapolis.

A High-Fiber Diet Does Not Prevent Colon Cancer

It was previously believed that a high-fiber diet reduced exposure of the intestinal wall to carcinogens by preventing constipation.

But: Several large studies have failed to find that fiber provides a protective effect...and there's no known link between constipation and colon cancer.

University of California, Berkeley Wellness Letter, 500 Fifth Ave., New York City 10110.

Magnesium Reduces Colon Cancer Risk In Men

Researchers at Japan National Cancer Center in Tokyo found that men who consumed at least 327 milligrams (mg) of magnesium in foods each day had 52% lower risk for colon cancer. The researchers did not investigate why this benefit was not found in women. Healthful foods high in magnesium include green leafy vegetables, whole grains, nuts and milk. Men at risk for colon cancer should make sure that their diets are high in magnesium or take 350 mg daily of magnesium.

Mark A. Stengler, NMD, licensed naturopathic medical doctor and leading authority on the practice of alternative and integrated medicine. He is founder and medical director of the Stengler Center for Integrative Medicine, Encinitas, California, and author of many books, including The Natural Physician's Healing Therapies (Bottom Line Books).

FDA Approves Prostate Cancer Vaccine

The vaccine Provenge, which was approved by the FDA to treat certain kinds of advanced prostate cancer, combines the patient's own immune cells with a specially developed protein to stimulate the immune system to fight the cancer. In clinical trials, it extended patients' lives by an average of 4.1 months. Most common side effects include chills, fatigue and fever.

Philip Kantoff, MD, director, Lank Center for Genitourinary Oncology, chief of solid tumor oncology and chief clinical research officer, Dana-Farber/Brigham and Women's Cancer Center, Boston.

Aspirin Fights Prostate Cancer

Prostate cancer patients were less likely to die when they were given an anticoagulant such as aspirin in addition to standard treatment (surgery or radiation).

Possible reason: The body's natural tendency is to cover cancer cells with platelets in the blood. The platelet covering protects cancer cells from the immune system, making it easier for the cells to survive. Anticoagulants interfere with this platelet function.

Kevin Choe, MD, PhD, assistant professor of radiation oncology at University of Texas Southwestern Medical Center at Dallas and leader of a study of prostate cancer, presented at a meeting of the American Society for Radiation Oncology.

Hormone Therapy for Prostate Cancer Raises Risk for Heart Disease

Treatment known as androgen-deprivation therapy (ADT), which shuts down production of male sex hormones, is part of the standard treatment for high-risk prostate cancer.

Problem: Multiple studies have linked ADT to heart risks.

Self-defense: Men on ADT for prostate cancer who do not have heart disease should discuss their risk with their physicians and closely monitor their cholesterol, blood-sugar and blood-pressure levels.

Men with existing heart disease also should be on low-dose aspirin if they can tolerate it.

Advisory from a panel of experts for American Heart Association, American Cancer Society and American Urological Association, published in *Circulation*.

How Men Can Avoid Prostate Cancer

Geovanni Espinosa, ND, director of the Integrative Urology Center at New York University Langone Medical Center in New York City. He is also a certified nutrition specialist, a licensed acupuncturist and registered herbalist with the American Herbalists Guild. Dr. Espinosa is the author of the naturopathy section in the book *1,000 Cures for 200 Ailments* (HarperCollins).

Prostate cancer is the most common malignancy among men in the US—in 2009, there were 192,280 new cases. In men over age 75, it is the most common cause of death due to cancer.

What all men need to know: You can't eliminate your risk for prostate cancer entirely, but men of any age can significantly reduce it with simple, natural approaches.

Prostate cancer prevention is especially smart for men who are at increased risk for the disease due to such factors as age (men age 65 or older account for 70% of cases) and/or family history (having a father or brother with prostate cancer doubles your own risk).

A little-known possible risk factor: Research is still inconclusive, but men whose mothers have had breast cancer also may be at increased risk for prostate cancer.

If you've been diagnosed with prostate cancer, the strategies described in this article are even more crucial. They help make your medical treatment more effective and may keep the malignancy from progressing or returning.

THE POWER OF LIFESTYLE

To give yourself the best possible chance of avoiding prostate cancer, the goal is to create an environment in your body in which malignant prostate cells cannot grow.

Important finding: In a study of 93 men whose early prostate cancer was treated with "watchful waiting"—no surgery, radiation or chemotherapy as long as the cancer wasn't growing—roughly half participated in an intensive lifestyle-modification program that included a plant-based diet and exercise while the other half did not. After a year, none of the men in the lifestyle program needed surgery or radiation to treat growth of their cancer, but six in the control group did.

STEP 1: EAT THE RIGHT FOODS

The first component of a prostate cancer prevention plan is to eat a plant-centered Mediterranean-type diet.

Good rule of thumb: Get carbohydrates from whole grains and legumes—both food types are rich in cancer-fighting antioxidants. Avoid products containing white sugar and refined flour. *Your diet should also include...*

•**Green, leafy vegetables**—especially crucifers (such as broccoli, cauliflower and watercress), which contain *indole-3-carbinol*, a chemical that has been shown to fight prostate cancer. Aim to eat three to five one-half cup servings daily.

•**Cooked tomatoes.** Tomatoes contain the anticancer carotenoid lycopene. Aim to eat three to five one-half cup servings weekly. Consuming them in tomato sauce is ideal—cooking the tomatoes makes lycopene more easily absorbed by your body. Avoid canned tomatoes, which may contain the harmful chemical *bisphenol A* (BPA). Choose jarred tomatoes instead. Watermelon and guava also contain lycopene.

•**No milk.** Avoid milk and other dairy products—including non- or low-fat products. In recent years, three studies have linked dairy intake with increased risk for prostate cancer.

•**Carefully chosen fish.** Many experts believe prostate cancer is an inflammatory condition, and omega-3 fatty acids in certain types of fish are natural anti-inflammatories.

Each week, eat about 12 to 18 ounces of smaller fish (such as mackerel, sardines and salmon) rather than large fish (including tuna and sea bass). Use a slow-cook method, such as baking, rather than grilling, in order to avoid carcinogenic *heterocyclic amines* (HCAs).

If you eat salmon: Choose "wild Alaskan" or "wild Pacific" salmon—it is less likely to contain contaminants, such as PCBs, than farmed salmon.

Caution: Avoid red meat. Some research has linked it to increased risk for prostate cancer. Stick with lean, free-roaming organic chicken and, if you do eat red meat, grass-fed beef.

STEP 2: TAKE SUPPLEMENTS

Research has found that certain supplements also help prevent prostate cancer.* *All men should take at least 2,000 international units (IU) of vitamin D daily and consult their doctors for advice on adding other supplements (all available at health-food stores)...*

•**Pectasol,** a form of modified citrus pectin, has been shown to slow rises in prostate-specific antigen (PSA)—a possible marker for cancerous cells—in men with prostate cancer. Animal studies suggest that pectasol inhibits prostate cancer cell growth. Men with prostate cancer or who are at high risk should take three capsules, twice a day (for a total of about 4.8 grams [g] daily).

Recommended brand: PectaSol-C made by EcoNugenics (800-308-5518, *www.econu genics.com*).

•**Vitamin E** is believed to have anti-cancer effects when both forms of the vitamin—alpha tocopherol and gamma tocopherol—are consumed. Take a 400 international unit (IU) supplement daily with both alpha and gamma tocopherol.

•**Zyflamend** is an extract of 10 different herbs, including green tea leaf, basil and ginger. A natural anti-inflammatory, it has been shown to keep precancerous prostate cells from turning malignant. Take one tablet, three times daily.

•**Fish oil supplements** help ensure an adequate level of inflammation-fighting omega-3s. Take 4,000 to 5,000 milligrams (mg) a day.

Caution: If you take blood-thinning medication, consult your doctor before using fish oil.

•**Indole-3-carbinol,** the cancer-fighting chemical found in cruciferous vegetables, is available as a supplement. Take 100 mg daily.

•**Curcumin,** a powerful natural anti-inflammatory, has been shown to inhibit prostate cancer cell growth. The spice turmeric contains curcumin—use it regularly. Or take curcumin

*Check with your doctor before taking these or any supplements. They may interact with prescription medication.

as a supplement—200 mg to 250 mg, two to three times daily.

STEP 3: EXERCISE AND CONTROL YOUR WEIGHT

Research has shown that prostate cancer patients who exercise have a better quality of life and live longer than those who don't—perhaps because a fit body burns glucose more efficiently, starving cancer cells of a nutrient they need.

My recommendation: Exercise 30 to 60 minutes five to six days a week. Mix moderate aerobics (such as jogging, swimming or riding an exercise bike) with resistance exercise (free weights and/or machines).

Infertile Men at Risk for Prostate Cancer

Infertile men are two-and-a-half times more likely to develop an aggressive form of prostate cancer. Men who are infertile should discuss prostate cancer risk with their doctors to determine if they should start being screened for the cancer at an earlier age.

Thomas J. Walsh, MD, assistant professor, department of urology, University of Washington School of Medicine, Seattle, and leader of a study of 22,562, published in *Cancer*.

Men Are at Risk for Breast Cancer

Among 28 men with at least one maternal relative with breast cancer, 80% did not know that they themselves were at increased risk for the disease.

Self-defense: Men, not only women, should discuss family history of breast cancer with their doctors and be alert to lesser-known breast cancer symptoms—nipple discharge or inversion, breast swelling and/or reddening or dimpling of the skin or nipple.

Eileen Thomas, PhD, RN, assistant professor, College of Nursing, University of Colorado Denver, Aurora.

Reason to Think Positive!

Testicular cancer patients who had positive thoughts showed improved mental health, in contrast to men who thought negatively or neutrally about their disease. The men who showed improvement wrote positively about their cancer in a journal for five weeks, writing things such as how the cancer had made them appreciate life more. Men with testicular cancer often become depressed and/or anxious because chemotherapy and radiation treatment for the disease may temporarily interfere with sexual performance and fertility. Expressing positive feelings about the experience can help to improve the quality of life, especially since this disease usually strikes younger men who will live a long time afterward.

Mark T. Morman, PhD, associate professor of communication studies and graduate program director, Baylor University, Waco, Texas, and coleader of a pilot study of 48 men with testicular cancer, presented at the International Communication Association Conference.

Why Cancer Patients Should See a Dentist

Cherry L. Estilo, DMD, a dental oncologist and an associate attending dentist at Memorial Sloan-Kettering Cancer Center in New York City. She specializes in the oral and dental management of patients with hematologic malignancies. Dr. Estilo has participated in research identifying the genetic basis for the development of head and neck cancers. She has also been involved in studying the oral complications related to head and neck cancer treatment.

Many adult cancer patients are surprised to learn that cancer treatments, such as chemotherapy and radiation therapy, can affect the mouth, teeth and gums.

Why: These therapies slow the growth of healthy cells in the mouth—impeding its ability to heal—as well as weaken the immune system and reduce the number of white blood cells that help defend against disease, making patients more prone to developing mouth infections.

Some patients may already have an abnormally low level of white blood cells due to their specific type of cancer (such as leukemia), making oral care particularly important.

Cancer treatment may also cause changes in the lining of the mouth and in the salivary glands, which can lead to *xerostomia* (dry mouth)...*mucositis* (inflammation of the mucous membrane in the mouth)...tooth decay...changes in taste...and generally painful mouth and gums.

According to the National Institute of Dental and Craniofacial Research, oral complications occur in almost all patients who receive radiation for head and neck cancer...in up to 75% of blood and marrow transplant recipients...and in nearly 40% of patients who receive chemotherapy for any type of cancer.

Most of these oral complications subside soon after treatment ends. However, high-dose radiation for head and neck cancer can cause lasting or permanent damage in the tissue of the mouth and the jawbone.

Example: A patient with a history of high-dose radiation to the head and neck who must undergo dental surgery or dental extraction has a risk of developing *osteoradionecrosis*, a rare and potentially severe complication that results in the death of bone tissue.

The good news: Oral care before and throughout cancer treatment can reduce or even prevent some of these complications.

TO MINIMIZE RISK FOR ORAL COMPLICATIONS

You can minimize your risk of developing oral complications from cancer treatment by receiving appropriate dental care and practicing good oral hygiene before, during and after treatment. *What all cancer patients should do...*

•**Discuss your risk for oral complications with your cancer doctor.** He/she may suggest that you get a complete dental evaluation from your dentist or from a dental oncologist (a dentist who is trained in dental and oral care for patients with cancer).

To find a dentist who is trained in treating cancer patients, ask your cancer doctor or check with other reputable resources, including the National Cancer Institute (800-422-6237, *www.cancer.gov*) or the National Comprehensive Cancer Network (215-690-0300, *www.nccn.org*).

Your cancer doctor may want to discuss with the dentist your treatment plan and any potential oral complications that may arise.

•**Get a complete dental evaluation prior to your cancer treatment.** Your dentist will do a thorough examination of your mouth, teeth and jawbone to identify problems that may arise during treatment. During your visit, discuss your risk for oral complications.

Important: If your dentist has identified teeth that might become problematic during or after cancer treatment, make sure that these issues are addressed at least one month prior to the start of chemotherapy to provide enough time for your mouth to properly heal before treatment begins.

If tooth extraction is required, wait at least two weeks or until adequate healing is accomplished before beginning cancer treatment.

•**Practice good home care.** Oral hygiene during and after treatment can reduce your chances of getting mouth sores, infections and tooth decay. Brush your teeth after every meal and at bedtime using a soft toothbrush and fluoride toothpaste.

If you are receiving high-dose radiation to the head and neck, prescription-grade toothpaste is recommended, such as Colgate PreviDent 5000 Plus, which has more fluoride than regular toothpaste. Floss once a day to remove plaque.

Your dentist may recommend a fluoride mouth rinse in addition to daily brushing or a fluoride gel to reduce the chances of getting tooth decay.

•**Keep your saliva up.** Saliva has antibacterial properties.

Best: Keep your mouth hydrated with water.

• **Follow your oral-care plan throughout your treatment and recovery.** In addition to getting regular dental checkups and practicing good oral hygiene, patients with a history of treatment for head and neck cancer should be evaluated by a dental oncologist at least twice a year even after treatment ends.

• **Take a moment every day to check your mouth for any changes or problems.** Notify your dentist immediately if you notice swelling, lumps, soreness, ulcerations, bleeding or a sticky, white film in your mouth, which may indicate infection.

• **Eat a healthful diet to prevent tooth decay.** While tooth decay is not a result of chemotherapy or high-dose radiation, dry mouth can increase risk for tooth decay. Avoid eating foods high in sugar. You may want to eat softer foods if your mouth is sore.

Alcoholic beverages should be avoided during treatment. If you smoke, it is especially important to stop during cancer treatment and to try smoking-cessation strategies as soon as possible.

Bonus: A well-balanced diet can keep you strong enough to endure cancer treatment and help your entire body to heal.

• **Use the "Popsicle technique."** To prevent mouth sores from developing, some oncologists recommend sucking on a sugar-free Popsicle or eating ice cubes or ice chips while chemotherapy is being administered. Ice not only acts as an anesthetic but hydrates as well.

Better Melanoma Treatment

In a five-year study of 250 people (average age 57) with melanoma (a serious form of skin cancer) that had spread to lymph nodes, those who received radiation therapy after surgery were 40% less likely to experience melanoma recurrence in the following two years than those who did not undergo radiation treatments. Radiation therapy destroys malignant cells that can remain after surgical removal of tumors.

If you have melanoma and are at high risk for recurrence: Ask your doctor whether radiation therapy would be appropriate for you.

Bryan Burmeister, MD, associate professor and director, radiation oncology, Princess Alexandra Hospital, Brisbane, Australia.

Melanoma More Common in Parkinson's Patients

When 2,106 adults with Parkinson's disease (average age 68) underwent skin cancer screenings, they were found to be more than twice as likely to have melanoma than adults of the same age in the general population.

Implication: Anyone with Parkinson's disease should receive routine full-body skin exams (as often as recommended by a dermatologist) and report any changes in the shape, color and/or size of moles to their physicians.

John Bertoni, MD, PhD, professor of neurological sciences, University of Nebraska Medical Center, Omaha.

Even Small Skin Moles Can Be Cancerous

Current guidelines from the American Academy of Dermatology, Skin Cancer Foundation and American Cancer Society state that only moles larger than a pencil eraser (about six millimeters) may indicate melanoma.

But: One recent study shows that 22% of invasive melanomas are smaller than that.

Best: You and your doctor should check all moles, regardless of size. In particular, small moles that are dark-colored with irregular borders should be checked. Give yourself a full body exam and be sure to check with your dermatologist.

Stuart M. Goldsmith, MD, dermatologist, Southwest Georgia Dermatology, Albany, Georgia.

Cancer Risk from Parking Lots and Driveways

Many asphalt driveways and parking lots in the US are sealed using coal-tar–based sealant.

Recent finding: The sealant wears off and is tracked into homes. House dust from ground-floor apartments near parking lots made with coal-tar–based sealants had concentrations of carcinogens that were, on average, 25 times higher than house dust from ground-floor apartments with other types of parking lot surfaces, such as unsealed asphalt pavement and concrete. To determine if a sealant is coal-tar–based, look for the Chemical Abstracts Service (CAS) number "65996-93-2" on the product's material safety data sheet (MSDS). You can find resources for locating the MSDS at *www.ilpi.com/msds* or inquire when you buy the sealant.

Barbara Mahler, PhD, hydrologist, US Geological Survey, Austin, Texas, and leader of a study of coal-tar dust in apartments in Austin, Texas, published in *Environmental Science & Technology.*

Folic Acid Alert

Recent studies have shown that people who regularly consume large amounts of folic acid (found in vitamins and enriched foods) may increase their risk for several forms of cancer, including colorectal and prostate. The government-recommended tolerable upper limit is 1,000 micrograms (mcg) a day.

At risk: People who take in a lot without realizing it.

Example: A daily multivitamin with 400 mcg of folic acid...a B-complex supplement with another 400 mcg...cereal with 400 mcg to 800 mcg...and flour-based products with 100 mcg to 200 mcg.

Joel Mason, MD, director, Vitamins and Carcinogenesis Laboratory, Jean Mayer USDA Human Nutrition Research Center on Aging, Tufts University, Boston.

Avoid Stress Before Cancer Therapy

A laboratory study finds that any type of stress can produce heat shock factor-1, a protein that may protect cancer cells from radiation and chemotherapy drugs. Additional research is under way.

Molecular Cancer Research.

Cancer-Fighting Virus

Cold viruses can be genetically altered to increase the activity of a tumor suppressor gene that slows cancer cell replication—a discovery that may lead to a new type of cancer therapy.

Nature.

Cancer vs. Alzheimer's

According to a recent study, Alzheimer's patients are less likely to develop cancer...and cancer patients are less likely to develop Alzheimer's. People who had Alzheimer's at the start were 69% less likely to be hospitalized for cancer after eight years than those who didn't have Alzheimer's. People who had cancer were 43% less likely to develop Alzheimer's after five years than those who didn't have cancer. The links between the conditions may help researchers discover new treatments.

Catherine M. Roe, PhD, research assistant professor, neurology, Washington University School of Medicine, St. Louis, and author of a study based on data from the Cardiovascular Health Study, published online in *Neurology*.

Calcium May Protect Against Cancer

In a seven-year study of more than 490,000 adults, women who consumed the most calcium (1,881 milligrams [mg] daily, on average) were 23% less likely to develop cancers of the digestive system (such as colorectal or stomach cancer) than those who consumed the least calcium. Men who consumed the most calcium (1,530 mg daily, on average) had a 16% lower risk.

Self-defense: Aim to eat several servings daily of calcium-rich foods (such as low-fat dairy products, leafy green vegetables, navy beans and calcium-fortified orange juice) and/or take a calcium supplement.

Yikyung Park, ScD, staff scientist, National Cancer Institute, Bethesda, Maryland.

Soda May Raise Pancreatic Cancer Risk

People who drank two or more sugar-sweetened soft drinks a week had an 87% higher risk for pancreatic cancer than people who drank less soda, found a recent study.

Reason: Unclear. It could mean that people who drink a lot of soda have poor health habits in general, raising their risk for cancer.

Also: People who drank fruit juice—which includes many nutrients and typically has less sugar than soft drinks—did not carry the same cancer risk.

Mark A. Pereira, PhD, MPH, associate professor, School of Public Health, University of Minnesota, Minneapolis, and leader of a study of 60,524 people, published in *Cancer Epidemiology, Biomarkers Prevention*.

Body Weight Linked To Pancreatic Cancer

Researchers compared the body mass index (BMI) of 2,170 adults with pancreatic cancer to that of 2,209 adults without.

Result: Those who were overweight (BMIs of 25 to 29) or obese (BMIs of 30 or greater) were up to 55% more likely to develop pancreatic cancer than those with healthy BMIs (18.5 to 24.9).

Theory: Excess fat increases insulin levels, which promotes cell growth in the pancreas—possibly including cancerous cells.

Self-defense: Track your BMI at the National Heart, Lung and Blood Institute Web site, *www.nhlbisupport.com/bmi*.

Alan A. Arslan, MD, assistant professor, New York University Langone Medical Center, New York City.

Estrogen and Gallbladder Cancer

Gallbladder cancer affects women more than men. In animal studies, lowering estrogen (by removing the ovaries) has been shown to prevent gallbladder tumors. It's possible that estrogen-lowering drugs could be used to treat this cancer in humans.

Proceedings of the National Academy of Sciences.

Lonely Disease?

In patients with some cancers, those who rate high on loneliness tests tend to produce larger amounts of vascular endothelial growth factor, a substance that promotes tumor growth.

Psychosomatic Medicine.

Keep the Toxic Chemical BPA Out of Your Food

Frederick S. vom Saal, PhD, Curators' Professor of biological sciences at the University of Missouri, Columbia. He is a leading researcher on the effects of BPA and has conducted dozens of studies on this topic.

Were you relieved by the FDA's recent about-face on *bisphenol-A* (BPA), the toxic chemical that can leach out of plastic containers and into food? At last, the agency has expressed "some concern" regarding the dangers of this ubiquitous contaminant. With luck, the FDA's new interest in BPA is not too little too late—but meantime, steps can be taken to protect yourself.

BPA is used in many plastic food and beverage containers, particularly those made of hard, clear polycarbonate plastic. BPA is also an additive in polyvinyl chloride (PVC) plastic, which is used in some plastic food wraps.

Surprising news: BPA is in the epoxy resins found in the lining of almost all cans used by the food industry (including baby formula cans!). In fact, canned food is the primary food source of BPA for adults.

The problem: BPA molecules that escape their chemical bonds can migrate into the foods and beverages they contact, especially if the container is heated or the food inside is acidic. We then ingest the BPA—thereby increasing our risk for numerous health problems. There's even BPA on the coated paper from cash registers—the toxin gets into our bodies when we touch the paper and then handle the food we're about to eat. BPA can also be absorbed through the skin.

Frederick S. vom Saal, PhD, Curators' Professor of biological sciences at the University of Missouri and a leading BPA researcher, explained that this chemical has estrogen-like effects on the body. It acts as an endocrine disruptor, interrupting our hormonal patterns —and actually reprogramming our genes. Roughly 1,000 published, peer-reviewed studies have linked BPA to negative health consequences. *These include...*

- **Breast cancer, ovarian cysts and uterine fibroids in females** (and prostate cancer, sexual dysfunction and altered sperm in males).
- **Type 2 diabetes and its precursor, insulin resistance.**
- **Heart disease as well as heart rhythm abnormalities.**
- **Liver disease.**
- **Thyroid dysfunction.**
- **Obesity and greater accumulation of fat in cells.**

Unborn babies, infants and children are especially susceptible to BPA's harmful effects because they are still growing. *Exposure before birth and/or during childhood has been linked to...*

- **Birth defects.**
- **Cognitive problems, including learning deficits.**
- **Behavioral problems, such as hyperactivity disorders.**
- **Early puberty in females.**
- **Increased risk for cancer in adulthood.**

How much is too much? The EPA estimates that exposure of up to 50 micrograms (mcg) of BPA per kilogram (kg) of body weight per day is safe. However, recent studies suggest that even a tiny fraction of this amount—as little as 0.025 mcg/kg per day—may be dangerous.

Dr. vom Saal said, "No matter what you might hear from the plastics industry, which is trying to convince consumers that BPA is safe, hundreds of published papers show that BPA is a toxin with no safe levels."

Scary: When the CDC studied urine samples of more than 2,500 Americans age six and older, 93% of those tested had BPA in their urine.

BPA SELF-DEFENSE

Here are Dr. vom Saal's suggestions for minimizing your exposure to BPA...

- **Avoid canned foods as much as you can.**

Note: It does not help to store cans in the refrigerator or to use canned goods soon after you buy them. The harm is already done even before the cans reach the market because high heat must be used to sterilize the food during canning.

Exceptions: Several manufacturers—including Eco Fish, Eden Organic, Edward & Sons, Muir Glen, Oregon's Choice Gourmet Albacore and Wild Planet—have begun using BPA-free cans for some of their products. (See a manufacturer's Web site for information on its BPA-free canned products, or contact the company directly.)

• **Choose cardboard over metal.** Cardboard cartons (such as those used for juice or milk) and cardboard cylindrical "cans" (such as those used for raisins) are generally better options than metal cans—but they are not ideal because they may contain some recycled paper (which is loaded with BPA)...or they may be lined with a resin that contains BPA.

Best: Opt for foods that are fresh or frozen or that come in glass bottles or jars or in foil pouches.

• **Never give canned liquid formula to an infant.** Powdered is much safer.

• **When microwaving, never let plastic wrap come in contact with your food.** If a product has a plastic film covering that is supposed to be left in place during microwave cooking, remove the film and replace it with a glass or ceramic cover instead.

• **Transfer prepackaged food to a glass or ceramic container before cooking,** even if the instructions say to microwave the product in the plastic pouch it comes in.

• **Check the triangle-enclosed recycling numeral on plastic items that come in contact with foods or beverages**—storage containers, water pitchers, baby bottles, sippy cups, utensils and tableware. The numeral "7" indicates a plastic that may or may not contain BPA. To be safe, Dr. vom Saal said, "If you see a numeral '7' and it doesn't say BPA-free, assume there is BPA." The letters "PC" stamped near the recycling number are another indication that the plastic contains BPA.

• **Recheck what's in your cupboards.** Those new travel mugs? They might be made from number-seven plastic.

• **Plastics labeled number two or five, which also are often used for food containers, do not have BPA.** But they may contain other potentially harmful chemicals that can leach out, especially when heat breaks down the molecular bonds of plastic. To be safe, wash all plastic kitchenware in cold to room-temperature water with a mild cleanser, not in the dishwasher. Never microwave plastic containers—not even those labeled microwave-safe, such as frozen entrée trays. Instead use a glass or ceramic container. Before putting hot soup or gravy into plastic containers to freeze, first allow it to cool. Throw out any plastic kitchenware that is scratched, chipped or discolored—damaged plastic is most likely to leach chemicals.

• **Do not assume that plastics with no triangle-enclosed numeral are safe.** Dr. vom Saal cautioned, "Manufacturers know that consumers are looking for BPA, so they're taking identifying numbers off their products and packaging." Don't fall prey to such tricks.

Skip the Tanning Salon

Tanning beds cause cancer. In a recent finding, people who started using tanning beds or sunlamps before age 30 increased their risk for melanoma, the deadliest kind of skin cancer, by 75%. The International Agency for Research on Cancer recently classified tanning beds as "carcinogenic to humans."

University of California, Berkeley Wellness Letter, 500 Fifth Ave., New York City 10110.

Nonsmokers and Lung Cancer

Rebecca Shannonhouse, editor, *Bottom Line/Health,* Boardroom Inc., 281 Tresser Blvd., Connecticut 06901.

Nearly one out of every 15 homes in the US contains a silent killer. You can't see it or smell it. But radon (a naturally occurring radioactive gas) is the second-leading cause (after smoking) of lung cancer deaths.

Recent developments: The World Health Organization (WHO)—a United Nations–sanctioned international authority on public health—recommended late last year that indoor radon levels not exceed 2.7 pico Curies per liter (pCi/L). And in the US, a report recently released by the President's Cancer Panel encourages the EPA to consider lowering its current "action level" of 4 pCi/L for radon exposure.

To determine how much radon is in your home, R. William Field, PhD, a leading expert on radon and professor at the University of Iowa in Iowa City, suggests that you…

• **Perform short-term testing.** Place two radon units side by side in the lowest lived-in level of your home (typically for 48 hours). Do not open your windows on the floor being tested. After the allotted time, mail them to the laboratory specified on the package for results.

Cost: About $20. If either test shows elevated radon, do a long-term test for 90 days or more for your average year-round exposure.

Cost: About $25 to $30.

• **Reduce radon.** If levels are high, hire a qualified radon-mitigation contractor to install a subslab depressurization system—a vent-fan connected to suction pipes draws radon away from below the house and releases it outdoors.

Cost: $800 to $2,500. Some health-care savings accounts can be used to pay for radon mitigation.

Rising Thyroid Cancer Rates

Thyroid cancer diagnoses are on the rise—increasing by about 6% a year in the US. About 37,000 cases of thyroid cancer were diagnosed in 2009, up from 18,400 in 2000.

One reason for the increase: Medical scans are identifying thousands of extremely small thyroid tumors that otherwise would go undetected.

Possible causes of thyroid cancer: Obesity…radiation exposure from medical scans, especially during childhood.

The late Elaine Ron, PhD, senior investigator, division of cancer epidemiology and genetics, National Cancer Institute, Bethesda, Maryland.

Blood Pressure Drugs Increase Cancer Risk

In a recent study, people who used an angiotensin-receptor blocker (ARB), such as *losartan* (Cozaar) or *telmisartan* (Micardis), for an average of four years had a 25% higher incidence of lung cancers—and 8% to 11% more cancers overall—than people who did not use the drugs. ARBs can trigger the development of new blood vessels, which speeds tumor growth.

Self-defense: Talk to your doctor about possibly switching to an alternative drug.

Ilke Sipahi, MD, is assistant professor of medicine, Case Western Reserve University, Cleveland, and lead researcher of a meta-analysis published in *The Lancet Oncology.*

CT Scan? When to Say No

Richard Semelka, MD, professor and vice chairman for quality and safety, department of radiology, University of North Carolina Hospitals, Chapel Hill, author of eight textbooks and an expert on the hazards of medical radiation.

In a recent study in *Archives of Internal Medicine* (AIM), researchers estimated that the radiation from CT scans performed in the US in a single year could lead to 29,000 future cases of cancer—66% of them in women.

Many different kinds of diagnostic screenings use radiation these days. Might these tests be doing more harm than good? Richard

Semelka, MD, is vice chairman for quality and safety in the department of radiology at University of North Carolina Hospitals and one of the first internationally recognized radiology experts to speak out on the potential hazards of medical radiation. He said that, in many cases, the immediate benefits of a CT scan—which pairs X-rays with computers to produce three-dimensional images—do outweigh its long-term risks.

But: Far too often, CT scans are done even when there is no compelling reason or when a safer test could be used instead. "Ideally, physicians would do thorough risk/benefit analyses before ordering any tests, but this rarely happens. Given radiation's risks, patients must consider whether they really need that CT or not," Dr. Semelka cautioned.

Here's what you need to know to protect yourself from the dangers of medical radiation...

WHEN TO SAY YES

There is no question, Dr. Semelka said, that in certain types of emergencies or when you may have certain serious diseases, a CT scan is invaluable. *If your doctor recommends a CT scan, don't hesitate if you have...*

• **Possible internal injuries**—for instance, when an accident may have caused significant trauma to the brain, organs or blood vessels.

• **Facial trauma.** The test could help map future surgical reconstruction.

• **Possible symptoms of a potentially deadly problem,** such as a heart attack, stroke, aneurysm, blood clot, severe pneumonia or interstitial lung disease (inflammation of the tissue that surrounds the lungs' tiny air sacs).

• **A suspected complex bone problem**—for instance, a major fracture of a complex location, such as the hip—if a traditional X-ray has not provided sufficient information.

WHEN TO ASK ABOUT OTHER OPTIONS

In situations other than the above, before you agree to a CT scan, Dr. Semelka suggested first discussing these points...

• **Vulnerability of tissues to be scanned.** In the AIM study, the areas most sensitive to radiation were the abdomen and pelvis and, to a lesser degree, the chest and head. So you can assent without much worry to a CT of the leg or arm....but before scanning the torso or head, your doctor should clearly explain why the test is necessary.

• **Alternate ways to diagnose**—based on your symptoms, medical history, risk factors, etc.—and the best test for confirming that particular problem.

For instance: Suppose you have severe abdominal or pelvic pain. If your doctor suspects kidney stones, a CT is most appropriate. If an inflammatory condition such as appendicitis seems probable, a CT may be the easiest way to make the diagnosis—but often magnetic resonance imaging (MRI) can reveal the problem without exposing the patient to radiation. And although CT scans often are done to look for cancer, many malignancies (such as some abdominal cancers) are shown as well or even better with MRI.

• **Previous radiation exposure.** Radiation risk is cumulative, so be sure that your current doctor is aware of any CT scans you've had in the past—and whenever possible, provide copies of those results. If another scan is suggested within a year of a previous CT, ask if it is safe to wait before repeating the test.

• **Amount of radiation involved.** Ask the doctor how many images will be taken and whether that number can be reduced without compromising accuracy. Also, request a referral to a radiology facility that uses up-to-date equipment—many newer CT machines use significantly less radiation than older models. If your doctor is not sure about the quality of a local facility's equipment, ask him or her to find out.

• **Your age.** The younger you are, the more likely it is that a CT scan is not worth its risks.

Examples: A young woman's breasts are more sensitive to radiation than an older woman's, so a CT of the lungs is potentially more harmful...and a heart CT generally is less appropriate for a younger woman because her risk for heart disease is low.

•**Shields.** Using an AttenuRad breast shield during a chest CT reduces radiation delivered to the breasts by up to 57% without significantly changing the quality of the images. Shields also are available to protect the eyes, gonads and thyroid gland from radiation when other areas are being scanned. When you schedule your CT, ask whether shields are provided—and if they are not, find a center where they are.

•**Protection in a pill?** The dietary supplement BioShield-Radiation (888-606-8883, *www. bioshieldpill.com*) purportedly protects against radiation by providing multiple antioxidants to combat free radicals. Dr. Semelka said that the information available on this product is too preliminary to recommend it, though research is ongoing. If you want to try this product, discuss it with your doctor.

WHEN TO SAY NO THANKS

Tell your doctor that you prefer to skip a CT scan if none of the above situations apply and if you…

•**Could instead have a safer test**—one that does not use radiation.

Examples: Gallstones are easily seen with ultrasound. In general, MRI is best in cases of soft-tissue injury, such as a torn ligament or tendon…injury to the spinal cord, such as disk herniation…a suspected brain tumor…and sometimes for complex fractures in joints.

•**Are pregnant.** Radiation may cause harm to the fetus.

•**Suspect that a doctor or hospital is guarding against a lawsuit**—and that's the primary reason for the CT recommendation. "Many physicians worry that if they miss anything, they could get sued for malpractice. Covering all bases with a CT scan is a defensive weapon against potential legal action," Dr. Semelka explained.

Say to your doctor, "I understand that there are no guarantees with health care. Please weigh my concerns about radiation and my likelihood of having this condition you are looking for, then suggest which tests you think that I should undergo."

Coffee May Fight Endometrial Cancer

When researchers studied the diets and health of 23,356 women (ages 55 to 69), those who drank at least 2.5 cups of coffee daily had a much lower risk for endometrial cancer than those who drank no coffee over a 20-year period. Decaffeinated coffee is believed to offer the same benefit.

Theory: Coffee helps metabolize sugar—thus fighting obesity, which plays a role in endometrial cancer.

If you're at risk for endometrial cancer (due to such factors as obesity and diabetes): Ask your doctor about drinking a few cups of coffee daily.

Stefano Uccella, MD, researcher, department of obstetrics and gynecology, University of Insubria, Varese, Italy.

Fight Cancer with Sweet Potatoes

Sweet potatoes contain carotenoids, including beta-carotene, which help lower risk for cardiovascular disease.

Also: According to a study, diets that include three or more servings a week of carotenoid-rich vegetables, such as sweet potatoes, may reduce the risk for stomach cancer by as much as 57%. Sweet potatoes are rich in dietary fiber…and they are a good source of vitamins A, B and C.

Best: Store sweet potatoes in a dry, unrefrigerated bin. Scrub them and trim woody portions before baking, broiling, roasting or microwaving.

Environmental Nutrition, 800 Connecticut Ave., Norwalk, Connecticut 06854.

Broccoli Sprouts May Protect Against Stomach Cancer

When 48 adults infected with the bacterium *Helicobacter pylori* (H. pylori)—a major cause of stomach cancer—ate about 2.5 ounces daily of fresh broccoli sprouts or alfalfa sprouts for eight weeks, H. pylori levels were significantly lower in the broccoli sprouts group but were unchanged in the alfalfa group.

Theory: The protective effects may be due to sulforaphane, a compound produced by broccoli plants to defend against predators. Broccoli sprouts are available at health-food stores and online.

Jed Fahey, ScD, faculty research associate, department of pharmacology, Johns Hopkins School of Medicine, Baltimore.

Selenium May Reduce Bladder Cancer Risk

Researchers at the Spanish National Cancer Research Center have found that people with high levels of selenium in their bodies had a 39% reduced risk for bladder cancer. The study did not look at sources of selenium or doses. To increase your intake of selenium, eat about six Brazil nuts (one of the richest dietary sources of selenium) daily or take 200 micrograms (mcg) daily of selenium.

Mark A. Stengler, NMD, licensed naturopathic medical doctor and leading authority on the practice of alternative and integrated medicine. He is founder and medical director of the Stengler Center for Integrative Medicine, Encinitas, California...author of many books, including *The Natural Physician's Healing Therapies* (Bottom Line Books).

More from Mark Stengler, NMD...

Does IP6 Protect Against Cancer?

IP6—the antioxidant *inositol hexaphosphate*—has been around as a nutritional supplement since the 1980s—and has mainly been promoted as an anticancer nutrient and an antioxidant to prevent heart disease. But IP6's use as a cancer-prevention supplement is mainly a result of animal and test tube studies. Due to the lack of studies in humans, I do not recommend it, especially since there are so many other natural substances that have been studied and found to reduce inflammation.

How IP6 can help: Studies have shown that IP6 reduces urinary calcium oxalate levels, which helps prevent kidney stones. It also binds to metal ions, such as zinc, calcium and iron, in the digestive tract, making them less bioavailable, which may be helpful for someone with a genetic problem in which any of these metals accumulate in the body.

Vitamins and Minerals Protect Against Bladder Cancer

Researchers led by Cancer Council Victoria in Australia found that older people who consumed the largest amounts of vitamin E (at least 193.4 milligrams [mg] daily) were 34% less likely to develop bladder cancer than those with the lowest intake. A high intake of phosphorus (1,557 mg daily) was associated with a 51% reduction in bladder cancer risk. Carotenoids, niacin and vitamin D were also found to reduce risk. To get enough of these nutrients, consume vegetables that are high in these vitamins and minerals, such as alfalfa sprouts, celery and onion.

M.T. Brinkman, et al., "Minerals and Vitamins and the Risk of Bladder Cancer," published in *Cancer Causes and Control*.

Vitamin K and Cancer Risk

For the first time, researchers have found a link between vitamin K and risk for non-

Hodgkin's lymphoma, cancer of the immune system. Mayo Clinic researchers found that people with higher dietary intake of vitamin K had a 45% lower risk for the cancer than those with lower vitamin K intake. Vitamin K supplements did not provide the same benefit.

Best dietary sources of vitamin K: Kale, broccoli, spinach and collard greens.

Mark A. Stengler, NMD, licensed naturopathic medical doctor and leading authority on the practice of alternative and integrated medicine. He is founder and medical director of the Stengler Center for Integrative Medicine, Encinitas, California, and author of many books, including *The Natural Physician's Healing Therapies* (Bottom Line Books).

Free Housecleaning For Cancer Patients

The nonprofit organization Cleaning for a Reason provides maid service at no cost, once a month for four months, to patients in treatment for any kind of cancer. There are currently 650 partners (primarily professional cleaning companies) volunteering in all 50 sates and Canada. To check for services in your area, all 877-337-3348 or visit *www.cleaningforareason.org.*

Mike Farney, executive director, Cleaning for a Reason, Lewisville, Texas.

24

Cutting-Edge Cures

Reset Your "Body Clock"

For most of us, our bodies need a day or two to adjust when we travel across time zones or change the clock. But increasing evidence now shows that chronic (or even occasional) interruptions in our circadian rhythms—the 24-hour cycles that regulate sleep and wakefulness—may affect our health more than we thought.

What's new: The brain used to be considered the body's only biological "clock." Now researchers are finding that *many* cells in the body have "clock genes" that regulate their activity—for example, organs such as the liver also have cycles.

WHEN BODY CLOCKS FALTER

Exposure to light is one of the main factors for maintaining, or changing, our daily rhythms. And our modern society has essentially turned night into day with near-constant exposure to lights, TVs, computers and other electronic gadgets. In many cases, our bodies haven't adapted, and it's putting us at increased risk for health problems.

Age is also a factor. Older adults tend to have a weaker *circadian orchestration of physiology,* which means the body's clocks are less able to work together—a problem that has been linked to heart disease.

What you can do: Here's how to help manage your body's internal clocks so that you minimize your risk for health problems, such as...

HEART ATTACK

More than half of heart attacks occur in the six hours between about 6 am and noon. The greater frequency probably is due to several circadian factors, including body position—most people experience about a 10-to-25-point increase in systolic (top number) blood pressure when they rise from bed in the morning. What's more, people who have a heart attack

Steve A. Kay, PhD, dean and Richard C. Atkinson Chair in the division of biological sciences at the University of California, San Diego, where he is also a Distinguished Professor of Cell and Developmental Biology.

in the morning are likely to suffer more damage to the heart than those who have heart attacks later in the day.

Caution: In most people, blood pressure rises in the morning, then dips slightly in the afternoon and falls during sleep. However, some people don't have these periodic declines. Known as "non-dippers," they're more likely to have a heart attack than those who experience normal cycling.

Simple self-defense: Get out of bed slowly. In addition, because high blood pressure is a leading risk factor for heart attack, people who take blood pressure–lowering medication may benefit from timing it so that they get the greatest reduction in the morning.

Example: The blood pressure medication *verapamil* (such as Verelan PM) is meant to be taken at bedtime. The active ingredient isn't released during the first hours of sleep (when blood pressure is already low)—more is released in the morning, the time when blood pressure rises. Other drugs that are designed to provide greater benefit when taken at night include timed-release versions of *diltiazem* (Cardizem LA) and *propranolol* (InnoPran XL).

ASTHMA

People with asthma are more likely to need emergency treatment between 10 am and 11 am than at other times of the day, research has shown. The use of rescue inhalers also increases during the morning.

Reason: Lung movements are reduced during sleep and soon after waking up. This impairs the elimination of mucus, which can lead to congestion and difficulty breathing several hours later.

Simple self-defense: If you have asthma and use a bronchodilator, such as one containing *theophylline* (Uniphyl), talk to your doctor about taking your last dose of the day a few hours before bedtime. This allows the active ingredients to increase through the night and reach peak levels in the morning.

DROWSINESS

Feel drowsy after lunch? Blame your circadian rhythms. It's normal for body temperature,

blood pressure, metabolism and cognitive abilities to decline in the afternoon.

The peak mental hours for most adults are from about 7 am or 8 am until early afternoon. This is followed by a brief (one- to two-hour) dip, after which energy rises again until later in the evening.

Simple self-defense: If your job and lifestyle allow it, take a brief (20- to 30-minute) nap in the afternoon. Or, if that's not possible, try to schedule less demanding tasks during the "dip" period.

Smartphone Apps: A Smart Way to Stay Healthy

Joseph C. Kvedar, MD, founder and director of the Partners HealthCare Center for Connected Health in Boston. He also is a board-certified dermatologist and associate professor of dermatology at Harvard Medical School. *http://chealthblog.connected-health.org*

Health care used to be more of an episodic endeavor, meaning that we mostly dealt with it when we had to—when we were sick. Now, computers and constant connectivity are supporting health care's shift to being more of a continuous endeavor—aided by thousands of consumer health applications, or "apps," that we can download to our smartphones.

That's the opinion of Harvard Medical School associate professor Joseph C. Kvedar, MD, founder and director of Partners Health-Care Center for Connected Health. (The term "connected health" refers to technology-enabled programs and potential new strategies in health-care delivery.) Of course, no app can substitute for regular care from your doctor, Dr. Kvedar said. But you can use health-related apps to motivate yourself to follow a healthy lifestyle…better manage your medical condition…and give your doctor more complete information on your health status.

Currently, most apps are for iPhones, though Android, BlackBerry, Palm, iPod Touch and iPad also have their share—and the universe of apps for all types of smartphones is expanding rapidly. So if the specific apps below are not available for your device, search your apps store for something similar.

Apps can help you manage a chronic health condition…

•**Allergy Alert** provides a four-day forecast of allergy, asthma, cold-and-cough and ultraviolet index levels for your area.

•**BP Buddy** logs 60 days of home-monitored blood pressure readings (plus heart rate and stress levels)—important info to share with your doctor.

•**OnTrack Diabetes** tracks glucose levels, blood pressure, pulse, weight, exercise, diet and medications…and produces graphs or reports for your doctor.

•**Pillbox** helps you stay on schedule in taking all your medications and supplements.

Also: You can search a database for medication information.

Exercise apps make workouts more fun and more effective…

•**RunKeeper Pro** records your runs using your smartphone's built-in GPS capabilities. Whether you jog, walk, cycle or ski, you can see your distance, pace, path traveled and calories burned…then later sync data to the *www.runkeeper.com* Web site to track your progress.

•**MoboVivo Workout** provides a wide selection of exercise videos—ballet, yoga, belly dancing and more—that you can use to work out wherever you go.

Weight-loss apps keep you motivated, connected and informed…

•**WiScale** is an app that uses the Withings Internet-connected body scale ($159 at *www.withings.com*) to track your weight and body mass index and transfer the information automatically to your smartphone. It includes a social dimension—you share information and motivation with a community, joining virtual forces to engage in healthier behaviors. "It's like attending a weight-loss group without going in person," Dr. Kvedar said.

•**Fast Food Calorie Counter** lists calories, fat, carbs, fiber and protein content of thousands of menu items from dozens of popular restaurant chains (including some that you might not relegate to "fast food" status).

Educational apps help you diagnose a problem or handle an emergency…

•**uHear** reveals whether your hearing is in the normal range.

•**Emergency First Aid & Treatment Guide** tells you what to do in case of burns, frostbite, seizures and more…and how to use emergency medical equipment, including a defibrillator.

Many apps are free, while others typically cost from $1 to $10—so the financial damage is slight if you end up not liking an app that you have downloaded.

But beware: The FDA does not regulate health-related apps, and some may be the modern equivalent of snake oil. (Do any of us really believe that the blue light generated by an iPhone can smooth away wrinkles?) As Dr. Kvedar pointed out, "With any app, if it seems too good to be true, it probably is."

What Doctors Didn't Know 25 Years Ago— New Science

Dennis Gottfried, MD, an assistant clinical professor of medicine at the University of Connecticut School of Medicine, Farmington, and an internist with a private practice in Torrington, Connecticut. *www.drdennisgottfried.com*. He is the author of *Too Much Medicine: A Doctor's Prescription for Better and More Affordable Health Care* (Paragon House).

W hat if your doctor had advised you for years to follow a certain treatment or lifestyle practice but later told you that the advice had been found to be harmful or outdated? That's exactly what has happened numerous times over the past several years. Science is always changing.

Dennis Gottfried, MD, is a leading expert on medical research. He identified some of the most significant and interesting medical advances that have occurred during the past quarter century.

Some represent frightening realizations. For example, millions of women had been treated for decades with hormone replacement therapy (HRT) for hot flashes and other menopausal symptoms. Then, in 2002, a Women's Health Initiative study showed that HRT increased a woman's risk for life-threatening conditions such as heart attack, stroke and breast cancer.

But there were other developments that received far less fanfare. *For example...*

CATARACT FIX IN ONE DAY

By age 80, more than half of all Americans either have a cataract or have had cataract surgery.

By the late 1960s, surgeons had developed techniques to remove the damaged lens of the eye. But patients who had cataracts removed could see only if they wore thick, Coke bottle–style glasses. They also had to stay in the hospital—and lie almost completely still—for five or six days. In 1981, the FDA approved the first implantable lens so that thick glasses were no longer needed after surgery.

Now: Cataract surgery is one of the most common surgical procedures in the US—and it's almost always done at outpatient centers.

The lens of the eye is removed via an incision that's usually no longer than one-eighth inch. An artificial lens is slipped through the opening. The incision then usually closes on its own, without stitches. Vision in the corrected eye is typically improved within two weeks. Implantable lenses continue to evolve—even bifocal implants are now available.

"KEYHOLE" SURGERIES

A few decades ago, most surgeries were "open" procedures, requiring large incisions and lengthy hospital stays and recovery times.

Now: Most surgeries are done using laparoscopes, which allow the area being operated on to be seen through a telescope-like tube that is connected to a video camera. Such minimally invasive "keyhole" surgery is routinely performed for gallbladder removal, appendectomies, hernia repairs, gynecological surgery and many orthopedic procedures. The incisions can be as small as five millimeters in length and generally result in reduced blood loss, less pain and shorter hospital stays—or no hospital stay at all.

CT DANGERS

Computed tomography (CT) scans, which were introduced in 1972, have revolutionized our ability to detect tumors and other abnormalities in virtually every part of the body.

However, the precision offered by CT scans has come with an unexpected cost—Americans are now exposed to more radiation from medical diagnostic tests than people anywhere else in the world.

The National Cancer Institute estimates that radiation exposure from CT scans done in 2007 alone eventually will result in 29,000 cancers and 15,000 cancer deaths.

Now: Because the diseases caused by medical radiation take decades to develop, we're just beginning to see the consequences of excessive testing with radiation-producing imaging scans such as CTs.

Important: Don't assume that you need a scan just because your doctor ordered it. Question every scan. Ask if the diagnosis can be made in some other way.

Also important: Ask the imaging center for a digital copy of your scan. It's usually free of charge. Having a copy may help you avoid unnecessary duplicate scans if you later get treated at a different hospital.

"KILLER" EGGS

For decades, it was widely believed that eating eggs would increase one's cholesterol levels. It's true that eggs (or, more specifically, yolks) contain a significant amount of cholesterol—213 milligrams (mg) in one large egg. So it seemed logical that eating eggs would greatly increase blood-cholesterol levels.

Now: We know that you do not have to avoid eggs to protect your heart. In fact, some doctors now frequently recommend that their patients eat eggs as a good source of protein and other nutrients. For the majority of people, most of the cholesterol in the body is not affected by diet. Most of the cholesterol that comes from diet is converted in the liver from the saturated fats and trans-fatty acids in our food.

Most importantly, no studies have found any connection between eggs and the development of heart disease.

Exception: People with existing cardiovascular disease or hard-to-control cholesterol should limit their egg consumption to no more than a few eggs a week or eat egg whites only.

BETTER THAN BUTTER?

Margarine was initially developed as a low-cost alternative to butter. By the mid-1970s, the consumption of margarine worldwide was about 25% greater than that of butter. Later, when manufacturers touted margarine's health benefits—the trans fat in margarine was supposedly healthier than the saturated fat in butter—sales rose even more.

Now: Nutritionists agree that margarines with high levels of trans fat are linked to various health risks. For example, such margarines elevate LDL "bad" cholesterol just as much as saturated fat and promote inflammation in the body, one of the underlying causes of heart disease.

Stick margarine contains the most trans fat, while many soft-tub margarines contain less than 0.5 g trans fat per serving, which appears as "zero trans fat" on the label.

Best: Benecol Spread or Promise activ Light Spread. They contain modified plant extracts that can reduce cholesterol by about 15%.

THREE EXTRA YEARS OF LIFE

Perhaps the greatest medical advance in the past 25 years has been our successful effort against cardiovascular disease. Although cardiac disease is still the leading cause of death in the US and stroke is the third, the death rate from these diseases has dramatically declined. According to the American Heart Association, cardiac deaths dropped 36.4% from 1996 to 2006, and over the past 25 years, death from strokes has been cut in half. The average American has gained more than three years of added life expectancy from these advances!

Sophisticated cardiac surgeries and procedures have played a role, but prevention has been the overwhelming reason for our improved cardiovascular statistics. Fewer adults now smoke, and blood pressure drugs are more

effective and more widely taken. Research has shown that cholesterol-lowering statins—beginning with the first FDA-approved statin, lovastatin (Mevacor), in 1987—decrease cardiac death by 35%.

Caution: About one-third of Americans are obese—a known risk factor for many serious conditions, including diabetes. Ultimately, the increased cardiac deaths related to diabetes could erase the advances of the last few decades.

Stem Cell Breakthroughs

Jan Nolta, PhD, director of the University of California at Davis Stem Cell Center and Research Program. Dr. Nolta has authored or coauthored more than 75 scientific papers as well as 15 book chapters related to stem cells. She is the editor of the textbook *Genetic Engineering of Mesenchymal Stem Cells* (Springer).

U ntil recently, most of the news about stem cells focused on those derived from human embryos. These so-called "undifferentiated" cells have been heralded for their potential to treat—or even cure—diseases ranging from Alzheimer's and Parkinson's to diabetes and spinal cord injuries.

Embryonic stem cells are capable of producing heart cells, blood cells, brain cells—or any one of the more than 200 other types of specialized cells in the body. Although research related to embryonic cells is promising, it still is preliminary and has been performed only on laboratory animals. Human embryonic stem cell clinical trials will not begin for at least one year—and embryonic stem cells remain controversial, because some people believe that it is unethical to use the cells for medical purposes.

Now: Researchers are discovering new uses for adult stem cells, which have long been used in transplants (from the patient's own bone marrow or blood…or from the bone marrow of someone who is a genetic match) to treat leukemia, lymphoma and, more recently, as an adjunct therapy for advanced malignancies of the prostate, kidney and bladder.

LATEST BREAKTHROUGH

Researchers at the University of California at Davis have for the first time identified adult bladder stem cells—which might be used in the future to regenerate replacement bladder tissue in people whose bladders are too small or don't function properly, such as adults with spinal cord injuries or bladder cancer. These findings were reported in *The American Journal of Physiology-Renal* online.

Other exciting research: Elsewhere, hundreds of recent clinical trials in the US and around the world show that adult stem cells found in specific tissues and organs, such as the heart, muscles and bones—or "harvested" from the patient's blood or bone marrow—can treat a variety of medical conditions, including congestive heart failure, rheumatoid arthritis and multiple sclerosis.

At the UC Davis Stem Cell Center, we often refer to adult stem cells as the "paramedics of the body"—that's because they move very quickly to areas of tissue damage and secrete substances that repair tissue and improve blood flow.

Future research at our center will study the use of adult stem cells for, among other problems, repairing heart tissue after a heart attack…and restoring restricted blood flow in peripheral artery disease (PAD), a blockage in the arteries, occurring mainly in the legs.

Some of the current research in these two areas…

HEART DISEASE

A review article in *The Journal of the American Medical Association* cited more than 30 studies that have been conducted using adult stem cells in people who have had heart attacks or who suffer from cardiovascular disorders.

How they work: Adult stem cells from the bone marrow or blood may generate compounds, including proteins, that stop cell death and promote the body's own capacity to regenerate blood vessels.

Results have included fewer deaths from heart disease…an 18% improvement in the strength of the heartbeat, on average…less severe angina (chest pain)…fewer arrhythmias (abnormal heart rhythms)…slower rates of new arterial blockage…and better daily functioning.

PERIPHERAL ARTERY DISEASE

About 10 million Americans suffer from peripheral artery disease. When the disease advances to the point where pain in the lower legs is nearly constant, and leg wounds and ulcers won't heal, the condition is called *critical limb ischemia* (CLI). CLI affects 1.4 million Americans. Every year, 100,000 people with CLI lose a toe, foot or a leg to amputation.

Latest development: Researchers at Northwestern University Feinberg School of Medicine are studying 75 people with CLI for whom all standard therapies, including angioplasty (the use of a balloon-tipped catheter to open blocked arteries), had been unsuccessful.

Half the CLI patients were given a drug that stimulated the release of CD34+ cells (a type of adult stem cell) from their bone marrow. The cells were then collected via an intravenous line, and a sophisticated machine "purified" that mixture to increase the concentration of CD34+ cells. The patients were injected intravenously with the cells. Researchers hope the cells will accumulate in—and help repair—the damaged arteries as well as attract other adult stem cells to the area.

Other promising research…

AUTOIMMUNE DISEASES

In the 1990s, doctors began to use stem cell transplants to treat autoimmune diseases, in which the white blood cells of the body's immune system attack a particular organ or type of tissue—for example, the joints in rheumatoid arthritis…the coverings (sheaths) of nerves in multiple sclerosis…and the pancreas in type 1 diabetes. The transplants were performed to generate new white blood cells that would not attack the body.

Recent clinical studies have used adult stem cells to repair tissue damaged by…

• **Crohn's disease.** Two-thirds of the 21 patients treated had complete remission of this form of inflammatory bowel disease.

• **Lupus.** Nearly two-thirds of the 26 patients treated were "event-free" for five years from the symptoms of this autoimmune disease. Lupus can attack the skin, joints, heart, lungs, blood, kidneys and brain.

•**Multiple sclerosis.** Of 21 patients, none had progression of this neurological disease over two years, and 62% were improved.

FINDING A CLINICAL TRIAL

To learn more about participating in a clinical trial using adult stem cells, consult the National Institutes of Health's Web site, *www. clinicaltrials.gov.*

Targeted Cancer Therapy

Christopher Taylor Barry, MD, PhD, an associate professor of surgery at the University of Rochester Medical Center in Rochester, New York. A pioneer in IRE procedures, he is a member of the American Society of Transplant Surgeons and The Transplantation Society and has authored numerous professional articles in such journals as *Nature Biotechnology, Journal of Gastroenterology and Hepatology* and the *American Journal of Transplantation.* Dr. Barry reports that he has no financial interest in or special arrangements regarding the NanoKnife or AngioDynamics, its maker.

A "shocking" new treatment that some doctors believe offers hope to cancer patients with tumors that would have been inoperable in the past is now being used in 16 medical centers across the US.

Specially trained doctors can now use long, needlelike probes to deliver high-voltage bursts of electricity to tumors that are difficult to remove surgically. The minimally invasive procedure, known as *irreversible electroporation* (IRE), targets cancer cells that are then engulfed and removed by the body's immune system.

Intended benefits: Because IRE doesn't involve traditional "open" surgery, patients may experience little pain after the procedure. Some of them go home from the hospital the same day. Because the treatment generates little heat and the probes are precisely positioned through tiny incisions in the skin, there's a very low risk for damage to nearby nerves, blood vessels or organs.

Anecdotal evidence based on procedures that have been performed using IRE shows that this approach has proved successful in treating cancers of the liver, kidneys, pancreas, prostate and lungs. Thus far, the device has been used to perform about 300 procedures worldwide. In the future, it may be used for treating many different types of cancer, including malignancies of the breast and brain.

Important caveat: The device that is used to administer IRE, known as a NanoKnife, has not yet undergone randomized studies comparing it with other treatments—an important step in scientific research. Some doctors are concerned about the lack of clinical data.

MORE PRECISION, LESS PAIN?

Traditional cancer treatments, such as surgical removal or the destruction of cells with extreme heat (radiofrequency ablation) or cold (cryoablation), are somewhat imprecise, even in skilled hands. These procedures not only can damage some of the healthy tissue that surrounds the tumor, but also result in scar tissue that causes pain.

With IRE, it's now possible to attack tumors on an almost unthinkably small ("nano") scale. The electrical pulses punch very tiny holes in the walls of cancer cells and cause them to die. However, because of the lack of a head-to-head comparison with other techniques, it is unclear whether less pain is involved or precision is superior with IRE.

The NanoKnife has received FDA approval for soft-tissue ablation (removal) based on a regulatory provision that allows expedited approval without rigorous scientific testing. The approval was granted because the NanoKnife was deemed sufficiently similar to another medical device currently in use—one that is used to destroy tissue during heart operations.

Use of IRE is not intended to replace older cancer treatments. For now, it's mainly used for treating cancers that aren't readily removed with other procedures. It gives doctors an additional tool when treating tumors that are smaller than 5 cm (approximately 2 inches), are located in hard-to-reach areas or that can't be removed without a high risk of damaging nearby structures.

WHO MAY BENEFIT

The expected precision of IRE, and the fact that it may be less likely to produce scar tissue or damage healthy tissue than other procedures, means that there may be a lower risk for complications.

Example: Men who undergo prostate surgery often suffer from impotence or urinary incontinence because of damage to critical nerves. This damage has thus far been less likely with IRE.

In the future, IRE could become an important treatment for patients who can't withstand the trauma of major surgery. It's performed under general anesthesia but is much faster than traditional surgery and less physically taxing.

However, the anesthesia must be "deep" to keep patients completely immobile during the procedure. Otherwise, the probes could shift and potentially damage healthy tissue or fail to destroy portions of the tumor. Potential complications include inadvertent perforation of an organ or tissue, hemorrhage or infection.

HOW IT WORKS

Once the patient is anesthetized, a computed tomography (CT) scanner or ultrasound device is used to guide the placement of the probes. The doctor then uses a foot pedal to generate electrical bursts (each one lasting less than 100-millionths of a second) that kill the cancer cells within a particular area.

IRE treatment can cover an area that measures about 3 cm by 4 cm in less than four minutes. It's less effective for tumors larger than 5 cm. The standard treatment consists of a series of 90 electrical pulses.

Because this technology is so new, it is not yet widely available in the US. It's being used, and studied, in Europe and Australia.

Not all insurers cover the cost of treatment with IRE. Some cite a current lack of scientific evidence when declining claims for coverage.

Treatments for Liver Cancer

Howard J. Worman, MD, professor of medicine, pathology and cell biology at the Columbia University College of Physicians and Surgeons in New York City. He is the author of *The Liver Disorders and Hepatitis Sourcebook* (McGraw-Hill).

Primary liver cancer (known as *hepatocellular carcinoma*) is widely considered to be one of the deadliest malignancies.

But there's a glimmer of hope for the estimated 22,000 Americans who are diagnosed with this type of cancer each year. In the US, the five-year survival rate for people with primary liver cancer more than tripled from 4% to 13% during the years 1992 to 2005.

There is no single reason for the improved prognosis. Screening tests that allow for earlier diagnoses, such as ultrasound, are now more widely used than in the past. Also, liver transplants are more prevalent than they used to be, which can also increase survival times—and, in some cases, even result in a total cure.

Another important development: While primary liver cancer has long been associated with people who have a history of excessive alcohol use and infection with hepatitis B or C, there are also lesser-known risk factors. *What you need to know...*

ARE YOU AT RISK?

Most liver cancers in the US are secondary—they originate in other parts of the body (including the breast, colon or lung) and then spread to the liver. Only a small percentage of malignancies, known as primary cancers, originate in the liver.

In the US, an average man's lifetime risk of developing primary liver or intrahepatic bile duct cancer (which develops in bile duct branches in the liver) is about one in 100. For an average woman, the lifetime risk is lower, about one in 217. It is thought that men have higher risk because they are more likely to engage in behaviors, such as heavy drinking, that can lead to liver cancer.

Hidden risks: Cirrhosis (scarring) of the liver, often caused by excessive alcohol consumption, is a major risk factor. Infection with hepatitis B or C raises a person's risk for liver cancer because both types of hepatitis damage the liver.

Most people with cirrhosis or hepatitis experience no obvious symptoms for many years, so they can develop liver cancer before they even know that they have a serious risk factor.

Symptoms of hepatitis B include dark urine, abdominal pain or loss of appetite...for hepatitis C, symptoms include liver tenderness, fever and nausea. Symptoms often do not develop until cirrhosis complications occur. Both hepatitis B and C are transmitted primarily through unprotected sex with an infected partner (though less commonly for hepatitis C)...sharing contaminated needles or having had a blood transfusion before blood supply screening was routine...and coming into contact with contaminated blood (usually in a health-care setting).

Lesser-known risk factors: These include nonalcoholic fatty liver disease, in which obesity and/or other factors cause the liver to accumulate large amounts of fat. It affects up to one of every five Americans.

Diabetes also increases the risk for liver cancer. So does hemochromatosis (a hereditary disorder affecting iron absorption and storage). These three conditions can cause cirrhosis over time, thus increasing risk for liver cancer.

SHOULD YOU BE TESTED?

Early-stage liver cancer often causes no symptoms or vague ones, such as unexplained weight loss, poor appetite, nausea and vomiting. In later stages, symptoms include abdominal swelling, upper abdominal pain and/or jaundice.

By the time many patients are diagnosed—sometimes when a doctor can actually feel a mass in the abdomen or when imaging tests reveal an abnormality—the cancer has spread throughout the liver and treatment options are limited.

Red flag: More than 90% of patients with liver cancer have cirrhosis of the liver. Everyone who has been diagnosed with cirrhosis should undergo at least one (and sometimes two) abdominal ultrasounds annually.

Also important: The alpha-fetoprotein (AFP) blood test. Normal levels should be below 10 nanograms per millimeter (ng/mL) of blood. In people with hepatitis and/or liver cancer, levels will sometimes be as high as 500 ng/mL.

If you have nonalcoholic fatty liver disease, diabetes or hemochromatosis: Ask your doctor if you should have a blood test to detect abnormalities in liver enzymes. Anyone with an abnormal reading may need additional tests, such as ultrasound, to determine if a liver malignancy is present.

BEST TREATMENTS

The odds of recovering from liver cancer are highest when there are no more than three small tumors that can be surgically removed.

The challenge: Since the majority of patients with liver cancer also have cirrhosis, there may not be enough healthy liver to permit a surgeon to remove any additional tissue. In this case and if the tumors are small, a liver transplant is the best option. The five-year survival rate following a liver transplant is about 60%. But many patients are already too ill from the liver malignancy to benefit from a transplant.

NONSURGICAL OPTIONS

For now, surgery and liver transplant are the only possible cures for liver cancer. *However, other treatments can prolong survival and reduce pain and other symptoms...*

•***Sorafenib*** (Nexavar) is the first chemotherapeutic drug that can help patients with liver cancer. Until now, chemotherapy was ineffective because the liver naturally breaks down and eliminates chemicals, including medications for treating cancer. Sorafenib was approved by the FDA for this use in 2007.

Recent finding: Among 602 patients with advanced primary liver cancer, those who took sorafenib twice daily lived almost three months longer, on average, than those who did not take the drug. In some patients, tumors stopped growing for more than three years. Possible side effects, such as diarrhea and fatigue, tend to be mild.

• **Radiofrequency ablation,** in which needle-like probes are inserted through the skin into liver tumors, uses heat to destroy cancer cells. The tumors eventually grow back, but this treatment can give patients—including those on waiting lists for a liver transplant—a little more time.

• **Chemoembolization,** like radiofrequency ablation, kills cancer cells and shrinks tumors. The difference is that a chemotherapeutic drug is used rather than heat. The drug is injected into the arteries that carry blood to the tumor. It may be combined with radiofrequency ablation for better results. But chemoembolization is not a cure—the tumors eventually regrow.

• **Radiation treatments,** including microsphere selective radiation, in which tiny, radioactive beads (similar to the "seeds" that are sometimes used to treat prostate cancer) are inserted into the liver near tumors, have not been shown to increase survival times. However, radiation is sometimes used to shrink tumors in order to reduce pain and other symptoms.

Treatment Advances For Thyroid Cancer

Robert C. Smallridge, MD, professor of medicine, chair of endocrinology and a deputy director of the Mayo Clinic Cancer Center in Jacksonville, Florida. He has published more than 140 scientific papers on the prevention and treatment of thyroid disorders.

More people are getting diagnosed with thyroid cancer than ever before. The National Cancer Institute estimates that there will be 44,670 new cases in the US this year—more than double the number of individuals diagnosed a decade ago.

SYMPTOMS OF THYROID CANCER

When cancer occurs in the thyroid, a butterfly-shaped gland located at the base of the neck, symptoms may include hoarseness…swallowing difficulties…pain in your neck or throat and/or a lump near or on the thyroid.

Latest development: In addition to recent advances in treatment, there are simple steps that we all can take to help reduce our risk for this disease.

THYROID TUMORS ON THE RISE

Many thyroid tumors are detected when people undergo computed tomography (CT) scans for unrelated reasons or other imaging tests, such as an ultrasound examination of the carotid (neck) artery in an older adult. Because these imaging tests are being used with increasing frequency, this may explain the rise in thyroid cancer diagnoses.

However, many experts believe that there is an increase in the actual number of thyroid cancers as well. *Even though the exact cause of this malignancy is unknown, risk for the disease has been linked to…*

• **Radiation exposure.** People who grew up anywhere in the US—but especially in the Southwest—in the 1950s, when nuclear weapons were tested aboveground in Nevada, may be at increased risk for thyroid cancer as older adults. In addition, radiation therapy was used widely and unwisely during that period for medical conditions such as enlarged thymus glands and tonsils or even acne.

• **Environmental toxins,** including *polychlorinated biphenyls* (PCBs)—compounds found in such materials as some plastics, oil-based paint and carbonless copy paper—have been shown to disrupt function of endocrine glands, including the thyroid. Such toxins may contribute to rising malignancy rates.

WHAT YOU CAN DO

To guard against thyroid cancer…

• **Use caution with radiological tests.** Radiological procedures—including CT scans, which typically expose the patient to higher levels of radiation than other imaging tests—contribute to a person's total radiation exposure over his/her lifetime. Excessive radiation exposure increases risk for cancer, especially malignancies of the thyroid when it is the area being scanned. The thyroid gland is highly sensitive to the effects of radiation.

Self-defense: When a CT scan or other radiological test is prescribed by your doctor, ask whether the test is truly necessary. Sometimes a nonradiation-producing test, such as an ultrasound, can be used instead. Avoid getting dental X-rays as a part of routine care. When you do have dental X-rays, be sure to shield the thyroid. Some dental offices provide lead-lined aprons that cover this area in addition to the chest and torso.

• **Get your thyroid checked.** Whenever you see your doctor for a physical exam, he should palpate the thyroid to check for growths.

Self-defense: If you were exposed to an unusual amount of radiation as a youngster (for example, via radiation therapy to the head, neck or chest area), your regular thyroid check should also include an ultrasound examination of the gland.

Small lumps, known as nodules, in the thyroid are common (up to 50% of people have them by middle age) and are usually benign. However, if you have a history of radiation exposure, thyroid nodules are far more likely to be malignant.

• **Consider genetic testing.** A type of thyroid malignancy that can run in families, known as *medullary cancer*, occurs in 5% to 10% of people with thyroid cancer.

Self-defense: If someone in your family (especially a first-degree relative, such as a parent, sibling or child) has been diagnosed with medullary thyroid cancer, ask your doctor about receiving a blood test for the RET proto-oncogene. Mutations in this gene indicate increased risk for medullary thyroid cancer. If the test is positive, the thyroid should be removed to prevent cancer from developing.

TREATMENT ADVANCES

Thyroid cancer is generally treated by removing the cancerous area of the thyroid gland (and surrounding tissue) or the entire gland. Until recently, it was common to follow this surgical procedure with treatment with radioactive iodine (RAI), which is swallowed as a liquid or capsule, to destroy thyroid remnants that may include malignant cells.

New approach: When the risk for recurrence is low—for example, in younger patients (under age 45) who had small tumors of the most common type of thyroid cancer, known as *papillary cancer*—the American Thyroid Association has found little evidence to support the use of RAI. In fact, the group's 2009 treatment guidelines do not recommend this extra step for these patients.

This approach contrasts with that for older people, who may be undertreated for thyroid cancer.

Important recent finding: A paper in the journal *Cancer* reported that thyroid cancer patients over age 65 in the US tend to have larger, more extensive cancers than younger patients but are one-third less likely to receive RAI even though it is recommended for them.

In addition, a small percentage, about 5%, of papillary tumors are aggressive and deserve more extensive treatment no matter what the patient's age. Increasing evidence shows that testing cells from the tumor before surgery can identify these dangerous cancers by their genetic signature.

Recent discovery: A Johns Hopkins study of 190 people found that papillary tumors with the so-called BRAF gene were more likely to have spread before surgery and posed a greater risk for recurrence.

Most thyroid cancers don't come back after surgery and RAI treatment, but monitoring is essential to detect the 5% to 10% that recur. One procedure involves the use of a scan to see whether a small dose of radioactive iodine is absorbed by tissues anywhere in the body—once thyroid tissue has been removed, radioactive iodine should not be absorbed at all.

But some thyroid cancer cells stop "taking up" iodine, making them hard to spot. Doctors have developed more sensitive tests that measure *thyroglobulin*, a protein that all thyroid cells secrete. A blood test for thyroglobulin can be combined with a neck ultrasound exam to monitor for recurrence. Positron emission tomography (PET) scans also have been used to find remnants of thyroid cancer in nearby lymph nodes after surgery.

Five-year survival rates for all types of thyroid cancer range from 83% to 94%.

MEDICATION BREAKTHROUGHS

Progress has been made against the 10% of thyroid cancers that are considered to be the most aggressive because they grow rapidly and don't respond to standard treatment. New approaches include drugs that target biochemical processes that the cells need to survive.

The most promising, a group of drugs called *tyrosine kinase inhibitors*, block a protein that is overactive in thyroid cancer cells. Several are on the market for other cancers, but none are yet approved by the FDA for thyroid cancer. In one study, the cancers stopped growing for more than six months in about half of treated patients and actually shrank in 15% of patients.

One of these drugs, *pazopanib* (Votrient), targets growth factors to shut down new blood vessels that feed the tumor. Mayo Clinic researchers recently reported that aggressive thyroid cancers stopped growing or shrank over a period of one to 23 months in two-thirds of 37 patients. Because pazopanib may cause serious side effects, such as excessive bleeding, the drug is not recommended for people with less aggressive, slow-growing thyroid tumors.

To learn about clinical trials for advanced thyroid cancer, go to *www.clinicaltrials.gov*.

Cold Therapy Kills Cancer Cells

Peter J. Littrup, MD, vice-chair for radiology research and director of interventional radiology, Barbara Ann Karmanos Cancer Institute, and professor of radiology, urology and radiation oncology, Wayne State University School of Medicine, both in Detroit. Dr. Littrup is a founder of the American Cancer Society's National Prostate Cancer Detection Project.

Most of the promising new cancer treatments are complicated and hard to understand for those of us who don't have advanced degrees in chemistry, but here's one that's quite simple and effective— killing cancer cells by freezing them. Called cryotherapy, the technique has been in use for decades for some very specific problems (for instance, a type of prostate surgery), but recently, more precise technology has brought it to a new level. This led some doctors to ask, why can't we do this elsewhere in the body? It turns out that they can, and that may be very good news for some cancer patients.

We're at a tipping point with cryotherapy, says Peter Littrup, MD, vice-chair for radiology research and director of interventional radiology at the Barbara Ann Karmanos Cancer Institute in Detroit. In this country, 120 hospitals now use cryotherapy to treat cancer, though it still has far to go before it becomes a standard of care. *He discussed some of the exciting new developments...*

COLD KILLS CANCER CELLS

Many cancers that once required extensive open surgery now can be treated with this type of "thin needle surgery." Cryotherapy (also known as cryosurgery or cryoablation) uses extreme cold generated by liquid nitrogen or argon gas to destroy abnormal tissue. The procedure is far safer, less painful and easier to recover from than heat ablation techniques that burn the tumor and/or open surgery.

Dr. Littrup said that today's extremely thin "cryoprobes" (needlelike tubes that deliver the freezing gas) are so small that they can be inserted through tiny pencil-point-sized nicks in the skin. New imaging technology lets doctors target tumors with great accuracy, providing a better road map for treatment, as Dr. Littrup puts it.

Here's how a cryotherapy procedure works: The patient is lightly sedated. Using guided imaging such as ultrasound, computed tomography (CT) or magnetic resonance imaging (MRI), the radiologist inserts the cryoprobes at carefully selected locations within a tumor, where they deliver freezing gas that causes a ball of ice crystals to gradually develop around the probes. In this way, cancerous tissue is frozen and destroyed with minimal harm to nearby healthy tissue. When it thaws, the tissue is naturally and safely absorbed by the body and may initiate an immune response. Cryotherapy can be safely repeated as often as necessary to local tumors and can be combined with standard surgery, chemotherapy, radiation and hormone therapy and potentially immune therapy.

WHO CAN BE HELPED BY CRYOTHERAPY?

Cryotherapy has become a primary treatment for some types of cancer (specifically prostate, liver and renal cell carcinoma, which is a type of kidney cancer, and also breast and bone tumors) and may someday provide a treatment option for cancers that are inoperable or that fail to respond to standard treatment. It is helpful as a localized treatment for elderly patients and cancer patients who also have medical problems such as heart disease but who aren't healthy enough to undergo the rigors of more dramatic surgery.

Dr. Littrup summarized the advantages of cryotherapy:

Excellent visualization and targeting of a tumor, which is a distinct benefit compared to heat ablation techniques. Imaging techniques now provide doctors with a superb picture of the ice treatment zone during and after the procedure. With three-dimensional breast MRI imaging, for example, interventional radiologists can see and measure a tumor in the breast, then insert probes accordingly and monitor how the resulting "ice ball" grows and destroys the cancer.

Fewer side effects. Because it is minimally invasive, cryotherapy largely eliminates the bleeding and pain associated with surgery. The tiny incision has less chance of infection.

Shorter recovery time. Cryotherapy is usually an outpatient procedure, and patients heal faster with minimal scarring and may even return to normal activities the next day.

At $10,000 to $15,000 or so per procedure, it is less expensive than many other cancer therapies (chemotherapy can cost double or more per month), but it is considered experimental—Medicare covers it, but not all insurance carriers will. Another limitation is that little is known about the long-term effectiveness—it's hard to tell whether all cells are destroyed and there is concern that it may miss microscopic cells that can't be seen with imaging techniques. (This is also quite true of heat ablation and surgical treatments.) And there's some danger of collateral damage to the surrounding area if it is not adequately protected.

THE FUTURE OF CRYOTHERAPY

Be aware that this cutting-edge treatment is still new in cancer treatment and not widely available. Additional large-scale, multicenter studies are needed to confirm its long-term effectiveness in controlling cancer and improving survival.

You can find a board-certified interventional radiologist (the type of doctor who performs cryotherapy) in your area at the Web site of the Society of Interventional Radiology (*http://doctor-finder.sirweb.org/*). If you have cancer, cryotherapy may well be a promising treatment option to explore with your physician.

Ovarian Cancer: Life-Saving Discoveries

Krishnansu S. Tewari, MD, associate professor of gynecologic oncology at the University of California, Irvine Medical Center. Dr. Tewari is the principal investigator for the Gynecologic Oncology Group at UCI, and cochair of the Clinical Trials Protocol Review & Monitoring Committee at UCI's Chao Family Comprehensive Cancer Center.

Ovarian cancer is known as a deadly malignancy that typically causes no symptoms or ones that are so subtle they are easily overlooked. For this reason, the cancer is already widespread in 75% of newly diagnosed cases.

Now: Tests are being developed that help detect ovarian cancer before it reaches advanced stages—and scientists are hopeful that a breakthrough treatment will extend survival times in women diagnosed with the disease.

Recent developments that could help save your life or that of someone you love...

WHO IS AT GREATEST RISK

No one knows what causes ovarian cancer. But it is known that risk increases with age—90% of cases occur after age 45—as well as with...

•**Ovulation.** Every time an egg ruptures through the surface of the ovary during normal ovulation, the body repairs the damage.

Each repair brings the possibility of DNA mutations that can set the stage for ovarian cancer. That's why taking a break from ovulation—by using birth control pills, for example, or having children—reduces the risk for ovarian cancer.

Who can benefit: Women of child-bearing age who do not have contraindications to birth control pills and are at high risk for ovarian cancer.

• **Genetic susceptibility.** Women who carry an inherited mutation in the BRCA1 and BRCA2 genes (most commonly associated with breast cancer) are 10 to 27 times more likely to develop ovarian cancer than women without this mutation.

Women who should consider testing for BRCA mutations: Those who are of Ashkenazi Jewish descent—they are at increased risk for breast cancer and ovarian cancer... those who have multiple relatives affected by cancer, especially ovarian and breast...and/or have a first-degree relative, such as a parent, sibling or child, who developed any cancer before age 50.

Important: Having a mutation means an increased risk, not a guarantee of cancer.

In addition to increasing surveillance—via ultrasound and a blood test for the protein cancer antigen 125 (CA-125)—women with genetic susceptibility may want to consider having their ovaries and fallopian tubes removed. Fallopian tubes also are susceptible to developing cancer from BRCA mutations. This surgery, known as *salpingo-oophorectomy* (SO), is recommended only if a woman has completed childbearing or when she reaches age 35—the age at which most women have decided whether they want to have children.

Because small bits of tissue could be left behind, SO significantly reduces, but doesn't eliminate, the risk for ovarian cancer. This surgery may sound drastic, but many women prefer this approach to living with an elevated threat of cancer.

What's new: Researchers have found a new genetic marker of ovarian cancer—a mutation on a variant of the cancer gene known as KRAS.

In one study, the KRAS variant was present in more than 25% of women with ovarian cancer.

What's more, the KRAS variant was present in 61% of women with ovarian cancer who did not have BRCA1 or BRCA2, adding a new piece to the genetic cancer puzzle. More clinical research is needed before the test for the KRAS gene variant can be approved by the FDA.

WHAT'S NEW IN DETECTION

If a suspicious ovarian tumor is discovered—during a pelvic exam or ultrasound, for example—a gynecologist will usually order a CA-125 blood test. Typically, high levels of CA-125 protein in these women signal the presence of ovarian cancer. The test also is used to screen for cancer in women with known genetic mutations and to catch signs of cancer recurrence after treatment.

However, the test has not been used for general screening of women without tumors because it has a high rate of false positives—even regular menstruation can increase CA-125 levels. False positives often lead to unnecessary and expensive follow-up testing, occasionally surgery and, of course, fear and distress for the patients.

What's new: An effective and low-cost way to use CA-125 to screen for ovarian cancer in the general population. An eight-year study followed more than 3,000 postmenopausal women (ages 50 to 74) who had no family history of breast or ovarian cancer. Researchers took a baseline reading of CA-125, and then the women were categorized by risk level based on a mathematical model called the Risk of Ovarian Cancer Algorithm (ROCA). Each woman ended up with her own CA-125 profile, which was used to determine when additional testing was warranted. For example, if an individual woman's CA-125 increased by a certain amount, then she would get an ultrasound.

Exciting finding: Among the more than 3,000 women studied, this method of CA-125 testing found three invasive ovarian cancers, which were detected at an early stage. If approved for general use, this method will provide a cost-effective way to screen women for ovarian cancer, just as the Pap test screens for cervical cancer.

Another new development: The OVA1 blood test was recently approved by the FDA. OVA1 is a panel of five marker proteins, including CA-125, which are combined to give an overall composite score, like a cancer risk report card. OVA1 is used in women with a tumor to assess whether it is likely to be malignant and whether biopsies/surgery should be recommended or avoided.

In some cases, oncologists order three tests —OVA1, CA-125 and another test called HE4, which detects an additional ovarian cancer marker —to determine whether a mass is likely to be malignant. Because OVA1 gives a composite score, not an individual value for each of the five proteins, it can be helpful to also order CA-125 individually.

EXCITING TREATMENT ADVANCE

This is the first year in more than a decade that a breakthrough has occurred in the treatment of ovarian cancer. Up to now, ovarian cancer has typically been treated only with surgery and chemotherapy.

What's new: Research has shown that a drug called *bevacizumab* (Avastin)—also used to treat malignancies such as those of the colon and breast—delays the progression of advanced ovarian cancer. Bevacizumab is an antiangiogenic drug, which starves tumors by preventing the growth of new blood vessels.

Women who took bevacizumab during and up to 10 months after chemotherapy lived an average four months longer than those not taking it.

Bevacizumab is not FDA approved for ovarian cancer but can be used for this condition at a doctor's discretion. For this reason, insurance may not cover the cost of the drug—a year's supply can exceed $50,000. The drugmaker is expected to apply soon for FDA approval to use bevacizumab in the treatment of ovarian cancer.

GET THE BEST CARE

• **If you have one or more symptoms of ovarian cancer and they don't subside with treatment, ask for proof of the diagnosis.** For example, if your doctor says that you have a urinary tract infection, ask if a urine culture was performed. Don't give up until your symptoms improve.

• **If your doctor suspects ovarian cancer, be sure to see a gynecologic oncologist to confirm the diagnosis.** These doctors have specialized training that helps ensure your best chances for survival. To find a specialist in your area, consult the Women's Cancer Network (*www.wcn.org/findadoctor*).

• **If you are diagnosed with ovarian cancer,** try to get treated at one of 40 Comprehensive Cancer Centers in the US that are designated by the National Cancer Institute (NCI). These centers provide cutting-edge therapy and offer access to clinical trials. To find an NCI-designated cancer center near you, go to *http://cancercenters.cancer.gov/cancer_centers/index.html.*

Prevent Arm Swelling After Breast Cancer Surgery

Gwen White, PT, physical therapist and lymphedema specialist with Kaiser Permanente in Portland, Oregon, and coauthor of *Lymphedema: A Breast Cancer Patient's Guide to Prevention and Healing* (Hunter House).

If you have breast cancer, you may already be familiar with the condition lymphedema. This condition—which involves mild to extreme swelling, usually in the arm—can cause significant pain, loss of arm function, disfigurement and emotional distress. Symptoms can develop soon after surgery or may appear months or even years later. According to the National Cancer Institute, as many as 56% of breast cancer patients experience it within two years after surgery.

Good news: A recent Spanish study suggests that physical therapy (PT) provided soon after breast cancer surgery can significantly reduce the risk of developing lymphedema. One group of breast cancer patients who did not have lymphedema received typical instruction on prevention strategies...a second group got instruction plus three sessions of PT per week for three weeks. After one year, 25% of the instruction-only group had developed lymphedema—compared with only 7% of the PT group.

Physical therapist Gwen White, PT, coauthor of *Lymphedema: A Breast Cancer Patient's Guide to Prevention and Healing* and a lymphedema specialist at Kaiser Permanente in Portland, Oregon, explains how PT helps…

• **Lymphedema lesson.** The lymphatic system, which is part of the immune and circulatory systems, helps clean the body's tissues and maintain its balance of fluids. It includes vessels that carry lymph fluid through the body, plus nodes that filter out waste. White explained that, if part of the lymphatic system is damaged, lymph fluid can accumulate in nearby tissues, triggering severe swelling, increasing infection risk and eventually causing skin to thicken and harden. Breast cancer patients are at risk because one or more lymph nodes are typically removed during a mastectomy or lumpectomy and because radiation therapy can produce scar tissue—and both these factors can interrupt lymph flow.

• **What happens in PT.** Specially trained physical therapists in the US use the same techniques to prevent and treat lymphedema as the Spanish researchers used. Many insurance policies cover PT—check with your carrier. Generally therapy includes…

Manual lymph drainage: This gentle massage technique moves lymph fluid away from areas that are swollen or at risk for swelling and into areas where it can drain normally. During the 45- to 60-minute massage, the therapist "presses no harder than she would on a newborn baby's head," said White.

Caution: Deep-tissue massage must be avoided, as it can bring on lymphedema even years after surgery.

Scar tissue massage: Surgery and radiation can leave inflexible scars that inhibit lymph flow. Massage techniques using heavier pressure stretch and soften scar tissue.

Lymph drainage exercises: Specific exercises, done in sequence, help pump lymph fluid through the lymphatic pathways. A typical routine includes pelvic tilts, partial sit-ups, neck rotations, shoulder shrugs, elbow bends and wrist circles.

Self-care instruction: PT patients learn lymphedema-minimizing strategies for home use, including self-massage…exercises…abdominal breathing (which acts as a pump to stimulate lymph flow)…hydration, diet and weight control…infection avoidance…stress reduction…use of a compression garment (a special sleeve that limits lymph accumulation)…and application of elastic Kinesio tape, which lifts the skin to promote lymph flow.

• **Prevention policy problem.** Given the Spanish study's findings about PT's effectiveness in preventing lymphedema, you would think that all breast cancer patients would get PT—but that's not happening. "Ideally, patients would be referred for PT before or shortly after surgery…but doctors tend to send patients to PT only if signs of lymphedema occur," White said.

Self-defense: Don't wait for lymphedema to develop. Even if you show no signs of it after breast surgery, ask your doctor for a referral to a physical therapist with expertise in lymphedema…or find one through the National Lymphedema Network (800-541-3259, *www.lymphnet.org*).

If any symptoms do appear, alert your physician without delay. Unless treated promptly, lymphedema can worsen quickly and eventually become chronic. The area may not look swollen at first, so watch for warning signs—a sensation of fullness, heaviness, heat, numbness or "pins and needles" in the arm, hand, breast or side of the torso.

Put Your PSA Score To Good Use

John Davis, MD, assistant professor, department of urology, The University of Texas MD Anderson Cancer Center, Houston.

Cancer screening is a surprisingly controversial topic these days as public health officials, epidemiologists and academic researchers attempt to sort out questions about whether screening tests actually save many lives and, if so, at what cost. Right near the top of the list of tests being so questioned is the PSA blood test as a screening tool for prostate cancer.

Whether men with no special risk factors should undergo this test is a complicated issue that we won't try to settle here, but there remain a significant number of men who either want or need to have regular PSA tests. For them, the MD Anderson Cancer Center at the University of Texas has developed a tracking system that helps patients assist their doctors in spotting warning signs of prostate cancer. It's helpful, easy to use and free.

MAKE TEST RESULTS MEANINGFUL

John Davis, MD is assistant professor in the department of urology at the University of Texas MD Anderson Cancer Center in Houston and one of the architects of this new tool. Dr. Davis said that the tracking system can help make PSA tests more valuable and meaningful for those who choose to have them.

When this simple tool is maintained and discussed by doctor and patient, it enhances the value of the PSA test in several ways…

• **It provides a clear, easily stored record that can be quickly consulted.**

• **It can serve as a reminder that it is time to have your annual test.**

• **It lets the extent and speed** (called "velocity") of any rise in PSA be easily seen over time. This helps the doctor evaluate how meaningful the rise may be and provides an opportunity to recommend other tests to determine whether the patient has cancer. It is important to keep track of velocity, since studies have linked it—not just the actual level of PSA—to the risk of death from prostate cancer. If the velocity is high, Dr. Davis said, the patient can be treated earlier and more aggressively.

The tool is a simple, two-page form on which patients and/or doctors can record basic information, including the patient's name and age, the doctor's name, dates of tests and the results in nanograms of PSA per milliliter of blood. You can print a copy at *www.mdanderson.org/publications/focused-on-health/issues/images/psa-20tracking-20tool.pdf.*

538

PSA TEST—WHO NEEDS IT?

While this is a question you should discuss with your own doctor, Dr. Davis is of the opinion that men should begin annual PSA testing at age 50 unless there are particular risk factors. These include being of African descent or having a close relative (father, brother or son) with prostate cancer. There also is some evidence that a diet high in fat—especially animal fat—increases risk.

If any of those risk factors describes you, Dr. Davis recommends having your first PSA test at age 45.

Regenerative Medicine— Breakthrough Technology Grows Human Organs And Tissue

Anthony Atala, MD, director of the Institute for Regenerative Medicine and chair of the department of urology at Wake Forest University Baptist Medical Center in Winston-Salem, North Carolina. He also is the author or editor of eight books, including *Principles of Regenerative Medicine* (Academic Press) and the author of more than 250 medical journal articles.

If you heard about scientists growing body parts in a laboratory, you might assume that it's something out of science fiction. But such "regenerative medicine" is now occurring—and it will undoubtedly play an important role in the future of medical care.

Landmark breakthrough: Nine children and teenagers with a congenital defect that prevented their bladders from functioning properly received regenerated (laboratory-grown) bladders beginning in 1998. They have been followed for an average of seven years, and their bladders are continuing to function.

Anthony Atala, MD, director of Wake Forest University's Institute for Regenerative Medicine, one of the country's leading regenerative medicine research facilities, answered questions about this cutting edge research.

• **Where are we in the development of regenerative medicine?** Much of the existing research has been conducted on animals, such as mice and rats. But we also know that there is a constant "turnover" of cells in the human body—that is, the growth of new cells and the regeneration of tissue after injury.

For example, if a person's liver is damaged in a car accident and half of the organ must be removed, the liver can regenerate. If you take an X-ray of the same patient nine months later, the liver is fully regrown. Since we know that many parts of the human body are able to regenerate, our goal is to enhance that function to treat certain injuries and diseases.

• **What is unique about regenerative medicine's capacity for healing?** Because the damaged or diseased body part is completely replaced, it has the potential to cure rather than manage illness. Regenerative medicine also will help solve organ shortages—the lengthy waiting period for a transplantable organ, such as a kidney, liver or heart, that sometimes ends in the patient's death if an organ does not become available. And because regenerated organs can be grown from a patient's own cells, there is less risk for organ rejection, a significant problem in transplants.

• **Besides accident victims, what types of patients could potentially benefit most from regenerative medicine?** People with diabetes or kidney, liver or heart failure are among the prime candidates. Others include patients who need replacement bone, muscle, ligament and tendon during surgery, and burn patients who don't have enough healthy skin for grafting.

• **How exactly are new organs and body tissues grown?** Many methods are being tested and developed, but the most commonly used technique has already been utilized to create implantable bladders in humans (described earlier). This method is also being used in the laboratory to grow other organs, such as kidneys and livers, and structures, including the esophagus, blood vessels and heart valves.

For the regenerated bladders, the first step involved taking a small tissue sample—about half the size of a postage stamp—from the diseased organ. Cells from the sample were mixed with growth factors (naturally occurring substances capable of stimulating cell growth and reproduction) so that the cells would multiply in the lab.

Those cells were then layered onto a scaffold-like structure (or mold) that had the same shape as the diseased organ and was made out of materials that are compatible with the human body.

The cell-covered scaffold was then placed in an ovenlike device or incubator that reproduced the conditions inside the human body—the same temperature and the same combination and concentration of biological elements. After approximately six to eight weeks, the cells had grown into tissue and the regenerated organ was ready to be implanted. It was removed from the incubator and placed in the patient by suturing it to the diseased organ. The scaffolding gradually degraded, and the new tissue integrated with the body.

• **How is regenerative medicine currently being used?** The process I just described was used to create the implantable bladders for children and teenagers with stiff, poorly functioning bladders. Previously, this defect was fixed by using a section of intestine to fashion a pouch to hold urine. But because intestinal tissue is not designed for such a use—but rather to absorb and excrete waste—this procedure increased the risk for osteoporosis, kidney stones and cancer. The recipients of the regenerated bladders have fully functioning bladders without the side effects produced by the old procedure.

Clinical trials focusing on implantable bladder technology are now being conducted at about 10 US research centers. The next step will be to make the technology available for widespread use.

In another case, cells from ear cartilage were used to formulate an injectable gel to repair the bladder sphincter in women with a type of severe stress incontinence called intrinsic sphincter deficiency. This single injection was far more effective in producing continence than the existing procedure, which involves repeatedly injecting collagen (derived from cow carcasses) into the neck of the bladder.

•**What are the greatest challenges scientists face in the development of regenerated organs and tissue?** The least difficult processes involve flat organs, such as the skin and cartilage in some areas of the body. The next level of difficulty is a hollow organ, such as the bladder or stomach, which consists of many different cell types and must "respond" on demand (for example, the bladder must expand to hold urine, and the stomach expands when food is consumed).

The most difficult is a solid organ, such as a kidney or heart, which has the greatest number of cells and requires the most blood supply. Ensuring that a regenerated organ has a sufficient blood supply is a major challenge.

•**Which human organs and tissues are being studied most for regeneration?** At Wake Forest Institute, scientists are working on the regeneration of more than 20 different types of organs and tissues. For example, blood vessels for heart bypass surgery (which now are harvested from leg veins) and heart valves (which are currently replaced with the heart valves of pigs) are being engineered.

To treat battlefield injuries, we're developing new skin to repair burns and heal wounds without scarring. Meanwhile, attempts are being made to replace a human ear, engineer new muscle and grow fingers and limbs. Cellular therapies, such as the creation of insulin-producing cells from the pancreas to treat diabetes and the production of red blood cells to treat anemia, are also being investigated in the lab.

An exciting development in this area is the recent discovery of a new source of stem cells from amniotic fluid and placental tissue—a readily available, fast-growing stem cell that we have used in the laboratory to create muscle, bone, fat, blood vessel, nerve and liver cells. A "bank" of such cells could provide 99% of the US population with perfect genetic matches for organ transplantation.

•**You haven't mentioned lungs or eyes—are there any developments happening there?** Yes. The Wake Forest laboratory is currently involved in efforts to engineer lung tissues and cornea tissues.

•**How close are we to actually deriving the benefits of such treatments?** Most of the developments in regenerative medicine are not yet ready for clinical use, but there may well be applicable results, such as engineered heart valves and blood vessels, during the next decade.

New Research On Diabetes

M. William Lensch, PhD, affiliate faculty, Harvard Stem Cell Institute, HHMI/Children's Hospital Boston, Harvard Medical School.

We're accustomed to thinking of viruses as "bad guys" that the world would be better without—but now that scientists have used a virus to transform a non-insulin-producing pancreatic cell into one that produced insulin, we may need to reconsider that position. Adding to the achievement is that the "programming" of the cell was done without use of sometimes controversial stem cells. This is a major breakthrough in the field of regenerative medicine, which aims to regrow or repair missing or damaged tissue.

In the study, which was published in the journal *Nature*, Douglas A. Melton, PhD, co-director of the Harvard Stem Cell Institute, and his fellow researchers used a modified virus to activate three key genes in non-insulin-producing pancreatic cells in mice. Within three days, the "infected" cells started producing insulin—far faster than the several weeks it's known to take to transform stem cells into specific organ tissues.

The findings are incredibly exciting for other researchers in the field of regenerative medicine as well. "This paper really got a lot of people's attention," says M. William Lensch, PhD, affiliate faculty at the Harvard Stem Cell Institute, who wasn't himself involved with Melton's research. "It expands the possible universe of where regenerated cells can come from and how to get there—that's exciting."

Though remarkable, it's important to note that this type of cell reprogramming is still a long way from becoming a viable mainstream treatment—it has yet to be tried in humans, and long-term safety is still to be determined. Nonetheless it deserves attention because of the thinking behind it—the idea that you can quickly, relatively easily and with no political debate, change a cell that's close to what's needed into exactly what's needed, perhaps to treat cancer, liver disease, cardiovascular disease and more.

Contact Lens to Heal Blindness

Nick Di Girolamo, PhD, associate professor, NHM-RC, director of ocular research, Centre for Infection and Inflammation Research, School of Medical Sciences, University of New South Wales, Australia.

Contact lenses have been used to correct vision for a long time—but what if you could wear one that would actually help heal blindness? This kind of healing contact lens is exactly what researchers at the University of New South Wales in Sydney, Australia, have created to restore vision to three legally blind patients who had damaged corneas. What's really intriguing is that the researchers used stem cells from the patients' own eyes as part of the healing process.

STEM CELLS FOR EYE REPAIR

Yes, stem cells are what did the trick. The cornea is constantly replenished from a bank of stem cells. In each of these patients, however, that bank had been depleted or damaged.

The researchers began by taking a small tissue biopsy of the cornea that contained stem cells from each patient's healthy eye, plus a blood sample which was used to create a serum to nourish the stem cells. The cells were placed on a therapeutic contact lens and immersed in the serum, taking about 10 days to grow sufficiently to cover the lens. A surgeon then scraped each patient's cornea to remove abnormal cells, after which the lens was placed on the damaged eye in a procedure that took about a half hour. The lens remained in place for two weeks, during which time the stem cells transferred to the damaged cornea, eventually creating a healthy corneal surface. Vision improved for all three patients, one of whom even went from being legally blind to passing a vision test for a driver's license. Since the technique is new, there is no long-term experience to know if the change is permanent, but the effects in this study have thus far lasted beyond the eight to 13 months of follow-up.

EASY TO EXPAND UPON

One really exciting aspect of this particular course of treatment is that it is actually very low-tech and therefore easy for physicians to learn and perform, says Nick Di Girolamo, PhD, director of ocular research at the University of New South Wales and lead researcher in this project. "The simplicity of this technique means that it can ultimately be performed anywhere in the world," he says, "providing it is performed under sterile conditions by an experienced ophthalmic surgeon with proper facilities to culture cells." The cells and serum are the patient's own, so there's no need for immunosuppressive drugs, and the procedure itself is quick, so there is minimal time in the hospital.

Keep in mind that this treatment is still very, very new—only those three patients have had it so far. Much more research and follow-up need to be done before it can be used everywhere. Still, for the millions who suffer from cornea-related vision loss, this research could make the future look bright, indeed.

Gripping Trick for Neuro Patients

Alexander Aruin, PhD, DSc, professor of physical therapy and bioengineering, University of Illinois at Chicago, associate professor of physical medicine and rehabilitation, Rush Medical College, and director, Knecht Movement Science Laboratory, Chicago.

The simple act of lifting a glass to enjoy a drink can be a challenge for elderly people and for those suffering from neurological disorders, such as multiple sclerosis

(MS), Parkinson's disease, stroke or peripheral neuropathies. These conditions interfere with neuromuscular communication, and people end up overcompensating for their lack of sensitivity of touch and motor control by grasping too forcefully when trying to lift an object—so they may end up breaking the object they are trying to grasp. It's frustrating, fatiguing and even can be dangerous (if a glass shatters, for instance)—but new research offers an innovative approach to solving the problem.

A LIGHT TOUCH

Recently, a team of researchers at the University of Illinois at Chicago published a study demonstrating how effectively a simple maneuver can help patients gain better control over their grip—all it takes is a light touch on the wrist with the other hand (details below). An earlier study had used this technique with stroke patients—the Illinois team tried it with MS patients, and it worked. The patients were able to soften and better manipulate their grips to perform the task at hand (which, in the study, was to lift a cup that was outfitted with sensors to measure grip strength).

Alexander Aruin, PhD, DSc, lead author of the study, explained that various sensors in the joints, muscles and other parts of the body feed *proprioceptive information* (having to do with your ability to sense the position and location of the body and its parts) into the brain. Age and certain neurological conditions can cause these sensors to break down, resulting in the common problem of overgripping. Researchers found that involving the other hand gives your brain information from more sensory receptors, thus improving the likelihood that the nervous system will respond efficiently.

This technique is easy, safe and costs nothing to try...but Dr. Aruin cautions that the research involved only those with moderate—not severe—impairment. *Here's how to do it...*

• **Before lifting an object,** reach over with your other arm, lightly placing the index finger of that hand on the inner wrist of the arm with which you will be lifting the object.

• **Now,** to lift an object, wrap your hand around it...but without trying to move it—yet.

• **Keeping the index finger on the wrist at all times,** lift the object and use it (if that's the plan—for instance, to sip from a cup) and then, with your index finger remaining on your wrist, put the object down.

• **Once the task is fully completed,** remove your gripping hand from the object and then remove the finger from your wrist.

It may take a few attempts to get this to work for you, but keep practicing...when you start to feel that your arms are working together in a sort of gentle ballet and your grip is softer than before but controls the object successfully, you've got the hang of it!

Brain Wave Therapy For Pain, Parkinson's And Other Conditions

Celeste De Bease, PhD, medical psychologist and bioneurofeedback therapist, based in Bala Cynwyd, Pennsylvania.

People with epilepsy, Parkinson's disease, *attention deficit disorder* (ADD) or addictions may be able to learn how to "think themselves better" by altering their brain waves to improve their symptoms. A new form of treatment called neurotherapy (also known as neurofeedback) is similar to biofeedback but has a unique focus on controlling brain wave activity rather than skin temperature, heart rate, breathing and muscle tension.

Neurotherapy is now used with a wide scope of health issues, including not only those listed above but also autism, chronic pain, post-traumatic stress disorder, depression and anxiety. Medical psychologist and bioneurofeedback therapist Celeste De Bease, PhD, explains how.

HIGH-TECH MIND-BODY MEDICINE

According to Dr. De Bease, many neurological problems involve disordered brain waves. Neurofeedback helps patients learn to set them right.

The brain produces brain waves at varying electrical frequencies measured in hertz (cycles per second). (Just to compare, the current used for household electricity is 60 Hz here in the US.) *Brain wave electrical frequencies include...*

- **Delta**—1 to 3 Hz and the slowest of all, is mostly seen during sleep.
- **Theta**—4 to 7 Hz, a state of deep relaxation that can bring bursts of creative insight. It occurs during daydreaming and advanced meditation.
- **Alpha**—8 to 13 Hz, a pleasurable, relaxed state associated with being calm and lucid. it occurs in some forms of meditation and sometimes with dream sleep.
- **Beta**—14 to 30 Hz, is the frequency produced during normal waking activities, when you are processing information for daily living, problem solving and the like.
- **High Beta**—any Beta over 21 Hz, these waves show that the brain is in its racing mode associated with anxiety and tension.

Many patients with neurological problems tend toward either under- or over-arousal of the brain. Neurofeedback teaches methods to gain control by using video display (like a video game) images that correspond to different brain waves. Working with the therapist, people can learn ways to produce faster or slower waves. Even children can do this.

MIND CONTROL?

Dr. De Bease explained that people with ADD or depression, or who suffer from mental fog and lethargic thinking in general, benefit from learning how to speed up their brain waves—those who need to slow them down to calm over-arousal include people with compulsions, autism, post-traumatic stress disorder, chronic-pain disorders, epilepsy and insomnia. Parkinson's disease patients can benefit from slower brain waves that relax their nervous systems and contribute to better motor functioning.

Neurofeedback technology is continuing to evolve, Dr. De Bease said. Where there used to be just a few approaches, therapists now have many well-researched training protocols to work with, and their techniques become more customized as the science and training are refined. For instance, placement of electrodes varies depending on the issue being addressed—for people with ADD, Dr. De Bease said that she places electrodes on the scalp directly above the frontal cortex, which controls the function of paying attention.

PRACTICAL ADVICE

The goal of neurotherapy is to recognize how it feels to operate in the desired brain wave activity range and to then learn how to get there at will. Effective training typically takes 10 or more sessions, depending on the problem. Prices vary by area and may range from $50 to more than $100/session. Some health insurance plans cover neurofeedback for some conditions, but usually only after you get a diagnosis and prescription from your doctor.

Dr. De Bease calls neurotherapy "a powerful technique," but cautions that it is crucial to find a Biofeedback Certified Professional (BCP) who is well-trained specifically in this technique, especially in light of the fact that many who call themselves qualified have completed just a weekend training program. Look for a practitioner who is certified by the Biofeedback Certification Institute of America (*http://www.bcia.org/*). This means that, among other credentials, the practitioner has had 25 hours of practice mentored by a BCIA-approved practitioner and 100 patient/client sessions reviewed and approved by BCIA.

Neurofeedback can benefit healthy people, too. Dr. De Bease said she works primarily with medical conditions but knows many therapists who focus on performance enhancement, which includes training athletes, business professionals and even members of the military in the use of neurofeedback. Certainly this is a therapy worth looking into—it's noninvasive and drug-free, not terribly expensive, and may help with many conditions.

Jellyfish Treatment Makes You Smarter in Days

Mark A. Stengler, NMD, licensed naturopathic medical doctor and leading authority on the practice of alternative and integrated medicine. He is founder and medical director of the Stengler Center for Integrative Medicine, Encinitas, California, and associate clinical professor at the National College of Natural Medicine, Portland, Oregon. He is author of *The Natural Physician's Healing Therapies* (Bottom Line Books).

Scientists have found that a naturally occurring protein in one of the planet's oldest sea creatures—the jellyfish—might hold the key to improved memory and comprehension. The substance, *apoaequorin* (a-poh-ee-kwawr-in), found in the *Aequorea victoria* jellyfish species, has a unique way of working in the brain that is different from other natural memory enhancers. Many of my patients already are benefiting from it. Apoaequorin not only seems to reverse some of the effects of aging on the brain but also might help alleviate the effects of serious neurodegenerative diseases such as Alzheimer's disease, Parkinson's disease and ALS (Lou Gehrig's disease).

THE JELLYFISH CONNECTION

Scientists first discovered apoaequorin and its companion molecule, green fluorescent protein (GFP), in the Aequorea jellyfish, found off the west coast of North America, in the 1960s. The natural glow of GFP enables researchers to observe microscopic processes within cells that were previously invisible, such as how proteins are transported or how viruses enter cell membranes.

Apoaequorin, which binds to calcium and becomes luminescent once it does, has been used since the 1990s in a similar way to track the activity of calcium in the body's cells. In 2008, three researchers who played key roles in developing these chemical markers were awarded the Nobel Prize in Chemistry. Apoaequorin's value as a memory-boosting supplement also depends on its calcium-binding properties but in a different way. In the brain, calcium plays an important role in the chemical process that allows nerve cells to recharge

before firing. It has to be present in just the right amounts. If too much calcium builds up inside a nerve cell, it interferes with the nerve-firing process and causes the cell to die.

One of the key roles of calcium-binding proteins is to prevent the toxic buildup of calcium by removing excess calcium from the nerve cells. In the normal course of aging, beginning at around age 40, the number of calcium-binding proteins in our brain cells starts to decline, resulting in the gradual buildup of toxic calcium inside these cells. This leads to impaired cellular function and eventually brain damage as the toxic calcium kills off brain cells.

The symptoms of this age-related deterioration start slowly but then accelerate as we get older. Because apoaequorin is similar to the naturally occurring calcium-binding proteins in the brain, the theory is that by taking daily supplements, you can replace the calcium-binding proteins that are lost through the aging process—allowing your brain cells to function optimally again while also preserving them from the long-term toxic effects of excess calcium.

A "EUREKA" MOMENT

The jellyfish protein went from "scientific" discovery to "supplement for the brain" because of the efforts of Mark Underwood, cofounder of the biotech firm Quincy Bioscience, the company that makes Prevagen (888-814-0814, *www.prevagen.com*), the only commercially available form of apoaequorin. Underwood's "eureka" moment came when he was reading about an Australian swimmer who developed multiple sclerosis–like symptoms after being stung by a jellyfish. Underwood wondered what protected the jellyfish from its own venom…and whether apoaequorin's calcium-binding abilities could have neuroprotective properties.

His company conducted a number of studies in conjunction with the University of Wisconsin—Milwaukee that found that apoaequorin did seem to have a powerful protective effect on brain cells. In one study, 56 people ranging in age from 20 to 78 showed significant improvements in memory after taking 10 milligrams (mg) of Prevagen daily for 30 days. More than half the group reported gains in general memory and information retention… two-thirds did better at word recall…and 84% showed improvement in their ability to remember driving directions.

Most of my patients and others report that taking Prevagen helps them feel mentally sharper, improves their memory and gives them more mental energy. Some even say that their mood is enhanced and that they sleep more soundly.

HOW TO USE IT

Prevagen is best taken in the morning (because cognitive function is more important during the day than at night), with or without food. I recommend it for anyone over age 40 who wants to improve memory and focus. While 10 mg daily is the recommended starting dose, apoaequorin also is safe at higher doses. I recommend that my own patients who have suffered a noticeable decline in cognitive function start out with 10 mg daily for four weeks. If they don't notice an improvement in memory and focus, they can increase to 20 mg daily. Most of my patients benefit from taking 10 mg or 20 mg daily. Research has shown that Prevagen is safe to take with other memory-enhancing supplements, such as omega-3 fish oils, or medications, such as *donepezil* (Aricept). People with allergies to fish or shellfish can use it because jellyfish is neither.

The manufacturer of Prevagen is exploring apoaequorin's potential as a medical treatment for conditions such as Alzheimer's disease and Parkinson's disease.

Extreme Migraine Makeover

Among migraine patients who had forehead surgery to remove muscles at headache trigger sites, 57% reported permanent elimination of migraines (compared with 4% of a control group who had sham surgery)…and 84% had at least a 50% reduction in symptoms.

Side effects included temporary facial numbness and, rarely, very slight (and fixable) hollowing of the temples.

Bonus: The operation, similar to a forehead lift, reduced forehead wrinkles.

Good news: This surgery, which is now available, offers hope for migraine patients who want to avoid or do not respond to medication. Many insurance companies cover at least a portion of the cost.

Bahman Guyuron, MD, professor and chairman of the department of plastic surgery at University Hospitals Case Medical Center in Cleveland and author of seven studies on surgical treatment for migraine.

Help for Inflammation

The gastric bacterium *H. pylori* infects half of Americans over age 60 and is becoming antibiotic-resistant. This bacterium can weaken the stomach's protective coating, damaging cells and leading to chronic inflammation—which in turn increases risk for ulcers and stomach cancer.

Recent finding: Among lab animals infected with H. pylori, those that were fed a diet rich in the amino acid *glutamine* for 20 weeks had less stomach inflammation than those fed a standard diet. This suggests that extra glutamine in the diet could protect against gastric damage caused by H. pylori.

Next: Human studies are needed to determine whether supplements (sold in health-food stores as L-glutamine) protect against stomach maladies, including ulcers and cancer. In the meantime, talk to your doctor about the potential benefits of glutamine-rich foods, such as eggs, dairy, fish, chicken and beef.

Susan Hagen, PhD, associate director of surgery at Harvard Medical School and associate vice chair for research in the department of surgery at Beth Israel Deaconess Medical Center, both in Boston, and lead author of an animal study.

Music Sets Beat for Heart and Lungs

Luciano Bernardi, MD, professor of internal medicine, Pavia University, Pavia, Italy.

Some people love classical music, others prefer country—but regardless of our individual preferences, our bodies will respond to music in the same way. So much so, in fact, that new research from Italy demonstrates that music affects cardiovascular functioning and breathing in such a predictable way it may someday be used as a medical tool.

We're all familiar with how music can impact our emotions, whether energizing or soothing. Research has also established that music can be used to elicit a relaxation response useful for health purposes, for example for preoperative patients and others under stress. Now this study finds that the physiological responses music triggers were virtually identical for all people in the study group.

RESEARCH NOTES

The Italian study included 24 healthy participants, half of whom were experienced choir singers, and the rest with no music training at all. Participants listened in random order to short selections from five classical compositions, including Verdi's operatic aria "Nessun dorma" from Turandot and the orchestral adagio from Beethoven's "Ninth Symphony" (Symphony No. 9 in D minor). Although the participants said they had no particular emotional response or preference for any of the music selections, they all showed similar subconscious autonomic response, which also corresponded to the compositions both in degree and timing. For example, crescendos or swelling of the music induced skin vasoconstriction and increases in blood pressure and heart rates...and, in a more complex response, participants synchronized modulation of the cardiovascular system (through naturally occurring fluctuations in arterial pressure) with the rhythm of the music. Where other researchers have accomplished this with yoga

and prayer, this study achieved success by playing certain pieces of music.

Luciano Bernardi, MD, of Pavia University in Pavia, Italy, is lead author of the study. He said that the study shows that the physiological effects of music are predictable. For instance, he said, blood pressure "tends to follow the musical profile," dropping with slow meditative music and increasing at faster tempi. This provides a better understanding of how music works to affect the body and thus the role it could eventually fill therapeutically, Dr. Bernardi said. So it appears that we now have yet another instrument with which doctors can practice "the art" of medicine.

Promising Treatment for Painful Heels

Luca M. Sconfienza, MD, is a radiologist at Policlinico San Donato in Milan, Italy, and lead author of a study of 44 people, presented at a meeting of the Radiological Society of North America.

If you dread getting out of bed because it hurts to put weight on your heel (particularly in the morning or after standing for a long time), chances are that you have plantar fasciitis—persistent, painful inflammation of a large ligament on the bottom of the foot. Usually it is treated with rest, exercises, splints and arch supports...steroid injections...a series of shockwave treatments (often uncomfortable)...or surgery.

Encouraging: A recent study investigated a new single-treatment therapy. Under ultrasound guidance, after injecting local anesthesia, researchers repeatedly punctured affected areas with a needle, creating a bit of bleeding (which hastens healing by increasing blood flow to the area)...then injected an anti-inflammatory steroid.

Results: 95% of study participants were symptom-free within three weeks and remained so throughout the four- to six-month follow-up period.

Best: If you have severe plantar fasciitis that has not responded to noninvasive therapies, talk to your podiatrist about this technique, called dry-needling with steroid injection. More research is needed before it could become standard protocol—but results are promising.

New Treatment For Hemorrhoids

Michael Epstein, MD, a gastroenterologist in Annapolis, Maryland, and a founder and board member of Macedonia, Ohio-based MAX Endoscopy, *www.maxendoscopy.com*.

Hemorrhoids can make life miserable… and that's especially so if you have the ones that are internal, because these can cause problems that range from being very uncomfortable to actually being dangerous. Some people who have internal hemorrhoids don't even realize it (they may be found during a colonoscopy or blood in the stool may reveal their presence), but other people experience a great deal of pain.

Internal hemorrhoids may cause constipation, pain, itching, bleeding and even soiling. If they get large enough to extend through the anus (a condition called prolapse), they sometimes rupture and bleed. This type of hemorrhoid can be difficult to treat, but a new technology uses infrared energy to shrink them. Michael Epstein, MD, a gastroenterologist in Annapolis, Maryland, and one of the founders of the company that makes the medical device, MAX Endoscopy, explained how it works.

NEW & IMPROVED TECHNOLOGY

Face it, there's nothing pleasant about having hemorrhoids and the typical treatments are pretty awful, too. Most commonly, doctors treat internal hemorrhoids with a procedure that involves putting a tight rubber band around the base of the hemorrhoid inside the rectum, cutting off blood flow so that it shrinks and withers away. Since this is quite painful, it requires a local anesthetic and sometimes general anesthesia (which carries the usual risks). There also is a risk for excessive bleeding, and patients often have to stay overnight in the hospital for monitoring, which is expensive and inconvenient. Other treatment options include injection with a chemical solution (sclerotherapy), which shrinks up the bulging vein and also requires anesthesia…or surgical removal, which is usually reserved for larger, more serious hemorrhoids.

Dr. Epstein said that the new form of treatment for internal hemorrhoids is easier for both doctor and patient. It's a procedure performed with a fiber optic tool (with a lamp and a tiny video camera) that gets passed into the rectum, where it delivers bursts of infrared light to the tissue above the vein, coagulating the blood and thereby shrinking the tissue. The patient feels some heat and sometimes some minor discomfort, but it's over in just a few minutes. This can be done as outpatient surgery, even in the doctor's office (or as part of a colonoscopy, if the hemorrhoids are discovered that way and/or a patient is scheduled to have one), and the patient can go home immediately afterward and resume normal activities. Treatment typically costs about $300 and usually is covered by Medicare and most insurance companies.

New research sponsored by MAX Endoscopy found that 53 patients whose internal hemorrhoids were treated with the Infrared Coagulator experienced an average 87.6% reduction in six symptoms—pain, bleeding, itching, burning, prolapse and soiling.

Index

N

N-acetylcysteine (NAC), 344
Nalfon *(fenoprofen)*, 267
Napping, 246. *See also* Sleep
Narcolepsy, 249. *See also* Sleep
Nasacort *(triamcinolone acetonide)*, 333–334
Nasal cleansing, 334–335, 338–339
Nasalcrom *(cromolyn)*, 332
Nasal sprays, 332–333
National Council on Aging, 44
Natural treatments. *See also* Acupuncture; Herbs; Home remedies; Penny cures; Supplements; Therapy; specific conditions
  acupressure, 335, 379–381, 395–396
  for allergies, 331–332, 333–335
  body awareness and, 273–275
  boosting immunity, 342–344
  for cold sores, 394
  for digestive health, 364–365
  edible flowers as, 113
  for eyesight, 282–283
  for headaches, 267–271, 278
  for heartburn, 353–354
  for IBS, 352–353
  for sleep problems, 247–248
  to slow hearing loss, 301
  for snoring, 251–252
  for tooth care, 295–298
  for ulcers, 354–355
Naturopathic doctors (NDs), 10
Nausea
  acupressure in treating, 381
  from anesthesia, 13, 369
  aromatherapy for, 393
  ginger for, 106, 121, 365, 369, 390
  prevention and treatment, 365–366
Navigation, as brain booster, 75
Navy beans, 96
NDRIs (norepinephrine and dopamine reuptake inhibitors), 270
NEAT (non-exercise activity thermogenesis), 132–133
Neck
  aging appearance of, 324
  pain in, 261, 381, 395
Negotiations. *See also* Mediation
  for dental care, 33
  for medical costs, 28, 41
Nerve pain, 261–262, 432
Nervous system, 70, 132
Neti pots, 334–335, 338–339
Neurological disorders, 462, 541–542. *See also* specific conditions
Neuromonics Tinnitus Treatment, 307
Neurontin *(gabapentin)*, 69, 278
Neurotherapy, 542–543
News, reading, as brain booster, 76
Nexavar *(sorafenib)*, 530–531
Nexium *(esomeprazole)*, 270, 354
Niacin, 310, 469, 472, 488. *See also* Vitamin B
Niaspan, 472
Night sweats, 495
Nitrates, 58
Nitrostat *(nitroglycerin)*, 452
Non-GMO Project, 121
Noni juice, 113
Norpramin *(desipramine)*, 50
Norvasc *(amlodipine)*, 60
Nosebleeds, 301
Noses, caring for, 301, 309, 310. *See also* Nasal cleansing; Respiratory health; Smell
NSAIDs (nonsteroidal anti-inflammatories). *See also* specific

  for arthritis, 277, 402
  for back pain, 55, 260, 262
  causing nutrient depletion, 59–60
  diarrhea link to, 356
  hearing loss link to, 301
  heart failure and, 452
  herbs interacting with, 51
  interaction warnings, 48, 58, 489
  risks in taking, 69–70
  tinnitus caused by, 306
  ulcer link to, 355
Nurses, filing complaints against, 26
Nursing homes, 20, 238
Nutmeg, 378
Nutrients. *See specific*
Nutrition. *See also* Diet; Food and drink
  for aging gracefully, 327–328
  for avoiding hospital stays, 240
  on a budget, 97–99
  for healthy hair, 325, 326
  in hearing loss prevention, 303
  for skin health, 311–312
  supplements adding to, 99–101 (*see also* Supplements)
Nuts
  benefits of, 95, 98
  as headache trigger, 271
  as heartburn treatment, 389
  lowering blood pressure, 467
  lowering cholesterol, 107, 472
  peanut butter, 370
  as stress fighter, 181
Nytol, 62

O

Oats, 98–99, 108
Oat seed tea, 372
Obesity. *See* Weight; Weight control
Obstructive sleep apnea (OSA), 252
Occupational therapists (OTs), 19
Off-label drug prescriptions, 62
Oils, for healthful cooking, 105. *See also* specific types
Olive oil, 95, 105, 119
Omega-3s. *See also* Fish; Fish oil
  after heart attacks, 463
  eggs enriched with, 78
  flaxseed providing, 371
  hair affected by, 169, 326
  for heart failure patients, 452
  as immunity booster, 340
  joint health link to, 398–399
  as mood booster, 187
  in preventing hearing loss, 303
  for skin health, 312
Oncologists, choosing, 497
Onions, 270, 271, 378, 406
Opiates, 57. *See also* specific
Oracea, 310
Oral health. *See also* Periodontal disease; Teeth
  bad breath, 291–292
  bleeding gums, 293, 495
  burning mouth syndrome, 292–293
  cancer links to, 495, 510–512
  canker sores, 294
  cracked tongue, 293
  diabetes link to, 430, 446
  gum disease, 290–291
  holistic dentistry for, 296–298
  mouthwashes, 290–291
  receding gums, 293
  swallowing problems, 494–495
  tonsil stones, 291–292
Oranges, 79, 114
Orapred *(prednisolone)*, 448
Oregano, 382

Organization tips, 196–198
Oscillococcinum, 344
Osteoarthritis. *See also* Arthritis; Joint health
  blended medicine treatment for, 56
  defined, 397, 399
  pain caused by, 263, 277
  slowing progression of, 401–403
Osteomalacia, 102, 103
Osteomyelitis, 436–437
Osteoporosis. *See also* Bone health
  medications for, 62, 64
  in men, 420–421
  natural treatments for, 416–419, 422–424
  obesity link to, 419
Outpatient surgery, 25–26
Ovarian cancer, 160, 534–536. *See also* Cancer
Overcare, in medical ageism, 4–5
Oxazepam, 16
OxyContin *(oxycodone)*, 57, 359

P

PAD (peripheral artery disease), 482–484, 527
Paget's disease, 313
Pain. *See also* specific conditions
  body awareness in treating, 273–275
  drug-free relief for, 395–396
  myotherapy in treating, 275–276
  physical therapy for, 272–273
  pinched nerve, 261–262
  relaxation in managing, 268, 274, 275
  supplements in treating, 259, 261
  topical relief for, 278–279, 391
Painkillers. *See* NSAIDs; specific medications
Palm oil, 119
Pamelor *(nortriptylne)*, 69, 426
Pancreas health, 438
Pancreatic cancer, 514. *See also* Cancer
Pantethine, 459
Papaya, 377–378
Parking lots, sealant on, 513
Parkinson's disease, 86–87, 299, 359, 512
Parsley, 106–107, 370–371, 383
Passion flower, 244
Pasta seasonings, 473
Pathology reports, 496–497
Patient advocacy groups, 44
Patient rights, 9. *See also* Hospitals
Paxil *(paroxetine)*, 16, 52, 62, 66, 421, 426
Peanut butter, 370
Peat/peloid packs, 400
Pectasol, 509
Pelvic floor dysfunction, 363, 364
Penicillin, 58
Penlac *(ciclopirox)*, 266
Penny cures. *See also* Home remedies
  acupressure, 379–381
  antibiotic alternative, 387
  aromatherapy, 392–393
  arthritis treatment, 388
  fresh garlic versus bottled, 386
  for hiccups, 387
  for longevity, 390 (*see also* Meditation)
  for pain, 395–396
Pepcid *(famotidine)*, 48, 63, 87–88
Peppermint, 278, 372, 390, 393. *See also* Mint; Mint tea
Pepto-Bismol *(bismuth subsalicylate)*, 358